Lauren Gawne, Nathan W. Hill (Eds.)
Evidential Systems of Tibetan Languages

Trends in Linguistics
Studies and Monographs

Editor
Volker Gast

Editorial Board
Walter Bisang
Jan Terje Faarlund
Hans Henrich Hock
Natalia Levshina
Heiko Narrog
Matthias Schlesewsky
Amir Zeldes
Niina Ning Zhang

Editor responsible for this volume
Walter Bisang and Volker Gast

Volume 302

Evidential Systems of Tibetan Languages

Edited by
Lauren Gawne
Nathan W. Hill

DE GRUYTER
MOUTON

ISBN 978-3-11-063493-8
e-ISBN (PDF) 978-3-11-047374-2
e-ISBN (EPUB) 978-3-11-047187-8
ISSN 1861-4302

Library of Congress Cataloging-in-Publication Data
A CIP catalog record for this book has been applied for at the Library of Congress.

Bibliografische Information der Deutschen Nationalbibliothek
The Deutsche Nationalbibliothek lists this publication in the Deutschen Nationalbibliografie;
detailed bibliographic data are available on the internet http://dnb.dnb.de.

© 2018 Walter de Gruyter GmbH, Berlin/Boston
This volume is text- and page-identical with the hardback published in 2017.
Typesetting: Compuscript Ltd., Shannon, Ireland
Printing and binding: CPI books GmbH, Leck

♾ Printed on acid-free paper
Printed in Germany

www.degruyter.com

Contents

Nathan W. Hill and Lauren Gawne
1 The contribution of Tibetan languages to the study of evidentiality —— 1

Typology and history

Shiho Ebihara
2 Evidentiality of the Tibetan verb *snang* —— 41

Lauren Gawne
3 Egophoric evidentiality in Bodish languages —— 61

Nicolas Tournadre
4 A typological sketch of evidential/epistemic categories in the Tibetic languages —— 95

Nathan W. Hill
5 Perfect experiential constructions: the inferential semantics of direct evidence —— 131

Guillaume Oisel
6 On the origin of the Lhasa Tibetan evidentials *song* and *byung* —— 161

Lhasa and Diasporic Tibetan

Yasutoshi Yukawa
7 Lhasa Tibetan predicates —— 187

Nancy J. Caplow
8 Inference and deferred evidence in Tibetan —— 225

Other Tibetan languages

Marius Zemp
9 Evidentiality in Purik Tibetan —— 261

Juha Yliniemi
10 Copulas in Denjongke or Sikkimese Bhutia —— 297

Gwendolyn Hyslop and Karma Tshering
11 An overview of some epistemic categories in Dzongkha —— 351

Zoe Tribur
12 Observations on factors affecting the distributional properties of evidential markers in Amdo Tibetan —— 367

Hiroyuki Suzuki
13 The evidential system of Zhollam Tibetan —— 423

Katia Chirkova
14 Evidentials in Pingwu Baima —— 445

Index —— 461

Nathan W. Hill and Lauren Gawne
1 The contribution of Tibetan languages to the study of evidentiality

In his *Aṣṭādhyāyī* the great Sanskrit grammarian Pāṇini cryptically notes the grammatical encoding of information source with the words *parokṣe liṭ* 'one uses the perfect tense in reference to past action not linked to the present day and not witnessed' (Hock 2012: 93–101); so began the study of evidentiality.[1] Although Tibetan grammatical studies, like all domains of traditional Tibetan high culture, build upon Indian models, the Tibetan grammarians did not inherit an explicit awareness of evidentiality.

Alexandra Aikhenvald's 2004 monograph *Evidentiality* is the most thorough typological treatment of evidentiality to date, drawing on grammatical descriptions of over 500 languages (Aikhenvald 2004: xii). While Aikhenvald concedes that "evidentiality in Tibetan varieties was hardly mentioned" (Aikhenvald 2012: 467, Note 20) in her study, she does make reference to four Tibetan varieties, viz. Ladhaki, Amdo, Sherpa, and Lhasa. The World Atlas of Language Structures' (WALS) survey of evidentiality[2] draws on three of the same four Tibetan languages, omitting Lhasa, on the basis of the same secondary literature as Aikhenvald. There is scope both for increased documentation of Tibetan evidential systems and for typological work on evidentiality to make more ample use of the Tibetan data already available. Such work will deepen the understanding of specific Tibetan varieties and improve typological theorizing on evidentiality (cf. Hill 2013a: 51–52; Tournadre, this volume). By making the results of research on Tibetan evidential systems more conveniently accessible, the work in the reader's hands aids in filling these lacunae.

The title of this work and this introduction refer to the varieties of Tibetan spoken today as Tibetan languages (we discuss this terminology in §5 below). We follow Tournadre in drawing together this "well-defined family of languages derived from Old Tibetan" (Tournadre 2014: 107). As all families do, these languages demonstrate phonetically regular reflexes of historic forms, share a core vocabulary, and retain many elements of inherited grammar. As this volume

---

[1] Boas (1911: 43) often mistakenly receives credit for the earliest discussion of grammatical marking of information souce (e.g. Aikhenvald 2004: 12–13, 2014: 4).
[2] http://wals.info/feature/77A#2/16.6/148.7

Note: A list of abbreviations appears at the end of this chapter. Where possible, glosses in citations from other authors have been regularized to the Leipzig Glossing Rules.

demonstrates, despite their common features, these languages encode evidentiality in different ways, demonstrating the outcome of historical developments (see §4). Just as there is variation in how Tibetan languages have grammaticalised evidentiality, the speakers of these languages do not necessarily consider themselves as belonging to a single unified group. Tibetan language speakers reside in Tibet, other parts of China, India, Nepal, Bhutan, and Pakistan. Many Tibetan language speakers will not refer to themselves as Tibetan, but consider themselves to be a member of a specific cultural group, such as Sherpa, or Bhutia. In addition, not all Tibetan language speakers share the same Buddhist culture, e.g. the Purik and the Balti are predominantly Muslim (Zemp, this volume), and many Buddhist groups like the Yolmo have a synchronous indigenous tradition (Desjarlais 1992). This volume attempts to give some illustration of the diversity of Tibetan languages, with contributions on varieties from China, Nepal, India and Bhutan.

Lhasa Tibetan is far and away the best described Tibetan variety. Consequently, to the extent typologists make reference to Tibetan at all, they rely primarily on Lhasa Tibetan and traditions of its analysis, in particular 'conjunct-disjunct' and 'egophoric'. The three evidential categories of Lhasa Tibetan (called 'personal', 'experiential', and 'factual' in this introduction) serve as the point of departure in the exploration of other Tibetan varieties and in the study of the development of evidentials throughout Tibet's long literary history. This introduction describes in turn, the history of the study of Lhasa Tibetan evidentiality (§1), the use of Lhasa Tibetan in typological discussions (§2), the study of other Tibetan varieties (§3), and research on the historical development of Tibetan evidentials (§4). The contributions to this volume correspondingly present research on Lhasa Tibetan, typology, other Tibetan varieties, and the historical emergence of Tibetan evidentiality and we refer to these contributions throughout this introduction. In §5 we discuss the conventions and nomenclature of the volume overall. Throughout this introduction we offer a standardized terminology (personal, factual, and experiential) as equivalences to the terminology of specific authors, in order to facilitate comparison among authors and Tibetan varieties.

While we have given a definition of Tibetan, we have not given a definition of evidentiality. Aikhenvald's definition of evidentiality as "a grammatical expression of information source" (2015: 239) has a simplicity, and certainly has popularity. This rather narrow definition has perhaps led her to miss the nature of evidentiality in languages like Tibetan, which we discuss below. Tournadre and LaPolla (2014) also believe that Aikhenvald's definition is too narrow. After a survey of some Tibetan varieties, and beyond, they give a definition of "the representation of source and access to information according to the speaker's perspective and strategy" (Tournadre and LaPolla 2014: 240). The inclusion of 'access to information' and 'speaker's perspective' is intended to tease out some of the subtleties of personal evidentiality, which we discuss below. Attempting to find one definition of evidentiality that applies to all languages may prove elusive. As can be seen in this volume, even closely related languages may use cognate forms in very different ways. Similarly, linguists from different theoretical backgrounds may approach the question of evidentiality in different ways. We have not constrained our authors by asking them to employ a particular definition of evidentiality in their analyses.

As a related issue, attempting to articulate the relationship between evidentiality and other grammatical features, particularly those contextually-dependent features related to speaker stance, is unlikely to be a successful endeavor at the cross-linguistic level. Our authors expand on the interaction of evidentiality with other grammatical features as they see fit for a particular language. For many of our authors an understanding of modality, speaker perspective, and interrogativity within a particular language are vital to an understanding of evidentiality. For example, for Hyslop and Tshering (this volume) evidentiality is entirely subsumed within the epistemic system. In order to keep this introduction to a containable size, we focus on the grammatical categories of evidentiality specifically, but we also acknowledge that within a single language these cannot be understood in isolation from other features of the language.

1.1 The study of Lhasa Tibetan evidentiality

Research on Lhasa Tibetan evidentiality divides into three groups: 1. early pedagogical grammars, where evidentiality is treated more or less as a form of person agreement, 2. linguistic research where the three-term Lhasa system is analysed as reflecting binary settings of interacting features, 3. linguistic research where the three semantic categories encoded by the evidential system are described as isomorphic with the three morphosyntactic categories used to encode them. These three approaches broadly correspond with chronologically distinct stages in research on Tibetan evidentiality, and reflect an overarching movement away from *a priori* commitments to person and toward characterizations that are both structurally verifiable and motivated by usage in discourse. However, there are striking exceptions to the chronological pattern. While Yukawa Yasutoshi already championed the third approach in 1966, some typologists continue today to rely on outdated treatments of Tibetan evidential systems in discussions of person agreement (see Bickel and Nichols 2007: 223–224; Aikhenvald 2015: 257). Although a useful heuristic, the division of researchers among these three groups is somewhat arbitrary. No researcher unambiguously equates the Lhasa system with person agreement of the Indo-European type, to do so would be foolish. Concomitantly, until recently few researchers vehemently disavowed grammatical person.

As terms for the basic meanings that the Lhasa categories express, 'mood' or 'modality' (Takeuchi 1978; Tournadre 1996: 217; Denwood 1999: 119), 'evidentiality' (DeLancey 1992: 45; Tournadre 1996: 217; Denwood 1999: 119), and 'deixis' (Tournadre 1992; Beckwith 1992; Bartee 1996) have all enjoyed popularity. It would be meaningless to attempt to adjudicate among these terms, as no single rubric will ever capture the subtleties of the Lhasa Tibetan evidential system. In the current volume, most authors prefer the terminology of 'evidentiality', but as the reader will see, Tibetan varieties fail to support the claim that evidentiality "does not bear any straightforward relationship to truth, the validity of a statement or the speaker's responsibility" (Aikhenvald 2014: 44).

1.1.1 Early pedagogical grammarians

Early pedagogical grammars of spoken Lhasa or Central Tibetan attempt to describe the language's three evidential categories as person agreement. Authors themselves acknowledge the imperfect fit. Writing that personal *yod* "is more commonly used with the 1st person" (1894: 46), Graham Sandberg pointedly avoids the direct identification of this category with first person agreement. Vincent Henderson habitually translates the personal verb suffixes -*yin* and -*yod* as first person and the suffixes -*red* and -*ḥdug* as both second and third person, but he includes caveats along the lines that sometimes "*yin* is also heard with 2nd and 3rd persons" (1903: 33). Charles Bell continues to suggest that these suffixes indicate person agreement by offering paradigms such as *ṅas blug-gi-yod* 'I pour' (personal) and *khos blug-gi-ḥdug* 'He pours' (experiential) (1905: 37). Nonetheless, when writing about the use of the relevant forms as existential verbs rather than as tense suffixes, he also draws attention to the importance of evidence. He writes that as

> a general rule it may be said that *yod* [personal] means 'it is there, I saw it there and know that it is still there'; *ḥdug* [experiential] means 'I saw it there but I am not sure whether it is still there or not'; *yod-pa-red* [factual] means, 'I did not see it, but have heard that it is there'. (1905: 40)

Unfortunately, Bell's observations on the evidential meanings of the existential verbs languished for some time.[3]

---

[3] Writing more than 50 years after Bell, Roerich and Phuntshok remain exactly where Sandberg and Henderson left matters. They caution that the apparent association of certain suffixes with grammatical person is "rather irregular" (1957: 48) and underline that in the Tibetan verbal system "the persons are not distinguished" (1957: 48). Nonetheless, they identify the choice of evidential category with person agreement, noting that personal *yod* is used "for the first person singular and plural, and [experiential] *ḥdug* in the second and third persons" (1957: 49–50).

Like Bell, Chang and Shefts continue to treat the tense suffixes as marking person (1964: 25), while singling out the existential verbs for alternative treatment. Unlike Bell, they distinguish the latter in terms of certainty (1964: 18) rather than evidence. Also in keeping with the precedence of Bell, Goldstein and Nornang speak of person when describing the verbal suffixes (1970: 408–409) but in their discussion of existential verbs they distinguish experiential *ḥdug* "actual visual knowledge" from factual *yod-pa-red* "hearsay and knowledge other than visual" (1970: 23). Thus, altogether early pedagogical grammars never abandoned the attempt to characterize the Lhasa Tibetan verbal system in terms of person agreement, through time the importance of information source gradually emerged. In assessing the accuracy of these pedagogical treatments, one must bear in mind the classroom context, where a comprehensible oversimplification often commends itself.

1.1.2 Interacting binary features

A ramification of the early pedagogical treatments' identification of the Lhasa personal evidential category with first person agreement is the bifurcation of the three term Lhasa system into a two way opposition of personal (associated with first person) versus factual and experiential taken together (both associated with both second and third person). Such a tack precipitates the need to subsequently bifurcate factual and experiential without recourse to person agreement. Thus, it is no coincidence that to the limited extent Goldstein and Nornang (1970: 408/409) invoke source of knowledge they do so to distinguish between factual and experiential.

Whether out of deference to this pedagogical heritage or under the influence of a Jakobsonian penchant for binary features, many of the linguists who studied the Lhasa Tibetan verbal system in the latter part of the 20th century upheld this analysis of double bifurcation. Thus, Takeuchi Tsuguhito divides Lhasa Tibetan 'modus' into 内的 'inner' (personal) and 外的 'outer', with the latter subsuming 直接認識 'direct recognition' and 間接認識 'indirect recognition' (1978). Independently of Takeuchi and of each other, in 1992 a further three scholars describe the three Lhasa Tibetan evidential categories in terms of two binary contrasts. Scott DeLancey distinguishes "conjunct" (personal) and "disjunct", dividing the disjunct into "mirative" (experiential) and "non-mirative" (factual) (1992: 45). Nicolas Tournadre distinguishes between "égophoriques" (personal) and "hétérophoriques" auxiliaries (1992: 197), dividing the latter between "constatif" (experiential) and "assertif" (factual) (1992: 207).[4] Less clearly, Christopher

---

4 Since they have been influential outside of the study of Tibetan varieties, we return to DeLancey's 'conjunct-disjunct' (§2.1) and Tournadre's 'egophoric' (§2.2) in greater detail below.

Beckwith posits a primary distinction of 'personal deictic class' of "first versus second and third persons" (1992: 2) but recognizes "evidentials" (1992: 11) within the latter class. Ellen Bartee (1996) repeats DeLancey's account, as does Krisadawan Hongladarom, although she notes that his classification is "not wholly adequate" (1992: 1151). Philip Denwood's description of the Lhasa Tibetan three term evidential system as resulting from binary interactions of up to four independent factors 'person', 'evidentiality', 'viewpoint', and 'generality' (1999: 150) represents the apogee of a Jacobsonian binary approach. This machinery allows him to explain the use of the relevant morphemes in a wide array of contexts, but using a descriptive apparatus of 16 possible settings to account for three paradigmatically contrasting categories is excessive.

1.1.3 Three contrasting forms means three contrasting functions

The earliest published dedicated study of Tibetan evidentiality we are aware of is Yukawa Yasutoshi's 1966 article on *ḥdug*, a revised version of his 1964 master's thesis. He followed this study with overall treatments of Tibetan predicates in 1971 and 1975. Yukawa's approach is to treat each morphological suffix in turn in all of the syntactic positions in which it occurs, with a sensitivity to the interactional context. In the third of these publications he says the personal "話し手〈疑問文の場合は話し相手〉にとって身近に感じられる状態をあらわし [denotes a state with which the speaker (or the listener in interrogative sentences) feels familiar]" the factual "ある状態であることを客観的に断定する objectively asserts a certain state]" and the experiential is "ある状態を話し手（疑問文の場合は話し相手）の感覚で直接にとらえ [...] 場合に用いられる [used when the speaker (or the listener in interrogative sentences) directly perceives a certain state through the senses]" (1975: 4, p. 189 this volume). In addition, Yukawa notes that while in most constructions 'familiarity' is sufficient to warrant the use of the egophoric, the past suffix *-pa-yin* "この場合は、自分の子供であっても、このいい方をすることはできず、自分「または自分を含む集団」の行為についてだけ、こういえるのである [can only denote the speaker's own actions (or those of a group to which she belongs) and cannot be used, for example, to refer to the speaker's own child]" (1971: 194). With this observation Yukawa describes what many years later Garrett refers to as 'weak ego' versus 'strong ego' (2001: 178–205) and Tournadre refers to as 'wide scope' versus 'narrow scope' egophoric (2008: 296). Similarly, Yukawa shows an awareness of the distribution of evidential forms in questions over a decade before DeLancey's conjunct-disjunct account. Yukawa's contributions have long been overlooked in the English-language literature on Tibetan. To rectify this neglect Yukawa's 1975 article is here republished in English translation for the first time.

In Japan, Kitamura Hajime continues the third tradition, describing the personal as encoding what is "psycholinguistically nearer to the speaker" (1977: 25), the experiential as "psycholinguistically remote from the speaker" and "which the speaker or hearer has ascertained or is ascertaining by his experience" (1977: 26), and the factual as "generally known facts" (1977: 27).

Some researchers who had described Tibetan evidentials using person agreement or binary feature approaches move towards the three-way morphosyntactic contrast as a guide to describing contrasting evidential functions. Twenty years after the publication of their textbook, Chang and Chang return to the Lhasa Tibetan evidential system with an audience of linguists rather than students in mind. Although they do not explicitly characterize the Tibetan system as 'evidential', their discussion of the personal as "the habitual or customary basis of knowledge which has been personally acquired" (1984: 605), the experiential as "witness" (1984: 619), and the factual as "hearsay" (1984: 605) makes clear that these morphemes encode three types of information source. Similarly, Hongladarom moves from a binary 'conjunct-disjunct' description to describing Tibetan as having:

> a three way evidential distinction among *yöö* [personal], *tuu*, [experiential] and *yôôree* [factual] indicating the speaker's self knowledge, direct experience, and indirect source of information respectively. (1993: 52, emphasis in original).

Garrett arrives at the same analysis positing three "evidential categories in Lhasa Tibetan—ego [personal], direct [experiential], and indirect [factual]" (2001: x et passim). Schwieger (2002: 183) explicitly rejects the association of these evidential categories with agreement. Recent pedagogical grammars also stress that the Tibetan system encodes information source and not person agreement (Tournadre and Dorje 2003; Chonjore 2003).

The preoccupation of this discussion has been the general characterization of evidentiality in Lhasa Tibetan and an emphasis on the fact that Lhasa has a three term evidential system. This structure is most clear in the parallelism between the existential verbs *yod* (personal), *ḥdug* (experiential), and *yod-pa-red* (factual) and the present tense suffixes *-gi-yod* (personal), *-gi-ḥdug* (experiential), and *-gi-yod-pa-red* (factual). Probably one factor that impeded description of this system is the opacity of the system's symmetry in other parts of the verbal system. In particular, the placement of the suffixes *-yoṅ*, *-myoṅ*, and *-byuṅ* into the overall verbal paradigm requires further study. In their contributions to this volume both Hill and Caplow recommend that *bźag* be analyzed as a perfect experiential rather than a separate inferential evidential (as in DeLancey 1985: 65–67, 2003: 279; Tournadre 1992: 198, 207, 1996: 236–238; Tournadre and Dorje 2009: 140–144, 410, 413); Hill additionally suggests that the analysis of the semantics of inference as a combination of direct evidentiality with perfect tense is a useful framework for understanding phenomena in other languages.

Linguistic meaning is an emergent social practice, which no abstract characterization will fully succeed at capturing. Consequently, the task of describing the Lhasa evidential system does not end at realizing the inadequacy of approaches making reference to person or binary features. Instead, the contextual use of evidentials in conversation and narration is available for study at any level of granularity. Hongladarom (1993) offers a nuanced account of the contrasting use of *ḥdug* and *yod-pa-red* in conversation.

1.2 The use of Lhasa Tibetan in typological discussions

The wider typological literature fails to take note of the great majority of the research discussed in the previous section. Aikhenvald (2004) cites only works by DeLancey and one article by Tournadre (1994). Her lopsided attentiveness is characteristic of the citation of Tibetan research articles in the later decades of the 20th century and early 21st century; Google Scholar registers 141 citations of DeLancey (1986) and 81 citations of Tournadre and Dorje (2003)[5] as opposed to 15 for Hongladarom (1993) and none for Yukawa (1966).[6] Because of their influence, in the context of Tibetan's impact on the typological literature DeLancey's 'conjunct-disjunct' (§2.1) and Tournadre's 'egophoric' (§2.2) require treatment in detail.

1.2.1 Lhasa Tibetan as a conjunct-disjunct system

The discourse of 'conjunct-disjunct' began with an unpublished paper by Austin Hale (1971). In the decade before the publication of an updated version (Hale 1980) his framework was already influential among missionaries associated with the Summer Institute of Linguistics and scholars of Newar (Strahm 1975; Sresthacharya et al. 1971; Sresthacarya 1976); the published version (Hale 1980) became the *locus classicus* for this terminology. In this article Hale proposes conjunct-disjunct nomenclature for a patterning of verbal suffixes in Kathmandu Newar whereby first person declaratives and second person interrogatives are marked the same way, in contrast to first person interrogatives, second person declaratives and all

---

5 Combining the count for the English and French editions.
6 Google Scholar www.scholar.google.com accessed 29 December 2015.

third person forms. In (1) the first person verb is differentiated from the second and third person forms with a lengthening of the vowel.[7]

(1) a. *ji ana **wanā***
'I went there.' (conjunct)
(Hale 1980: ex. 1)
b. *cha ana **wana***
'You went there.' (disjunct)
(Hale 1980: ex. 2)
c. *wa **wana***
'He went there.' (disjunct)
(Hale 1980: ex. 3)

Hale's description of the system involves three major features. The first is that clauses with first person declarative subjects occur with the same form of the verb as clauses with second person subjects in question constructions (Hale 1980: 95) (cf. (2)).

(2) *cha ana **wanā** lā*
'Did you go there?' (conjunct)
(Hale 1980: ex. 4)

The second is that this pattern only holds when the subject is the 'true instigator' of the action. Impersonal verbs, which the subject has no control over, are never marked with a conjunct form (cf. (3)), not even for first person or interrogatives. That the 'disjunct' is not actually contrasting against anything in this context is one of the reasons this terminology is unhelpful.

(3) a. *jįį wa saa **tāla***
'I heard that noise.' (disjunct)
(Hale 1980: ex. 9)
b. *chąą wa saa **tāla***
'You heard that noise.' (disjunct)
(Hale 1980: ex. 9)
c. *wąą wa saa **tāla***
'He heard that noise.' (disjunct)
(Hale 1980: ex. 9)

This dimension of 'instigator-hood' means that for verbs other than the impersonal set (where they are always marked disjunct regardless of person) it is possible

---

[7] In citations from Hale (1980) the emphasis is ours.

to make a distinction for first person between actions that were done voluntarily (cf. (4a)) and those done involuntarily (cf. (4b)) (Hale 1980: 96). This distinction is possible because the conjunct form is used exclusively for voluntary actions, as discussed above.

(4) a. *jį̄į̄ lā* **palā**
 'I cut the meat (intentionally).' (conjunct)
 (Hale 1980: ex. 10)
 b. *jį̄į̄ lā* **pala**
 'I cut the meat (quite by accident).' (disjunct)
 (Hale 1980: ex. 11)

The third important feature of Hale's conjunct-disjunct is the way it interacts with indirect quote frames. The two examples below translate the same in English, but use different verb forms in Newar and have different co-referential relations. In (5) we give Hale's gloss and also include subscript referent notation.

(5) a. *wą̄ą̄ wa ana* **wanā** *dhakāā dhāla*
 'He$_i$ said that he$_i$ went there (himself).' (conjunct)
 (Hale 1980: ex. 5)
 b. *wą̄ą̄ wa ana* **wana** *dhakāā dhāla*
 'He$_i$ said he$_j$ (someone else) went there.' (disjunct)
 (Hale 1980: ex. 6)

The first utterance involves the person saying he went, while the second utterance is a person reporting on another person who went. Hale does not discuss how the choice of conjunct versus disjunct forms in these constructions intersect with impersonal verbs (cf. (3)), or with non-volitional acts (cf. (4)), but in a later treatment Hargreaves (2005: 17) demonstrates that the conjunct-disjunct pattern does not hold in such conditions, instead all forms are disjunct.

Six year prior to the publication of Hale's 1980 study Bendix wrote that (what would later be called) the conjunct expresses "the evidential category of intentional action" (Bendix 1974: 54) and emphasizes it "is evidential and not a first-person verb ending: it may occur with any person" (1974: 49). In 1980 Hale cites, but makes little use of Bendix' work. In contrast to Bendix, Hale frames his discussion of conjunct-disjunct marking in syntactic terms. Nonetheless, his description of the system's special treatment of the subject as 'true instigator' on the one hand and the treatment of impersonal verbs on the other hand, make clear that the choice of these suffixes is semantically motivated. Although Hale's 'conjunct' and 'disjunct' terminology persists in the treatment of Kathmandu Newar, the definition of these terms now takes its cue from Bendix. Hargreaves says that conjunct "suffixes will occur whenever the action is construed as intentional, and the actor/agent is also the evidential source reporting the action" (2003: 376) whereas disjunct "suffixes occur in all other finite environments" (2003: 376, also cf. Hargreaves 2005). Hale's recent work employs an *in extenso* quotation from Hargreaves as his definition of conjunct and disjunct; the quotation itself cites Bendix on the evidential nature of the system (Hale and Shreshta 2006: 55/56). Although originally framing his argument around person agreement, Hale now appears to agree that the Newar pattern is motivated by evidential semantics.

It is worth discussing Aikhenvald's perspective on the Newar verbal system, as she analyses both it and Lhasa Tibetan as conjunct-disjunct. Aikhenvald describes Newar as having an evidential system of three or more terms (2004: 291), but 87 pages earlier describes it as displaying "conjunct and disjunct person marking" (2004: 204, also see p. 124), a view she repeats in 2012 (p. 471). To say that Newar has a conjunct-disjunct system that expresses evidentiality poses no contradiction for Hale and Hargreaves, but Aikhenvald rejects the consensus view that Newar conjunct-disjunct is evidential marking by another name. Instead, she offers a purely syntactic definition of conjunct-disjunct marking[8] and contends that "[c]onjunct-disjunct person-marking systems are not evidential in nature" (2004: 127), a view she reiterates in 2015 with the words "[c]onjunct-disjunct systems do not mark information source" (2015: 257), in direct contrast with the views of both Hargreaves and Hale.

Citing Hale's 1980 article, DeLancey first mentions the possibility of considering Newar conjunct-disjunct marking in connection with the Tibetan verbal system (1985: 66, Note 5).[9] It was in 1990 that DeLancey first explicitly describes Tibetan as exhibiting a conjunct-disjunct system. He offers examples (6a–d) to show both that first person declaratives and second person interrogatives are marked the same way and that second person declaratives and first person interrogatives are marked the same way (corresponding to Hale's first feature).[10]

---

8 She defines conjunct-disjunct marking as "person-marking on the verb whereby first person subject in statements is expressed in the same way as second person in questions, and all other persons are marked in a different way (also used to describe cross clausal co-reference)" (2004: 391). More recently she concedes that person marking "may correlate with speaker's control in conjunct-disjunct [...] person-marking systems" (2015: 257, Note 17), i.e. in her view we paradoxically see here a person-marking system that does not mark person.
9 In an article published the following year (1986) he does not reiterate this observation, making no mention of 'conjunct-disjunct'; puzzlingly, it is this 1986 paper that Aikhenvald cites to claim that conjunct-disjunct agreement has nothing to do with evidentiality (2004: 127, 2015: 257).
10 DeLancey was by no means the first scholar to note the patterning of first person declaratives with second person interrogatives in Tibetan; this pattern was known at least as early as Yukawa (1966: 77).

(6) a. *ṅa   bod-pa   yin*
I   Tibetan   be.PER
'I am a Tibetan.'
b. *kho   bod-pa   red*
He   Tibetan   be.FAC
'He is Tibetan.'
c. *khyed-raṅ   bod-pa   yin-pas*
You   Tibetan   be.PER.INTERR
'Are you a Tibetan?'
d. *ṅa   rgya-mi   red-pas*
1SG   Chinese   be.FAC.INTERR
'Am I Chinese?'
(DeLancey 1990: 295)

DeLancey also points to the Tibetan distinction between first person actions done voluntarily (cf. (7a)) and those done involuntarily (cf. (7b)). Thus, the Tibetan evidentials also satisfy Hale's second feature.

(7) a. *ṅas   dkar-yol   bcag-pa-yin*
1SG   cup   broke.PST.PER
'I broke the cup (intentionally).'
b. *ṅas   dkar-yol   bcag-soṅ*
1SG   cup   broke.PST.TES
'I broke the cup (unintentionally).'
(DeLancey 1990: 300)

He offers examples (8a–d) to show the way that interactions with indirect quote frames parallel those of Newar as in Hale's third feature.

(8) a. *khos   kho   bod-pa   yin*
3SG.M.ERG   3SG.M   Tibetan   be.PER
'He is Tibetan.'
b. *khos   kho   bod-pa   yin   zer-gyis*
3SG.M.ERG   3SG.M   Tibetan   be.PER   say.IPFV
'He$_i$ says 3SG.M$_i$ is Tibetan.'
c. *khos   kho   bod-pa   red   zer-gyis*
3SG.M.ERG   3SG.M   Tibetan   be.FAC   say.IPFV
'He$_i$ says he$_j$ is Tibetan.'
d. *khos   ṅa   bod-pa   red   zer-gyis*
3SG.M.ERG   1SG   Tibetan   be.FAC   say.IPFV
'He says I am Tibetan.'
(DeLancey 1990: 295/296)

Although DeLancey has not distanced himself from Hale's 1980 presentation of conjunct-disjunct as explicitly as Hale himself has, DeLancey's approach to describing Tibetan with 'conjunct-disjunct' terminology has changed over time. First, DeLancey never committed himself to Aikhenvald's assertion that conjunct-disjunct is person agreement and categorically not evidential marking. Most explicitly in 2003 he rejects her account by referring to conjunct-disjunct as a "particular evidential pattern" (2003: 278). Earlier he referred to the Lhasa Tibetan verbal system as an "evidential system" (1990: 304) and "problematic as an example of verb agreement" (1992: 43). Second, he has begun to use Tournadre's 'egophoric' terminology in addition to Hale's 'conjunct-disjunct'. Citing personal communication with DeLancey in 2003, Tournadre claims that with regard to Tibetan DeLancey had been "convinced that the notion of 'egophoric' [...] was more appropriate than the opposition conjunct/disjunct" (2008: 284, Note 6). In print DeLancey has not embraced 'egophoric' in favour of 'conjunct-disjunct', but recently he treats the two frameworks as interchangeable, writing of "'conjunct-disjunct' or 'egophoric' systems" (2012: 550, 2015: 64).

The framework of 'conjunct-disjunct' is not popular among other researchers on Tibetan. Sun refers to the terms as "utterly unrevealing" (1993: 995). Garrett sees their use in reference to Lhasa Tibetan as "regrettable" pointing out that "for a language like Tibetan, in which the evidential opposition is ternary [...] rather than binary, as in Newari, two terms do not suffice" (2001: 209, Note 66). Tournadre (2008) devotes an entire study to rejecting 'conjunct-disjunct'; he notes his argument's "implications for typological studies" (2008: 284), and sketches the ramifications of such a rejection on Aikhenvald's evidential typology. In his contribution to this volume Tournadre elaborates that Aikhenvald

> has set up conjunct/disjunct marking and evidentiality as categorically different in nature whereas at least for the Tibetic languages, 'conjunct/disjunct' was just a provisional and inappropriate description of evidential phenomena. (Tournadre, p. 118 this volume).

Tournadre's remarks provide a convenient juncture for the exploration of Aikhenvald's treatment of Lhasa Tibetan.

Paradoxically Aikhenvald describes Lhasa Tibetan *ḥdug* (experiential) as both a "disjunct copula" (2004: 127) and a morpheme that "marks 'actual visual knowledge'" (2004: 284). If as she contends, "[c]onjunct-disjunct person-marking systems are not evidential in nature" (2004: 127, cf. 12, 146, 276), then a single morpheme cannot be both disjunct and evidential. Her inconsistent treatment of *ḥdug* reflects an ambivalence as to whether Lhasa Tibetan exhibits evidential marking (2004: 14, 28, 69) or conjunct-disjunct agreement (2004: 127, 134). This ambivalence persists into 2012, but perhaps with her inclining in favor of person. She hesitantly finds Tibetan evidentiality plausible.

> The case for ḫdug as a marker of information source appears to be likely [...] However, to make it fully convincing, it needs to be placed within the context of a full grammar of a language. (2012: 467)

She expresses dissatisfaction with Denwood's (1999) treatment, but does not draw on the full grammars of Kitamura (1977), M. Hoshi (1988), Chonjore (2003), nor Garrett's (2001) thesis etc., which all discuss the evidential nature of the Tibetan system. Her skepticism regarding ḫdug is curious, given that very few of the languages treated in her 2004 monograph are as well researched as Tibetan.[11] Most recently, in 2015, she reiterates both the view that Tibetan has conjunct-disjunct person marking (2015b: 257, Note 17) and the view that "[c]onjunct-disjunct systems do not mark information source" (2015b: 257)", but remains silent on Tibetan evidentiality.

In addition to Newar and Lhasa Tibetan, the terminology of conjunct-disjunct has appeared in the description of the Jirel (Strahm 1975), Sherpa (Schöttelndreyer 1980; Woodbury 1986; Kelly 2004), and Lhomi (Vesalainen and Vesalainen 1980) varieties of Tibetan, as well as Awa Pit and other Barbacoan languages (Curnow 2002a, 2002b),[12] Kaike (Watters 2006), Duna (San Roque 2008: 425), and Yongning Na languages (Lidz 2010: 14, 373–381). How closely an author draws comparison to Hale's description of Newar, and whether he or she characterizes 'conjunct-disjunct' in a particular language as syntactic agreement or semantically based evidential choices, of course, varies case to case. In general, as in the case of Newar, earlier descriptions (e.g. Schöttelndreyer 1980) are syntactic in approach, but more recent descriptions, such as Watters' of Kaike emphasize that "'person' is not the primary motivating factor behind the system, but rather, 'volitionality' and 'locus of knowledge'" (2006: 300). It is likely that the authors of the older more syntactic descriptions would now reformulate their presentation in light of more recent research. Even among the older descriptions, a definition of the conjunct as meaning that there is "an experiencer [...] who has been closely involved with the event of the main verb" (Vesalainen and Vesalainen 1980: 27) is more similar to Tournadre's description of the egophoric than to any type of person agreement.

---

[11] In the same 2012 article in which she holds high the bar for Lhasa's ḫdug as a marker of information source, Aikhenvald posits *le* as a mirative marker in Balti Tibetan on the basis of Bashir's (2010) treatment of a mere two examples.

[12] Dickinson's (2000) description of Tsafiki essentially uses the 'conjunct-disjunct' approach, although she uses the terminology 'congruent' and 'noncongruent'.

1.2.2 Lhasa Tibetan egophoric evidentiality

DeLancey's current identification of 'conjunct-disjunct' with 'egophoric' makes good sense in the context of Tournadre's initial coining of the term 'egophoric'. In 1992, Tournadre contrasts the "égophoriques" (personal) and "hétérophoriques" (experiential-factual) auxiliaries (1992: 197), dividing the latter between "constatif" (experiential) and "assertif" (factual) (1992: 207).[13] In subsequent publications "hétérophoriques" became "hétérophorique ou neutre" (1994: 151), and "neutres" (1996: 220). By 2001 he had cast off the binary perspective, describing "egophoric", "sensorial", and "assertive" as equal evidential categories (Tournadre and Jiatso 2001: 72). From then on DeLancey's 'conjunct' and Tournadre's 'egophoric' parted ways. For Tournadre 'egophoric' refers to a specific evidential category in Lhasa Tibetan, a category that this introduction refers to as 'personal' (as in Hill 2012, 2013a) and others call 'participant specific' (Agha 1993: 157) or 'self-centered' (Denwood 1999). See Gawne (this volume) for further discussion of egophoric/personal in Lhasa Tibetan as well as other Tibetan varieties.

The personal (egophoric) is used in Lhasa Tibetan if the speaker of a declarative sentence draws on her own personal information about something closely associated with her or her intentions. The following examples (9a–f) contrast the semantics of the personal with the factual (cf. (10a+b)) and experiential (cf. (10c–f)).[14]

(9) a. ṅa   rdo-rje   yin
    I, me   Dorje   be-PER
    'I'm Dorje.' (introducing oneself to a stranger)
   b. kho   ṅaḥi   bu   yin
    he   I, me-GEN   son, child   be-PER
    'He is my son.' (emphasizing his relationship to me, e.g. answering 'whose son is he?')
   c. ṅar   deb   ḥdi   yod
    I, me-DAT   book   this   be-PER
    'I own this book.' (seeing the book on a friend's table)

---

13 Tournadre's use of 'egophoric' differs profoundly from its meaning for Hagège (1982) or Dahl (2000).
14 These examples are adapted from Hongladarom (1993: 112), Schwieger (2002) and Hill (2013a). One could equally offer experiential equivalents of 10a-b, viz. ḥdi ṅa red-bźag '(I now see that) this is me' and kho ṅaḥi bu red-bźag '(I now see that) he is my son.'

d. *kha-lag ḥdi źim-po yod*
food this tasty be-PER
'This food is tasty.' (I find that it tastes good)

e. *ṅa na-gi-yod*
me sick-PRS-PER
'I'm (chronically) sick.'

f. *ṅa-tsho yar ḥgro-gi-yod*
we yonder go-PRS-PER
'We are going over there.'

g. *dge-rgan-gyis bod-yig bslab gnaṅ-gi-yod*
teacher-AGN Tibetan script teach do-PRS-PER
'The teacher teaches (me) Tibetan script.'

(10) a. *ḥdi ṅa red*
this me be-FAC
'This is me.' (presenting a group picture indicating one's place in a crowd)

b. *kho ṅaḥi bu red*
he I, me-GEN son, child be-FAC
'He is my son.' (emphasizing his correct identification, e.g. answering 'who is he'?)

c. *ṅar deb gcig ḥdug*
I, me-DAT book this be-TES
'(Oh,) there is a book for me.' (looking in an office pigeonhole)

c. *kha lag ḥdi źim-po ḥdug*
food this tasty be-TES
'This food is tasty.' (I know, because I am tasting it)

d. *ṅa na-gi-ḥdug*
me sick-PRS-TES
'I'm sick (at the moment).'

e. *ṅa-tsho yar ḥgro-gi-ḥdug*
we yonder go-PRS-TES
'(In my dream) we were going over there'.

f. *ṅa bod-yig slob-sbyoṅ byed-gi-ḥdug*
me Tibetan script study do-PRS-TES
'(In this scene of the home movie) I am studying the Tibetan script.'

These examples make abundantly clear that person agreement or its adaptation as 'conjunct-disjunct' has no explanatory value. The personal is perfectly compatible with third person (examples (9a, d, g)) and the first person is perfectly compatible with the experiential (examples (10a, c, d, e, f)). The supposed correlation of the personal evidence (egophoric) with first person subject is simply specious. Thus, "the coreference concepts of conjunct and disjunct are not appropriate" and instead the "semantic and pragmatic notion of 'egophoric' related to 'personal knowledge' [...] is better suited to interpret the linguistic facts" (Tournadre 2008: 304).

The Lhasa Tibetan personal evidential category has echoes in categories described for languages from other parts of the world (Loughnane 2009: 249–253; San Roque and Loughnane 2012: 157/158), some of which also passed through a phase of misidentification as person agreement or 'conjunct' marking. For example, W. M. Rule describes that when he and his wife

> first analysed the Foe language [of Papua New Ginea], we had this 1st [participatory] aspect classified as a 1st pers. subject-verb agreement [...] It was not until later, when we came across numbers of examples of sentences wherein the 1st aspect was used for actions which a 3rd person/s were doing [...] that I realised that the basic relationship was not between subject & the verb, but between the speaker & the verb. (Rule 1977: 71).

With the Lhasa and Foe cases in mind, it is clear that intensive language documentation needs to consider the interactional uses of grammatical forms in a range of interactional contexts.[15] In addition, whereas a contextualized example of evidential usage found in natural discourse is a fact to reckon with, grammaticality judgments are fallible opinions. For example, misled by the artificiality of elicitation, DeLancey (1990: 300) and Bartee (2011: 143) report that example (9e) (above) is ungrammatical.[16] Their example stands as a warning that readers must "feel entitled to explicitly doubt a direct statement about a language by someone who actually knows something about it" (DeLancey 2012: 538).

Aikhenvald does not discuss a category of personal (egophoric) evidentiality. Remarking that "complex evidentiality systems may involve further terms" (2004: 60), she mentions several of the relevant categories including the Foe "participatory" and the Kashaya "performative" (2004: 60–62), but these languages do not influence her typology (2004: 65) nor does she draw parallels between these categories and evidential usage in Newar and Lhasa Tibetan.[17]

---

15 One is entitled to wonder whether more intensive language documentation and comprehensive study will disprove observations such as that the "conjunct" of Awa Pit is "entirely person-based" (Curnow 2002a: 616) or that in sentences marked with the Kashaya "performative" the subject "is always the first person" (Oswalt 1986: 34). Subtle evidential nuances are hard to elicit.
16 Tournadre (1992: 203) appears to be the first to have reported example 9e.
17 Her more recent work (2012: 471, 2015: 257, Note 17) merely reiterates her long held opinions and reveals a lack of awareness of relevant work such as Tournadre (2008) and Loughnane (2009: 249–253).

In other quarters Tournadre's rejection of 'conjunct-disjunct' terminology has garnered attention and egophoric terminology is now proliferating among younger scholars (Post 2013; Daudey 2014a, 2014b; Knuchel 2015).[18] Nonetheless, closer scrutiny reveals Tournadre's insights have attracted fewer adherents than his terminology. In particular, the old analysis lives on in the -*ity* of 'egophoricity', a term Mark Post coined (2013: 107, 119, 127). He explicitly identifies the old outlook with the new term, referring to "person-sensitive T[ense]A[spect]M[ood] E[videntiality] marking in Lhasa Tibetan – 'a.k.a conjunct-disjunct marking' or 'egophoricity'" (2013: 107), unaware that the Lhasa personal (egophoric) is insensitive to person. Daudey reveals an unambiguous misunderstanding of Tournadre's position by referring to "evidentiality versus egophoricity" (2014a: 344) and incorrectly claiming that the "term egophoricity is used by Tournadre (2008)" (2014a: 358, Note 349). Knuchel likewise contradicts Tournadre's perspective at the same time as adopting his terminology.

> I opt for using Tournadre's (1991; 1996) term *egophoric*, with the contrasting *non-egophoric* where applicable. *Egophoricity* serves as the generic term for the category and *egophoric contrast* is used to include both values, egophoric and nonegophoric. (Knuchel 2015: 2 emphasis in original).

In an attempt to communicate ambivalence between the 'conjunct-disjunct' and 'egophoric' outlooks, San Roque et al. point out both that some have "proposed that egophoric markers are a special evidential category of 'ego' evidentiality" (2017: 137) and that by others "an 'information source' interpretation has been explicitly rejected" (2017: 137/138). Their formulation of "the phenomenon of egophoricity (conjunct/disjunct marking)" as "a typological category that has been closely linked to evidentiality" (2017: 122) reveals that they reject Tournadre's perspective. They identify 'conjunct/disjunct' and 'egophoricity' whereas Tournadre (2008) rejects this identification. Furthermore, if the personal (egophoric) is an evidential category, then to say that it is 'linked' to evidentiality is as confused as saying the House of Representatives maintains links to the US Government. In their efforts to weigh the merits of the two schools of thought San Roque et al. again betray a proclivity for Aikhenvald's perspective by not considering egophoric evidentiality to be on the same footing as 'classic' evidential morphemes.

> the view that egophoricity is a type of evidentiality is especially compelling for languages where EGO markers contrast paradigmatically with 'classic' evidential morphemes such as visual and

---

18 In a clear case, Post previously described Galo as having "a conjunct/disjunct system" (2007: 611), but later concludes that "it would seem appropriate to adopt Tournadre's terminology" (2013: 111).

other sensory markers ... However, for some egophoric languages there is less motivation for an evidential interpretation, as information source is not (otherwise) grammaticalised. (San Roque et al. 2017: 138, emphasis in original)

In claiming that egophoric marking which fails to contrast with 'classic' evidential morphemes provides less motivation for an evidential interpretation, they cling too firmly to existing typologies that fail to mention personal (egophoric) evidentiality.[19] If it is sensible to analyze some languages as exhibiting personal evidentiality, then the personal merits to stand among other evidential categories with cross-linguistic evidence of reoccurring semantics. The field of evidential typology has too long overlooked personal evidence. This volume provides ample evidence of this category, and its variation in a group of related languages.

The overall pattern of defining 'egophoric(ity)' in relation to Hale's (1980) definition of 'conjunct-disjunct' and then providing qualifications (Post 2013; Daudey 2014a, 2014b) repeatedly breathes fresh air into a defunct outlook and fulfills Tournadre's prophecy that "the phantom concept of conjunct/disjunct will haunt linguistic articles for a long time" (Tournadre 2008: 304). In his contribution to the current volume, Tournadre attempts to rectify the misunderstandings of his work, by again rejecting the view that egophoric and non-egophoric are contrasting members of a single category:

the term 'egophoric' ... never referred to a *system* but to a specific category of the Evidential/Epistemic system, used with many other categories. (Tournadre, p. 116 this volume, emphasis in original)

The application of the term 'egophoricity' and references to 'egophoric systems' is a hindrance to the understanding of the specific evidential forms in Tibetan varieties and analogous phenomena in other languages. In sum, those whom Tournadre convinced to drop 'conjunct-disjunct' should abstain from putting -*ity* on the egophoric.

Perhaps Tournadre's term 'egophoric' is partly to blame for engendering the misunderstandings of his perspective. The term has several disadvantages. First, it has been used for other purposes (by Hagège 1982 and Dahl 2000). Second, its derivative 'egophoricity' has become identical with 'conjunct-disjunct' (by Post 2013, Daudey 2014a, 2014b, Knuchel 2015, and San Roque et al. 2017). Third, as it contains the word 'ego', the first person singular subject pronoun of Greek and Latin, it will always imply first person. For these reasons this introduction prefers 'personal'.

---

19 To speak of 'egophoric languages' is odd, since one does not speak of 'aorist languages' or 'imperfective languages' but rather 'tense languages' and 'aspect languages'.

1.3 The study of other Tibetan varieties

As far as we are able to determine all Tibetan varieties exhibit grammaticalized evidentiality. In contrast to the extensive literature on Lhasa Tibetan evidentiality, comparatively little work has been done on other varieties. Some of this work appears in broader descriptive grammars, and may only obliquely make reference to the evidential categories of a particular language. However, specific studies of evidential systems are increasingly appearing (e.g. Sun 1993; Shao 2014). In this section we summarize the existing literature on evidentiality in Tibetan varieties beyond Lhasa, for this purpose it is convenient to treat languages in a rough geographic sweep from west to east. There is no reason to think that the geographic divisions correspond to stemmatic clades. We have attempted to be as comprehensive as possible in terms of the languages covered in this section, however with regards to each language we have not indicated the complete range of references available. This is particularly the case in regard to languages that have chapters in this book. We direct the reader to each chapter for a more detailed background on the literature regarding that language. The contributions of this volume are mentioned in turn under the appropriate geographic heading. In addition, two of our contributors offer cross-variety studies. Gawne compares the expression of personal evidentiality ("egophoric") in a suite of Tibetan varieties. Ebihara, taking her departure from form rather than meaning, explores the uses of cognates of *snaṅ* across varieties.

1.3.1 Western varieties

Balti is one of the first Tibetan varieties for which evidentiality was described. Read underlines the evidential opposition between *yodpa* and *yodsuk* as respectively "hearsay" and "seen by the speaker" (1934: 41). He also highlights evidential uses of the copula verbs when used with adjectives: *yod* "suggests personal experience" whereas *in* lacks this connotation (1934: 36). Read also describes *in* as an auxiliary verb in the formation of the perfect as used with the first person "on most occasions" (1934: 45), a description redolent of personal evidentiality. With this early account of Read's in mind, it is surprising that Tournadre and LaPolla (2014: 254, Note 27) cite Bielmeier (2000) as saying that Balti dialect does not mark evidentiality. Although Bielmeier does not use the term 'evidentiality' in his article, his treatment of 'semantic-pragmatic effects' is clearly about evidentiality. For example, his description of *jot* [*yod*] as indicating "subjective definite knowledge, acquired through previous personal experience" (2001: 56), refers very clearly to personal evidentiality. In his earlier monograph Bielmeier (1985) presents a number of paired verb tenses in which one of the two indicates visual information source (e.g. Imperfekt v. Beobachtetes Imperfekt, Duratives Präteritum v. Beobachtetes duratives Präteritum, Nezessitatives Präteritum v. Beobachtetes nezessitatives Präteritum). In all cases, the addition of a suffix -*suk* marks the 'Beobachtetes' ['observed'] member of the pair. Jones (2009) devotes a study to the experiential suffixes -*suk* and -*naŋ*. In the current volume Ebihara discusses evidential uses of *snaṅ* in Balti Tibetan among other varieties.

In Ladakhi, Francke (1901) presents most of those affixes which later authors regard as evidential, but rarely draws attention to their evidential meaning. However, he does remark that -*rag* "can only be used with verbs which denote a perception of the senses (with the exception of sight) or an action of the intellect" (1901: 29). Like other authors of his time period, he frequently sees evidentiality through the lens of grammatical person, e.g. remarking that -*pin* "is very much used in lively conversation, rather more for the first and second persons than for the third" (1901: 30), and noting an association of the third person with the suffixes -*song* and -*tog* (1901: 30/31). Koshal offers a complex presentation of the Ladakhi verbal system. In this account the Ladakhi verbal template is composed of a verb stem, an optional modal suffix, and is completed with a 'tense-aspect-orientation' suffix (1979: 193), in which 'orientation' may be understood as equivalent to evidential. The paradigm of 'tense-aspect-orientation' markers includes 33 forms (1979: 295–313). Koshal does not organize these 33 forms into subcategories.[20] In a pedagogical grammar, Norman (2001: 52/53) describes seven evidential or modal settings for the present tense (-*at* already known to the speaker, -*duk* seen, -*rak* felt or sensed, -*anok* general, -*at-ḍo* probably, -*at-kyak* inferred, and -*chen* indefinite)

---

20 Koshal's terminology for individual forms, e.g. "observed present continuous" (1979: 195) generally implies a categorization of the 33 forms into large categories, but this categorization is not seen through explicitly. In a typological work, Bhat, relying entirely on Koshal, describes Ladakhi as having six epistemic moods, viz. reported, observed, experienced, inferred, probable, and generic (1999: 72), four inference distinctions, and two narrative suffixes (1999: 73). Relying on Koshal (1979) and Bhat (1999), Aikhenvald describes Ladakhi as exhibiting "four evidentiality specifications", namely reported, observed, experienced (e.g. by feeling), and inferred (2004: 211). One is left to infer that Aikhenvald's radical simplification is based on Bhat's comment regarding the epistemic moods that "the first four suffixes are primarily evidential in nature and only the last two can be regarded as involving judgment" (1999: 72). Thus, rather than empirically consulting Ladakhi to formulate her typology, Aikhenvald makes her assumption that "expressing an appropriate information source and choosing the correct marking for it, has nothing to do with one's 'epistemic stance', point of view, or personal reliability" (2004: 5) a Procrustean bed in which she makes Ladakhi lie. One may also note that for Koshal the 'reportive' past is "based on direct and definite knowledge" (1979: 197). Thus, Bhat and Aikhenvald have radically misreported Koshal's description, distracted by a specious resemblance of terminology.

and four for the past tense (*-pin* performed by speaker, *-Ø* seen, *-tok* unseen, and *-kyak* inferred). In the Jakobsonian tradition, Zeisler describes a binary contrast between 'non-experiential knowledge' marked with *yot* and 'experiential knowledge' marked by *duk*, but proceeds to draw a further distinction within 'experiential knowledge' between visual evidence marked by *duk* and other sense evidence marked by *rak* (2004: 650). She places additional 'inferential markers' (*-ok*) and 'distance markers' (*-suk*, *-kyak*) outside of this system (2004: 653).

In contrast to the cases of Balti and Ladakhi, researchers have been slow to recognize evidentiality in Purik. Bailey's (1920) Purik sketch grammar makes no reference to evidentially or person agreement. In their function as auxiliaries of durative aspect Rangan describes *jot* and *duk* as respectively indexing first person and second/third person (1979: 87/88). This description of Purik evidentiality as person persists into the 21st century. According to Bielmeier (2000) the existential *jot* "occurs in statements where the speaker plays a role as participant [...] but not as subject" (2000: 87) and *duk* is used "in sentences where the speaker does not play a syntactico-semantic role as participant" (2000: 89). Sharma (2004) effectively repeats Rangan's description of *jot* and *duk* as auxiliaries, using the terminology "first person" and "non-first person" (2004: 94) but he adds the caveat that this distribution is "not adhered to strictly" (2004: 94/95). In this context, where the sophistication of analysis lags far behind that of descriptions of other Tibetan varieties, Zemp's detailed discussion of Purik evidentiality in the current volume is trail blazing.

1.3.2 Central varieties

Using Hale's (1971) 'conjunct-disjunct' paradigm, missionaries associated with the Summer Institute of Linguistics described the evidential systems of several Central Tibetan varieties spoken in Nepal, viz. Jirel (Strahm 1975), Sherpa (Schöttelndreyer 1980), and Lhomi (Vesalainen and Vesalainen 1980). As mentioned earlier, these early descriptions (e.g. Schöttelndreyer 1980) are generally syntactic in approach, but even among these older descriptions, a definition of the conjunct as meaning that there is "an experiencer ... who has been closely involved with the event of the main verb" (Vesalainen and Vesalainen 1980: 27) reflects personal evidentiality much more than any type of person agreement.

Sherpa received further attention in an article by Woodbury (1986), exploring the interaction of evidentiality and tense in lexical verb marking. He provides a very different account to the binary-focused conjunct-disjunct analysis presented in Schöttelndreyer (1980). Woodbury argues that the Sherpa form *nok* is used as a visual sensory evidential in the present tense (glossing with 'I see, have seen...') and an inferential evidential in the past (glossing with 'I hear, I infer...'). In the past, the form *suŋ* instead has sensory semantics. These two uses of *nok* can be attributed to it being used for 'immediate evidence', either evidence of the event itself taking place in the present, or the evidence of the aftermath of an event that allows the speaker to make an inferential claim. Woodbury also discusses *nok* as a future inferential, and *wi* as a 'gnomic', glossed with 'It is known'. Kelly (2004) draws on both traditions, outlining the semantics of each specific Sherpa evidential form, while also noting how it would be distributed in a conjunct/disjunct analysis. She discusses the *ĩ* verb suffix as a 'first-person conjunct' marking "a volitionally instigated event as having been directly experienced by a speaker" (Kelly 2004: 250). The form *suŋ* is a 'disjunct' used to "mark an event as having been directly witnessed by a speaker" (Kelly 2004: 250). Like Woodbury, Kelly (2004: 251/252) notes that *nok* can be used either as a visual sensory or inferential, but argues that instead of a tense-based distinction it is aspectual, with the sensory function in imperfective contexts and the inferential function in the perfective. Finally Kelly gives *wi* as gnomic (2004: 253), marking accepted ideas of how things happen. Tournadre et al. organize the evidential suffixes of Sherpa into paradigms. In their analysis in Sherpa "as in other Tibetic languages, there are three main types of evidentials: *factual* i.e., general or factual information, *sensory* [experiential] i.e., testimonial information (whereby the speaker is a witness), and *egophoric* [personal] i.e., based on the speaker's personal information" (Tournadre et al. 2009: 271 emphasis in original).

Kretschmar gives a very detailed description of the Tibetan dialect of South Mustang, but because she does not present an overview of the verbal paradigm it is difficult to gain an overall impression of the system. Her most clear description of evidentiality is in discussion of the copula verbs, which, as in all other Tibetan varieties, also serve as affixes in the verbal system. In her description the copulas distinguish only two evidential categories. The essential copulas *ra̱k* has "einen stärker konstatierenden Charakter [a strong reporting character]" (1995: 109) whereas with *ji̱n* "ein stärkeres persönliches Engagement zum Ausdruck kommt [a stronger personal committement is expressed]" (1995: 109). The existential copulas *ö̱* and its equivalent *ö̱ka ra̱k* express "persönliche Überzeugung [personal conviction]" whereas *du̱k* and its equivalent *öta rak* express "perönlich bezeugtes Wissen [personally certain knowledge]" (1995: 109).

In Melamchi Valley Yolmo, Hari presents the copula verbs in a table with a basic two-way distinction between "old or general knowledge" and "mirative/inferential forms" (2010: 63). She breaks down old or general knowledge further with '*yihn* being used for "truth, emphasized" and '*yeh* considered "neutral" (2010: 73). It is possible that the 'truth' that is being invoked in Hari's description is driven by a speaker's personal knowledge. Gawne (2014) argues that *ye* and *yin* (*yìmba* in the Lamjung variety) are egophoric (personal), although without the restriction on speaker relationship to subject that the Lhasa personal sometimes involves. The morpheme *dù* (Hari's 'mirative/inferential') is more prototypically a sensory evidential like its Lhasa Tibetan cognate. Hari (2010: 51) and Gawne (2014) also note that Yolmo has a general fact *òŋge*, which is not attested in other Tibetan varieties.

Central Tibetan varieties spoken inside of Tibet have received somewhat less attention than those of Nepal. Kretschmar (1986) describes the Drokpa dialect spoken in South West Tibet. She recognizes the same three evidential categories, personal, experiential, and factual, now familiar to the reader. In her account *yin* /jin/ (personal) "drückt das persönliche Engagement, die innere Regung des Sprechers aus [expresses a personal commitment to the inner emotion of the speaker]" (1986: 65) and *ḥdug* /tuk/ (experiential) expresses "die persönliche Kenntnis eines Geschehens [the personal knowledge of an event]" (1986: 65). The five suffixes /ö'/, /re'/, /ö:re'/, /te:/, /ö:te:/ "dienen zur Kennzeichnung einer allgemeinen Feststellung und zu distanzierter Beschreibung und werden ohne Unterschied gebraucht [are used to identify a general statement and distanced description and are used indiscriminately]" (1986: 65). It is surprising to see /ö'/ (presumably *yod*) among the factual suffixes. In addition, from a structural perspective the description of five suffixes with identical value is not possible. Hermann (1989) describes the Dingri dialect without making explicit reference to evidentiality. Her reference to grammatical person necessitates a 'conjunct-disjunct' style of presentation, although she shows no awareness of this tradition. The many details of its verbal system that resembles Lhasa, e.g. the formation of the present with *-ri ö̤:* (*ki-yod*) and *-ki-tuk* (*-ki-ḥdug*) and a "beobachtendes Präteritum [witnessing preterite]" formed with *-tšhuṅ (byuṅ)* and *soṅ (soṅ)* (1989: 72) succor an impression that this variety does encode evidential distinctions in its verbal system. Unfortunately, it is precisely in those aspects where the system least resembles Lhasa that the evidential components of its verbal system are most unclear. Haller (2000: 89) describes Shigatse as exhibiting three evidential categories, viz. volitional evidential, non-volitional evidential, and non-evidential, respectively cognate with the Lhasa personal, experiential, and factual.[21] Huber offers a description of Kyirong evidentiality (2005) in the tradition of binary feature opposition. Citing DeLancey (1986), she bifurcates the evidential settings into old and new knowledge (2005: 98).[22] Under 'old knowledge' she includes

---

[21] Note that this three-way contrast and the terminology for it he exactly repeats in his description of the Themchen dialect of Amdo (Haller 2004: 137).

[22] By describing 'old knowledge' and 'new knowledge' under the general rubric of 'evidentiality' (2005: 97), Huber makes clear that she disagrees with DeLancey's subsequent writings in which he sets up 'mirativity' in opposition to 'evidentiality' (1997, also cf. Hill 2012).

'generic knowledge' and 'personal experience'; under 'new information' she includes 'direct sensory evidence' and 'inference'. Huber does not justify the grouping together of these four evidential categories under the 'old' and 'new' rubrics on morphosyntactic grounds. A simpler and equally accurate account would flatten the description to four evidential categories of the same level. In general all four evidential options are available in each tense,[23] e.g. the imperfective distinguishes -kẽ: (generic knowledge), -ko-jø: (personal experience), -ko-nu: (direct sensory evidence), and -kojobajimbɛ (indirect evidence). The functional correspondence of the first three evidentials to the Lhasa factual, personal, and experiential is clear. However, the 'indirect' category is particular to Kyirong.

Denjongke, the Tibetan variety of Sikkim, has received very little study. Both in their use as present and future auxiliaries and in their use as copula verbs, Sandberg associates 'in with first person and be'/du' with second and third (1888: 19–21, 1895: 40–44). In the current volume, Yliniemi gives the first comprehensive treatment of Denjongke copulas and their evidential values.

Among the Tibetan varieties spoken in Bhutan, only Dzongkha is relatively well described. The early description of Dzongkha by Byrne (1909) is not currently available to us. In a much more recent work on Dzongkha, van Driem contrasts two evidential values, viz. "old, ingrained background knowledge which is or has become a firmly integrated part of one's conception of reality" typical of the equative copula 'ing and the existential copula yö, versus "knowledge which has been newly acquired" (1998: 127), typical of the equative copula 'immä and the existential copula dû. To identify this distinction with DeLancey's 'mirativity' (1997, 2001) would misunderstand van Driem profoundly (see van Driem 2015: 8/9). Van Driem describes the structural meaning of a language-internal contrast, whereas DeLancey imagines a typological category of crosslinguistic validity, and one distinct from evidentiality. In the current volume, Hyslop and Tshering further illustrate the evidential contrasts of Dzongkha. Although their analysis is fundamentally compatible with van Driem's they seek a terminology more in keeping with the Zeitgeist of functional and typological linguistics. Another Tibetan variety spoken in Bhutan, Chochangacha, has received almost no study. The recent article of Tournadre and Rigzin (2015) distinguishes three verbal categories that express experiential evidentiality, personal evidentiality and possibility. Atypically, Chochangacha uses yöt for the experiential existential copula and yöt-pi for the personal (Tournadre and Rigzin 2015: 64).

---

[23] In the aorist and future tenses she calls this evidential setting 'volitional' rather than 'personal experience' (2005: 98 et passim).

1.3.3 Eastern varieties

It is convenient to discuss eastern varieties according to division in terms of Tibet's traditional provinces of Amdo and Kham.

The three phased description of the study of Lhasa evidentiality employed above serves equally well for describing the history of research on the evidential systems of Amdo dialects. In the first phase, George de Roerich (1958) describes the Reb-gong dialect of Amdo (specifically the speech of the famous intellectual Dge-ḥdun chos-ḥphel, 1902–1951, cf. Stoddard 1985) in terms of verb agreement. For example, he gives *ṅa ȷ̑'o yŏ-jol'* (*ṅa ḥgro-gyin-yod*) 'je vais' [I go], *č"o ȷ̑'o yŏ-dïy* (*khyod ḥgro-gyin-ḥdug*) 'tu vas' [you go], etc. for *le present simple* (1958: 43) and *ṅa joṅ-nǒ-jin* (*ṅa yoṅ-ni-yin*) 'je suis venu' [I came], *č"o joṅ-nǒ-rel'* (*khyod yoṅ-ni-red*) 'tu est venu' [you came], etc. for one of three ways to conjugate *le passé accompli* (1958: 45). However, like the early researchers on Lhasa Tibetan, he makes clear that he is aware that what is at play here is not European style person agreement. For example, he notes that "[l]a conjugaison tibétaine – sauf quelques exceptions – ne connaît ni distinction de personne, ni distinction de nombre [Tibetan conjugation – with some exceptions – knows neither person distinctions nor number distinctions]" (1958: 43) and points out that "[e]xceptionnellement la forme *jin* s'étend aussi à la deuxième et troisième personne [exceptionally the *jin* form also extends to the second and third person]" giving the example *č"o joṅ-nǒ-jin* (*khyod yoṅ-ni-yin*) 'tu est venu' [you came] (1958: 45). A particular weakness of de Roerich's account of the Amdo verbal system is his failure to offer any semantic distinctions among the three ways of forming the *passé accompli*, which respectively exhibit *rel'*, *zïy*, and *t'a* as their exponents (1958: 45/46). Thus, Sun is justified in his criticism that in de Roerich's work the "evidential morphology is buried unanalyzed in his section on 'morphologie'" (Sun 1993: 948, Note 6).

Despite his criticism of de Roerich, Sun does not himself shake off reference to person. He recognizes a distinction between 'self person' and 'other person', which he equates with 'conjunct'/'disjunct' person marking.[24] His use of this distinction is however inconsistent. At times he appears to use 'self person' as a name for a morphological category, for example writing that "the volitional self-person forms (the default marking) represent direct knowledge of the volition" (1993: 961), but at other times 'self person' in his usage refers to a type of sentence regardless of how it is marked morphologically, for example he writes that

---

[24] Despite this equation of 'self person' and 'other person' with 'conjunct' and 'disjunct' respectively, Aikhenvald (2004: 45, 160, et passim), although she consulted Sun (1993), does not count Amdo Tibetan among those languages with conjunct-disjunct systems.

"[s]elf-person sentences containing such verbs are usually marked with the direct evidential" (1993: 692). From Sun's claim that "no particular evidential marking is employed for volitional self-person sentences" (1993: 958) one may surmise, along with Tribur (this volume), that the personal is zero-marked in Mdzo-dge Amdo.[25] Adding the 'personal', which he avoids describing as evidential, and omitting the 'quotative', which he includes although it does not pattern with the other evidentials,[26] the system he describes equates to three evidential settings in the past tense, 'personal' (unmarked), 'direct' ($t^hœ$), and 'indirect' ($zəg$), and two evidential settings in the present tense 'personal' (unmarked), and 'immediate' ($^hkə$). This updated version of Sun's description, with two evidential settings in the present and three in the past closely corresponds to Wang's (1995) account. Taking the binary approach, Wang contrasts first person and third person forms in the future (respectively -rgyu-yin and rgyu-red) and present (respectively -gi-yod and -ko-gi), but offers three options for the past, viz. a first person (-btaṅ-ṅa), third person (-btaṅ-gzig) and an additional third person form that is used if "the speaker has witnessed the action occurred" (1995: 61). As befits a pedagogical grammar Wang avoids the opaque terminology of 'conjunct-disjunct', but his 'first person' includes second person interrogatives (1995: 59/60 et passim), so his description is in keeping with the conjunct-disjunct tradition. Sung and Rgyal describe the future and present contrast as 'subjective' (-a or -yin) versus 'objective' (-gi or -red) (2005: 168). The more complex options available in the past they enumerate as 'subjective' (-a), 'objective' (-zig), 'witnessed' (-thal), and 'focused', with the fourth setting again offering 'subjective' (-ni-yin) and 'objective' (-ni-red) alternatives (2005: 205/206). Shao, in his description of the A-rig dialect, also takes a binary approach. He analyses the affixes into eight 'personal' (自我中心) and 12 'non-personal' (非自我中心) affixes (2014: 49/50). Among the 'non-personal' he further distinguishes some forms as 'witnessed' (亲见) and 'assertive/factual' (断言/事实) (2014: 49/50).

---

25 Nonetheless, Sun's comment that as "in other Tibetan dialects, the equative copulas jən [yin] and re [red]... carry inherent epistemological values: jən indicates that the reported situation is well-known to the speaker, otherwise re is used" (Sun 1993: 951, Note 10) suggests that personal evidentiality is sometimes explicitly morphologically indexed.
26 Although the "quotative morpheme se is, on both categorical and distributional counts, at variance with the other three evidential markers" (1993: 991), Sun lists it with the others because "it is quite common for evidentials not to constitute a unitary morphological category in a given language" (1993: 992). Such an analysis is unjustified, and his reliance upon the authority of others shows how one unjustified analysis may beget another. The cognates of se, decedents of Written Tibetan zer, are not normally considered evidential suffixes.

Ebihara's (2011) description is again similar, but she does not pursue person across all tenses but instead regards some tenses as encoding person and others as encoding evidentiality. She describes ten auxiliaries in Amdo, six of these forms she sets off in pairs of 'conjunct' and 'disjunct' forms across the three tenses 'future', 'progressive' and 'explanation' (2011: 58). Three of the four remaining suffixes she describes as evidential in value, two of which she identifies as 'past' (2011: 68). An odd facet of her analysis is that the evidential she describes as "used to express the event that the speaker performed, made somebody to perform, or is familiar with" (2011: 68) she does not identify with the 'conjunct'.

A step away from a binary account, Haller describes three distinct evidential categories across six tenses in the Themchen dialect (2004: 137). This description comes close to a structural account, but his terminological choices 'volitional evidentiell', 'nicht-volitional evidentiell', and 'nicht-evidentiell' are still cast in terms of binary contrasts. Making use of original fieldwork on the Mgo-log dialect, Zoe Tribur (this volume), discusses in detail the previous research of Sun, Haller, and Ebihara. She emancipates herself from the specters of both person agreement and binary classificatory schemes, using the terminology 'egophoric', 'direct' and 'indirect'.

The similarity of the Amdo evidential system to Lhasa Tibetan is a point of controversy. Sun (1993) emphasizes the ways in which the Amdo evidential system differ from that of Lhasa, pointing out that the evidential exponents in the two languages are not cognate and suggesting that the Mdzo-dge system is less pragmatically flexible than the Lhasa system. The dissimilarity is however not as obvious as he presents it. The Mdzo-dge system corresponds very closely to the Themchen, but Haller (2004: 137/138) describes Themchen with the same labels he uses for the three categories of Shigatse cognate to the Lhasa personal, experiential, and factual (*vide supra*). Likewise, Tribur judges that the Amdo evidential categories "appears to correspond closely to the Standard Tibetan system" (p. 416 this volume).

The evidential systems of Kham dialects have so far received very little attention. In her description of the Nangchen dialect of Kham, Causemann (1989) does not clearly organize the verbal inflections into paradigms and does not describe the function of each affix individually. Nonetheless, for all tenses she distinguishes a witnessed (beobachtete) from a neutral form, and within the neutral forms distinguishing a typically first person from a typically third person form (1989: 104–108). The morphological material is often what one expects from Lhasa dialect (*-yin*, *-yod*, and *-red* as auxiliary verbs) and the system is also often parallel. The auxiliary verbs ˄*äin* (*yin*) and *re* (*red*) are used in the formation of the future (in the suffixes *dži-*˄*äin* and *dži-re*), with the former associated with first person or third person if the speaker feels responsibility for the verbal action (1989: 88) and the latter used for second and third persons or impersonal verbs in the first person (1989: 88). The durative present distinguishes what could easily be called the personal *-kï-^o'* (*ki-yod*), factual *-ki-re*, and experiential *ki-da* and the past distinguishes personal *-le-^äin*, factual *-le-re*, and experiential *-thi:*. Causemann's description leaves many questions open, e.g. the difference between the formation of the past with V-*thi:* and V-*pa-thi:* (1989: 108). Schwieger describes the verbal system of Brag-g.yab Tibetan without making explicit reference to evidentiality. He describes the present tense as marked with the three suffixes /jö:/, /jö: re:/, and /ṅgi/; the first is used "in Verbindung mit der ersten Person [in connection with the first person]", the second "hat allgemeineren Charakter [has more general character]" and the third expresses "die persönliche Wahrnehmung der Handlung [the personal perception of the action]" (1989: 34). Thus, the present tense of this variety exactly parallels Lhasa Tibetan. His presentation of the other tenses is less clear, perhaps in part because of the adverse circumstances under which his fieldwork was carried out (1989: 7/8). Suzuki (this volume) offers a preliminary treatment of the evidential system of Zhollam Tibetan. His discussion is based entirely on elicited data and does not organize the affixes into paradigms. The evidential systems of Nangchen, Brag-g.yab, Zhollam, and other Kham varieties certainly merit further research.

The Baima language, which is not traditionally regarded as either an Amdo or Kham variety, serves as a fitting variety to conclude our discussion of research on Tibetan evidential systems aside from Lhasa. The evidential system of Baima, spoken at the border of Sichuan and Gansu, has received treatment in only one short article (Chirkova 2008). The author of that study, Katia Chirkova, returns in the current volume to the same topic, with much more detail provided by fresh fieldwork.

1.4 The historical development of Tibetan evidentials

According to many authorities the evidentials in Tibetan varieties arose independently in the recent past. According to Beckwith "there is not the slightest evidence for the existence of personal deictic class in the Old Tibetan verbal system" (1992: 9). DeLancey concurs that Lhasa Tibetan evidential marking "is a recent innovation" (1992: 49). In Hongladarom's words "there are no attested evidential contrasts […] in the classical language" (1993: 52). Tournadre holds that "[l]'opposition égophorique/neutre n'existe pas dans la langue littéraire [the egophoric/neutral opposition does not exist in the literary language]" (1996: 220,

Note 9). These authors overlook Takeuchi's observation that in Old Tibetan *yin*, an antecedent of the Lhasa Tibetan personal, is used to "話し手の判断，意志を強調している [emphasize the speaker's judgment and will]" (1990: 12); one may hope that the recent translation of Takeuchi's article into English will precipitate the careful examination of his evidence (2014: 410). Similarly, Denwood remarks that in Classical Tibetan *ḥdug* "usually has strongly the sense of discovery that it retains in Lhasa Tibetan" as a marker of the experiential (1999: 246). Hill confirms Denwood's observation in texts from the 13th century onward (2013b). From an investigation of *yod* and *ḥdug* in the 14th century *Rgyal-rabs gsal-baḥi me-loṅ*. Hoshi concludes that in its basic components the Lhasa system was already in place at that time (2010). In the context of a detailed description of the verbal system of the 15th century *Mi la ras paḥi rnam thar*, among many other insights Oisel (2013: 81) identifies the contrast between the copula verbs *yin* (personal in Lhasa) and *red* (factual in Lhasa). His contribution to the current volume traces the development of this 15th century evidential system into Modern Literary Tibetan and Lhasa. The continued exploration of evidential values across the history of Tibetan literature will no doubt remain a fruitful domain of research.

1.5 Notation and nomenclature

The authors who have contributed to this volume work in a diverse range of languages and approaches. We have exercised restraint in imposing an artificial univocality on the volume. In this section we discuss some of the notation and nomenclature that the reader will encounter. Although we have our own preferences, in general we have allowed the naturally arising heterogeneity to persist. In particular regard to evidentiality we have not constrained authors in terms of the names they give the evidential categories present in any language. As we mentioned in §1 the terminology in discussions of Tibetan evidentials has never been consistent, and authors from different research traditions have different preferences. Nonetheless, we have asked authors to avoid the term 'egophoricity' precisely to eschew the resulting confusion described in §2.2.

For transcription each author employs his or her own phonemic orthography for the specific variety in question. Transliteration of Written Tibetan follows Wylie, de Nebesky-Wojkowitz, or Library of Congress conventions. With regard to interlinear glossing, where conventions exist in the Leipzig Glossing Rules (LGR) (Comrie et al. 2008), authors attempt to conform to these standards. The conventions of the LGR offer little guidance for glossing evidentiality. Authors in this volume have their own glossing conventions, depending on what terminology they use and categories they identify.

With regard to identifying the different Tibetan varieties as languages, dialects or some other nomenclature, different terms relate to different perspectives. In this chapter we have used the term 'Lhasa Tibetan'; other researchers refer to Standard Tibetan. Although there are some differences between the two varieties (Róna-Tas 1985: 160/161), some researchers use these terms interchangeably. As mentioned earlier in this introduction, the title of this work and this introduction refer to the varieties of Tibetan spoken today as Tibetan languages. Other possible formulations include 'Tibetan dialects' and 'Tibetic languages'. Tournadre (2014) argues for the term 'Tibetic' because the diversity of languages descending from Old Tibetan parallels the Germanic languages or Romance languages, i.e. Tibetic is a language family. Tournadre's characterization of the diversity of this family is not in doubt, however, the term 'dialect' serves to designate the 'Chinese dialects' (also called Sinitic languages) and the 'Arabic dialects', which are also both language families of considerable age, size, and diversity. As the distinction between 'dialect' and 'language' is political rather than scientific, it is perhaps most legitimate to defer to the sense that Tibetans have of sharing a single language. It is for similar reasons of political solidarity that speakers of Arabic and speakers of Chinese respectively regard themselves as speaking but one language. Some would want to draw the line between languages and dialects such that two mutually intelligible forms of speech are refereed to as 'dialects'. Such an effort is not possible given the current state of knowledge on Tibetan varieties. Based as it is on the monolithic and sociolinguistically naïve notion of mutual intelligibility, such a division, even if possible, would still do violence to the full picture of Tibetan linguistic diversity. Even if one accepts the description of members of the family as 'languages' rather than as 'dialects', there is no *a priori* need for -ic rather than -an. It is true that many Indo-European subbranches end in -ic (Celtic, Germanic, Slavic, etc.) but others end in -an (Tokharian, Anatolian, Indo-Iranian). The difference between -ic and -an is of no significance in Europe and there is no need to make an issue of it in Asia. Thus, the choice among 'Tibetan dialect', 'Tibetan language' and 'Tibetic language' in this volume is left to the authors; the reader should merely note that these three designations refer to the same notion.

Abbreviations

1 first person, 2 second person, 3 third person, ABL ablative, AUX auxiliary, COP copula, DEM demonstrative, DIR direct, EGO egophoric, ERG ergative, EXPER experience, F female, FUT future, GEN genitive, HON honorific, IND indirect,

INT intentional, INTER interrogative, IPFV imperfective, LOC locative, LQ limiting quantifier, M male, NUTRAL neutral, PE perceptual evidential, PFV perfective, PRS present tense, PROX proximal, PST past tense, REC receptive, SG singular, VIS visible evidential, Q question, QOM quote marker.

References

Agha, Asif. 1993. *Structural form and utterance context in Lhasa Tibetan: grammar and indexicality in a non-configurational language.* New York: Peter Lang.
Aikhenvald, Alexandra Y. 2004. *Evidentiality.* Oxford: Oxford University Press.
Aikhenvald, Alexandra Y. 2012. The essence of mirativity. *Linguistic Typology* 16(3). 435–85.
Aikhenvald, Alexandra Y. 2014. The grammar of knowledge: a cross-linguistic view of evidentials and the expression of information source. In Alexandra Y. Aikhenvald and R. M. W. Dixon (eds.), *The Grammar of Knowledge: A Cross-Linguistic Typology*, 1–50. Oxford: Oxford University Press.
Aikhenvald, Alexandra Y. 2015. Evidentials: Their links with other grammatical categories. *Linguistic Typology* 19(2). 239–277.
Bailey, T. Grahame. 1920. *Linguistic Studies from the Himalayas.* London: Royal Asiatic Society.
Bartee, Ellen. 1996. Deixis and spatiotemporal relations in Lhasa Tibetan. Arlington: The University of Texas MA thesis.
Bartee, Ellen. 2011. The role of animacy in the verbal morphology of Dongwang Tibetan. In Mark Turin and Bettina Zeisler (eds.), *Himalayan Languages and Linguistics: Studies in Phonology, Semantics, Morphology and Syntax*, 133–182. Leiden: Brill.
Bashir, Elena. 2010. Traces of mirativity in Shina. *Himalayan Linguistics* 9(2). 1–55.
Beckwith, Christopher I. 1992. Deictic class marking in Tibetan and Burmese. In M. Ratliff and E. Schiller (eds.), *Papers from the First Annual Meeting of the Southeast Asian Linguistics Society*, 1–14. Tempe: Arizona State University, Program for Southeast Asian Studies.
Bell, Charles. 1905. *Manual of Colloquial Tibetan.* Calcutta: Baptist Mission Press.
Bendix, Edward. 1974. Indo-Aryan and Tibeto-Burman contact as seen through Nepali and Newari verb tenses. *International Journal of Dravidian Linguistics* 3.1, 42–59.
Bhat, D. N. S. 1999. *The Prominence of Tense, Aspect and Mood.* Amsterdam: John Benjamins.
Bickel, Balthazar and Johanna Nichols. 2007. Inflectional morphology. In T. Shopen (ed.), *Language typology and syntactic description*, 169–240. Cambridge: Cambridge University Press (Revised second edition).
Bielmeier, Roland. 1985. *Das Märchen von Prinzen Čobzaṅ.* Sankt Augustin: VGH Wissenschaftsverlag.
Bielmeier, Roland. 2000. Syntactic, semantic and pragmatic-epistemic functions of auxiliaries in Western Tibetan. *Linguistics of the Tibeto-Burman Area* 23(2). 79–125.
Boas, Franz. 1911. Introduction. In F. Boas (ed.), *Handbook of American Indian Languages*, 5–83. Part i. Washington DC: Smithsonian Institution.
Byrne, St. Quentin. 1909. *A Colloquial Grammar of the Bhutanese Language.* Allahabad: Pioneer Press.
Caplow, Nancy. This volume. Inference and deferred evidence in Tibetan. In L. Gawne & N.W. Hill (eds.) *Evidential systems of Tibetan languages*, 225–257. Berlin; Boston: Mouton de Gruyter.

Causemann, Margret (1989). *Dialekt und Erzählungen der Nangchenpas*. Bonn: VGH Wissenschaftsverlag.
Chang, Kun & Betty Shefts. 1964. *A Manual of Spoken Tibetan (Lhasa Dialect)*. Seattle: University of Washington Press.
Chang, Kun & Betty Chang. 1984. The certainty hierarchy among Spoken Tibetan verbs of being. *Bulletin of the Institute of History and Philology, Academia Sinica* 55. 603–635.
Chirkova, Katia 2008. 白马语示证范畴及其与藏语方言的比较 baimayu shizheng fanchou ji qi yu Zangyu fangyan de bijiao [Evidentials in Baima and Tibetan dialects compared] 民族语文 *Minzu yuwen* 3. 36–43.
Chirkova, Katia. This volume. Evidentials in Pingwu Baima. In L. Gawne & N.W. Hill (eds.), *Evidential systems of Tibetan languages*, 445–459. Berlin; Boston: Mouton de Gruyter.
Chonjore, Tsetan. 2003. *Colloquial Tibetan: a textbook of the Lhasa dialect with reference grammar and exercises*. Dharamsala: Library of Tibetan Works and Archives.
Comrie, Bernard, Haspelmath, Martin, & Bickel, Balthasar. 2008. Leipzig glossing rules. http://www.eva.mpg.de/lingua/resources/glossing-rules.php Retrieved 2015-06-07
Curnow, Timothy Jowan. 2002a. Conjunct/disjunct marking in Awa Pit. *Linguistics* 40(3). 611–627.
Curnow, Timothy Jowan. 2002b. Conjunct/disjunct systems in Barbacoan languages. In Jeanie Castillo (ed.), *Proceedings from the fourth Workshop on American Indigenous Languages*, 3–12. (Santa Barbara Papers in Linguistics 11). Santa Barbara: UCSB Department of Linguistics.
Dahl, Östen. 2000. Egophoricity in discourse and syntax. *Functions of Language* 7(1). 37–77.
Daudey, Henriëtte. 2014a. A grammar of Wadu Pumi. Melbourne: La Trobe University dissertation.
Daudey, Henriëtte. 2014b. Volition and control in Wădū Pǔmǐ. *Linguistics of the Tibeto-Burman Area* 37(1). 75–103.
DeLancey, Scott. 1985. Lhasa Tibetan evidentials and the semantics of causation. *Proceedings of the Eleventh Annual Meeting of the Berkeley Linguistics Society*. 65–72.
DeLancey, Scott. 1986. Evidentiality and volitionality in Tibetan. In Wallace L. Chafe and Johanna Nichols (eds.), *Evidentiality: the linguistic coding of epistemology*, 203–213. Norwood, N.J.: Ablex Pub. Corp.
DeLancey, Scott. 1990. Ergativity and the cognitive model of event structure in Lhasa Tibetan. *Cognitive Linguistics* 1(3). 289–321.
DeLancey, Scott. 1992. The historical origin of the conjunct-disjunct pattern in Tibeto-Burman. *Acta Linguistica Hafniensia* 25. 289–321.
DeLancey, Scott 1997. Mirativity: The grammatical marking of unexpected information. *Linguistic Typology* 1. 33–52.
DeLancey, Scott. 2001. The mirative and evidentiality. *Journal of Pragmatics* 33. 369–382.
DeLancey, Scott. 2003. Lhasa Tibetan. In Graham Thurgood and Randy J. LaPolla (eds.), *The Sino-Tibetan languages*, 255–269. London: Routledge.
Delancey, Scott. 2012. Still mirative after all these years. *Linguistic Typology* 16 (3). 529–564.
DeLancey, Scott. 2015. The Historical Dynamics of Morphological Complexity in Trans-Himalayan. *Linguistic Discovery* 13(2), 60–79.
Denwood, Philip. 1999. *Tibetan*. Amsterdam: John Benjamins.
Desjarlais, Robert R. 1992. *Body and emotion: the aesthetics of illness and healing in the Nepal Himalayas*. Philadelphia: University of Pennsylvania Press.
Dickinson, Connie. 2000. Mirativity in Tsafiki. *Studies in Language* 24(2). 379–421.

van Driem, George. 1998. *Dzongkha*. Leiden: Research CNWS, School of Asian, African, and Amerindian Studies.
van Driem, George. 2015. Synoptic grammar of the Bumthang language: A language of the central Bhutan highlands. *Himalayan Linguistics Archive* 6. 1–77.
Ebihara Shiho. 2011. Amdo Tibetan. In Yasuhiro Yamakoshi (ed.), *Grammatical Sketches from the Field*, 41–78. Tokyo: Research Institute for Languages and Cultures of Asia and Africa (ILCAA), Tokyo University of Foreign Studies.
Ebihara, Shiho. This volume. Evidentiality of the Tibetan Verb snang. In L. Gawne & N.W. Hill (eds.), *Evidential systems of Tibetan languages*, 41–59. Berlin; Boston: Mouton de Gruyter.
Francke, August Hermann. 1901. A Sketch of Ladakhi Grammar. *Journal of the Royal Asiatic Society of Bengal* (Part 1-History, Literature, etc.) 70(1), extra No. 2. 1–63.
Garrett, Edward John. 2001. Evidentiality and Assertion in Tibetan. Los Angeles: University of California dissertation.
Gawne, Lauren. 2014. Evidentiality in Lamjung Yolmo. *Journal of the South East Asian Linguistics Society* 7. 76–96.
Gawne, Lauren. This volume. Egophoric evidentiality in Bodish languages. In L. Gawne & N.W. Hill (eds.), *Evidential systems of Tibetan languages*, 61–94. Berlin; Boston: Mouton de Gruyter.
Goldstein, Melvyn C. and Nawang Nornang. 1970. *Modern spoken Tibetan: Lhasa dialect*. Seattle: University of Washington Press.
Hagège, Claude. 1982. *La structure des langues, Que sais-je?* Paris: Presses Universitaires de France.
Hale, Austin. 1971. Person markers: conjunct and disjunct forms. Topics in Newari Grammar I. 1–12. SIL.
Hale, Austin. 1980. Person markers: Finite conjunct and disjunct verb forms in Newari. In R. L. Trail (ed.), *Papers in South-East Asian linguistics*, Vol. 7, 95–106. Canberra: Australian National University.
Hale, Austin & Kedār P. Shrestha. 2006. *Newār (Nepāl Bhāśā)*. Munich: Lincom Europa.
Haller, Felix (2000). *Dialekt und Erzählungen von Shigatse*. Bonn: VGH Wissenschaftsverlag.
Haller, Felix (2004). *Dialekt und Erzählungen von Themchen: sprachwissenschaftliche Beschreibung eines Nomadendialektes aus Nord-Amdo*. Bonn: VGH Wissenschaftsverlag.
Hargreaves, David. 2003. Kathmandu Newar (Nepal Bhāśā). In Graham Thurgood and Randy J. LaPolla (eds.), *The Sino-Tibetan Languages*, 371–384. London: Routledge.
Hargreaves, David. 2005. Agency and intentional action in Kathmandu Newar. *Himalayan Linguistics* 5. 1–48.
Hari, Anna Maria. 2010. *Yohlmo Sketch Grammar*. Kathmandu: Ekta books.
Henderson, Vincent C. 1903. *Tibetan manual*. Calcutta: Inspector General of Chinese imperial maritime customs.
Hermann, Silke. 1989. *Erzählungen und Dialekt von Dinri*. Bonn: VGH wissenschaftsverlag.
Hill, Nathan W. 2012. 'Mirativity' does not exist: ḥdug in 'Lhasa' Tibetan and other suspects. *Linguistic Typology* 16(3). 389–433.
Hill, Nathan W. 2013a. Contextual semantics of 'Lhasa' Tibetan evidentials. *SKASE Journal of Theoretical Linguistics* 10(3). 47–54.
Hill, Nathan W. 2013b. ḥdug as a testimonial marker in Classical and Old Tibetan. *Himalayan Linguistics* 12(1). 1–16.
Hill, Nathan W. This volume. Testimonial perfect constructions: the inferential semantics of direct evidence. In L. Gawne & N.W. Hill (eds.), *Evidential systems of Tibetan languages*, 131–159. Berlin; Boston: Mouton de Gruyter.

Hock, Hans Henrich. 2012. Sanskrit and Pāṇini–Core and Periphery. *Saṃskṛtavimarśaḥ* 6: 85–102.
Hongladarom, Krisadawan. 1992. Semantic peculiarities of Tibetan verbs of being. In S. Luksaneeyanawin (ed.), *Pan-Asiatic Linguistics, Proceedings of the Third International Symposium on Language and Linguistics*, Vol. III. 1151–1162.
Hongladarom, Krisadawan. 1993. Evidentials in Tibetan: A dialogic study of the interplay between form and meaning. Bloomington: Indiana University dissertation.
Hoshi Izumi (星泉). 2010. 14 世紀チベット語文献『王統明示鏡』における存在動詞. 14 Seiki Chibetto-go bunken "ōtō meiji-kyō" ni okeru sonzaidōshi. [Existential verbs in the Rgyal rabs gsal ba'i me long, a 14th century Tibetan narrative]. 東京大学言語学論集 *Tōkyōdaigaku gengo-gaku ronshū* / *Tokyo University Linguistic Papers* 29(3). 29–68.
Hoshi Michiyo (星 実千代). 1988. 現代チベット語文法（ラサ方言）. *Gendai Chibetto-go bunpō (Rasahōgen)*. [Modern Tibetan grammar (Lhasa Dialect)]. Tokyo: ユネスコ東アジア文化研究センター Yunesuko Higashi Ajia Bunka Kenkyū Sentā.
Huber, Brigitte. 2005. *The Tibetan dialect of Lende (Kyirong)*. Bonn: VGH Wissenschaftsverlag.
Hyslop, Gwendolyn & Karma Tshering. This volume. An overview of some epistemic categories in Dzongkha. In L. Gawne & N.W. Hill (eds.), *Evidential systems of Tibetan languages*, 351–365. Berlin; Boston: Mouton de Gruyter.
Jones, Eunice. 2009. Evidentiality and Mirativity in Balti. London: SOAS, University of London MA thesis.
Kelly, Barbara F. 2004. A grammar of Sherpa. In C. Genetti (ed.), *Tibeto-Burman languages of Nepal: Manange and Sherpa*, 232–440. Canberra: Pacific Linguistics.
Kitamura Hajime. 1977. *Tibetan (Lhasa dialect)*. Tokyo: Ajia Afurika gengo bunka kenkyūjo.
Koshal, Sanyukta. 1979. *Ladakhi Grammar*. Delhi: Motilal Banarsidass.
Knuchel, Dominique. 2015. A comparative study of egophoric marking: Investigating its relation to person and epistemic marking in three language families. Stockholm: Stockholms universitet MA thesis.
Kretschmar, Monika. 1986. *Erzählungen und Dialekt der Drokpas aus Südwest-Tibet*. Sankt Augustin: VGH Wissenschaftsverlag.
Kretschmar, Monika. 1995. *Erzählungen und Dialekt aus Südmustang*. Bonn: VGH Wissenschaftsverlag.
Lidz, Liberty A. 2010. *A Descriptive Grammar of Yongning Na (Mosuo)*. Austin: University of Texas dissertation.
Loughnane, Robyn. 2009. A Grammar of Oksapmin. Melbourne: University of Melbourne dissertation.
Norman, Rebecca. 2001. *Getting Started in Ladakhi*. (2nd edition). Leh: Melong Publications.
Oisel, Guillaume. 2013. Morphosyntaxe et sémantique des auxiliaires et des connecteurs du Tibétain Littéraire. Paris: Université Sorbonne Nouvelle - Paris 3 dissertation.
Oisel, Guillaume. This volume. On the origin of the Lhasa Tibetan evidentials *song* and *byung*. In L. Gawne & N.W. Hill (eds.), *Evidential systems of Tibetan languages*, 161–183. Berlin; Boston: Mouton de Gruyter.
Oswalt, Robert L. 1986. The evidential system of Kashaya. In Wallace L. Chafe & Johanna Nichols (eds.), *Evidentiality: the linguistic coding of epistemology*, 29–45. Norwood, N.J.: Ablex Pub. Corp.
Post, Mark W. 2007. *A Grammar of Galo*. Melbourne: La Trobe University dissertation.
Post, Mark W. 2013. Person-sensitive TAME marking in Galo: Historical origins and functional motivation. In T. Thornes, E. Andvik, G. Hyslop & J. Jansen (eds.), *Functional-Historical Approaches to Explanation*, 107–130. Amsterdam: John Benjamins.

Rangan, K. 1979. *Purik Grammar*. Mysore: Central Institute of Indian Languages.
Read, Alfred F. C. 1934. *Balti Grammar*. London: Royal Asiatic Society.
de Roerich, George. 1958. *Le parler de l'Amdo: étude d'un dialecte archaïque du Tibet*. Rome: Istituto Italiano per il Medio ed Estremo Oriente.
Roerich, George & Lopsang Phuntshok. 1957. *Textbook of colloquial Tibetan: dialect of central Tibet*. Calcutta: Govt. of West Bengal, Education Dept., Education Bureau.
Róna-Tas, András. 1985. *Wiener Vorlesungen zur Sprach- und Kulturgeschichte Tibets*. Wien: Arbeitskreis für Tibetische und Buddhistische Studien, Universität Wien.
Rule, W. M. 1977. *A comparative study of the Foe, Huli and Pole languages of Papua New Guinea*. Sydney: University of Sydney.
San Roque, Lila. 2008. *An introduction to Duna grammar*. Canberre: The Australian National University dissertation.
San Roque, Lila, Floyd, Simeon, & Norcliffe, Elisabeth. 2017. Evidentiality and interrogativity. *Lingua*. 120–143.
San Roque, Lila & Robin Loughnane. 2012. The New Guinea Highlands evidentiality area. *Linguistic Typology* 16(1). 111–167.
Sandberg, Graham. 1894. *Hand-book of colloquial Tibetan*. A practical guide to the language of Central Tibet. Calcutta: Thacker, Spink and co.
Sandberg, Graham. 1888. *Manual of the Sikkim Bhutia Language or Dénjong Ké*. Calcutta: Oxford Mission Press.
Sandberg, Graham. 1895. *Manual of the Sikkim Bhutia Language or Dénjong Ké* (second and enlarged edition). London: Archibald Constable & Co.
Schwieger, Peter. 1989. *Tibetisches Erzählgut aus Brag-g.yab: Texte mit Übersetzungen, grammatischem Abriss und Glossar*. Bonn: VGH Wissenschaftsverlag.
Schwieger, Peter. 2002. Zur Funktion der verbalen Kongruenz im Lhasa-Tibetischen. In D. Dimitrov, U. Roesler, and R. Steiner (eds.), 175–184. *Sikhisamuccayah: Indian and Tibetan Studies*. Wien: Arbeitskreis für Tibetische und Buddhistische Studien, Universität Wien.
Schöttelndreyer, Burkhard. 1980. Person Markers in Sherpa. In S. A. Wurm (ed.), *Papers in Southeast Asian Linguistics No.7*, 125–130. Canberra: The Australian National University.
Shao, Mingyuan (邵明園). 2014. 安多藏语阿柔话的示证范畴 Anduo zangyu arou hua de shizheng fanchou [Evidentiality in A-rig Dialect of Amdo Tibetan]. Nankai: Nankai University dissertation.
Sharma, D. D. 2004. *Tribal Languages of Ladakh. Part III. A Descriptive Grammar of Purki and Balti*. New Delhi: Mittal Publications.
Sresthacharya, Iswaranand, Jagan Nath Maskey & Austin Hale. 1971. *Conversational Newari*. Kathmandu: Summer Institute of Linguistics, Institute for Nepal Studies, Tribhuvan University.
Sresthacarya, Iswaranda. 1976. Some types of reduplication in the Newari verb phrase. *Contributions to Nepalese Studies* 3(1). 117–127.
Stoddard, Heather. 1985. *Le mendiant de l'Amdo*. Paris: Société d'ethnographie.
Strahm, Esther. 1975. Clause Patterns in Jirel. In Austin Hale (ed.), *Collected Papers on Sherpa, Jirel*, 73–146. Kirtipur: Summer Institute of Linguistics.
Sun, Jackson T.-S. 1993. Evidentials in Amdo Tibetan. *Bulletin of the Institute of History and Philology, Academia Sinica* 63(4). 143–188.
Suzuki, Hiroyuki. This volume. The evidential system of Zhollam Tibetan. In L. Gawne & N.W. Hill (eds.), *Evidential systems of Tibetan languages*, 423–444. Berlin; Boston: Mouton de Gruyter.

Sung, Kuo-ming & Lha Byams Rgyal. 2005. *Colloquial Amdo Tibetan: A Complete Course for Adult English Speakers*. Beijing: China Tibetology Publishing House.
Takeuchi, Tsuguhito (武内紹人). 1978. 現代チベット語における文の構造. *Gendai Chibetto-go ni okeru bun no kōzō* [The structure of the sentence in modern Tibetan]. Kyoto: Kyoto University MA thesis.
Takeuchi, Tsuguhito (武内紹人). 1990. チベット語の述部における助動詞の機能とその発達過程 Chibetto-go no jutsubu ni okeru jodōshi no kinō to sono hattatsu katei / The semantic Function of Auxiliary verbs in Tibetan and their historical development. In Osamu Sakiyama and Akihiro Sato (eds.), *Asian Languages and General Linguistics*, 6–16. Tokyo: Sanseido.
Takeuchi, Tsuguhito (武内紹人). 2014. The function of auxiliary verbs in Tibetan predicates and their historical development. *Revue d'Etudes Tibétaines* 31. 401–415. (Translation of Takeuchi 1990).
Tournadre, Nicolas. 1992. La déixis en tibétain: quelques faits remarquables. In Morel M.-A. et Danon-Boileau L. (ed.), *La Deixis*, 197–208. Paris: Presses Universitaires de France.
Tournadre, Nicolas. 1994. Personne et médiatifs en tibétain. *Faits de langues* 3. 149–158.
Tournadre, Nicolas. 1996. *L'ergativité en tibétain: approche morphosyntaxique de la langue parlée*. Louvain: Peeters.
Tournadre, Nicolas. 2008. Arguments against the concept of 'conjunct'/'disjunct' in Tibetan. In B. Huber, M. Volkart & P. Widmer (eds.), *Chomolangma, Demawend und Kasbek, Festschrift für Roland Bielmeier*, 281–308. Saale: International Institute for Tibetan and Buddhist Studies.
Tournadre Nicolas. 2014. The Tibetic languages and their classification. In Nathan W. Hill and Thomas Owen-Smith (eds.), *Trans-Himalayan linguistics, historical and descriptive linguistics of the Himalayan area*, 105–130. Berlin: Mouton de Gruyter.
Tournadre, Nicolas. This volume. A typological sketch of evidential/epistemic categories in the Tibetic language. In L. Gawne & N.W. Hill (eds.), *Evidential systems of Tibetan languages*, 95–129. Berlin; Boston: Mouton de Gruyter.
Tournadre, Nicolas & Sangda Dorje. 2003. *Manual of standard Tibetan: Language and civilisation*. Ithaca: Snowlion Publications.
Tournadre, Nicolas & Sangda Dorje. 2009. *Manuel de tibétain standard: langue et civilisation*. Paris: Langues & mondes, L'Asiathèque.
Tournadre, Nicolas & Konchok Jiatso. 2001. Final auxiliary verbs in literary Tibetan and in the dialects. *Linguistics of the Tibeto-Burman Area* 23(3). 49–111.
Tournadre, Nicolas & Randy J. LaPolla. 2014. Towards a new approach to evidentiality: Issues and directions for research. *Linguistics of the Tibeto-Burman Area* 37(2). 240–263.
Tournadre, Nicolas & Karma Rigzin. 2015. Outline of Chocha-Ngacha. *Himalayan Linguistics* 14(2). 49–87.
Tournadre, Nicolas, Lhakpa Norbu Sherpa, Gyurme Chodrak & Guillaume Oisel. 2009. *Sherpa-English and English-Sherpa dictionary*. Kathmandu: Vajra Publication.
Tribur, Zoe. This volume. Observations on factors affecting the distributional properties of evidential markers in Amdo Tibetan. In L. Gawne & N.W. Hill (eds.), *Evidential systems of Tibetan languages*, 367–421. Berlin; Boston: Mouton de Gruyter.
Vesalainen, Olavi & Marja Vesalainen. 1980. *Clause Patterns in Lhomi*. Canberra: Pacific Linguistics, Australian National University.
Wang, Qingshan (王青山). 1995. *A Grammar of Spoken Amdo Tibetan*. Chengdu: Sichuan Nationality Publishing House.

Watters, David E. 2006. The conjunct-disjunct distinction in Kaike. *Nepalese Linguistics* 22. 300–319.
Woodbury, Anthony C. 1986. Interactions of tense and evidentiality: a study of Sherpa and English. In Wallace L. Chafe and Johanna Nichols (eds.), *Evidentiality: The Linguistic Coding of Epistemology*, 188–202. Norwood, NJ: Ablex.
Yliniemi, Juha. This volume. Copulas in Denjongke or Sikkimese Bhutia. In L. Gawne & N.W. Hill (eds.), *Evidential systems of Tibetan languages*, 297–349. Berlin; Boston: Mouton de Gruyter.
Yukawa Yasutoshi (湯川恭敏). 1966. チベット語のduuの意味 Chibettogo no duu no imi [The meaning of Tibetan duu]. 言語研究 *Gengo Kenkyū* 49. 77–84.
Yukawa Yasutoshi (湯川恭敏). 1971. チベット語の述部の輪郭 Chibettogo no jutsubu no rinkaku [Outline of Tibetan Predicates]. 言語学の基本問題 *Gengogaku no kihon mondai / Basic problems in linguistics*. Tokyo: 大修館書店 Taishūkan Shoten. 178–204.
Yukawa Yasutoshi (湯川恭敏). 1975. チベット語の述語 Chibettogo no jutsugo [The Predicates of Tibetan] アジア・アフリカ文法研究 *Ajia Afurika bunpō kenkyū / Asian & African Linguistics* 4. 1–14. Tokyo: ILCAA.
Yukawa Yasutoshi (湯川恭敏). This volume. Lhasa Tibetan Predicates. In L. Gawne & N.W. Hill (eds.), *Evidential systems of Tibetan languages*, 187–224. Berlin; Boston: Mouton de Gruyter. (Translation of Yukawa 1975).
Zeisler, Bettina. 2004. *Relative tense and aspectual values in Tibetan languages: A comparative study*. Berlin; New York: Mouton de Gruyter.
Zemp, Marius. This volume. Evidentiality in Purik Tibetan. In L. Gawne & N.W. Hill (eds.), *Evidential systems of Tibetan languages*, 261–296. Berlin; Boston: Mouton de Gruyter.

Typology and history

Shiho Ebihara
2 Evidentiality of the Tibetan verb *snang*

2.1 Introduction

This study analyzes the evidential usage of the Tibetan verb *snang* in spoken and written Tibetan. As is well known to Tibetologists, the Tibetan verb *'dug* (which originally meant 'to sit, remain, or stay') has a tendency to become an evidential marker. Thus far, a number of studies have shown the evidentiality of the verb *'dug* in many Tibetan dialects (Yukawa 1966; DeLancey 1986; Agha 1993; Hongladarom 1994; Tournadre 1996; Hoshi 1997; Häsler 1999; Garrett 2001; Hill 2012, etc.). In the Lhasa dialect of Central Tibetan *'dug* is described as a sensory evidential (Hill 2012: 329). In the same way as *'dug*, the verb *snang* also shows evidential senses in some dialects that are geographically widely distributed. *snang* originally meant 'to emit light, to be seen, appear' and was grammaticalized into an evidential marker. In contrast to *'dug*, *snang* has so far enjoyed little research attention, with the exception of a few publications (Suzuki 2006, 2012; Suzuki and Tshe ring 2009). Specifically, the geographical distribution and semantic variations of *snang* have not yet been investigated. This contribution presents a first attempt to consider the evidential use of Tibetan *snang* in a range of cases and to analyze its semantic variation, thus providing new data on the study of evidentials in Tibetan.

We will first provide an overview of the evidential usage of *snang* and consult the trace of evidential *snang* in Written Tibetan. Based on these data, the following points will be demonstrated: 1) the distribution of evidential *snang*, and 2) the semantic map of evidential *snang*.

2.2 The Tibetan verb *snang*

First, we will examine the basic meaning of *snang*. According to Jäschke (1949 [1881]), the verb *snang* generally means: (i) to emit light, to shine, to be bright; *shin tu mi snang ba'i mun pa* 'darkness entirely devoid of light', (ii) to be seen or perceived, to show one's self, to appear; *da lta rgyu zhig snang ngo* 'now an opportunity shows itself', (iii) =*yod pa*; *zer ba snang* 'it is said'. Since *yod pa* is one of the existential verbs in Tibetan, (iii) suggests that *snang* can be used as an existential verb. Although evidential meanings are not mentioned in dictionaries, descriptive studies show that *snang* is used as an evidential (sometimes an evidential-like) marker in some spoken Tibetan.

A typological study by Aikhenvald (2004: 271) notes that evidential specifications come from: (i) verbs of speech, (ii) verbs of perception, and, more rarely, from (iii) verbs of other semantic groups. Tibetan *snang* belongs to the second type.

2.3 Evidential *snang* in spoken Tibetan

We examine some examples of evidential meanings of *snang* in the following Tibetan dialects.

Western Archaic Tibetan
    Balti (Tyakshi)
    Balti (Turtuk)
    Balti (Khaplu)

Amdo Tibetan
    dPa' ris
    Thewo

Kham Tibetan
    Dongwang
    rGyalthang
    Bathang
    Budy
    Zhollam

Shar Tibetan
    sKyangtshang

Central Tibetan
    Reting
    Nyimachangra
    Drigung
    Penpo

Aikenvald (2004: 65) classifies evidential meanings into six types: (i) visual, (ii) sensory, (iii) inferential, (iv) assumptive, (v) hearsay, and (vi) quotative. Evidential *snang* in spoken Tibetan is related to (i) visual, (ii) sensory, and (iii) inferential. In what follows, we will see examples from each dialect.

2.3.1 Western Archaic Tibetan

Western Archaic Tibetan (Róna-Tas 1966, Bielmeier 1985) is spoken in north India and Pakistan and includes Ladakhi, Purik, and Balti. In Balti, *snang* is used as an evidential marker. The data from three dialects of Balti are shown here. Read classifies *naŋ* as a verb and said it "implies to be, in the sense of 'apparently is' or 'looks' to be" (1934: 61). Bielmeier (1985: 101) classifies -*aŋ* (suffix form of *naŋ*) as an auxiliary verb, and in the glossary, he repeats the explanation of Read (1934).

On the other hand, evidential *snang* is not attested in Ladakhi (Koshal 1979; Norman 2001) and Purik (Rangan 1979). In Ladakhi, *duk* (visual evidential) and *rak* (non-visual evidential) are used as evidential markers.

2.3.1.1 Tyakshi dialect of Balti

Tyakshi is one of the Balti dialects spoken in North India. The Tyakshi data are taken from the present author's field notes. In this dialect, *naŋ* (as well as its negative form *medaŋ*) is used as an evidential marker. This verb can be used as (a) an existential verb (expressing existence and possession), and (b) an auxiliary in both adjective and verb clauses, and marks 'speaker's sensory evidential' (both visual and non-visual).

The verb *naŋ* contrasts with another existential verb *jot*, which marks 'speaker's knowledge.'

Tab. 1: Existential Verbs in Tyaksi Dialect.

	Affirmative	Negative
Sensory evidential	naŋ	medaŋ
Speaker's knowledge	jot	met

The first two examples show *naŋ* and *jot* used as existential verbs. Example (1) illustrates that *naŋ* can indicate both visual and non-visual evidence. On the other hand, *jot* can show speaker's knowledge, as in (2).

(1) *firola*   *kʰyi*   *naŋ.*
    outside   dog   snang
    'There is a dog outside.' (speaker sees or hears a dog barking)

(2) *ŋa=la*   *naŋ*   *tɕi*   *jot.*
    1SG=DAT   house   one   yod
    'I have a house.' (speaker has known about this fact)

The next examples are *naŋ* and *jot* used in adjective clauses.[1] In these examples, *naŋ* appears as an auxiliary verb following the adjectives. The consultant for this dialect added that example (3) is suitable for the speech of foreigners who come to Turtuk (a village where Balti is spoken) for the first time, and (4) is for the speech of native people who are familiar with the place.

(3) *turtuk gaçe naŋ.*
Turtuk beautiful *snang*
'Turtuk is beautiful.' (speaker sees, suitable for foreigner's speech)

(4) *turtuk gaçe jot.*
Turtuk beautiful *yod*
'Turtuk is beautiful.' (speaker is familiar with the place, suitable for native people's speech)

naŋ can express both visual and non-visual evidence (smell, taste, feel), as in (5)–(8).

(5) *gaçe naŋ.*
beautiful *snang*
'It's beautiful.' (visual)

(6) *ṭi ẓimbo naŋ.*
smell tasty *snang*
'It smells good.' (smell)

(7) *Paju jaŋmo naŋ.*
salt light *snang*
'It's not salty.' (taste)

(8) *graxmo naŋ.*
cold *snang*
'It's cold.' (feel)

The following examples are *naŋ* and *jot* used in verb clauses. After a verb, *naŋ* appears as a suffix *-aŋ*, as in (9).

(9) *ɲima nub-aŋ.*
sun set-*snang*
'The sun is setting.' (visual)

---

[1] The term adjective here is used for referring the words belonging to the noun class which derive from stative verbs by affixation or reduplication.

Example (10) is an expression used when the speaker knows that something is biting her because she can feel it, or sees a dog biting. Example (11) is an expression used when the speaker knows that someone is talking like this because she can hear it.

(10) *kʰyi   kʰril-aŋ.*
　　　dog   bite-*snang*
　　　'A dog is biting.' (feel or visual)

(11) *do-tsok   zer-aŋ.*
　　　this-like talk-*snang*
　　　'[He is] talking like this.' (hear)

2.3.2 Turtuk dialect of Balti

Turtuk is one of the Balti dialects spoken in North India. The Turtuk data are also taken from the present author's field notes. In this dialect, *naŋ* (as well as its negative form *meraŋ*) is used to express sensory evidential (visual and non-visual). In contrast, *jot* (as well as its negative form *met*) is used to express speaker's knowledge. *naŋ* is used as an existential verb, and an auxiliary in both adjective and verb clauses, as in (12)–(16).

Tab. 2: Existential Verbs in the Turtuk Dialect.

	Affirmative	Negative
Sensory evidential	*naŋ*	*meraŋ*
Speaker's knowledge	*jot*	*met*

(12) *diga   naŋ.*
　　　here   *snang*
　　　'[Something] is here.' (visual)

(13) *gontɕa   gaɕe   naŋ.*
　　　clothes   beautiful *snang*
　　　'The clothes are beautiful.' (visual)

(14) *tri   ʑimpo   naŋ.*
　　　smell   delicious *snang*
　　　'It smells good.' (smell)

(15) *tɕa   tronmo   naŋ.*
    tea   hot   *snang*
    'The tea is hot.' (feel)

(16) *kʰo   oŋ=ŋaŋ.*
    3SG   come=*snang*
    'He is coming.' (visual)

2.3.3 Khaplu dialect of Balti

Khaplu (Khapalu) is one of the Balti dialects spoken in Pakistan. The Khaplu data are taken from Sprigg (2002), who wrote a Balti dictionary. Sprigg defines *nang* as '(seem to) be' and *met-nang* as '(apparently) is not' (Sprigg 2002: 113, 120). Sprigg (2002) does not provide further explanations or examples of *nang* and *met-nang*.

Tab. 3: Existential Verbs in Khaplu Dialect.

	Affirmative	Negative
'(seem to) be'	*nang*	*met-nang*
'be, is, are, exist, have'	*yot*	*met*

2.3.4 Amdo Tibetan

Amdo Tibetan is spoken in the north-eastern part of Tibet. In Amdo Tibetan, *snang* is seldom used; the use of *snang* as an evidential verb is attested only in dPa' ris [χwari] and Thewo.

2.3.4.1 dPa' ris dialect

dPa' ris is one of the dialects of Amdo Tibetan. This dialect is spoken in the north-eastern end of the Qinghai-Tibet highlands. The dPa' ris data are taken from Ebihara (2012: 153–156). In dPa' ris, *ɲaŋ* (as well as its negative form *menaŋ*) is used as an existential verb (expressing existence and possession), and an auxiliary verb. *ɲaŋ* is mostly used in events concerning the third person (when the speaker does not know the person well), but in some cases is used for events concerning the first person (such as physical phenomena or newly discovered information). That is to say, these verbs are used for non-egophoric expressions, as in (17)–(20).

(17) htandzən=na χʷiɕʰa ṇaŋ.
    PSN=LOC   book   snang
    'Tandzin has a book.'

(18) ndə=na   χʷiɕʰa menaŋ.
    this=LOC book   snang.NEG
    'The book is not here.'

(19) ntʰoŋ-sʰa   menaŋ.
    drink-place snang.NEG
    Literal translation: 'There is no place [for me] to drink.'
    More natural translation: 'I cannot drink.'

(20) ŋə   χʷiɕʰa ndə=na   ṇaŋ.
    1SG.GEN   book   this=LOC snang
    'My book is here!' (This expression focuses on the newly discovered information after searching for the book)

Another existential verb *jol* (as well as its negative form *mel*) is mostly used in events where the first person is relevant and questions the second person. That is to say, *jol* is used for egophoric expressions.

(21) ŋɔ: χʷiɕʰa jol.
    1SG.DAT   book   yod
    'I have a book.'

(22) tɕʰo   χʷiɕʰa ə-jol.
    2SG.DAT   book   Q-yod
    'Do you have a book?'

This verb *jol* can be followed by an auxiliary verb =*kʰə* 'state, attribution,' while *jok* =*kʰə* is used in the same situation as *ṇaŋ*. In my research, there is no difference between these two existential expressions, and they are interchangeable in all examples. Furthermore, in native speakers' intuition they have the same functions.

(23) htandzən=na χʷiɕʰa jok=kʰə.
    PSN=LOC   book   yod=AUX
    'Tandzin has a book.'

(24) ntʰoŋ-sʰa   mek=kʰə.
    drink-place yod.NEG=AUX
    Literal translation: 'There is no place [for me] to drink.'
    More natural translation: 'I cannot drink.'

(25) ŋə   χʷiɕʰa   ndə=na   jok=kʰə.
     1SG.GEN   book   this=LOC   yod=AUX
     '(My) book is here!' (This expression focuses on the newly discovered information after searching for the book)

These three series of existential expressions are summarized in Tab. 4 below.

Tab. 4: Existential Verbs in dPa' ris Dialect.

	Affirmative	Negative
Egophoric	jol	mel
Non-egophoric	n̥aŋ	menaŋ
	jok=kʰə	mek=kʰə

The verbs n̥aŋ/menaŋ are also used as part of the 'progressive' auxiliary verb (=kʰə n̥aŋ/=kʰə menaŋ), and a second part of verb serialization (V n̥aŋ/V menaŋ), as in (26).

(26) ŋa   tɕʰamba   hok   n̥aŋ.
     1SG   a.cold   catch   snang
     'I caught a cold.'

2.3.4.2 Thewo dialect

Tournadre and Jiatso (2001: 87) pointed out that nɔ̃ (WT: snang) is used in Thewo, corresponding to 'dug in Standard Tibetan. Unfortunately, this study does not demonstrate any sentence including snang.

2.3.5 Kham Tibetan

Evidential snang is found in several Kham Tibetan dialects: Dongwang, rGyalthang, Bathang, Budy, and Zhollam. All of these dialects are spoken in southern Kham.

2.3.5.1 Dongwang dialect

The Dongwang data are taken from Bartee (2007). In Dongwang n̥õ (as well as its negative form ma-n̥õ) expresses the "direct visual evidential (imperfective)," and contrasts with tʰi, which is the "visual evidential (perfective)" (Bartee 2007: 369/370). She says, "[t]he imperfective direct visual evidential n̥õ has likely arisen from WT <snang> 'to feel' or 'to sense.' It is used when the time of speech and the time of the event are identical" (2007: 369). First, she shows sentences with the third person and second person subject.

(27) $kʰə^{55}$ $tɕʰe^{55}tɕi^{53}$ $^ndʐa^{13}$ n̥õ.
    3SG.ABS   tired   look.like   snang
    'She looks tired.' (speaker is looking at her)
    (Bartee 2007: 369)

(28) $kʰə^{55}$ na^{13} de   n̥õ.
    3SG.ABS   sick   CONT   snang
    'He is sick.' (speaker has seen him or is looking at him)
    (Bartee 2007: 370)

(29) $ɕe^{55}$ $ŋɯ^{55}ɕi^{11}$ $gæ^{53}$ de   n̥õ.
    2SG.ABS   sweat   VBZR   CONT   snang
    'You are sweating.' (speaker sees)
    (Bartee 2007: 369)

She then adds that "n̥õ sometimes occurs in clauses with non-control verbs and first person S or A argument," and explains example (30) as follows.

> In the portion of text expressed by (54)[=(30) in the present article], the speaker is relating events that had happened to her while she was unconscious. This is not like the mirative use of an evidential, as the hearsay in the third clause in (54) indicates that these events were related to her by others. Thus it is their visual knowledge that is being coded. (Bartee 2007: 370)

(30) gc^{55} $wõ^{53}$ $dʑe^{55}ŋa^{53}$ me^{13} $rõ^{13}$ $ʂə^{53}$ $ɾæ̃$ n̥õ
    minute   fifteen   NEG.COP.SELF   COND   die   INGRESS   snang
    bu^{353} $təi^{53}$ la   ma-n̥õ   sə.
    breath   one   even   NEG-snang   HS
    'If (we) had been fifteen minutes (later when we arrived at the hospital), I would have died. They say that (I) didn't have any breath whatsoever.'
    (Bartee 2007: 370)

2.3.5.2 rGyalthang dialect

The rGyalthang data are taken from Hongladarom (2004, 2007). According to Hongladarom (2007: 26), the existential copula n̥ã̄ŋ marks the speaker's new and unexpected knowledge (mirativity), and contrasts with other existential copulas: ndô, ndô rê, jŷ, jŷ rê. The dimensions of contrasts are summarized in Tab. 5.

Tab. 5: rGyalthang Existentials (Hongladarom 2007: 27).

	ndô	jŷ	ndô rê	jŷ rê	ŋāŋ
Participant perspective	SELF	SELF	OTHER	OTHER	–
Animacy	ANIM	INANIM	ANIM	INANIM	–
Evidentiality	–	–	VIS	NONVIS	–
Mirativity	–	–	–	–	MIR

(31) khũə̯-la   ɲēi   dʑēpa   ŋ̊āŋ.
     3SG-DAT   money   many   snang
     'He has a lot of money.' (speaker just found out)
     (Hongladarom 2007: 28)

(32) khũənata-la   tā   dʑēpa   ŋ̊āŋ.
     3PL-DAT   horse   a.lot   snang
     'They have many horses.' (speaker just found out)
     (Hongladarom 2007: 28)

(33) khũə-la   dēwā   ŋ̊āŋ.
     3SG-DAT   intelligent   snang
     'He is intelligent.' (I just discovered it)
     (Hongladarom 2007: 35)

(34) tʂhā   khȳ   ɲi-ŋ̊āŋ.
     water   boil   NEG-snang
     'There's no boiled water.' (I just found out)
     (Hongladarom 2004: 4)

2.3.5.3 Bathang dialect

The Bathang data are taken from Hongladarom (2004). She mentions that the existential verb ŋ̊òʔ marks a 'specific, mirative statement' and 'inference' when accompanying a 'be' verb (Hongladarom 2004: 7). Gesang and Gesang (2002: 89) give an example of *snang* in Bathang, but do not explain its specific meaning and function.

The first example marks the 'mirative' and the second is an example with combined '*be+snang*' that marks 'inference.'

(35) jâŋə̀   mā   tɕĩʔ   ŋ̊òʔ.
     up.there   person   one   snang
     'There is a person up there.' (I just found out)
     (Hongladarom 2004: 7)

(36) ʔâlā   khə̄y   tshūŋ   jăpò   rê   n̥ò?.
    this.year their   business good   be   *snang*
    'Their business is good this year.' (I could tell from the evidence)
    (Hongladarom 2004: 7)

2.3.5.4 Budy dialect

The Budy data are taken from Suzuki (2006). He mentions that n̥ō marks "inference from the situation" (Suzuki 2006: 6).

(37) tsʰəpa: ˈpoʔ nə   ˋn̥ò.
    rain   fall   *snang*
    'It seems that it has rained.' (speaker found the ground wet)
    (Suzuki 2006: 6)

2.3.5.5 Zhollam dialect

The Zhollam dialect of Gagatang Tibetan is spoken in southern Kham. The Zhollam data are taken from Suzuki (2012).² He mentions that n̥ɔŋ (as well as its negative form ˊmi-n̥ɔŋ) is mainly employed as follows: (1) copulative usage: equational and/or identificational functions for non-self-oriented speech without any specific evidentiality (example (38)); (2) existential usage: for both the existence of the subject and the speaker's intimate awareness of that existence (example (39)); (3) evidential usage as a verbal suffix: to represent the visual experience of a speech (examples (40) and (41)). He added that of these usages, the first usage is unique to the Zhollam dialect among the Tibetan dialects.

(38) khy-Ø   ˊpi:-Ø   n̥ɔŋ.
    3-ABS   Tibetan-ABS   *snang*
    'S/he is Tibetan.'
    (Suzuki 2012: 4)

(39) ˋna kʌ   ˊmə ⁿdo   ˋtsə:-Ø   ˆjuʔ-n̥ɔŋ.
    here   person   one-ABS   exist-*snang*
    'Here is one person.' (existential) (speaker saw from a window a person in the room)
    (Suzuki 2012: 7)

---

2 Also see Suzuki, this volume.

(40) ˊɕiŋ-Ø   ʰkẽ-mə-n̥ɔŋ.
    field-ABS   dry-PF- snang
    'The field has become dry.' (speaker has seen the dry field)
    (Suzuki 2012: 11)

(41) ˊtʌ mʌ   p̃ʰoŋ-Ø   ˆkʰoŋ tɕʌ-Ø.   ˊmʌ- ʰtʌ-n̥ɔŋ.
    recently   tree-ABS   peach-ABS   NEG-bear-snang
    'The tree did not bear peaches recently.' (speaker has seen the tree not bearing peaches)
    (Suzuki 2012: 11)

2.3.6 Shar Tibetan

Suzuki and dKon mchog Tshe ring (2009) note the evidential use of *snang* in the sKyangtshang dialect of Shar Tibetan spoken in Songpan in the Sichuan province. In this dialect, ^ʰ*nɔŋ* is used as an existential verb (expressing existence and possession). In sentences with third person subjects, ^ʰ*nɔŋ* is used to indicate the speaker's affirmation of the event, as in (42). When the other existential verb *joʔ* (WT *yod*) is used, inference based on a judgement of the situation is indicated, as in (43). Thus, speaker affirmation of ^ʰ*nɔŋ* contrasts with inference.

(42) ⁿkʰo: ɣɵʔ   nɛ   °pʰaʂ   ᵒʰnɔŋ   gə.
    house   under   suffix   pig   NEG-bear-snang   gi
    'There is a pig under the house (speaker has known about this fact)'

(43) ⁿ̥kho: ɣɵʔ   nɛ   °pʰaʂ   °joʔ   ɦdzə   reʔ.
    house   under   suffix   pig   yod   particle   COP
    'There is a pig under the house (speaker guesses it because s/he hears the voice)'

2.3.7 Central Tibetan

Tournadre and Jiatso (2001: 85/86) point out that *nãŋ* (WT: *snang*) is used in four dialects: Reting, Nyimachangra, Drigung (Nomad), and Penpo, in Central Tibetan, corresponding to *'dug* in standard Tibetan. Unfortunately, this study does not give any sentence including *snang*.

2.4 *snang* in written Tibetan

Evidentiality in written Tibetan is difficult to attest. Some scholars insist that evidentiality is attested in neither Old Tibetan[3] nor Classical Tibetan[4] (Zeisler 2000: 40) and some scholars say that evidentiality is attested in written Tibetan (Hoshi 2010; Hill 2013; Takeuchi 2015 etc.). For example, Hoshi (2010) suggests the difference between *yod* and *'dug* (sensory evidential) can be found in *Rgyal rabs gsal ba'i me long*.

In the case of *snang*, although the existence of evidential *snang* is not clear in Written Tibetan, some scholars mention the evidential usage in Written Tibetan (Bacot 1948; Yamaguchi 1998). Bacot (1948: 72) defines the construction *kyi snang ba* (-*kyi snang*-NMLZ) as 'seems to.' He provides the following example.

(44) *byed kyi   snang ba/*
do.IPF-*kyi*   *snang*-NMLZ
'Est faisant. Paraît faire.'
(translation by Bacot (1948: 72), glosses mine)

Yamaguchi (1998: 353) explains the constructions *yin par snang* (COP-NMLZ.DAT *snang*) and *yod par snang* (exist-NMLZ.DAT *snang*) in written Tibetan. He says these expressions have the same meaning as *yin par 'dug* (COP-NMLZ.DAT *'dug*) and *yod par 'dug* (exist-NMLZ.DAT *'dug*), which mark 'inference.' The following examples show the construction with *snang* used as 'inference.'

(45) *snyug rum   dgon par   gsheg pa ni*
Snyug rum   temple.DAT   go-NMLZ-TOP

lo   gnas brtan gyis   gus par
Lo   elder.monk-ERG   respect-NMLZ.DAT

ma byas pa'i   rgyu mtshan gyis
NEG-do.PF-NMLZ.GEN   reason-ERG

yin par   snang ngo /
COP-NMLZ.DAT   *snang*-SFP
'ニュクルム僧院にお行きになったのは、ロの長老が丁重にしなかったという原因によってそうなったかのようである。
[It seems to be because the elder monk in Lo did not pay respect that he went to *Snyug rum* temple].'
(*Deb ther sngon po*, Yamaguchi 1998: 354; English translation and glosses mine)

---

3 Mid-7th–end of 10th century.
4 11th–19th century.

(46) yab   sras   gnyis la   'dod pa
     father.HON son.HON   2-DAT   opinion

   mi mthun pa yang   *yod par*   *snang ngo /*
   NEG-correspond-NMLZ-also   exist-NMLZ.DAT   *snang*-SFP
   '父子二人の間に一致しない主張も実はあったらしいのである。'
   [There seems to be a difference of opinions between the father and his son].'
   (*Deb ther sngon po*, Yamaguchi 1998: 354; English translation and glosses mine)

When searching through texts, it is difficult to distinguish between the meanings 'appear' and 'exist' in Written Tibetan. For example, in the next example, which is from the Old Tibetan text of the treaty inscription of 821/822, Li and Coblin (1987: 79/80) translate *snang* as 'appear,' but it might also be interpreted as 'exist.'

(47) yul   gnyis kyi   bar na   dud   rdul ni   myi snang //
     country   2-GEN   between-LOC   smoke   dust-TOP   NEG-*snang*
   'Between the two countries smoke and dust (i.e. warfare) shall not appear.'
   (translation from Li and Coblin 1987: 79/80, glosses mine)

Regarding the use of *snang* in written Tibetan, it is interesting that in *Rgyal rabs gsal ba'i me long* (written in the 14th century), in his concluding remarks, the author mentions the policy of writing this book as follows:

> *snang skad dang/ gda' skad go dka' ba rnams bcos te gsal bar byas/*
>
> 'The speech of *snang* and speech of *gda'*, which are not easily understood have been corrected and made clear.' (the text is from Sa skya pa Bsod nams rgyal mtshan 1981, translation by the present author)

Both *snang* and *gda'* are existential verbs and grammaticalized as evidential markers in spoken Tibetan dialects. *gda'* is used in the Kham and Hor dialects (Tournadre and Jiatso 2001: 87). *snang skad* 'speech of *snang*' and *gda' skad* 'speech of *gda'*' seem to be varieties of Tibetan with the final endings *snang* and *gda'*. Presumably, these expressions might be thought of as dialectal variations, and are thus considered not standard for Written Tibetan. The statement suggests the possible trace of *snang* as a verb ending in the 14th century.

2.5 Conclusion

The evidential usages of *snang* in spoken and written Tibetan have been discussed above. We can see that evidential *snang* is widely used in modern Tibetan dialects. These areas are mapped in Fig. 1. It is worth noting that evidential *snang* ranges from the western to the eastern ends of the Tibetan speaking area. Geo-linguitsic analysis suggests that the use of evidential *snang*, which can be traced back to Old and Classical Tibetan, remains in the peripheral areas of Tibetan speaking area. As there is insufficient data regarding *snang* in Central Tibetan, its function is at present unclear, as is the reason for its isolated location in this area.

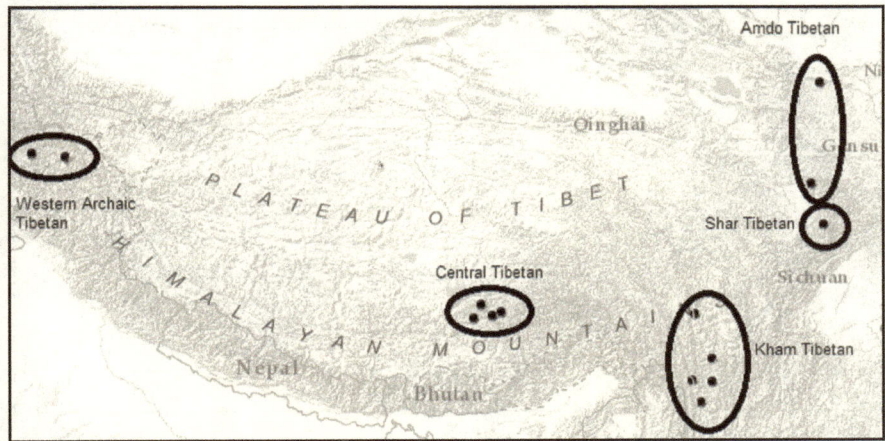

Fig. 1: Distribution of Evidential *snang*.

In the examples of several Tibetan dialects, we can see five evidential and evidential-like meanings/functions as shown below. The names of each dialect are mentioned in parentheses, though the meanings/functions in Thewo and five dialects of Central Tibetan are not clearly known. Speaker affirmation of *snang* in sKyangtshang, which contrasts with inference, does not show clear sources of information, and is thus not included in the following:

(i)   Visual (Dongwang)
(ii) Sensory (Tyakshi, Turtuk, Khaplu)
(iii) Inferential (Budy)
(iv) Non-Egophoric (dPa' ris, Zhollam)
(v)   Mirative (rGyalthang, Bathang)

After examining the evidence of a variety of Tibetan dialects, I have arrived at a semantic map for the meanings/functions of evidential *snang*. The semantic map is "a method for describing and illuminating the patterns of multifunctionality of grammatical morphemes that does not imply a commitment to a particular choice among monosemic and polysemic analyses" (Haspelmath 2003: 212).

This map is shown in Fig. 2. This diagram shows that visual and sensory meanings occur when the speaker sees the events, and the mirative then derives from these evidentials. Inference occurs when the speaker sees the result of the event. Lastly, the non-egophoric meaning has no participation in the event-result frame.

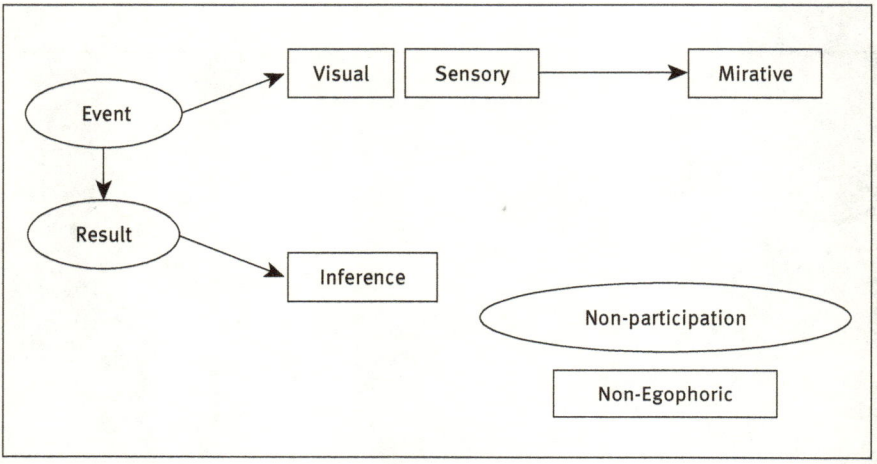

Fig. 2: The Semantic Map of the Meanings/Functions of Evidential *snang*.

In this study, examples of Written Tibetan could not be fully investigated, so that more research is required on the usage of *snang* in written texts, particularly concerning constructions such as *yod par snang, yin par snang, cing snang, gi snang,* and *V snang*. Figure 1 shows us that the geographical distribution of evidential *snang* is quite widely ranging. This distribution might have some connection to the historical development of *snang*. It is desirable that from this distribution, research on Written Tibetan will make the historical development and grammaticalization process of evidential *snang* clear in future.

Acknowledgments: Great thanks go to the consultants of Balti and Amdo Tibetan. This study is based on my presentation in the panel on Tibetan Evidentiality at the 24th conference of SEALS. I also thank the organizers and participants of the panel. I am grateful for many comments in the presentation, which were helpful for revising this chapter. In particular, Nicholas Tournadre and Hiroyuki Suzuki suggested useful resources for this study. Izumi Hoshi and Satoko Shirai also gave me valuable advice.

This study was supported by a Grant-in-Aid for Scientific Research funded by the Japan Society for the Promotion of Science "Formation of the oldest layer of Tibetan and its formational transition" headed by Tsuguhito Takeuchi

(2012–2017, project number 24242015), Linguistic Dynamics Science Project 2 (project for building an international network of collaborative research on endangered linguistic diversity) headed by Toshihide Nakayama.

Abbreviations

1 first person, 2 second person, 3 third person, ABS absolutive, AUX auxiliary verb, COND conditional, CONT continuative, COP copula, DAT dative, ERG ergative, GEN genitive, HON honorific, HS hearsay, IMP imperative, IPF imperfective, LOC locative, NEG negative, NMLZ nominalizer, PF perfective, PL plural, PSN personal name, Q question, SELF self, SFP sentence, final particle, SG singular, TOP topicalizer, VBZR verbalizer, WT Written Tibetan

- Affix boundary ; = Clitic boundary

References

Agha, Asif. 1993. *Structural form and utterance context in Lhasa Tibetan: Grammar and indexicality in a non-configurational language*. New York: Peter Lang.
Aikenvald, Alexandra Y. 2004. *Evidentiality*. New York: Oxford University Press.
Bacot, Jacques. 1948. *Grammaire du Tibétain littéraire*. Paris: Librairie d'Amérique et d'Orient.
Bartee, Ellen. 2007. *A grammar of Dongwang Tibetan*, University of California, Santa Barbara doctoral dissertation.
Bielmeier, Roland. 1985. *Das Märchen vom Prinzen Čobzaṅ. Eine tibetische Erzählung aus Baltistan. Text, Übersetzung, Grammatik und westtibetisch vergleichendes Glossar.* (Beiträge zur tibetischen Erzählforschung, 6.) St. Augustin: VGH Wissenschaftsverlag.
DeLancey, Scott. 1986. Evidentiality and volitionality in Tibetan. In Wallace Chafe & Johanna Nichols (eds.), *Evidentiality: The linguistic coding of epistemology*, 203–213. Norwood, NJ: Ablex Publishing Corporation.
Ebihara, Shiho. 2012. Preliminary field report on dPa'ris dialect of Amdo Tibetan. In Tsuguhito Takeuchi & Norihiko Hayashi (eds.), *Historical Development of the Tibetan Languages: Proceedings of the Workshop B of the 17th Himalayan Languages Symposium*, 149–161. Kobe: Kobe City University of Foreign Studies.
Garrett, Edward. 2001. *Evidentiality and assertion in Tibetan*. University of California, Los Angeles doctoral dissertation.
Ge sang Ju mian & Ge sang Yang jing 格桑局冕 & 格桑央京. 2002. *Zangyu fangyan gailun* 《藏语方言概论》 [An introduction to Tibetan dialects]. Beijing: Minzu Chubanshe 民族出版社.
Haspelmath, Martin. 2003. The geometry of grammatical meaning: Semantic maps and cross-linguistic comparison. In Michael Tomasello (ed.), *The new psychology of language*, vol. 2, 211–242. Mahwah, NJ: Lawrence Erlbaum.
Häsler, Katrin Louise. 1999. *A grammar of the Tibetan Dege (Sdege) dialect*. University of Bern doctoral dissertation.

Hill, Nathan. 2012. "Mirativity" does not exist: ḥdug in "Lhasa" Tibetan and other suspects. *Linguistic Typology* 16(3). 389–433.

Hill, Nathan. 2013. ḥdug as a testimonial marker in Classical and Old Tibetan. *Himalayan Linguistics* 12(1). 1–16.

Hongladarom, Krisadawan. 1994. Historical development of the Tibetan evidential tuu. Paper presented at the *Tibetan linguistics workshop, 26th international conference on Sino-Tibetan languages and linguistics*, October, National museum of ethnology: Osaka, Japan.

Hongladarom, Krisadawan. 2004. Development of evidentials in various dialects of Kham Tibetan. Paper presented at the *Evidentiality workshop*, September 30, organized concurrently with the *37th International Conference on Sino-Tibetan Languages and Linguistics*, University of Lund, Sweden.

Hongladarom, Krisadawan. 2007. Evidentiality in Rgyalthang Tibetan. *Linguistics of the Tibeto-Burman Area*, 30(2). 17–44.

Hoshi, Izumi 星泉. 1997. *Chibettogo Rasahōgenniokeru jutsugono imino kijutsuteki kenkyū* 《チベット語ラサ方言における述語の意味の記述的研究》 [Descriptive study on meanings of predicates in Lhasa dialect of Tibetan]. Tokyo University doctoral dissertation.

Hoshi, Izumi 星泉. 2010. 14 seiki Chibettogobunken ōtōmeijikyōniokeru Sonzaidōshi 14 世紀チベット語文献『王統明示鏡』における存在動詞 [Existential Verbs in the Rgyal-rabs Gsal-ba'i Me-long, a 14th century Tibetan narrative]. *Tokyo University Linguistic Papers 29*. 29–68.

Jäschke, H. A. 1949 [1881]. *A Tibetan-English dictionary*. London: Lowe and Brydone.

Koshal, Sanyukta. 1979. *Ladakhi Grammar*. Delhi: Motilal Banarsidass.

Li, Fang Kuei & Coblin, South W. 1987. *A study of the old Tibetan inscriptions*. Taipei: Institute of history and philology, Academia Sinica.

Norman, Rebecca. 2001. *Getting Started in Ladakhi*. (2nd edition). Leh: Melong Publications.

Rangan, K. 1979. *Purik Grammar*. Mysore: Central Institute of Indian Languages.

Read, Alfred F. C. 1934. *Balti Grammar*. London: Royal Asiatic Society.

Róna-Tas, A. 1966. *Tibeto-Mongolica: the Tibetan loanwords of Monguor and the development of the archaic Tibetan dialects*. The Hague: Mouton.

Sa skya pa Bsod nams rgyal mtshan. 1981. *Rgyal rabs gsal ba'i me long*. Beijing, Mi rigs dpe skrun khang.

Sprigg, Richard Keith. 2002. *Balti-English English-Balti dictionary*. Richmond: Routledge Curzon.

Suzuki, Hiroyuki 鈴木博之. 2006. Senseiminzokusōrō Chibettogo shohōgenniokeru snangno imi 川西民族走廊・チベット語諸方言におけるsnangの意味 [The meaning of snang in Tibetan dialects of the ethnic corridor in West Sichuan]. Paper presented at the *9th meeting of Tibeto-Burman Linguistic Circle*, July 17, Kyoto University, Japan.

Suzuki, Hiroyuki. 2012. Multiple usages of the verb 'snang' in Gagatang Tibetan (Weixi, Yunnan). *Himalayan Linguistics*, 11(1). 1–16.

Suzuki, Hiroyuki & dKon mchog Tshe ring 鈴木博之・供邱澤仁 2009. Hyaru Chibettogo Songpan Shanba [sKyangtshang] hōgenniokeru snangno yōhō ヒヤルチベット語松潘・山巴 [sKyangtshang] 方言におけるsnangの用法 [The Usage of snang in Songpan sKyangtshang dialect of Shar Tibetan]. In Onishi, Masayuki 大西正幸 & Kazuya Inagaki 稲垣和也 (eds.) *Chikyūken Gengo Kijutsu Ronshū*《地球研言語記述論集》1. 123–132.

Takeuchi, Tsuguhito. 2015. The function of auxiliary verbs in Tibetan predicates and their historical development. *Revue d'Etudes Tibétaines*, 31. 401–415.

Tournadre, Nicholas. 1996. *L'ergativité en Tibétain: Approche morphosyntaxique de la langue parlée*. Leuven: Peeters.

Tournadre, Nicholas & Konchok Jiatso. 2001. Final auxiliary verbs in literary Tibetan and in the dialects. *Linguistics of the Tibeto-Burman Area* 24(1). 49–111.

Yamaguchi, Zuihō 山口瑞鳳. 1998. *Chibettogo bungo bunpō* 《チベット語文語文法》 [Grammar of written Tibetan]. Tokyo: Shunjūsha 春秋社.

Yukawa, Yasutoshi 湯川恭敏. 1966. Chibettogono duu no imi チベット語のduuの意味 [The meaning of Tibetan duu]. *Gengo Kenkyū* 《言語研究》 [Journal of the Linguistic Society of Japan] 49. 77–84.

Zeisler, Bettina. 2000. Narrative conventions in Tibetan languages. The issue of mirativity. *Linguistics of the Tibeto-Burman Area*, 23(2). 39–77.

Lauren Gawne
3 Egophoric evidentiality in Bodish languages

3.1 Introduction

A common feature of evidentiality in Tibetan and related languages is a category that has been given a number of names, including 'egophoric' (Tournadre 2008), 'ego' (Garrett 2001), 'participant specific' (Agha 1993: 157), 'self-centred' (Denwood 2000), 'personal' (Hill 2012, this volume), 'personal knowledge' (van Driem 1998) and 'personal experience' (Huber 2005). As these names indicate, this evidential category is used when the source of information is the speaker's own knowledge state, rather than some external sensory perception, or public consensus.

While this category appears to share some similarities with evidential categories in other language families, there is yet to be any clear demonstration that there is a category with an equivalent breadth of use in other language families. Therefore, in a discussion of evidentiality in Tibetan languages, the category of egophoric evidential is an important topic. This chapter offers a description of egophoric evidentiality in Tibetan and related languages in relation to the cross-linguistic literature on evidentiality.

I begin by examining Standard Tibetan[1] (§2), as the Standard Tibetan egophoric is the most comprehensively described, and also appears to have some of the most specific restrictions on its use. I then look at discussions of egophoric and egophoric-like categories in other Tibetic languages (§3), before a brief discussion of the diachronic development of this category (§4). The egophoric in all of these Tibetic varieties indicates speakers' own knowledge as the evidential source, but the breadth of scope for that knowledge, and what it contrasts with differs among languages. I then look at discussions of egophoric categories in Bodish languages that are not part of the smaller Tibetic family (§5). The existence of egophoric categories in these languages indicates that it may be a larger areal feature, or perhaps the result of contact with Tibetic varieties. I then look briefly at the relationship between egophoric evidentials and the phenomenon of conjunct/disjunct and egophoricity (§6), before looking at how egophoric evidentials compare to similar categories in other language families (§7).

---

[1] Some of the authors I discuss in relation to Standard Tibetan refer to Lhasa Tibetan, or simply Tibetan. While I use the term Standard Tibetan to discuss all of these varieties, I acknowledge that there are differences between the 'Standard' and 'Lhasa' varieties (Róna-Tas 1985: 160/161).

Before I begin, a brief note on terminology is required. In this study I discuss the egophoric evidential category. I use the terms egophoric, and egophoric evidential(s) interchangeably. These need to be distinguished from 'egophoricity' (San Roque, Floyd, and Norcliffe 2015, forthcoming), and the older term 'conjunct/disjunct' (Hale 1980). Egophoric evidentiality is not necessarily related to these grammatical patterns, but has a history intertwined with them. DeLancey (1986, 1990, 1992) uses the terminology of 'conjunct/disjunct' in his analysis of Tibetan egophoric and perceptual evidentiality, which has influenced later typological work that draws on Tibetan (cf. Aikhenvald 2004). The term 'egophoricity' (derived from the use of egophoric in Tibetan) has been adopted by San Roque, Floyd, and Norcliffe (forthcoming, see also San Roque, Floyd, and Norcliffe 2015) for more contemporary discussions of a similar set of features that occur cross-linguistically. DeLancey (2012: 555) has now adopted 'egophoricity' in place of his earlier 'conjunct/disjunct' terminology for his work on Tibetan. Other Tibetic languages have been discussed under the rubric of conjunct/disjunct, particularly Sherpa (Schöttelndreyer 1980, Kelly 2004) and Amdo Tibetan (Ebihara 2010), although Tibetic researchers normally do not situate their analyses in these terms (see Tournadre 2008). Throughout this chapter egophoric specifically refers to the evidential category. I will mention egophoricity or conjunct/disjunct as per the original author where it is relevant, particularly in §6. I do not use the term egophoric for these patterns, but for the specific evidential category for which the term was originally coined (Tournadre 1991).[2]

3.2 Egophoric in Standard Tibetan

Egophoric is one of a number of evidential distinctions marked in Standard Tibetan, with sensory and factual evidential categories and a reported speech evidential particle also found in the language. The evidential distinctions are most often encoded in the copula verbs or auxiliary verb, with the auxiliary forms often

---

[2] This is somewhat different to the sense of 'egophoric' found in Dahl's (2000) discussion of Swedish, English and Spanish. Dahl's (2000: 37) definition states that "[e]gophoric reference is defined as reference to speech act participants (SAP) and generic reference", where generic references are used as a SAP in something like the English generic 'you'. Standard Tibetan 'egophoric' can include non-SAPs, but they are not 'generic'. The Tibetan egophoric is a specific distribution of grammatical forms in relation to a particular person or persons considered to hold a particular knowledge state.

related to the copulas. These forms may also encode tense or aspectual information (Tournadre 2008; Tournadre and Dorje 2003). Some authors prefer different terminology for these categories, for example in this volume Hill, Caplow and Yliniemi use the term 'personal' instead of 'egophoric', while Garrett (2001) uses 'ego'. Hill refers to the sensory as the 'testimonial', Garrett prefers the term 'direct' and I use 'perceptual' (see Gawne 2016). The term 'egophoric' was first coined by Tournadre (1991, 1996); Tournadre and Dorje give a clear description:

> Certain auxiliary verbs are associated only with *the first person* (singular or plural), irrespective of the function of that person in the sentence, i.e., as subject, object or complement. The use of an "egophoric" auxiliary expresses the speaker's knowledge or personal intention, often directly implied in the event that is being described. (Tournarde and Dorje 2003: 93, original emphasis)

This definition captures the primary importance of the first person (the 'ego' of the 'egophoric') but a later discussion by Tournadre and LaPolla (2014) goes into more detail, and demonstrates how it is infeasible to consider evidentiality, particularly egophoric evidentiality, as marking an objective source of information. Instead, it is best to think about "the speaker's representation of her *access* to the information represented in the utterance" (Tournadre and LaPolla 2014: 242 original emphasis). Egophoric evidentiality is therefore about a speaker's access to her own knowledge state regarding the information in the utterance. Egophoric evidentiality is marked on copula verbs and a related set of auxiliary verbs. Forms with egophoric semantics in Standard Tibetan include the existential copula <yod>, the equative copula <yin> and the receptive <byung>, as well as auxiliaries for future < V-gi-yin>, present <V-gi-yod>, past <V-pa-yin> and perfect <V-yod> (Garrett 2001: 11).

In example (1), the speaker's access to this knowledge is through personal knowledge of her own actions.

(1) nga-s   moṭa   btang-gi.***yod***
    I-ERG   car   drive-IPFV.**EGO**
    'I drive the car.'[3]
    (Tournadre 2008: 297)

---

[3] Interlinear glossing have been regularized across quoted examples where possible to meet the Leipzig Glossing Rules. A list of abbreviations is given at the end of the chapter. All examples are given in Roman script, with the transliteration maintained from the original author's example and only regularized where clear non-standard forms can be replaced with the appropriate IPA symbol, e.g. S > ʃ.

One of the most important features of Tournadre and Dorje's definition of egophoric evidentiality is that the speaker is drawing on her own personal information about her own state, or something that is very closely associated with her. This does not exclusively mean first-person marking, as the 'first person' element can be any part of the sentence, or in some contexts, absent altogether. For example, from Tournadre (2008: 295–297), we see that the egophoric copula used for the person's own actions as in (1) above, but also for the actions of other people, but only if they are closely related to the speaker (2).

(2) nga-'i   bu.mo-s   moṭa   btang-gi.**yod**
    I-GEN   daughter.ERG   car   drive-IPFV.**EGO**
    'my daughter drives the car.'
    (Tournadre 2008: 297)

The example below offers a way to tease out this specific feature of Tibetan egophoric. Example (3) was originally given by DeLancey (1986: 204), who argued that all three English translations could be feasible. The example was reanalysed by Garrett (2001: 102), who argued that the sense in (3a) is not possible with an egophoric evidential:

(3) bod-la   g.yag   **yod**
    Tibet-LOC   yak   **EGO**
    a) ??'There are yaks in Tibet.'
    b) 'I have yaks in Tibet.'
    c) 'My yaks are in Tibet.'
    (DeLancey 1986: 204 [question marks from Garrett 2001: 102])

DeLancey argues (1986: 204) that speakers of Standard Tibetan will accept meaning (3a) if they have had long term exposure to and knowledge of the presence of yaks in Tibet. This is part of a tangentially related argument about the status of the sensory evidential as a mirative marker, and therefore the egophoric as decidedly non-mirative. Garrett argues that no speaker of Standard Tibetan would accept (3a), but would find both (3b) and (3c) felicitous. Garrett's analysis fits with an understanding of egophoric *yod* only occurring in situations where the speaker has a personal connection to the yaks. Standard Tibetan egophoric does not just encode personal knowledge though extended exposure, but may also be used because of some real personal link to the content of the proposition, even sometimes when the speaker is not overtly expressed in the clause.

Egophoric in Standard Tibetan can only be used for first person when the speaker did something over which she had control. This means that non-volitional actions (such as 'see', as opposed to the volitional 'look') for first person are not marked with egophoric but with direct perception (4).

(4) nga-s   mthong-song/*mthong-pa-yin
    I-ERG   see-DIR.PST/*see-EGO.PST
    'I saw it.'
    (Garrett 2001: 18)

It is in this regard that the issue of 'access' is important in the understanding of the egophoric. A speaker must have access to her own knowledge to be able to use the egophoric, and in non-volitional situations that access is not available.

Volitionality is an important feature of most egophoric forms in Standard Tibetan because it establishes the importance of the cognitively active individual. Of course, the status of volitionality in pure copula contexts is perhaps not so relevant; in example (3) above it is not necessary that I wish intentionally for the yaks to belong to me. Volitionality does appear to be relevant to actions however, and as I will discuss below, is relevant to the discussion of egophoric evidentiality in other varieties.

Tournadre (2008) and Garrett (2001), amongst others, have broadly conceptualized egophoric as having two different levels, depending on how strictly the 'first person' component is evoked. The usage in example (1) would be 'narrow' scope as the egophoric is for a first-person subject, while example (2) above is referred to by Tournadre (2008: 296) as 'wide' scope egophoric, as the speaker is not the subject. Tournadre also notes that the *pa.yin* egophoric evidential can only be used exclusively with first person subjects, which he refers to as the 'narrow' scope egophoric (2008: 296). Tournadre has more recently come to call these 'weak' (or 'assumptive' – see Tournadre and LaPolla 2014: 225) and 'strong', as per Garrett (2001: 178–206). This distinction is useful for Standard Tibetan, and will become more relevant when we compare the egophoric categories found in other Tibetan varieties.[4]

---

4 Garrett (2001) identifies a number of situations where the egophoric copula does not exhibit the type of evidential behaviour discussed above. One such context is embedded clauses (Garrett 2001: 106–107, also Chang and Chang 1984: 610), where the *yin* form is always used, and there are no restrictions based on subject, volitionality or evidential status. Instead of egophoric semantics as an inherent property of these lexical forms the egophoric sense arises from interaction. I will not pursue Garrett's (2001) line of argument in any more detail, suffice to say that it illustrates some of the difficulties with analysing egophoric evidentiality. The notion of 'default' forms occurs in descriptions of copula forms in other Tibetic varieties (e.g. Rgyalthang, Hongladarom 2007: 22 and Yolmo, Gawne 2013: 197–201), and is relevant to our understanding of the origins of the egophoric category (§4).

There is one particular exception to the volitionality feature, which is the form *byung*. Tournadre calls this form a 'receptive egophoric' (Tournadre 2008; Tournadre and Dorje 2003: 557). This egophoric is used when the speaker has experienced the event first-hand, but as the goal or recipient of the action.

(5) khos   nga-la   kha-par   btang   byung
    3SG   1SG-DAT   phone   call   EGO.REC
    'He phoned me.'
    (Tournadre and Dorje 2003: 147)

This form is derived from a lexical verb meaning 'happened, occurred, arose' and is used for events about which the speaker has personal knowledge, because she was involved, but there is an absence of volitionality as she did not perform the volitional act. The evidential source of the receptive egophoric is personal experience, like all other egophoric forms discussed, but the access is not of personal volitional action as it is for the other egophoric uses discussed above. This form is a good illustration of Tournadre and LaPolla's (2014: 241) argument that source of evidence and access to knowledge need to be separated out. In receptive egophoric constructions the source is personal experience, but the access is that of a receptor and therefore not necessarily volitional participant. The receptive egophoric is also attested in Diasporic Common Tibetan *tʃuŋ* (Caplow 2000: 37, this volume), Rgyalthang Tibetan *ɕaŋ* (Hongladarom 2007: 32), Dinri *tšhuṅ* (Hermann 1989), the Drakyap County variety of Khams *tɕu:n* (Schwieger 1989: 30–31), and Zhollam Tibetan -ཆོ (Suzuki, this volume). Outside the Tibetic family a similar phenomenon is found in Awa Pit, a Barbacoan language of Colombia and Ecuador (see §7 for more detail).

Throughout this discussion I have been referring to the speaker's knowledge state in reference to declarative utterances. Interrogative structures in Standard Tibetan are constructed on an 'anticipation rule', where the speaker asks a question using the evidential form that she believes her addressee will most likely use in his response (Tournadre and LaPolla 2014; Garrett 2001: 230). The presence of an egophoric evidential and the anticipation rule may result in egophoricity patterning, which I discuss in more detail in §6, however as I also show in that section this is not always the case. The anticipation rule works with any of the evidential forms in Standard Tibetan, and other Tibetic languages where evidentiality occurs. This interrogative structure is not always clearly described for Tibetic languages, and the nature of its use in discourse is still poorly understood. In Lamjung Yolmo it appears to involve a combination of presumption based on general expectation of knowledge state, and context-specific knowledge-state tracking (Gawne 2016), and it is likely that this is how it also operates in other Tibetic varieties. The anticipation rule does not exclusively relate to use of the egophoric evidential category, as any evidential type can be anticipated, or avoided if the language allows that possibility.

3.3 Egophoric in other Tibetic languages

Tournadre (2014: 112) notes that the presence of the 'auxiliary verbs' *yin* and *yod* is a common feature across Tibetic languages. Beyond the literature on Standard Tibetan, there are a number of Tibetic languages that have evidential categories similar, but not identical, to the egophoric discussed above. In this section I draw on descriptions of Tibetic varieties including Diasporic Common Tibetan (§3.1), Kyirong (§3.2), Yolmo (§3.2), Denjongke (§3.3), Zhollam (§3.5) and Dzongkha (§3.6). I will also discuss Amdo Tibetan (§3.4), which has been described by some as having an egophoric categories and by others as not, but still demonstrates features that are relevant.

I use Tibetic to refer to what is often described as the 'Tibetan dialects' (see Tournadre 2014 and the introduction to this volume), which all derive from a common ancestor. The Tibetic family is generally thought to sit within the larger Bodish grouping, which also includes languages from the Qiang and Rgyalrongic groups, amongst others (Shafer 1966: 3). In §5 I look at two languages from this larger Bodish area that have a demonstrated egophoric category.

Tournadre (2014) groups the Tibetic languages in a geographic continuum based on genetic similarly, taking into account geographic and historical factors. Table 1 lists the languages discussed in this section and their place within Tournadre's classification.

Tab. 1: Classification of the Tibetic languages in this chapter as per Tournadre (2014).

Language	Classification
Standard Tibetan	Central section
Diasporic Common Tibetan	Central or Western section
Kyirong	South-Western section
Yolmo	South-Western section
Denjongke	Southern section
Amdo	North-Eastern section
Zhollam	South-Eastern section
Dzongkha	Southern section

The languages in this discussion therefore account for a diverse collection of sub-groups within the Tibetic family. The languages in this study were not randomly selected, instead they were drawn from the small, but growing, body of available literature on Tibetic languages, particularly more recent work where there is specific attention paid to evidentiality. Until more detailed documentation of evidential forms and their use is available for more Tibetic languages a systematic areal typology will not be possible.

Figure 1 is a map of the languages described in this section, and the non-Tibetic languages discussed in §5. Tibetic languages are indicated with darker points, while Kurtöp and Wadu Pumi are the two non-Tibetic languages and marked with lighter grey points. Geolocations are mostly taken from Glottolog (Hammarström et al., 2015). Zhollam was added based on the location of the village Suzuki (this volume) mentions. Standard Tibetan is indicated as being located in Lhasa, even though I discussed the problems with this in Note 1. Just as the classification within the Tibetic subgroups was varied, the languages discussed in this chapter come from a wide geographical area.

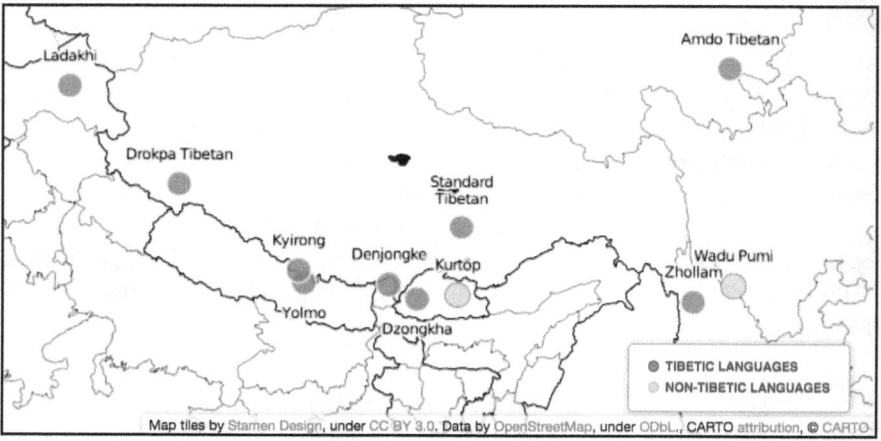

Fig. 1: A map of languages discussed in this study.

Although there is much detail that could be discussed with regard to the egophoric in all of these languages, I focus specifically on descriptive features that illustrate differences to other known types of egophoric evidentiality or enrich our understanding of the category. While describing the use of the egophoric in these languages I demonstrate a broader definition of egophoric than that used for discussions of Standard Tibetan. Other Tibetic languages that have been identified as having an egophoric evidential form include the Spiti, Khunu-Töt (upper Kinnaur) and Garzha group of dialects (Western Tibetan) (Tournadre and LaPolla 2014; for Spiti see also Hein 2007). More documentation of the copula verb forms in these Western Tibetan varieties needs to be published to ensure we have a clear idea of their function. Kretschmar (1986) has also observed that *yin* in the Drokpa dialect spoken in South West Tibet "drückt das persönliche Engagement, die innere Regung des Sprechers [expresses a personal commitment to the inner emotion of the speaker]" (p. 65), indicating that her use of 'speaker emotion' is similar to what other egophoric literature terms 'speaker knowledge' (see §3.1. for Caplow's analysis of Diasporic Common Tibetan). Kretschmar also mentions Southern Mustang *yin* can be used with all persons as with other copulas, however "in emotionalem oder emphatischem Sinn gebraucht wird [is used in more emotional or emphatic sense]" (1995: 110), which indicates that it may be founded more on personal knowledge than the other copulas. Sherpa also has a cognate that has been described using a conjunct/disjunct model (Kelly 2004: 250). That it is used with 'first person volitional actors' in declarative sentences indicates that it is an egophoric, however the description is brief and does not give insight into any variation that might be useful for this chapter. The vast majority of modern descriptions of Tibetic languages include description of a feature that is either called 'egophoric' or is called something else but appears to behave similarly. It should also not be assumed that egophoric evidentiality is found in all Tibetic languages with evidential systems.

3.3.1 Diasporic Common Tibetan

Caplow (2000, this volume) discusses the evidential semantics of a variety of Diasporic Common Tibetan (called Drokpa Tibetan in her earlier work) spoken by a man who lived in Nepal and India, and whose parents were from southwest Tibet. Caplow details three forms that fall within a category she calls 'personal evidentials'; *yìn*, *yö̀ʔ* and *tʃuŋ*. The 'personal' category is used when the speaker "was involved in the state, action or event described" (Caplow 2000: 25). All examples given indicate that these forms can only be used with first person subjects or non-first person subjects to create an effect of intimacy, except for *tʃuŋ*, which acts as a receptive egophoric for experiencer situations including the recipient as well as experiencer of non-volitional actions. Therefore, *yin* and *yö̀ʔ* appear to have a more narrow range of functions than in Standard Tibetan, while *tʃuŋ* can be used similarly to its cognate <byung>.

Caplow (2000: 29) observes that one difference between *yìn* and *yö̀ʔ* is that *yìn* has a higher degree of 'speaker consciousness'. In (6) both utterances mean that the speaker is tall, however the use of *yö* indicates a personal fact, while *yin* has an additional sense that the speaker has come to accept this fact about himself.

(6) ŋa̱ sŭkpo ri̱ŋpo **yö?/yi̱n**
    1SG body tall PF.AUX/CPF.AUX
    'I am tall'
    (Caplow 2000: 27, ex 33)

When used as verbal auxiliaries the use of *yö?* produces something more like a factual statement while *yin* indicates an intention (7).

(7) sa̱nnyi ŋa̱ do̱-gi **yö?/yi̱n**
    tomorrow 1SG go-IMPF PF.AUX/CPF.AUX
    'tomorrow I'm going (fact)'/ 'tomorrow I'll go (intention)'
    (Caplow 2000: 35, ex 56)

This distinction is not reported in other languages where these forms are cognates, but fits with a general pattern of intentionality of action being an important feature of egophoric forms. In this case, one form *(yi̱n)* has a stronger intentionality than the other *(yö?)*.

Diasporic Common Tibetan has a receptive egophoric *tʃuŋ*, which is cognate with the Standard Tibetan receptive <byung> discussed in §2.

(8) cʰī=gi ŋa̱=la mö(k) **tʃuŋ**
    dog=ERG 1SG=DAT bite REC.AUX
    'the dog bit me...'
    (Caplow 2000: 37, ex 61)

The receptive egophoric in Diasporic Common Tibetan can also be used to mark the speaker if they are the experiencer of a non-volitional action, such as with a non-control verb (9). This usage is also described for Standard Tibetan in Yuwaka (1975/this volume).

(9) ⁿda̱ŋgoŋ ŋa̱ ri̱ː **tʃuŋ**
    yesterday 1SG fall REC.AUX
    'yesterday I fell...'
    (Caplow 2000: 37, ex 60)

3.3.2 Kyirong and Yolmo

Kyirong is a Southern Tibetan variety spoken in Tibet, just north of the border with Nepal, and is closely related to Yolmo, which is spoken in Nepal. Due to their physical proximity and shared linguistic features, I discuss these two languages in the same section. It is worth noting, however, that even these closely related varieties still have differences in the distribution and use of egophoric copulas. Huber discusses the category of 'personal experience' in Kyirong, which is used when "the speakers has (...) personally experienced the action or event he is referring to" (2005: 98), although as example (10) shows, these forms can also be used for states. In Huber's analysis the main dichotomy in Kyirong is between old and new information. Under 'old information' Huber includes 'generic knowledge' along with 'personal experience', in contrast to the 'new knowledge' category, which includes 'direct sensory evidence' and 'inference.' Example (10) is one Huber gives to contrast the generic knowledge (GENER) with the personal experience (EXPER):

(10) *kʰø̄:*   *ātɕī*   *barō*   *jĩ:/jø:*
    he.GEN   sister   rich   COP.GENER/EXPER
    'his sister is rich'
    (Huber 2005: 99)

The generic *jĩ:* form is used for something generally accepted, and the speaker does not even need to know the person to make the observation. In (10) with the *jĩ:* form this would mean that many people in the village know about, and discuss, the sister's wealth. In contrast, *jø:* is for contexts where the speaker has personal experience of the fact (Huber 2005: 99), so for (10) with *jø:* the speaker may have been to the sister's house and saw she had many expensive goods, or saw her with a large amount of money. Huber does not indicate that the speaker has to have any particular relation to the person being spoken about, indicating that the Kyirong egophoric category is about a speaker's personal knowledge, but the access is not restricted only to those the speaker has a close personal connection to. This is even broader than the 'broad scope' egophoric for Standard Tibetan, which can only insert include states and actions of that which the speaker has a connection to. The term 'broad' is not really relevant here, as the 'broad/narrow' scope distinction refers to whether the actor is first person ('narrow'), or simply connected to the speaker ('broad'), which is a distinction in terms of the speaker's access to the knowledge rather than source of knowledge, which is personal knowledge or experience in all contexts.

The use of the egophoric in Kyirong is similar to what is found in Yolmo, with the relationship between the speaker and the speech content not a feature of the category, with focus instead on the speaker's knowledge state. Example (11) comes from AL, a speaker of the Lamjung variety of Yolmo, participating in the Family Story picture task (San Roque et al. 2012), where she describes a man carrying corn:

(11) màgi **yìmba**
    corn COP.EGO
    'it is corn'
    (AL 091108-01 01:14)[5]

The egophoric here does not indicate any relationship between AL and the corn in the image, or the man carrying it. Instead it is a way for her to establish for her interlocutors (a younger cousin and a research linguist) that this is a general statement, and it is not sufficiently novel or focal to warrant the use of a perceptual evidential. This is not to say that she could not use the perceptual evidential if the context warranted, as I discuss in Gawne (2013). Hill (2013b) also demonstrates for Standard Tibetan that any evidential form can be used given the right interactional context. Yolmo does not have the same 'general fact' category that is found in Standard Tibetan and other Tibetic varieties. This is possibly a factor in why the Yolmo egophoric form has a broader distribution than the Standard Tibetic cognate. Of all the languages with an egophoric, in Yolmo the 'personal knowledge' component is much weaker than in varieties where it is in contrast with a clear factual, gnomic or 'non-egophoric' category.

That the egophoric in Yolmo and Kyirong behaves in a similar fashion should not be surprising, as they are closely related Tibetan varieties. It is probable that some of the variation in egophoric semantics is due to the time depth of the distance between different varieties, as I discuss in §4 below. This does not mean that the forms behave exactly the same in both varieties. For example, Yolmo *yìmba* is cognate with the Kyirong *jĩ:*, but does not share the expectation that other people share knowledge of the content marked.

3.3.3 Denjongke (Sikkimese Bhutia)

Denjongke is also known as Sikkimese Bhutia and is spoken in Sikkim, making it the only Tibetic language of India discussed in this chapter. Yliniemi (this volume), like Hill (2012) and Caplow (this volume), prefers to use the term 'personal'

---

[5] Examples of Lamjung Yolmo are drawn from my work. Each example includes a reference with the speaker initials and the archival file number of the recording, which is also the date. Naturalistic examples also include a time code. The corpus is archived with Paradisec (catalog.paradisec.org.au/collections/LG1/).

over 'egophoric' in his discussion of Denjongke. Similar to Yolmo, the personal copulas in Denjongke refer less to the speaker's involvement in an event, and more to the speaker's state of knowledge. In example (12) below, the speaker does not have any personal relationship to the teacher under discussion:

(12) khõː   lópø: ĩ́ː
 he.HON teacher COP
 'he is a teacher'
 (Yliniemi, this volume)

The Denjongke personal forms, equative ĩ́? and existential jə̀? are contrasted with the familiar sensorial du?, but also with a neutral copula bɛ?. This means that while the Denjongke personal forms have quite a broad distribution like other Southern Tibetic languages, the neutral form covers some of the semantic space that the egophoric covers in Yolmo. For example, in Lamjung Yolmo a speaker can use the egophoric to talk about historical events, as there is no other evidential form that is preferred. In Denjongke, however, "[i]t seems impossible to gain personal knowledge of distant historical events" (Yliniemi, pp. 317–318, this volume) and instead the neutral form is used.

3.3.4 Amdo Tibetan

Amdo Tibetan represents a large group of dialects, spoken in the northeast of Tibet. There have been descriptions of the evidential systems of a number of these dialects including Mdzod dge (Sun 1993), Them chen (Haller 2004), Gonghe (Ebihara 2011), and Mgo log (Tribur, this volume). Here I focus on Sun's (1993) analysis, which predates much of the discussion of egophoric evidentiality, and how this contrasts with subsequent analyses. Some of the variation in the analyses may be due dialect differences among the varieties of Amdo discussed, but some arise from different understandings about the nature of evidentiality, and the role of the egophoric category within a Tibetan evidential system.

Sun's description of evidentiality in Amdo Tibetan does not initially appear to involve a form that includes an egophoric, but in his description of the relationship between certain verbal suffixes and person, he observes that there is a distinction in which forms are used based on "a fluid dichotomous distinction" (1993: 955) between 'self-person' and 'other person'. 'Self-person' utterances are made using the 'neutral' =nə form, in contrast to direct perception =tʰœ, hearsay =zəg and an 'immediate event' =ʰkə. Thus, in utterances about the self, the 'neutral' form is used, and it is not used with third person subjects (Sun gives no clear evidence of what happens with second person subjects). As with the relationship between evidential forms and person in other languages, this is not a grammatical restriction, but an interaction of the semantics of the evidential forms with the context and the other evidential forms in the paradigm.

The neutral =nə is not used when there is a negative form or auxiliary verb, which is why Sun (1993: 958) argues that it is more or less a neutral form for when a verb requires a suffix. If this analysis best reflects the situation in Amdo it gives an insight into the type of evidential environment in which an egophoric form may arise. Garrett's (2001: 106) identification of the 'neutral' uses of the Standard Tibetan egophoric in contexts like conditional clauses indicate a link to Old and Classical Tibetan where the forms that are now used as egophoric were used in contexts with no egophoric evidential sense. Although Sun refers to these forms as neutral, Aikhenvald analyses the use of this form and argues that the neutral's use of intentional and purposeful acts indicates 'overtones of evidentiality' (2004: 326).

That the 'neutral' does in fact have features in common with the egophoric is supported in later analyses of the Amdo system. These later analyses draw on a wider range of suffixes, for example Tribur (this volume) includes discussion of epistemic forms that occur in the same paradigm and Haller (2004: 137) includes compositional forms that Sun (1993) omits. Haller (2004: 137) describes an -a form, which has a similar distribution and function to Sun's (1993) =nə, being used with volitional actions. Haller calls this form a "volitional evidential" ("volitional evidentiell"). Haller argues that the volitional verb will always be marked as an evidential as the speaker can only perform an event volitionally if she has knowledge of her actions (2004: 138).

Ebihara calls the same -a evidential "speaker performed" (2010: 68, 2011: 68/69), arguing that it is used "to express the event that the speaker performed, made somebody to perform, or is familiar with" (2010: 68). This definition is much more clearly in line with the egophoric than the analyses from Sun (1993), and focuses more on the speaker rather than the volitional focus of Haller (2004). Ebihara (2010: 69/70) also argues that there are copula verbs, separate from the verbal auxiliaries discussed until now, with a conjunct/disjunct distinction with jən (cognate with Standard Tibetan yin) and re (cognate with Standard Tibetan red). She does not report on the full usage of these forms, but it appears that an egophoric variation exists that shows similar distribution to that in Standard Tibetan in the copula series.

Tribur discusses the verbal auxiliaries, including a category of 'egophoric evidence' which she says pertains to "knowledge of one's own intentions" (this volume). This is a more narrow definition, pertaining specifically to intention, rather than personal knowledge through familiarity. This is sympathetic to Haller's (2004: 137) analysis of the form being grounded in 'volitional' action. Tribur also argues that verbal declarative clauses that end with a bare stem are also zero-marked egophoric utterances. This fits with her larger argument that the egophoric category in the Mgo log dialect was original the unmarked form, which is why it continues to be so in negation and interrogation in varieties like the Mdzo dge dialect in Sun (1993), and why it is still unmarked in all contexts for a small number of dialects. Tribur argues that "as the non-egophoric evidential categories (direct and indirect evidence) developed, egophoric emerged as a distinct coherent evidential category in response" (p. 379, this volume). This is similar to the historical development of the egophoric in Standard Tibetan that I discuss in §4.

Amdo Tibetan has forms that are cognate with the evidential forms in other Tibetan languages. It also has a set of suffixes that do not obviously come from Tibetan forms such as *yin* or *yod* that are known to be egophoric in other dialects. The use of =nə or -a in different dialects of Amdo Tibetan provide an insight into the nature of egophoric evidentials within the larger evidential system of a language. Egophoric evidentials do not operate in semantic independence, but as part of a larger set of evidential choices, which may affect their nature in different languages.

3.3.5 Zhollam

Zhollam is a small Khams variety, spoken in northwestern Yunnan. The evidential system in Zhollam is built around an egophoric/non-egophoric distinction (Suzuki, this volume). There are no other specific evidential categories that the egophoric can contrast with, such as sensory or gnomic, which is what we also see for other varieties with an egophoric/non-egophoric distinction, including Denjongke (§3.3). As Suzuki observes, we should think of this as an A/not-A type distinction, rather than the A vs. B type distinction we see in languages like Standard Tibetan, Kyirong, Yolmo and Sherpa. The declarative egophoric *ji̇̃* is cognate with many of the other Tibetic egophoric forms discussed in this study, while the non-egophoric ȵɔŋ is a cognate of the Written Tibetan etymon: *snang*. The form <snang> is well-attested in a number of Tibetic varieties, where it means 'to shine', and is often extended to mean 'to seem' or 'to appear' (Suzuki 2012, Ebihara, this volume). Zhollam Tibetan is the only variety attested to date where this form is extended to use in a copula construction. Its use as a non-egophoric gives a sense of "objective statement of the fact", in comparison to the egophoric which expresses a relationship to the referent in the utterance:

(13) ˉkhɣ-ø˗   pi:-ø̃   ȵɔŋ
     3.ABS   Tibetan-ABS COP[N.EGO]
     's/he is Tibetan'
     (Suzuki, this volume)

(14) ⁻khγ-ø´   pi:-ø̄   jĭ
     3.ABS   Tibetan-ABS   COP[EGO]
   's/he is Tibetan (so we are the same ethnic group).'
   (Suzuki, this volume)

As with many Tibetic languages, a related set of verbal auxiliaries with the same semantic functions are also found in Zhollam. This therefore also includes a set of non-egophoric suffixes.

Zhollam's contrast between an egophoric and a non-egophoric is unusual, but it is perhaps not the only language that makes this distinction. Haller (2000: 75/76) argues that the main copula evidential contrast in the Shigaste variety of Tibetan is between *jì*, which is used for the speaker's established knowledge, and *pi̱ȩ*, which is used for information outside of the speaker's established knowledge.

Zhollam also has a receptive egophoric suffix -ɕɔ̃, which is a cognate of Standard Tibetan <byung>. This is used, according to Suzuki (this volume: 440) to mark "an external factor which influences the speaker". Although Suzuki does not talk about -ɕɔ̃ in relation to volitionality, it occurs in his examples where the speaker does not have any control over the event.

3.3.6 Dzongkha

Dzongkha is the national language of Bhutan, and has a large number of second-language speakers. The copulas of identity '*ing* and '*immä* and those of existence/location/attribution *yö* and *dû* have similar semantic distribution to those seen for other Tibetan languages, with the first in each pair having a more egophoric function and the second having a more sensory evidential function. Van Driem (1998: 127) describe this as a difference between "assimilated" and "acquired" knowledge, with the focus being on the knowledge state of the individual, rather than a gnomic knowledge state of a larger group of people.

Van Driem's (1998: 136) discussion of the interaction of copula evidential semantics and subject person illustrates one way that Dzongkha appears to vary from other languages discussed. Second person subjects cannot be talked about with an 'assimilated' (egophoric) evidential, "Even a mother speaking to her own son whom she has raised and nurtured from birth cannot grammatically replace (…) *dû* with (…) *yö*" (1998: 136) in the sentence below:

(15) chö   j'ârim   dû/*yö
     2SG   beautiful   COP/*COP
   'you are beautiful'
   (van Driem 1998: 135)

This restriction on the use of egophoric with second person subject is in contrast with the same utterance with the son as a third person subject, which is acceptable with the egophoric. Van Driem argues that this is because "knowledge about a second person referent is by definition objective" (1998: 136), but none of the other languages discussed above have been described as having this specific restriction on the use of the egophoric. The choice of egophoric or other evidential may interact with other pragmatic factors regarding the possibly face-threatening nature of referring to assimilated knowledge over observed knowledge in interaction in Dzongkha. It is possible that this restriction is a form of face-saving politeness in Dzongkha, with the egophoric seen as too personal or intimate for second person subjects, even those well known by the speaker. More corpus-based work with other Tibetan varieties may demonstrate lower use of egophoric for second person subjects, without it being the kind of overt restriction that van Driem indicates.

Van Driem (1998: 129) also notes that the use of the acquired knowledge form *'immä* instead of the 'assimilated' knowledge form indicates a degree of sudden realisation, and gives example (18) where the speaker has just realized that a long-time acquaintance has taken to stealing:

(16) 'eng   chö   'âu   **'immä**   bô   te
     oh   2SG   thief   COP   PART   PART
     'Oh... so, you are a thief'
     (van Driem 1998: 129)

This is similar to the 'assimilated knowledge' dimension of the broad scope egophoric contrasting with a perceptual evidential giving rise to contextual mirative sense that is discussed for other languages above. Hyslop and Tshering (this volume) argue that the mirative sense is a key feature of this copula.

Hyslop and Tshering (this volume) also discusses two progressive aspect suffixes that are distributed based on egophoric semantics. Hyslop and Tshering argue that the form *-do* is used in egophoric contexts, and the form *-dê* is used in other contexts, which she labels 'alterphoric', for non-first-person actions (as per Post 2013).

(17) nga   to   z'a-***do***
     1.SG   cooked.rice   eat-PROG.**EGO**
     'I am eating.'
     (Hyslop and Tshering, this volume)

(18) kho   to   z'a-***dê***
     3.SG   cooked.rice   eat-PROG.N.**EGO**
     'I am eating.'
     (Hyslop and Tshering, this volume)

The use of the egophoric can be extended to uses with non-first-person. In such uses it asserts the speaker's inclusion in the event, perhaps as a witness or participant.

This analysis of the distribution of progressive aspect suffixes in Dzongkha is one of the few examples of a Tibetic language with an egophoric category that is not a direct cognate with the copula forms <yin, yod, byung> discussed so far, except perhaps for the Amdo Tibetan neutral =*nə/-a*. These aspect markers are also one of only a small number of instances where there is an egophoric/non-egophoric distinction, rather than the egophoric form contrasting with a number of other evidential or epistemic forms (see also the binary distinction in Zollam).

3.4 The diachronic development of egophoric evidentiality

The diachronic development of egophoric evidentiality can offer a possible understanding of the variation we see in different languages. The origins of egophoric semantics in Tibetan are slowly becoming clearer, as more detailed study is being undertaken relating to the historical basis of evidentiality in Tibetan. Tournadre and Jiatso (2001: 66) argue that the egophoric evidential sense is only found in modern Tibetan and was not present in Classical Tibetan. While the cognate forms existed at that time, they were functionally distinct, acting exclusively as syntactic copulas.

Takeuchi's (1990, 2015) analysis gives a different perspective. In his analysis of Old Tibetan, *yin* began to be used in contrast to a final particle *-o*. In this contrastive position *yin* was used to emphasize the speaker's will. Over time these were grammaticalized into regular contrastive meanings. Something outside the speaker's will, and therefore external, would be marked with the *-o* particle (19), which was distinguished from something inside the speaker's will, which was therefore internal, marked with *yin* (20) (Takeuchi 2015: 410). In (19) the speaker has no control over Zu-tse's loyalty. In (20), however, the speaker is making a choice to send medicine. Other examples of the use of *yin* from this time also relate to the speaker and her own willful actions.

(19) *zu tse glob a nye 'o*
 'Zu-tse is loyal.'
 (Takeuchi 2015: 409)

(20) *zhang klu bzang gi yi ge la nad cabs che rab ches byung nas/*
*sman snga ma skur ba //**yin** no/*
'Since it was [written] in Zhang-klu-bzang's letter that [your] sickness is very serious, I will immediately send medicine.'
(Takeuchi 2015: 410)

Therefore it appears that something similar to 'egophoric' semantics arose earlier in the use of *yin* than Tournadre and Jiatso's (2001) analysis indicates. This is also supported by Hoshi (2010), who argues that the kinds of distinctions found in modern Tibetan between *yod* and *'dug* can be found in the 14th Century narrative *Rgyal-rabs Gsal-ba'i Me-long*.

Oisel's (2013: 81) investigation of the biography of Milarepa by Gtsang smyon he ru ka (1452–1507) demonstrates the form *yin* was used in contexts that capture the personal knowledge of the speaker. This appears to be supported by an example where the use of the form *yin* expresses the personal information of the speaker (glossing translated from French):

(21) | *de.nas* | *da* | *bar* | *'di.kar* | *bsdad-pa+yin-nam* |
|---|---|---|---|---|
| then | now | until | here | stay(PST)-REL.AUX-Q |
| *zer* | *de.ka* | **yin**-*te* | *khyed-rnams* | *za-r* |
| say | this | **be**-CONN | 2PL | eat(PRES)-OBL |
| *rung-ba-'i* | *zas* | *med* | *byas-pas* | |
| suit-NOM-GEN | food | not.have | say(PST)-CONN | |

'Ensuite, (les chasseurs demandèrent :) [...] Es-tu resté là jusqu'à maintenant ? C'est cela, dis-je. Mais je n'ai rien à manger qui vous convienne. ['Then (hunters asked) "have you stayed there until now?" "That's it" I say, "but I have nothing to eat that suits you."]'
(Oisel 2013: 81)

In this example, the speaker is the main speech act participant, making this usage appear similar to the narrow scope of egophoric use found in Standard Tibetan today (§2). Oisel observes that the speaker does not have to be the subject, and the distribution of egophoric at this time was more like what we find in modern varieties such as Kyirong and Yolmo today.

Oisel's analysis is more than commensurate with Hill's (2013a) analysis of *'dug*, the perceptual evidential with which the egophoric forms are in contrast in many Tibetic languages. Hill (2013a) has also argued that evidentiality became a feature of Tibetan as early as the 12th Century.

This timeline indicates a possible source of the split between Standard Tibetan and its very specific form of egophoric evidentiality, and languages like Kyirong and Yolmo where the cognate forms can be used in more flexible ways. The more specific Standard Tibetan usage is likely to have arisen after the Southern languages like Kyirong already diverged with the more general distinction outlined in Takeuchi's (1990) analysis. It is also possible that they diverged when there were no evidential properties to their cognates of *yin*, and acquired the semantics via contact, as languages further afield like Dzongkha and Kurtöp may have.

Oisel (this volume) looks at the origins of the 'receptive egophoric' and 'sensorial', arguing that this distinction arose in the use of Middle Tibetan lexical verbs *byung* 'to come' versus *song* 'to go'. The direction verbs shifted to relate the participation and the state of awareness of the speaker in the actions in an utterance. The semantic distinction between the receptive and sensorial may have been grammaticalized in different ways at different times, and may not occur in the same place in related languages.

As the analysis of historical texts from a variety of locations becomes more sensitive to the origins of evidentiality in Tibetan, and we build a more sophisticated understanding of the areal distribution of egophoric evidentiality and related phenomena this picture will become clearer.

3.5 Egophoric in non-Tibetic languages of the Tibetosphere

As egophoric evidentiality becomes more commonly acknowledged in descriptions of Tibetic languages, the term is also being applied to features of non-Tibetic languages. In this section I discuss Kurtöp and Wadu Pumi, two languages within the Tibeto-Burman family that are outside of the Tibetic group.

To date there are only a small number of examples of the use of 'egophoric' for a grammatical feature other than the copula forms that are cognates of the Standard Tibetan copulas *yin* and *yod*. Non-Tibetic languages that are described as having egophoric forms have so far been confined to the Tibeto-Burman family, although the term 'egophoricity' has been applied to a much broader range of languages (see §6 below). It would not be surprising if the list of languages outside the Tibetic group, and outside Tibeto-Burman, that are described as having 'egophoricity' continues to grow, but these languages may not necessarily have a category of egophoric evidentiality.

3.5.1 Kurtöp

In Kurtöp (East Bodish), Hyslop refers to the perfective suffix *-shang* an egophoric. Hyslop observes that *-shang* is used for "direct, personal evidence of a given event" and also notes that it encodes certainty, as well as "the expectation that the interlocutor does not share the knowledge" (2011: 589). This final property is not discussed for other languages with grammatical egophoric forms, except for Yuwaka (1975/this volume), who notes that in Standard Tibetan *yo 'o-red* is used either because the speaker "presupposes that the listener does not know" or "informs the listener".

Hyslop gives an example of the 'egophoric' *-shang* with a third person subject (24).

(22) tshé   o-ning   'au-rang   shakhwi   tshui   ge-**shang**
     DEM   3.PROX-ABL   where-EMPH   hunting.dog   look.for   go-PFV.EGO
     'And then (they) went everywhere looking for the hunting dog'
     (Hyslop 2011: 591)

Nothing in this example indicates that the speaker has any close connection with the subject of this narrative, indicating once again a 'broad' egophoric that focuses more on speaker knowledge about the event rather than the speaker's personal relationship to the propositional content. This makes the notion of egophoric in Kurtöp similar to that found in Kyirong and Yolmo. It is possible that the Kurtöp egophoric is closer to something like the Amdo Tibetan neutral in Sun's (1993) analysis, that exhibits a dimension of egophoric evidentiality in some contexts, or perhaps it is a more defused type of egophoric the language obtained through contact with Dzongkha, which is used by speakers of Kurtöp for communication outside of their community (Hyslop 2011: 19).

3.5.2 Wadu Pumi

Wadu Pumi (Qiangic) has a verb system with a suffixing alternation that has been described in Daudey (2014) as marking an egophoric/non-egophoric distinction. This distinction is marked on copula forms, some auxiliary verbs and a set of verbal inflective suffixes. The verbal suffix forms also mark features of aspect and modality. Daudey observes that the egophoric "denotes the involvement of the speaker in an action" (2014: 335), however the existence of egophoric existential verbs indicates that the function is broader than just participation, and marks the speaker's personal knowledge:

(23) ế ə̀-pú zôŋ tɕə̂=**ɖàw**
  1.SG this-under exist.AN:EGO:1SG say=IPFV:N.EGO
  '"Yes, I'm here," (she) said.' (PC04w.2.7)
  (Daudey 2014: 299)

Unlike the majority of Tibetic languages, Wadu Pumi has a specific category of non-egophoric markers, used when the speaker is talking about events she did not participate in, actions she performed without control or volition, or the states of others. Non-egophoric is a category that exists only marginally in the literature on Tibetic languages (see §3.6 above for Zhollam), instead the other evidential oppositions are used in all contexts where the egophoric is not. The Wadu Pumi evidential paradigm does not appear to cover as broad a semantic space as systems found in Tibetic languages (for example there is no factual, and the visual evidential semantics are only implied in the absence of a perfective inferential form = *si*) and instead it appears that the non-egophorics fill this semantic space.

Daudey notes that there are variations in egophoric and evidential preferences in different genres of language, and the speaker can chose to use an egophoric form or not for pragmatic effect, usually to align themselves, or distance themselves from their interlocutor. For the set of examples below Daudey observes that "[w]hereas the statement with *dzə̂* is a neutral statement, the statement with *djaw* implies that the speaker knows very well that the addressee knows the fact expressed in the statement" (2014: 348).

(24) *nĭŋ* *thóŋmə́* ***dzə̂***
  2SG Pŭmĭ be:N.EGO
  'You are Pŭmĭ.' (EL)
  (Daudey 2014: 348)

(25) *nĭŋ* *thóŋmə́* ***djàw***
  2SG Pŭmĭ be:EGO:2SG
  'You are Pŭmĭ.' (you know that very well yourself!) (EL)
  (Daudey 2014: 348)

Example (25) is about speaker knowledge, but it is speaker knowledge of another person's knowledge state. Daudey does not indicate whether the speaker must know her interlocutor well to use this form. If she does then perhaps this is a usage of egophoric similar to the 'broad' scope in Standard Tibetan. If it can be used with any interlocutor then this particular function is quite different to anything described for Tibetic languages to date.

3.6 Egophoric, egophoricity and conjunct/disjunct

Throughout this chapter I have used the terms egophoric, and egophoric evidential(s). These need to be distinguished from 'egophoricity' (San Roque, Floyd, and Norcliffe 2015, forthcoming), and 'conjunct/disjunct' (Hale 1980). This is not because egophoric evidentiality is necessarily related to these patterns, but (as I discuss in §1) because the term 'egophoricity' was derived from the egophoric. At its most basic, egophoricity in a language involves first person declaratives sharing grammatical marking (often, but not always, evidentiality motivated) with second person interrogatives, in contrast with the other persons, as schematized in Fig. 2 below. In each language this may be affected by a number of other features including volitionality, tense or interactional context.

Declaratives   **Interrogatives**

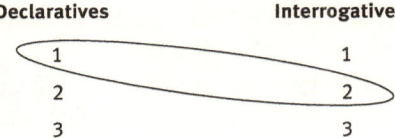

  1   1
  2   2
  3   3

Fig. 2: An abstract representation of egophoricity as per San Roque et al. (forthcoming).

The discussion of egophoric evidentiality in this study indicates that we might often see a split in the evidentiality used in declaratives for first person in contrast with second and third. This is an overgeneralization of course, as we have seen that in many Tibetic varieties speakers can use egophoric forms with non-first-person referents, as it is the speakers knowledge state, rather than their participation, that is marked. Also, with the Tibetic systems discussed here, it is possible to use forms other than egophoric with first person. To achieve the distribution in Fig. 2, the language additionally requires a mechanism such as the 'anticipation rule' (Tournadre and LaPolla 2014; Garrett 2001: 230, Gawne 2016), whereby the person asking the question is required to use the evidential form most likely in the answer.

Widmer's (2015) discussion of Dolakha Newar (Central Himalayan) and Bunan (Kinauri) indicates that conjunct/disjunct systems in those languages arose from first/second/third person distinctions collapsing into self/other epistemic distinction. I demonstrated in §4, the egophoric distinction in the Tibetic cognate forms does not appear to have come from a person-marking collapse, but the development of a set of contrasts in the verbal system. While different origins do not necessarily result in different types of systems, the range of variation in egophoric forms in Tibetic languages indicates that any demonstration of a system of egophoricity, would also be varied in its patterning.

The presence of egophoric evidentiality does not necessarily mean that a language will have a system of egophoricity. For example in §5.2 I discuss Kurtöp as a language with an egophoric evidential category, but for interrogative constructions a specific interrogative particle is used instead (Hyslop 2011: 263, 574–587):

(26) *wo   zhâa   yo?*
     DEM.PROX   what   Q.COP
     'What is this?'
     (Hyslop 2011: 264)

In more recent work Hyslop (2014) introduces another question particle *shu*. Hyslop argues that the difference between them is that *yo* is used when the speaker expects their interlocutor to know the answer to a question and *shu* when they do not, or for rhetorical questions (she glosses *shu* as DBT, 'doubt'). The contrast indicates that something like an 'anticipation rule' is required for tracking the likelihood your interlocutor has knowledge to answer a question. The Kurtöp form does not explicitly anticipate the source of knowledge (for example, egophoric knowledge or perceptual knowledge), as would be necessary to produce an egophoricity patterning.

With further cross-linguistic examination of the egophoric evidential category, and growing interest in the concept of egophoricity, it may be that there is a frequent co-occurrence of egophoric evidentiality and a feature like the 'anticipation rule'. Even if this turns out to be true, researchers should not conflate the specific egophoric evidential category with the epiphenomenal patterning of egophoricity.

3.7 Egophoric compared to similar categories in other language families

Looking beyond the Tibeto-Burman languages discussed above, we find evidential categories in other language families that share some similarities with the egophoric category. While these language groups have categories with similar features to the Tibetan egophoric, they are more constrained in their domains of use. In this section I discuss the 'participatory' category found in a variety of languages in Papua New Guinea, the 'performative' in Kashaya, a Pomoan languages of North America, and the 'conjunct' in Barbacoan languages of South America. The categories described for all of these languages privilege the speaker's own knowledge of an event or state. They do vary on what can be marked, and what these forms can contrast with. None have the breadth of usage of the egophoric found in Tibetic languages, and are mostly confined to use with first-person participants. Note that in this section I focus specifically on epistemic or evidential categories that are similar to the egophoric discussed above. For discussion of 'conjunct/disjunct' or 'egophoricity' see §6.

An evidential category found in Papua New Guinea (PNG) is the 'participatory' evidential, discussed by Rule (1977) in relation to Foe, and also by San Roque and Loughnane (2012) in their survey of evidentiality in a range of languages of the area. The participatory is a category used when the speaker knows the evidence because she performed, or is performing the action. Out of the eleven languages examined, San Roque and Loughnane (2012) identify Oksapmin (of the Ok-Oksapmin family), Fasu (West Kutubu) and Foe (East Kutubu) as languages with participatory evidentials, indicating that in the area it is not genetically constrained. Example (29) from the Oksapmin language illustrates the participatory (PCP):

(27) nuxut   gəl   ml   di-**pa**
     1DU   cut   do(TR)(.SEQ)   eat.PFV-**PCP.FP.PL**
     'We cut it up and ate it {I did it}.'
     (Oksapmin, San Roque and Loughnane 2012: 122)

While San Roque and Loughnane argue that the PNG participatory can be considered to be part of an egophoric category of evidentiality, the participatory is not entirely like the Tibetan egophoric. The egophoric can be used for states and attributes as well as actions, giving it a much broader range of uses. The broad scope egophoric in Standard Tibetan, and the egophoric in many other varieties can also be used with non-first person subjects, which makes the function of the PNG form much narrower, as it is about the speaker's knowledge through undertaking an action. Thus the PNG participatory evidentials are much more specific in their semantic parameters and interactional function. What Oksapmin, Foe and Fasu share with Tibetan though is that the participatory contrasts with other categories of sensory evidentials. Oksapmin has a single 'visual-other' and Foe has both a 'seen' and an 'unseen (other sense)' form. This means that, like the Tibetan egophoric, these participatory forms are doing more than just marking that the speaker was a witness of something, but highlighting a level of personal involvement. This is because the existence of the sensory evidential creates a divide where the participatory is used predominantly for first person declaratives and the sensory is used for second and third person, because the speaker has sensory evidence of their actions.

In Fasu, Foe and Oksapmin the participatory category also includes a factual usage (San Roque and Loughnane 2012). 'Factual' is another evidential type initially observed by Rule (1977), which San Roque and Loughnane define for Oksapmin as "signifying events for which the speaker has accumulated evidence of various types throughout his or her life, where this evidence is assumed to be shared by or accessible to others" (2012: 122).

(28) jəxe   awxen-il   ixile   dik   jox
     so   grandparent-PL   3PL.POSS   time   DEF
     kukumi   jox [...]   i=ma   jox=si   moxe-**sxe**
     brideprice   DEF   DEM.DST=REL   DEF=INSTR   buy-**PCP.FP.PL.HAB**
     'So, in the elders' time, they used to pay the bride price (with pig's teeth, bows, arrows, axes and stone axes,) with these things.'
     (Oksapmin, San Roque and Loughnane 2012: 122)

The addition of the 'factual' dimension brings the participatory closer to the egophoric in some regards, as it is not just referring to a single event, but accumulated knowledge. On the other hand, the assumption that others share this information has not been described as a feature of egophoric semantics in Tibetic languages, which exclusively focus on the status of the speaker's knowledge state (except Kyirong, as discussed in §3.2). In San Roque and Loughnane's (2012) analysis the 'factual' category appears to only exist as an extension of the participatory, indicating that they may, in fact, be simply a single areal category. In comparison, Tibetan varieties have separate factual categories, like the Standard Tibetan *red* (Garrett 2001; Tournadre 2008) and Lamjung Yolmo *òŋge* (Gawne 2013). The factual in the Papuan languages is predicated on the knowledge of other interactional participants, similar to the Tibetic factuals. The Tibetan egophoric, in contrast, is specifically about the knowledge state of a single person, usually the speaker in declaratives, and does not rely on this knowledge being shared with others.

As well as the work in PNG there have been descriptions of 'personal' evidentials in Northern American languages. Oswalt (1986) describes a 'performative' evidential in Kashaya (Pomoan) used by speakers to show that they know what they know because they are performing, or have performed an action. The performance does not even have to be particularly recent, example (31) below was spoken many years after the event:

(29) mi·-li   ʔa   me-ʔ-el-   pʰak'úm-**mela**
     there-visible   I   your-father-OBJ   kill-perform
     'Right there I killed your father.'
     (Oswalt 1986: 35)

This performative is, like the languages of PNG, more limited than the range of uses of the 'egophoric' in Tibetan. The performative can also have an extended use to indicate that something is a general fact, which is similar to the personal-factual forms for PNG languages.

Mithun (1999) mentions that Kashaya shares this category with Central Pomo,[6] but it is not found in related Pomoan languages, indicating a smaller cluster than that found for the participant-factual in languages of PNG and the egophoric in Tibetan languages. Thus it appears that there are similar phenomena cross-linguistically, where there is an evidential form that indicates the speaker has personal knowledge of the event. It also appears that cross-linguistically speakers use this form over visual evidence as the most personal category of evidence. One major factor that appears to influence the scope of egophoric categories in different languages are the markers they contrast with. The fewer other evidential or epistemic distinctions it is in contrast with, the broader its application will be. For example, as we saw for Yolmo (§3.2), the egophoric has quite a wide scope, taking on the function that the factual has in a language like Standard Tibetan (§2).

Descriptions of two Barbacoan languages of South America include mention of a category that has different names, but a similar function; the 'conjunct' in Awa Pit (Curnow 2002) and the 'congruent' in Tsafiki (Dickinson 2000). In Tsafiki the congruent is used to indicate that the information in the proposition is "congruent with the speaker's general knowledge", in contrast to a 'non-congruent' form that is used for information that is not congruent with the speaker's general knowledge, which includes the actions and states of non-first-person subjects and non-volitional actions of the speaker. The addressee's knowledge-state is the focus for questions. The speaker cannot extend the congruent to a non-first-person subject who she knows well, and whose actions or states may be congruent with the speaker's knowledge, in contrast to what we saw for Standard Tibetan and many of the other varieties, particularly Kyirong and Yolmo.

The conjunct form in Awa Pit does not appear to be cognate with the Tsafiki form (Curnow 2002: 612) although they share a similar distribution. One of the main differences between the two languages is that volitionality does not affect the conjunct in Awa Pit, and the disjunct form is not invoked in the case of non-volitional actions (Curnow 2002: 615). This means that the distribution of conjunct is exclusively with the speaker in declarative utterances, and the addressee

---

[6] Mithun (1999) states this category is for "first hand personal experience," although she also mentions that this experience is usually 'visual' so perhaps this is not so closely tied to first person as what we saw in Kashaya and is more of the visual evidential type.ˇcʰémul-*ya* 'it rained (I know because I was there and saw it)' (Mithun 1999: 181). Neither Central Pomoan nor Kashayan personal evidential appear to be affected by the volitionality of the action.

in questions. Awa Pit has a specific 'conjunct-undergoer' form for past tense first person objects (Curnow 2002: 218). Instead of the regular -*w* verbal suffix, the form -*s* is used. The marking of the participation of the speaker, even as a participant other than the actor is similar to the receptive egophoric discussed for Standard Tibetan (§2) and Diasporic Common Tibetan (§3.1.).

(30) *Demetrio=na   tit-ma-ti-s*
Demetrio=TOP   cut-COMP-PST-CONJ:under
'Demetrio cut me.'
(Curnow 2002: 618)

The conjunct-undergoer has an additional function, where the suffix is present, but there is no first-person referent for it to cross-reference in intransitive, stative and copulative constructions. In these cases conjunct marking "indicates that the action or state affected a conjunct entity, even though that entity is not an argument of the verb indicating the action or state" (Curnow 2002: 620).

(31) *alu   ki-ma-ti-s*
rain   do-COMP-PST-CONJ:under
'(I was on my way to bathe,) it rained on me.'
(Curnow 2002: 620)

The use of the conjunct-undergoer indicates that this utterance relates to the speaker. In this way it is similar to the 'broad scope' egophoric in Tibetan.

3.8 Conclusion

Egophoric evidentiality, as broadly defined, appears to be common in Tibetic languages, and may also be found in Bodish languages that are within the Tibetosphere, such as Kurtöp and Wadu Pumi. Although similar to other evidential categories, particularly those found in languages of Papua New Guinea and North American Pomoan languages, the use of egophoric is not limited to personal knowledge though performance of actions and thus can be used with more than just first person actors.

Although many of the Tibetic languages discussed in §3 appear to have an egophoric category more often than not using cognates of *yin* or *yod*, the use of the egophoric as described for Standard Tibetan appears to be more limited in distribution compared to the egophoric in other varieties.

Table 2 below includes all of the Tibetic languages discussed in this chapter, and the additional two Bodish languages, which are also part of the Tibeto-Burman family, but not so closely related. In this table I indicate a number of features discussed throughout this study. The first is whether there was an egophoric category attested (either by that name, or another), the second is whether that category included at least one form that was cognate with a Standard Tibetan egophoric (*yin, yod* or *byung*), the third is whether any scope restrictions were mentioned regarding the speakers' relationship with the subject in the event, that is, does it require some kind of narrow/broad scope relationship to the subject, or can the speaker refer to any subject with the egophoric, the fourth is the attested presence of a receptive egophoric and the final category is whether the language has a specific non-egophoric form. I have not added a cross in any cell unless the original author explicitly stated that something was not the case. The egophoric for Amdo Tibetan is left as an unresolved question-mark as it is not clear if the variation between the descriptions from Sun (1993) and Tribur (this volume) are a result of different analyses or dialect variation.

Tab. 2: Summary of discussion.

Language	Family	Egophoric category attested	Egophoric cognate with ST	narrow/wide distinction mentioned	receptive egophoric mentioned	specific non-egophoric
Standard Tibetan	Tibetic (Central)	✓	n/a	✓	✓	✗
Diasporic Common Tibetan	Tibetic (Central or Western)	✓	✓		✓	✗
Kyirong	Tibetic (South-Western)	✓	✓			✗
Yolmo	Tibetic (South-Western)	✓	✓			✗
Denjongke	Tibetic (Southern)	✓	✓			✗
Amdo	Tibetic (North Eastern)	?	n/a			✗
Zhollam	Tibetic (South-Eastern)	✓	✓		✓	✓
Dzongkha	Tibetic (Southern)	✓	✓	✓	✗	✓
Kurtöp	East Bodish	✓	n/a			
Wadu Pumi	Qiangic	✓	n/a	✓		✓

As this table demonstrates, there is a lot of variation in the use of the egophoric category in Tibetic varieties, and further documentation of languages of this area will undoubtedly reveal more points of difference as well as similarities.

It is possible that work in other language families will demonstrate that there are grammatical categories similar to egophoric evidentiality. It already appears that the phenomena described in a number of languages of Papua New Guinea may have features in common with Tibetic egophoric categories. Likewise, languages of North America may have features with semantics similar to those in Tibetan languages.

The language-specific chapters in this book have demonstrated that researchers are developing a more sophisticated understanding of evidentiality, and how it is used as a grammatical resource by speakers. This language-specific work allows us to build a more comprehensive typological understanding of phenomena like egophoricity. The more detailed our understanding of egophoric in many different varieties of Tibetan becomes, the more we can observe such similarities and differences, particularly between closely related varieties, which can help us tease out nuanced features of egophoric use.

Abbreviations

1 first person, 2 second person, 3 third person, ABL ablative, ALT alterphoric, AN animate, AUX auxiliary, CONJ conjunct, CONN connector, COP copula, CPF conscious personal fact, DAT dative, DEM demonstrative, DEF definite, DIR direct, DO direct object, DST distal, DU dual, EGO egophoric, EMPH emphatic, ERG ergative, EXPER experience, FP far past, GEN genitive, GENER generic, HAB habitual, HM experienced, IND indirect, INSTR instrumental, IPFV imperfective, LOC locative, N non, NOM nominative, OBL oblique, PART particle, PCP participatory, PF personal fact, PFV perfective, PL plural, POSS possessive, PRES present tense, PROG progressive, PROX proximate, PST past tense, REC receptive, REL relative, SEQ sequential, SG singular, TOP topic, TR transitive, UNDER undergoer, Q question.

Acknowledgements: An earlier version of this contribution was presented during the 'Evidential systems in Tibetan languages' workshop at the 24th Meeting of the South East Asian Linguistics Society in Yangon (May 27–28 2014), thanks to all the participants at the workshop for their feedback. Thanks also to Barbara Kelly, Rachel Nordlinger, Nicolas Tournadre, Tom Owen-Smith and Nathan Hill with whom I had many discussions in relation to this topic, and thanks to Nathan W. Hill and Nancy Caplow for reading drafts of the paper. Thanks also to the speaker of Lamjung Yolmo who tolerated many questions from me as I attempted to grapple with egophoric evidentiality in their language. The work on Lamjung Yolmo was funded by the Australian Research Council Discovery Project (0878126) "Language and Social Cognition: The Design Resources of Grammatical Diversity" and the Alma Hanson Scholarship at The University of Melbourne. An earlier version of this chapter was written while I was at NTU, Singapore as a Centre for Liberal Arts and Social Sciences (CLASS) funded Postdoctoral Research Fellow.

References

Aikhenvald, Alexandra Y. 2004. *Evidentiality*. Oxford: Oxford University Press.
Agha, Asif. 1993. *Structural form and utterance context in Lhasa Tibetan: grammar and indexicality in a non-configurational language*. New York: Peter Lang.
Caplow, Nancy J. 2000. *The epistemic marking system of émigré Drokpa Tibetan. Unpublished manuscript*. University of California. Santa Barbara. Retrieved from http://lingtechcomm.unt.edu/~njcaplow/
Caplow, Nancy. This volume. Inference and deferred evidence in Tibetan. In L. Gawne & N.W. Hill (eds) *Evidential systems of Tibetan languages*, 187–224. Berlin; Boston: Mouton de Gruyter.
Chang, Kun, and Betty Chang. 1984. The certainty hierarchy among Spoken Tibetan verbs of being. *Bulletin of the Institute of History and Philology, Academia Sinica* 55(4). 603–635.
Curnow, Timothy. 2002. Conjunct/disjunct marking in Awa Pit. *Linguistics* 40(3). 611–627.
Dahl, Östen. 2000. Egophoricity in discourse and syntax. *Functions of Language* 7(1). 37–77.
Daudey, Henriëtte. 2014. *A grammar of Wadu Pumi*. (PhD), Melbourne: La Trobe University PhD thesis
DeLancey, Scott. 1986. Evidentiality and volitionality in Tibetan. In W. L. Chafe and J. Nichols (eds.), *Evidentiality: the linguistic coding of epistemology*, 203–213. Norwood, N.J.: Ablex Publishing Corporation.
DeLancey, Scott. 1990. Ergativity and the cognitive model of event structure in Lhasa Tibetan. *Cognitive Linguistics* 1(3). 289–321.
DeLancey, Scott. 1992. The historical origin of the conjunct-disjunct pattern in Tibeto-Burman. *Acta Linguistica Hafniensia*, 25. 289–321.
DeLancey, Scott. 2012. Still mirative after all these years. *Linguistic Typology* 16(3). 529–564.
Denwood, Philip. 2000. *Tibetan*. Amsterdam: John Benjamins.
Dickinson, Connie. 2000. Mirativity in Tsafiki. *Studies in language* 24(2). 379–421.
van Driem, George. 1998. *Dzongkha*. Leiden: Research School CNWS.
Ebihara, Shiho. 2010. Amdo Tibetan. In Y. Yamakoshi (ed.), *Grammatical Sketches from the Field*, 41–78. Tokyo: Research Institute for Languages and Cultures of Asia and Africa.
Ebihara, Shiho. 2011. Amdo Tibetan. *Tokyo University of Foreign Studies grammatical sketches from the field*. 41–78.
Ebihara, Shiho. This volume. Evidentiality of the Tibetan Verb snang. In L. Gawne & N.W. Hill (eds.), *Evidential systems of Tibetan languages*, 41–59. Berlin; Boston: Mouton de Gruyter.
Garrett, Edward John. 2001. *Evidentiality and Assertion in Tibetan*. Los Angeles: University of California PhD thesis.

Gawne, Lauren. 2013. *Lamjung Yolmo copulas in use: Evidentiality, reported speech and questions*. Melbourne: University of Melbourne dissertation.
Gawne, Lauren. 2016. Questions and answers in Lamjung Yolmo Questions and answers in Lamjung Yolmo. *Journal of Pragmatics* 101(31–53). doi: http://dx.doi.org/10.1016/j.pragma.2016.04.002
Hale, Austin. 1980. Person markers: Finite conjunct and disjunct verb forms in Newari. In R.L. Trail (ed.), *Papers in South-East Asian linguistics* (Vol. 7), 95–106. Canberra: Australian National University.
Haller, Felix. 2000. *Dialekt und Erzählungen von Shigatse*. Bonn: VGH Wissenschaftsverlag.
Haller, Felix. 2004. *Dialekt und Erzählungen von Them chen: sprachwissenschaftliche Beschreibung eines Nomadendialektes aus Nord-Amdo*. Bonn: VGH Wissenschaftsverlag.
Hammarström, Harald, Robert Forkel, Martin Haspelmath and Sebastian Bank. 2015. *Glottolog 2.5*. Leipzig: Max Planck Institute for Evolutionary Anthropology. (Available online at http://glottolog.org, Accessed on 2015-09-30.)
Hein, Veronika. 2007. The mirative and its interplay with evidentiality in the Tibetan dialect of Tabo (Spiti). *Linguistics of the Tibeto-Burman Area* 30(2). 195–214.
Herrmann, Silke. 1989. *Erzählungen und Dialekt von Diṅri*. Bonn: VGH Wissenschaftsverlag.
Hill, Nathan W. 2012. 'Mirativity' does not exist: ḥdug in 'Lhasa' Tibetan and other suspects. *Linguistic Typology* 16(3). 389–433.
Hill, Nathan W. 2013a. 'ḥdug as a testimonial marker in Classical and Old Tibetan. *Himalayan Linguistics* 12(1). 1–16.
Hill, Nathan W. 2013b. Contextual semantics of 'Lhasa' Tibetan evidentials. *SKASE Journal of Theoretical Linguistics* 10 (3):47–54.
Hill, Nathan W. This volume. Perfect experiential constructions: the inferential semantics of direct evidence. In L. Gawne & N.W. Hill (eds.), *Evidential systems of Tibetan languages*, 131–159. Berlin; Boston: Mouton de Gruyter.
Hongladarom, Krisadawan. 2007. Evidentiality in Rgyalthang Tibetan. *Linguistics of the Tibeto-Burman Area* 30(2). 17–44.
Hoshi, Izumi. 2010. 14世紀チベット語文献『王統明示鏡』における存在動詞. / *Existential Verbs in the rGyal-rabs gSal-ba'i Me-long, a 14th Century Tibetan Narrative*. 東京大学言語学論集 (Tokyo University Linguistic Papers), 29(3). 29–68.
Huber, Brigitte. 2005. *The Tibetan dialect of Lende (Kyirong)*. Bonn: VGH Wissenschaftsverlag.
Hyslop, Gwendolyn. 2011. *A grammar of Kurtöp*. Eugene: The University of Oregon PhD thesis.
Hyslop, Gwendolyn. 2014. On the category of speaker expectation of interlocutor knowledge in Kurtöp. *Proceedings of the 40th Annual Meeting of the Berkeley Linguistics Society (BLS 40)*, 201–214. Berkeley: Berkeley Linguistics Society.
Hyslop, Gwendolyn & Karma Tshering. This volume. An overview of some epistemic categories in Dzongkha. In L. Gawne & N.W. Hill (eds.), *Evidential systems of Tibetan languages*, 351–365. Berlin; Boston: Mouton de Gruyter.
Kelly, Barbara F. 2004. A grammar of Sherpa. In C. Genetti (ed.) *Tibeto-Burman languages of Nepal: Manange and Sherpa*, 232–440. Canberra: Pacific Linguistics.
Kretschmar, Monika. 1986. *Erzählungen und Dialekt der Drokpas aus Südwest-Tibet*. Sankt Augustin: VGH Wissenschaftsverlag.
Kretschmar, Monika. 1995. *Erzählungen und Dialekt aus Südmustang*. Bonn: VGH Wissenschaftsverlag.
Mithun, Marianne. 1999. *The languages of native North America*. Cambridge, UK; New York: Cambridge University Press.

Oisel, Guillaume. 2013. *Morphosyntaxe et semantique des auxiliaires et des connecteurs du Tibetain Litteraire*. Paris: Universite Sorbonne Nouvelle - Paris 3, PhD thesis.
Oisel, Guillaume. This volume. On the Origin of the Lhasa Tibetan Evidentials song and byung. In L. Gawne & N.W. Hill (eds.), *Evidential systems of Tibetan languages*, 161–183. Berlin; Boston: Mouton de Gruyter.
Oswalt, Robert L. 1986. The evidential system of Kashaya. In W. L. Chafe and J. Nichols (eds.), *Evidentiality: the linguistic coding of epistemology*, 29–45. Norwood: Ablex Publishing Corporation.
Post, Mark W. 2013. Person-sensitive TAME marking in Galo: Historical origins and functional motivation. In Tim Thornes, Eric Andvik, Gwen Hyslop & Joana Jansen (eds.), *Functional-Historical Approaches to Explanation*, 107–130. Amsterdam; Philadelphia: John Benjamins Publishing Company.
Róna-Tas, András. 1985. *Wiener Vorlesungen zur Sprach- und Kulturgeschichte Tibets*. Vienna: Arbeitskreis für Tibetische und Buddhistische Studien, Universität Wien.
Rule, W.M. 1977. *A comparative study of the Foe, Huli and Pole languages of Papua New Guinea*. Sydney: University of Sydney.
San Roque, Lila, and Loughnane, Robin. 2012. The New Guinea Highlands evidentiality area. *Linguistic Typology* 16(1). 111–167.
San Roque, Lila, Simeon Floyd & Elizabeth Norcliffe. 2015. Evidentiality and interrogativity. *Lingua*. Advance online publication. doi:10.1016/j.lingua.2014.11.003.
San Roque, Lila, Simeon Floyd & Elisabeth Norcliffe. forthcoming. *Egophoricity*. Amsterdam: John Benjamins.
San Roque, Lila, Lauren Gawne, Darja Hoenigman, Julia Colleen Miller, Stef Spronck, Alan Rumsey, Alice Carroll, and Nicholas Evans. 2012. Getting the story straight: Language fieldwork using a narrative problem-solving task. *Language Documentation and Conservation* 6. 135–174.
Schöttelndreyer, Burkhard. 1980. Persons markers in Sherpa. *Pacific Linguistics* A53. 125–130.
Schwieger, Peter. 1989. *Tibetisches Erzählgut aus Brag-g.yab: Texte mit Übersetzungen, grammatischem Abriss und Glossar*. Bonn: VGH Wissenschaftsverlag.
Shafer, Robert. 1966. *Introduction to Sino-Tibetan*. Wiesbaden, Harrassowitz.
Sun, Jackson T.-S. 1993. Evidentials in Amdo Tibetan. *Bulletin of the Institute of History and Philology*, 63(4). 143–188.
Suzuki, Hiroyuki. 2012. Multiple usages of the verb snang in Gagatang Tibetan (Weixi, Yunnan). *Himalayan Linguistics*, 11(1). 1–16.
Suzuki, Hiroyuki. This volume. The evidential system of Zhollam Tibetan. In L. Gawne & N.W. Hill (eds.), *Evidential systems of Tibetan languages*, 423–444. Berlin; Boston: Mouton de Gruyter.
Takeuchi, Tsuguhito. 1990. チベット語の述部に置ける助動詞の昨日と園発達 方栄 Chibetto-go no jutsubu ni okeru jodōshi no kinō to sono hattatsu katei / The semantic Function of Auxiliary verbs in Tibetan and their historical development. In Sakiyamo and Sato (eds.), *Asian Languages and General Linguistics*, 6–16. Tokyo: Sanseido.
Takeuchi, Tsuguhito. 2015. The function of auxiliary verbs in Tibetan predicates and their historical development. *Revue d'Etudes Tibétaines* 31. 401–415.
Tournadre, Nicholas. 1991. The rhetorical use of the Tibetan ergative. *Linguistics of the Tibeto-Burman Area* 14(1). 93–107.
Tournadre, Nicholas. 1996. *L'ergativité en Tibétain Moderne*. Paris/Leuven: Peeters Publishers.
Tournadre, Nicholas. 2008. Arguments against the concept of 'conjunct'/'disjunct' in Tibetan. In Brigitte Huber, Marianne Volkart and Paul Widmer (eds.), *Chomolangma, Demawend*

und Kasbek, Festschrift für Roland Bielmeier, 281–308. Saale: International Institute for Tibetan and Buddhist Studies.

Tournadre, Nicholas. 2014. The Tibetic languages and their classification. In T. Owen-Smith & N. Hill (eds.), *Trans-Himalayan linguistics, historical and descriptive linguistics of the Himalayan area*, 105–130. Berlin: Mouton de Gruyter.

Tournadre, Nicholas, and Sangda Dorje. 2003. *Manual of standard Tibetan: Language and civilisation*. Ithaca: Snowlion Publications.

Tournadre, Nicholas & Konchok Jiatso. 2001. Final auxiliary verbs in literary Tibetan and in the dialects. *Linguistics of the Tibeto-Burman Area* 24(1). 49–111.

Tournadre, Nicholas, and Randy J. LaPolla. 2014. Towards a new approach to evidentiality: Issues and directions for research. *Linguistics of the Tibeto-Burman Area* 37(2). 240–263.

Tribur, Zoe. This volume. Observations on factors affecting the distributional properties of evidential markers in Amdo Tibetan. In L. Gawne & N.W. Hill (eds.), *Evidential systems of Tibetan languages*, 367–421. Berlin; Boston: Mouton de Gruyter.

Widmer, Manuel. 2015. The transformation of verb agreement into epistemic marking: evidence from Tibeto-Burman. In Jürg Fleischer, Elisabeth Rieken & Paul Widmer (eds.), *Agreement from a diachronic perspective*, 53–73. Berlin: De Gruyter.

Yliniemi, Juha. This volume. Copulas in Denjongke or Sikkimese Bhutia. In L. Gawne & N.W. Hill (eds.), *Evidential systems of Tibetan languages*, 297–349. Berlin; Boston: Mouton de Gruyter.

Yukawa Yasutoshi 湯川恭敏. 1975. チベット語の述語 Chibettogo no jutsugo [The Predicates of Tibetan] アジア・アフリカ文法研究 *Ajia Afurika bunpō kenkyū / Asian & African Linguistics* 4. 1–14. Tokyo: ILCAA.

Yukawa Yasutoshi 湯川恭敏. This volume. Lhasa Tibetan Predicates. In L. Gawne & N.W. Hill (eds.), *Evidential systems of Tibetan languages*, 187–224. Berlin; Boston: Mouton de Gruyter.

Nicolas Tournadre
4 A typological sketch of evidential/epistemic categories in the Tibetic languages

4.1 Introduction

This chapter provides a typological overview of evidential categories found in the Tibetic languages. The most complex evidential systems are attested in three regions of the world: the Tucanoan and Nambikwaran language families of Amazonia; the East Kutubuan language family spoken in Papua New Guinea (see Aikhenvald 2004; Guentchéva and Landaburu 2007) and, as we will see, the Tibetic languages, spoken on the Tibetan plateau and in the Himalayas. The term 'Tibetic' denotes a well-defined compact family of languages derived from Old Tibetan (see Tournadre 2008, 2014) which constitutes a 'close-knit sub-group' of the Sino-Tibetan macro-family (Sun 2014).[1] The Tibetic languages, called until recently "Tibetan dialects", are mutually unintelligible. They are spoken across a large area that spans six countries: China, India, Bhutan, Nepal, Pakistan and Myanmar.

In the last three decades, numerous studies have discussed evidentiality, a fundamental feature of this language family. However, another important dimension of the verb systems of Tibetic language family is epistemicity. For various reasons (some ideological, some perhaps related to scientific fashion), epistemic modalities have not received sufficient attention in the literature on Tibetic languages. The evidential systems of some languages are relatively well documented, including Standard Tibetan (Garrett 2001; Tournadre 1996a; Tournadre and Dorje 2003; Mélac 2014), Kyirong (Huber 2005), Amdo (Sun 1993; Sung and Lha 2005), Ladakhi (Koshal 1982), Balti (Ebihara this volume) and Sherpa (Kelly 2004; Tournadre et al. 2009). Epistemic modalities, on the other hand, still need fundamental research in most Tibetic languages. Some authors (e.g. Aikhenvald 2004; de Haan 1999) insist on maintaining a clear-cut distinction between epistemic and evidential markers. However as shown by Tournadre and LaPolla (2014), these two domains are very closely related and they may indeed function as a continuum. The continuity between epistemic and evidential marking is

---

[1] Other scholars call this family 'Tibeto-Burman' or 'Trans-Himalayan'.

Note: I am grateful to Nathan W. Hill, Lauren Gawne and an anonymous reviewer for their sound comments and useful suggestions. Many thanks also to Diana Lewis for correcting the manuscript.

DOI 10.1515/9783110473742-004

particularly clear in Tibetic languages. Thus, I here refer to Evidential/Epistemic systems (E/E systems). As well as evidential and epistemic marking, various specific speech acts such as promising, warning and suggesting may also be marked, marginally, in the verbal systems of the Tibetic languages.

It is convenient to classify Tibetic E/E systems as essentially conveying three types of grammatical information: a) evidentiality, b) epistemicity, c) specific speech acts. These types of marking occur in the same paradigmatic slot of the verb, and may be analysed within the general concept of "authorial stance" (see Alonso Almeida 2012).

For the notion of 'evidential', I use the definition proposed by Tournadre and LaPolla that evidentiality refers to "the representation of source and access to information according to the speaker's perspective and strategy" (2014: 241). This definition makes a clear distinction between 'source' and 'access'. In the Tibetic languages, both source and access to information are grammaticalized.

For epistemicity, the definition proposed by Nuyts is useful:

> Epistemic modality is [...] an evaluation of the chances that a certain hypothetical state of affairs under consideration (or some aspect of it) will occur, is occurring, or has occurred in a possible world which serves as the universe of interpretation for the evaluation process, and which, in the default case, is the real world (or rather, the evaluator's interpretation of it) [...] (2001: 21).

De Haan makes the following claim:

> Epistemic modality and evidentiality both deal with evidence, but they differ in what they do with that evidence. Epistemic modality *evaluates* evidence and on the basis of this evaluation assigns a confidence measure to the speaker's utterance. This utterance can be high, diminished, or low. An epistemic modal will be used to reflect this degree of confidence. An evidential *asserts* that there is evidence for the speaker's utterance but refuses to interpret the evidence in any way. (1999 emphasis in original)

While this view seems correct in general, we will see that in the Tibetic languages, some epistemic markers do both operations: they *assert* a type of evidence, i.e logical or sensory inference, and *evaluate* this evidence.

In order to capture the specificity of Tibetic evidentiality, one must thus take into consideration the relation between the three components of the E/E systems: evidential *sensu stricto*, epistemic marking and some specific speech acts.

4.2 General characteristics of E/E systems in Tibetic languages

The Tibetic E/E systems are associated with a number of typological characteristics that play a crucial role in the functioning of these systems. Among these characteristics, one should mention: E/E marking on the verb, restriction of E/E categories to declarative and interrogative sentences, the anticipation rule in interrogative sentences, marking on the main clause, flexibility of E/E marking, correlations with tense-aspect markers, correlations between E/E categories and person, and correlations between E/E categories and memory activation (see Tournadre and LaPolla 2014). I discuss these in turn below.

4.2.1 E/E marking on the verb

In the Tibetic languages, both evidential and epistemic marking appears on the verb as an auxiliary, a clitic or a suffix.[2] It is also conveyed by copulative and existential verbs. As we shall see below, the marking strategies are the same in all the Tibetic languages. Since predicative adjectives[3] have many verbal properties in these languages, E/E marking may also occur on adjectives, but it is never marked on any other lexical categories such as nouns or adverbs. Evidential and epistemic suffixes may co-occur. In that case, the epistemic suffix normally precedes the evidential one.

The paradigm of E/E categories conveyed by verbs is essentially available in the main clause, but it is generally absent in subordinate clauses (see Chang et al. 1964; Tournadre and Dorje 1998, 2009: 76, 142; Garrett 2001; DeLancey 2012).

4.2.2 Restriction of E/E categories to declarative and interrogative sentences

Evidential markers occur only in declarative and interrogative sentences and do not appear in commands. The absence of evidential marking in the imperative or its limitation to declarative and interrogative sentences is however not specific to Tibetic languages and seems to be attested in "an overwhelming majority of languages" (Aikhenvald 2004: 250). In the Tibetic languages, the set of evidentials in interrogative sentences is usually the same as the set used in declarative sentences, contrary to many languages throughout the world which have "reduced systems of evidential in questions" (Aikhenvald 2004: 242). Unlike evidentials, most epistemic markers are not compatible with questions in the Tibetic languages (see Vokurková 2008, see also §5.5 below).

---

2 In some cases, they may appear at the clausal level.
3 For example in Amdo, the adjectives *yag*, "beautiful", *ring* 'long', *'khyag* 'cold' (outside), which have comparative and superlative suffixes also take verbal auxiliaries when they are used as predicates.

4.2.3 The anticipation rule in interrogative sentences

The isomorphism of evidential categories in declarative and interrogative sentences is attributable to the anticipation rule in interrogative structures in Tibetic languages. In the case of questions, the speaker must anticipate the source and access to information that is available to the addressee. Accordingly, she chooses an auxiliary or copulative verb that can be used by the addressee in his answer (see Tournadre 1992: 204, 1996b: 220; Tournadre and Dorje 2003). The anticipation rule may be best explained by the pragmatic notions of 'empathy' (Kuno 1987) and 'perspective' (Tournadre and LaPolla 2014).

Although the addressee may always use in his answer the auxiliary or the copulative verbs proposed by the current speaker, he is not obliged to. This characteristic is not unique to Tibetic languages. According to Aikhenvald in languages from a wide variety of families "evidentials in an interrogative clause reflect the information source of the addressee" (2004: 245). However, Aikhenvald's formulation lacks an important feature: the evidential does not *reflect* the source (since the source and access are not precisely known), but *presupposes* the addressee's information source and/or access and *anticipates* the use of the appropriate evidential marker in the question. For the Tibetic languages, some authors have interpreted the rule of anticipation as a fundamental feature of so called 'conjunct markers' (§6); however, the anticipation rule applies to any of the evidential markers (see examples in §5.4).

4.2.4 Flexibility of E/E marking

The choice of evidential or epistemic markers is flexible and depends on the speakers' communicative intention and is also related to memory activation, as shown by Tournadre and LaPolla (2014); E/E marking is not purely 'automatic' or 'objective'. Many authors note this flexibility in the use of the E/E markers (Hongladarom 1993; Bielmeier 2000; Vokurková 2008; Oisel 2013; Gawne 2013; Hill 2013b; Tournadre and LaPolla 2014). This flexibility, related to the communicative intention, is one of the arguments against the notions of 'conjunct/ disjunct' being applied to Tibetic languages (for a refutation of these notions in Tibetan see Tournadre 2008).

4.2.5 Correlations with tense-aspect markers

E/E categories depend on the various tenses and aspects. The number of evidential markers is usually higher in the past than in the present and future. The same auxiliaries may be used (together with different connectives/ nominalizers) in the various tenses and aspects, but they often convey slightly different values. For example in Ü-Tsang and northern Kham, the sensory auxiliaries *'dug* and *gda'* are used in the progressive present and in the completed past but they convey respectively a 'sensory' meaning and a 'sensory inferential' meaning (see Tournadre and Jiatso 2001).

4.2.6 Correlations between E/E categories and person

Among the striking characteristics of the E/E systems are the correlations between the access to information and the first, second or third persons. These patterns are motivated by pragmatic and cognitive features. By and large person correlations have either gone unnoticed (see §5.1 for the endopathic function of the sensory marker) or conversely have been magnified (see §5.2 for the egophoric markers) and considered as instances of 'person marking' and agreement.[4]

4.3 Morphology of E/E systems

From a diachronic point of view, evidentiality and epistemicity emerged in Classical Tibetan, and possibly even as early as Old Tibetan (see Oisel 2013; Hill 2013a). The emergence of evidentiality is probably related to the grammaticalization of deixis (see Tournadre 1992; Oisel 2013; Hill 2013a; Shao 2014). Evidential and epistemic markers are derived from copulative, existential and motion verbs and, to a lesser extent, modal verbs (see Tournadre and Jiatso 2001). These verbs have been grammaticalized into copulas and auxiliary verbs. The auxiliaries may occur alone after the verb but are often accompanied by a relator, which corresponds either to a nominaliser or to a connective linking the auxiliary to the lexical verb. Synchronically, auxiliaries and relators are often fused together and one may analyse these forms as suffixes or verb endings (see Zeisler 2004). In most cases, evidential and epistemic marking now appears as a suffix or even as a series of suffixes. However, these suffixes still sometimes retain some autonomy and have an intermediary status between auxiliary and suffix. From a diachronic and comparative point of view, it is better to use the concept of auxiliary even if, from a strictly synchronic point of view 'verb endings' or 'verb suffixes' would often be more appropriate.

Evidential and epistemic marking continues in all the modern languages, but most auxiliaries are not the same as those used in Classical Tibetan and are

---

[4] Person correlations are probably frequent in various fields of the world languages but they have not received much attention. See Mélac (2014: 438, 492, 493).

specific to the modern languages. As pointed out by a number of authors (Sun 1993; Bielmeier 2000; DeLancey 2012), modern evidential systems are not cognate and "do not always correspond in morphological structure" (DeLancey 2012: 555). However, the modern Tibetic E/E systems share a fundamental semantico-cognitive strategy as well as an auxiliation strategy.

I propose the following general abstract structure for the verb predicate in the Tibetic languages:

*(DIR)-(NEG)-**VERB**[INFL]-(REL)- **(**NEG/PQ**)**-**AUX**-(FQ/TAG/JUS)

As mentioned in Section 1, evidential and epistemic markers are closely related at both the morphosyntactic and the semantic level. The chart below shows that the evidential and epistemic copulas in Standard Tibetan (Lhasa Tibetan) are made of the same verbs: *yin* 'to be', *red* 'to be' and *yod* 'to exist'. Note that these copulas are either simple (see e.g. *yin* or *yod*) or compound (see *yin.pa.red* or *yod. pa red.*).

Here all the examples in the various Tibetic languages appear in the traditional orthography and are accompanied by a phonological transcription only when the pronunciation is not obvious. The choice of a Classical orthography is to facilitate the comparison among languages and to show the tight relations between these languages and Classical Tibetan, even when it is not obvious.[5]

Evidential copulas	Epistemic copulas
yin (EGO)	*a.yin* (EPI3+NEG), *yin.pa. 'dra* (EPI2)
	yin.'gro (EPI1)
yin.pa.red (CORR)	*yin.gyi.red* (EPI2)
yin.pa.yod (MNEM)	*yin.sa.red* (EPI2)
yod (EGO)	*a.yod* (EPI3+NEG), *yod.pa. 'dra* (EPI2)
	yod. 'gro (EPI1)
yod.pa.red (CORR)	*yod.kyi.red* (EPI2)
yod.red (FACT)	*yod.sa.red* (EPI2)

The parallelism between evidential and epistemic marking continues outside the copula system, being also reflected in the morphology of auxiliaries. In the chart

---

[5] Thus a knowledge of Kham phonology immediately tells us that Dongwang /ze/ is regularly derived from *yod*, but only this transliteration allows one to compare it easily with Central Tibetan equivalent /yö/ (yod) or Amdo /yot/, /yol/.

4 A typological sketch of evidential/epistemic categories in the Tibetic languages

below, both evidential and epistemic auxiliaries of Standard Tibetan are built with the existential copulas *'dug* and *yod*.

Evidential auxiliaries	Epistemic auxiliaries
V-*gi. 'dug* (PROG+SENS)	V-*pa. 'dug* (FUT+EPI3+SENS+INF)
V-*gi.yod* (PROG+EGO)	V-*pa.yod* (FUT+EPI3+MNEM)

Many Tibetic languages exhibit this kind of parallelism between epistemic and evidential markers. Some Tibetic languages have developed very rich paradigms. Let us illustrate the paradigm of evidential and epistemic equative copulas found in Standard Tibetan. We find in this language the following 14 equative copulas (*red, red.bzhag, yin.da.yin, yin.pa.red, yin.pa.yod, a.yin, yin. 'gro, yin. 'gro'o, yin.pa. 'dra, yin.gyi.red, yin.sa.red, yin, yin-za, red-za*), which all correspond to the English verb 'to be' but encode addition grammaticalized E/E categories.

(1) *bu.mo **red*** '(it) is a girl' [FACT]
(2) *bu.mo **red.bzhag*** '(Oh, I see!), (it) is a girl' [SENS INF]
(3) *bu.mo **yin.da.yin*** 'Of course, (it) is a girl' [EPI3]
(4) *bu.mo **yin.pa.red*** '(Oh so), (it) was a girl!' (I did not think so) [CORR]
(5) *bu.mo **yin.pa.yod*** '(it) is/was a girl, (as far as I can remember)' [MNEM]
(6) *bu.mo **a.yin*** 'I strongly doubt (it) is a girl!' [EPI3+NEG]
(7) *bu.mo **yin. 'gro*** '(It) may be a girl!' [EPI1]
(8) *bu.mo **yin. 'gro'o*** '(It) is maybe not a girl!' [EPI1+NEG]
(9) *bu.mo **yin.pa. 'dra*** '(It) is probably a girl! (from what I can see)' [EPI2+ SENS]
(10) *bu.mo **yin.sa.red*** '(It) is probably a girl! (It) is a girl' [EPI2+ SENS]
(11) *bu.mo **yin.gyi.red*** '(It) is probably a girl!' [EPI2+ FACT]
(12) *bu.mo **yin*** '(I) am a girl' or in a marked sentence '(it) is *my* girl/daughter' [EGO]
(13) *bu.mo **yin-za*** '(I) am a girl, (she) says'
(14) *bu.mo **red-za*** '(they) say that (it) is a girl'

The sentences above are made with *bu.mo* 'girl' followed by a simple copula or a compound copula (in bold). Even though, most of these copulas are very frequent, some of them are not well described in the literature. In particular, the 'mnemic' *yin.pa.yod*, the 'self-corrective' *yin.pa.red* and the 'epistemic' forms which display a number of very fine semantic nuances, have received little attention. The same E/E paradigms are attested with the auxiliary verbs. For details, see Tournadre and Dorje (2003: 461–465) and Vokurková (2008).

4.4 Core categories of the evidential and epistemic systems

4.4.1 Sensory

All the Tibetic E/E systems have sensory markers.[6] Thus the grammaticalization of sensory perception plays a central role in the Tibetic languages. However, the sensory perception often involves various senses as well as some kind of inference. Thus sensory is closely related to the notion of inference. As noted in Tournadre and LaPolla "in many cases, the perception requires various types of senses and inferences, so the use of the evidential markers is generally much more complex than can be captured by simply saying, for example, 'visual sensory'" (2014: 258).

The choice of one sense or another depends on the semantics of the predicate. For example, presenting an object (cloth, food, sound, etc.) to somebody, in Standard Spoken Tibetan one may ask:

(15) *snying.rje.po*   *'dug-gas*
     beautiful   COP.SENS-Q
     'Is it beautiful?'

(16) *zhim.po*   *'dug-gas*
     tasty   COP.SENS-Q
     'Is it good?'

(17) *dri.ma*   *'dug-gas*
     smell   COP.SENS-Q
     'Is there a (bad) smell?'

(18) *'jam.po*   *'dug-gas*
     soft   COP.SENS-Q
     'Is it soft?'

(19) *snyan.po*   *'dug-gas*
     nice to hear   COP.SENS-Q
     'Is it nice to hear?'

The speaker invites the addressee to look at her dress (cf. (15)), to taste the dish (cf. (16)), to smell the object (cf. (17)), to touch the cloths (cf. (18)), to listen to the sound (cf. (19)).

---

[6] According to Bielmeier (2000), Balti might be the only language that lacks a sensory evidential, but recently Ebihara (2014) has shown that this language has also developed sensory markers in the Turtuk and Tyakshi dialects.

As mentioned earlier, very often, a sensory marker implies several senses:

(20) *me   chen.po   cig   'dug*
     fire   big   a   COP.SENS
     'There is a big fire.'

The speaker sees the fire, but at the same time smells it, and feels the smoke in her eyes, experiencing the fire through a number of different senses at once.

In a strict sense, purely sensory markers are related to the perception of on-going situations and thus associated with progressive aspect or a present state. Sensory markers are also attested with past completed events and, in that case, they usually imply that the speaker has witnessed the entire scene.

For obvious cognitive reasons, sensory markers do not occur with the future tense, nor do they occur with the resultative perfect. In the first case, it is impossible to witness an event which has not (yet) taken place and in the latter, one perceives only the result of an event and not the entire event itself. In these cases, inferential markers are used as we will see below.

4.4.2 Inferential

Inferential markers[7] also play a very important role in the Tibetic E/E systems. They frequently occur in the perfect and future as shown in the examples below from Standard Tibetan:

(21) *char.pa   btang-pa.'dug*[8]
     rain   LV-FUT.SENS.INF.EPI
     'It's likely to rain.'

(22) *char.pa   btang-bzhag*
     rain   LV-PERF.SENS.INF
     'It has rained.'

Both (21) and (22) imply visual evidence and inference. The first example may be uttered in a situation when the speaker notices dark clouds and *deduces* that is likely to rain in the near future. In the second sentence, the speaker has only seen

---

7 The term inferential here essentially refers to 'sensory inferential' following Aikhenvald (2004). Logical inference falls into the category of 'assumed evidentials' (see below).
8 In Lhasa, the auxiliary *'dug* may be dropped in affirmative sentences but is necessarily present in questions. As noted by N. Hill (2012: 399), the form is not structurally a future as in V-*gi.yin/ gi.red* but rather a present corresponding literally to "there is (a *clue*) to rain"

the wet ground and can *infer* that it has rained. It is worth mentioning that in (21), the grammatical semantics conveys sensory, inferential and epistemic meanings, while in (22), the epistemic dimension is absent: the speaker makes a statement based on his sensory inference and has no doubt that it has rained. This is true even if he is wrong and if for example, the ground is wet because it has been watered by the neighbours.

In some Tibetic languages, inferential markers also occur with the present tense.

4.4.3 Assumed

Another macrocategory attested in all the Tibetic languages is 'assumed evidential'. This category is based on evidence "other than visible results" and may include logical reasoning, assumption, general or even personal knowledge (see Aikhenvald, 2004: 63).[9] Aikhenvald adds: "the more the speaker has to rely on reasoning based on knowledge or on common sense, the more chance there is that an assumed evidential will be used" (2004: 3).

The main characteristic of the assumed evidential is that it is based on neither sensory nor inferential evidence, but on the *speaker's knowledge* and it conveys either information about events or situations that she knows well or general knowledge. Thus, the source of this type of statement is normally the speaker, but the access to information is not specified. The assumed evidential just like the inferred evidential does not imply any doubt (Aikhenvald 2004: 175). The term "assumed evidential" is problematic in the case of the Tibetic languages because it implies in English some doubt ("I assume that") and other terms might be more convenient such as "certificative" or "authoritative", but I will keep the term 'assumed evidential' in this chapter. In the various Tibetic languages, assumed evidentials subsume different subcategories such as 'assumptive' (see Oisel 2013), 'factual' (Tournadre and Dorje 1998, 2003) and 'egophoric' (see below).

4.4.4 Hearsay and reported speech

Another important category found in the Tibetic languages is hearsay and reported speech. Normally this evidential category is marked with a clitic and does not appear in the same syntactic slot as other evidential forms. One of the major features of hearsay and reported speech marking in the Tibetic languages is that this evidential category may combine with various other evidentials. Thus sentences

---

9 Aikhenvald does not mention personal knowledge.

which convey reported speech may double mark the access to information: a) the actual speaker's access to information and b) the reported speaker's access to information (see Tournadre and LaPolla 2014: 245/246).

In a number of modern languages such as Ü-Tsang (see Tournadre and Dorje 2003; Haller 2000), Amdo (Haller 2004; Sun 1993; Sung and Lha-Byams-rgyal 2005), and northern Kham (Gesang and Gesang 2002; Häsler 1999), the quotative marker is derived from the verb of speech *zer* 'to say' found in Classical Tibetan. In languages such as Ladakhi or Dzongkha, another form derived from the Classical Tibetan form *lo* is used to indicate reported speech or hearsay and is found in Balti (Sprigg 2002), Kyirong (Huber 2005), Yolmo (Gawne 2013) and Dzongkha (van Driem 1998). Another hearsay marker /tṣa/ in Dongwang Tibetan is derived from the Classical Tibetan verb *grag* 'to sound' (Bartee 2007: 374). I do not discuss subcategories of hearsay and reported speech, although there is variation in these categories across the Tibetic languages.

4.4.5 Epistemic

The last major category of these E/E systems is epistemic marking which plays a very significant role in the Tibetic languages. In these languages, unlike European languages, modal verbs are not used to express epistemic modalities. The equivalents of modality adverbs (such as 'perhaps', 'maybe', 'likely', 'probably', 'certainly', etc.) as well as epistemic cognition verbs (such as 'guess', 'believe', 'suppose', etc.) are not used as frequently as in European languages (see Vokurková 2008; Melac 2014). From a morphological point of view, the form and the number of epistemic markers in Tibetan languages vary quite a lot across varieties, but they all appear in the same morphosyntactic slot as the evidential markers, i.e as verb suffixes.

As noted earlier, since most studies have concentrated upon evidentiality, further research is still needed to describe the epistemic paradigm for most Tibetic languages. There are very few studies that deal with epistemic markers and these works are mostly devoted to Standard Spoken Tibetan and to Amdo. For Standard Spoken Tibetan see Tournadre and Dorje (1998, 2003), Mélac (2014) and particularly Vokurková (2008), the only monography entirely devoted to epistemic markers. For Amdo, see Sung and Lha-Byams-rGyal (2005) and Shao (2014).

One of the reasons that might explain the scarcity of research in that field is that epistemic markers are less frequent than evidential markers. According to Mélac's corpus, evidential markers appear in average every 12 seconds, i.e 300 times in one hour[10] (Mélac 2014: 383), while epistemic markers appear in average

---

10 or every 22 words.

only 15 times per hour (Mélac 2014: 211). Despite this big difference in frequency, epistemic markers constitute a rich paradigm in most Tibetan languages and the number of epistemic markers seems even higher than the number of evidential markers. Vokurková (2008: 348/349) lists altogether 19 evidential suffixes and 48 epistemic suffixes for the various tense-aspect categories. A word of caution is in order regarding the division of suffixes into evidentials and epistemics; epistemic markers often convey additional evidential meanings. On the one hand purely evidential suffixes (that are not associated with any evaluation or uncertainty) and, on the other hand, 'epistemic suffixes' which primarily indicate epistemic values, i.e the speaker's degree of certainty, but may additionally convey evidential meaning based on several types of inferences, either sensory or logical. Here are two examples from Vokurková (2008).

(23) *khong-la   dga'.rogs   yod.pa.'dra*
     3SG.HON-DAT lover   exist (EPI2+INF)
     'She probably has a boyfriend'

(24) *khong-la   dga'.rogs   yod.'gro*
     3SG.HON-DAT lover   exist (EPI1+ ASM)
     'She maybe has a boyfriend'[11]

Examples (23) and (24) differ in the degree of certainty. The speaker is more confident about her statement in (23) than in (24), but the two examples also differ in the types of inferences made by the speaker. Vokurková provides the following comment for (23): "[it corresponds to a] sensory inference: the speaker can often see her with the same person"; and for (24): "[it is a] logical inference: she is twenty, so the speaker guesses she has a boyfriend" (2008: 119).

Some epistemic markers such as *a.yin, yod.'gro, a-yong,* etc. inherently convey a negative polarity, without the presence of a negative morpheme, as in (25):

(25) *em.chi   cig   yod.'gro'o*
     doctor   IND   exist-EPI1+NEG
     "it is improbable that we'll find a doctor (here); I really doubt we'll find a doctor (here)"
     (Tournadre and Dorje 1998).

---

[11] I have modified the translation. Vokurková uses the adverb "probably", however, the degree of certainty conveyed here is less certain than in the previous example and thus it is better rendered in English by 'maybe'. Generally Vokurková (2008) translates EPI1 by both 'probably' and 'maybe'.

4.4.6 Summary of the core categories

Thus we may summarize the core (macro) categories of evidential and epistemic found in the Tibetic verb systems: (a) sensory, (b) inferential, (c) assumed, (d) quotative, (e) epistemic. Each of these categories may be subdivided into several subcategories. In section 8, we will also mention some marginal categories of the Tibetic systems, related to various speech act categories such as the benefactive and preventive futures.

4.5 Specific categories and subcategories

Each of these five categories may be subdivided into several subcategories. We will examine some of these subcategories and see how they may differ in the various languages.

4.5.1 Subcategories of sensory markers

The category of 'sensory' may receive various marking depending on the language. In many central and southern languages such as Ü-Tsang, Sherpa, and Dzongkha, the present and perfect marking of the sensory is derived from the verb *'dug*[12] 'to sit', while in Hor and several northern Kham dialects it is derived from the verb *gda'* with a similar meaning.[13] Another form, derived from *snang* 'to shine, to appear', is used for the sensory access marker in Phenpo (central Tibet), in the Pari (Hwari) dialect of Amdo, in many Kham dialects such as Bathang, Rgyalthang, Dongwang, in some languages of the northeast region such as Thewo, Cone, Drugchu, Sharkhok and Khöpokhok in Gansu and Sichuan (see Suzuki 2012), as well as in the Turtuk and Tyakshi dialects of Balti (see Ebihara this volume). In Amdo, the suffix *gi* is used.[14] The sensory markers *'*gi*, used in the Kham Derge dialect, as well as the Dzongkha *mas are not attested in Classical Tibetan. In the completed past, auxiliaries derived from *thal* 'to go'

---

12 The form *'dug* had already acquired evidential meaning in Classical Tibetan (Hoshi 2010; Hill 2012, 2013a; Oisel 2013).
13 The cognate *gdan* means 'seat', 'cushion'.
14 *gi* is probably a relator and the auxiliary (whether *gda'* or *'dug*) has been lost. Even in Lhasa Tibetan, affirmative sentence may drop the auxiliary and use only the relator gi: *khong yong-gi ('dug)* "he is coming". However, the auxiliary is obligatory in negative and interrogative sentences.

(Kham, Amdo) and *song* 'to go' (Ü, Tsang, Sherpa) are frequently attested to convey a sensory meaning.

The category of 'sensory' refers here to both 'external' and 'internal' sensory accesses to information. This category is attested in all the major Tibetan languages. The information referred to may be acquired through the sensory channels of the five senses of sight, sound, touch, smell, and taste, but may also be used for 'internal sensory' or 'endopathic' (the latter term coined in 1996a: 226 and 1996b) access to information. Endopathic marking encodes inner sensations such as cold, pain and hunger, as well as emotions such as fear and anger. Of course the speaker may lie when using a sensory marker and has not necessarily seen or experienced the event referred to.

'Endopathic' markers are formally identical to the 'external sensory' markers. The external sensory and the endopathic functions always exhibit different syntactic behaviours: the former are normally used in declarative sentences with 2nd and 3rd person "subject" while the latter are used with 1st person "subject".[15] The reason is clearly pragmatic: one cannot be a witness of oneself, except in some specific situations. For example, to say 'I am eating' or 'I am writing', Tibetan languages do not use sensory markers simply because it would entail 'I see myself eating', 'I see myself writing'. If the speaker sees himself in a mirror, in a dream, or in a movie, then the use of a sensory with the first person is perfectly acceptable. Conversely, the endopathic function is naturally associated with the first person since, only the speaker may directly perceive hunger, headache, fear, or some other internal state. He may only infer other people's experiences of these sensations.[16]

Some Tibetan languages, such as Ladakhi, Tö Ngari, and Spiti-Khunu-Garzha (Tournadre and LaPolla 2014; Hein 2007), make a distinction between 'visual' and 'non-visual sensory' (i.e gustative, auditory, tactile, olfative). These languages mark the visual with the auxiliary *'dug*, while the non-visual evidential is indicated by an auxiliary derived from *grag* 'to sound'. In these systems, as one could expect, the endopathic (or 'inner sensory') function is always marked by the non-visual evidential.

Some Tibetan languages such as Dzongkha have a special 'participatory-sensory' marker *yi* to convey the fact that the speaker has either witnessed or consciously taken part in an action or a situation. Van Driem calls this marker

---

[15] Aikhenvald (2004), who extensively mentions the so called 'conjunct-disjunct' opposition in relation to person, overlooks the strong correlation in declarative sentences between the sensory markers and persons.

[16] In questions, both external and endopathic sensory markers follow the anticipation rule.

"witnessed past" (1992, 1998: 267–270). Nonetheless, as we have seen earlier in the Tibetic languages 'sensory' markers normally do not occur with first person.[17] In order to designate the markers that normally occur both with 1st person (the speaker is a participant of the event, see example (28)) and with 2nd or 3rd person (the speaker is a witness of the event, see example (29)), I propose the term 'participatory-sensory'[18] for the marker *yi* in Dzongkha.

(26) *nga   lto   da ci las   za-da-yi*
     1SG   meal   already   eat-PAST-PSENS
     'I have already taken my meal.'
     (van Driem 1992: 243).

(27) *da   mo-gis   om   de   'bo-da-yi*
     now   3SGF-ERG   milk   that   spill-PAST-PSENS
     'Now she's spilt the milk.'
     (van Driem 1992: 243).

The 'participatory-sensory' category attested in Dzongkha is one of the major differences with many Tibetic languages such as Standard Tibetan or Amdo, for which the sensory category is not normally used with the 1st person in declarative sentences (see section 4.1)

4.5.2 Subcategories of inferential markers

Inferential meanings may be divided into 'sensory inferentials' and 'logical inferentials' (see Tournadre and Dorje 1998, 2003). Following Aikhenvald (2004), I apply the label 'inferential' by default to the sensory inferentials. Other types of inferentials, based on general knowledge and on logical deductions, are normally conveyed by factual or assumptive markers. As noted by Garrett (2001: 36–51) for Standard Spoken Tibetan, epistemic and inferential values may overlap. It is sufficient here to say, that the existence of 'sensory inferential' vs. 'inferential factual/assumptive' is attested across the Tibetic area.

---

[17] Except for the endopathic function and other specific situations.
[18] The term 'participatory' is used to describe some evidential markers of Papua New Guinea that are related to the participation of the 1st person (see San Roque and Loughnane 2012).

4.5.3 Subcategories of assumed, egophoric markers

As mentioned above, egophoric markers constitute a subtype of assumed evidentials. The category of 'egophoric' has recently attracted a growing attention in the community of linguists (see Gawne 2013; San Roque et al. 2017). The term '*égophore*' was coined by Claude Hagège (1982), and meant that 'ego' as a deictic center is a fundamental property of linguistic systems.[19] It did not refer to the grammatical phenomenon now known as 'egophoric' in the Tibetan languages and did not apply to any particular language or language group. The term 'egophoric' was used by Tournadre (1991) with an entirely different definition to describe a specific phenomenon found in Standard Tibetan. The use of an 'egophoric' auxiliary expresses the speaker's personal knowledge. The speaker is often directly implied involved in the event that is being described (see Tournadre and Dorje 2003: 93), "Egophoric auxiliaries are used with first person occurring overtly, covertly [...] regardless of its function in a given clause (subject, object, indirect object, locative complement)" (Tournadre 2008: 296). The *egophoric* is equivalent to 'personal knowledge' (van Driem 1998; DeLancey 1990), 'self-person' (Sun 1993), 'personal experience' (Huber 2005) or 'ego evidentiality' (Garrett 2001). While the semantic characteristic of egophoric is personal knowledge, the correlation of egophoric marking with 1st person (in declarative sentences) has attracted the attention of some researchers. However, it should be emphasized that the correlation of a marker with 1st person in Tibetic languages is not restricted to egophoric. For example, endopathic marking is normally only compatible with 1st person in declarative sentences. This is also true for benefactive futures (see below) which cannot be considered 'egophoric', although they are restricted to 1st persons. The reason is that benefactive futures do not convey personal knowledge but correspond to a proposal made by the speaker for the benefit of the addressee.

There are various subtypes of egophorics (see e.g. Tournadre 1996b, 2008): 'intentional egophoric', 'habitual egophoric', 'receptive egophoric' and 'experiential egophoric'. However, all these markers correspond to the definition above: they all indicate the speaker's personal knowledge and are all used with first person in declarative sentences. That is, the speaker is always the default interpretation even though in some cases, egophorics do appear with 3rd person

---

19 *Égophore* is a hyperonym for a few other notions related to the deictic center: *chronophore, exophore,* and *endophore,* which included the subcategories of *autophorique, anaphorique, cataphorique* and *logophorique.*

subject in declarative sentences when the speaker is either involved in the event or intimately related to the subject. Tournadre (2008: 296) describes a distinction between "narrow scope" and "wide scope" egophoric markers: the former type of egophoric auxiliary (or linking verb) designates only the 1st person itself, while the latter indicates not only the 1st person but also any entity (person or object) closely connected to the first person (such as a relative, close friend, or possession).

Egophoric markers are found in Tibet (Ü-Tsang, Tö-Ngari, Kham and Amdo, etc.) but do not generally appear in the Tibetan languages in the southern and western Himalayas. For example, Dzongkha *ʔin* (< *yin*) and *yod* do not convey an egophoric meaning in the sense defined above, unlike the related markers *yin* and *yod* found in Ü-Tsang, Amdo and Kham. The possibility of an interrogative sentence is a good test to distinguish the two concepts. Let's compare Dzongkha (30, 32) and Standard Spoken Tibetan (31, 33):

Dzongkha
(28) kho   mi   phyugpo   ʔin-na
     3SGM   man   rich   COP.ASM-Q
     'Is he a rich man?'[20]

Standard Spoken Tibetan
(29) *?kho   (mi)   phyug.po   yin-pas
     3SGM   (man)   rich   COP.EGO-Q
     Intended meaning: 'Is he a rich man?'[21]

Dzongkha
(30) kho-lu   tig.rub   yod-ga
     3SGM-DAT   money   COP.ASM-Q
     'Does he have money?'

On a similar example, van Driem gives the following commentary: "the sentence is appropriate if the speaker knows that the person to whom he is speaking is a long-time friend [...] who has personal knowledge of [his] financial affairs" (1998: 142).

The same use in Standard Spoken Tibetan would not normally be acceptable.

---

[20] Dzongkha examples are inspired by van Driem (1992: 117 and 130).
[21] In order to translate the question, one has to use a factual *red-pas* or an inferential *red-'dug-gas*.

(31) *?khong-la   dngul   yod-pas
    3SG.HON-DAT   money   COP.EGO-Q
    Intended meaning: 'Does he have money?'

In order to be appropriate, one should use either the factual *yod.red-pas* or the sensory *'dug-gas*.

As noted by for Yolmo evidentiality: "'ego' form [...] is similar to the standard Tibetan egophoric, but also has some major differences" (Gawne 2013: iii). Let us compare Yolmo with Standard Spoken Tibetan:

Yolmo
(32) /ngómbu   yìmba/
    sngon.po   yin.pa
    green   COP.ASM
    'It is green.'
    (Gawne 2013: 154)

Standard Spoken Tibetan
(33) *?*sngon.po*   yin*
    blue/green   COP.EGO
    Intended meaning: 'It is green.'

In fact, the only normal interpretation in Standard Spoken Tibetan is 'I am blue/green'. In order to translate the Yolmo sentence, one would have to use the factual marker and say: *sngon.po red*. The same would be true for the following example:

(34) /dì   hããs   yìmba/
    'di   /hããs/   *yin.pa*
    this   duck   COP.ASM
    'This is a duck.'
    (Gawne 2013: 169)

Again the use of the egophoric *yin* would not be acceptable in Standard Spoken Tibetan. The use of /yìmba/ in Yolmo emphasizes the speaker's (good) knowledge, but it does not entail that this knowledge is personal or specific to the speaker and hence restricted to first person. Yolmo, just as Ladakhi and Dzongkha, does not have an egophoric category *per se*. Rather than describing this as 'weak egophoric' it is more appropriate to use another label such as "assumptive". Historically, egophorics have evolved from the markers *yin* and *yod* which conveyed an assumptive meaning in Classical Tibetan (see Oisel 2013). Thus we probably have the following grammaticalization pattern: *neutral > emphatic >*

assumptive > or authoritative egophoric. The two copulas *yin* and *yod* are found in nearly all the modern Tibetic languages but they reflect different stages of this grammaticalization.

4.5.4 Subcategories of epistemic markers

Here I do not examine the subcategories of epistemic markers in details. Epistemic may be divided according to the degree of certainty. Vokurková (2008) proposes a threefold scale from low to high certainty: EPI1 'maybe/perhaps, it's possible that X', EPI2 'it's (im)probable/(un)likely that X' and EPI3 'it's very (im)probable/(un)likely that X'. As mentioned in §4.4 some epistemic markers also convey evidential meanings.

The main markers used to convey epistemic modalities in the Tibetic languages are derived from the verb *'gro* 'to go' (Ü, Tsang, Ladakhi), *'dra* 'to seem' (Ü, Tsang) and *'ong* 'to come' (Dzongkha). The copulative verb *red* (in combination with various relators) suffixed to the copulative verb *yin* or to the existential verb *yod* also conveys an epistemic meaning: *yin gyi red* (Ü), *yin.rgyu.red* (Am), *yin.ni.red* (Am) *yod.kyi.red* (Ü), *yod.rgyu.red* (Amdo), *yod.ni.red* (Amdo). In Lhasa Tibetan, a dubitative marker indicating a very low probability is a compound of the copulative verb with the prefixed interrogation: *a yin* (Ü) "I doubt X is", *a.yod* (Ü) 'I doubt X has'. The compound made of the verb *yong* is also attested for the dubitative: *a.yong* (Ü) "I doubt X has" (see Tournadre and Dorje 2003: 313).

Apart from these frequent constructions, one also encounters specific constructions attested only in some localities. That is the case of the Amdo suffix *na-thang* (Sung and Lha 2005) derived from the verb *thang* 'to be clear' or the Ladakhi *thig 'dug* form probably derived from the *thig (pa)* 'prediction'.

4.5.5 The anticipation rule applied to the various categories

The anticipation rule mentioned in section 2 is often described for egophoric markers (see also §6 on 'conjunct'), but in fact, it applies to all E/E categories. Here are some examples from Standard Spoken Tibetan:

4.5.5.1 Egophoric
In declarative sentences, the egophoric existential verb is used by default with the 1st person in declarative sentences and may not appear with 2nd or 3rd persons.

(35) nga-la   dngul   yod
    1SG-DAT   money   COP.EGO
    'I have money.'

The same existential verb *yod* is used in anticipation with the 2nd person in interrogative sentences.

(36) rang-la   dngul   yod-pas
    2SG-DAT   money   COP.EGO-Q
    'Do you have money.'

4.5.5.2 Endopathic sensory

In declarative sentences, the endopathic sensory marker *kyi ('dug)* is used by default with the 1st person and may not appear with 2nd or 3rd persons.

(37) nga   grod.khog   ltogs-kyi ('dug)
    1SG   stomach   be hungry-UNCP+ENPT
    'I am hungry.'

The same form (*kyi.'dug*) is used by anticipation with the 2nd person in interrogative sentences.

(38) rang   grod.khog   ltogs-kyi.'dug-gas
    2SG   stomach   be hungry-UNCP+ENPT -Q
    'Are you hungry.'

4.5.5.3 External sensory

In declarative sentences, the sensory copula is used by default with the 2nd and 3rd persons.

(39) rang   snying.rje.po   'dug
    2SG   pretty   COP.SENS
    'You are pretty!'

The same copula is used by anticipation with the 1st person in interrogative sentences.

(40) nga   snying.rje.po   'dug-gas
    1SG   pretty   COP.SENS-Q
    'Am I pretty?'

For some events, the speaker's access to information is cognitively limited. That is the case of the verb *skyes* 'to be born' because the speaker cannot have witnessed her own birth and she has to rely on reported speech or assumption. Thus, in

Standard Spoken Tibetan, in order to say: 'I was born there', one usually employs the factual.

(41) nga   chab.mdo-la   skyes-pa.red
     1SG   PR.N-DAT   be born-PAST.CMP.FACT
     'I was born in Chamdo.'

The most usual way to ask 'where were you born?' is to anticipate the answer and use the factual auxiliary:

(42) rang   ga.par   skyes-pa.red
     2SG   where?   be born-PAST.CMP.FACT
     'Where were you born?'

(43) *?rang   ga.par   skyes-song
     2SG   where?   be born-PAST.CMP.SENS
     'Where were you born?'

Evidentials are normally compatible with direct question markers (DQ) but they exhibit a lower compatibility with tag markers (TQ) or emphasis markers (EM). Epistemic markers are much less compatible with DQ, TQ and EM than the evidentials. This phenomenon has not received much attention so far. For example in Standard Spoken Tibetan, the DQ marker *pas/gas* is compatible with most evidential copulas and auxiliaries: *red-pas* (factual), *yin-pas* (egophoric), *'dug-gas* (sensory), *red.'dug-gas* (sensory inferential) but **yin.pa.yod-pas* (mnemic), **yin. pa.red-pas* (self-corrective). They are usually not compatible with most epistemic: !*yin.pa.'dra 'dug-ga*, !*yin.mdog kha.po 'dug-ga* (EPI2), **yin-pa 'dra-pas* (EPI2), **yod. kyi.red-pas* (EPI2), **a.yin-pas* (EPI3), etc.

The tags *(pa/ga)* which may be translated by 'isn't it' and express the search for a consensus show similar restrictions with evidentials and epistemic copulas or auxiliaries: *red-pa* (factual), *yin-pa* (egophoric), *'dug-ga* (sensory), *red.'dug-ga* (sensory inferential) but **yin.pa.yod-pa* (mnemic), **yin.pa.red-pa* (self-corrective), **a.yin-pa* (EPI3), etc. The emphatic marker *da* shows similar restriction to the tags.

4.6 The controversy concerning 'conjunct/disjunct systems'

Tibetic evidential systems have sometimes been described as 'conjunct/ disjunct' systems. Austin Hale in his study on Kathmandu Newari (1980) proposed the notion of 'conjunct' *versus* 'disjunct'. Post (2013) summarized Hale's idea in the following way. The 'conjunct' set is normally employed in: (a) simple first person declarative sentences, (b) simple second person interrogative sentences, (c) complex speech report constructions in which the matrix verb subject is co-referential with the complement clause subject. These three behaviours correspond respectively to (a) *declarative C/D pattern*, (b) *interrogative C/D pattern* and (c) *quotative C/D patterns* (see Tournadre 2008).

Additionally, as mentioned by Post, one "of the most common factors identified [as associated with 'conjunct'] has been the *volition or intention of an actor*" (2013: 109 emphasis in original). Intentionality appears in DeLancey's definition: "conjunct forms occurs with first person subjects in statements and second person subjects in question which refer to an intentional act" (2001: 372). However the opposition conjunct/disjunct has been defined in various ways, some authors ignoring intentionality or quotative patterns as part of C/D patterns. For example, Aikhenvald gives the following definition: "[it refers to] person-marking on the verb whereby first person subject in statements is expressed in the same way as second person in questions, and all other persons are marked in a different way (also used to describe cross clausal co-reference)" (2004: 391). DeLancey (1986, 1990, 1992, 2001, 2012) has popularized the notion of conjunct/disjunct in many of his articles devoted to Lhasa Tibetan using the structural notion of 'conjunct' instead of the semantico-cognitive notion of 'egophoric' (see above). Schöttelndreyer (1980) and Kelly (2004) have applied the notion of conjunct/disjunct to Sherpa, another Tibetic language. This notion has also been used in some 'second-hand data' typological works such as Aikhenvald (2004) and thus has received some wider attention.

In some recent publications, DeLancey (2001, 2012) has implicitly suggested using the terms 'conjunct/disjunct patterns/systems' and 'egophoric systems' as synonyms: "The analysis of Tibetic verbal 'conjunct/disjunct' or 'egophoric' systems requires reference to aspect, evidentiality and mirativity, volitionality, and person" (DeLancey 2012: 550), despite the fact that the two notions reflect two very distinct approaches. Moreover, the term 'egophoric' (Tournadre 1991, 1996b; Tournadre and Dorje 2003) never referred to a *system* but to a specific category of the Evidential/Epistemic system, used with many other categories.[22]

Many linguists who have worked on Tibetic languages such as van Driem (1998), Garrett (2001), Haller (2000, 2004), Sun (1993), Gawne (2013), Mélac (2014), etc., avoid both the terms 'conjunct/disjunct' and the analysis these

---

[22] In earlier works, I have sometimes used the opposition 'egophoric' vs 'heterophoric' (Tournadre 1996). Some authors (Sun 1990; Bartee 2007, etc.) have also used 'self' vs 'other'. However, egophoric is not opposed to one single notion but to all the other categories (sensory, factual, inferential, epistemic, etc.) of the E/E systems, see Tournadre (2008).

terms imply. Some authors such as Sun (1993), Tournadre (2008), Bartee (2007), among others, explicitly reject the notion of conjunct/disjunct as relevant for describing Tibetic languages. Sun writes that his terms 'self person' and 'other person'

> are related to, but not identical with, the structurally-based labels 'conjunct' vs 'disjunct'. [...]. Since the distinction involves more than mere structural co-reference, more self-evident labels should be sought, probably along the lines of such semantically-based terms as *shenzhi* 'thoroughly integrated knowledge' [...] or Tournadre's term egophoric. (1993: 955/956, Note 15).

For a summary of the conjunct/disjunct controversy, see Tournadre (2008) and Bartee (2007).

The conjunct/disjunct interpretation is essentially a syntactic approach related to the coreference/non-coreference pattern of the '1st person subject'. The C/D system approach is inadequate and fundamentally differs from the present approach to the Tibetic E/E systems for the following main reasons:

a) It is structural/syntactic in nature and not motivated by semantico-cognitive parameters
b) It is binary in nature, while E/E systems attested in the Tibetic languages comprise a fairly large paradigm of forms and functions (see §3)
c) The use of conjunct/disjunct categories is largely automatic and compulsory unlike the use of egophoric, sensory and inferential categories, which may depend on the speaker's perspective (see Tournadre and LaPolla 2014).
d) It is based on the notion of person coreference patterns, while in our approach the 'person agreement' is a secondary effect of semantico-cognitive concepts related to the evidential source and access to information.
e) The 'conjunct' category is not primarily defined by its specific semantic meaning unlike the category of 'egophoric' (see §5.3).
f) The conjunct/disjunct pattern or system is a *complex category* that usually manifests itself in three heterogeneous patterns: 'the declarative pattern', 'the interrogative pattern' and 'the quotative pattern'.

As we have seen above (in §2 and §5.5) the 'conjunct' set is not only employed in first person declarative sentences but also in second person interrogative sentences is not specific to the so-called conjunct/disjunct pattern. This anticipation rule applies to all the evidential categories in Tibetic languages. The 'quotative conjunct/disjunct pattern' can also be described in the framework of 'hybrid indirect speech' which more accurately explains these phenomena (see Tournadre and Dorje 2003; Tournadre 2008).

Despite their irrelevance for Tibetic languages, conjunct/disjunct systems have misled some typologists who have constructed various theories on the basis of these concepts. Aikhenvald concluded for example that "conjunct/ disjunct systems primarily mark speech act participants" and that "historically any evidentiality strategy, except for demonstratives and conjunct disjunct person marking can develop into a grammatical evidential" (2004: 146). She has set up conjunct/disjunct marking and evidentiality as categorically different in nature whereas at least for the Tibetic languages, 'conjunct/disjunct' was just a provisional and inappropriate description of evidential phenomena.

4.7 The controversy over mirativity

The concept of 'mirative' (DeLancey 1997, 2001; Hein 2007; Aikhenvald 2012) used for Lhasa Tibetan is also at the centre of a controversy (see Hill 2012; DeLancey 2012). DeLancey applies this term to Lhasa Tibetan (or SST) and van Driem describes Dzongkha with the superficially similar terminology 'newly acquired information' (Driem 1998: 196).

Aikhenvald (2012: 437) proposes the following values falling under the 'mirativity' label:
(i) sudden discovery, sudden revelation or realization (a) by the speaker, (b) by the audience (or addressee), or (c) by the main character;
(ii) surprise (a) of the speaker, (b) of the audience (or addressee), or (c) of the main character;
(iii) unprepared mind (a) of the speaker, (b) of the audience (or addressee), or (c) of the main character;
(iv) counterexpectation (a) to the speaker, (b) to the addressee, or (c) to the main character;
(v) information new (a) to the speaker, (b) to the addressee, or (c) to the main character.

DeLancey (2012) defended the idea that *'dug* in Lhasa Tibetan has a fundamental mirative meaning. Discussing the sentence,

(44) *bod-la   g.yag   'dug*
    Tibet-DAT   yak   COP.SENS
    'There are yaks in Tibet.'

DeLancey considered that "no Tibetan could ever say [it]" (2012: 551). He continues:

> It is not the case that what is being expressed here is simply that the speaker has direct perceptual evidence for the statement. If that were the case, anyone who has seen a yak in

Tibet – which would include a great many Tibetans – could, and, one would expect, normally would, use this construction to report this fact. (DeLancey 2012: 551).

It is true that this sentence is a little weird (because it is expected that people have seen yaks in Tibet) and needs a special situation to be uttered.[23] However, the awkwardness is not a linguistic issue but rather an *extralinguistic* issue. A slight change in the formulation would make the sentence perfectly acceptable from a pragmatic point of view, as shown below:

(45) bod-la   'brong   'dug
    Tibet-DAT   wild yak   COP.SENS
    'There are wild yaks in Tibet (I saw some)'

(46) la.dwags-la   g.yag   'dug
    Tibet-DAT   yak   COP.SENS
    'There are yaks in Ladakh' (I saw many yaks while I was there)

The problem with DeLancey's formulation above is the implication that if the speaker has seen something and the language has a visual evidential, then she is compelled to use this form ("he could [...] and normally would use this construction").[24] Here lies a crucial error in DeLancey's conception of Tibetic evidential systems. The fact that a speaker has witnessed an event does not oblige her in any way to use a sensory marker. The choice of an evidential is quite flexible and depends on the speaker's perspective and discursive strategy (see Tournadre and LaPolla 2014). In other words, there is no contradiction between Hill's description of *'dug* as a sensory evidential and the tendency for speakers to conventionally fail to use the sensory evidential in certain situations, even when they have sense access to information conveyed in the sentence; in such situations the speaker *chooses* to emphasize something other than the sensory source of the evidence.

As Hill (2012: 403) rightly points out, the endopathic function of the sensory *'dug* in sentences such as *nga na-gi 'dug* 'I am sick' does not normally insist on the novelty of this information. It is nevertheless true that in Tibetic languages

---

[23] Such a situation could however be found. For example, a Tibetan from south India who made a visit to Tibet and came back to Karnataka could easily say this sentence to some young Tibetans brought up in India, who thought that there were no longer yaks in Tibet. Although this kind of sentences seems odd at first, there are many improbable situations that could prompt a speaker to utter one (cf. Hill 2013: 48–49).
[24] His argument is a little surprising since DeLancey aims at showing that the mirative reading is more appropriate than the direct perception reading, but in this case, according to him, neither readings is possible.

one often encounters sensory evidentials with connotations of new information. Huber (2002: 142) used the term 'mirative function' to describe the copula /nukpa/ (< 'dug.pa) found in Kyirong Tibetan.

(47) /Amo   dimi   di:la   nukpa/
     a ma   *lde.mig* *'di-la* *'dug-pa*
     mother   key   here   COP.SENS
     'Oh, the key is here!' (I have been looking everywhere for it)

Huber rightly considers that the mirative is just one of the functions of the direct sensory marker /nug/ (< *'dug*), followed here by a tag /pa/. In Spiti-Khunu-Garzha and Ladakhi both visual sensory (*'dug*) and non-visual sensory (*grag*) (see §5.1) may additionally convey mirative overtones, but in any case, mirativity is not their primary function.

DeLancey seems to now agree that although in Tibetic languages many forms have connotations of 'new information' mirativity is not grammatical category per se. He writes that "Zeisler and Hill are correct in pointing out that despite its strong mirative connotations, the immediate evidence category in Tibetic languages is, strictly speaking, an evidential category, and thus, by definition not a pure mirative" (2012: 554). Thus, the 'mirative controversy' is perhaps close to resolution compared to the controversy over 'conjunct/ disjunct systems' versus E/E systems, which require entirely different views of the Tibetic verbal systems.

Let us now examine the notion of 'newly acquired information', related to mirativity, which van Driem uses to describe Dzongkha (1992, 1998). Van Driem defines the markers ʔ*in* and ʔ*in.pas* as 'assimilated' versus 'acquired knowledge', writing that "The form ʔ*in* expresses old, ingrained background knowledge[25] which is or has become a firmly integrated part of one's conception of reality, whereas the form ʔ*in.pas* expresses knowledge which has been newly acquired" (van Driem 1992: 112, 1998: 127). I partly disagree with van Driem's description and will endeavour to show that ʔ*in.pas* expresses inferential access to information. The mirative interpretation or newly acquired information is a secondary meaning. Consider the following example:

(48) *khyod-kyis*   *blta-ba.cin*   *kho*   *mi*   *phyugpo*   *in.pas-ga*
     2SG -ERG   look at-if   3SG   man   rich   COP-Q
     'Do you consider him a rich man?'
     (van Driem 1992: 117)

---

[25] I proposed above (§5) that this category be treated as 'assumptive'.

If ʔin.pas (/immä/) expressed newly acquired knowledge, then it would not appear in the question above. The speaker asks the hearer about information which he may not have yet acquired! In fact, the speaker explicitly asks the hearer to answer his question by using an inference based on external evidences. Consider another sentence.

(49) nga   ʔin.pas
     1SG   COP.INFR
     'It's me'
     (van Driem 1992: 117)

This utterance may be pronounced when the speaker recognizes herself on a fuzzy photograph because she has spotted her hat or shoes on the picture (van Driem 1992: 117).

The corresponding sentence in SST would be:

(50) nga   red-bzhag
     1SG   COP.INFR
     'It's me'

In this situation, we are dealing with a visual *inference*, which may have a mirative overtone. However, this overtone is not always present. Let's consider for example another situation: somebody is shown a class picture and asked to *recognize* one of the students on the picture (for example the addressee). The speaker knows that the addressee is one of the students on the picture and thus in that case it involves a recognition and does not (usually) imply any surprise. Yet in both Dzongkha and Standard Tibetan, the copulas which will be used are again the inferential forms, respectively *in.pas* and *red-bzhag*.

Thus, ʔin.pas in Dzongkha cannot be a mirative marker per se, but rather an inferential marker that can be used in new information contexts.

4.8 Marginal categories of the evidential and epistemic systems

The richness and complexity of the Tibetic E/E systems is not restricted to the categories examined so far. In some languages, one finds other categories that play a marginal role but tell much about the semantico-cognitive and pragmatic principles that govern these systems. Most of these categories have yet to receive sufficient attention, although they are an integral part of E/E systems and could shed light on the functioning of these systems.

4.8.1 Self-corrective and mnemic

Some languages have a form called 'self-corrective' by Tournadre and Dorje (1998, 2003) and 'erroneous belief' by Huber (2002: 141). The self-corrective may be glossed as: 'I thought X was Y but it isn't.'
Here is a Kyirong example.

(51) /nga-ni: kho cahpa yöbitsi/
nga-ni kho rgyags.pa yod.pa'i.rtsi
1SG-TOP 3SG fat COP.CORR
'(And) I thought he was fat' (but he isn't).
(Huber 2002: 143)

Here is an example in Standard Spoken Tibetan:

(52) ai'i tshe.ring-la mo.ṭa yod.pa.red[26]
oh PR.N-DAT car COP.CORR
'Well well, so Tshering has a car!' (I thought it was not the case)

Another underdescribed category of the Tibetic verb systems is the mnemic (Tournadre and Dorje 1998, 2003: 339; Vokurková 2008: 198/199, 203). In Standard Spoken Tibetan, the mnemic is marked by a series of endings such as *yin.pa.yod*, *yod.pa.yod*. These markers indicate that the speaker has only a vague recollection of what he is saying. Vokurková describes the mnemic in the following way: "The speaker remembers something but he is not absolutely sure because, often, some time has elapsed since it happened, Therefore, they can be translated in English by such expressions as 'I remember that (perhaps)' or 'I think that it is like this (but do not remember it well)'" (2008: 198). The following example was recorded by Vokurková (2008: 198) in Lhasa:

(53) gri ngas 'khyer-yod.pa.yod
knife 1SG.ERG bring-PERF.EPI3
'I'm pretty sure I brought that knife.'

She provides the following comment: "For a picnic, the speaker has brought a lot of things but he is not absolutely sure whether he has the knife" and adds: "Although the speaker is quite sure when uttering the above sentence, he may follow: "Oh, I haven't, I am wearing another jacket today. It's in the other one."

---

26 Note that the corrective copula *yod pa red* is pronounced [jø? pa re?] and should not be confused with the factual copula *yod-red* [jo: re?], which on etymological grounds is also sometimes spelled *yod-pa-red* (cf. Hill 2010).

This mnemic is quite common in the spoken language of Lhasa though less frequent than some other types of epistemic endings (e.g. *yod. 'gro, yod.pa. 'dra*). Bartee mentions the existence of the marker /dʐã⁵³/ in Dongwang Kham with a similar meaning: "[T]he validational dʐã⁵³ indicates that the speaker has a vague recollection regarding the statement s/he is making" (2007: 378).

(54) *kho-a   a-ka   'dug* /dʐã wu-ɕa/
     3SG +DAT child   COP   VAL VAL
     'She has children (I seem to recall).'

4.8.2 Experiential

Another category which occurs in some languages is the 'experiential' past. It is derived from the verb *myong* 'to taste' and is often attested in the Tibetic languages of the high plateau (Ü-Tsang, Amdo, Kham). This form conveys the meaning of V *guo* in Chinese, or V(*ta*-form) *koto ga aru* in Japanese; it corresponds in English to "X has already done the verbal action". The auxiliary *myong* appears alone only with the 1st person and conveys an egophoric meaning, but when it occurs with 2nd and 3rd person, it is always followed by evidential or epistemic auxiliaries.

Other marginal categories are attested in the Tibetic languages, but they are hard to detect because their frequency is much lower than that of major evidential and epistemic markers.

4.8.3 Preventive, deontic, benefactive and autolalic futures

In Standard Spoken Tibetan, a 'preventive future', which is marked by the auxiliary *yong* 'to come', is frequently used to indicate a warning about a coming danger or risk. Although it has sometimes been described as an imminent danger, it is not always the case (Tournadre and Jiatso 2001).

(55) *gzab.gzab   byas-na   ma.gtogs   zag-yong*
     careful   LV(make)-if   otherwise   fall-FUT.PREV
     'Be careful, otherwise, you/it will fall down.'

A 'deontic future' *rgyu.yin/rgyu.red* is also attested in Standard Spoken Tibetan. It corresponds in English to 'have yet to', 'still need to' (see Tournadre 1998; Vokurková 2008; Tournadre 2015).

Again in Ü-Tsang, a form called 'benefactive future'[27] is frequently attested. It is formed with the auxiliaries *dgos* 'must', *chog* 'to be allowed to', and *yong* 'to come'. The speaker offers to perform an action for the benefit of the addressee. This construction only appears with a 1st person subject in the ergative (see Tournadre 2015):

(56) ngas   khong-la   zhus-dgos/chog
     1SG.ERG   3SG.HON-DAT   tell.HON-FUT.BEN
     'I'll tell him (on your behalf).'

The next examples is a very specific form of future described by van Driem for Dzongkha:

> There is a special future form, the autolalic future, which expresses the intent of the first person subject. The autolalic future is only used when thinking to oneself in Dzongkha about what one intends to do. The form is never uttered, unless one is talking to oneself, and is always in the first person singular. The autolalic future also occurs in narrative, in direct quotation of someone's thoughts, and is marked by the ending *-ge-no*, which originally derives from the adhortative suffix. (1998: 363)

(57) /tama   nga   sa-geno/
     lta ma   nga   za-ge.no
     later   1SG   eat-FUT.auto
     'I'll eat later.'

These various types of future (benefactive, preventive, deontic, etc.) have largely been overlooked in the description of Tibetic E/E systems. The existence of a benefactive and a preventive form in the verb paradigm shows that speech acts play a significant role in the functioning of the Tibetic verb systems.

4.8.4 Intentionality and animacy

In a number of languages, such as Ü-Tsang, Amdo and Kham, evidentiality interacts with the semantic categories of 'intentionality' and 'animacy'. DeLancey noted the significance of volitionality (i.e intentionality) for Lhasa Tibetan and elaborated a 'cognitive model':

> My exposition so far may suggest that the Lhasa verbal system separately encodes two semantic parameters beside aspect, evidentiality and volitionality. [...] But this analysis fails to explain certain odd facts about the data, in particular the restriction of the marking of the volitionality distinction to conjunct [i.e. egophoric] contexts and the plurifunctionality of

---

[27] I have previously called it 'allocentric future' (Tournadre and Dorje 1998, 2003).

song, which appear to encode direct evidence as opposed to inference in disjunct clause [all except egophoric, i.e. sensory, inferential, factual, etc.], and non volitionality as opposed to volitionality in conjunct clauses. A unitary account of the semantics of *song* requires that we reinterpret the volitionality distinction as reducible to an evidential one. Here the association of the conjunct form with the first person is a crucial clue. For to describe an act as volitional is to say that the actor performs an intentional act of volition [...], which is the occasion of his acting. And only the agent of this act of volition can have direct knowledge of it. (1990: 302)

On the basis of DeLancey's 'cognitive model' and his proposal to integrate volitionality (intentionality)[28] in the evidential system, Tournadre (1996: 169/170) expanded this model by including various perfect forms (1996: 250/251) and related it to the case system to the 'trajectory model'.

The last sentence of DeLancey's statement is quite important. Within the present conception of E/E system, I would rephrase it in the following way: only the speaker, who is both the source of the statement and the agent, has access to his own intention. Other agents' intentions are never accessible to the speaker.

The grammatical category of intentionality, associated with egophoric markers, plays a major role in Central Tibetan, Amdo and some Kham languages but it is not pervasive in the Tibetic languages. For example, it is grammaticalized neither in Dzongkha nor in Ladakhi.

In a few languages, evidential auxiliaries manifest an animacy split. That is the case, for example, in Donwang Tibetan (Bartee 2007). Bartee writes:

The Donwang existential forms [...] have fours forms due to an animacy split. For this reason, they are more complex than those reported in other Tibetan dialects. [...] In clauses expressing possession, the animacy of the possessed argument conditions speakers' choice of /ze/ [<*yod*] versus /ⁿdo/ [< *'dug*], while the possessor argument conditions speakers' choice regarding SELF/OTHER considerations. (2007: 139/140, emphasis in original)

The list of the Tibetic E/E categories mentioned in this chapter is of course not exhaustive. Further research may reveal still new forms and categories.

4.9 Conclusions

Aikhenvald (2004) mentions briefly four Tibetic languages (Lhasa Tibetan, Amdo, Sherpa, and Ladakhi) but she was unaware of their genetic proximity. Her

---

28 It is important to distinguish [+/-control] a lexical property of the verb and intentionality, a grammatical property which is marked by auxiliaries. The term volitional applies sometimes to both and is thus ambiguous. That is why, following Bielmeier (personal communication) I use the term 'control' for the verb class and 'intentional' for the auxiliary.

typological work is based on second-hand data, and on materials that present very different conceptions and terminologies for the description of evidential systems. This heterogeneity in the descriptions has led to the mistaken conclusion that the Tibetic languages have entirely different systems. For example, Ladakhi she classifies as a complex "four choice evidential system" (Aikhenvald 2004: 53), Amdo a "three term evidential system" (2004: 45), while Lhasa Tibetan (2004: 127) and Sherpa (2004: 127) she does not even consider evidential and treats as 'conjunct/disjunct systems'. This kind of misinterpretation is the risk of second-hand typology, even when it is practised by excellent typologists. In fact, describing those four languages in such a way gives no impression of the real complexity of the Tibetic evidential and epistemic systems.

In this study, I have tried to present a typological sketch of evidentiality in the family of languages derived from Old Tibetan. All the Tibetic languages have E/E systems which share fundamental features and semantico-cognitive categories: sensory, inferential, assumed, quotative and epistemic. Each of these categories may have several subtypes. E/E systems interact not only with tense and aspect but also with person and are sensitive to illocutionary force.

The E/E systems found throughout the Tibetic area differ in a number of ways. For example egophoric markers are not found everywhere in the Tibetic area and seem to have developed essentially in the languages of Tibet. Egophoric markers do not form a 'system' but are just one category of some evidential and epistemic systems. The egophoric corresponds to the last stage of a grammaticalization process. Outside Tibet, in the southern and western Himalayas, one finds the more archaic 'assumptive' (or 'weak egophoric') evidentials.

Sensory evidential markers may have distinct values in the Tibetic languages. Some languages distinguish visual from non-visual sensory. Both sensory and inferential markers may convey a mirative overtone, but mirativity is not a central category of the Tibetic E/E system. There are about fifty Tibetic languages spoken in China, India, Bhutan, Pakistan, Nepal and Myanmar. Of these languages, only a few have been described in some details. We now have ideas about the functioning of evidentiality in Ü, Tsang, Tö-Ngari, Amdo, Dzongkha, Northern Kham, Spiti, Sherpa, Ladakhi, Lhoke (Sikkim), Kyirong, Dongwang Kham, Yolmo, Chocha-ngacha and the languages in this volume, but detailed descriptions of evidentiality and epistemicity are still lacking for most languages. Even in the languages, which have been largely documented, the interaction between evidential and epistemic markers has not received sufficient attention. This language family, which allows for a diachronic analysis over a millennium, has made and will make a very important contribution to the typological understanding of evidentiality.

Abbreviations

ASM assumptive, BEN benefactive, CMP completed aspect, COP copula, CORR self-corrective, DAT dative, DIR directional, EGO egophoric, ERG ergative, ENPT endopathic sensory, EPI epistemic, EPI 1 epistemic of the 1st degree, EPI 2 epistemic of the 2nd degree, EPI 3 epistemic of the 3rd degree, FACT factual, FQ Final question marker, FUT future, INFL inflection, INFR inferential, JUS Jussive LOC locative, LV light verb, MNEM mnemic, NEG negation, PERF perfect, PQ preverbal question marker, PREV preventive, PR.N proper noun, PSENS participatory sensory, POST postposition, Q question marker, REL relator, SENS sensory, UNCP uncompleted aspect, VAL validation

References

Aikhenvald, Alexandra Y. 2004. *Evidentiality*. Oxford: Oxford University Press.
Aikhenvald, Alexandra Y. 2012. The essence of mirativity. *Linguistic Typology* 16(3). 435–85.
Alonso Almeida, F. 2012. Sentential evidential, adverbs and authorial stance in a corpus of English computing articles. *Revista española de lingüística aplicada* 25(1). 15–32.
Bartee, Ellen. 2007. A Grammar of Dongwan Tibetan. Santa Barbara: PhD Thesis, University of California.
Bielmeier, Roland. 2000. Syntactic, semantic, and pragmatic-epistemic functions of auxiliaries in Western Tibetan. *Linguistics of the Tibeto-Burman Area* 23. 79–125.
Chang, Kun et al. 1964. *A manual of spoken Tibetan (Lhasa Dialect)*. Seattle: University of Washington Press.
DeLancey, Scott. 1986. Evidentiality and volitionality in Tibetan. In Wallace L. Chafe & Johanna Nicholas (eds.), *Evidentiality: the linguistic coding of epistemology*, 203–213. Norwood, NJ: Ablex Publishing Corporation.
DeLancey, Scott. 1990. Ergativity and the cognitive model of event structure in Lhasa Tibetan. *Cognitive Linguistics* 1(3). 289–321.
DeLancey, Scott. 1992. The historical origin of the conjunct-disjunct pattern in Tibeto-Burman. *Acta Linguistica Hafniensia* 25. 289–321.
DeLancey, Scott. 1997. Mirativity: The grammatical marking of unexpected information. *Linguistic Typology* 1. 33–52.
DeLancey, Scott. 2001. The mirative and evidentiality. *Journal of Pragmatics* 33. 369–382.
DeLancey, Scott. 2012. Still mirative after all these years. *Linguistic Typology* 16(3). 529–564
van Driem, George. 1992. *The grammar of Dzongkha*. Thimphu: Royal Government of Bhutan.
van Driem, George. 1998. *Dzongkha*. (Languages of the greater Himalayan region). Leiden: Research School CNWS, School of Asian, African, and Amerindian Studies.
Ebihara, Shiho. This volume. Evidentiality of the Tibetan Verb *snang*. In Lauren Gawne & Nathan W. Hill (eds.), *Evidentiality in Tibetic languages*, 41–59. Berlin & Boston: Mouton de Gruyter.
Garrett, Edward J. 2001. *Evidentiality and Assertion in Tibetan*. PhD thesis, Department of Linguistics, University of California, Los Angeles.
Gawne, Lauren, 2013. *Lamjung Yolmo copulas in use: Evidentiality, reported speech and questions*. PhD thesis, The University of Melbourne, Melbourne.

Gesang Jumian 格桑居冕 & Gesang Yangjing 格桑居冕 2002. 藏语方言概论 *Zangyu fangyan gailun* [Tibetan Dialects]. Beijing: 民族出版社 Minzu Chubanshe.

Guentchéva, Zlatka & Jon Landaburu. 2007. *L'énonciation médiatisée II - Le traitement épistémologique de l'information: illustrations amérindiennes et caucasiennes.* (Bibliothèque de l'Information Grammaticale, 63). Louvain: Peeters.

de Haan, F. 1999. Evidentiality and epistemic modality: Setting boundaries. *Southwest journal of linguistics* 18. 83–101.

Hagège, C. 1982. *La structure des langues, Que sais-je?* Paris: Presses Universitaires de France.

Hale, Austin. 1980. Person markers: Finite conjunct and disjunct verb forms in Newari. In R. L. Rail (ed.), *Papers in South-East Asian linguistics*, 95–106. Canberra: Australian National University.

Haller, Felix. 2000. *Dialekt und Erzählungen von Shigatse.* Bonn: VGH Wissenschfttsverlag GmbH.

Haller, Felix. 2004. *Dialekt und Erzählungen von Themchen.* (Beiträge zur tibetischen Erzählforschung 14). Bonn: VGH Wissenschaftsverlag.

Häsler, Katrin Louise. 1999. *A grammar of the Tibetan Dege (sde dge) [kham] dialect.* Inauguraldissertation der Philosophish-Historischen Fakultät der Universität Bern. Zürich: Selbstverlag.

Hein, Veronika. 2007. The mirative and its interplay with evidentiality in the Tibetan dialect of Tabo (Spiti). *Linguistics of the Tibeto-Burman Area* 30(2). 195–214.

Hill, Nathan W. 2010. A note on the phonetic evolution of yod-pa-red in Central Tibet. *Linguistics of the Tibeto-Burman Area* 33(1). 93–94.

Hill, Nathan W. 2012. 'Mirativity' does not exist: ḥdug in 'Lhasa' Tibetan and other suspects. *Linguistic Typology* 16(3). 389–433.

Hill, Nathan W. 2013a. ḥdug as a testimonial marker in Classical and Old Tibetan. *Himalayan Linguistics* 12(1). 1–16.

Hill, Nathan W. 2013b. Contextual semantics of 'Lhasa' Tibetan evidentials. *SKASE Journal of Theoretical Linguistics* 10(3). 47–54.

Hongladarom, Krisadawan. 2007. Evidentiality in Rgyalthang Tibetan. *Linguistics of the Tibeto-Burman Area* 30(2). 17–44.

Hoshi, Izumi. 2010. 14 世紀チベット語文献『王統明示鏡』における存在動詞. [Existential verbs in the Rgyal rabs gsal ba'i me long, a 14th century Tibetan narrative]. 東京大学言語学論集 (Tokyo University Linguistic Papers) 29(3). 29–68.

Huber, Brigitte. 2005. *The Lende sub-dialect of Kyirong Tibetan: A grammatical description with historical annotations.* Bonn : VGH Wissenschaftsverlag.

Kelly, Barbara F. 2004. A grammar of Sherpa. In Carol Genetti (ed.), *Tibeto-Burman languages of Nepal: Manange and Sherpa*, 232–440. Canberra: Pacific Linguistics.

Koshal, Sanyukta. 1982. *Conversational Ladakhi.* Delhi : Motilal Banarsidass.

Kuno, Susumu. 1987. *Functional syntax: Anaphora, discourse and empathy.* Chicago: The University of Chicago Press.

Mélac, Eric. 2014. L'évidentialité en anglais - approche contrastive à partir d'un corpus anglais-tibétain. PhD thesis. Paris III, Sorbonne Nouvelle.

Nuyts, Jan. 2001. *Epistemic modality, language, and conceptualization: a cognitive-pragmatic perspective.* Amsterdam: John Benjamins.

Oisel, Guillaume. 2013. *Morphosyntaxe et semantique des auxiliaires et des connecteurs du Tibetain Litteraire*, PhD thesis, Universite Sorbonne Nouvelle - Paris 3, Paris.

Post, Mark W. 2013. Person-sensitive TAME marking in Galo: Historical origins and functional motivation. In T. Thornes, E. Andvik, G. Hyslop & J. Jansen (eds.), *Functional-Historical Approaches to Explanation*, 107–130. Amsterdam: John Benjamins.

San Roque, L, S. Floyd, & E. Norcliffe. 2017. Evidentiality and interrogativity. *Lingua*. 120–143.

San Roque, L, & R Loughnane. 2012. The New Guinea Highlands evidentiality area. *Linguistic Typology* 16(1). 111–167.
Schöttelndreyer, Burkhard. 1980. Person Markers in Sherpa. In S. A. Wurm (ed.), *Papers in Southeast Asian Linguistics No.7*, 125–130. Canberra: The Australian National University.
Shao, Mingyuan (邵明園). 2014. 安多藏语阿柔话的示证范畴 Anduo zangyu arou hua de shizheng fanchou [Evidentiality in A-rig Dialect of Amdo Tibetan]. Nankai: Nankai University dissertation.
Sprigg, R. K. 2002. *Balti-English, English-Balti dictionary*. London: Routledge
Sun, Jackson, T.-S. 1993. Evidentials in Amdo Tibetan. *Bulletin of the Institute of History and Philology* 63(4). 143–188.
Sun Jackson, T.-S. 2014. *Phonological Profiles of Litttle-studied Tibetic varieties*. Taipei: Institute of linguistics, Academia Sinica.
Sung, Kuo-ming & Lha Byams rgyal. 2005. *Colloquial Amdo Tibetan*. Beijing: China Tibetology Publishing house.
Suzuki, Hiroyuki. 2012. Multiple usages of the verb *snang* in Gagatang Tibetan (Weixi, Yunnan). *Himalayan Linguistics* 11(1). 1–16.
Tournadre, Nicolas. 1991. The rhetorical use of the Tibetan ergative. *Linguistics of the Tibeto-Burman Area* 14(1). 93–107.
Tournadre, Nicolas. 1992. La déixis en tibétain: quelques faits remarquables. In Morel M.-A. et Danon-Boileau L. (eds.), *La Deixis*, 197–208. Paris, PUF.
Tournadre, Nicolas. 1996a. *L'ergativité en Tibétain moderne: Approche morphosyntaxique de la langue parlée*. (Bibliothèque de l'Information Grammaticale 33). Paris & Leuven: Peeters.
Tournadre, Nicolas. 1996b. Comparaison des systèmes médiatifs en tibétain central, lada- khi, dzongkha et amdo. In Zlatka Guentchéva (ed.), *L"Enonciation médiatisée (Bibliothèque de l'Information Grammaticale, 35)*, 195–213. Paris & Leuven: Peeters.
Tournadre, Nicolas. 2008. Arguments against the concept of 'conjunct'/'disjunct' in Tibetan. In B. Huber, M. Volkart, P. Widmer, P. Schwieger (eds.), *Chomolangma, Demawend und Kasbek. Festschrift für Roland Bielmeier zu seinem 65. Geburtstag*, Band 1, 281–308. Halle (Saale): International Institute for Tibetan and Buddhist Studies GmbH.
Tournadre, Nicolas. 2014. The Tibetic languages and their classification in T. Owen-Smith & Nathan W. Hill (eds.), *Trans-Himalayan Linguistics: Historical and Descriptive Linguistics of the Himalayan Area*, 105–130. Berlin: Mouton de Gruyter.
Tournadre, Nicolas. 2015. The future tenses in the Tibetic languages. In Guentchéva (ed.), *Diachronic and dialectal perspectives, Aspectuality and temporality: theoretical and empirical issues*. Amsterdam: Benjamins.
Tournadre, Nicolas & Sangda Dorje. 1998. *Manuel de tibétain standard*. Paris: l'Asiathèque, [re- ed. 2003, 2009]
Tournadre, Nicolas & Sangda Dorje. 2003. *Manual of Standard Tibetan*. Ithaca, New York: Snowlion. [translation of *Manuel de tibétain standard*, 1998]
Tournadre, Nicholas & Konchok Jiatso. 2001. Final auxiliary verbs in literary Tibetan and in the dialects. *Linguistics of the Tibeto-Burman Area* 24(1). 49–111.
Tournadre, Nicolas & Randy J. LaPolla. 2014. Towards a new approach to evidentiality: Issues and directions for research. *Linguistics of the Tibeto-Burman Area* 37(2). 240–263.
Tournadre, Nicolas, Lhakpa Norbu Sherpa, Gyurme Chodrak & Guillaume Oisel. 2009. *Sherpa-English and English-Sherpa dictionary*. Kathmandu: Vajra Publication.
Vokurková, Zuzana. 2008. Epistemic modalities in Spoken Standard Tibetan, PhD Thesis, University of Prague and Paris 8.
Zeisler, Bettina. 2004. *Relative tense and aspectual values in Tibetan languages: a comparative study*. Berlin & New York: Mouton de Gruyter.

Nathan W. Hill
5 Perfect experiential constructions: the inferential semantics of direct evidence

Man kann viel sehn, wenn man zwei Augen hat und nicht blind ist und die Sonn scheint.
—Marie

5.1 Introduction

In his typological categorization of evidential systems, Thomas Willett observes that "the primary evidential parameter expressed in natural language is that of **direct evidence** versus **indirect evidence**" (1988: 57 emphasis in original); he sees evidence from the senses as a sub-type of 'direct' and 'inferring' as one sub-type of 'indirect' (1988: 57). In a more recent typological categorization, Alexandra Aikhenvald divides the world's evidential categories into six "recurrent semantic parameters" (2004: 63), viz. visual, sensory, inference, assumption, hearsay and quotative (2004: 65); although "a number of these six parameters can be subsumed under one evidential specification" (2004: 64), she does not observe crossover between the visual and inferential. In a similar vein, Scott DeLancey holds that "direct vs. indirect evidence is the fundamental evidential distinction" (2012: 540), and Hengeveld and Olbertz assert that "a case of direct perception" and "a case of inference on the basis of perception" are "two completely different cases when seen from the evidential perspective" (2012: 495). Agreement with the dominant perspective that starkly separates sensory evidence from inference is not universal. Tournadre remarks that "l'inférentiel est un type de « testimonial » particulier, puisqu'il implique une opération construite à partir d'une *constatation* (d'indices, de traces, etc)" (1994: 158 emphasis in original). Similarly, de Haan classifies inference along with sense evidence as a sub-type of direct evidence (2001: 195). According to his semantic analysis the "inferential evidential has certain elements in common with [...] sensory evidentials (such as visual evidentiality)" (2001: 193).

To the extent that any inference pertains to the world outside, for biological reasons this inference will originate with a sense perception. One must presume that the authors who see no overlap between perception and inference do not espouse

---

Note: I would like to thank the British Academy and the European Research Council for support during the course of this research. Abbreviations appear at the end of this chapter. In Tibetan, any noun phrase not specified for case should be construed as absolutive.

an analysis that totally precludes the use of sense perceptions in the drawing of inferences, but rather they draw an empirical generalization on the basis of the distribution of language specific structural morphosyntactic categories. A possible paraphrase of this perspective is that all languages with grammaticalized evidentials fail to employ the evidential category used for (non-inferential) direct perception in inference contexts. This essay assumes such a paraphrase is a fair reflection of a view Willett, Aikhenvald, DeLancey, and Hengevel and Obertz share.

A number of previously published descriptions of languages, showing interactions between direct evidence and inference appeared prior to Willett (1988). Rule (1977: 71–75) describes an evidential category of 'visual evidence' in Foe that is distinct from both 'seen' and 'deduced'; this category exactly strides Willett's unbreachable chasm. Willett appears unaware of Rule (1977), but Aikhenvald accommodates the Foe system, putting the 'seen', 'visual evidence' and 'deduced' respectively into her 'visual', 'inference' and 'assumptive' parameters (2004: 63). Gordon (1986: 76, Note 4) notes in Maricopa the use of a lexical verb *yuu* 'see' in inference contexts. Although both Willett (1988: 68) and Aikhenvald (2004: 275) cite Gordon's work, they appear to have overlooked the relevant footnote and its importance. Watahomigie et al. (1982: 395) report an evidential system in Hualapai, which systematically collapses inference and direct evidence in certain contexts. Willett and Aikhenvald take no notice of the Hualapai system.[1] The perfect experiential construction found in Sherpa, Duna, Oksapmin, Bogaia, and 'Lhasa' Tibetan, in which the conjunction of sensory evidence and perfect tense[2] gives rise to the semantics of inference, provides further counter-evidence to the dominant perspective.[3] Cognizance of the perfect experiential construction in these five languages permits its recognition also in Kham and Kashaya.

---

[1] In another case of interaction between direct evidentiality and inference, Matses has a binary evidential opposition between conjecture and non-conjecture, in which direct experience and inference constitute the two sub-specfications of non-conjecture. Relying on Aikhenvald (2004), Fleck distinguishes three evidential categories: experiential (*-o*, *-onda*, *-denne*), inferential (*-ak*, *-nëdak*, *-ampik*, *-nëdampik*) and conjecture (*-aṣh* and *-nëdaṣh*) (2007: 593), but his own description of the co-occurence constraints of these suffixes belies this analysis. Whereas the "conjecture suffixes, *-aṣh* and *-nëdaṣh*, cannot combine with any of the other evidential inflections" (2007: 602) "one of the experiential suffixes (*-o*, *-onda*, or *-denne*) must be used directly after the inferential suffix" (2007: 599). So, Matses has two evidential categories (conjecture and non-conjecture), of which conjecture is mono-morphemic, whereas non-conjecture is bi-morphemic, the first morpheme specifying time from event to detection and the second morpheme specifying time from detection to report. Thus, inferential and experiential belong to the same evidential specification.

[2] Through this essay I use 'tense' as equivalent to Greek *chrónos* or Latin *tempus*, i.e. I do not intend 'tense' as opposed to 'aspect'.

[3] Willett (1988) and Aikhenvald (2004) cite the article of Woodbury (1986) on Sherpa, but without realizing that his description vitiates their overall typologies.

The goal of this essay is emphatically not to demonstrate that 'perfect experiential' is a novel typological category, rather its modest aim is to correct a common misunderstanding of the relationship between inference and direct evidence present in the works of others. Because the goal is negative the ontological status of 'inference' and 'direct evidence' as categories in the conception of previous researchers is immaterial. As Nāgārjuna argued long ago, to show that the view of another is inconsistent, whether internally inconsistent or contradicted by observation, it is unnecessary to commit to the validity of the terms of the debate, but suffices to manipulate these terms in a way analogous to the interlocutor. Lest the promotion of the 'perfect experiential' as a productive conceptualization of these language specific phenomena take on the air of a newly discovered platonic form, a general adumbration of the tasks and limits of linguistic typology within the context of recent methodological discussions precedes discussion of the proposed application of the term 'perfect experiential' in particular languages.

5.1.1 Terminological and theoretical preliminaries

Linguistic typology faces the hurdle of employing cross-linguistic terminology to compare the grammatical categories of individual languages as definable in *sui generis* structural terms. Broadly speaking there are two current approaches to this challenge. One school posits pre-established universal grammatical categories that particular languages instantiate (Dixon 2010; Newmeyer 2007, 2010). Researchers operating in this tradition refrain from making explicit the ontological status of these categories or the epistemological means of accessing them. The alternative school accepts the structuralist position that "all linguistic categories are language specific" (Lazard 2012: 249) and makes cross linguistic comparisons on the basis of 'intuitive conceptual frameworks' (Lazard 2012: 250) or 'comparative concepts' (Haspelmath 2010a). Newmeyer is critical of this latter approach, noting that Haspelmath employs thematic roles among his comparative concepts, and that "there is no construct as murky in ANY subdivision of linguistic theory as that of 'thematic role'" (2010: 689 emphasis in original).[4] Haspelmath offers the pragmatic but unpersuasive reply that "problems with such semantic

---

[4] Newmeyer cites Dowty's observation that thematic roles are also beset with onotological and epistemological problems, namely "(i) lack of agreement among linguists as to which thematic roles exist, and (ii) the lack of any effective way to independently justify the assignment of noun phrases to thematic roles in particular sentences" (Dowty 1989: 70). Rather than dismissing thematic roles in a spasm of aporia, as this quote might imply he does, Dowty instead proposes an account of thematic roles using model theoretic semantics.

roles have never arisen in a typological context" and typology "is happy to limit its generalizations to clear cases of agents, patients, and recipients" (2010b: 697). Haspelmath does not specify how we can know whether a particular case of an agent, patient, etc. is clear. If roles are messy and contested but no typologists complain, this speaks more to the phlegmatic disposition of typologists than it does to the suitability of semantic roles as methodological tools.

An appeal to semantics implies the need for a semantic theory; Newmeyer points to the dozens of incommensurate semantic theories in circulation as evidence of the uphill battle facing Haspelmath's comparative concepts (2007: 139). The problem is worse than Newmeyer presents—although semantics thrives as a sub-discipline of linguistics, Bloomfield's objection that "the study of language can be conducted without special assumptions only so long as we pay no attention to the meaning of what is spoken" (1933: 75 and 139–157) remains unanswered. If, as Bloomfield suggests, semantics is itself an impossibility, then Haspelmath's comparative concepts are doomed to remain loose, vague, and indeterminate. The typologist has no means by which to understand his own most effective tools. It is as if a chemist, having added a droplet to a beaker of liquid, observes the liquid turn red, and confidently declares the droplet to contain acid, despite readily admitting that he does not know (even cannot know) the composition of the liquid, let alone why it changes red.

But language is not a chemical. Linguists lack labs or machines to determine the presence or non presence of a particular purported meaning; in the words of Haspelmath "pre-established categories don't exist" (2007). Language, as a social institution (Sapir 1921: 2), presents methodological hurdles analogous to other cultural practices studied in a cross-cultural perspective. Consequently, Haspelmath's comparative concepts draw inspiration from the comparative study of wedding dress and legal systems (2010a: 681).⁵ In 2003–2004 Harvard's Tozzier Library hosted an exhibition of footwear across cultures and ages. The visitor who hoped to behold shoeicity itself left disappointed, but his naïveté and no curatorial failing engendered his disappointment.

When a linguist chooses a semantic label for a morphosyntactic phenomenon, he does this on analogy to the use of that label in the description of other languages.

---

5 In reply to this point, Newmeyer cites a comment of Greenberg's that because "language as a subject matter possesses certain peculiarities such as the arbitrariness of the relation between form and meaning" (1973: 59) the use of linguistic methodology in other disciplines have been unsuccessful. This reply misses the point. Haspelmath does not encourage anthropologists to use the methods of linguistics, but he encourages linguists to use the methods of anthropologists. Newmeyer's observation that attempts at applying the comparative method to social institutions such as mythology, religion, and law "all resulted in failure" (2010: 693), reveals ignorance of recent research in historical linguistics and comparative mythology (e.g. Watkins 1995 and Witzel 2012).

5 Perfect experiential constructions: the inferential semantics of direct evidence — 135

If a student working on a far-flung language finds a grammatical phenomenon he is unsure how to describe, he rummages through the linguistic literature for analogues to serve as inspiration. This groping for labels results in terminological choices that in hindsight may seem unfortunate. For example, in Classical Tibetan 'terminative' refers to a case with the allomorphs *-tu*, *-du*, *-r*, and *-su* that is used for destinations of movement or transformations, equivalent to 'to', 'into' or 'as' in English (Hill 2011: 19–35), but cases known as 'terminative' in other languages such as Basque *-ra-ino* or Hungarian *-ig* instead correspond in meaning to English 'up to' or 'until' (Creissels 2008: 610, 619). Since the relationship between *signifiant* and *signifié* is arbitrary no harm need arise from such situations. The use of the term 'aorist' to describe verbal forms of very different meaning in Greek and Tuareg poses no danger either to the classicist who knows that *élthon* 'went' is an aorist or to the Berberist who knows that *əqqəl* 'will return' is an aorist (Belkadi 2013: 137). On the other hand, the typologist lives in ubiquitous and constant danger of presuming that *élthon* and *əqqəl* are incarnations of a 'true aorist'.[6] There is no grammatical category in any language that refers to the same concept as the grammatical category of another language for the simple reason that the two categories will face differing structural oppositions; to speak of a 'true evidential' (DeLancey 2001: 376), 'true mirative' (DeLancey 2012: 553), or 'true egophoricity' (DeLancey 2012: 555), etc. is always a mistake.

To have any concrete meaning the chain of analogies a typological term gestures to must be moored to a particular phenomenon in a particular language. To say of *ni* and *kyaṅ* in Classical Tibetan that they are similar in function to *wa* and *mo* in Japanese is more succinct, accurate, and verifiable than to say that *ni* is a 'subject particle' (Miller 1970: 90), 'Isolationspartikel' (Hahn 1996: 63), 'topicalizer' (Beyer 1992: 275), or whatever. The typologist should serve as matchmaker in such a case between the Tibetologist and the Japanologist. By aggregating observations on phenomena in diverse languages the typologist lowers the transaction cost for an investigator looking at a tidbit in one language to find a tidbit in another that he might find interesting. For typology to provide a milieu to assist those confronting the analysis of a specific language in understanding what they witness with greater insight, that is goal enough. For this purpose he assembles a menagerie, a cabinet of curiosities that may be more or less skillfully curated. The temptation remains imminent to slip from describing *ni* to describing subjecthood, topicality, or whatever, but subjecthood and topicality are not things in the world; *ni* and *wa* are.

---

[6] The danger is mitigated in cases such as 'aorist' where the non-equivalence of the meaning is obvious. The temptation to believe that the ergative in Tibetan and Basque are 'the same thing' is much greater, and consequently more dangerous, than the temptation to think that the 'terminative' in these two languages is 'the same thing'.

The more in focus remain the realia underpinning the analogies implicit in the use of a semantic label for a morpho-syntactic phenomenon, the more explicit and rigorous typology becomes and the more helpful this discipline renders itself to students of the world's languages. I accept Haspelmath's methodology and undertake to employ it, while bearing in mind that comparative concepts are not linguistic entities and their elaboration is not a contribution to linguistics; they are manners of speaking, convenient fictions, conceits, precise only if reducible to the pair-wise comparison of bits of the grammars of specific languages.

With this methodological orientation in place the account of the 'perfect experiential' construction begins. The label 'perfect experiential' is built on the model of such terms in traditional grammar as 'perfect subjunctive' and 'aorist imperative'. No terminological choice precludes misunderstanding, but traditional terms of this type have the benefit of implying the conjunction of two categories (for example aorist and imperative) that are both members of superordinate categories (tense and mood), with both subordinate and superordinate categories well defined using language internal distributional criteria. Furthermore, although the literature is not innocent of meditations on aoristicity (Culioli 1980), traditional terms present themselves more clearly as arbitrary labels than their younger kin (ergative, anti-passive, etc.). The 'perfect experiential' takes as its paragon the suffix -*bźag* in 'Lhasa' Tibetan.

5.1.2 The perfect, direct perception, and inference

Comrie, who defines the perfect as encoding "the continuing present relevance of a past situation" (1976: 53), notes a correlation between the perfect and inferentials. In Bulgarian, Georgian, and Estonian "the Inferential form for the Past Tense consists of a Past Participle plus the Present Tense of the verb 'to be', i.e. a form [...] characteristic of the perfect" (1976: 110). He explains that with

> the perfect, a past event is related to a present state, in other words the past event is not simply presented per se, but because of its relation to a present state. With the inferential, the past event is again not presented simply per se, rather it is inferred from some less direct result of the action (e.g. a second-hand report, or prima facie evidence, such as the wetness of the road leading to the inference that it has been raining, even when the raining itself has not been directly witnessed). Thus the semantic similarity (not, of course, identity) between perfect and inferential lies in the fact that both categories present an event not in itself, but via its results. (1976: 110)

In Comrie's example of witnessing wetness on the road the source of evidence is visual and the tense is perfect. In such a case, inference is the direct summation of the semantics of direct evidence and the semantics of the perfect.

Even in English sensory evidence when combined with perfect tense can yield inferential semantics. On entering the living room the night before Easter a parent, who sees torn bits of chocolate wrappers and chocolatey paw prints across the carpet, might say:

(1) *I **see** the dog **has found** the Easter chocolates.*

The use of the verb 'see' in example (1) ensures that this construction encodes visual evidence, and yet, the proposition 'the dog found the Easter chocolates' is an inference.[7] English is not a language with paradigmatic obligatory encoding of information source. Nonetheless, English is relevant because it shows that in principle inferential readings are latent in the semantics of seeing. One "cannot deny the fact that sentences like *I see that you are a liar* contain a direct indication to the speaker's source of evidence, i.e. the senses" (Usoniene 1999: 217).

Visser's general observation that "evidential meanings seem to be in line with the meaning of the tenses they are fused with, obeying the rules of logic" (2015: 308) applies without any obstacle to the interaction of direct witness and perfect. In the Duna perfect experiential, inferential semantics are "completely predictable given the usual meaning of the individual forms" (San Roque 2008: 379). Volkart (2000) spells out this predictability with reference to the perfect experiential in Tibetan.

> Now if you say 'I can see it' with reference to something which is still in progress [...], this means that what you see is the process or event itself. If, on the other hand, you say 'I can see it' with reference to something that has been completed in the past [...], this means that the event must have some effect or result in the present time, since the notion of 'seeing it' can only refer to present results, but not to an action already completed. (2000: 143)

If one sees 'that something has happened,' one sees evidence in the present that the action took place in the past, and that the state of the world produced by the action continues into the moment of observation, i.e. one infers that the event took place in the past on the basis of evidence in the present.

---

[7] The inferential reading of the verb 'see' with a subordinate clause in the perfect is not obligatory. The host of a party might say to a guest upon arrival: "I see that you've brought your Belgian boyfriend along" (BNC), with the boyfriend in full view. The present progressive is also compatible with both inferential and direct readings. In a sentence such as "I see you're weaving a rug" the 'direct evidence' reading is triggered in a situation such as this: a student fails to arrive at a meeting. Another student locates him in the weaving studio, saying with a tone of indignation, 'We expected you to be at the meeting in room three, but I see you are weaving a rug'. For the inferential reading both guest and host are in a living room. The guest sees a loom in the corner, approaches it, and says to his host 'I see you're weaving a rug'.

It is misplaced to object that inference is a cognitive operation relating premises and conclusion, pointing to the process of reasoning to arrive at a conclusion, whereas 'direct perception' does not point to the speaker's reasoning process but directly to the evidence. On the one hand, since all experience is mediated by the sense organs, perception of an object as a Gestalt is always 'inferred'. On the other hand, when Arthur Eddington watched the solar eclipse of 29 May 1919 from the island of Príncipe, he directly perceived the correctness of Einstein's general theory of relativity. Tournadre and LaPolla emphasize the arbitrary nature of the distinction between 'direct evidence' and 'inference' by drawing attention to four scenarios which showcase the ambiguity.

a. If we see smoke over a forest and say: 'There is a fire', is it sensory visual (and/or olfactory) or is it inferential based on seeing smoke (visual)? What we see is actually the smoke not the fire.

b. If we look at a map and say: 'Melbourne is near Sydney', we might use a visual evidential looking at the map, but the map is not the reality. You need inference and the knowledge of the scale to draw conclusions concerning the distance.

c. If we hear a sound on the roof and say 'It is raining', is it direct evidence or an inference based on the type of sound made by the rain drops?

d. When the speaker sees somebody moving in a particular way and says: 'He is coming', it is also an inference based on the perception that the general direction of movement is toward the speaker. It can also be a confirmation that the person is actually coming, that is, the speaker knew somebody was to come and on seeing the person says the utterance as a confirmation, which could involve a different form of evidential marking. (2014: 258)

If a researcher decides a priori which scenarios constitute direct perception and which constitute inference, he studies only his own opinions. Instead, a semantic analysis should emerge empirically from the use in natural language of an identifiable morpho-syntactic category. Such an investigation makes clear the intimate contacts both between perfects and inferentials and between sensory evidentials and inferentials.

5.2 Previously noted perfect experiential constructions

The use of sensory evidentials for inferential semantics in specific tense and aspect constructions is attested in Sherpa, Duna, Oksapmin, Bogaia, and 'Lhasa' Tibetan. Because the description of the relevant phenomena in

Sherpa (a Tibetan dialect), and Duna, Oksapmin, and Bogaia (three languages of Papua New Guinea) has yet to garner controversy, it suffices here to summarize the findings of previous researchers. In contrast, although the majority of scholars describe *-bźag* as a perfect experiential in 'Lhasa' Tibetan, others see it as exhibiting a dedicated 'inferential' evidential category. The investigation here concurs with the majority of investigators.

5.2.1 Sherpa

Woodbury (1986) points out that the Sherpa form *nok* is used as a visual sensory evidential in the present tense (glossing with 'I see, have seen...') and an inferential evidential in the past (glossing with 'I hear, I infer...')

(2) *ḍaa saa-p mi ti yembur-laa de-ki-**nok***
   rice eat-NMLZ man he Kathmandu-DAT stay-HE
   'The man who is eating rice lives in Kathmandu.' (I see, ... have seen)
   (Woodbury 1986: 191)

(3) *'jon-ki 'ti 'kuršiŋq 'ti dzo-**nok***
   John-ERG the chair it build-PI
   'John built the chair.' (I infer ... I hear ...)
   (Woodbury 1986: 93)

He attributes these two uses of *nok* to it being used for 'immediate evidence', either evidence of the event itself taking place in the present, or the evidence of the aftermath of an event that allows the speaker to make an inferential claim. Kelly (2004: 251/252) notes that *nok* can be used either as a visual sensory evidential in imperfective contexts and an inferential perfective contexts. Tournadre et al. classify *-no'* as sensory in all tenses (see Tab. 1). To them the inferential meaning of sensory evidentials in the perfect tense is apparently self explanatory.

Tab. 1: Sherpa tense and evidential affixes according to Tournadre et al. (2009: 271/272).

	Present (general)	Present (progressive)	Past (simple)	Perfect	Future
Egophoric	giwi'	inwe'	win	niwe'	in/up
Factual	uza	inweza	uza	niweza	uza
Sensory	gino'	inno'	sung	no'	---

5.2.2 Duna

The Duna suffix -*rua* furnishes the next example of the perfect experiential construction. In Duna "the visual evidential -*rua* is used as a primary inflection in reference to states that are assumed to be ongoing at the time of utterance" (San Roque 2008: 380). When it is attached to the -*a* base of verbs with a stative meaning this suffix "marks states that the perceiver observed to be the case before the time of utterance" (San Roque 2008: 317, cf. example (4)). The -*a* base is broadly associated with imperfective aspect (San Roque 2008: 275).

(4) *phekeriti-tia, [...]   khao   rindi-ta   **ra-rua***
    factory.lw-PL   redskin   ground-LOC   be/put-STAT.VIS.P
    'Factories, [...] they exist in European places {I saw}.'
    (San Roque 2008: 317)

However, when applied to the -*o* base (associated with perfective aspect) of action verbs "the verb is independently specified as perfective with respect to 'now', and -*rua* is added to give extra information about how the speaker knows that this event took place; they have seen something that suggests it" (San Roque 2008: 379). In other words, in this construction an action occurred in the past with results that carry forward until the time of the utterance, a typical perfect scenario. To be clear, the -*o* stem is perfective in opposition to the imperfective -*a* stem; it is the combination of the -*o* stem with -*rua* that yields a perfect-like construction. The speaker witnesses not the event itself, but merely its result (examples (5) and (6)).

(5) *rowa   hundi   **ro-rua***
    fire   disappear   be.PFV-STAT.VIS.P
    'The fire had gone out {I saw}.'
    (San Roque 2008: 380)

(6) *anda-ta   hoa-ya-roko,   Metai yeria   aye-ya   **ngo-rua.***
    house-LOC   come-DEP-SW.SIM   PSN   chestnut gather-DEP go.PFV-STAT.VIS.P
    '[I] was coming to the house, Metai had gone to gather chestnuts {I saw}.'
    (San Roque 2008: 380)

The use of the English pluperfect in the translations of examples (5) and (6) makes clear that the action took place first, the speaker witnessed the resulting state later, and later still (at the time of speaking) the speaker reports the action to a listener, employing a visual evidential. With this construction Duna presents a perfect experiential, the intersection of visual evidence and the perfect yielding the semantics of inference.

5.2.3 Oksapmin

To express inference Oksapmin uses the verb *x-* 'to be' in an auxiliary construction marked for visual evidence and perfective aspect in one of the three past tenses (far past, yesterday past, today past); the subordinate verb is marked in the personal evidential category (Loughnane 2009: 428–430).[8] Examples (7) and (8) demonstrate this construction.

(7) mlo-s=a   ej   [ku   muk   ixil   sik   ap
    come.up-SEQ=LINK gosh woman group 3p sick(Eng) house
    m-tpul=a   xu-ja]   **x-n-gwel**
    PRX.O-close(.SEQ)=LINK go.PFV-PER.TODP.PL be-PFV-VIS.YESTP
    'I came up and saw that the ladies had already shut the health centre and gone.'
    (Loughnane 2009: 428)

(8) wanxe=si   wanxe=si=a   awat   x-t-ja
    a.lot=WITH a.lot=WITH=EMPH   decorate.self   DO-PFV-PER.TODP.PL
    x-n-gopa=li=o
    be-PFV-VIS.FP.PL=REP=EMPH
    '(It was seen that) lots and lots (of people) had decorated themselves.'
    (Loughnane 2009: 428)

The use of the English pluperfect in the translations of examples (7) and (8) makes clear that the action took place first, the speaker witnessed the resulting state later, and later still (at the time of speaking) the speaker reports the action to a listener, employing a visual evidential.

Without the auxiliary *x-* 'be' the past perfective visual implies that the speaker was a direct witness to the event, as seen in examples (9) and (10).

(9) a   go   apuŋ=xe   i=xi-m   **əpli-n-gwel**
    HES   2s   yesterday=FOC like.that=DO-SEQ   come-PFV-VIS.YESTP
    'Hey, (I saw that) you came like this too yesterday.'
    (Loughnane 2009: 257)

---

[8] 'Lhasa' Tibetan also neutralizes in favor of the personal in subordinate clauses (cf. Chang and Chang 1984: 607–608; DeLancey 1990: 298).

(10) de=nuŋ   s-pti=o   **n-p-n-gwe**
    WHICH=TO   go-IPFV.PL(.PRS)=QUOT   1/2.O-tell-PFV-VIS.TODP.PL
    '(I saw that) they told us "where are you going?"'
    (Loughnane 2009: 285)

Although the Oksapmin auxiliary construction with *x-* is structurally qute distinct in its formation from the use in Duna of *-rua* with base *-o* verbs, both constructions intersect explicitly morphological marking of sensory evidence and explicit morphological marking of perfective aspect to yield inferential meaning.

5.2.4 Bogaia

San Roque and Loughnane draw attention to the possibility of an inferential interpretation of the visual evidence marker *-ki* in Bogaia when used with past tense verbs (2012: 128, 156).

(11) ho   mabaro   wagan   **mogona=ki**
    [3SG   pig   hunt   go.PST=VIS]
    'He has gone to hunt pigs. (I saw him go.)', or 'I see evidence that he went.'
    (San Roque and Loughnane 2012: 128, citing Seeland 2007: 9 and Seeland, personal communication)

Although San Roque and Loughnane (2012: 128) describe the verb form as 'past' they offer an English translation in the present perfect. In this case again perfect aspect and visual evidence, the perfect experiential, may give rise to an inferential interpretation, although this interpretation is not obligatory. Thus, Bogaia confirms that semantic inference can be grammatically expressed with a visual evidential.

5.2.5 'Lhasa' Tibetan

The suffix *bźag* in 'Lhasa' Tibetan provides a fifth example of a direct evidential marker used for inferential semantics.[9] Table 2 presents an overview of the

---

[9] Ideally one should draw a distinction among the language of the city of Lhasa itself, other dialects of Central Tibet, and the *lingua franca* of the Tibetan diaspora (Miller 1955; Róna-Tas 1985: 160–161). However, because previous authors do not clearly maintain these distinctions, it is not possible to do so here. In order to keep the ambiguity of the underlying language in focus I write 'Lhasa' with single quotes.

5 Perfect experiential constructions: the inferential semantics of direct evidence

Tab. 2: 'Lhasa' Tibetan copula systm (top) and verbal conjugation (bottom).

	Existential copula	Equational copula	
Personal	yod	yin	
Factual	yod-pa-red	red	
Experiential	ḥdug	red-bźag	
	Future	**Present**	**Past**	**Perfect**
Personal	V-gi-yin	V-gi-yod	V-pa-yin	V-yod
Factual	V-gi-red	V-gi-yod-pa-red	V-pa-red	V-yod-pa-red
Experiential	---	V-gi-ḥdug	V-soṅ	V-bźag

'Lhasa' Tibetan verbal system and the place of *bźag* in this system.[10] The conclusion that the use of V-*bźag* in 'Lhasa' Tibetan undermines the preconception that inference and sense evidence require encoding with separate categories rests on the analysis of V-*bźag* as a perfect experiential (cf. Yukawa 1971: 190 *inter alios*). In contrast, DeLancey (1985: 65–67, 2003: 279) and Tournadre and Dorje (2009: 140–144, 410, 413) propose that *bźag* marks a separate 'inferential' category. For the analysis of V-*bźag* in 'Lhasa' Tibetan as a perfect experiential to stand secure, these alternative analyses call for reply.

5.2.5.1 DeLancey's analysis of Tibetan V-*bźag*

DeLancey's opinion that "in a true evidential language" direct perception and inference "could not be in the same grammatical form" (2012: 536), is compatible with his own analysis of the 'Lhasa' Tibetan verb. In 1985, when writing about the meaning of V-*bźag*, DeLancey contrasts this morpheme with V-*pa-red*, and V-*soṅ*, citing examples (12), (13), and (14).

(12) bsod-nams-kyis   thaṅ-kha   **bkal-pa-red**
    Sonam-ERG   Thangka   hang-PST:FAC
    'Sonam hung up a Thangka' (based on report or inference)
    (DeLancey 1985: 65)

---

[10] The analysis in Tab. 2 reflects my own understanding of the Tibetan verbal system. In nonfinite clauses the difference among the three evidential moods is often neutralized in favor of the personal (cf. note 8). This paper will not discuss the constructions V-*byuṅ*, V-*myoṅ*, V-*yoṅ*, V-*pa-ḥdug*, etc. which, although essential parts of a complete picture of the 'Lhasa' verb, are not relevant to the current discussion.

(13) *bsod-nams-kyis*   *thaṅ-kha*   **bkal-soṅ**
Sonam-ERG   Thangka   hang-PST:EXP
'Sonam hung up a Thangka' (based on direct perception)
(DeLancey 1985: 65)

(14) *bsod-nams-kyis*   *thaṅ-kha*   **bkal-bźag**
Sonam-ERG   Thangka   hang-PRF:EXP
'Sonam hung up a Thangka' (inferred from direct perception of the hanging Thangka)
(DeLancey 1985: 66)

Discussing the difference between the meaning of V-*bźag* and V-*soṅ* DeLancey refers to

> the inadequacy of a simple notion of direct evidence here, for there are clearly two distinct types of direct perception which can be distinguished: direct perception of the actual event being reported, and direct perception of the subsequent state which directly resulted from that event. (DeLancey 1985: 67).

DeLancey correctly describes the semantics of V-*bźag* and V-*soṅ*, but because he contrasts two past tense forms (V-*pa-red* and V-*soṅ*) with a perfect tense form (V-*bźag*), he interprets a tense distinction as an evidential distinction. His account is only possible because he conflates the past and perfect tenses, ignoring several terms of the verbal paradigm, in particular V-*yod-pa-red*, the perfect equivalent of V-*pa-red*.

DeLancey overlooks many publications that treat V-*bźag* as a perfect. According to Sandberg V-*pa-yin* and V-*pa-red* reflect "what the French would style the Past Indefinite" whereas V-*yod* and V-*ḥdug* are an "expression of the perfect tense active" (1894: 53). Goldstein and Nornang classify V-*yod*, V-*yod-pa-red*, and V-*bźag* as 'present perfect', distinct from V-*pa-yin*, V-*pa-red*, and V-*soṅ*, which they label 'past' (1970: 408). Yukawa clearly identifies V-*bźag* as a perfect experiential.

> 完了動詞にduuがつくと、その行為がおこったことが現在目前のことがらから歴然としていることもあらわす。つまり，何らかの感覚で感じられるわけである。なお，肯定形はšaaを用いる。

> When it comes to *ḥdug* in the perfect, it describes the fact that evidence of the action that occurred is now before the eyes, i.e. that one experiences a sensation in some way. For the unnegated form *bźag* is used. (Yukawa 1971: 190)

Yukawa also describes V-*yod* and V-*yod-pa-red* as having perfect semantics (1971: 189/190). Kitamura describes V-*pa-yin*, V-*pa-red*, and V-*soṅ* as 'past' (1977: 31/32) and V-*yod*, V-*yo-pa-red*, and V-*bźag* as 'present perfect' (1977: 33). Chang

5 Perfect experiential constructions: the inferential semantics of direct evidence — 145

Tab. 3: 'Lhasa' Tibetan copula system (top) and verbal conjugation (bottom) according to Tournadre and Dorje (2009: 410).

	Existential copula	Essential copula		
Personal	*yod*	*yin*		
Factual	*yod-pa-red*	*red*		
Testimonial	*ḥdug*	---		
Revelatory	---	*red-bźag*		

	Future	Present	Past	Perfect
Personal	V-*gi-yin*	V-*gi-yod*	V-*pa-yin*	V-*yod*
Factual	V-*gi-red*	V-*gi-yod-pa-red*	V-*pa-red*	V-*yod-pa-red*
Testimonial	---	V-*gi-ḥdug*	V-*soṅ*	---
Inferential	---	---	---	V-*bźag*

and Chang identify V-*yod*, V-*yo-pa-red*, and V-*bźag* as the 'present perfect' (1984: 620–622); they describe -*bźag* as having the semantics of "first-hand experience" (Chang and Chang 1984: 621). Hoshi describes V-*pa-yin*, V-*pa-red*, and V-*soṅ* as 'completed non-durative' (完了-非継続相) and V-*yod*, V-*yod-pa-red*, and V-*bźag* as 'completed durative' (完了-継続相) (1988: 187/188).[11] Tournadre also clearly distinguishes V-*pa-yin*, V-*pa-red* and V-*soṅ* as 'aorist' and V-*yod*, V-*yod-pa-red*, and V-*bźag* as 'perfect' (1996: 245). Denwood likewise distinguishes V-*pa-yin*, V-*pa-red* and V-*soṅ* as 'past' (1999: 142–149) and V-*yod*, V-*yod-pa-red*, and V-*bźag* as 'perfect' (1999: 158–161). Volkart (2000) points out that an inferential meaning of a perfect experiential is found not only in 'Lhasa' Tibetan, but in a number of Central Tibetan dialects. Apparently unaware of this tradition of scholarship, in his most recent discussion of V-*bźag*, DeLancey essentially repeats his 1985

---

[11] I see 'completed durative' (完了-継続相) as equivalent to Comrie's "continuing present relevance of a past situation" (1976: 53), i.e. the textbook definition of 'perfect', but the reader may note that Hoshi uses the term 完了, normally identified with English 'perfect', in her terminology both for the past (V-*pa-yin*, V-*pa-red* and V-*soṅ*) and the perfect (V-*yod*, V-*yod-pa-red*, and V-*bźag*).

Tab. 4: Re-presentation of 'Lhasa' Tibetan verbal system emphasizing morphological links among revelatory, inferential and testimonial.

	Existential copula	Essential copula		
Personal	yod	yin		
Factual	yod-pa-red	red		
Testimonial	ḥdug	---		
Revelatory	---	(red-ḥdug)		
	Future	Present	Past	Perfect
Personal	V-gi-yin	V-gi-yod	V-pa-yin	V-yod
Factual	V-gi-red	V-gi-yod-pa-red	V-pa-red	V-yod-pa-red
Testimonial	---	V-gi-ḥdug	V-soṅ	---
Inferential	---	---	---	(V-ḥdug)

discussion;[12] he continues to ignore V-*yod*, and V-*yod-pa-red* and fails to recognize the perfect and past as separate tenses (2003: 227/228).[13]

Just as the semantics of the experiential "is an inevitable consequence of its position in a paradigm where it contrasts with other epistemic categories, the personal and generic" (DeLancey 2012: 554), so too the semantics of the 'Lhasa' Tibetan perfect tense is an inevitable consequence of its position in a paradigm where it contrasts with the future, present, and past. Returning to DeLancey's examples about hanging up Thangkas, if verb tense is held constant, the three evidential categories contrast in the past with the triplet of examples (15), (16), and (17) or in the perfect with the triplet of examples (18), (19), and (20).

Past

(15) ṅas   thaṅ-kha   **bkal-pa-yin**
     me-ERG   Thangka   hang-PST:PRS
     'I hung up a Thangka' (I know; I did it)

---

[12] DeLancey does change other elements of his analysis of the 'Lhasa' Tibetan verbal system, for example introducing the terminology 'conjunct-disjunct' (2003: 278–280). These changes draw his analysis further out of step with other researchers on Tibetan (cf. Tournadre 2008).

[13] As recently as 2012 DeLancey appears to regard 'Lhasa' Tibetan as having a separate 'inferential' category (2012: 536). Although he does not mention V-*bźag* or explicitly posit any other inferential marker in 'Lhasa' Tibetan, he does comment that "the immediate category contrasts with the personal and inferential categories" (DeLancey 2012: 554).

(16) *bsod-nams-kyis thaṅ-kha **bkal-pa-red***
     Sonam-ERG   Thangka   hang-PST:FAC
     'Sonam hung up a Thangka' (I know; people know)

(17) *bsod-nams-kyis thaṅ-kha **bkal-soṅ***
     Sonam-ERG   Thangka   hang-PST:EXP
     'Sonam hung up a Thangka' (I know; I saw)

Perfect

(18) *ṅas   thaṅ-kha **bkal-yod***
     me-ERG   Thangka   hang-PRF:PRS
     'I have hung up a Thangka.' (I know; I did it)

(19) *bsod-nams-kyis thaṅ-kha **bkal-yod-pa-red***
     Sonam-ERG   Thangka   hang-PRF:FAC
     'Sonam has hung up a Thangka' (I know; people know)

(20) *bsod-nams-kyis thaṅ-kha **bkal-bźag***
     Sonam-ERG   Thangka   hang-PRF:EXP
     'Sonam has hung up a Thangka' (I know; I saw)

If one distinguishes the past and perfect tenses, the apparent contrast between a 'direct' V-*soṅ* and an 'inferred' V-*bźag* disappears. Instead, both V-*soṅ* and V-*bźag* encode witnessed evidentiality and the difference in their semantics is the different between the past and the perfect.

5.2.5.2 Tournadre and Dorje's analysis of Tibetan V-*bźag*

Tournadre and Dorje posit five evidential categories in their analysis of the 'Lhasa' Tibetan verbal system: personal, factual, testimonial, revelatory, and inferential (2009: 140–144, 410, 413). Table 3 summarizes their presentation of the verbal system.[14] In this analysis three evidential categories, testimonial, revelatory, and inferential, are in complementary distribution. The testimonial occurs as an existential copula and as a suffix of the past and present. The revelatory and the inferential are also in complementary distribution: the revelatory occurs only as an essential copula and the inferential occurs only as a perfect verb ending. In contrast, the personal and assertative occur as existential copula,

---

[14] In an inconsequential terminological adjustment to agree with the overall usage here, I change 'egophoric' to 'personal'. 'Egophoric' is an unattractive neologism and implies some special relationship with the first person (*ego*), but all Tibetan evidentials can occur with any of the grammatical persons (Hill 2013b).

essential copula, and as suffixes of the present, past, perfect, and future. From a methodological perspective, if two categories are in complementary distribution it is possible to unite them as a single category (Harris 1951: 303–309). Until Tournadre and Dorje make explicit their reasoning for separating the inferential and relevatory from the testimonial, the distribution of the relevant forms compels their unification.

In addition to improving the overall elegance of the analysis, there are morphological reasons for combining the testimonial, revelatory, and inferential. As seen in Tab. 3, the revelatory essential copula *red-bźag* shares the component '*bźag*' with the inferential perfect ending V-*bźag*. This formal similarity suggests a special relationship between the revelatory and the inferential. Tournadre and Dorje's inferential and relevatory evidential categories also bear formal links with the testimonial, which Tab. 3 fails to capture. The interrogative form of *red-bźag* is *red-ḥdug*, and it is negated as *red-mi-ḥdug* (cf. Tournadre and Dorje 2009: 411). An alternative form of the perfect inferential is V-*ḥdug*, and V-*bźag* itself is negated as V-*mi-ḥdug* (Kitamura 1977: 33; Chang and Chang 1984: 620; Hoshi 1988: 286–291; Tournadre and Dorje 2009: 140).[15] If one presents the 'Lhasa' verbal system in tabular form again, emphasizing these formal ties among the revelatory, inferential, and testimonial (cf. Tab. 4), the desirability of uniting all three together as a single category is readily apparent. Amending Tournadre and Dorje's analysis to account for these distributions results in Tab. 2 above.[16]

5.2.5.3 Tibetan V-*bźag* is a perfect experiential

Having considered in turn the arguments of DeLancey and Tournadre and Dorje that V-*bźag* is an inferential marker, it is convenient to summarize the case that V-*bźag* is a perfect experiential. DeLancey arrives at his analysis by omitting several components of the Tibetan verbal paradigm. For Tournadre and Dorje the inferential is in complementary distribution with the testimonial and revelatory. Taken together the testimonial, inferential, and revelatory are used in the same morpho-syntactic environments as the personal and factual evidential categories. Consequently,

---

[15] Tournadre (1996: 245) and Denwood (1999: 159–160) distinguish V-*bźag* and V-*ḥdug* as having somewhat separate meanings. However, as seen, Yukawa (1971: 190), Chang and Chang (1984: 620), and Tournadre and Dorje (2009: 140, 411) reject such a distinction. Given the discussion in Volkart (2000) and Denwood (1999: 159) it seems likely that V-*bźag* is the form used in the city of Lhasa itself whereas V-*ḥdug* is current in other parts of Central Tibet (cf. Note 9).

[16] Tournadre and LaPolla (2014: 241) refer to *ḥdug* as 'sensory' and *red-bźag* as 'sensory (inferential)' this choice of terminology implies that Tournadre now agrees with the analysis proposed here.

structuralist methodology leads to the inevitable conclusion that it is a mistake to distinguish the inferential and revelatory from the testimonial. The morphological content of the forms in question further buttresses this conclusion; the morpheme ḥdug appears in all three. These considerations all weigh in favour of positing only three evidential categories for 'Lhasa' Tibetan, viz. personal, factual, and testimonial. More specifically, the suffix V-bźag patterns paradigmatically like a perfect testimonial, it has morphological links with the testimonial (via V-ḥdug and V-mi-ḥdug), and its inferential meaning precisely sums the semantics of the testimonial and the perfect; V-bźag is a perfect experiential with a derived use to express inferences.

5.3 Newly proposed examples of the perfect experiential

The perfect experiential constructions in Sherpa, Duna, Oksapmin, Bogaia, and 'Lhasa' Tibetan, by undermining confidence in the iron-clad boundary between direct perception and inference, inspire an open-mindedness that constructions hitherto described in some other fashion may also permit analysis as perfect experientials. The morphemes *oleo* in Kham and *-qa* in Kashaya present such cases.

5.3.1 Kham

Watters describes *oleo* in Kham not as a visual evidential but as a mirative marker (2002: 288–296). Nonetheless, equipped with knowledge of the perfect experiential in other languages, it is possible to resolve those objections that DeLancey (2012: 535–538) and Hengeveld and Olbertz (2012: 495/496) raise to my (Hill 2012: 420/421) analysis of *oleo* as a visual evidential.

Hengeveld and Olbertz draw attention to examples (21) and (22) in Kham (2012: 495), which Watters (2002: 292) analyzes as showing mirativity,[17] but which I understand as consistent with an analysis in terms of sense evidence (Hill 2012: 421). According to Hengeveld and Olbertz (2012: 495/496) example (21) "is clearly a case of direct perception" and example (22) is "a case of inference" (Hengeveld and Olbertz 2012: 495).

---

[17] Hengeveld and Olbertz agree with Watters that these examples merit the moniker 'mirative' (2012: 495), but they redefine what is meant by this label (2012: 498 *et passim*); i.e. they disagree with DeLancey and Watters about the grammatical meaning that *oleo* in Kham exhibits.

(21) *mənlal-lai   tə   "e   babəi   mənlal*
    Manlal-OBJ FOC   hey   man   Manlal
    *nə-kə   zə   ci   syã:-də **u-li-zya-o**   oleo   sani"*
    DIST-at   EMP   CEP   sleep-NF 3S-be-CONT:NML MIR   CONFIRM
    (I said) to Manlal, "Hey man, Manlala, he's right there sleeping, see!"

(22) *ŋa-khurja   **ŋa-sə-məi-wo**   oleo*
    my-knife   1S-CAUS-lose-NML   MIR
    'I lost my knife!' (I just discovered it)
    (Watters 2002: 292 example 19)[18]

These two sentences share a common morphological element and a common semantic element. The common morphological element is the *oleo* construction. The common semantic component is direct perception. There is also a morphological and a semantic difference between the two sentences. Example (21) includes the marker of continuous aspect *-zya* (Watters 2002: 89) and refers to present time. In contrast, since "the default aspect for this paradigm is the perfective, which is unmarked" (Watters 2002: 89) the lack of *-zya* in example (22) indicates perfective aspect and the sentence refers to past time.[19] The inferential reading in Kham emerges as an interaction of direct evidence with certain tense or aspect categories.

In his argument against *oleo* as a marker of direct evidence, DeLancey contrasts example (21) with example (23). For DeLancey example (21) is used "when the information being related is perceived at first hand" and example (23) a statement "based on inference [...] said when the speaker first discovered traces showing that the leopard had eaten his dog" (DeLancey 2012: 536).

(23) *a-kə   zə   o-kəi-wo   oleo*
    here-at EMP   3sg-eat-NML MIR
    'He ate [him] right here!'
    (DeLancey 2012: 536, cf. Watters 2002: 291)

DeLancey rightly surmises that I see no obstacle to analyzing (23) as visual evidence "because, after all, the speaker did see SOMETHING" (DeLancey 2012: 536

---

18 There is an ambiguity in Watters translation as to whether the knife or the fact of loss is the antecedent of 'it'.

19 The reader may object that 'perfective aspect' (with reference to past time) is not a 'perfect', so *oleo* used with perfective aspect cannot be a 'perfect testimonial'. This objections places too much significance on Watter's terminological choices. Example (22) is indubitably an instance of "continuing present relevance of a past situation" (Comrie 1976: 53). Thus, *oleo* used with a verb unmarked for aspect jointly express perfect semantics, even if Kham has no morphosyntactic category for which 'the perfect' is a tempting label.

5 Perfect experiential constructions: the inferential semantics of direct evidence — 151

emphasis in original). The same aspectual contrast observed between examples (21) and (22) also obtains between (21) and (23); consequently, the same explanation is available. Example (23), where the speaker infers that a leopard has eaten a dog and expresses this inference with *oleo* in the perfective aspect, is parallel to example (1), where the speaker infers that a dog has eaten Easter chocolates and expresses this inference with 'see' in the English present perfect.

In the Kham examples (22) and (23) the direct perception is not the perception of an action or a presence, but of an absence. As DeLancey puts it, "the speaker is a direct witness to the proposition he states in (5) [= 21], and is explicitly not in (6) [=(23)]" (2012: 536). Whether or not witness of absence, of nothingness, is indeed direct perception is a philosophical question, and we "must leave to philosophers the task of clarifying the status of semantic, i.e. conceptual categories considered independently of their linguistic embodiment" (Lazard 1999: 105); in language such things happen. The Classical Tibetan example (24), in which two brothers discover that their younger brother has been eaten by a tiger, is narratively close to the Kham example (23). Just as in the Kham example the dog owner did not witness the leopard consuming his dog, in the Tibetan example the two brothers did not witness the eating of their sibling but only its after effects, nonetheless the passage uses the direct evidential marker *ḥdug*, which DeLancey himself now analyses in 'Lhasa' Tibetan as an 'immediate evidential' (2012: 554).[20]

(24) *bltas-pa-na / nu-bo tha-chuṅ stag-gis zos-te / śa-daṅ*
look-NMZ:CV younger.brother younger tiger-AGN eat-CV flesh-ASS
khrag-gis kun-tu bsgos nas/ rtsog-rtsog ltar
blood-AGN everywhere-TRM stain-CV filth like-TRM
ḥdug-par *mthoṅ-nas*
is-TES:NMZ:TRM see-CV
'When they looked (his older brothers) saw, that the younger brother had been eaten by a tiger, that everywhere was filthily stained with flesh and blood'
(Hahn 1996: 191, my translation)

Tuyuca is yet another language in which the visual witness of absence is a valid means to express an inferred act of feline violence. In a situation very close to the leopard slaying a dog in Kham, or the tiger eating a young prince in Tibetan,

---

[20] DeLancey claims that in Classical Tibetan *ḥdug* is not an evidential marker but instead a verb 'sit' (1992: 52). It is unclear how he would analyze *ḥdug* in example (24). For further discussion of testimonial evidentiality in Classical Tibetan see Hill (2013a).

in Tuyuca one can relate the inferred slaying of a dog by a jaguar with a visual evidential.

> On one occasion a man returned from his field and, using a visual evidential, told me that a jaguar had killed his dog. In astonishment, I asked him if he had seen the event. He said that he had not [...] he *saw* marks on the ground where the jaguar had dragged him off. (Barnes 1984: 263 emphasis in original).

Unfortunately Barnes does not provide the original sentence that the man said to her.

Putting aside the predatory activities of big cats, the use of negated direct evidentials shows that seeing an absence is still seeing. In the 'Lhasa' Tibetan example (25) the speaker sees the absence of shelves.

(25) thab ḥdiḥi steṅ-la ña skam-paḥi phyir-du
 hearth this-GEN above-OBL fish dry-GEN in.order-to
 grab **mi-ḥdug**
 method not-exist-EXP
 'There are no shelves over the fire for the drying of fish.'
 (Lewin 1879: 71, exercise 61, example 6)

In English it is also possible to see absences, as examples (26) and (27) show.

(26) *But the second my eyes cleared floor level I* **saw** *that the relics* **had gone***!* (BNC)

(27) *I* **see** *that y you* **weren't there** *at that meeting on* ... (Looking at the minutes of a previous meeting) (BNC)

If the experiential in Tibetan, the visual evidential in Tuyuca, and the verb 'see' in English can encode the visual witness of absence, there is no reason a priori that this possibility should escape *oleo* in Kham.

DeLancey offers no evidence for his claim that "in a true evidential language" examples (21) and (23) "in the context in which they were made, could not be in the same grammatical form" (2012: 536). If his view is accurate than the possibility remains open that like English, neither Tibetan, Tuyucan, nor Kham are 'true' evidential languages. In the absence of a discussion of how a 'true evidential language' differs from other types of evidential languages, an effort to ponder DeLancey's intention would drift into speculation (cf. §1.1 above).

DeLancey's contention that the 'Lhasa' Tibetan equivalents of (21) and (23) would be effected in two distinct evidential categories, respectively the 'direct evidential' and 'inferential' (2012: 536), is only true if one follows his analysis of the Tibetan verbal system, rejected above (§2.5.1). Examples (28) and (29) provide translation into 'Lhasa' Tibetan of the Kham examples (21) and (23); *contra* DeLancey these two sentences use the same experiential evidential category, the difference between V-*gi-ḥdug* and V-*bźag* being one of tense and not evidence (cf. §2.5).

(28) *gzigs   pha-gir   **gñal-gyi-ḥdug***
    leopard there-OBL sleep-PRS-TEST
    'The leopard is sleeping over there'

(29) *ḥdir   kho   **bzas-bźag***
    here-OBL he   eat-PRF-TEST
    '(The leopard must have) eaten him right here'
    (cf. example 24 for an analogous example in Classical Tibetan also in the experiential)

In sum, Watters does not provide evidence sufficient to preclude the analysis of *oleo* as a direct evidential; until such evidence is in hand the conclusion that *oleo* marks the 'mirative' is premature and *oleo* should not serve as the prime example of "mirativity as a separate category" (Aikhenvald 2004: 211).[21] Whatever future research on Kham may yield, those who do fieldwork on this language would do well to not enter upon their work with the preconception that direct evidence and inference are irreconcilably opposed. The published examples of *oleo* admit themselves to analysis as direct evidentials.

5.3.2 Kashaya

Oswalt (1961, 1986) describes Kashaya as a language that has eight evidential categories in the 'spontaneous' tense. He distinguishes two types of inferential evidentials: 'inferential I' the suffix -*qa* and 'inferential II' the suffix -*bi*. In his 1961 contribution Oswalt draws both syntactic and semantic distinctions between these two suffixes (1961: 243/244), but in his 1986 contribution he presents them as semantically identical but distinct in distribution, with -*qa* occurring in main clauses and -*bi* occurring only in subordinate clauses.

Oswalt's description of inferential suffixes in Kashaya is equivocal and methodologically unsatisfactory. After reporting that -*bi* occurs predominantly in subordinate clauses (1986: 41), he discusses -*bi-w* "where -w is probably the Absolutive" as the "most common nonsubordinating combination" (1986: 42). Thus, Oswalt is unsure of whether -*w* is the Absolutive and there are other non-subordinating

---

[21] Examples of *oleo* in Kham constitute four of the seven examples that Aikhenvald uses to illustrate 'mirativity as a separate category' (2004: 211–214). As for the one example of =*(a)m* given from Cupeño, Aikhenvald more recently admits there "is unfortunately no way the exact status of =*(a)m* can be ascertained" (2012: 467). Her remaining two examples are from Tariana (cf. Hill 2012: 425–426).

combinations into which -*bi* enters, which he refrains from enumerating. One non-subordinating combinations into which -*bi* enters is -*bi-qa*; "no difference has been determined for the meaning of this form versus either suffix separately" (1986: 42). In gross violation of the 'one form one meaning' principle, the speaker of Kayasha is burdened with three equivalent ways of expressing inference in finite clauses: *bi-w*, -*qa*, and -*bi-qa*; it must be a difficult language to master.

Based on Oswalt's account, de Haan unites -*qa* and -*bi* as one inferential category in his discussion of Kashaya evidentiality (2001: 198). This unification is not justifiable. Such a unification would be possible only if the two suffixes together patterned similarly to other evidential suffixes. Since the suffix -*bi* is mostly restricted to subordinate clauses, if -*qa* were precluded from subordinate clauses, then together the two evidentials would pattern like other evidential categories such as visual -*ya*, which occurs in both finite and subordinate clauses. However, because Oswalt does not preclude the use of -*qa* in subordinate clauses, such a unification is not permissible.

Perhaps it is premature to use Kashaya at all in typological discussions of evidentiality until its structural description is more precisely formulated. I nonetheless indulge in a few remarks on the basis of Oswalt's examples. Almost all examples of 'Inferential I' have English translations with a present perfect and the context normally requires visual evidence (examples (30)–(33)).

(30) *mu* **cohtoc^{h}q^h**
 mu cohtoc-qa
 he leave-INFER.I
 'He has left' (Said on discovering that the person is no longer present)
 (Oswalt 1986: 38)

(31) ʔahq^{h}a **p^{h}ímaqam = t'o**
 river they-must-have-gone-across
 'They must have gone across the river' (This was judged from the tracks)
 (Oswalt 1961: 244)[22]

(32) *kalikak^h* *dima:* **s'i -qa-c'-q^h**
 book holding make-cause-self-INFER.I
 'He has had a picture taken of himself holding a book'
 (Oswalt 1986: 39)

---

[22] Oswalt does not segment the verb form *p^{h}ímaqam* but underlines the 'q' to note it as the inferential-I form (1961: 244).

(33) **sinamqʰ**
 drown-INFER.I
 'He must have drowned'
 (Oswalt 1961: 243)

(34) *sapa·tu   mít́ónṭolowa·du   tala·qʰ*
 shoes   that-are-rubbing-sore-on-his-toes   he-must-be-wearing
 'He must be wearing shoes that are rubbing sore spots on his toes'
 (This was deduced form the person's manner of walking in new shoes)
 (Oswalt 1961: 244)

In examples (30) and (31) the translation makes the visual nature of the evidence explicit. In example (32) the evidence is "the existence of the picture, which the speaker has seen" (de Haan 2001: 200). Example (33) is said when "the speaker saw the body cast up on a beach or floating in the water" (Oswalt 1961: 243). Example (34) does not have an English present perfect in the translation, but does make the source of visual evidence explicit.

According to Oswalt *qa-* marks evidence from senses other than vision and hearing "to a certain extent" (1986: 38); he offers example (35) as evidence.

(35) *cuhni: **muʔtʻa-qʰ***
 bread   cook-INFER.I
 '[I smell that] bread has been cooked'.
 (Oswalt 1986: 38).

However, it is noteworthy that example (35) also employs the present perfect tense in the English translation. If 'Inference-I' is used for smell, taste, and touch in general, then one ought to be able to say 'I smell that the vegetables are cooking' using this evidential. In the absence of an example of 'Inference-I' used in habitual or imperfective contexts, nothing in Oswalt's description precludes the conclusion that *-qa* is a morpheme that encodes the overlap between sense evidence and perfect tense, another example of the perfect experiential.

5.4 Conclusion

With due allowance for the anthropomorphism this study concurs with de Haan that languages "can choose how they wish to treat the inferential evidential" (2001: 194). Willett, Aikhenvald, DeLancey, and Hengeveld and Olbertz are mistaken in their belief that "direct vs. indirect evidence is the fundamental evidential distinction" (DeLancey 2012: 540), as the perfect experiential in Sherpa, Duna,

Oksapmin, Bogaia, and 'Lhasa' Tibetan shows. Disabused of this misconception it is possible not only to dismiss the objections of DeLancey (2012) and Hengeveld and Olbertz (2012) to the analysis of *oleo* in Kham as a direct evidential, but to potentially describe *-qa* in Kashaya as yet another perfect experiential. Apart from these six perfect experientials, Foe, Maricopa, Hualapai, and Matses reveal other types of interaction between direct evidence and inference.

Abbreviations

1s first singular, 3s third singular, ASS associative, AUX auxiliary verb, BNC British National Corpus, CAUS causative, CEP counter-expectation particle, CONFIRM confirmative, CONT continuous aspect, CV converb, DEP dependent, EMP emphatic, EMPH emphatic, ERG ergative, EVID evidential marker, FAC factual, FOC focus, FP far past, HE habitual evidential, HES hesitation, INFER-I inferential evidential 1, IPFV imperfective, LINK prosodic linker, NF non-final marker, NML nominalizer, NMZ nominalizer, MIR mirative, O object, OBJ objective, P previous evidence, PAST past, PER personal-factual evidential in Oksapmin or personal in Tibetan, PFV perfective, PI past inferential, PL plural, PRF perfect, PRS present, PRX proximal, PSN personal name, QUOT quote, REP reported evidential, SEQ sequential, SIM simultaneous, SS same- subject/reference marker, STAT stative, SUBJ subject marker, SW switch, EXP experiential, TRM terminative, TODP today past, VIS visual evidence, YESTP yesterday past.

References

Aikhenvald, Alexandra. 2004. *Evidentiality*. Oxford: Oxford University Press.
Aikhenvald, Alexandra. 2012. The Essence of Mirativity. *Linguistic Typology* 16(3). 435–485.
Barnes, Janet. 1984. Evidentials in the Tuyuca Verb. *International Journal of American Linguistics* 50(3). 255–271.
Belkadi, Aicha. 2013. Aspect and mood in Berber and the aorist issue. *SOAS Working Papers in Linguistics* 16. 27–150.
Beyer, Stephen. 1992. *The Classical Tibetan language*. New York: State University of New York
Bloomfield, Leonard. 1933. *Language*. New York: Henry Holt and Company
Chang, Kun & Betty Chang. 1984. The certainty hierarchy among Spoken Tibetan verbs of being. *Bulletin of the Institute of History and Philology, Academia Sinica* 55(4). 603–635.
Comrie, Bernard. 1976. *Aspect: an introduction to the study of verbal aspect and related problems*. Cambridge: Cambridge University Press.
Creissels, Denis. 2008. Spatial Cases. In Malchukov, A. & A. Spencer (eds.), *The Oxford Handbook of Case*, 609–625. Oxford University Press.
Culioli, Antoine. 1980. Valeurs aspectuelles et opérations énonciatives: l'aoristique. In J. David and R. Martin (eds.), *La notion d'aspect*, 181–193. Paris: Klincksieck.

DeLancey, Scott. 1985. Lhasa Tibetan evidentials and the semantics of causation. *Proceedings of the Eleventh Annual Meeting of the Berkeley Linguistics Society*. 65–72.
DeLancey, Scott. 1990. Ergativity and the cognitive model of event structure in Lhasa Tibetan. *Cognitive Linguistics* 1. 289–321.
DeLancey, Scott. 1992. The historical status of the conjunct/disjunct pattern in Tibeto-Burman. *Acta Linguistica Hafniensia* 25. 39–62.
DeLancey, Scott. 2001. The mirative and evidentiality. *Journal of Pragmatics* 33. 369–382.
DeLancey, Scott. 2003. Lhasa Tibetan. In G. Thurgood and R. LaPolla, *The Sino-Tibetan Languages*, 270–288. London: Routledge.
DeLancey, Scott. 2012. Still mirative after all these years. *Linguistic Typology* 16(3). 529–564.
Denwood, Philip. 1999. *Tibetan*. Amsterdam: John Benjamins.
Dixon, Robert M. W. 2010. *Basic linguistic theory*. Oxford: Oxford University Press
Dowty, David R. 1989. On the semantic content of the notion 'thematic role'. In Gennaro Chierchia, et al (eds.), *Properties, types, and meaning*, vol. 2: *Semantic issues*, 69–129. Dordrecht: Kluwer.
Fleck, David W. 2007. Evidentiality and double tense in Matses. *Language* 83(3). 589–614.
Goldstein, Melvyn C. & Nawang Nornang. 1970. *Modern spoken Tibetan: Lhasa dialect*. Seattle: University of Washington Press.
Gordon, Lynn. 1986. The Development of Evidentiality in Maricopa. In Wallace Chafe & Johanna Nichols (eds.), *Evidentiality: the linguistic coding of epistemology*, 75–88. Norwood: Ablex Publishing Corporation.
Greenberg, Joseph H. 1973. Linguistics as a pilot science. In Eric Hamp (ed.), *Themes in linguistics: The 1970s*, 45–60. The Hague: Mouton.
Hahn, Michael. 1996. *Lehrbuch der klassischen tibetischen Schriftsprache*. Swisttal-Odendorf: Indica et Tibetica Verlag.
de Haan, Ferdinand. 2001. The Place of Inference within the Evidential System. *International Journal of American Linguistics* 67(2). 193–219.
Harris, Zellig S. 1951. *Structural linguistics*. Chicago: University of Chicago Press.
Haspelmath, Martin. 2007. Pre-established categories don't exist: Consequences for language description and typology. *Linguistic Typology* 11: 119–132.
Haspelmath, Martin. 2010a. Comparative concepts and descriptive categories in cross-linguistic studies. *Language* 86(3). 663–687.
Haspelmath, Martin. 2010b. The interplay between comparative concepts and descriptive categories (Reply to Newmeyer). *Language* 86(3). 696–699.
Hengeveld, Kees & Hella Olbertz. 2012. Didn't you know? Mirativity does exist! *Linguistic Typology* 16(3). 487–503.
Hill, Nathan W. 2011. The allative, locative, and terminative cases (la-don) in the Old Tibetan Annals. In Imaeda, Yoshiro & Kapstein, Mathew (eds.), *New Studies in the Old Tibetan Documents: Philology, History and Religion*, 3–38.Tokyo: Research Institute for Languages and Cultures of Asia and Africa, Tokyo University of Foreign Studies.
Hill, Nathan W. 2012. 'Mirativity' does not exist: ḥdug in 'Lhasa' Tibetan and other suspects. *Linguistic Typology* 16(3). 389–433.
Hill, Nathan W. 2013a. ḥdug as a testimonial marker in Classical and Old Tibetan. *Himalayan Linguistics* 12(1). 1–16.
Hill, Nathan W. 2013b. Contextual semantics of 'Lhasa' Tibetan evidentials. *SKASE Journal of Theoretical Linguistics* 10(3). 47–54.

Hoshi, Michiyo 星 実千代 1988. 現代チベット語文法（ラサ方言）*Gendai Chibetto-go bunpō (Rasa hōgen)*. Tokyo: ユネスコ東アジア文化研究センター Yunesuko Higashi Ajia Bunka Kenkyū Sentā.

Kelly, Barbara F. 2004. A grammar of Sherpa. In C. Genetti (ed.), *Tibeto-Burman languages of Nepal: Manange and Sherpa*, 232–440. Canberra: Pacific Linguistics.

Kitamura, Hajime. 1977. *Tibetan: Lhasa Dialect*. Tokyo: Asia Africa Gengo Bunka Kenkyūjo, Tokyo Gaikokugo Daigaku.

Lazard, Gilbert. 1999. Mirativity, evidentiality, mediativity, or other? *Linguistic Typology* 3. 91–109.

Lazard, Gilbert. 2012. The case for pure linguistics. *Studies in Language* 36(2). 241–259.

Lewin, Thomas Herbert. 1879. *A manual of Tibetan*. Calcutta: G. H. House, at the Baptist mission press.

Loughnane, Robyn. 2009. A Grammar of Oksapmin. Melbourne: University of Melbourne dissertation.

Miller, Roy Andrew. 1955. The Independent Status of Lhasa dialect within Central Tibetan. *Orbis* 4(1). 49–55.

Miller, Roy Andrew. 1970. A Grammatical Sketch of Classical Tibetan. *Journal of the American Oriental Society* 90(1). 74–96.

Newmeyer, Frederick J. 2007. Linguistic typology requires crosslinguistic formal categories. *Linguistic Typology* 11(1). 133–57.

Newmeyer, Frederick J. 2010. On comparative concepts and descriptive categories: A reply to Haspelmath. *Language* 86(3). 688–695.

Oswalt, Robert L. 1961. A Kashaya grammar (Sothwestern Pomo). Ph.D. Dissertation, University of California, Berkeley.

Oswalt, Robert L. 1986. The evidential system of Kashaya. In Wallace Chafe & Johanna Nichols (eds), *Evidentiality: The Linguistic Coding of Epistemology*, 29–45. Norwood, NJ: Ablex Publishing Corporation.

Róna-Tas, András. 1985. *Wiener Vorlesungen zur Sprach- und Kulturgeschichte Tibets*. Vienna: Arbeitskreis für Tibetische und Buddhistische Studien, Universität Wien.

Rule, W. M. 1977. *A comparative study of the Foe, Huli, and Pole languages of Papua New Guinea*. Sydney: University of Sydney.

San Roque, Lila. 2008. *An introduction to Duna grammar*. Canberre: The Australian National University dissertation.

San Roque, Lila & Robyn Loughnane. 2012. The New Guinea Highlands evidentiality area. *Linguistic Typology* 16(1). 111–167.

Sandberg, Graham. 1894. *Hand-book of colloquial Tibetan: a practical guide to the language of Central Tibet*. Calcutta: Thacker, Spink and co.

Sapir, Edward. 1921. *Language: An Introduction to the Study of Speech*. New York: Harcourt, Bruce and company.

Seeland, D. 2007. Bogaia Affixes. Unpublished manuscript.

Tournadre, Nicolas. 1994. Personne et médiatifs en tibétain. *Faits de langues* 3. 149–158.

Tournadre, Nicolas. 1996. *L'ergativité en tibétain: approche morphosyntaxique de la langue parlée*. Paris: Peeters.

Tournadre, Nicolas. 2008. Arguments against the Concept of 'Conjunct'/'Disjunct' in Tibetan. In Brigitte Huber, et al. (eds.), *Chomolangma, Demawend und Kasbek: Festschrift für Roland Bielmeier zu seinem 65. Geburtstag*, 281–308. Halle: International Institut for Tibetan and Buddhist Studies.

Tournadre, Nicolas & Sangda Dorje. 2009. *Manuel de tibétain standard*. 3rd edition. Paris: L'asiathèque.
Tournadre, Nicolas & Randy J. LaPolla. 2014. Towards a new approach to evidentiality: Issues and directions for research. *Linguistics of the Tibeto-Burman Area* 37(2). 240–263.
Tournadre, Nicolas, Lhakpa Norbu Sherpa, Gyurme Chodrak & Guillaume Oisel. 2009. *Sherpa-English and English-Sherpa dictionary*. Kathmandu: Vajra Publication.
Usoniene, Aurelia. 1999. Perception Verbs Revisited. *Working Papers* (Dept. of Linguistics, Lund University) 47. 211–225.
Visser, Eline. 2015. Tensed evidentials: A typological study. *Linguistic Typology* 19(2). 279–325.
Volkart, Marianne. 2000. The meaning of the auxiliary morpheme '*dug* in the aspect systems of Central Tibetan dialects. *Linguistics of the Tibeto-Burman Area* 23(2). 127–153.
Watahomigie, Lucille J., Foriqire Berder, Akira Y. Yamimoto, Elnora Mapatis, Fosie Manakaja & Malinda Powskey. 1982. *Hualapai Reference Grammar*. Los Angeles: American Indian Studies Center, UCLA.
Watkins, Calvert. 1995. *How to kill a dragon: aspects of Indo-European poetics*. New York: Oxford University Press.
Watters, David E. 2002. *A grammar of Kham*. Cambridge: Cambridge University Press.
Willett, Thomas. 1988. A cross-linguistic survey of the grammaticalization of evidentiality. *Studies in Language* 12. 51–97.
Witzel, Michael. 2012. *The origins of the world's mythologies*. Oxford: Oxford University Press.
Woodbury, Anthony C. 1986. Interactions of tense and evidentiality: a study of Sherpa and English. In Wallace L. Chafe & Johanna Nichols (eds.), *Evidentiality: The Linguistic Coding of Epistemology*, 188–202. Norwood, NJ: Ablex Publishing Corporation.
Yukawa, Yasutoshi 湯川恭敏. 1971. チベット語の述部の輪郭 Chibettogo no jutsubu no rinkaku [Outline of Tibetan Predicates]. 言語学の基本問題 *Gengogaku no kihon mondai / Basic problems in linguistics*. Tokyo: 大修館書店 Taishūkan Shoten. 178–204.

Guillaume Oisel
6 On the origin of the Lhasa Tibetan evidentials *song* and *byung*

6.1 Introduction

This contribution presents the emergence of some Lhasa Tibetan evidentials from Middle Tibetan deictic motion verb and other. More specifically, it traces the origin of the 'receptive egophoric' and 'sensorial' past tense markers *byung* and *song* from the Middle Tibetan verbs *byung* 'to come forth, to occur' and *song* 'to go'. Hongladarom (1995) also mentions the origin of these evidentials, but without providing philological details of the these verbs as they are used throughout Tibet's literary history. I fill this gap by presenting three verbal systems that display discrete stages in this evolution: Middle Tibetan (a 15th century biography), Modern Literary Tibetan (2 genres, newspapers and tales), and Lhasa Tibetan. Although Modern Literary Tibetan is not diachronically intermediate between Middle Tibetan and Standard Colloquial Tibetan, its generic conservatism allows it to be used as such.[1]

---

[1] Since deictic verbs are an important element in the emergence of the evidential system in Middle Tibetan and the full establishment of evidentiality in Lhasa Tibetan, it is useful to define both motion verbs and evidentiality for the purpose of this study. There are at least two types of motion verbs in typological studies: verbs indicating motion toward a landmark 'to come' and verbs indicating motion away from a landmark 'to go' (Fillmore 1997: 77–102; Nakazawa 2007: 59–82). Evidentiality is defined as "the representation of source and access to information according to the speaker's perspective and strategy" (Tournadre and LaPolla 2014: 240).

Note: This contribution derives from a few chapters from my PhD thesis (University of Paris 3, La Sorbonne-Nouvelle, 2013), but additionally includes data from another Modern Literary Tibetan corpus as well as data from Lhasa Tibetan. A preliminary version of this paper was presented at the 24th Meeting of Southeast Asian Linguistics Society (SEALS 24) at Yangon University in May 2014. I would like to thank Nathan W. Hill (SOAS), Lauren Gawne (SOAS) and the anonymous reviewers for their very useful comments. I also thank Ray Denning (my former colleague and friend from Xi'an Jiaotong University, China) for reviewing my English.

6.2 Middle Tibetan

In this section, using examples drawn from a 15th century biography of Milarepa (1052–1135), by Tsang Nyön Héruka, from Central Tibet's Tsang region,[2] I present four Middle Tibetan[3] verbs, which occur both as lexical motion verbs and as auxiliary verbs. This corpus has two advantages. First, it is a well-known text, copied and printed in different editions on the Tibetan Plateau through the centuries and more recently translated into many languages.[4] Second, the narration of Milarepa's life is lively and the context of events is clear. This contextual clarity allows us to easily interpret the meaning of grammatical forms, notably those which convey motion and evidentiality.

6.2.1 Deictic versus relative deictic lexical verbs

In general a Tibetan transitive and controllable verb has four stems, traditionally called 'present' (*lta da*), 'past' (*'das-pa*), 'future' (*ma-'ongs-pa*), and 'imperative' (*skul tshig*). Almost all verbs have only one form for each of these stems (e.g. 'kill' *gsod, bsad, gsad, sod*). However, the deictic verb 'to go' exhibits the peculiarity of distinguishing more forms in the past than in the present. This verb has one present stem *'gro*, but both *phyin* and *song* as past stems. In contrast, the verb 'come' has one present *'ong* (with *yong* as a variant spelling) and one past *'ongs* (sometimes spelt *yongs*). Hereafter I avoid the traditional terminology 'present' and 'past' (Gyurmé 1994: 182–194), preferring the more accurate 'imperfective' and 'perfective' (Zeisler 2004: 315–468). Here I focus on the behavior of the perfective forms *phyin, song, 'ongs/yongs,* and *byung,* laying to one side the imperfective stems *'gro* and *'ong*.

A look at a few passages reveals that verbs *phyin* and *song* 'to go' correlate to some extent with the grammatical person of the subject. The verb *phyin* is generally used with the first person, as in examples (1) and (2). But, it may also be used with the third person, in particular when the speaker is not present, as in (3). As for *song,* it occurs only with the third person, as in (4).

(1) nga sngon.la **phyin**-pas thog.mar yum-dang mjal
    I before **to go(perf.)**-CO first wife-ASS meet(hon.)
    '**I went** ahead and first met the lama's wife.'
    (Mila 2.2) (Quintman 2010: 74)

---

[2] Quintman (2010), Larsson (2012).
[3] For the term 'Middle Tibetan' see Zeisler (2004: 216–222).
[4] I consult the version published in Dharamsala (Rus pa'i rgyan can 1994).

6 On the origin of the Lhasa Tibetan evidentials *song* and *byung* — 163

(2) *phag.phyi-la   nga-yang   **phyin***
    servant-OBL   I-THEM   **go(perf.)**
    '(One day) **I accompanied** my master (to the lower valley of Tsa where he was invited to preside over a great wedding feast).'
    (Mila 1.3) (Quintman 2010: 27)

(3) *pe.ta-s   mthong-ste   myur.du   a.ma-'i   sa-r   **phyin**-nas*
    Peta-ERG   see-CO   rapidly   mother-GEN   place-OBL   **go(perf.)**-CO
    'Seeing [the calamity that filled the area outside], **Peta rushed** to my mother ...' [The speaker, Mila, was not present in the village when his sister Peta saw his spell of black magic.]
    (Mila 1.3) (Quintman 2010: 34)

(4) *de.nas   Bha.ri.ma   na.re   tsha.bo   rang   'dir   re.zhig   sdod-cig*
    then   Bharima   QUO   nephew   you   here   a moment   stay(imp.)-IMP
    nga-s   sangs.rgyas-la   gnang.ba   zhus-   'ong-gis   zer
    I-ERG   Buddha-OBL   permission   ask(perf.)-AUX-PRM   say
    ***song**-ba.las   gnang.ba   thob-ste*
    go(perf.)-CO   permission   obtain-CO
    'Then Bharima said, "Nephew, stay here a moment. I will ask for permission from the Buddha." [Lit.: I promise I am going to ask] **She went** to make her request and was granted permission.' [The speaker is Rechungpa seeing Bharima in his vision/dream.]
    (Mila 1.1) (Quintman 2010: 12)

As for the verb *'ongs* 'to come', it is used with both the first person, as in example (5), and the second and third person, as in examples (6) and (7). Thus, the verb *'ongs* does not indicate any opposition based on person deixis. In contrast, the verb *byung* 'to come forth, to occur', only occurs with the third person, as in (8).

(5) *bla.ma-'i   rin.po.che   da   bdag-gis   **'ongs**-pa*
    Lama-GEN   precious   now   I-ERG   **come(perf.)**-NMLZ
    *dam.pa-'i   chos-la   **'ongs**-nas*
    pure-GEN   teaching-OBL   come(perf.)-CO
    'Precious Lama, I am here now [Lit: **I came** now], (**I**) **came** here for the genuine dharma, (but have done only evil deeds).'
    (Mila 2.2, translation mine)

(6) *khyod   dang.po   lan   zhig   yul-du   **'ongs**-pa-'i*
    you   first   time   ART   village-OBL   **come(perf.)**-NOM-GEN
    gtam   zhig   byung-nas   lo   mang-du   song
    story   ART   be(perf.)-CO   year   several-OBL   elapse(perf.)
    'It was said that **you** once **returned** to the village, but that was many years ago.'
    (Mila 2.7) (Quintman 2010: 139)

(7) khyed   mi   yin-nam   'dre   yin   zer
    you(hon.)   man   be-Q   demon   be   say
    nga   mi.la thos.pa.dga'   yin   byas-pas
    I   Mila Thöpaga   be   say(perf.)-CO
    skad   ngo.shes-te   nang-du   **'ongs**   nga-la   'jus-nas
    voice recognize-CO   inside-OBL **come(perf.)** I-OBL   embrace(perf.)-CO
    'Are you a man or a ghost?" she asked. "I am Mila Töpaga," I replied.
    Recognizing my voice, **she came** in and embraced me...'
    (Mila 2.7) (Quintman 2010: 142)

(8) nga-la   sngar   slob.ma   ji.snyed.cig   **byung**-ste
    I-OBL   before   disciple   so many   **come(perf.)**-CO
    'So **many disciples came to me** in the past (or I had so many disciples).'
    (Mila 1.3, translation mine)

The following table summarizes the foregoing analysis according to person and subject. Where there is no x the verb does not occur in the corpus.

Tab. 1: Motion verbs in Middle Tibetan according to person and subject in declaratives.

Subject (Agent)	song 'to go away from'	byung 'to come toward'	phyin 'to go away from'	'ongs 'to come toward'
1st person			x	x
2nd /3rd person	x	X	x	x

Despite the correlation of these verbs with grammatical person, their distribution should not be confused with agreement. Instead, we see a contrast between verbs that can take the speaker as subject (agent), i.e. *phyin* and *'ongs*, and those that cannot, i.e. *song* and *byung*.[5] The reason that *song* and *byung* are incompatible with a first person agent is that these two verbs already indicate other relationships

---

5 In order to avoid the mismatch of the tripartite terminology of person with the bipartite distinction that Tibetan draws, it is tempting to instead refer to Speech Act Participant (SAP) and Non-Speech Act Participant (non-SAP) (see Kuno and Kaburaki 1977[1975]: 652 and 660; Ebert 1987; Agha 1993: 93). However, since the question of whether the hearer is a speech act participant is not relevant to the discussion at hand, I find it more convenient to simply refer to the 'speaker' and 'non-speaker'. Potential confusion with J. L. Austin's speech act theory is another reason to avoid the SAP terminology. Note that the speaker as the observer of the speech situation must be distinguished from the speaker as a participant of the sentence (SAP). This distinction, unknown in the literature on SAP, is similar to the distinction between *locuteur* and *énonciateur* in Ducrot (1980), or *énonciateur* and *locuteur* in Desclés and Guentchéva (2000).

between the speaker and the verbal action, namely *song* indicates movement away from the speaker while *byung* indicates movement toward the speaker.[6]

Motion always occurs in reference to locations. In the case of the verbs *song* and *byung* the speaker herself serves as the location of reference. I refer to these two verbs as 'personal deictic' verbs. In contrast, the verbs *phyin* and *'ongs* make reference to some imagined location that is only contextually specified, like the English verbs 'come' and 'go'. I refer to these verbs as 'relative deictic' verbs.

To return to the textual examples discussed above, for the verb *phyin* 'to go (relative deictic)' in (1), (2) and (3), the motion is away from a non-specific location, whereas, in (4) with the verb *song* 'to go (personal deictic)', the motion is away from the speaker's oneiric vision. As for the verb *'ongs* 'to come (relative deictic)', the motion is toward the lama's residence in (5), the village in (6) and the cave in (7). In contrast, for the verb *byung* 'to come forth (personal deictic)' in (8), the motion is toward the speaker. The speaker is in the semantic role of the beneficiary.

One should ward against too tight a conceptualization of personal deixis. The deixis may be real or fictive. Real deixis occurs if the speaker (the observer) is present, where 'real' is understood as relative to the discourse in question and not some external *ontos*. Fictive deixis refers to a "deictic projection" which implies a "fictive observer" (Diessel 2012; Lyons 1977: 579; Jakobson 1957; Fillmore 1997). One may further subcategorize fictive deixis into 'oneiric', 'hypothetical', and 'fake'. For oneiric deixis the speaker is conscious in a dream or vision (cf. (4)). For hypothetical deixis the speaker imagines her presence in a situation (cf. (9)). For fake deixis the speaker dissembles in order to induce a reader or listener to imagine a specific scenario (cf. (10)).

(9) nan.tar   ma-**song**-na   khang.ba   yang   nged   dbang-bas
    really   NEG-**leave(perf.)**-CO house   also   ours   sovereignty-CO
    ma.smad-tsho   phyi-r   songs
    mother and children-PL   outside-PL go(imp.)
    'If (I see) all of you **haven't** really **left** the house, the house will be ours. You, mother and your children, get out!'
    (my translation)

---

[6] These verbs are also used as essential and existential aspectual copulas in Milarepa's biography. The verb *byung* and *song* indicate the past perfective. They imply the following features: identification, categorization or characterization (Oisel 2013: 88–90). The verb *'ong* (or *yong*) indicates the imperfective or the future. It also indicates the following features: identification, categorization or characterization. It also occurs in a complex copula construction *yin.'ong* (or *yin.yong*) to indicate an epistemic meaning/strong probability 'must be' (Mila 1.3, 2.2) which became the copula *yong* (strong probability) versus *yin.'gro* (weak probability) in Lhasa Tibetan.

(10) *mi.la shes.rab rgyal.mtshan   lho   rdzas   mang.po   khyer-te*
     Mila Sherab Gyaltsen   south   merchandise   a lot   bring-CO
     *byang   stag.rtse-'i   phyogs-su   tshong-la   **song-nas***
     north   Taktse-GEN   surrounding-OBL   sell(pres.)-CO   **leave(perf.)**-CO
     'Mila Sherab Gyaltsen having brought numerous goods from the South, **set out** to sell them in the vicinity of Taktse in the North.' [Mila the narrator who is not born yet did not see the scene of his father leaving hence the notion of fictive/fake deixis.]
     (Mila 1.1) (Quintman 2010:18)

In brief, the verbs *phyin* 'to go' and *'ongs* 'to come' do not depend on a fixed deictic landmark, but a relative deictic one. The latter explains why *phyin* may occur with both speaker and non-speaker. In contrast, the speaker does not appear with the verb *song* because one cannot in principle move away from oneself, i.e. *nga phyin* 'I left' occurs but **nga song* does not. For the same reasons there are many examples of the speaker used with the verb *'ongs*, but not with the verb *byung*, i.e. *nga 'ongs* 'I came' occurs but **nga byung* does not.

It would be convenient to have a label for each of the verbs *byung, song, 'ongs,* and *phyin*. I propose to respectively call *byung* and *song* cislocative (toward me, the speaker) and translocative (away from me), i.e. when there is a personal deictic landmark. I call *'ongs* and *phyin* respectively ventive (toward this person or place) and andative (away from this person or place), i.e. when there is a relative deictic landmark. This proposed terminology combines the terminology of the "cislocative" versus "translocative" used in Amerindian languages (e.g. Lounsbury 1953; Adelaar 2006; Montgomery-Anderson 2008) and the equivalent opposition of "venitive/ventive" versus "andative/itive" used by Africanists (e.g. Jungraithmayr and Mohlig 1983).[7] The following table exhibits the proposed analysis.

Tab. 2: Motion verbs in Middle Tibetan according to type of motion and deixis.

Motion	translocative	cislocative	andative	ventive
landmark	personal deixis		relative deixis	
lexical verb	*song* 'to go way from'	*byung* 'to come toward'	*phyin* 'to go way from'	*'ongs* 'to come toward'

---

[7] See also more recently Hooper (2002) and O'Connor (2004) for Polynesian and Amerindian languages, respectively.

Having considered the use of motion lexical verbs in Middle Tibetan, the following discussion presents the use of these same forms as secondary verbs.

6.2.2 Personal deictic and relative deictic secondary verbs

The use of the same four verbs as secondary verbs (i.e. the trailing verbs of a serial verb construction)[8] supports the preceding account of a system of double orientation based on personal and relative deixis.

(11) *gtad*   **'*ongs***   *pa.lags*
 lexical verb   **secondary verb**   auxiliary verb construction
 'to direct toward'   **VENITIVE PERFECTIVE**   HUMILIFIC PERFECTIVE
 '[…] I came to (the Lama to receive dharma) [lit.: I came toward].'
 (Mila 2.1) (Quintman 2010: 51)

(12) *log*   **'*gro***   *grabs.byed*   *cing.'dug*
 lexical verb   **secondary verb 1**   secondary verb 2   auxiliary verb construction
 'to return'   andative imperfective   'to be about to'   SENORY PROGRESSIVE
 '(My companions) were (all) preparing to leave [lit.: were about to return].'
 (Mila 1.3) (Quintman 2010: 30)

These motion secondary verbs are in general combined with other motion lexical verbs or metaphorical motion verbs. The table below shows the secondary verb constructions which mark motion and the perfective. Imperfective forms are quite rare in the corpus and lie outside the scope of this study.

---

8 At least in Tibetan one must distinguish between secondary verbs and auxiliary verbs (Gyurmé 1994: 205; Vokurková 2008: 295–321). Secondary verbs primarily function to further specify the meaning of the lexical verb whereas auxiliary verbs mark tense, aspect, and mood. Secondary verbs precede auxiliary verbs (Oisel 2013: 155–156, 226–227). On the distinction between serial verb constructions and auxiliary verb constructions see DeLancey (1991) and Anderson (2006): 11–15). For a typological census of serial verb constructions see Aikhenvald and Dixon (2006) and its critique in Paillard (2013).

Tab. 3: Motion Secondary Verb Constructions in Middle Tibetan.

Motion	translocative	cislocative	andative	ventive
landmark	personal deixis		relative deixis	
scondary verb constructions	*V.-te+song V.-song	V.-pa+byung V.-byung	V.-nas+phyin V.-phyin	V.-nas+'ongs V.-'ongs

*Only in Old Tibetan

By analogy with their respective lexical motion verbs, I label the secondary verbs *song* and *byung* translocative (cf. (13)) and cislocative (cf. (14)) respectively. I name the secondary verb *phyin* and *'ongs* andative (cf. (15)) and ventive (cf. (16)). In addition, there is a subtle difference between the example (15) and (16) related to speaker volition.

(13) *kho.rang   yang   dgod-cing   thon-**song**-ngo*
 he   also   laugh-CO   go out-TRAN.PERF-CP
 'laughed too and then **went away**.' [The robber walked away from Mila, the speaker, who is meditating inside the cave.]
 (Mila 2.7) (Quintman 2010:139)

(14) *sring.mo-yang   thon-**byung**-ste*
 sister-THEM   go out-CIS.PERF-CO
 '[...] my sister **came over** and [...].' [She came toward the speaker.]
 (Mila 1.3) (Quintman 2010: 29)

(15) *phyir   thon-**phyin**-te*
 outside   go out-AND.PERF-CO
 '**Stepping out** [...] (I thought ...).' [Against his will, the speaker walked away from the Lama who told him to get out.]
 (Mila 2.2) (Quintman 2010)

(16) *phyir   thon-'**ongs**-te*
 outside   go out-VEN.PERF-CO
 '(Unable to respond) I **went outside**.' [The speaker was eager to get leave before the Lama allowed him to. The speaker heads off to his next destination: the house of another master.]
 (Mila 2.2) (Quintman 2010:68)

In examples (13–16), the secondary verbs combine with the verb *thon* 'to go out'. Translocative and cislocative secondary verbs can also occur in combination with the lexical verbs listed in Tab. 6. It is convenient to group these verbs semantically under the rubrics 'motion', 'motion up' and 'metaphorical motion'.

Tab. 4: List of verbs which can be combined with the cislocative and translocative.

	secondary verb	
	cislocative	translocative
	chapter, number of occurrences	chapter, number of occurrences
lexical verb		
motion		
sleb(s) 'to arrive'	1.1 (1), 1.3 (1), 2.7 (3)	
byon 'to arrive; to go, to set out'	2.1 (1), 2.2 (2)	2.9 (1)
log 'to return'	1.3 (1), 2.2 (1)	1.3 (3), 2.1 (1), 2.7 (1)
gtad 'to direct toward'	2.3 (1)	
bros 'to run away'		2.7 (2)
bsnams 'to take away'		2.2 (1)
'phur 'to fly'	2.7 (1)	
motion up		
langs 'to get up'	1.3 (1)	
shar 'to raise'	2.5 (1)	
'dzegs 'to climb'		1.3 (1)
spungs 'to pile up'		1.3 (1)
metaphorical motion		
zer 'to say'	2.4 (1), 2.7 (2), 2.9 (1)	
gnang 'to give'	1.3 (1), 2.1 (1), 2.2 (1), 2.3 (1)	
gzigs 'to look'		2.2 (2)

Example (17) with the verb *gzigs* 'to look' is quite instructive regarding the functioning of the translocative secondary verb *song*. The eyes of the lama look away from the speaker, so the translocative *song* rather than cislocative *byung* is used.

(17) bla.ma   gzims.khang-gi   yang.thog-na   zhal   shar-la   gzigs-nas
      lama   room-GEN   terrace-OBL   face   east-OBL   look(hon.)-CO
      thugs.dam-la.bzhugs-'dug-pas   phyag-dang   dar.yug
      sit in meditation practice(hon.)-AUX.COM   salutation-ASS   bolt silk
      phul-bas   zhal   nub-tu   gzigs-**song**
      of offer(hon.past)-CO   face   west-OBL   look(hon.)-**TRAN.PERF**
      nub-nas   phul-bas   lho-r   gzigs-**song**-ba.la
      west-ABL   offer(hum.past)-CO   south-OBL   look(hon.)-TRAN.PERF-CO
      'The lama was on the upper terrace of his residence, **looking to** the east, and seated in meditation practice. I offered prostrations and the bolt of silk, but **he turned to look toward** the west. I prostrated from the west, but **he turned to look toward** the south.'
      (Mila 2.2) (Quintman 2010: 74/75)

The distribution of the andative and ventive secondary verbs (*phyin* versus *'ongs*) is more restricted. They occur with motion verbs but not the motion up or metaphorical motion verbs.

Tab. 5: List of verbs that can be combined with the ventive and andative.

	secondary verb	
	ventive	**andative**
	chapter, occurrence	chapter, occurrence
lexical verb		
motion		
sleb(s) 'to arrive'	1.3 (1), 2.1 (2)	
bros 'to run away'		2.7 (1)
log 'to return'	1.3 (2), 2.2 (1)	1.3 (1), 2.9 (1)
lam.du zhugs 'to go on the way'		1.3 (1)
gtad 'to direct toward/away'	2.1 (1), 2.2 (1)	1.3 (2), 2.2 (1)
khyer 'to bring'	2.2 (1), 2.5 (1), 2.7 (2)	
'phur 'to fly'	2.7 (1)	

Having presented the lexical and secondary uses of motion verbs in Middle Tibetan and shown that they exhibit a double system of orientation based on personal and relative deixis, I now examine how this system developed in two varieties of Modern Literary Tibetan.

6.3 Modern Literary Tibetan

For this section, two different corpora have been used. The first one is *The Facetious Tales of the Corpse* (hereafter '*Tales*'), translated from Tibetan to French by Françoise Robin (2005) and published under the French title *Les contes facétieux du cadavre*. The Modern Literary Tibetan version used by Robin is based on a Chinese version, itself based on an earlier Tibetan version (Robin 2005). The *Tales* reflect a literary style specific to the Amdo region. Like the biography of Milarepa for Middle Tibetan, *Tales* tells lively stories, with many motion verbs and evidentials. Unlike the first person narration of Milarepa's biography the *Tales* has an omniscient third person narrator, as a consequence it makes extensive use of fictive deixis with the motion verbs and 'indirect' sensorial *song* (on which see below).

The second corpus is collected from newspapers and social media written in India and the US (Radio Free Asia, Tibet Information Network, Tibet Times, etc.) (for details see Oisel 2013: 59/60). The main reason for referring to this kind of corpus is the use of evidentials as well as motion verbs therein. In these text, the speaker is the reporter or interviewer (i.e. a real deixis).

6.3.1 Relative deictic and sensorial

In *Tales*, the Middle Tibetan deictic opposition with the perfective is no longer relevant. The language of *Tales* does not use *phyin*, so there is no contrast between *song* and *phyin*; we may thus drop the terminology of andative and ventive. As a lexical verb *song* has a translocative meaning relying on relative deixis, as in (18) and (19). It is also used as a secondary verb for marking a translocative motion based on relative deixis, as in the example (20). Contrary to Middle Tibetan, it is also used as a sensorial auxiliary verb when it is combined with non-motion lexical verbs, as in (22). Consequently, the verb *byung* indicates a cislocative motion based on a relative deixis, and not on a personal deixis, as in example (20). It is thus used in a way similar to the Middle Tibetan ventive, *'ongs*, which is still used in this variety of Literary Tibetan, as in example (21).

— Lexical Verb *song* (relative deixis, translocative)

(18) nyin   gcig   nu.bo   **don.grub-kyis**   rgyags.bro   bskyal-nas
     day   one   younger brother   **Thöndrup-ERG**   supply   carry-CO
     der   song-ste/   phu.bo-dang   mnyam.du   bsdad/
     there   go(perf.)-CO   elder brother-ASS   with   stay
     'One day his younger brother **Thöndrup went** there carrying some supplies and stayed with him.' [landmark: the narrator]
     (Robin 2005: 27)

(19) gros.byed-rgyu-r   da.bar.du   **nga-tsho**   lhan.cig   **song**-nas
     discuss(pres.)-NMLZ.-OBL   till now   I-PL   together   go(perf.)-CO
     ltad.mo   mang.po   mthong/
     spectacle   a lot   see
     'They said: "Till now **we have walked along** together (lit.: **went** together) and have seen a lot of scenery."' [landmark: the seven brothers]
     (Robin 2005: 44)

— Secondary Verbs *song* versus *byung* (translocative versus cislocative)

(20) *de.ma.thag   gser   nya   gcig-tu   sprul-nas*
     immediately   golden   fish   one-OBL   turn into-CO
     *chu'i   gzhung-la **bros-song**/*
     water-GEN   inside-OBL **flee(perf.)-TRAN.PERF**
     de.nas   sgyu.ma.mkhan   spun   bdun.po   yang
     then   magician   brother   the seven   also
     *sram   bdun-la   sprul-nas   **ded-byung** /*
     otter seven-OBL   turn into-CO   **pursue-CIS.PERF**
     'As soon as he turned into a golden fish, he **fled away** into the water. The seven magician brothers also turned into seven otters and **pursued him**.'
     [landmark with *song*: the narrator; landmark with *byung*: the fish]
     (Robin 2005: 33)

— Secondary Verb *'ongs* (cislocative)

(21) *de'i   sngon-la   phug.ron   dkar-po   zhig   brag   khung*
     this-GEN   before   pigeon   white   ART   cave   hole
     *'di   nang la   **'phur-'ongs**-pa   gang.na   yod/*
     this   inside-OBL   **fly-CIS.PERF**.NMLZ   where   be located
     'Where is the white pigeon who **flew to** this cave earlier (i.e. it flew to you)?' [the seven brothers asking Nagarjuna -landmark- in the cave]
     (Robin 2005: 35)

— Auxiliary verb *song* (sensorial)

(22) *sgyu.ma   sprul.sgyur-gyi   man.ngag   lhag.chad*
     magic   emanation-GEN   instruction   entirely
     *nor.gsum   med-par   **shes-song***
     this   inside-OBL   **know-SEN.PERF**
     '**He** thus **knew** the instructions for the magic in their entirety and without error.' (Narrator speaking)
     (Robin 2005: 29)

The following table summarizes the use of the lexical and secondary motion verbs based on relative deixis in *Tales*, as presented in the examples above (cf. (18–21)). This table can be compared with the Tab. 3 in order to see the diachronic differences.

Tab. 6: *Lexical and secondary motion verbs in* Tales.

	translocative	cislocative	
	song	*byung*	*'ongs*
Agent		relative deixis	
speaker	(19)		
non-speaker	speaker 'fictive deixis' (18, 20)	(20)	(21)

In newspapers, the relative deictic system also combines with an evidential system (Oisel 2013: 201–249). The auxiliary verb *song* indicates a sensorial evidential with verbs of saying (cf. (23)). In Middle Tibetan, this type of metaphorical motion verb was used with the cislocative *byung* (Oisel 2013: 94). This contrast further illustrates that the auxiliary verb *song* no longer indicates a translocative meaning (away from me), but rather a sensory value. In newspapers, *song* occurs neither as a lexical verb nor as a secondary verb indicating motion, perhaps because the Middle Tibetan verb *song* has been replaced in these functions by *phyin*, as in Lhasa Tibetan.

The verb *byung* is also used as a secondary verb, but it indicates a cislocative motion based on a relative deixis with (metaphorical) motion verbs, as in (24). It may also indicate the inchoative aspect (appearance of something) with specific verbs implying a state, as in (25). In this case only, *byung* may be combined with evidential final auxiliaries.

The verb *'ongs* does not occur in Newspaper, in contrast to the *Tales*.
— Auxiliary Verb *song* (Sensorial)
(23) ngo.rgol.byed   dgos-pa-'i [...]   rgyu.mtshan
     demonstrate(imperf.) must-NMLZ-GEN   reasons
     'grel.brjod.gnang-**song**
     explain(hon)-**SEN.PERF**
     '[In addition, a Tibetan named Dorje] **explained** [...] why they should demonstrate.'

— Secondary Verb *byung* (Relative Deixis, Cislocative)
(24) nye.char   phyi.zla 6-pa'i   nang   bal.yul-gyi   dmag.dpon
     recently   month 6-NMLZ-GEN   in   Nepal-GEN   the general
     pi.yar jang thwa.pa-dang   rgya.nag [ ] -gi   dmag.dpon
     Piyar Jung Thapa-ASS.   China-GEN   the General
     ka'o gang chung   gnyis   mjal.'phrad-**byung**-skabs   rgya.nag-gis
     Cao Gang Chuan   two   meet(hon.)-**CIS.PERF**.CO   China-ERG
     bal.yul-la   dmag.rogs   bya-rgyu-'i   khas.len.byas-yod.pa.red
     Nepal-OBL   military aid   do(fut.)-NOM-GEN accept(perf.)-FAC.PT
     'Recently in June 2004, when the Nepalese General Piyar Jung Thapa and Chinese General Cao Gang Chuan **met each other**, the Chinese government agreed to provide military aid to Nepal.' [landmark: the two generals]

— Secondary Verb *byung* + Auxiliary Verb (Inchoative + Evidential)
(25) rtse.gras-ru   khag   bzhi   bdams.thon-**byung**-'dug
     best-OBL   team   four   be selected-**INC-SEN.PT**
     'Four teams **have been selected** as the best (ones).' [inchoative + sensorial perfect]

The data presented in this section show that the motion system in Modern Literary Tibetan is now based on relative deixis. The system of Middle Tibetan based on the distinction between personal deixis and relative deixis is defunct. Some of the

Middle Tibetan motion verbs have acquired new functions, notably for marking evidentiality (*song*), and other Middle Tibetan motion verbs have become obsolete (*phyin* in *Tale*s, *'ongs* in newspapers): these developments are partly due to the influence of Amdo and Lhasa Tibetan, accordingly. Having said so, let us see how the system appears in Colloquial Lhasa Tibetan.

6.4 Colloquial Lhasa Tibetan

The corpus used in the last section is extracted from the *Manual of Standard Tibetan* (Tournadre and Dorje 2003) as well as from Denwood (1999). The specificity of the system of Lhasa Tibetan consists of the grammaticalization of the egophoric (versus the sensorial). The egophoric is an evidential category marking several functions: self-awareness, intentionality, empathy, personal knowledge and personal involvement (Tournadre and Dorje 2003; Tournadre and LaPolla 2014; Gawne, this volume). These functions essentially depend on the tense-aspect of the predicate, the controllability of the lexical verb, and the semantic role of the speaker.

6.4.1 Sensorial versus egophoric

In colloquial Lhasa Tibetan, the Middle Tibetan translocative *song* became a sensorial. Tournadre calls it a *testimonial* (Tournadre and Dorje 2003). A sensorial "specifies that the speaker was himself witness to what he is stating. The testimony is usually visual, but also based on hearing or any of the other senses (touch, smell or taste)" (Tournadre and Dorje 2003: 558). Contrary to Middle Tibetan, *song* in Lhasa Tibetan is used with many verbs, not only motion verbs. When used with verbs of motion, the translocative meaning is still apparent, as in (26).

(26) *rta   zhon-nas   phyin-***song**
horse   team-CO   go(perf.)-**SEN-PERF**
'He went by horse (went riding a horse).'
(Tournadre and Dorje 2003: 351)

With verbs of action (cf. (27+28)) and state (cf. (29)), *song* indicates that the speaker states she saw the whole process or some point of it, i.e. it marks sensory access.

(27) *char.pa   babs-song*
rain   come down(perf.)-**SEN-PERF**
'It rained' [I saw the rain falling at some point between when it started raining and when the rain stopped.]'
(Tournadre and Jiatso 2001: 72)

(28) *sa.yom   brgyabs-**song***
     earthquake   VBR(perf.)-**SEN-PERF**
     'There was an earthquake.' [I was there and felt it, i.e. the whole event.]
     (Tournadre and Jiatso 2001: 72)

(29) *nyi.ma   nang-la   bsdad-**song***
     Nyima   home-OBL   stay(perf.)-**SEN-PERF**
     'Nyima stayed at home.' [I saw s/he staying at some point of it during the relevant interval.]
     (Tournadre and Dorje 2003: 152)

In contrast, with change of state verbs (cf. (30–32)), the sensorial indicates cessative aspect (disappearance of something); the sensory value is neutralized. Example (30), marked with *song* and expressing cessative aspect is the opposite of example (36), marked with *byung* and expressing inchoative aspect (appearance of something). In the same way, example (31), with *song*, is aspecutally opposite to example (37), with *byung*. One can still see here a correlation between a motion away from the speaker (translocative) and the cessative aspect and between a motion toward the speaker (cislocative) and the inchoative aspect.

(30) *nga-s   brlags-**song***
     I-ERG   lose-**SEN-PERF**
     'I've lost it.'
     (Tournadre and Dorje 2003: 200)

(31) *nga-s   brjed-**song***
     I-ERG   forget-**SEN-PERF**
     'I forgot.'
     (Tournadre and Dorje 2003: 200)

(32) *shing.tog   nyo-shul.ring.kar   tang.ga.ril   rku.ma.la.shor-**song***
     fruit   buy(pres.)-CO   bicycle   be stolen-**SEN-PERF**
     'Our bicycle **was stolen** while we were buying fruits.'
     (Tournadre and Dorje 2003: 315)

As for the Middle Tibetan cislocative *byung*, in Lhasa Tibetan it becomes a *receptive egophoric* evidential auxiliary "which is used only in the past, implies that the subject-speaker of a sentence has undergone the action [or the state], has perceived it (involuntarily) or has been its goal/the recipient of it" (Tournadre and Dorje 2003: 557, 199; square brackets are mine). Contrary to Middle Tibetan, in Lhasa Tibetan *byung* is used with various verbs, not only motion verbs.

One can still see the deictic cislocative motion (toward the speaker) in the receptive egophoric use, as in the example (33) and (34), even if that directionality is also incorporated into the semantics of the main verbs.

In the first example, the motion is metaphorical. Tournadre defines these examples as "the speaker has been the recipient of it" (Tournadre and Dorje 2003: 169).

(33) kho-s   nga-la   kha.par+btang-**byung**
he-ERG me-OBL phone+VBR-**REC.EGO.PERF**
'He phoned **me**.'
(Tournadre and Dorje 2003: 172, 200)

(34) khong   nga-'i   rtsa-la   phebs-**byung**
he(hon.) me-GEN place-OBL come(hon.)-**REC.EGO.PERF**
'He came **to my** place.'
(Tournadre and Dorje 2003: 173)

However, *byung* is not a cislocative based on deixis as in Middle Tibetan. In example (35), the motion is toward the hospital and not toward the speaker, but, the speaker is still implicated. In other words, *byung* works like the Middle Tibetan ventive (*'ongs*) which implies a relative deixis. Tournadre defines it as "the subject-speaker has undergone the action" (Tournadre and Dorje 2003: 169).

(35) khong-gis   nga sman-khang-la khrid-**byung**
he(hon.)-ERG me hospital-OBL take someone(perf.)-**REC.EGO.PERF**
'He took **me** to the hospital.'
(Tournadre and Dorje 2003: 200)

In examples (36) and (37) *byung* expresses an inchoative aspect. In (36) the speaker perceived the object in question (sensorial). In (37) the speaker has undergone a state (endopathic). Contrast the following two examples with (30) and (31).

(36) khong-gis   nga sman-khang-la khrid-**byung**
he(hon.)-ERG me hospital-OBL take someone(perf.)-**REC.EGO.PERF**
'He took **me** to the hospital.'
(Tournadre and Dorje 2003: 200)

(37) lam.khag-nas   brnyed-**byung**
road-ABL find-**REC.EGO.PERF**
'I found it on the road.'
(Tournadre and Dorje 2003: 180)

(38) *nga-s*   *dran-**byung***
   I-ERG   remember-**REC.EGO.PERF**
   'I remembered.'
   (my fieldwok)

Denwood (1999: 145) noticed that, with the perfective negation *ma-*, the auxiliary verb *-byung* may imply that the speaker unsuccessfully tried to do something, as in (38). This example can be compared with example (39) in which the sensorial *-song* is used with the same negation.

(39) *nga*   *dran-**ma-byung***
   I   remember-**NEG-REC.EGO.PERF**
   'I didn't remember (though I tried).'
   (my fieldwok)

(40) *nga*   *dran-**ma-song***
   I   remember-**NEG-SEN.PERF**
   'It didn't occur to me.'
   (my fieldwok)

With the foregoing examples of *byung* in mind, the reader may question the appropriateness of referring to this auxiliary as egophoric when it has clear cislocative and inchoative meanings. The reason for this choice of terminology is that the main access to information for sentences in which *byung* occurs, as for the egophoric in general is *self-awarenes*. The speaker is necessarily involved even if the first person pronoun *nga* 'I' is omitted, as in (40).

(41) *kho-tsho-s*   *nyan-**ma-byung***
   he-PL-ERG   listen-**NEG-REC.EGO.PERF**
   'They didn't listen to me.'
   (Denwood 1999: 143)

The receptive egophoric is less grammaticalized than the sensorial, i.e. the distinction between the receptive egophoric and cislocative is not as easy to draw as that between the sensorial and the translocative. Additional evidence that *byung* is less grammaticalized than *song* is that the egophoric value of *byung* can be 'neutralized' when it is combined with the sensorial, witness the following set of constructions with *-byung* versus *-byung+song*. In (41) *byung* is an egophoric used as a final auxiliary verb. The egophoric indicates here a self-awareness access as well as a cislocative motion based on deixis. In contrast, in (42) *byung* is a cislocative based on relative deixis sed as a secondary verb with the final auxiliary verb *song* (sensorial). In both (41) and (42), the motion that *byung* suggests is metaphorical. In (41) the metaphorical motion is toward the speaker, whereas in (42) it is toward the non-speaker; the speaker is explicitly not involved.

(42) [receptive egophoric]
V + *dgos-byung* 'I had to' (Tournadre and Dorje 2003: 256–258)
V + *'dod- byung* 'I wanted to' (Tournadre and Dorje 2003: 330)
V + *long-byung* 'I got time to' (Tournadre and Dorje 2003: 370)
V + *rgyu-byung*, V + *yag-byung* 'I have been able to' (Tournadre and Dorje 2003: 336/337)

(43) [receptive/cislocative + sensorial]
V + *dgos-byung-song* 'he had to' (Tournadre and Dorje 2003: 256–258)
V + *'dod-byung-song* 'he wanted to' (Tournadre and Dorje 2003: 330)
V + *long-byung-song* 'he got time to' (Tournadre and Dorje 2003: 370)
V + *rgyu-byung-song*, V + *yag-byung-song* 'he has been able to' (Tournadre and Dorje 2003: 336/337)

In (42), the first two complex verb constructions show the possibility of combining at least two secondary verbs with an auxiliary verb. The secondary verb *dgos* 'to need/must' and *'dod* 'to desire' are followed by the secondary verb *byung* 'to come forth, to occur' and the auxiliary verb *song* 'to go'. Such combinations of multiple secondary verbs should thus be taken into consideration in future research on Tibetan secondary verb constructions (see also the examples (11) and (12)). Another point meriting additional attention is the inchoative aspect conveyed either by a secondary verb (42) or by a final auxiliary verb (cf. (36+37)). Contrary to evidentiality which is only marked on the final auxiliary verb, aspect may be marked on any verbs: lexical, secondary or auxiliary.

A final mysterious use of *song* and *byung* merits presentation here. In conjunction with a very limited number of lexical verbs, in particular *ha go* 'understand', *song* indicates a proximal past (43) and the *byung* a distal past (44)[9] (Tournadre and Dorje 2003: 200; Tournadre and Jiatso 2001: 73).[10] One would probably expect the translocative (away from) *song* to imply a distal past and the cislocative (towards) *byung* a proximal past, but that is not the case. I do not have an explanation for these usages.

---

[9] See also Denwood (1999: 144) for the same examples with the ergative.
[10] Bourdin (2002: 187) shows that in Ben (dialect of Togo), the translocative *daa* is used as a distal past and in French, the cislocative *venir de* as a proximal past (*passé récent*).

(44) *(da)   nga(s)   ha.go-**song***
    (he)   I-(ERG)   understand-SEN.PERF
    'I have understood (right now)/Now I understand.'
    (my fieldwok)

(45) *nga(s)   ha.go-**byung***
    I-(ERG)   understand-REC.EGO.PERF
    'I understood (before).'
    (my fieldwok)

I have shown in this section the use of the sensory *song* and the receptive (cislocative) egophoric *byung*. The next section considers the use of the other two motion verbs *phyin* 'to go' and *yong* 'to come', the latter originating from *'ongs/yongs*.

6.4.2 Motion and evidentiality

The Middle Tibetan andative *phyin* and ventive *yong* continue in use in Lhasa Tibetan as lexical motion verbs. In contrast to in Middle Tibetan, in Lhasa they are obligatorily followed by evidential auxiliary verbs. The motion suggested by these two verbs is no longer based on relative deixis, as in Middle Tibetan, but rather personal deixis, because the evidentials in question (sensorial *song* and egophoric *byung*) indicate the speaker as deictic landmark. In example (45), the bird moved away from the speaker, whereas, in (46), the bird moved toward the speaker.

(45) *bya   phur-**phyin**-song*
    bird   fly(perf.)-TRAN-SEN.PERF
    'The bird flew **away from me**.'
    (Tournadre and Jiatso 2001: 91)

(46) *bya   phur-**yong(s)**-byung*
    bird   fly(perf.)-CIS-REC.EGO.PERF
    'The bird flew **away toward me**.'
    (Tournadre and Jiatso 2001: 91)

The perfective stems *phyin* and *yong* are not available as secondary verbs. Thus, the sentences, ?*ngas brjed phyin song* 'I forgot' and ?*ngas dran yong byung* 'I remembered', do not seem to be possible. However, Tournadre and Jiatso (2001: 92) show that the imperfective equivalents of these sentences are attested, viz. *nga brjed 'gro gis* 'I forget' (cessative + sensorial) and *nga dran yong gis* 'I remember' (inchoative + sensorial). Nonetheless, this construction is not available for all verbs. In particular, *brlags 'gro* 'I am losing' (cessative) is possible, but not **brnyed yong* 'I am finding' (inchoative) (Tournadre and Jiatso 2001: 92).[11] This restriction seems to be due to the aspectual configuration: the progressive does not fit with *brnyed* 'to find'.

6.5 Typological context

Evidentials that come from spatial-motion morphemes are attested in other languages, for example in Euchee, an isolate language of North America:

> The auditory evidential marker -ke in Euchee is cognate with the locative suffix ke meaning 'yonder', 'way over there' (Linn 2000: 318). According to Linn, the semantic connection between the two is to do with distance: 'the action is so far away that it can only be heard and not seen.' (Aikhenvald 2004: 275)

In Meithei, the inferential *-ləm* (Chelliah 1997:224) comes from Proto-Tibeto-Burman **lam* 'path, road' (Matisoff 1991: 389/390), according to Aikhenvald (2004: 275). In addition, Hooper (2002) shows that in Tokelauan (Polynesian) the directional particle *mai* (*venitive*, toward the speaker) may also indicate a visual evidential with some classes of verbs. Except for the deictic/locative/directional markers quoted above, Aikhenvald (2004: 271–287; 2011) also mentions, the "rare" use of motion verbs. In Dulong (LaPolla 2003: 679), the motion verbs *jì* 'go' and *lùŋ* 'ascend' became direction and tense-aspect as well as evidential markers: visual *jì* versus non-visual *lùŋ*.

For his part, de Haan draws a tight link between evidentially and deixis (1999, 2005).

> I propose to add evidentiality to the category deixis as an example of *propositional deixis*. An evidential grounds an action or event with respect to the speaker, just as a demonstrative grounds an object with respect to the speaker. In other words, the relation between a proposition and an evidential is analogous to the relation between a noun (phrase) and a demonstrative. (De Haan 2005: 29, emphasis in original)

Reciprocally, as mentioned above (§1.1), the lack of deictic center does not imply an observer, so non deictic sources can lead to assumptive or factual evidentials (Oisel 2013: 34, 229–235).

---

11 Note that *ngas brlags song* 'I lost' (30) and *brnyed byung* 'I found' (36) both occur.

6.6 Conclusions

Middle Tibetan uses a personal deictic (*song* and *byung*) versus relative deictic (*phyin* and *'ongs*) secondary verb system. Modern Literary Tibetan uses a relative deictic auxiliary system (*song* versus *byung/'ongs*). It has grammaticalized the perfective sensorial from the deictic translocative *song*. The sensorial occurs with non-motion verbs. Colloquial Lhasa Tibetan uses an evidential auxiliary system (*song* versus *byung*). It has grammaticalized the egophoric. The receptive egophoric comes from the deictic cislocative *byung*. The evidential system can be combined with a secondary verb system indicating motion (*phyin* and *yong*). Deixis and evidentiality are closely related in Tibetan. Thus, Tibetan supports de Hann's perspective (1999, 2005) that evidentiality is a deictic category.[12]

For future research, it will be necessary to analyze and to compare through the centuries the imperfective forms *'gro* 'to go' and *'ong* 'to come' (as well as its variant *yong*), forms which are quite rare in my Middle Tibetan corpus.[13]

Abbreviations

ABL ablative case, AND andative, ART indefinite article, ASS associative case, CIS cislocative, CO connective/clause linker, CP conclusive particle, EGO egophoric, ERG ergative case, FAC factual, GEN genitive case, hon honorific word, IMP imperative particle, imp imperative stem, imperf imperfective stem, INC inchoative aspect, Lit literally, NEG negation, NOM nominalizer, OBL oblique case, PERF perfective aspect, perf perfective stem, PL plural particle, PRM promise particle, PT perfect aspect, QUO quotative particle, REC receptive, SEN sensory, THEM thematizer, TRAN translocative, VEN ventive

References

Adelaar, Willem F. H. 2006. The vicissitudes of directional affixes in Tarma (Northern Junín) Quechua. In Rowicka, G. J. & Carlin, E. B. (eds.), *What's in a verb? Studies in the verbal morphology of the languages of the Americas*, 121–142. Utrecht: LOT.

Agha, Asif. 1993. *Structural Form and Utterance Context in Lhasa Tibetan*. New York: Peter Lang Publishing, Inc.

---

[12] But, some other evidentials may not necessarily be related to it. Aikhenvald (2004: 284/285) has mentioned some evidentials which may originate from epistemic meanings (i.e. modality).
[13] For *yong* in Modern Literary Tibetan see Oisel (2013: 243–246). For *'gro* and *yong* in Lhasa see Vokurková (2008: 230–239, 274–282) and Tournadre and Jiatso (2001: 89–96).

Aikhenvald, Alexandra Y. 2004. *Evidentiality*. Oxford: Oxford University Press.
Aikhenvald, Alexandra Y. 2011. The grammaticalization of evidentiality. In Narrog, Heiko & Heine, Bernd (eds.), *The Oxford Handbook of Grammaticalization*. (Oxford Handbook in Linguistics), 605–613. Oxford: Oxford University Press.
Aikhenvald, Alexandra Y. & Dixon, R. M. W. (eds.). 2006. *Serial Verb Constructions. A Cross-linguistic Typology*. Oxford: Oxford University Press.
Anderson, Gregory D. S. 2006. *Auxiliary verb constructions*. Oxford: Oxford University Press.
Bourdin, P. 2002. The grammaticalization of deictic directionals into modulators of temporal distance. In Wischer, I. & Diewald G. (eds.), *New reflections on grammaticalization*, 181–200. Amsterdam & Philadelphia: John Benjamins Publishing Company.
Chelliah, S.L. 1997. *A Grammar of Meithei*. Berlin: Mouton de Gruyter.
Desclés, Jean-Pierre & Guentchéva, Zlatká. 2000. Enonciateur, locuteur, médiateur, in Aurore Monod-Becquelin & Philippe Erikson (eds.), *Les Rituels du Dialogue*, 79–112. Nanterre: Société d'Ethnologie.
DeLancey, Scott. 1991. The Origins of Verb Serialization in Modern Tibetan. *Studies in Language* 15(1). 1–23.
Denwood, Philip. 1999. *Tibetan*. Amsterdam & Philadelphia: John Benjamins Publishing Company.
Diessel, Holger. 2012. Deixis and demonstratives. In Claudia Maienborn, Klaus von Heusinger, Paul Portner (eds.), *An International Handbook of Natural Language Meaning*, Vol. 3, 2407–2431. Berlin: Mouton de Gruyter.
Ducrot, Oswald. 1980. Esquisse d'une théorie polyphonique de l'énonciation. In *Le Dire et le Dit*, 171–233. Paris: Minuit.
Ebert, Karen H. 1987. Grammatical marking of speech act participants in Tibeto-Burman. *Journal of Pragmatics* 11. 473–482.
Fillmore, Charles J. 1997. Coming and going. In *Lectures on Deixis*, 77–102. Stanford, CA: CSLI.
Gyurmé, Kesang. 1994. *Le clair miroir. Enseignement de la grammaire tibétaine* (traduction et adaptation et commentaires de Heather Stoddard et Nicolas Tournadre). Arvillard: Editions Prajña.
De Haan, Ferdinand. 1999. *Visual evidentiality and its origins*. Manuscript, University of New Mexico.
De Haan, Ferdinand. 2005. Encoding speaker perspective: Evidentials. In Z. Frajzyngier & D. Rood (eds.), *Linguistic diversity and language theories*, 379–397. Amsterdam & Philadelphia: John Benjamins Publishing Company.
Hongladarom, Krisadawan. 1995. On the emergence of epistemic meanings: A study of Tibetan deictic motion verbs. *Mon-Khmer Studies* 25. 15–28.
Hooper, Robin. 2002. Deixis and aspect: The Tokelauan directional particles *mai* and *atu*. *Studies in language* 26(2). 283–313.
Jakobson, Roman [1957] 1971. Shifter, verbal categories, and the Russian verb. In: R. Jakobson. *Selected Writings*, vol. 2, 130–147. The Hague: Mouton.
Jungraithmayr, H. & Johann G.W. Möhlig (eds.). 1983. *Lexikon der Afrikanistik*. Berlin: Reimer.
Kuno, Susumu & Etsuko Kaburaki [1975] 1977. Empathy and Syntax. *Linguistic Inquiry* 8(4). 627–672. (First published in *Harvard Studies in Syntax and Semantics* 1. 1–73)
LaPolla, Randy. 2003. Dulong. In Thurgood & LaPolla (eds.), *The Sino-Tibetan Languages*, 674–684. London: Routledge.
Larsson, Stefan. 2012. *Crazy for Wisdom: The Making of a Mad Yogin in Fifteenth-Century Tibet*. Leiden: Brill.

Linn, Mary S. 2000. *A grammar of Euchee (Yuchi)*. PhD. dissertation. University of Kansas.
Lounsbury, Floyd G. 1953. *Oneida Verb Morphology* (Yale University Publications in Anthropology 48). New Haven: Yale University Press.
Lyons, John 1977. *Semantics*. 2 vols. Cambridge: Cambridge University Press.
Matisoff, James A. 1991. Areal and universal dimensions of grammatization in Lahu. In Traugott, E.C. & Heine, B. (eds.), *Approaches to Grammaticalization*, vol. 2, 383–453. Amsterdam: John Benjamins.
Montgomery-Anderson, Brad. 2008. *A Reference Grammar of Oklahoma Cherokee*. PhD dissertation, University of Kansas.
Nakazawa, Tsuneko. 2007. A typology of the ground of deictic motion verbs as path-conflating verbs: the speaker, the addressee, and beyond. *Poznań Studies in Contemporary Linguistics* 43(2). 59–82.
O'Connor, Loretta. 2004. Going getting tired: 'associated motion' through space and time in Lowland Chontal. In M. Achard & S. Kemmer (eds.), *Language, Culture and Mind*, 181–198. Stanford: CSLI publications.
Oisel, Guillaume 2013. *Morphosyntaxe et sémantique des auxiliaires et des connecteurs du tibétain littéraire: étude diachronique et synchronique,* Doctoral dissertation, Université de la Sorbonne nouvelle-Paris III.
Paillard, Denis. 2013. Les constructions verbales en série en khmer contemporain. *Faits de langues* 41(1). 11–39.
Quintman, Andrew. 2010. *The Life of Milarepa*. New York: Penguin classics.
Robin, Françoise. 2005. *Les Contes facétieux du Cadavre*. L'Asiathèque. Paris.
Rus pa'i rgyan can. 1994. *Rnal 'byor gyi dbang phyug chen po mi la ras pa'i rnam mgur* (The life and the songs of Milarepa). Tibetan cultural printing press, Dharamsala.
Tournadre, Nicolas & Konchok Jiatso. 2001. Final auxiliary verbs in literary Tibetan and in the dialects. Person and Evidence in Himalayan Languages. [Special Issue]. *Linguistics of the Tibeto-Burman Area* 24(1). 177–239.
Tournadre, Nicolas & LaPolla, Randy. 2014. Towards a new approach to evidentiality: issues and directions for research. *Linguistics of the Tibeto-Burman Area* 37(2). 240–263.
Tournadre, Nicolas & Sangda Dorje. 2003. *Manual of Standard Tibetan*. Ithaca, New York: Snow Lion.
Vokurková, Zuzanna. 2008. *Epistemic Modalities In Spoken Standard Tibetan*. Ph.D. dissertation. Filozoficka Fakulta Univerzity Karlovy – Université Paris 8.
Zeisler, Bettina. 2004. *Relative tense and aspectual verbs in Tibetan Languages*. Berlin & New York: Mouton de Gruyter.

Lhasa and Diasporic Tibetan

Yasutoshi Yukawa (Translation by Nathan W. Hill)
7 Lhasa Tibetan predicates

7.1 Introduction

This contribution provides an overview of Tibetan predicates.[1] The structures of Tibetan predicates per se are not overly complex. However, non-Tibetans find it relatively difficult to grasp the meanings expressed by the various predicate structures. When discussing the Tibetan language, the term 'predicate' should be taken to refer to the immediate constituents of a sentence that occur at the end of the sentence and can alone constitute a sentence. In Tibetan, all other constituents are not essential elements of the sentence and do not occur in a grammatically determined order.[2] The following includes an outline of Tibetan predicates while classifying them by structure.

7.2 Predicates of type I auxiliary verbs

The term 'type I auxiliary verb' refers to auxiliary verbs that denote the existence of an object or its existence in a certain state.[3] Type I auxiliary verbs take on different phonetic forms in affirmative sentences, negative sentences, polar questions

---

[1] This outline is based on research conducted at the Toyo Bunko. The informants were Tshering Dolma and Sonam Gyatso. In particular, Sonam answered various questions, thus helping me to revise the content of this article.
[2] In Yukawa (1971) entire sentences such as དེབ་གཅིག་ཡོད་རེད་ ^teb `žig 'yoo-re 'There is one book' are regarded as predicates. However, an immediate constituent may occur between དེབ་གཅིག་ ^teb `žig 'one book' and ཡོད་རེད་ 'yoo-ree 'there is', which does not lead to a change in the grammatical function of the sentence. Therefore, the previous conceptualization is not appropriate; in the example in question only ཡོད་རེད་ 'yoo-ree should be regarded as the predicate.
[3] These verbs can be used for any given time range if the speaker is clearly aware of the existence at the present moment (in other words, if the sentence can be asserted).

Note: This chapter is a translation of Yukawa (1975). The editors thank the Research Institute for Languages and Cultures of Asia and Africa at the Tokyo University of Foreign Studies for permission to publish this translation. We also thank Ulatus for preparing the translation of the original article under the auspices of the European Research Council funded project "Beyond Boundaries: Religion, Region, Language and the State" (ERC Synergy Project 609823 ASIA). As Yukawa (1975) is itself a revision of Yukawa (1971), the editors have tacitly incorporated material from the earlier paper where helpful.

(yes–no questions), and nonpolar (*wh*-questions) or choice questions. Their various forms are shown in the following table:

Tab. 1: Inflection of type I auxiliary verbs

Affirmative	ཡོད་ yöö	ཡོད་རེད་ 'yoo-ree	འདུག duu	ཡོང yoŋ	བྱུང čuŋ
Negative	མེད་ mää	ཡོད་མ་རེད་ 'yoo^maree	མི་འདུག ^minduu	མི་ཡོང་ 'meyoŋ	མ་བྱུང 'mačuŋ
Polar question	ཡོད་པས་ ^yöbää	ཡོད་རེད་པས་ 'yoo^rebää	འདུག་གས་ ^dugää	ཡོང་ངས་ ^yoŋää	བྱུང་ངས་ ^čuŋää
Nonpolar/choice question	ཡོད་ yöö	ཡོད་རེད་ 'yoo-rää	འདུག doo	ཡོང yoŋ	བྱུང čuŋ

Next, let us demonstrate the meanings of these auxiliary verbs using specific examples. First ཡོད་ *yöö*, མེད་ *mää* etc., denote the existence of an object with which the speaker (or the listener in interrogative sentences) feels familiar at a given time (not necessarily at the present).

(1) ང་ར་དེབ་ཡག་པོ་ཞིག་ཡོད།
    'ŋaa   ^teb   'yago   žig   yöö.
    me.DAT   book   good   a   is
    'I have a good book.'

(2) ང་ར་ཕྲུ་གུ་གཉིས་ཡོད།
    'ŋaa   ¯bugu   ¯ñii   yöö.
    me.DAT   child   two   is
    'I have two children.'

Examples (1) and (2) are ordinary statements, because the speaker is referring to an essentially familiar object or person as familiar. A legitimate sentence is also formed when ང་ *ŋaa* is replaced with a different pronoun or noun phrase.

(3) ངའི་གྲོགས་པོར་དེབ་ཡག་པོ་ཞིག་ཡོད།
    'ŋää   'ţogoo   ^teb   'yago   žig   yöö.
    me.GEN   friend   book   good   a   is
    'My friend has a good book.'

(4) ངའི་ཨ་ཅག་ལགས་ལ་ཕྲུ་གུ་གཉིས་ཡོད།
    'ŋää   `ažaa-laa-la   ¯bugu   ¯ñii   yöö.
    me.GEN   elder.sister-DAT   child   two   is
    'My elder sister has two children.'

In (3) the speaker feels familiar with the fact that the friend has a good book. For example, the speaker may expect that the friend would be willing to lend the book upon request, thus expressing familiarity concerning the book. Indeed, this sentence particularly occurs when the friend is a close one. Similarly, example (4) may be used when the speaker expresses familiarity with the fact that her own elder sister has children.

There is no need for ཡོད་ *yöö* to express possession; it may also express simple existence, if the situation is compatible with the semantics of the verb.

(5) ཕ་གིར་དེབ་ཡག་པོ་ཞིག་ཡོད།
 ⁻pagee ^teb   'yago žig yöö.
 yonder book   good   a   is
 'There is a good book over there.'

Example (5) is used if the speaker feels familiar with the fact that the book exists, for example, if she placed it over there.

Next, ཡོད་རེད་ *'yoo-ree*, ཡོད་མ་རེད་ *'yoo^maree*, etc., denote the objective existence of an object that was not directly perceived through the senses (or is not specified as such) at a given time.

(6) ཁོང་ལ་དེབ་དེ་ཡོད་མ་རེད།
 ⁻koŋ-la ^teb   'te   'yoo^mare.
 he-DAT   book   that   NEG.is
 'He does not have that book.'

(7) ང་ར་དེབ་དེ་ཡོད་རེད།
 'ŋaa   ^teb   'te   'yoo-ree.
 me.DAT   book   that   is
 'I have that book.'

Example (6) is an ordinary statement, denoting that a certain person does not have a particular book, whereas (7) is used if the speaker wishes to emphasize the objective nature of the existence. Therefore, it often includes a somewhat special nuance. For example, it can be used to suggest that there is an especially good or rare book (i.e., emphasizing its objective existence).

Next, འདུག་ *duu*, etc., indicate that the speaker has directly perceived the existence of an object through the senses (sight, hearing, touch, etc.) at a given time (present or past).[4]

---

[4] In general, existential verbs are rarely used when describing a future state, because at the present moment, the speaker can assert that an object will exist at a future point in time only in very limited cases, for example, when asserting that she has a class the following day. Because of its meaning of sense perception འདུག་ *duu* is never used when describing a future state.

(8) ཕ་གི་ར་མེ་ཏོག་འདུག
 ⁻pagee ^medoo duu.
 yonder flowers is
 'There are flowers over there.'

(9) གསང་སྤྱོད་ག་པར་འདུག ཕ་གི་ར་འདུག་གས
 `saŋžöö 'kabaa doo? ⁻pagää ^dugää?
 restroom where? is over.there is.Q
 'Where is the restroom? Over there?'

(10) དེབ་ཡག་པོ་ཞིག་འདུག
 ^teb 'yago žig duu.
 book good a is
 'There is a good book.'

In (8) the speaker is referring to flowers that she has already seen and knows to exist or flowers that are visible at the present moment. The question in (9) is often used when the addressee has gone to a restroom before the speaker, who wants to know where that restroom is.⁵ Example (10) shows that འདུག *duu* does not only indicate that the speaker simply perceives an *existence* through the senses. This sentence is used when the speaker has read the book well enough to know that it is good.

The speaker may also use རང་ *'ŋaa...* when indicating that she perceived the existence through the senses.

(11) རང་དངུལ་འདུག
 'ŋaa ⁻ŋüü duu.
 I.DAT money is
 'I have money.'

This sentence is used, for example, when the speaker reaches into her pocket, touches the money, and realizes it is there.

The next auxiliary verb ཡོང་ *yoŋ* is actually a pair of homonyms in which one expresses an existence about which the speaker has seen or heard in the past, whereas the other expresses a future existence (prediction).

---

5 The speaker might instead ask གསང་སྤྱོད་པར་ཡོད་ `saŋžöö 'kabaa yöö?, if she is in the addressee's house. In other words, if she presupposes that the addressee feels familiar with the location of the restroom. The speaker might also have asked གསང་སྤྱོད་པར་ཡོད་རེད་ `saŋžöö 'kabaa 'yoo-rää?, if she presupposes that the addressee does not feel that familiar with the location of the restroom and is likely not to have visited it previously.

(12) བོད་ལ་གཡག་མང་པོ་ཡོད།
    ^pöö-la   `yaa   'maŋgo   yoŋ.
    Tibet-DAT yak   many   is
    'There were many yaks in Tibet.'

(13) སང་ཉིན་ག་རེ་ཡོང་།
    ¯sañin   'kare   yoŋ?
    tomorrow what?   is
    'What will happen tomorrow?'

Lastly, བྱུང་ *čuŋ* indicates that the speaker acquired a certain object in the past, or rather, that an object happened to come into her possession.

(14) ཁ་སང་སྨན་ཏོག་ཙམ་བྱུང་།
    ¯kääsa   ¯män   `dää-ze   čuŋ.
    yesterday   medicine some   is
    'Yesterday, I got some medicine.'

In addition, type I auxiliary verbs also have negative interrogative forms, such as མེད་པས་ ^*mäbää* (cf. མེད་ *mää*) and མི་འདུག་གས་ '*mindu-gää* (cf. མི་འདུག་ ^*minduu*).

It is also possible to say ཨ་ཡོད་ ¯*a-yöö* 'I wonder if there is/was...' (present or past) and ཨ་ཡོང་ ¯*a-yoŋ* 'I wonder if there will be...' (future), as well as ཡོད་རེད་ *'yoo^redaa* 'There is...' (assertive). However, unlike ཡོད་ *yöö*, the use of ཨ་ཡོད་ ¯*a-yöö* is not restricted to familiar existences, but it denotes conjectural questions about existences in general.

7.3 Predicates of nouns (or noun phrases) and type II auxiliary verbs

Here the term 'type II auxiliary verb' refers to auxiliary verbs that denote an attribute in a similar manner to 'is' or 'was.' The affirmative, negative, polar question, and non-polar/choice question that are forms of the type II auxiliary verbs are shown below:

Tab. 2: Inflection of type II auxiliary verbs

Affirmative	ཡིན་	རེད་
	yin	ree
Negative	མིན་	མ་རེད་
	män	^maree
Polar question	ཡིན་པས་	རེད་པས་
	^yinbää	^rebää
Nonpolar/choice question	ཡིན་པུ་	རེད་
	'yin-baa	rää

Of these, ཡིན་ yin, etc., denote a state that exists at a given time and with which the speaker (or the listener in interrogative sentences) feels familiar.

(15) ང་སློབ་གྲྭ་འདིའི་སློབ་ཕྲུག་ཡིན།
'ŋa ⁻labḍa 'dii `labṭuu yin.
I school this.GEN student is
'I am a student of this school.'[6]

(16) ཁྱེད་རང་སུ་ཡིན་པས།
⁻keraŋ ⁻su 'yin baa?
you who? is Q
'Who are you?'

The auxiliary ཡིན་ 'yin can also be used in the second or third person if the speaker deems the thing or person referred to a familiar state.

(17) མོ་ཊ་འདི་ཡག་པོ་ཡིན།
'moḍa 'di 'yago yin.
car this good is
'This car is good.'

(18) ཁོང་སློབ་ཕྲུག་ཡིན།
⁻koŋ `labṭuu yin.
he/she student is
'He is a student.'

(19) ཁྱེད་རང་གི་ནོག་ལགས་བདེ་པོ་ཡིན་པས།
⁻keraŋ-gi 'oo-laa 'debo ^yinbää?
you-GEN younger.sibling well is.Q
'Is your younger brother (or sister) well?'

Sentence (17) is used, for example, when the speaker is boasting about her own car. In (18) the person denoted by ཁོང་ ⁻koŋ is often a family member or a close friend, but the essential meaning here is that the speaker feels familiar with the fact that the person is a student. Its use does not depend on whether the person

---

[6] In sentences like (15) ཡིན་ 'yin does not denote a state at the present moment, but it expresses the state of being a student as a continuous and unchanging state. When an adverb of time is added, ཡིན་ yin expresses the continuous and unchanging state that exists in the given time range. Therefore, one can also say ད་ལྟ་སློབ་ཕྲུག་ཡིན་ `tanda `labṭuu yin '(I am) a student now', དང་པར་ཏུ་སློབ་ཕྲུག་ཡིན་ 'daŋiŋ 'par-tu `labṭuu yin '(I was) a student until last year', སང་ཉིན་ནས་སློབ་ཕྲུག་ཡིན་ ⁻saŋiŋ nää `labṭuu yin '(I will be) a student from tomorrow', etc.

denoted by ཁོང་ ⁻koŋ is close to the speaker (because ང་ 'ŋa 'I' is not always used with ཡིན་ yin), but it depends on whether the speaker feels familiar with the situation as a whole. As a result, the person denoted by ཁོང་ ⁻koŋ tends to be someone close to the speaker.

In contrast, རེད་ ree, etc. denote an objective state that exists at a given time.

(20) ཁོང་གི་ཟླུམ་སུའི་སྲས་མོ་རེད།
    ⁻koŋ-gi   ⁻žam   ⁻süü   ⁻säämo   rää?
    he-GEN   wife   who?-GEN   daughter   is.Q
    'Whose daughter is his wife?' or 'Who are his wife's parents?'

(21) ཁོང་སློབ་ཕྲུག་རེད།
    ⁻koŋ   ˋlabṭuu   ree.
    he/she   student   is
    'He is a student.'

The auxiliary རེད་ ree can also be used to refer to a state associated with the speaker or listener when emphasizing this state as an objective one.[7]

(22) ཁྱེད་རང་འདི་ལྟར་ཡིན་ནའང་དགེ་རྒན་རེད་པས།
    ⁻keraŋ   ˆtenḍää   'yin-nää   'gegän   ˆrebää?
    you   thus   but   teacher   is.Q
    'And yet you are a teacher?' or 'And you call yourself a teacher?'

(23) ཁྱེད་རང་སློབ་ཕྲུག་རེད།
    ⁻keraŋ   ˋlabṭuu   ree.
    you   student   is
    'You are a student.'

Sentence (23) is used, for example, to tell the listener that he is a student, thus must study harder.

(24) ང་སློབ་ཕྲུག་རེད།
    'ŋa   ˋlabṭuu   ree.
    me   student   is
    'I am a student.'

---

[7] It is uncommon to make an assertion about a listener regardless of whether the assertion is positive or negative; however, it is possible to do so when emphasizing an objective fact. Naturally, རེད་ ree is used in such cases.

Whereas a sentence such as (15) above is used to simply report that the speaker is a student (a fact she is imminently familiar with), sentence (24) is used, for example, when the speaker is invited to gamble or asked to marry but wishes to refuse, because as a student, such an action would be wrong or impossible. Here the meaning is attained by describing something that the speaker would normally feel familiar with as an objective state. In other words, the speaker objectively emphasizes the fact that she is a student; thus, the meaning of the sentence subsumes a nuance of obligation associated with being a student. Indeed, in addition to obligation, the meaning of the sentence could include a feeling of pride or inferiority because the speaker is still not fully an adult.

In addition to the forms given in Tab. 2, type II auxiliary verbs also include the following negative interrogative forms: མིན་པས་ ^*mänbää*, མིན་སུ་ *'män-baa* (cf. མིན་ *män*), མ་རེད་པས་ *'mare-bää*, and མ་རེད་ ^*marää* (cf. མ་རེད་ ^*maree*). They also occur in the following forms: འ་ཡིན་ ⁻*a-yin* 'I wonder...', རེད་པ་ *'reba* 'It must be', རེད་བཟར་ *'redaŋ* 'It is, isn't it?', and རེད་ད་ ^*redaa* 'asserts a state'. Unlike ཡིན་ *yin*, etc., the use of འ་ཡིན་ ⁻*a-yin* is not restricted to states with which the speaker or listener feels familiar. Moreover, there are no forms such as *⁻*a-ree* or *'*yinba*. Furthermore, these auxiliary verbs form predicates in conjunction with nouns and noun phrases.

7.4 Predicates of adjectives and type I (and type II) auxiliary verbs

Adjectives (or adjectival phrases) can form predicates by combining with type I or type II auxiliary verbs. However, the instance of ཡོང་ *yoŋ* that expresses a past event does not have this function.

Both adjective + ཡིན་ *yin* and adjective + ཡོད་ *yöö* denote a state with which the speaker (or the listener in interrogative sentences) feels familiar; however, the former indicates an unchanging state, whereas the latter indicates a temporary state. For example, sentence (25a) expresses an unchanging state, whereas (25b) implies that the speaker feels well at the given time, but may have been unwell (or was unwell) at other points in time. Used by the speaker to refer to herself either (25a) or (25b) simply mean she is healthy, presenting a familiar state as something familiar. However, adjective + ཡིན་ *-yin* can also be used to refer to a third person (cf. (26)) when the speaker feels familiar with the state being described and is therefore often used when the third person is someone close to the speaker.[8]

---

8 Editor's note: Yukawa does not mention whether ཀོང་བདེ་པོ་ཡོད་ ⁻*koŋ 'debo yöö* is possible.

(25) a. ང་བདེ་པོ་ཡིན།
    'ŋa   'debo   yin.
    me   well   is
   b. ང་བདེ་པོ་ཡོད།
    'ŋa   'debo   yöö.
    me   well   is
    'I am well.'

(26) ཁོང་བདེ་པོ་ཡིན།
    ⁻koŋ   'debo   yin.
    he   well   is
    'He is well.'

It is important to note that the familiar state expressed by ཡོད་ *yöö* must have a specific relevance to the speaker, because ཡོད་ *yöö* cannot express a *general* state regardless of how familiar the speaker feels. For example, if the speaker wants to say, 'It is cold today,' then she cannot use (27).

(27) *དེ་རིང་གྲང་མོ་ཡོད།
    *'teriŋ   'ʈaŋŋo   yöö.
    today   cold   is
    *'Today is cold.'

Adjective + རེད་ *ree* objectively asserts a certain state (and in interrogative sentences asks whether that assertion can be made.)

(28) a. ཁོང་བདེ་པོ་རེད།
    ⁻koŋ   'debo   ree.
    he   well   is
    'He is well.'
   b. ང་བདེ་པོ་རེད།
    'ŋa   'debo   ree.
    me   well   is
    'I am well.'

Sentence (28a), referring to a third person, simply expresses an objective state; (28b), used by the speaker to refer to herself, objectively emphasizes the fact that she is healthy and could contain a nuance of pride or self-deprecation in that the speaker is so busy that she wants to become ill but cannot. It could also be used to emphasize the fact that she is healthy after being told to visit a doctor. Since a speaker is normally familiar with her own well-being, ཡིན་ *yin* and ཡོད་ *yöö* are more usual verbs to use (cf. (25a)).

Adjective + ཡོད་རེད་ *'yoo-ree* informs (or asks) the listener (or the speaker in interrogative sentences) about a certain state that he does not know about; generally, neither the speaker nor addressee can observe the state at the present moment.

(29) a. ཨོ་ས་ཀ་ལ་གྲང་མོ་ཡོད་རེད།
   Osaka-la   'ṭaŋŋo   'yoo-ree.
   Osaka-DAT   cold   is
 b. ཨོ་ས་ཀ་ལ་གྲང་མོ་རེད།
   Osaka-la   'ṭaŋŋo   ree.
   Osaka-DAT   cold   is
   'Osaka is cold.'

When (29a) is used to make the general statement that Osaka is cold, the speaker may have experienced this state before. However, when used to describe a present state, the speaker has, for example, heard this information from someone else or on the radio. In (29b), the speaker makes a general assertion about a continuous and unchanging state.[9] Accordingly, ཡོད་རེད་ *'yoo-ree* is not used to state a general truth. For example, if the speaker wants to state the general truth that summer is hot one cannot say (30a), which either presupposes that the listener does not know that summer is hot (perhaps occasionally acceptable in jest) or informs the listener what summer is like somewhere else; to communicate the general truth, normally known to the listener, one must use (30b).

(30) a. དབྱར་ག་ཚ་པོ་ཡོད་རེད།
   ⁻yaaga   ⁻cabo   'yoo-ree.
   summer   hot   is
 b. དབྱར་ག་ཚ་པོ་རེད།
   ⁻yaaga   ⁻cabo   ree.
   summer   hot   is
   'The summer is hot.'

Adjective + འདུག་ *duu* is used when the speaker (or the listener in interrogative sentences) directly perceives a certain state through the senses and experience some

---

[9] It is possible to use རེད་ *ree* irrespective of whether the listener knows about the subject; in either case རེད་ *ree* is used by the speaker to assert her opinion.

type of emotion or feeling; འདུག་ duu is often used with adjectives that describe subjective phenomena (such as hot and cold).

(31) a. དེ་རིང་གྲང་མོ་འདུག
'teriŋ 'ṭaŋŋo duu.
today   cold   is
b. དེ་རིང་གྲང་མོ་རེད།
'teriŋ 'ṭaŋŋo ree.
'It is cold today.'

Sentence (31a) refers to the speaker's own perception, whereas (31b) is generally used while observing the temperature on a thermometer. Thus, it is also possible to say the following:

(32) ང་གྲང་མོ་འདུག
'ŋa 'ṭaŋŋo duu.
me   cold   is
'I am cold.'

In sentence (33), the speaker is not simply stating that the flower is red (རེད་ ree would be used in this case), but that she experienced a (not necessarily good) feeling about this 'redness.'

(33) མེ་ཏོག་འདི་དམར་མོ་འདུག
ˆmedoo 'di   ˉmaamo duu.
flower this red   is
'This flower is red.'

This point is further illustrated through the following comparison:

(34) a. མི་ཕ་གི་ནག་པོ་འདུག
'mi   ˉpagi   'nago   duu.
person   yonder   black   is
b. མི་ཕ་གི་ནག་པོ་རེད།
'mi   ˉpagi   'nago   ree.
person   yonder   black   is
'That person has a dark complexion.'

Generally, (34a) is used when the speaker personally observes the complexion and feels that it is dark, whereas (34b) is used to assert that the person's complexion is dark rather than light; consequently, the person described in (34a) tends to have a much darker complexion than the person described in (34b). Thus, it is not per se that འདུག་ *duu* is used when the property denoted by the adjective can be confirmed by observation, but rather its use is deeply imbued with the speaker's own perception. In addition, འདུག་ *duu* is still used in such cases, even when describing a familiar state; (32) is another example of this, as is (35):

(35) a. ང་བདེ་པོ་འདུག
    'ŋa   'debo   duu.
    me   well   is
    I'm (feeling) good.
b. ཁོང་བདེ་པོ་འདུག
    ⁻koŋ   'debo   duu.
    he   well   is
    'He is (looking) good.'

When བདེ་པོ་ *'debo* occurs with འདུག་ *duu* and describes the speaker (35a), it can mean that the speaker feels good because it is cool or because she has begun to recover from an illness. When used to describe the state of a third person (35b), it infers that the person has a healthy complexion and looks well.

Now, འདུག་ *duu* does not occur with adjectives such as གོར་གོར་ *'googoo* 'round'. Of course, we determine whether an object is round through the sense of sight. However, in this case, the shape of the object is captured objectively because one hardly experiences a compelling sense of roundness when viewing an object.

All three verbs (ཡོད་རེད་ *'yoo-ree*, རེད་ *ree*, and འདུག་ *duu*) describe a state at a given time and they do not necessarily refer to the present moment. Example (36) conveniently contrasts these three verbs as used with adjectives.

(36) a. ཁོང་གི་སྲུང་མ་མཛེས་པོ་ཡོད་རེད།
    ⁻koŋ-gi   ⁻žam   'zeebo   'yoo-ree.
b. ཁོང་གི་སྲུང་མ་མཛེས་པོ་རེད།
    ⁻koŋ-gi   ⁻žam   'zeebo   ree.
c. ཁོང་གི་སྲུང་མ་མཛེས་པོ་འདུག
    ⁻koŋ-gi   ⁻žam   'zeebo   duu.
    he-GEN   wife   beautiful   is
    'His wife is beautiful.'

In the first sentence (36a), the speaker is informing someone who is not well acquainted with the woman that she is beautiful. In the second sentence (36b), the question of whether the woman is beautiful has been raised and the speaker asserts that she is beautiful. In the final sentence (36c), the speaker sees the woman and experiences a compelling sense of beauty.

Adjective + ཡོང་ *yoŋ* denotes a state that the speaker thinks will occur in the future, whereas adjective + བྱུང་ *čuŋ* denotes a passive state experienced by the speaker (or the listener in interrogative sentences) in the past.

(37) སང་ཉིན་གནམ་གཤིས་ཡག་པོ་ཡོང་།
⁻sañin ˋnamšii 'yago yoŋ.
tomorrow weather good is
'I am sure the weather will be good tomorrow.'

(38) a. ཁ་སང་བདེ་པོ་ཡིན།
⁻kääsa 'debo yin.
yesterday well is

b. ཁ་སང་བདེ་པོ་བྱུང་།
⁻kääsa 'debo čuŋ.
yesterday well is
'I felt well yesterday.'

Whereas with ཡིན་ *yin* (38a, cf. 25a) the state of 'feeling well' is captured as a continuous and unchanging state, thus implying that although the speaker may feel unwell at the present moment, she did not feel unwell during the relatively long period of the past to the previous day, in contrast, with བྱུང་ *čuŋ* (38b) the implication is that the speaker does not normally feel that well, but happened to feel well on that particular day; བྱུང་ *čuŋ* expresses that a certain state befell the speaker (or the listener in an interrogative sentence), rather than occurring as the result of her effort.[10]

Of course, in addition to the affirmative form, the other forms shown in Tabs. 1 and 2 can also be used with adjectives.

Adjectives can occur in superlative form (for example, ཡག་པོ་ *'yago* becomes ཡག་ཤོས་ *'yagšöö* 'the best') in which case they are used as normal adjectives. Adjectives also occur in comparative form (for example, ཡག་པོ་ *'yago* becomes ཡག་ག་ *ya-ga*). However, when these comparative forms occur with affirmative འདུག *duu*, then for example, *ya-ga duu* becomes ཡག་ག་ *'ya-gaa*. In contrast, there is a separate

---

10 Moreover, when viewed in this light, the བྱུང་ *čuŋ* that follows a noun and the བྱུང་ *čuŋ* that follows an adjective can be regarded as the same linguistic unit. However, although the state that befalls the speaker usually involves acquisition of an object, བྱུང་ *čuŋ* can also be used, for example, in the event of an earthquake. This use of བྱུང་ *čuŋ* vividly illustrates the notion of a befallen state. When a state expressed by a certain adjective befalls the speaker, she does not produce this state through conscious efforts or intentions, but she experiences it.

comparative form in which ཡག་པོ་ 'yago becomes ཡག་གི་ 'yaagi by combining with the gi infinitive (see §7), although this construction only occur with རེད་ ree.

(39) a. འདི་པ་གི་ལས་ཡག་ག
     'di ⁻pagi lää 'ya-gaa.
  b. འདི་པ་གི་ལས་ཡག་གི་རེད།
     'di   ⁻pagi lää   'yaagi ree.
     this that   than better is
     'This is better than that.'

7.5 Predicates of negative verb forms

There are some Tibetan verbs for which the perfect and imperfect stems (both single-syllable) can be distinguished. For example, the verb 'to eat' has two separate forms བཟས་ ^sää (perfective) and ཟ་ 'sa (imperfective), and the verb 'to go' occurs as ཕྱིན་ `čin (perfective) and འགྲོ་ `do (imperfective). Those verbs that lack this distinction employ a single invariant stem in both perfective and imperfective contexts. A perfect stem negated with the མ་ ma prefix indicates that the speaker (or a group to which she belongs) did not (of her own will) perform a certain action in the past.[11]

(40) ཁ་སང་མ་ཕྱིན།
     ⁻kääsa   `mačin.
     yesterday NEG.went
     'I did not go yesterday.'

(41) ཁ་ལག་མ་བཟས།
     `kalaa   ^masää.
     food   NEG.ate
     'I did not eat food.'

This construction indicates that the speaker failed to perform the action out of her own will, such as a situation in which she did not eat because she did not want to eat, i.e. it describes the speaker's own past action.

---

11 The negative prefix མ་ ma when it precedes verbs beginning with /p, t, k, ǩ, ṭ, č, c, ȓ, ḷ, ŋ, ñ/ is pronounced voiceless as /m̥a/. However, in this study, <ma> is used for both /ma/ and /m̥a/.

7.6 Predicates of verbs and sentence-final particles

Here the term 'sentence-final particle' refers to the three particles that denote an interrogative meaning; that is, པས་ *bää*, པ་ *baa*, and ག་ *gaa*. First, when པས་ *bää* follows a perfective verb stem (or མ་ *ma* + perfective verb stem), it forms an interrogative predicate that inquires whether the listener (or a group to which he belongs) performed a certain action in the past, i.e. it is used for polar questions.

(42) ཁྱེད་རང་ཁོང་གི་གཟིམ་ཤག་ལ་ཕེབས་པས།
 ⁻keraŋ ⁻koŋ-gi ˆsimšaa-la ˋtää bää?
 you he-GEN house.HON-DAT go.HON Q
 'Did you go to his house?' (honorific)

(43) ཞལ་ལག་མཆོད་པས།
 ˆšälaa ˋčöö bää?
 food.HON eat.HON Q
 'Did you eat?' (honorific)

(44) དེབ་དེ་བཀློག་པས།
 ˆteb 'te ˋloo bää?
 book that read Q
 'Did you read that book?'

When པ་ *baa* occurs with a perfective verb, it forms a predicate expressing a non-polar question (*wh*-question) that inquires about an action performed by the listener (or a group to which he belongs) in the past.

(45) ཁྱེད་རང་ག་རེ་བྱས་ནས་མ་ཕེབས་པ།
 ⁻keraŋ 'kare-ˆčää-nää ˋmapee baa?
 you why? NEG.go Q
 'Why didn't you go?' (honorific)

(46) ཕེབས་པ། མ་ཕེབས་པ།
 ˋpee baa? ˋmapee baa?
 go.HON Q NEG.go.HON Q
 'Did you go or didn't you go?'

(47) ག་རེ་བཟས་པ།
 'kare ˆsää baa?
 what eat Q
 'What did you eat?'

(48) དེབ་ག་གི་ཀློག་པ།
 ^teb 'kagi `loo baa?
 book which read Q
 'Which book did you read?'

When ག gaa occurs with a perfective verb, it forms a polar or nonpolar question (*wh*-question) requesting the listener's opinion about the speaker's future action (or that of a group to which she belongs).

(49) ང་འགྲོ་ག
 'ŋa `čin gaa?
 me go Q
 'Should I go?'

(50) ང་ག་པར་འགྲོ་ག
 'ŋa 'kabaa `čin gaa?
 me where? go Q
 'Where should I go?'

In addition, there is another instance of ག gaa, which from a semantic viewpoint accords with that described above. When this ག gaa follows an imperfective stem, it forms a nonpolar question (*wh*-question) requesting the listener's opinion about a future action performed by the listener (or a group to which he belongs) or a group to which the listener and speaker belong.[12]

(51) ང་གཉིས་ག་པར་འགྲོ་ག
 ^ŋañii 'kabaa 'ḍo gaa?
 we.two where? go Q
 'Where should we (two) go?'

(52) ཁྱེད་རང་ཚོ་ག་རེ་མཆོད་ག
 ¯keraŋ-co 'kare `čöö gaa?
 you-PL what? eat.HON Q
 'What will you (plural) eat?' (honorific)

---

12 In the case of verbs for which the perfective and imperfective forms cannot be distinguished, this construction requests the listener's opinion regarding an action performed by the speaker, the listener, or the speaker and listener: དེབ་ག་གི་ཀློག་ག ^teb 'kagi `loo gaa? 'Which book shall I read' or 'Which book will you read?' However, when ག gaa occurs with an honorific verb, it is not used as a question about the speaker's own action: ག་རེ་མཆོད་ག 'kare 'čöö gaa? 'What will you have?' or 'What shall we eat?' (honorific). In Tibetan, when referring to an action that will occur in the future, the speaker can use an honorific expression even if she is one of the actors, provided that the listener is also an actor. This is why 'What shall we eat?' is a possible interpretation.

7.7 Predicates of verbs and auxiliary verbs

Here the term 'auxiliary verb' refers to type I auxiliary verbs (except the past form of ཡོད་ *yöö*) and སོང་ *soŋ*, ཚར *čoo*, ཆར *caa*, བྱུང *ñoŋ*, and འདུག *duu*. First, let us examine sentences in which these auxiliary verbs follow a perfective verb stem. When ཡོད *yöö* follows a perfective verb stem, the predicate indicates a state in which the results of a past action still remain and with which the speaker (or the listener in interrogative sentences) feels familiar. Accordingly, the person who performed the action is someone with whom the speaker has a close relationship (including the speaker herself).

(53) ངས་བཟས་ཡོད།
 ˊŋää   ˆsää   yöö.
 me-ERG eat   is
 'I have eaten.'

(54) ཕྲུག་གུ་འདི་བཟས་ཡོད།
 ˉbugu 'di ˆsää   yöö.
 child this eat   is
 'This child has already eaten.'

(55) དེ་དུས་དེབ་དེ་བཀློག་ཡོད་པས།
 ˆtetüü   ˆteb   'te   ˋloo   ˆyöbää?
 that.time book   that   read   is.Q
 'Had you already read the book at that time?'

Sentence (53) is used, for example, when the speaker politely refuses food because she has already eaten, asserts that she is not or will not be hungry, or apologizes for eating someone else's food. Sentence (54) is a case where a third person who performed the action has a close relationship with the speaker, e.g. a mother speaking about her infant son; either he has already finished his dinner or has eaten so much he cannot eat more. Sentence (55) is possible as a question when the listener is being asked about a certain book in an oral examination; it shows that perfective verb form + ཡོད *yöö* is not only used when the action occurred at a point in time before the present moment but also when the action occurred earlier than a point of time in the past.[13]

---

[13] The possibility of a pluperfect reading also exists for perfective verb + ཡོད་རེད *'yoo-ree* or འདུག *duu*. Note that these constructions are only rarely used to refer to an action that occurred before a point of time in the future, because it is difficult to assert the completion of this action at the present moment. They can be used when describing definite plans such as when you want to say that you "will have finished work" when someone arrives tomorrow.

When ཡོད་རེད་ 'yoo-ree follows a perfective verb form, the clause expresses an action that occurred in the past, the result of which can be presumed or known to remain in some form; the predicate denotes that the state described is objective and not directly perceived through the senses.

(56) ཚང་མ་ཕེབས་ཡོད་རེད།
⁻caŋma `pee   'yoo-ree.
everyone come.HON is
'Everyone is here.' (honorific)

(57) ཁོང་གིས་ཞལ་ལག་མཆོད་ཡོད་རེད།
⁻koŋ-gi   ˆšälaa   `čöö   'yoo-ree.
he/she-ERG   food.HON eat.HON   is
'He will have already eaten (it seems).'

(58) དེབ་པ་གིར་བྲིས་ཡོད་རེད།
ˆteb   ⁻pagee   ˆṭii   'yoo-ree.
book   yonder.DAT   write   is
'It is written in that book.'

The assertion in (57) is based on the assumption that the man has already eaten, because it is past dinner time, which implies that it would not be rude to visit him now. In (58), the speaker is teaching the listener something that she knows to be true.

This form can also be used to refer to the speaker herself if it denotes an objective state. In particular, it is normal to use such a sentence when the speaker cannot accomplish the action according to her own will. Sentence (59) denotes that the action of 'getting used to' has occurred. It is often used because the speaker cannot 'get used to something' of her own will.

(59) ང་ལས་ཀ་འདི་འདྲ་ལ་གོམས་ཡོད་རེད།
'ŋa   'lääga   ˆdinḍää-la   ˆkom   'yoo-ree.
me   job   like.this-DAT get.used.to   is
'I am used to this kind of job.'

In addition, when འདུག་ duu follows a perfective verb, the predicate denotes a action the result of which is directly perceived through the senses. However, བཞག་ šaa is used in affirmative sentences.

(60) ཁྱི་འདི་ཤི་བཞག
⁻ki   'di   ⁻ši   šaa.
dog   this   die   is
'This dog has died.'

(61) དེ་འདྲ་བྲིས་མི་འདུག
ˆdendää   ˆḍii   ˆminduu.
like.that written NEG.is
'Such a thing has not been written.'

Example (60) is used when the speaker is looking at or touching a dog lying on the ground, and (61) is used when she is looking at the section of a book being referred to.

This form can also be used when describing the speaker's own action if she feels the result of a past action at the present moment or perceives (through the senses) a change in herself that has occurred external to her own will.

(62) ཁ་ལག་བཟས་བཞག
`kalaa   ˆsää   šaa.
food   eat   is
'(Come to think of it) I have already eaten.'

(63) དྲག་བཞག
ˆṭaa   šaa.
recover is
'I have recovered.'

In (62), the speaker has forgotten that she had already eaten and recalls this when she attempts to eat again but does not feel hungry. In this case, the notion that the speaker 'discovered' something is permissible. However, this nuance is external to the idiosyncratic meaning of the verb + འདུག *duu* (བཞག *šaa*) construction and can be explained through the situation in which the speaker (who ought to know that she has already eaten) claims to have perceived this anew through a different sense; a situation that cannot arise unless forgetfulness has occurred. In (63), something has happened to the speaker that is external to her will and can be perceived because she feels well at the present moment (cf. examples (74) and (81)).

Next, when ཨ་ཡོད ˉa-yöö follows a verb, it expresses a meaning similar to "I wonder..." (about a past event) and bears no relation to whether the speaker feels familiar with the event.

(64) ཁོང་ཕེབས་ཨ་ཡོད
ˉkoŋ   `pee   ˉa-yöö.
he/she   go   is
'I wonder if he has arrived.' (honorific)

Next, when བྱུང *čuŋ* follows a perfective verb form, it expresses the notion that a certain action somehow befell or happened to the speaker (or the listener in interrogative sentences). Also note that *ču* (still written བྱུང) is the form that is generally used in an affirmative sentence.

(65) ཁོང་གིས་དེབ་བཀློག་བྱུང་།
 ̄koŋ-gi ˆteb ˋloo ču.
he-ERG book read is
'He read the book.'

(66) ཁོང་གིས་མཆོད་བྱུང་།
 ̄koŋ-gi ˋčöö ču.
he-ERG eat.HON is
'He ate with us' (honorific).

(67) བྱིའུས་འབྲས་བཟས་བྱུང་།
ˆčiüü ˆḍää ˆsää ču.
small.bird-ERG rice eat is
'The rice was eaten by a small bird.'

Sentence (65) may express various states. The person may have read the book for the speaker, read it upon the request of the speaker, or inconvenienced the speaker by reading it aloud in her vicinity. Examples (66) and (67) exhibit the same types of interpretations; in (66) the speaker feels herself benefited by the dinner guest's presence, in (67) she is annoyed at the bird's activity.

Incidentally, བྱུང་ *čuŋ* can be used when none of the above conditions are present, that is, if the nature of the verb is such that it denotes an action directed toward the speaker as in example (68)[14] and (69). However, this usage is limited to situations where 'directionality affecting the speaker' is rather specific. It cannot be used to say, 'I lost my father.'

(68) ཁོང་ཕེབས་བྱུང་།
 ̄koŋ ˋpee ču.
he come.HON is
'He came.' (honorific)

(69) ཡི་གེ་ལྔ་འབྱོར་བྱུང་།
'yigi 'ŋa 'žoo ču.
letter five receive is
'Five letters arrived.'

Now, even when the event described relates to the speaker, it expresses a change that befell or happened to the speaker, as the following examples show.

---

[14] Sentence (68) can also be used when the person was invited by the speaker or caused inconvenience by his/her arrival; although these uses appear to differ, the meaning of ཕེབས་བྱུང་ ˋ*pee ču* is the same.

(70) ཁོང་མཐོང་བྱུང་།
    ¯koŋ   ¯toŋ   ču.
    he   see   is
    '(I) saw him.'

(71) དཔྱ་ཨོ་ས་ཀ་ལ་སླེབས་བྱུང་།
    'tanda   Osaka-la   `lee   ču.
    now   Osaka-DAT arrive is
    '(I) just arrived in Osaka.'

(72) ཐུབ་བྱུང་།
    `tub   ču.
    able is
    '(I) did it' (could do it).

(73) ང་ན་བྱུང་།
    'ŋa   'na   ču.
    me   ill   is
    'I fell ill.'

If the speaker becomes ill, she uses (73). However, when the speaker has recovered from an illness she may use (74); it implies that she did not recover naturally but was treated by a doctor or with medicine. Although it is easy to interpret illness as a state that befalls the speaker, recovery can be interpreted in two ways: either as a naturally occurring state or a state that is achieved through some external factor (that is, a factor that befalls the speaker, also cf. example 63).

(74) དྲག་བྱུང་།
    ^ṭaa   ču.
    recover is
    '(I) recovered.'

Because use of བྱུང་ *čuŋ* includes the nuance that the event has occurred because of some external factor, asking someone who had caught a cold the following question would generally not be appropriate.[15]

---

[15] Such a sentence might be used if the illness is ongoing and the speaker has not seen the listener for a while. Furthermore, in terms of nuance, this sentence implies that the 'recovery' has happened as a whole or that the person has made a complete recovery.

(75) དྲག་བྱུང་ངས།
    ^ṭaa   ^čuŋää?
    recover is-Q
    '(Have you) recovered?'

The correct way to ask someone if they have recovered from a cold is as follows:

(76) དྲག་འདུག་གས།
    ^ṭaa   ^dugää?
    recover is-Q
    '(Are you) feeling better?'

Next, the auxiliary verb སོང་ *soŋ* (normally *so* in the affirmative, which is still written སོང་, མ་སོང་ *'masoŋ* in the negative, སོང་ངས་ ^*soŋää* in polar questions, and སོང་ *soŋ* in nonpolar/choice questions) indicates that the speaker directly perceived a certain past action through the senses at the time that this action was performed.

(77) སུ་གཞས་བཏང་སོང་།
    ⁻su   ^šää   ⁻daŋ   soŋ?
    who?   song   sang   is
    Who sang the song?

(78) ཁོང་ཕེབས་སོང་།
    ⁻koŋ   `pee   so.
    he   came.HON   is
    'He came.' (honorific)

(79) ཁོང་ཕེབས་སོང་ངས།
    ⁻koŋ   `pee   ^soŋää?
    he   come.HON   is-Q
    'Did he come?'

Sentence (78) is used when the speaker was present and saw the person arrive (or guessed from a noise); in (79) the speaker asks whether the addressee saw him come.

The form སོང་ *soŋ* can also be used to denote an action performed by the speaker or the listener if the action is perceived objectively.

(80) ང་སྔོན་ལ་སླེབས་སོང་།
    'ŋa   ⁻ŋän-la   `lee   so.
    me   earlier-DAT   arrive   is
    'I got there earlier.'

(81) ང་དྲག་སོང་།
 'ŋa ^ṭaa   so.
 me   recover is
 'I have recovered.'

(82) ཆམས་པ་བརྒྱབ་སོང་།
 ⁻čaŋba ^ğab so.
 cold   get   is
 '(I) caught a cold.'

Sentence (80) is used, for example, in a race when two people cross the finish line roughly at the same time and then contest who crossed the finish line first. Thus, the speaker in this case is stating an objective fact. Sentence (81) simply means that the speaker has recovered (cf. examples (63) and (74)). Sentence (82) is used, for example, when the speaker goes outside after being in a warm room and sneezes. Let us compare (82) with the following sentence.

(83) ཆམས་པ་བརྒྱབ་བྱུང་།
 ⁻čaŋba ^ğab ču.
 cold   get   is
 '(I) caught a cold.'

Sentence (83) suggests that such an event happened to the speaker because of an external factor and is often used when the speaker is confined to her bed with a cold. It is not used when the speaker experiences a minor symptom such as a sneeze. In example (84), if climbers reach the top of a mountain and say (84a) it simply means 'we are at the top,' but if they say (84b) then it includes a strong nuance of relief about finally making it to the summit.

(84) a. སླེབས་སོང་།
     ˋlee so.
   b. སླེབས་བྱུང་།
     ˋlee   ču.
     arrive   is
     'We arrived.'

In general, the auxiliary verb སོང་ soŋ is used quite frequently.

Next, when ཆོག čoo (negative form མི་ཆོག ^me čoo) occurs, the speaker is reasoning that it would be permissible for her to perform a certain action.

(85) ངས་ཉ་ཤ་འདི་བཟས་ཆོག
 ^ŋää   ˈňaša   'di   ^sää   čoo.
 me-ERG fish.meat this   eat   is
 'I may eat this fish.'

Next, ཚར ⁻caa indicates the completion of an action performed by the speaker.

(86) ངས་དེབ་འདི་ཀློག་ཚར།
　　　^ŋää　　^teb　'di　`loo　⁻caa.
　　　me-ERG　book　this　read　is
　　　'I have finished reading this book.'

Although ཆོག `čoo and ཚར ⁻caa also exist as main verbs, in these constructions the forms in question are used as auxiliary verbs.

Next, let us examine sentences in which auxiliary verbs follow imperfective stems. First, when མྱོང ñoŋ (negative form མ་མྱོང 'mañoŋ, polar question མྱོང་ངས ^ñoŋää, and nonpolar/choice question མྱོང ñoŋ) follows an imperfective stem, the predicate marks the speaker's (or the listener's in interrogative sentences) experience, thus indicating that she "has done" something.

(87) ང་བོད་ལ་འགྲོ་མ་མྱོང་།
　　　'ŋa　^pöö-la　'do　'mañoŋ.
　　　me　Tibet-DAT　go　NEG.is
　　　'I have never been to Tibet.'

Next, when འདུག duu follows an imperfective stem, it produces a meaning similar to 'let's' (or 'let's not' when it is preceded by the negative marker མ་ ma).

(88) ཁོང་གི་གཟིམས་ཤག་ལ་ཐད་འདུག
　　　⁻koŋ-gi　　^simšaa-la　　`tää　du.
　　　he/she-GEN　house.HON-DAT　go.HON　is
　　　'Let's go to his/her house.' (honorific)[16]

7.8 Predicates of infinitives and auxiliary verbs

The term 'infinitives' is here used as a general name for all forms in which connective morphemes, such as པ་ ba and གི་ gi, directly follow verb stems. I will call each of these respectively the པ་ ba infinitive, the གི་ gi infinitive, etc.

The པ་ -ba infinitive, which is formed from the perfect stem (e.g. བཟས ^sää becomes བཟས་པ ^sää-ba), can take the auxiliary verbs ཡིན yin, རེད ree, and ཡོད yöö. Expressions affixed with ཡིན yin express the past actions of the speaker (or the speaker's group). Note that པ་ཡིན -ba-yin cannot, for example, refer to the actions

---

[16] As discussed in Note 12, in Tibetan, the speaker can still use an honorific form (in this case ཐད `tää) even if she is involved in the action provided that the listener is also an actor.

of the speaker's child or others with whom the speaker is familiar (as can ཡིན་ yin alone).

(89) ང་དེབ་པ་གི་སློག་པ་ཡིན།
ŋa ˆteb ⁻pagi ˋloo-ba yin.
I book yonder read-INF is
'I read that book.'

(90) ཕྱིན་པ་ཡིན།
ˋčin-ba yin.
went- INF is
'(I) went.'

While ཡིན་ män may take the place of ཡིན་ yin with negatives, in a question about the past actions of an interlocutor, the verb + final particle པས་ bää (for polar questions) or པ་ baa (for nonpolar questions) are used, as we saw in section 5.

When the པ་ ba infinitive occurs with རེད་ ree, the speaker knows (regardless of through what means) about someone's past action that has had some lasting effect in the present.

(91) ངའི་པ་ལགས་རྒྱ་གར་ལ་གཤེགས་པ་རེད།
'ŋää ⁻baa-laa 'ğagaa-la ˋšaa-ba ree.
me-GEN father-hon. India-DAT die-INF is
'My father died in India.'

(92) ཁོང་གིས་བཟས་པ་རེད།
⁻koŋ-gi ˆsää-ba ree.
he-ERG ate-INF is
'He ate it.'

Sentence (91) is not used to mean that the speaker witnessed the final moment (in that case one would say, གཤེགས་སོང་ ˋšaa so), but rather means that the results of the death have had some lasting effect in the present (as with verb + ཡོད་ yöö, etc., note that this is not a direct effect). Sentence (92) is used, for example, as an answer to a question about what happened to the food that was left on the table. However, this sentence is not used to assert that the speaker saw the man eat the food but to state that the food was gone because the man ate it. The form verb + ཡོད་རེད་ 'yoo-ree discussed above indicates that a certain action occurred in the past and denotes its direct result. For example, བཟས་ཡོད་རེད་ ˆsää 'yoo-ree implies that a person ought to be full because he/she has eaten, whereas the པ་ ba infinitive + རེད་ ree indicates that a certain action occurred and that its influence affects the current situation in some way. Therefore, (92) includes the nuance that the food has gone.

Furthermore, the པ་ *ba* infinitive formed from an imperfective verb form can occur with རེད་ *ree* but not ཨིན་ *yin*. In this case, the predicate expresses a habit or tendency.

(93) ཡག་པོ་ཟ་བ་རེད།
ˊyago ˆsaa ree.
well eat is
'(He) eats a lot.'

However, because the perfective and imperfective forms of regular verbs cannot be distinguished, a single infinitive can have more than one meaning:

(94) ཁོང་གིས་ཞེ་དྲགས་ཀློག་པ་རེད།
ˉkoŋ gi ˊsheḍaa ˋloo-ba ree.
he-ERG very read is
'He reads a lot' or 'He read a lot.'

This could either mean that the man is a keen reader or it implies that his extensive reading in the past is affecting his current situation.[17] In a question, རེད་ *ree* may be replaced with རེད་པས་ *rebää* or རེད་ *rää*, but there are two types of negative forms.

---

[17] The question arises whether these two cases of ཀློག་པ་རེད་ ˋloo-ba ree are homonyms. In the first meaning, the speaker knows about a past action and feels its effects in some form at the present moment, whereas in the second, the speaker describes a person's habitual action. However, even in the second meaning, the speaker must have some form of knowledge of the person's past actions. Moreover, neither of the meanings includes the notion that the speaker has directly observed the action. Thus, these cases of ཀློག་པ་རེད་ ˋloo-ba ree do not appear to be homonyms, but a unified form in which the speaker (while recalling a past action) recognizes the continuation and effects of that past action in some form at the present moment. Furthermore, it is reasonable to conclude that the expression includes cases that focus more on the point of time in the past or the state at the present moment. To be sure, there are times when the speaker uses (94) without thinking about which point in time she is focusing on. In other words, it is uninterrupted and continuous.

One may note that ཀློག་པ་རེད་ ˋloo-ba ree has two negative forms མ་ཀློག་པ་རེད་ ˋmaloo-ba ree, which may be translated 'He did not read' and ཀློག་པ་མ་རེད་ ˋloo-baˆmaree which denotes habitual action. However, the different position of མ་ *ma* suffices to explain the difference between these two forms in structural terms. Moreover, note that in the case of habitual actions, this form can also be used to refer to an action before or after the given point in time if it is included in the habit: ཁ་སང་ཁོང་ཕེབས་པ་མ་རེད་ ˉkääsa ˉkoŋ ˋpee-ba ˆmaree, which explains that, 'Yesterday was the day that he does not come' and སང་ཉིན་ཁོང་ཕེབས་པ་མ་རེད་ ˉsaŋin ˉkoŋ ˋpee-ba maree, which explains that, 'Tomorrow is the day that he does not come.'

(95) a. ཁོང་ཁ་སང་མ་ཡིབས་པ་རེད།
   ⁻koŋ   ⁻kääsa   ˋmapee-ba   ree.
   he/she yesterday NEG.come-INF is
b. ཁོང་ཁ་སང་ཡིབས་པ་མ་རེད།
   ⁻koŋ   ⁻kääsa   ˋpee-ba   ˆmaree.
   He/she yesterday come-INF NEG.is
   'He did not come yesterday.'

Whereas the former implies 'did not come' in the normal sense (with, of course, the nagging sense of a lasting effect), the latter has the sense that yesterday was (simply) not the day that the person came.

Next, where ཡོད་ *yöö* is affixed to the perfective པ་ *ba* infinitive, it expresses an inference as to someone's apparent past action(s).[18]

(96) ཁོང་ཕྱིན་པ་ཡོད།
   ⁻koŋ   ˋčin-ba   yöö.
   he/she come-INF is
   'It seems like he went.'

Unlike the case wherein ཡོད་ *yöö* affixes directly to the stem, this has no relation as to whether said action can be regarded as familiar.

As mentioned above in the discussion of the པ་ *-ba* infinitive plus རེད་ *ree*, there are also examples where the པ་ *-ba* infinitive is created from the imperfect stem (when affixing to single-syllable stems, e.g. ཟ་ ˋ*sa*, འགྲོ་ ˊ*do*, or བྱེད་ ˊ*če* 'do', these take forms such as ཟབ་ ˆ*saa*, འགྲོབ་ ˆ*doo*, and བྱེདཔ་ ˆ*čää*), and when these are affixed with ཡོད་ *yöö* or འདུག་ *duu*, they become predicates expressing inference.[19] Examples affixed with ཡོད་ *yöö* express general inferences about past or future actions, whereas those affixed with འདུག་ *duu* express the case where the basis for an inference about a future action is understood directly from one's own senses.[20]

---

18 In this case, འདུག་ *duu* is not used, since the inferential meaning of the construction is incompatible with the sensory evidence encoded by འདུག་ *duu*. If one had seen a past event one would know it occurred and not speculate about whether or not it occurred.
19 Now, ཡོད་རེད་ *yoo-ree* does not follow the imperfective པ་ *ba* infinitive. The omission can be understood as semantically motivated; when making an inference, it is likely that the speaker either regards the event as something familiar (thus making the inference familiar) or perceives through the senses the evidence on which the inference is based.
20 The reason why the པ་ *ba* infinitive + འདུག་ *duu* cannot be used to make inferences about past events is explained in Note 18. Conversely, the པ་ *ba* infinitive + འདུག་ *duu* can be used when discussing future events because, quite naturally, although a future action itself cannot be confirmed, any amount of evidence suggesting that a certain action will be performed can be directly perceived through the senses.

(97) བོད་འགྲོ་བ་ཡོད།
  ⁻koŋ   ^doo   yöö.
  he/she come-INF is
  'It looks like he will go.' or 'It looks like he went.'

(98) བོད་དེ་རིང་ཁ་ལག་ཟ་བ་འདུག
  ⁻koŋ 'teriŋ `kalaa ^saa duu.
  he/she today food eat-INF is
  'It looks like he will eat the food today.'

Note that the བ་ *ba* infinitive, in addition to its functions in the formation of predicates, also has nominal uses.

(99) མི་ཕེབས་པ་དེ་སུ་རེད
  'mi   `pee-ba   'te   ⁻su rää?
  person come.HON-INF that who is.Q
  'Who was that person who came?' (honorific).

(100) བོད་ནས་ཕེབས་པའི་མི་
  ^pöö nää `pee-bää   'mi.
  Tibet from come.HON-INF.GEN person
  'The person who came from Tibet.' (honorific)

In sentence (99) ཕེབས་པ་ `pee-ba* is used as an adjective (cf. མི་ནག་པོ་དེ་ 'mi 'nago 'te 'that black-skinned person'). In sentence (100) ཕེབས་པ་ `pee-ba* occurs as a noun. This is the reason why I have chosen to regard these forms as 'infinitive' predicates.

Next, the གི་ -gi infinitive, which is formed from the imperfect stem (e.g. ཟ་ 'sa → ཟ་གི་ 'sagi, འགྲོ་ 'do → འགྲོ་གི་ 'dogi), may take ཡིན་ yin, རེད་ ree, ཡོད་ yöö, ཡོའོ་རེད་ yoo-ree, or འདུག་ duu.

The གི་ -gi- infinitive affixed with ཡིན་ yin expresses a future action on the part of the speaker (or the group to which she belongs).[21]

(101) སང་ཉིན་ནས་སློབ་སྦྱོང་ཡག་པོ་བྱེད་ཀྱི་ཡིན།
  ⁻sañin-nää `lobžoŋ ´yago ´čegi yin.
  tomorrow-ABL study good do-INF is
  'I will study hard from tomorrow.'

(102) ཟ་གི་ཡིན།
  'sagi yin.
  eat-INF is
  '(I) will eat.'

---

21 It deserves emphasis that this construction can never be used with actions of a third or second person (except of course for interrogative sentences for the second person).

While མིན་ *män* takes the place of ཡིན་ *yin* with negatives, in a question about the actions of an interlocutor, polar questions, rather than using the གི་ *gi* infinitive + ཡིན་པས་ ^*yinbää*, take the form གི་ *gi* infinitive + པས་ *bää*, whereas the nonpolar questions take the form ག་ *-gaa*, as shown in section 5.

(103) ཁྱེད་རང་སློབ་གྲྭ་བསྡད་ཀྱི་པས།
 ‾*keraŋ* ‾*labḍaa* ‾*täägi* *bää*?
 you school go-INF Q
 'Will you go to school?'

(104) ཕ་གིར་བསྡད་ཀྱི་པས།
 ‾*pagee* ‾*täägi* *bää*?
 over.there go.INF Q
 'Are you going to go there?' or 'Shall we go?'

(105) ག་པར་བསྡད་ག
 ‾*kabaa* ˋ*tää* *gaa*?
 where? go Q
 'Where will you go?'

When རེད་ *ree* follows the གི་ *-gi* infinitive, this expresses an objective action in the future or something that lasts from the present into the future.

(106) ཁོང་སང་ཉིན་ཕེབས་ཀྱི་རེད།
 ‾*koŋ* ‾*sañin* ‾*peegi* *ree*.
 he/she tomorrow come.INF is
 'He will come tomorrow.' (honorific)

(107) རི་པིན་ལ་ཆར་པ་མང་པོ་བབ་ཀྱི་རེད།
 ´*ribin-la* ´*čaaba* ´*maŋgo* ‾*daŋgi* *ree*.
 Japan-DAT rain lots.of fall.INF is
 'Lots of rain falls in Japan.'

(108) ཁོང་དེབ་ཞེ་དྲགས་ཀློག་གི་རེད།
 ‾*koŋ* ^*teb* ´*šeḍaa* ‾*loogi* *ree*.
 he book a.lot read.INF is
 'He reads a lot of books.'

(109) ང་ཡག་པོ་ཟ་གི་རེད།
 ´*ŋa* ´*yago* ´*sagi* *ree*.
 me a.lot eat.INF is
 'I eat a lot' or 'I am a big eater.'

As indicated by sentence (107–109), in addition to a straightforward future this form is also used to express generic facts.²² With negatives, རེད་ ree is replaced by མ་རེད་ ^maree, in polar questions it becomes རེད་པས་ ^rebää and in nonpolar questions རེད་ rää. The form *^mapeegi ree does not exist.²³

Next, when the གི་ gi infinitive is followed by ཡོད་ yöö, this forms a predicate that expresses a habitual, repetitive, or sustained action on the part of the speaker (or in a question, on the part of the interlocutor) at a certain point in time.

(110) ང་ད་ལྟ་དེབ་སློག་གི་ཡོད།
ˋŋa ˈtanda   ^teb   ⁻loogi   yöö.
me   now   book   read.INF is
'I am reading a book at the moment.'

(111) ཁོང་ཕེབས་དུས་ང་དེབ་སློག་གི་ཡོད།
⁻koŋ   ˋpee-düü   ˋŋa   ^teb   ⁻loogi   yöö.
he/she come-time   me   book   read.INF is
'When he came, I was reading.'

(112) ཁྱེད་རང་གིས་ག་རེ་གནང་གི་ཡོད།
⁻keraŋ-gi   ˈkare   ⁻naŋgi   yöö?
you-ERG   what?   do(hon.).INF is
'What are you doing?' (honorific)

---

22 Note that in Japanese 6時におきる is used to say both 'I get up at 6' and 'I will get up at 6' although the former denotes a genetic action and the latter denotes a future action.

The attentive reader may wonder how (94) and (108) differ when they both refer to habitual actions. According to the informants, for (94) it is likely that the speaker somehow got to know this fact in the past and states that the man reads a lot as a present continuation of this action. Conversely, in (108), the speaker avoids the question of whether she confronted this fact in the past by describing the action as an incomplete and certain event. Therefore, the speaker makes the latter statement with a certain degree of conviction and a nuance of deep interest.

23 As discussed in Note 17 it is possible to say ཁ་ལག་བཟོས་པ་མ་རེད་ ⁻kääsa ⁻koŋ ˋpee-ba ^maree, but it is not possible to say *⁻kääsa ⁻koŋ ⁻peegi ^maree. The གི་ gi infinitive + རེད་ ree categorically expresses a definite action that is not complete and is within the scope of a given time if a time marker is present or for an unrestricted period of time if a time marker is not present. Then, it expresses such a habit when it denotes an action within a period of time that is effectively unrestricted such as ཉིན་ལྟར་རེ་བཞིན་ ˋŋindaareši 'every day'. Conversely, when the བ་ ba infinitive + རེད་ ree denotes a habit, it captures an action as a continuation of a past action and thus expresses a more temporary and unstable habit allowing an action to be expressed as if it were a part of a habit, even if it occurred on a certain day. Accordingly, the use of the གི་ gi infinitive + རེད་ ree gives a sense that the speaker is more interested in that habit and has more conviction.

(113) དལྟ་ཁ་ལག་ཟ་གི་ཡོད།
     'tanda   `kalaa   'sagi   yöö.
     now   food   eat.INF is
     '(I am) eating now.'

(114) ཉིན་ལྟར་སློབ་གྲྭ་འགྲོ་གི་ཡོད།
     ŋindaa   ˉlabṭaa   'ḍogi   yöö.
     every.day school   go.INF   is
     '(I) go to school every day.'

(115) ད་ནིང་གི་དབྱར་ཀ་ཉིན་ལྟར་རེ་བཞིན་རྒྱལ་རྒྱབ་ཀྱི་ཡོད།
     'daŋiŋ-gi   ˉyaaga   'ŋindaareši   ˉǧää   'ǧaagi   yöö.
     last.year-GEN summer   everyday   swim   swim.INF is
     'I swam day in and day out last summer' or 'I was swimming every day last summer.'

In negative cases, ཡོད་ yöö is replaced by མེད་ mää.

Next, affixing ཡོད་རེད་ 'yoo-ree to the གི་ gi- infinitive results in a predicate that expresses a habitual, repetitive, or sustained action at a certain point in time that is *not* understood directly from one's own senses.

(116) སློབ་སྦྱོང་བྱེད་ཀྱི་ཡོད་རེད་པས།
     `lobčuŋ   'čegi   'yooˆrebää?
     studying   do.INF   is.Q
     'I guess he is studying, right?'

(117) ཁོང་ད་ལྟ་སློབ་སྦྱོང་བྱེད་ཀྱི་ཡོད་རེད།
     ˉkoŋ   'tanda   `lobžoŋ   ˊčcgi   ˊyoo-ree.
     he/she now   studying   do.INF is
     'He is studying now.'

(118) ཁྱེད་རང་ཡོང་དུས་ཕྲུག་གུ་འདི་སློབ་གྲྭ་འགྲོ་གི་ཡོད་རེད།
     ˉkeraŋ   `peetüü   ˉbugu   'di   ˉlabṭaa   'ḍogi   'yoo-ree.
     you   come.time child   this school   go.INF   is
     'This child will be at school when you come here.'

This construction is also used to describe the speaker's own action as an objective fact:

(119) དེ་དུས་ང་ཡང་ཀ་བྱེད་ཀྱི་ཡོད་རེད།
     ˆtetüü   'ŋa   'yaŋ   'lääga   'čegi   'yoo-ree.
     that.time me   also   work   do.INF   is
     'I will be working at that time.'

Affixing འདུག་ duu to the གི་ gi- infinitive results in a predicate that expresses a given action at a certain point in time that has been understood directly from one's own senses. However, in a case where the གྱི་ *gi* infinitive is affixed with the affirmative འདུག་ *duu*, the form *-gii* (still written གྱི་ etc.) is used instead.

(120) ཁོང་དུ་གི
    ⁻*koŋ*   ^*ŋugii*.
    he/she   cry.INF
    'He is weeping.'

(121) ཁོང་གིས་ད་ལྟ་ཞལ་ལག་མཆོད་གྱི
    ⁻*koŋ-gi*   '*tanda*   ^*šälaa*   ˋ*čöögii*.
    he/she-ERG   now   food   eat(hon.).INF.is
    'He is eating now.' (honorific)

(122) མི་ཕ་གི་ག་རེ་ཟེར་གྱི་འདུག
    '*mi*   ˋ*pagii*   '*kare*   '*segi*   *doo*?
    person   yonder   what?   say.INF   is.Q
    'What is that person saying?'

This construction can also be used with the first person as shown below:

(123) ངས་ཡག་པོ་ཟ་གི
    ^*ŋää*   '*yago*   ^*sagii*.
    me.ERG   well   eat.INF.is
    'I eat a lot.'

(124) ང་མགོ་ན་གི
    '*ŋa*   '*go*   ^*nagii*.
    me   head   ill.INF.is
    'I have a headache.'

Sentence (123) produces the sense that the speaker is viewing her own behavior from the outside, whereas (124) is used when the speaker perceives (through the senses) the occurrence of an event that is beyond her control.

Although the རྒྱུ་ *ğu* infinitive is often used as a verbal noun denoting the target of a verb, apart from this, its use in predicates is relatively uncommon. It is used in the following three situations, viz. with ཡིན་ *-yin*, རེད་ *-ree*, and མ་བྱུང་ ´*mačuŋ*.

When ཡིན་ *yin* affixes to the རྒྱུ་ *ğu* infinitive, created from the imperfect stem plus རྒྱུ་ *ğu* (e.g. ཟ་ ´*sa* → ཟ་རྒྱུ་ ´*sağu*, འགྲོ་ ´*do* → འགྲོ་རྒྱུ་ ´*doğu*), this form expresses the speaker's intention to perform an action in future the that she has not yet initiated.

(125) ངའི་གི་དེ་འབྲི་རྒྱུ་ཡིན
    ´*ŋa*   ´*yige*   ´*te*   ´*ṭiğu*   *yin*.
    me   letter   that   write.INF   is
    'I have still to write that letter.'

(126) ཁ་ལག་ཟ་རྒྱུ་ཡིན།
   'ŋa   `kalaa   'saǧu   yin.
   me   food   eat.INF is
   'I am still to eat.'

When རེད་ *ree* follows the རྒྱུ་ *ǧu* infinitive, it is often used to refer to the planned actions of the second or third person.[24]

(127) ཁོང་ཕེབས་རྒྱུ་རེད།
   ⁻koŋ   ⁻peeǧu   ree.
   he/she   arrive.INF is
   'He is still to arrive.'

There is no negative or interrogative equivalent of རྒྱུ་ཡིན་ *ǧu-yin* or རྒྱུ་རེད་ *ǧu-ree*.[25]

Next, when མ་བྱུང་ *mačuŋ* affixes to the རྒྱུ་ *ǧu* infinitive, this forms a frequently used predicate that expresses a past action that the speaker did not take because of an external agency.

(128) ཁ་སང་ཇ་ཉོ་རྒྱུ་མ་བྱུང་།
   ⁻kääsa   ´ča   ´ñoǧu   ´mačuŋ.
   yesterday tea   buy.INF   NEG.is
   'I did not get to buy tea yesterday.'

(129) ཁ་སང་ཟ་རྒྱུ་མ་བྱུང་།
   ⁻kääsa   'saǧu   'mačuŋ
   yesterday eat.INF   NEG.is
   'I did not get to eat yesterday.'[26]

However, when we look at ཟ་རྒྱུ་བྱུང་ *saǧu čuŋ*, we find that this is not the affirmative equivalent of ཟ་རྒྱུ་མ་བྱུང་ ´*saǧu´mačuŋ* but takes the meaning that the speaker was able to acquire something to eat (ཟ་རྒྱུ ´*saǧu*).

---

[24] Note that the རྒྱུ་ *ǧu* infinitive has a completely different meaning when it occurs with རེད་ *ree*, as in འགྲོ་རྒྱུ་རེད་ *'doǧu ree* 'no choice but to go,' 'have to go', or འགྲོ་རྒྱུ་མ་རེད་ *'doǧu ^mare* 'must not go'. Etymologically speaking, རྒྱུ་ *ǧu* originally denoted the nominal form or target of a verb. Therefore, this usage of རྒྱུ་ *ǧu* has diverged to form two different meanings in modern Tibetan. Because a semantic category exclusively shared by both uses of རྒྱུ་ *ǧu* cannot be presumed, this pair constitutes pure homonyms at the synchronic level.

[25] Apparently, a child may be corrected for producing a sentence such as ཟ་རྒྱུ་མིན་ *'saǧu män*.

[26] The difference between this form and མ་བཟས་ ^*masää* observed in section 4 is that མ་བཟས་ ^*masää* implies that the speaker did not eat of her own will, whereas the རྒྱུ་ *ǧu* infinitive + མ་བྱུང་ *'mačuŋ* implies that circumstances did not allow the speaker to eat.

The ཀྱིས་ *zii* infinitive, formed by affixing ཀྱིས་ *zii* to the imperfect stem (e.g. ཟ་ ˊ*sa* → ཟ་ཀྱིས་ ˆ*sazii*, འགྲོ་ ˊ*ḍo* → འགྲོ་ཀྱིས་ ˆ*ḍozii*) may be affixed with ཡོད་ *yöö*, ཡོད་རེད་ ˊ*yoo-ree*, or འདུག་ *duu*. Affixing ཡོད་ *yöö* forms a predicate that expresses familiarity with respect to the intention of the action.

(130) དབེ་ཕྲུག་གིས་སློབ་སྦྱོང་བྱེད་ཀྱིས་ཡོད།
 ˊ*ŋää*   ⁻*bugu*   ˋ*lobžoŋ*   ˆ*čezii*   *yöö*.
 me.ERG child   study   do.INF   is
 'My child will study (intention).'

Affixing ཡོད་རེད་ ˊ*yoo-ree* expresses the objective existence of an intention, whereas affixing འདུག་ *duu* implies that such a plan is understood directly from one's own senses. The fact that the ཀྱིས་ *zii* infinitive is not treated the same way as normal nouns can be understood from a comparison of the following two sentences.

(131) ང་རྒྱ་ནག་ལ་འགྲོ་ཀྱིས་ཡོད།
 ˊ*ŋa*   ˆ*ğanaa-la*   ˆ*ḍozii*   *yöö*.
 me   China-DAT   go.INF   is
 'I plan to go to China'

(132) ངར་དེབ་ཅིག་ཡོད།
 ˊ*ŋaa*   ˆ*teb*   *žig*   *yöö*.
 me.DAT book   a   is
 'There is one book for me.'

First, there is the difference between ང་ ˊ*ŋa* 'I' and ངར་ ˊ*ŋaa* 'for me'. Second, if འགྲོ་ཀྱིས་ ˆ*ḍozii* were a noun, then the phrase རྒྱ་ནག་ལ་འགྲོ་ཀྱིས་ ˆ*ğanaa la ḍozii* should be impossible.

The འདོད་ *döö* infinitive, which can be created by affixing འདོད་ (n)*döö* to the imperfect stem (e.g. ཟ་ ˊ*sa* → ཟ་འདོད་ ˆ*sandöö*, འགྲོ་ ˊ*ḍo* → འགྲོ་འདོད་ ˆ*ḍondöö*), may also take ཡོད་ *yöö*, ཡོད་རེད་ ˊ*yoo-ree*, and འདུག་ *duu* and expresses the hopeful desire (to do something). Their respective semantic differences are the same as those in the case of the ཀྱིས་ *zii* infinitive. However, there are two ways for the speaker herself to express desire:

(133) ང་བོད་ལ་འགྲོ་འདོད་ཡོད།
 ˊ*ŋa*   ˆ*pöö-la*   ˆ*ḍondöö*   *yöö*.
 me   Tibet-DAT go.INF   is
 'I want to go to Tibet.'

(134) ང་བོད་ལ་འགྲོ་འདོད་འདུག
 ˊ*ŋa*   ˆ*pöö-la*   ˆ*ḍondöö*   *duu*.
 me   Tibet-DAT go.INF   is
 'I want to go to Tibet.'

The former expresses a somewhat rational desire, whereas the latter expresses a kind of inner desire 'that springs from the heart.'

7.9 Other predicates

There are various forms for giving orders or asking favors. Often used, as expressions for ཟ་ ´sa, for instance, are the rather rough imperative ཟོས་ ˆsöö ('Eat!') (with མ་ཟོས་ ´masöö for the negative imperative 'Don't eat!'), the rather softer imperative ཟོས་ཤིག ˆsöö ši and the polite request form རོགས་གནང་ -roo naŋ, which is suffixed to the honorific form of verbs that have such or the imperfect stem of verbs that do not.

(135) མཆོད་རོགས་གནང༌།
     `čööroo   naŋ.
     partake.INF   do
     'Please partake' (e.g., of a meal)

(136) ཀློག་རོགས་གནང༌།
     `looroo   naŋ.
     read.INF   do
     'Please read.'[27]

For the sense of 'please don't ...' there are two options:

(137) མ་མཆོད་རོགས་གནང༌།
     `mačöö-roo   naŋ.
     NEG.partake-INF   do
     'Please do not partake.'

(138) ཀློག་མ་གནང་རོགས་གནང༌།
     `loo   ¯manaŋ-roo   naŋ.
     read   NEG.do-INF   do
     'Please do not read.'

Generally in this construction, if a verb is to be negated with མ་ ma, in order to make the usage honorific the verb is accompanied by the suffix གནང་ ¯naŋ, with མ་ ma prefixed to གནང་ ¯naŋ. This particular case is odd in so far as, although one

---

[27] The verb མཆོད་ `čöö 'partake' is the honorific equivalent of 'eat'; ཀློག་ `loo 'read' has no honorific form and when necessary may be affixed with གནང་ ¯naŋ (the honorable form of a verb meaning 'to do') to form ཀློག་གནང་ `loo ¯naŋ 'do please read'.

does not say *`loo ⁻naŋ-roo naŋ`, the second གནང་ ⁻naŋ does appear in the negative version.

Although there are various other predicate constructions, we will not touch on these here.

7.10 Some features of Tibetan predicates

The features of Tibetan predicates, in a word, are complicated.

For example, ཡིན *yin* affixes to nouns or adjectives to express a situation that feels familiar to the speaker (or in the case of a question, to the interlocutor). When affixed to the པ་ *-ba* or གྱི་ *-gi* infinitive, it expresses only the actions of the speaker. While we cannot completely rule out the possibility of explaining why this is so from the difference between a static state and the inherent dynamism that accompanies this difference, grammatically speaking, it may be best to consider these two instances of ཡིན *yin* as separate entities. In other words, it would seem better not to think of the latter ཡིན *yin* as a separate auxiliary verb but rather that the entire construction linked with the infinitive should constitute a variant (i.e., inflection category) of each verb.

Next, the structure of predicates that give affirmative, negative, or interrogative expression to certain actions do not necessarily correspond clearly with one another.

a) འགྲོ་གི་ཡིན།
 ´ḍogi yin. '(I) will go.'
 འགྲོ་གི་པས།
 ´ḍogi bää? 'Will you go?'
 ག་པར་འགྲོ་ག
 ´kabaa ´ḍo gaa. 'Where will you go?'

b) ཕྱིན་པ་ཡིན།
 ´čin-ba yin. '(I) went.'
 མ་ཕྱིན།
 ´mačin. '(I) did not go.'
 འགྲོ་རྒྱུ་མ་བྱུང་།
 ´ḍoğu ´mačuŋ. "

c) ཕྱིན་པ་རེད།
 ´čin-ba ree. '(He) went.'
 མ་ཕྱིན་པ་རེད།
 ´mačin-ba ree. '(He) did not go.'
 ཕྱིན་པ་མ་རེད།
 ´čin-ba ˆmaree. "

Here, the examples in a) lack any clear correspondence between the affirmative and interrogative uses, whereas those in b) lack a clear correspondence between the affirmative and negative usages. Finally, comparing b) and c), we find that though there are two types of negatives for the actions of a speaker and a third party, their respective structures are completely inconsistent.

7.11 Concluding remarks

Finally, let us consider what overall we may learn from the semantics of Tibetan predicates.

First, while researching Tibetan predicates, I have sensed the diversity of ways in which we organize real world phenomena and our own thoughts through a language. Not one of the aforementioned expressions includes a range of meaning that corresponds to those of English or Japanese. Such a situation is logically inevitable; nonetheless, when we actually engage in this type of research, its extent is revealed beyond our expectations.

Furthermore, only research on the structure and meaning of predicates has allowed us to clearly recognize that the semantic unities that give meaning to the concepts of internal linguistic factors are not purely objective; to varying degrees they also include subjective factors. It is also clear that the Tibetan language offers a rich variety of expressions that are governed by these subjective factors. In other words, when researching the meaning of these linguistic units, it is important to objectively identify what types of subjective elements express various events and, both objectively and subjectively, clarify the qualities upon which the concept of a semantic unit is grounded.

The second aspect that I have learned from Tibetan predicates is that when researching the meaning of a certain linguistic unit, it is generally not possible to reach an accurate conclusion about it without focusing on the unit itself. That is, it is not possible to accurately describe the meaning of that linguistic unit by inferring it from the meaning of another linguistic unit. For example, when the speaker refers to her own past action 'I ate,' she uses བཟས་པ་ཡིན་ ^*sää-ba yin* (བཟས་པ་ མིན་ ^*sää-ba män* cannot be used here), whereas the negation of the speaker's past action can be expressed by the two forms མ་བཟས་ ^*masää* and ཟ་རྒྱུ་མཆུང་ *'saǧu 'mačuŋ*, which have different meanings. Incidentally, this clearly shows that certain divisions exist in some cases, but not in others. In other words, the meanings of linguistic units correspond conceptually to individual semantic unities, thereby showing that individual research must be conducted for each one. Indeed, I do not propose that research on the meaning of other linguistic units is not useful as a reference. In fact, it goes without saying that the results of describing the meanings of ཡོད་ yöö, མེད་ mää, etc. in nominal and adjectival predicates was extremely helpful when looking into the meaning of their verbal counterparts. However, it is important to avoid superficial analogies by clearly recognizing that there is no reason why a difference in the meaning between two linguistic forms must also exist in other situations. In addition, it is theoretically invalid for a certain quality included in a semantic unit corresponding to a certain linguistic unit to also exist in an identical form in a semantic unit corresponding to a different linguistic unit.

April 27, 1975

References

Yukawa Yasutoshi 湯川恭敏. 1971. "チベット語の述部の輪郭 Chibettogo no jutsubu no rinkaku [Outline of Tibetan Predicates]" 言語学の基本問題 *Gengogaku no kihon mondai / Basic problems in linguistics*, 178–204. Tokyo: 大修館書店 Taishūkan Shoten.

Yukawa Yasutoshi 湯川恭敏. 1975. チベット語の述語 Chibettogo no jutsugo [The Predicates of Tibetan] アジア・アフリカ文法研究 *Ajia Afurika bunpō kenkyū / Asian & African Linguistics* 4: 1–14.

Nancy J. Caplow
8 Inference and deferred evidence in Tibetan

8.1 Introduction

The Tibetan system of epistemics and evidentials is among the most rich and complex observed in the languages of the world. For Diasporic Common Tibetan, the system is comprised of at least twenty distinct markers, which fall into eight categories. All markers within the system are epistemics, expressing degree of certainty, while some are also evidentials, expressing source of information. The primary epistemic opposition is between the categories of certainty and non-certainty, while the primary evidential opposition is between direct evidence and indirect evidence.

The CURRENT PERCEPTION marker *dųk* ('*dug*), in the present perfect construction, indexes deferred evidence. It tells the listener that he can be certain about the content of the proposition, and that the speaker has verified a past action or event through perception of present traces. Inference is a secondary, entailed reading. If the speaker wishes to explicitly index the mental process of drawing an inference, she can choose from among a set of markers of non-certainty, which also indicate the basis of inference. This contrast between deferred evidence and inference is also observed in Lhasa. By considering the overlapping and cross-cutting relationships of the epistemic-evidential system as a whole, the morpheme *bzhag* is re-analyzed as a unique, dedicated marker of DEFERRED PERCEPTION, rather than a marker of inference.

The variety of Tibetan described here can be referred to as Diasporic Common Tibetan (DCT). It is typical of the language that might be encountered in Dharamsala, Kathmandu, or other émigré Tibetan communities. 'Common Tibetan' comes from the literal translation of *spyi skad* 'common language'. The modifier 'diasporic' distinguishes the variety spoken in Nepal, India, and more far-flung communities from that spoken in Central Tibet. 'Diasporic Common Tibetan' also

---

Note: I am grateful to Karma Dönden Lama for the patience, insight, careful explanations, and good cheer he brought to our discussions of the Tibetan language. Carol Genetti, Alexandra Aikhenvald, Edward Garrett, and B. Alan Wallace offered comments on a much earlier paper from which much of this material was drawn (Caplow 2000). The current chapter was greatly improved by thoughtful input from Willem de Reuse, Nicolas Tournadre, Nathan W. Hill, Lauren Gawne, and an anonymous reviewer. I would also like to thank Tsering Gonkatsang of the University of Oxford for helpful discussion during the 14th IATS seminar in June 2016. I incorporated many – but not all – of the suggestions offered to me, so any inaccuracies that may remain are due to my own misinterpretation.

distinguishes this dialect from other potential diasporic varieties that linguists might wish to describe (e.g., 'diasporic Amdo Tibetan').

Some scholars (e.g., Tournadre and Dorje 2003, Vokurková 2008) use the terms 'Standard Tibetan' or 'Spoken Standard Tibetan' for *spyi skad*, but I prefer the word 'common', as it cannot be said that a 'standard' form of Tibetan exists. Nonetheless, we are all referring to the same variety of the language. Tournadre and Dorje describe Standard Tibetan as a variety of Central Tibetan (*dbus.skad*) which has arisen as a *lingua franca* in and around Lhasa. It must be distinguished from 'Lhasa Tibetan', which more narrowly characterizes the dialect spoken in Lhasa city proper, with its own particular grammatical features (2003: 25/26). Vokurková further explains that – given its historic political, economic, and cultural significance – the city of Lhasa has always attracted speakers of Amdo, Kham, and other varieties of Tibetan. Thus, *spyi skad*, as spoken in and around Lhasa, has incorporated phonological, lexical, and grammatical features from diverse sources. In modern-day diasporic communities, speakers from different regions of the Tibetan language area comprise a larger percentage of the population than they do in Lhasa, and have thus had a concomitantly greater influence on *spyi skad*. This influence accounts for differences between 'Standard Tibetan' spoken in Central Tibet, and 'Standard Tibetan' spoken in the diaspora (2008: 11, 80/81). These differences include specific lexical items and grammatical structures. What I call 'Diasporic Common Tibetan' is thus equivalent to what Vokurková would call 'Standard Tibetan as spoken in the diaspora'.[1]

Like other varieties of modern spoken Tibetan, an integral component of the grammar of DCT is its rich and intricate system of obligatory main-clause-final epistemic-evidential linking verbs and auxiliaries. These markers are densely packed with syntactic, semantic, and pragmatic information. They index tense, aspect, volitionality, and "person", and provide information to the listener regarding the speaker's source of knowledge, degree of certainty (whether or not the proposition has been verified by some source of evidence), and degree of "engagement" (whether the speaker chooses to present an intimate or remote view of the action, event, or state presented in the clause).

In this chapter I contrast two semantic-pragmatic categories of the epistemic-evidential system of DCT: deferred evidence, and inference. In previous research on other varieties of Tibetan, these two categories have not been clearly distinguished or described. The difference between them is highlighted here, as they are considered within the larger framework of the epistemic-evidential system as a whole. These findings are then extended to Lhasa/Spoken Standard Tibetan

---

[1] According to Vokurková (2008: 80), there are approximately one and a half million speakers of 'Spoken Standard Tibetan', or *spyi skad;* about 130,000 of them live in the diaspora.

(Lhasa/SST),[2] where I re-analyze the morpheme *bzhag* as a marker of DEFERRED PERCEPTION rather than inference.

Background information is provided in Section 8.2 below. An overview and schematic representation of the complete system of DCT epistemic-evidential markers is presented in Section 8.3. Markers of perception are discussed in Section 8.4, followed by a discussion of markers of inference in Section 8.5. The distinction between deferred perception and inference in Lhasa/SST is discussed in Section 8.6. A summary and conclusions are offered in Section 8.7.

8.2 Background

In Section 8.2.1 below I provide background information on the variety of Tibetan described here, and explain the transcription and transliteration conventions used. A brief overview of the syntactic functions of Tibetan epistemics and evidentials is provided Section 8.2.2, followed by definitions of key terms in Section 8.2.3.

8.2.1 Data

This study is based on narrative and elicitation data collected during a 1998–1999 linguistics field methods class at the University of California Santa Barbara, supplemented during the following year by further elicitation and discussion. My language consultant, Karma, was born in 1975, and was in his mid-20s at the time I worked with him. His parents were born in the Mount Kailash area of southwestern Tibet, but in 1959 or 1960 emigrated to northwestern Nepal, where Karma was born. They settled with other members of their family in a Tibetan community not far from Simikot. When Karma was five or six years old his family moved to Kathmandu, settling in the Tibetan community around Boudhanath. He attended several Tibetan boarding schools in Nepal and India. He studied Written Tibetan and English in school, but outside of school used DCT, Nepali, and Hindi for day-to-day communication. He speaks English fluently, though at the time I worked with him he did not have native-speaker proficiency in some structures and categories. He was then a student at Santa Barbara City College, in Santa Barbara, California.

---

[2] The term 'Lhasa Tibetan' has been used rather loosely by some scholars to refer to language data from Lhasa City, the broader Central Tibetan area, and/or the diasporic community (Hill 2013b: note 2, following Miller 1955 and Róna-Tas 1985: 160/161). Rather than attempt to distinguish these varieties here, I instead conflate them under the term 'Lhasa/SST'.

Karma identifies his family origin and his native language as *'brog.pa,* which refers to a community whose livelihood is based on nomadic pastoralism and animal breeding. In terms of linguistic classification, though, the variety of Tibetan Karma speaks is best identified not as the *'brog.pa* dialect but as a diasporic variety of Common Tibetan, which is a reflection of the speech communities in which he grew up. The strongest evidence for this classification is the set of epistemic and evidential markers he uses. These are very different from those described for the Drokpas of southwest Tibet by Kretschmar (1986), and are quite similar in both form and function to those in use by speakers of central Tibetan varieties – referred to by previous researchers as Lhasa or Spoken Standard Tibetan (Lhasa/SST) (Tournadre and Dorje 1998, 2003; Tournadre 2014) – and in other diasporic communities (Vokurková 2008).

Differences between Diasporic Common Tibetan and Lhasa/SST occur in specific lexical items, in the morphosyntax of past tense constructions with *[pa] yin* and *[pa] red,* and also in the form and function of some of the epistemic-evidential markers, which are discussed below.[3] Karma was conscious of these differences, and pointed them out to me.

Examples are presented here in the IPA, except that I use [y] rather than [j] for the voiced palatal glide, and [ö] rather than [ø] for the front rounded vowel. The transcription is roughly phonemic, though some phonetic distinctions have been preserved. In monosyllabic words, the vowel is marked for high tone (e.g., [ā]) or low tone (e.g., [a̱]). In disyllabic words the second syllable (σ_2) usually has neutral tone, so I leave the vowel unmarked; if σ_1 is high then σ_2 is low by comparison, and if σ_1 is low then σ_2 is high by comparison. Syllables with an initial tense, or slightly glottalized, consonant (marked with an apostrophe, C') or a final glottal stop (ʔ) have falling tone. For some words tone was not transcribed during elicitation and so has not been indicated; it is not immediately relevant to the focus of this study. Suffixes (-) and clitics (=) are also generally not marked for tone.

For Written Tibetan, I generally follow the Extended Wylie Transliteration Scheme developed by the University of Virginia's Tibetan and Himalayan Library (www.thlib.org), based on Wylie (1957), except that I prefer to use a period "." rather than a blank space to represent boundaries between syllables. This leaves the blank space available to mark word boundaries.

8.2.2 Syntactic functions of the epistemics

In independent or main clauses, epistemic markers in Tibetan simultaneously serve both semantic-pragmatic and syntactic functions. The semantic-pragmatic function is the epistemic or evidential meaning.

---

[3] Vokurková (2008: 80/81) also notes these distinctions.

Syntactically, when an epistemic occurs with a lexical verb predicate, it functions as an auxiliary verb, which I gloss as AUX. Together with the form of the verb stem⁴ and its aspect suffix, the epistemic contributes to indexing tense and aspect. When an epistemic occurs with other predicate types, it functions as a linking verb. Following Payne (1997: 114), I consider a linking verb which occurs with predicate nominals to be a copula (COP). A linking verb which occurs with existential, locative, possessive, and attributive predicates is not, per Payne's narrow definition, a copula. In these cases I gloss the linking verb as ELPA (for existential-locative-possessive-attributive). Scholars of other varieties of Tibetan have used terms such as "equative auxiliary verb" and "existential auxiliary verb" (e.g., Bielmeier 2000), "équatif" and "existentiel" (e.g., Tournadre 1996a), or "essential copula" and "existential copula" (e.g. Tournadre and Dorje 2003); Garrett (2001) adopted the terms COP and ELPA following Caplow (2000).

Epistemics are glossed here to reflect and distinguish their dual semantic-pragmatic and syntactic functions. For instance, in (1), with a predicate nominal, I gloss *yin* as CPK;COP,⁵ and in (2), with a lexical verb predicate expressing volitionality and future tense, I gloss the same marker as CPK;AUX.

(1) ང་སློབ་ཕྲུག་ཡིན།
    ŋa̱   lōbṭuk   y*i*n
    1.SG   student   **CPK;COP**
    'I am a student.'
    (*copular function*; V/50)⁶

(2) ང་མོ་ཊ་གསར་པ་ཉོ་གི་ཡིན།
    ŋa̱   mo̱ta   sārpa   nyṳ̄-gi   y*i*n
    1.SG   car   new   buy-IPFV **CPK;AUX**
    'I'm going to buy a new car.'
    (*auxiliary verb function*; V/33)

---

4 For many verbs, Old and Classical Tibetan distinguished four verb stem forms: past, present, future, and imperative. In modern spoken varieties of the language – including Diasporic Common Tibetan – these distinctions have merged to a greater or lesser degree. Some verbs are invariable, others may have two or three stem forms, and some retain the four-way distinction.
5 See the table of abbreviations at the end of this chapter.
6 "V/50" identifies field notebook and page number. Examples from narratives collected by me or by my classmates in the field methods course are identified with the narrative title and a number referring to the intonation unit, clause, or sentence. Some examples are identified only by the date of elicitation or discussion.

8.2.3 Definitions: Evidentials and epistemics

The definitions I use for the terms "evidential" and "epistemic" are generally consistent with those found in the typological literature and in characterizations of other varieties of Tibetan. I regard evidentials as grammaticized markers which encode source of information, and epistemics as grammaticized markers which encode degree of certainty.

I adopt a listener-oriented perspective in interpreting the semantic-pragmatic information provided by these markers. That is, evidentials can be regarded as answering the question: "How do *you* know?" The answer might be: "Because I saw it for myself", or "Because it happened to me personally", or "Well, everyone knows that", or "So-and-so told me." Likewise, epistemics can be regarded as answering the question: "Can I really take your word for it?" And the answer might be a definitive "Yes, it's been verified", or a more reserved "Well, it's true as far as I know, but it hasn't been confirmed". Thus when I refer to 'degree of certainty', I do not mean how certain the speaker is in her own mind that the claim she is making is true. Rather, I mean how certain the speaker is advising the listener *he* can be about whether her statement is accurate, or valid, or true.

There can be considerable semantic overlap in these categories, and epistemic and evidential information is often fused in a single form. In the rich paradigmatic system of Diasporic Common Tibetan, all of the markers can be called epistemics, since they encode epistemicity.[7] Some of these markers can also be called evidentials, since they encode evidentiality. A handful are ambiguous in terms of their evidential status: sometimes they indicate that some unspecified source of information exists, and sometimes they express only certainty or non-certainty, with no evidential meaning.

Markers of inference are a focus of this chapter. I demonstrate that there is a distinction between inference based on results vs. inference based on reasoning. Both can be evidentials, but in Diasporic Common Tibetan the former is expressed by a secondary interpretation of a marker of certainty, while the latter is expressed by a set of markers of non-certainty. This contrast is even more explicit in Lhasa/Spoken Standard Tibetan (Lhasa/SST), which has a unique form, *bzhag*, to express inference based on results.

---

[7] I regard 'degree of certainty' as spanning the full continuum, from certain to speculative. This differs from some interpretations (despite similar terminology), where epistemics are apparently considered to encode only degree of non-certainty – that is, distinctions between possibility, probability, inference, guessing, and the like.

8.3 An overview of epistemics and evidentials in Diasporic Common Tibetan (DCT)

The complete system of epistemics and evidentials in DCT is presented in Fig. 1. This schematic framework highlights the distinctions and the overlaps of semantic-pragmatic categories. The focus of this chapter is the cross-cutting relationship between the *perceptual* epistemics in Ellipse (a), and the markers of *inference* in Box 6. Crucially, *dųk* (Written Tibetan *'dug*) – which functions in DCT as a marker of CURRENT PERCEPTION – is a marker of certainty, falling within Box 2. In contrast, the markers of inference express non-certainty, and fall within Box 3. Note that the Lhasa/SST form *bzhag* (in square brackets) occupies the same space as *dųk*. *bzhag* has been described by previous researchers as a marker of inference, but by extension of the present analysis, I argue that it is best analyzed as a marker of DEFERRED PERCEPTION.

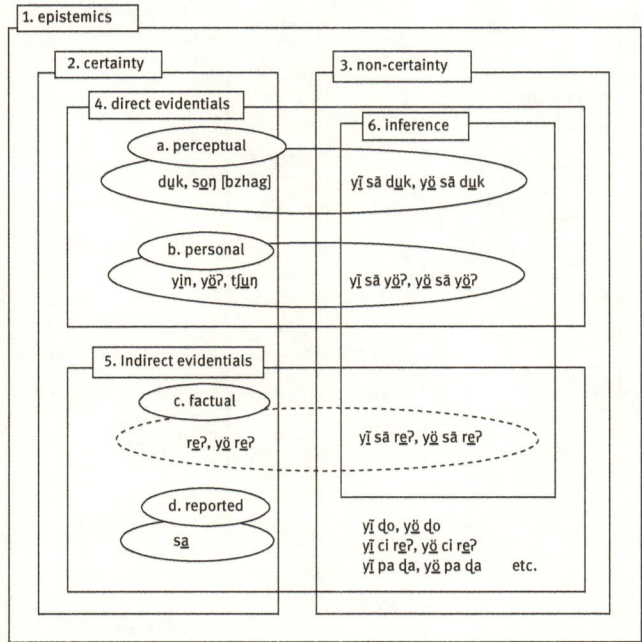

Fig. 1: Epistemics and evidentials in Diasporic Common Tibetan.[8]

---

8 *bzhag* is included here to show its position within the epistemic-evidential system as a whole, but it is in square brackets because it is used in Lhasa/SST, but not in DCT.

As shown, the complete DCT system includes twenty unique evidential markers; these are morphologically, semantically, and syntactically distinct, and are in paradigmatic relationship. They fall into eight categories, or terms:[9] perceptual, personal, factual/unspecified, reported, inference based on perceptual evidence, inference based on personal knowledge, inference based on fact/unspecified evidence, and non-evidential markers of conjecture. Glosses for the individual markers are provided in Tab. 1 below. Their semantic-pragmatic function and syntactic distribution are discussed in detail in Caplow 2000.

Tab. 1: Meaning of DCT's epistemic-evidential markers.

	1.1.1 Markers of certainty/verified			1.1.2 Markers of non-certainty/unverified		
	Form	**Abbr**	**Gloss**	**Form**	**Abbr**	**Gloss**
Direct evidentials	dụk	CP	CURRENT PERCEPTION	yị̃ sā dụk	INFR.CP	INFERENCE BASED ON CURRENT PERCEPTION
	soŋ	PP	PAST PERCEPTION	yö̃ sā dụk		
	yö?	PK	PERSONAL KNOWLEDGE	yị̃ sā yö?	INFR.PK	INFERENCE BASED ON PERSONAL KNOWLEDGE
	yịn	CPK	CONSCIOUS PERSONAL KNOWLEDGE	yö̃ sā yö?		
	tʃuŋ	HM	"HAPPENED TO ME"			
Indirect evidentials	rẹ?	SF	SIMPLE FACT	yị̃ sā rẹ?	INFR.UE	INFERENCE BASED ON UNSPECIFIED EVIDENCE
	yö rẹ?	GS	GENERAL STATE	yö̃ sā rẹ?		
	sa̱	RPT	REPORTED			
Non-evidentials				yị̃ ḍo	GES	"I GUESS"
				yö̃ ḍo		
				yị̃ ci rẹ?	THNK	"I THINK…"
				yö̃ ci rẹ?		
				yị̃ pa ḍa	SMS	"IT SEEMS THAT…"
				yö̃ pa ḍa		

---

[9] Aikhenvald (2004) regards systems of five or more terms to be large and uncommon among the world's languages. The Tibetan epistemic-evidential system is particularly rich and complex.

The outer-most box in Fig. 1, Box 1, is labeled *epistemics*. Every element in the entire system provides the listener with information regarding the truth-reliability of the propositional content – that is, whether it has been verified or not.

The primary distinction in this system is between the morphologically simple forms which express a high degree of certainty, and the set of lexicalized, structurally varied, morphologically complex forms which express inference, conjecture, probability, possibility, and the like. The markers of *certainty* (everything within Box 2) tell the listener that the propositional content has been verified. Markers of *non-certainty* (everything within Box 3) tell the listener that the propositional content has not been verified.

Box 4 is labeled *direct evidentials*. The markers within this box indicate that the speaker has first-hand knowledge to support her claim. This source of information may be perceptual or personal. Box 5 is labeled *indirect evidentials*. Forms within this box mean that the speaker's source of information is either widely known, or is something she was told by another person. A speaker can use an indirect evidential when she lacks first-hand knowledge, or when she chooses not to highlight it.

Box 6 is labeled *inference*. These morphologically complex forms tell the listener that the content of the proposition was determined via the cognitive process of inference, or deductive reasoning. Four of these markers indicate that the speaker's inference is based on perceptual or personal evidence; the other two tell the listener that the speaker's inference is based on something which is generally known, or that the speaker does not care to highlight her perceptual or personal evidence. As all of the markers of inference are within Box 3, they are markers of non-certainty, advising the listener that the content of the proposition has not been verified.

The ellipses in Fig. 1 reflect four categories of evidential marking: a. perceptual, b. personal, c. factual, and d. reported. The *perceptual* evidentials indicate that verification of the assertion derives from the speaker's own perceptual evidence (e.g., visual or internal). There are two perceptual evidentials of certainty (*du̱k* and *so̱ŋ*) and two perceptual evidentials of non-certainty (*yĩ̱ sā du̱k* and *yö sā duk*, which mark inference based on perception). The corresponding Written Tibetan (WT) spellings are *'dug, song, yin sa 'dug, and yod sa 'dug*.

The personal[10] evidentials assure the listener that he can take the speaker's word for it because she was a participant in or has 'insider' knowledge about the action, event, or state described. There are three morphologically simple personal evidential markers of certainty (*yi̱n, yö̱ʔ,* and *tʃu̱ŋ*; WT *yin, yod,* and *byung*) and two morphologically complex personal evidential markers of non-certainty

10 Some scholars use the term "egophoric".

(*yī̃ sā yö̃?* and *yö̃ sā yö̃?*, which mark inference based on personal knowledge; WT *yin sa yod* and *yod sa yod*).

The *factual* evidentials *rẽ?* and *yö̃ rẽ?* (WT *red* and *yo'o red, yog red* or *yod pa red*) are flexible in terms of their evidential status; the dashed line of the ellipse is intended to reflect this. On the one hand, they can indicate that evidence providing verification of the proposition exists, but this evidence will not be specified by the speaker. On the other hand, they can be used when no such source of information exists, in which case they function as epistemics, but not as evidentials.

There is only one *reported* evidential, *są* (WT *zer*), which apparently marks both reported speech and hearsay. In the data I have available, it functions as a marker of certainty, indicating that the proposition has been verified.

Finally, in the bottom right corner of the figure are the morphologically complex markers of non-certainty which are not markers of inference. Since they do not offer any evidential basis to support the speaker's conjecture, they are epistemics but not evidentials. My DCT data includes the two markers of guessing (*yī̃ ḍo* and *yö̃ ḍo*; WT *yin 'gro, yod 'gro*), the two markers meaning 'I think [that]...' (*yī̃ ci re?* and *yö̃ ci re?*; WT *yin kyi red, yod kyi red*), and the two markers meaning 'It seems [that]...' (*yī̃ pa ḍa, yö̃ pa ḍa*; WT *yin pa 'dra, yod pa 'dra*). Karma's translations 'I guess' and 'I think' should not be taken literally; there are lexical verbs that mean 'I guess' and 'I think' to express that. These forms can just as readily be translated as something like 'I suppose' or 'perhaps'. (They could be grouped as an eighth evidential term, indicating supposition).

Nearly all earlier work on Tibetic languages has focused on the morphologically simple forms, which are generally considered to comprise the complete set of evidentials. An exception is Vokurková (2008), which systematically investigates both morphologically simple and morphologically complex epistemics in Lhasa/SST. Though she categorizes these markers differently in several significant ways and draws different conclusions, her data is consistent with and supports the sets, subsets, and relationships I describe above.

Considering the simple and complex markers together provides perspective on the organization of the system as a whole, from which I conclude that it is primarily epistemic rather than evidential. That is, all of the markers encode epistemicity (certainty, verification), but not all of them consistently encode evidentiality (source of information or evidence). This poses a challenge to Aikhenvald's claim (2003, 2004) that evidential meaning is primary, and that epistemic readings arise only as a secondary semantic extension; in DCT, these meanings are concurrent, due to the intersection of the grammaticized expression of evidentiality and epistemicity.

Within the epistemic system, the set of evidential markers transects the domains of certainty and non-certainty. Furthermore, the set of inference markers transects the domains of 'direct' and 'indirect' evidentials, categories proposed by Willett (1988) and widely accepted as fundamental cross-linguistically. Willett strictly classifies markers of inference as indirect evidentials, which does not seem to be the case in Tibetan.

8.4 Perceptual markers of certainty in DCT

In Diasporic Common Tibetan, there are two perceptual evidentials which index certainty. These markers tell the listener that the speaker's claim has been verified by perceptual evidence. *dųk* (CP) expresses CURRENT PERCEPTION, and *sǫŋ* (PP) marks PAST PERCEPTION. When *dųk* is used with a past verb stem (when such a distinct form exists) or in a past tense context, it yields an interpretation of deferred evidence. Lhasa/SST has a third perceptual evidential, *bzhag*. As discussed in Section 6, *bzhag* serves as a unique, dedicated marker of DEFERRED PERCEPTION.

dųk (CP) essentially tells the listener 'you can believe what I'm telling you because I'm observing it right now'.[11] *sǫŋ* (PP) tells the listener 'you can believe what I'm telling you because I saw it happen'. In both cases, 'perception' most commonly refers to visual observation, but it can also refer to auditory observation (though not olfactory[12]) or to physical sensation or personal feelings. *dųk* and *sǫŋ* are most commonly used to describe the activities of others since the speaker does not usually observe herself.[13]

Syntactically, *dųk* functions as an ELPA linking verb (with existential, locative, possessive, or attributive predicates) and also as an auxiliary verb (with lexical verb predicates); it never functions as a copular linking verb, COP. *sǫŋ* functions only as an auxiliary verb.

The functions of *dųk* and *sǫŋ* are described in Sections 8.4.1 and 8.4.2 below.

---

[11] My gloss of *dųk* as CURRENT PERCEPTION suggests observation coinciding with the time of speech, but this is not strictly the case. *dųk* is also appropriate if the speaker has recently (say, within the past few hours) witnessed the state or event reported, and is relating this specific instance of observation to the hearer. This idea of specificity is consistent with what Goldstein and Narkyid (1984: xvi) have noted for Lhasa/SST.
[12] For Lhasa/SST, Tournadre (this volume) observes the use of *'dug* with olfactory evidence.
[13] Both *dųk* and *sǫŋ* can be used to describe the speaker's own actions to create a sense of remoteness from the event (Caplow 2000).

8.4.1 *du̱k* (CURRENT PERCEPTION; CP)

The function of *du̱k* is illustrated below: as an ELPA linking verb in Section 8.4.1.1; as an auxiliary in present imperfective sentences in 8.4.1.2; and as an auxiliary in present perfect sentences in 8.4.1.3, where it yields a semantic-pragmatic interpretation of deferred evidence.

8.4.1.1 *du̱k* as an ELPA linking verb

In the two sentences below, *du̱k* is used with an existential predicate. Example (3) is from a narrative Karma told about an encounter his father and uncle had with a leopard. The sentence in (4) would be an appropriate response to the question 'What is there to eat?', if bread were visibly available.

(3) དེ་ཁོང་གཉིས་ཀྱིས་ཨོ་ཏ་གཟིག་འདུག་ལབ་ནས།
te̱   kʰondzo   nyi=gi   "(w)o̱ta̱   si̱k   **du̱k**"   lap   =ne
then   3.PL   DU=ERG   wow   leopard   **CP;ELPA** say   =SUB
'Then the two of them said, "Oh, wow, there's a leopard," and ...
(*existential predicate; Leopard Story,* VI/57)

(4) བག་ལེབ་འདུག
pa̱ylep   ***du̱k***
bread   **CP;ELPA**
'There is bread.'
(*existential predicate;* 6/8/00)

du̱k occurs with a locative predicate in (5), a possessive in (6), and an attributive in (7) and (8). Perception is visual in these examples, except in (8) where it is physical or tactile.

(5) ཁོའི་རྒྱབ་ལ་འདུག
kʰō   nye̱:   kyab=la   **du̱k**
3.SG.M   1.SG.GEN   back=LOC   **CP;ELPA**
'He is behind me.'
(*locative predicate;* IV/107)

(6) ཉི་མ་ལ་པེ་ཤག་ཏོག་ཙམ་འདུག
nyima=la   peʃak   te:s   **du̱k**
[name]=DAT   money   little.bit   **CP;ELPA**
'Nyima has some money.'
(*possessive predicate;* V/39, VI/49)

(7) རྟ་དེ་ཆེན་པོ་འདུག
    *t'ā   tẹ   tʃʰēmpo **dųk***
    horse DEF big   CP;ELPA
    'The horse is big.'
    (*attributive predicate;* IV/51)

(8) ཉལ་ཁྲི་འབོལ་པོ་འདུག
    *nyạ:tị   bõ:βo **dųk***
    bed   soft   CP;ELPA
    'The bed is soft.'
    (*attributive predicate;* IV/69)

In (9), *dųk* is used when describing an internal sensation which cannot be observed by another person.[14]

(9) ང་སྐྱིད་པོ་འདུག
    *ŋạ   cipo   **dųk***
    1.SG happy CP;ELPA
    'I'm happy.'
    (*attributive predicate;* IV/83)

8.4.1.2 *dųk* as an auxiliary in the present imperfective

When *dųk* is used in a construction following the imperfective suffix (IPFV) *-gi-~-ki*, the action or event described by the clause is understood to be taking place at the time of speech; i.e., to indicate present tense. When it follows a past verb stem (for verbs which have such a distinct form), the clause takes on a perfect reading, and the CURRENT PERCEPTION epistemic *dųk* conveys a sense of 'deferred evidence', as discussed in Section 8.4.1.3 below.[15]

In (10) *dųk* is used in an explicit case of visual perception. In (11) and (12), perception is expressed through the speaker's choice of epistemic.

---

14 Tournadre coined the term "endopathic" for such states (1996a: 226; 1996b: 195, 206).
15 *dųk* is not used with clauses that describe actions, events, or states which occur in the future; obviously a speaker cannot have perceptual evidence for an event that has not yet occurred.

(10) ངས་འཇའ་མཚོན་གི་འདུག
    ŋyẹ: dʒa̱   thōŋ-gi   **du̱k**
    1.SG.ERG rainbow   see-IPFV   **CP;AUX**
    'I see a rainbow.'
    (*overt perception*; IV/65)

(11) ཁོ་ཟ་གི་འདུག
    kʰō   sa̱-gi   **du̱k**
    3.SG.M eat-IPFV **CP;AUX**
    'He's eating.'
    (*intransitive verb*)

(12) ཁོ་ཡི་གེ་འབྲི་གི་འདུག
    kʰō   yi̱ge   ṯi-gi   **du̱k**
    3.SG.M letter   write-IPFV **CP;AUX**
    'He's writing a letter.'
    (*transitive verb*; IV/61)

The CURRENT PERCEPTION marker is appropriate with auditory evidence, as well as specific information one has just been informed of. Karma says that a speaker could use *du̱k* in (13) under a variety of scenarios: (*i*) if she sees the rain falling outside; (*ii*) if she hears the rain falling outside; (*iii*) if someone has just walked into the house from outside and the speaker sees that he is wearing a coat dripping with rain; (*iv*) if someone has just told her that it is raining outside. In scenarios (*ii*) and (*iii*), the speaker could also choose to use a marker of inference, as in (14).

(13) ཆར་པ་འབབ་གྱི་འདུག
    tʃārpa   pa̱p-ki   **du̱k**
    rain   fall-IPFV **CP;AUX**
    'It's raining.'
    (*visual, evidence, auditory evidence, specifically informed*; 1/27/99)

(14) ཆར་པ་འབབ་གྱི་ཡོད་ས་རེད།
    tʃārpa   pa̱p-ki   **yö̱ sā re̱?**
    rain   fall-IPFV **INFR.UE;AUX**
    'It's raining.'
    (*inference*; 1/27/99)

du̱k is also appropriate with endopathic verbs expressing personal sensation, obligation, and desire – circumstances in which the speaker's perception is a physical sensation or internal feeling which cannot be confirmed by another person. Examples (15) and (16) illustrate personal sensation.

(15) ང་ན་གི་འདུག
    ŋa   ne-gi   **du̯k**
    1.SG be.sick-IPFV **CP;AUX**
    'I'm sick.'
    (*physical sensation, endopathic*; VI/50)

(16) ང་གྲོད་ཁོག་ལྟོགས་ཀྱི་འདུག
    ŋa   toqo   to-gi   **du̯k**
    1.SG stomach be.hungry-IPFV **CP;AUX**
    'I'm hungry.'
    (*current perception, endopathic*; 1/20/99)

8.4.1.3 *du̯k* as an auxiliary in the present perfect

When *du̯k* follows a past verb stem (when such a distinct form exists), the construction yields a sense of deferred evidence – that is, the speaker observes some present trace of an action or event that was completed in the past. This use of *du̯k* can be interpreted as perfect aspect; the extension from present perception to present temporal relevance is quite natural. In (17) the speaker did not witness the girl's tumble, but arrived on the scene to see her already lying on the ground.

(17) མོ་རིལ་འདུག
    mo   ri: **du̯k**
    3.SG.F fall.PST **CP;AUX**
    'She has fallen./She fell.'
    (*perfect aspect, deferred evidence*; IV/47)

The epistemic options available to a speaker are illustrated in example (18). If *du̯k* is used, the speaker is saying 'I see the letter and I know he's the one who wrote it, though I didn't see him write it'. This is a case of deferred evidence; it would be appropriate if, for instance, the speaker recognized her friend's handwriting. With *soŋ* (PAST PERCEPTION) the speaker is saying 'I know this because I saw him while he was writing it', with *tʃuŋ* (HAPPENED TO ME) the speaker is saying 'I know he wrote a letter, because I received it', and *re?* (SIMPLE FACT) means 'I just know this is true'. Karma explained that *re?* could be chosen even if the speaker *did* see her friend write the letter, or sees the letter itself, or was told about the event by someone else, but opts not to express this source of knowledge to her listener; thus *re?* is unspecified for evidentiality.

(18) ཁོ་ཡི་གེ་བྲིས་ འདུག མོང་ ཚུང་ རེད།
     kʰȭ   *yige*   *ṭi:*   *dṳk*   / *soŋ*   / *tʃuŋ*   / *re?*
     3.SG.M.ERG   letter   write.PST   **CP;AUX**   / **PP;AUX**   / **HM;AUX**   / **SF;AUX**
     'He has written a letter./He wrote a letter.'
     (*perfect aspect/past tense; epistemic options*; IV/61, V/64)

This analysis of *dṳk* as indicating deferred evidence follows de Reuse's (2000) work on the San Carlos variety of Western Apache. In this dialect, the deferred evidence marker *lék'eh* is used when "the speaker did not have evidence for the event at the time that it occurred, but the speaker gained evidence for it at a later time". In (19), for instance, the speaker did not see the collision she refers to, but saw the result. Similarly, the context for (20) is that a family set up their campsite in the dark, not knowing where they were, and hit the trail again before daybreak. When they looked back on their campsite in the light, they realized it was a graveyard.

(19) *Nt`é shih nabil lizgohi lék'eh*
     'There had been a car accident/collision.'
     Western Apache; de Reuse 2000:(6):[1]

(20) *Áí n`íí nanezna` leshijeedyú nohwiheskaa lék'eh*
     'We had slept in a graveyard!'
     Western Apache; de Reuse 2000:(6):[1]

Extrapolating from current perceptual evidence to knowledge of a past event necessarily entails the mental process of inference. However, I argue here that inference is not the epistemic meaning of *dṳk* in this construction. Rather, the consistent emphasis of *dṳk* is on the speaker's current perceptual evidence, and the certainty of her claim.

To specifically index the mental process of reaching a conclusion by reasoning, the speaker can draw instead from a dedicated subset of epistemics: the six morphologically complex markers of inference discussed in Section 5 below. As demonstrated there, some of these markers are direct evidentials, while others are not. But they all inform the listener that the speaker's assertion has not been verified, and that it is based on deduction.

Correlates of WT *'dug* are apparently employed as markers of deferred evidence in several other varieties of Tibetan. Volkart (2000) discusses *'dug* in Kagate, Southern Mustang, Jirel, Lhomi, and Sherpa. She, too, notes its use in the perfect aspect, and concludes that inference based on perception is implicit in most such occurrences.

8.4.2 *soŋ* (PAST PERCEPTION; PP)

Consistent with its semantic meaning, *soŋ* adds an inherent sense of past perfective tense-aspect. Thus, it only occurs after the past stem form of a verb (when such a distinct form exists; otherwise in a past tense context); it never follows the imperfective marker *-gi~-ki*, and is never used with clauses describing present or future actions or events. Examples (21) and (22) illustrate the use of *soŋ* with past visual and aural observation. In (21) Karma is narrating his description of the Pear Story (Chafe 1980) which he had just watched on video.

(21) ཕྲུ་གཞོན་གཞོན་ཅིག་སི་ཀལ་བཏང་ནས་སླེབས་སོང་།
    pu   ʃenʃen tʃik sekal taŋ=ne   lɛp   **soŋ**
    boy young   one   bicycle VBLZR=SUB come **PP;AUX**
    'A young boy came riding a bike.'
    (*visual evidence*; Pear Story, 8)

(22) ཁོས་ང་ལ་ཟ་ལབ་སོང་།
    kʰö̃   ŋa̠=la   sa̠   lap   **soŋ**
    3.SG.M.ERG 1.SG=DAT eat tell.PST **PP;AUX**
    'He told me to eat.'
    (*auditory evidence*; IV/61, V/64)

8.5 Markers of inference in DCT

The morphologically simple perceptual evidentials *du̠k* and *soŋ* discussed above are markers of certainty, advising the listener that the speaker's proposition has been verified; these are plotted in Box 2 of Fig. 1. The morphologically complex markers of non-certainty, plotted in Box 3, indicate that the proposition has not been verified. These include markers of inference (in Box 6), as well as markers of guessing and possibility (outside of Box 6). My focus here is on DCT's three pairs of inference markers, which are unique in their intersection with evidentiality.

Of particular interest are the two forms ending in *du̠k*, which tell the listener that the speaker's inference, or deduction, is based on perceptual evidence. The existence and the function of these forms helps us to refine our understanding of the simple epistemic *dụk* (CURRENT PERCEPTION) when it expresses deferred evidence (described in Section 8.4.1.3 above), as it would not make sense to have both simple and complex forms with the exact same meaning and function. The primary meanings of the simple form are certainty and perception; inference is only a secondary reading, invoked by the construction in which it occurs. This clarification in turn contributes to refining our analysis of Lhasa/SST *bzhag*, discussed in Section 8.6.

Examples (23) through (25) below demonstrate that the morphologically complex markers of inference specifically index the mental process of deductive reasoning. Here, A comments to B that B's brother is taller than B. B then responds that his father is taller than his brother, leading A to comment that the father must therefore be taller than B, too. The speaker's selection of *yọ̈ sā rẹ?* tells the listener that she has inferred the statement asserted in (25); a marker of non-certainty is appropriate since the proposition has not been verified.

(23) ཆོད་ཀྱི་ཇོ་ཇོ་ཆོད་ལས་རིང་ར་ཡོད་རེད།
  cʰö?=gi   *tʃödʒö*   *cʰö=le*   *riŋan*   **yọ̈ rẹ?**
  2.SG=GEN   older.brother   2.SG=COMP   taller   **GS;ELPA**
  'Your older brother is taller than you.'
  (*A speaking to B*; 2/3/99)

(24) རའི་ཨ་པ་(རའི་)ཇོ་ཇོ་ལས་རིང་ར་ཡོད་རེད།
  ŋyẹ: *āpa*   *(ŋye:)*   *tʃödʒö=le*   *riŋan*   **yọ̈ rẹ?**
  1.SG.GEN   father   1.SG.GEN   older.brother= COMP   taller   **GS;ELPA**
  'My father is taller than my older brother.'
  (*B's response to A*; 2/3/99)

(25) ཨ་པ་ཡང་ཆོད་ལས་རིང་རང་ཡོད་ས་རེད།
  āpa   *yaŋ*   *cʰö=le*   *riŋan*   **yọ̈ sā rẹ?**
  father   also   2.SG= COMP   taller   **INFR.UE;COP**
  'Oh, so [I infer] your father is also taller than you.'
  (*A's inference*; 2/3/99)

The complete set of DCT's morphologically complex markers of inference are shown in Tab. 2 below. Unless the predicate of the clause includes a lexical verb, they consist of two of the simple epistemics linked by the intervening morpheme *sā*. The first element must be *yịn* or *yọ̈?*, and the final element must be *dụk*, *yọ̈?*, or *rẹ?*.

Tab. 2: Complex markers of inference (INFR) in DCT.

Predicate type	Direct evidentials		Unspecified evidence/ non-evidential
	Perceptual evidence	Personal evidence	
Predicate nominals	yı̃ sā dụk	yı̃ sā yö̱?	yı̃ sā rę?
ELPA predicates	yö̱ sā dụk	yö̱ sā yö̱?	yö̱ sā rę?
Lexical verb predicates	V sā dụk	V sā yö̱?	V sā rę?
	V yö̱ sā dụk	V yö̱ sā yö̱?	V yö̱ sā rę?
	V yı̃ sā dụk	[V yı̃ sā yö̱?][16]	V yı̃ sā rę?

With non-lexical verb predicates, inference markers function as linking verbs. Forms beginning with *yin* are used with predicate nominals; forms beginning with *yö?* are used with ELPA predicates.[17] With lexical verb predicates, the choice between *yin* and *yö?* forms is governed primarily by tense and aspect. For past tense clauses, the locus of inference – whether the speaker is drawing an inference about the subject or the predicate of the clause – also plays a role in epistemic choice.

The final morphological component of these complex epistemics indicates the basis of inference. Forms ending in *dụk* indicate that the speaker's inference is drawn from perceptual evidence, just as the simple epistemic *dụk* marks CURRENT PERCEPTION. Similarly, the forms ending in *yö?* indicate that the speaker's inference is drawn from some type of personal knowledge, just as the simple epistemic *yö?* marks PERSONAL KNOWLEDGE. Finally, the complex epistemics ending in *rę?* do not specify the basis of inference, just as the SIMPLE FACT simple epistemic is appropriate when the speaker cannot or does not choose to specify the source of her evidence; she is only advising her speaker that her claim is based on this mental process and has not been verified.

The evidentials *yı̃ sā dụk*, *yö̱ sā dụk*, and *V sā dụk* are thus glossed here as INFR.CP, for 'inference based on current perception', and *yı̃ sā yö̱?*, *yö̱ sā yö̱?*, and *V sā yö̱?* as INFR.PK, for 'inference based on personal knowledge'. The sometime-evidentials *yı̃ sā rę?*, *yö̱ sā rę?*, and *V sā rę?* are glossed as INFR.UE, for 'inference based on unspecified evidence'.

---

[16] This form is not attested in my data, but I think would be confirmed with further elicitation.
[17] Goldstein and Nornang (1970: 35) also note this pattern, though for complex epistemics of possibility and probability; they do not address markers of inference.

8.5.1 Inference markers as linking verbs (COP and ELPA)

Complex epistemics beginning with *yin* are used with predicate nominals in an equational clause, as illustrated by the inference marker in (26).

(26) ཁོ་གི་རྩམ་བོད་པ་ཡིན་ས་རེད།
    kʰō=gi   *ceme*   *pọpa*   *yịn sā rẹ?*
    3.SG.M=GEN   wife   Tibetan   INFR.UE;COP
    '[I infer] His wife is Tibetan.'
    (*predicate nominal; inference, unspecified evidence*; V1/100)

Existential, locative, possessive, and attributive predicates occur with complex epistemics beginning with *yö?*. In (27), the speaker asserts the existence of a tiger based on current perceptual evidence. In (28), the speaker tells her listener that she has inferred the existence of a tiger at a particular location. The basis of inference is unspecified.

(27) ཞིང་གི་ནང་ལ་སྟག་འདུག
    ʃīnge: *naŋ=la*   *t'āk*   *dụk*
    field.GEN   inside=LOC   tiger   CP;ELPA
    'In the field, there's a tiger.'
    (*existential, simple epistemic, current perception*; IV/81)

(28) ཞིང་གི་ནང་ལ་སྟག་ཡོད་ས་རེད།
    ʃīnge: *naŋ=la*   *t'āk*   *yọ̈ sā rẹ?*
    field.GEN   inside=LOC   tiger   INFR.UE;ELPA
    '[I infer] In the field, there's a tiger.'
    (*existential, inference based on unspecified evidence*; VI/25)

A locative predicate is illustrated below. The CURRENT PERCEPTION marker of certainty in (29) would be appropriate if the speaker actually saw her friend at the house at the time of speech. The morphologically complex forms index noncertainty. With *yọ̈ sā rẹ?* in (30), the speaker indicates that she is drawing an inference about the friend's whereabouts, without specifying what type of evidence her inference is based on. The use of *yọ̈ sā dụk* in (31) would be appropriate if, for instance, the friend's car is parked out in front of the house. The speaker infers that her friend is at home and specifies that this inference is based on current perceptual evidence; *yọ̈ sā dụk* is thus an evidential.

(29) ཁོ་ནང་ལ་འདུག
    kʰō   *naŋ=la*   *dụk*
    3.SG.M   home=LOC   CP;ELPA
    'He's at home.'
    (*third person subject, simple epistemic, current perception*; V/94)

(30) ཁོ་ནང་ལ་ཡོད་ས་རེད།
  kʰō *naŋ=la* **yö̱ sā rẹ?** / **yịn sā rẹ?*
  3.SG.M home=LOC **INFR.UE;ELPA**
  '[I infer] He's at home.'
  (*simple epistemic, inference based on unspecified evidence*; V/94)

(31) ཁོ་ནང་ལ་ཡོད་ས་འདུག
  kʰō *naŋ=la* **yö̱ sā dụk**
  3.SG.M home=LOC **INFR.CP;ELPA**
  '[I infer] He's at home.'
  (*simple epistemic, inference based on perception*; V/94)

Similar choices are illustrated for a possessive predicate in the following. The scenario Karma offered here is that we imagine my brother is visiting, Karma sees his Mercedes Benz car keys on the table, and he infers that my brother owns a Mercedes. Both (32) and (33) are acceptable, but (33) tells the listener explicitly that the inference is based on perceptual evidence. The marker of guessing in (34) would be appropriate if the statement were simply conjecture.

(32) ཁོའི་ཇོ་ཇོ་ལ་Mercedesཡོད་ས་རེད།
  kʰō̱ *tʃö̱zo=la* 'Mercedes' **yö̱ sā rẹ?**
  3.SG.GEN brother=DAT [LUXURY.CAR.BRAND] **INFR.UE;ELPA**
  '[I infer] His brother has a Mercedes.'
  (*possessive, inference based on unspecified evidence*; VII/45)

(33) ཁོའི་ཇོ་ཇོ་ལ་Mercedesཡོད་ས་འདུག
  kʰō̱ *tʃö̱zo=la* 'Mercedes' **yö̱ sā dụk**
  3.SG.GEN brother=DAT [LUXURY.CAR.BRAND] **INFR.CP;ELPA**
  '[I infer] His brother has a Mercedes.'
  (*possessive, inference based on current perception*; VII/45)

(34) ཁོའི་ཇོ་ཇོ་ལ་Mercedesཡོད་འགྲོ
  kʰō̱ *tʃö̱zo=la* 'Mercedes' **yö̱ dro**
  3.SG.GEN brother=DAT [LUXURY.CAR.BRAND] **GES;ELPA**
  '[I guess] His brother has a Mercedes.'
  (*possessive, guess*; VII/45)

The marking of inference with an attributive predicate is illustrated below. The speaker's use of *dụk* in (35) indicates that she is certain about the size of the horse, based on current perceptual evidence. The complex epistemic of non-certainty in (36) indicates inference based on unspecified evidence, while that in (37) indicates inference based on current perception. Karma suggested the latter would be appropriate if the speaker hadn't seen the horse itself, but was looking at a very large footprint or a pile of very large horse droppings. (He clarified that yö̱ sā re̱? would also be acceptable in this specific scenario, but it is simply less informative.)

(35) རྟ་དེ་ཆེན་པོ་འདུག
 t'ā te̱ tʃēmpo **du̱k**
 horse DEF big **CP;ELPA**
 'The horse is big.'
 (*attributive predicate*; IV/51)

(36) རྟ་དེ་ཆེན་པོ་ཡོད་ས་རེད།
 t'ā te̱ tʃēmpo **yö̱ sā re̱?**
 horse DEF big **INFR.UE;ELPA**
 'The horse is big.'
 (*attributive predicate; inference, unspecified evidence*; VI/103)

(37) རྟ་དེ་ཆེན་པོ་ཡོད་ས་འདུག
 t'ā te̱ tʃēmpo **yö̱ sā du̱k**
 horse DEF big **INFR.CP;ELPA**
 'The horse is big.'
 (*attributive predicate; inference, current perception*; VI/104)

These examples highlight the contrast between the morphologically simple marker of certainty which indexes current perception, and the morphologically complex markers of non-certainty which explicitly index the mental process of deduction.

8.5.2 Inference markers as auxiliaries

The use of markers of inference with lexical verb predicates in the present tense and past tense is illustrated in Sections 8.5.2.1 and 8.5.2.2, respectively. Inference markers are also used with the future tense, but that is not considered here.

8.5.2.1 Lexical verb predicates in the present tense

With lexical verb predicates expressing present tense actions and events, an inference marker beginning with *yö̱* is used. The structure of the clause is similar for the simple and complex epistemics: the present form of the verb stem is followed by *-gi~-ki* (the imperfective suffix) and then the epistemic marker.

In (38) – seen above as (13) – the CURRENT PERCEPTION evidential conveys certainty, indicating that the information has been verified. The epistemic in (39) expresses inference based on unspecified evidence, while the evidential in (40) expresses inference based on perceptual evidence. The latter could be chosen if the speaker observed a wet umbrella or her friend's dripping coat.

(38) ཆར་པ་འབབ་གྱི་འདུག
    tʃārpa   *pap-ki*   **du̱k**
    rain   fall-IPFV   **CP;AUX**
    'It's raining.'
    (*certainty, current perception*; 1/27/99)

(39) ཆར་པ་འབབ་གྱི་ཡོད་ས་རེད
    tʃārpa   *pap-ki*   **yö̱ sā re̱?**
    rain   fall-IPFV   **INFR.UE;AUX**
    '[I infer] It's raining.'
    (*inference based on unspecified evidence*; 1/27/99, 6/13/00)

(40) ཆར་པ་འབབ་གྱི་ཡོད་ས་འདུག
    tʃārpa   *pap-ki*   **yö̱ sā du̱k**
    rain   fall-IPFV   **INFR.CP;AUX**
    '[I infer] It's raining.'
    (*inference based on current perception*; 6/13/00)

The following sentences are also in the present tense. The morphologically simple forms in (41) are evidential markers of certainty; with *du̱k* the speaker assures the listener that she has current perceptual evidence to verify her assertion, while with *yö̱?* the speaker can claim that the friend is eating since they are in the same room or are eating together. In (42) the speaker infers that her friend is eating but doesn't elaborate on how she came to this conclusion, while in (43) she specifies that her inference is based on some personal insider knowledge. This would be appropriate if the speaker had seen or talked to her friend previously and had some idea what her plans were.

(41) ཁོ་ཟ་གི་   འདུག   / ཡོད
    kʰō   *sa̱-gi*   **du̱k**   **/ yö̱?**
    3.SG.M   eat-IPFV   **CP;AUX**   **/ PK;AUX**
    'He's eating.'
    (*certainty, current perception/personal knowledge*; V/71)

(42) ཁོ་ཟ་གི་ཡོད་ས་རེད
    kʰō   *sa̱-gi*   **yö̱ sā re̱?**
    3.SG.M   eat-IPFV   **INFR.UE;AUX**
    '[I infer] He's eating.'
    (*inference based on unspecified evidence*; IV/21, V/71, VI/21)

(43) ཁོ་ཟ་གི་ཡོད་ས་ཡོད།
　　　 kʰō　　*sa-gi*　　***yö̱ sā yö̱?***
　　　 3.SG.M　　eat-IPFV　　INFR.PK;AUX
　　　 '[I infer] He's eating.'
　　　 (*inference based on personal knowledge*; VIII/6/11)

8.5.2.2 Lexical verb predicates in the past tense

The structure of the past tense is also similar for the simple and complex epistemics: the past stem form of the verb is directly followed by the epistemic auxiliary. Forms with *yö̱?* can have a perfect aspect reading.

In the past tense clauses below, the speaker uses an evidential marker of certainty based on perception in (44), and a morphologically complex marker of inference in (45).

(44) ཆར་པ་བབས་སོང་།
　　　 tʃārpa　　*pap*　　***soŋ***
　　　 rain　　　 fall　　　PP;AUX
　　　 'It rained.'
　　　 (*certainty, past perception*; 1/27/99)

(45) ཆར་པ་བབས་ཡིན་ས་རེད།
　　　 tʃārpa　　*pap*　　***yi̱n sā re̱?***
　　　 rain　　　 fall　　　INFR.UE;AUX
　　　 '[I infer] It rained.'
　　　 (*inference based on unspecified evidence*; 1/27/99, 6/13/00)

The following past tense examples illustrate the contrast between subject focus and predicate focus, as well as differences in the basis of inference. The scenario here involves the speaker's friend Pasang and his purchase of rice. In (46), the speaker sees rice on the table or in the cupboard and infers that Pasang is the one who bought it, since Pasang previously said he would do so, or since he went off to the market to buy food. There is no question that the rice has been bought, as it can be seen; what must be inferred is who bought it. Karma offered such comments here as: "I'm more sure *he* bought it rather than someone else" and "I see it at *his* place, or with *him*". In (47), the speaker sees Pasang coming from the market with his bag, and a friend asks her what's in Pasang's bag. The speaker doesn't know for certain since she can't see the purchase, but she infers that Pasang has bought rice since he said he would do so. Here there is no doubt about the subject, and it is the action which is in question and must be inferred. An appropriate context for (48) would be if the speaker had insider knowledge about Pasang's likely purchase – for instance, if the speaker were organizing a party and had given Pasang instructions to buy the needed rice, or if the speaker had seen Pasang at the rice stall at the market. The change in word order in (49) maintains focus on the rice, which is now the subject of the clause. I translate this into English with a passive construction in an attempt to reflect this. The inference in this case is based on current perceptual evidence.

(46) པ་སངས་ཀྱིས་འབྲས་ཚོས་ཡིན་ས་རེད། །
    pāsaŋ=gi   ɖe: nyö: **yi̱n sā re̱?**
    [NAME]=ERG rice buy.PST **INFR.UE;AUX**
    '[I infer] Pasang bought the rice.'
    (*inference, subject focus*; VII/79, VIII/4–5, 9, 22–27)

(47) པ་སངས་ཀྱིས་འབྲས་ཚོས་ཡོད་ས་རེད། །
    Pāsaŋ=gi   ɖe: nyö: **yö̱ sā re̱?**
    [NAME]=ERG rice buy.PST **INFR.UE;AUX**
    '[I infer] Pasang bought the rice/has bought the rice.'
    (*inference, predicate focus*; VII/79, VIII/4–5, 9, 22–27)

(48) ཁོས་འབྲས་ཚོས་ཡོད་ས་ཡོད།
    khö̃:   ɖe: nyö: **yö̱ sā yö̱?**
    3.SG.M=ERG rice buy.PST **INFR.PK;AUX**
    '[I infer] He bought the rice/has bought the rice.'
    (*inference, predicate focus, insider knowledge*; VII/79, VIII/4–5, 9, 22–27)

(49) འབྲས་ཁོས་ཚོས་ཡིན་ས་འདུག
    ɖe: khö̃=gi   nyö: **yi̱n sā du̱k**
    rice 3.SG.M=ERG buy.PST **INFR.CP;AUX**
    '[I infer] 'The rice was bought by him.' ('He bought the rice.')
    (*inference, subject focus*; VIII/25)

8.6 Inference and deferred perception in Lhasa/SST

In Section 8.4.1.3 above I demonstrated that, in Diasporic Common Tibetan, a speaker can use the morphologically simple CURRENT PERCEPTION evidential *du̱k* after the past stem form of a verb as a marker of certainty, telling the listener that she perceives traces of an event which was completed in the past. This yields a present perfect tense-aspect reading. The emphasis of *du̱k* here is on certainty and perception, consistent with its other uses. That the speaker came to know the information expressed in the clause through deduction is beside the point; inference is only a secondary interpretation.

In contrast, in Section 8.5, I showed that DCT has a dedicated set of morphologically complex markers of non-certainty which explicitly tell the listener that the speaker's assertion is founded on the mental process of inference. One pair of these markers – *yĩ sā dụk* and *yö̃ sā dụk* – specify that the speaker's inference is based on current perceptual evidence. These markers, too, can be used after the past stem form of a verb to describe an action or event which was completed in the past. The emphasis of *yĩ sā dụk* and *yö̃ sā dụk* is that the speaker's assertion has not been verified, and that it is based on deduction; inference is a primary meaning.

This comparison has helped to tease apart the semantic-pragmatic distinctions between these two morphosyntactic constructions. These findings can be directly extended to Lhasa/SST, permitting a refinement in our understanding of the morpheme *bzhag* in contrast to other markers.

8.6.1 *bzhag* as a marker of DEFERRED PERCEPTION

The place of *bzhag* within the Tibetan epistemic-evidential framework is illustrated in Fig. 1, where it is included (in square brackets) with *dụk* and *soŋ* as a morphologically simple marker of certainty, and an evidential marker of perception. *bzhag* (transcribed by some authors as *shạg*, and variously transliterated as *bzhag ~ bśag ~ shag ~ zhag*) is not used in DCT, a dialect difference which Karma was conscious of, and pointed out to me.

Previous researchers (DeLancey 1984, 1985, 1990; Tournadre 1994, 1996a, 1996b; Bartee 1996; Tournadre and Dorje 2003: 168; Vokurková 2008; and Oisel 2013) have identified *bzhag* as a marker of inference. Representative characterizations are provided by DeLancey: *bzhag* "reports inference from directly perceived evidence (1985: 66) and "marks a clause as a report of an event whose occurrence the speaker infers from present traces" (1990: 299).

I argue here that while *bzhag* entails inference, its emphasis is not on expressing inference; instead *bzhag* exactly parallels DCT's *dụk*[18] and is more appropriately glossed as DEFERRED PERCEPTION. This is consistent with the analysis by Hill (this volume) of *bzhag* as the 'perfect testimonial', with inference as a derived, secondary interpretation. The examples of *bzhag* provided by DeLancey,

---

18 In fact, Karma, educated in Written Tibetan at boarding schools in Nepal and India, explicitly pointed this equivalence out to me (VII/11). Further evidence of the equivalence of *dụk* and *bzhag* comes from the use of the sequence *re dụk* in DCT where Lhasa/SST uses *red bzhag*. Some scholars consider this sequence to express surprise, and Tournadre and Dorje (2003: 460) refer to it as a 'revelatory' epistemic.

Tournadre, Vokurková[19] and others can all be adequately accounted for from this perspective.

In the DCT sentences in (50) below, the PAST PERCEPTION evidential *soŋ* indicates that the speaker observed her friend's fall at the time it happened, while the CURRENT PERCEPTION evidential *duk* in (51) indicates that the speaker observed evidence of the fall after the fact.

(50) ཁྱེད་རིལ་སོང་།
    *cʰö̱ʔ   ṛi: **soŋ***
    2.SG fall.PST **PP;AUX**
    'You fell.'
    (*past activity, past observation, perfective aspect*; IV/45)

(51) ཁྱེད་རིལ་འདུག
    *cʰö̱ʔ   ṛi: **du̱k***
    2.SG fall.PST **CP;AUX**
    'You have fallen./You fell.'
    (*past activity, current observation; perfect aspect*)

The corresponding Lhasa/SST sentences are provided in (52) and (53) (in DeLancey's original transcription). *bzhag* (his *bśag*) serves the same function as *du̱k*; the speaker has current perceptual evidence of a completed activity or event.

(52) *k'yeraŋ ril **soŋ***
    you   fall **PFV;EVIDENTIAL**
    You fell down. *(I saw it.)*
    Lhasa; DeLancey 1984(8)

(53) *k'yeraŋ ril **bśag***
    you   fall **PFV;INFERENTIAL**
    You fell down. *(So I infer.)*
    Lhasa; DeLancey 1984(9)

In contrasting the following pair of sentences, DeLancey (1990: 299) says that (54) would be appropriate if the speaker witnessed the event, and (55) would be appropriate if the speaker inferred what happened upon observing shards on the kitchen floor, knowing that the subject had been in the room moments before.

---

[19] In the examples from these authors which follow, abbreviations have been regularized as much as possible to be consistent with those used elsewhere throughout this study.

(54) kho=s   dkaryol   bcag-**song**
    s/he=ERG   cup   broke-**PFV;EVIDENTIAL**
    S/he broke the cup.
    Lhasa; DeLancey 1990: 299(23)

(55) kho=s   dkaryol   bcag-**zhag**
    s/he=ERG   cup   broke-**PRF;INFERENTIAL**
    S/he broke the cup.
    Lhasa; DeLancey 1990: 299(24)

Tournadre (1994) and Vokurková (2008: 117) also describe *bzhag* as a marker of inference or deduction based on observation of traces of a completed event. Per Tournadre, in (56) the speaker witnessed her friend's actual departure; in (57) she infers he has departed based on some current evidence – for instance, his horse is gone, or the lights are extinguished. (The English translations here are mine.)

(56) kho   phyin-**song**
    il.ABS aller.PST-**AOR;CONST**[20]
    'Il est parti.' (Je l'ai vu partir.)
    [I saw that] 'He left.'
    (*past, witnessed*; Tournadre 1994: 152(2.c))

(57) kho   phyin-**shag**
    il.ABS aller.PST-**INFR**
    'Il est parti.' ([Je deduis qu']il est parti.)
    [I infer that] 'He [has] left.'
    (*past, deduced*; Tournadre 1994: 152(2.d))

In (58), from Vokurková, the speaker can see the girl carrying her school bag in the morning; in (59) the girl's school bag is no longer present at home.

(58) bu.mo   'di   slob.grwa-r   'gro   **-gis (gi.'dug)**
    girl   this   school-OBL   go.PRS   **-IPFV;SENSORY**
    'The girl is going to school.'
    (*present, direct evidential, sensory*; Vokurková: 2008: 112(104.b))

---

20 AOR = aoriste [aorist]; CONST = constatif [witnessed].

(59) *bu.mo   slob.grwa-r   phyin-**bzhag***
    girl   school-OBL   go.PST-**PRS.PRF;INFR**
    'The girl has (just) gone to school.'
    (*past, direct evidential, inference*; Vokurková: 112(104.c))

The correspondence of *bzhag* with *dụk* (WT *'dug*) has been observed by others. For spoken Lhasa/SST, Vokurková (2008: 117) says that the inferential meaning conveyed by *bzhag* can also be indicated by *'dug*. Oisel (2013: 237) notes that in modern literary Tibetan both *'dug* and *bzhag* are used; he calls this construction "l'inférentiel sensoriel" [sensory inferential]. According to Chonjore (2003: 253), *bzhag* is the "typical Lhasa colloquial form" while *'dug* is the literary form. He calls both forms "reportative" verb endings.

8.6.2 Markers of inference in Lhasa/SST

Like DCT, Lhasa/SST has a complete set of morphologically complex markers of inference, some of which are evidentials and some of which are not. Forms from Vokurková (2008: 266ff. and 282ff.) are shown in Tab. 3 below. There is a morphological asymmetry in the Lhasa/SST forms: the non-evidential markers of inference are based on *sa*, while the sensory and egophoric markers of inference are based on *bzo*, meaning 'shape'.[21] Vokurková (2008: 150) notes that the *sa* forms are rare in Lhasa/SST, and very frequent in diasporic and non-Central varieties.

Tab. 3: Complex markers of inference in DCT and Lhasa/SST.

Basis of inference	DCT	Lhasa/SST[22]
unspecified evidence/non-evidential	yī̃ sā rẹ?, yö̃ sā rẹ?	pa yin sa red, yod sa red[23]
sensory evidence (SENS)	yī̃ sā dụk, yö̃ sā dụk	pa yin bzo 'dug, yod bzo 'dug
speaker knowledge (EGO)	yī̃ sā yö̃?, yö̃ sā yö̃?	(pa yin bzo yod), yod bzo yod

---

[21] If this asymmetry existed historically in the DCT forms, it has been phonetically regularized.
[22] In Lhasa/SST, *pa* occurs in many of the epistemics beginning with *yin*. This morpheme is dropped in DCT and in other varieties.
[23] Vokurková (2008: 267) interprets her examples as showing that these forms have a sensory connotation, in spite of the *red* ending, which usually indicates factual evidence. However, I think she has overlooked the fact that the speaker may choose a *red* form if she does not wish to emphasize the perceptual basis of inference. Thus I categorize Lhasa/SST *yod.sa.red* and *pa.yin. sa.red* as indicating unspecified evidence or as non-evidential.

The following example illustrates the use of a Lhasa/SST *sa* form to express inference based on olfactory evidence. Although there is sensory evidence in this case, the speaker has chosen to use the default non-evidential inference marker here. (Another factor in this particular example is that *'dug* forms do not seem to be used with olfactory evidence.)

(60) *phun.tsogs=kyis   kha.lag   bzos   yod.sa.red*
     [NAME]=ERG   meal   make.PST   INFR.UE;AUX[24]
     'It seems Phuntsog has cooked.'
     ("the speaker can smell it"; Vokurková 2008: 150 (188))

A similar example from DCT is shown below, where a marker of inference is required when the speaker's evidence is olfactory. If the speaker sees the dinner burning, as in (61), *duk* is appropriate, but if she only smells it, then Karma says *yö sā re?* must be used instead, as in (62).

(61) ཤ་ཚིག་གི་འདུག
     ʃā   tsik-ki   duk
     meat   burn-IPFV   CP;AUX
     'The meat is burning.'
     (*visual perception*; 1/27/99)

(62) ཤ་ཚིག་གི་ཡོད་ས་རེད
     *ʃā   tsik-ki   *duk   / yö sā re?*
     meat   burn-IPFV   *CP;AUX   / INFR.UE;AUX
     [I infer] 'The meat is burning.'
     (*olfactory perception, inference based on unspecified evidence*; 1/27/99)

Consideration of these morphologically complex markers of non-certainty and inference helps to refine our understanding of the semantics and pragmatics of *bzhag*. As noted above, most previous researchers have simply identified *bzhag* as a marker of inference. But if we accept this definition, then when we consider the epistemic-evidential system as a whole, as I do here, we are prompted to ask why Tibetan should have two morphologically very different forms which both express inference, and to wonder about the potential difference between them. The answer, I argue, is that *bzhag* is best interpreted not as a marker of inference, but as a dedicated marker of DEFERRED PERCEPTION. The construction in which *bzhag* is used expresses deferred evidence. *bzhag* indexes certainty, perception,

---

[24] Vokurková glossed this form as "perf+epi 2+sens": present perfect+ a rather high degree of certainty+ sensory evidence.

and evidence available after the fact, while the morphologically complex forms index the mental process of deduction.

8.7 Summary and conclusions

In Diasporic Common Tibetan, the CURRENT PERCEPTION marker *duk* encodes both epistemic and evidential meaning. *duk* tells the listener that he can be certain about the speaker's statement, and that it is supported by perceptual evidence.

When *duk* follows the past form of a verb stem (or occurs in a past context), the tense-aspect of the clause can be interpreted as present perfect, and the construction yields a sense of deferred evidence. That is, the speaker has evidence after the fact; she observes some present trace of an action or event that was completed in the past.

Logically, in order to draw a conclusion about a past event from existing evidence, the speaker must necessarily have drawn an inference. However, the fact that inference has occurred does not mean that the speaker must choose an epistemic marker which indexes that mental process. *duk* here is intended to provide the listener with information about certainty and perception, and not about the speaker's thought process. Inference is implied, but it is not the primary information expressed by the construction.

Alternatively, if the speaker wishes, she can choose from a rich set of morphologically complex markers which explicitly index the mental process of inference. These forms express non-certainty (advising the listener that the assertion has not been verified), and they indicate whether the inference is based on perceptual information, personal information, or on generic or unspecified information.

This distinction between the epistemic-evidential categories of deferred evidence and inference becomes even more clear in Lhasa/SST. The epistemic-evidential system in this variety of the language includes *bzhag*, a unique, dedicated marker of DEFERRED PERCEPTION. The semantic-pragmatic function of *bzhag* parallels that of DCT *duk*: it indexes certainty and perception, and inference is secondary and implied. Like *duk*, *bzhag* contrasts with a set of morphologically complex epistemics which explicitly convey the mental process of inference and the basis of inference.

The meaning and function of both DCT *duk* and Lhasa/SST *bzhag* is illuminated only by contrasting them with the morphologically complex markers of inference. This analysis thus demonstrates that epistemic and evidential markers are most clearly understood when they are considered in the context of the complete system in which they exist, and that these two grammatical categories are inextricably interwoven.

Abbreviations

Epistemic-evidential markers are in bold.

ABS absolute, **AUX** auxiliary verb, COMP comparative, **COP** copula linking verb, **CP** current perception, **CPF** conscious personal fact, DAT dative, DEF definite article, **DP** deferred perception, DU dual, **ELPA** existential locative possessive attributive linking verb, ERG ergative, GEN genitive, **GES** guess, **GS** general state, **HM** it happened to me, **INFR** inference, **INFR.CP** inference based on current perception, **INFR.PK** inference based on personal knowledge, **INFR.UE** inference based on unspecified evidence, IPFV imperfective, LOC locative case, M masculine, OBL oblique, PFV perfective, PL plural, **PP** past perception, PRF perfect, PRS present, PST past (verb stem form), **RPT** reported, **SF** simple fact, SG singular, **SK** speaker knowledge, **SMS** it seems..., **THNK** I think..., VBLZR verbalizer.

References

Aikhenvald, Alexandra. 2003. Evidentiality in typological perspective. In Alexandra Aikhenvald & R. M. W. Dixon (eds.), *Studies in evidentiality*, 1–31. Amsterdam: John Benjamins.

Aikhenvald, Alexandra. 2004. *Evidentiality*. Oxford: Oxford University Press.

Bartee, Ellen. 1996. Deixis and spatiotemporal relations in Lhasa Tibetan. Arlington, TX: University of Texas at Arlington MA thesis.

Bielmeier, Roland. 2000. Syntactic, semantic, and pragmatic-epistemic functions of auxiliaries in Western Tibetan. *Linguistics of the Tibeto-Burman Area* 23(2). 79–125.

Caplow, Nancy J. 2000. The epistemic marking system of émigré Dokpa Tibetan. Santa Barbara, CA: University of California Santa Barbara Unpublished manuscript. 12 September.

Chafe, Wallace L. (ed.). 1980. *The Pear Stories: Cognitive, cultural, and linguistic aspects of narrative production*. Norwood, NJ: Ablex.

Chonjore, Tsetan, with Andrea Abinanti. 2003. *Colloquial Tibetan: A textbook of the Lhasa dialect*. Dharamsala: Library of the Tibetan Works and Archives.

DeLancey, Scott. 1984. Categories of non-volitional actor in Lhasa Tibetan. In A. Zide, D. Magier, & E. Schiller (eds.), *Proceedings of the conference on participant roles: South Asia and adjacent areas*, 58–70. Bloomington: Indiana University Linguistics Club (IULC).

DeLancey, Scott. 1985. Lhasa Tibetan evidentials and the semantics of causation. *Proceedings of the 11th Annual Meeting of the Berkeley Linguistics Society*, 65–72. Berkeley: Berkeley Linguistics Society.

DeLancey, Scott. 1990. Ergativity and the cognitive model of event structure in Lhasa Tibetan. *Cognitive Linguistics* 1(3). 289–321.

de Reuse, Willem J. 2000. The "deferred evidence" particle in Western Apache. Paper presented at the 3rd Annual Workshop on American Indigenous Languages (WAIL), University of California Santa Barbara, 14-16 April.

Garret, Edward. 2001. Evidentiality and assertion in Tibetan. Los Angeles, CA: University of California Los Angeles dissertation.

Goldstein, Melvyn C. & Nawang L. Nornang. 1970. *Modern spoken Tibetan: Lhasa dialect* (Bibliotheca Himalayica, Series II, Vol. 14). Kathmandu: Ratna Pustak Bhandar.
Hill, Nathan W. 2013a. *ḥdug* as a testimonial marker in Classical and Old Tibetan. *Himalayan Linguistics* 12(1). 1–16.
Hill, Nathan W. 2013b. Contextual semantics of 'Lhasa' Tibetan evidentials. *SKASE Journal of Theoretical Linguistics* 10(3). 47–54.
Hill, Nathan W. This volume. Perfect testimonial constructions: the inferential semantics of direct evidence. In Lauren Gawne & Nathan W. Hill (eds.), *Evidential Systems of Tibetan Languages*, 131–159. Berlin; Boston: Mouton de Gruyter.
Kretschmar, Monika. 1986. *Erzählungen und Dialekt der Drokpas aus Südwest-Tibet*. Sankt Augustin: VGH-Wissenschaftsverlag.
Miller, Roy Andrew. 1955. The independent status of Lhasa dialect within Central Tibetan. *Orbis* 4(1). 49–55.
Oisel, Guillaume. 2013. Morphosyntaxe et semantique des auxiliaires et des connecteurs du tibétain littéraire: étude diachronique et synchronique. Université Sorbonne Nouvel - Paris 3 dissertation.
Payne, Thomas E. 1997. *Describing Morphosyntax: a guide for field linguists*. Cambridge University Press.
Róna-Tas, András. 1985. *Wiener Vorlesungen zur Sprach- und Kulturgeschichte Tibets*. Vienna: Arbeitskreis für Tibetische und Buddhistische Studien, Universität Wien.
Tibetan and Himalayan Library. http://www.thlib.org/reference/transliteration/#!essay=/thl/ewts
Tournadre, Nicolas. 1994. Personne et médiatif en tibétain. *Faits de langues* 3. 149–158.
Tournadre, Nicolas. 1996a. *L'érgativite en Tibétain. Approche morpho-syntaxique de la langue parlée*. Louvain/Paris: Peeters.
Tournadre, Nicolas. 1996b. Comparaison des systèmes méditatifs en tibétain central, ladakhi, dzongkha et amdo. In Zlatka Guentchéva (ed.), *L'Enonciation médiatisée* (Bibliothèque de l'Information Grammaticale 35), 195–213. Louvain/Paris: Peeters.
Tournadre, Nicolas. 2014. The Tibetic languages and their classification. In Thomas Owen-Smith & Nathan Hill (eds.), *Trans-Himalayan linguistics: Historical and descriptive linguistics of the Himalayan area*, 105–130. Berlin: Mouton de Gruyter.
Tournadre, Nicolas & Sangda Dorje. 1998. *Manuel de Tibétain Standard: langue et civilisation*. Paris: L'Asiathèque.
Tournadre, Nicolas & Sangda Dorje. 2003. *Manual of Standard Tibetan: Language and civilization*. Ithaca: Snow Lion.
Vokurková, Zuzana. 2008. Epistemic modalities in Spoken Standard Tibetan. Filozofická Fakulta Univerzity Karlovy and Université Paris 8 dissertation.
Volkart, Marianne. 2000. The meaning of the auxiliary morpheme '*dug* in the context of the aspect systems of some Central Tibetan dialects. *Linguistics of the Tibeto-Burman Area* 23(2). 127–153.
Willett, Thomas. 1988. A cross-linguistic survey of the grammaticalization of evidentiality. *Studies in Language* 12. 51–97.
Wylie, Turrell. 1959. A standard system of Tibetan transcription. *Harvard Journal of Asiatic Studies* 22. 261–267.

Other Tibetan languages

Marius Zemp
9 Evidentiality in Purik Tibetan

9.1 Introduction

Purik is spoken by around 100,000 people (predominantly Shia Muslims) in the area with the same name around its hub, Kargil town in the western part of Ladakh (Jammu & Kashmir, India). Not much is known about the history of Purik. The area was Tibetanized probably over 1200 years ago. Ever since, Purik's eastern and northern neighbors Ladakh and Baltistan have tended to attract much more interest from both native and foreign scholars (see Zeisler 2004). As a consequence, most of the Purikpas I met when I first came to Kargil did not believe me when I expressed my intent to describe their language, telling me that it was probably Balti or Ladakhi I was interested in. I hope that they will not feel this way about their language anymore if they see the many respects in which its thorough analysis proves crucial for our understanding of the evolution of evidentiality in Tibetan.[1]

Tournadre and LaPolla (2014) note that the phenomena observed in different Tibetan varieties warrant a definition of evidentiality broader than Aikhenvald's (2004) and suggest the inclusion of the speaker's "access to information" in addition

---

[1] The Purik data presented here are my own. I collected them on several field trips between 2004 and 2010 and was able to complete my PhD thesis (Zemp 2013) on the grammar of that variety of Tibetan in December 2013 and defend it in February 2014. The present study will not make reference to the previous work on Purik, i.e. Konow (1909), Bailey (1920), Rangan (1979), Sharma (2004), and Purig (2007).

Note: The present chapter is dedicated to the loving memory of my main language consultant Syed Abbas of Doqs, Gongma Kargil. I am thankful to him and his whole family for treating me like one of their own. My thanks are also owed to my other main consultants Syed Mehdi of Doqs and Kacho Shabir Jawed of Yabgo, Gongma Kargil. I am also indebted to the Swiss National Science Foundation (SNSF) for repeatedly funding my description of Purik. The SNSF's Early Postdoc. Mobility fellowship P2BEP1_159046 "The resultative reanalysis of Proto-Tibetan and the evidence from Old Tibetan" has given me the opportunity to come to Kobe, Japan, to put my reconstruction of the Proto-Tibetan verbal system on a more solid basis. I am thankful to Tsuguhito Takeuchi for kindly inviting me to work with him and for his great support ever since. Finally, I owe my thanks to the anonymous reviewer and to the editors for their valuable comments on earlier drafts of this contribution. Needless to say that I assume sole responsibility for the views proposed here as well as any remaining errors.

DOI 10.1515/9783110473742-009

to its "source".² However, even if we accept that broader definition of evidentiality, we are still left with the problem that, of the two opposed existential copulas, it is only *duk* (Written Tibetan *'dug*³) that offers an evidential meaning, indicating directly attested information. The contrasting copula *jot* (WT *yod*) neither synchronically encodes nor at any time in its history encoded an evidential notion.⁴ Instead, while its 'factual' meaning is clearly 'epistemic' today, Purik *jot* still reflects the epistemically neutral 'factual' function it used to serve when it was still the only existential copula of the language, that is, before any evidential or epistemic notions were encoded in the verbal morphology. As soon as *yod* became contrasted by the 'testimonial'⁵ *'dug*, however, it became 'epistemicized'⁶ into emphasizing that it indicates facts, which is what *jot* has been doing ever since. It is important to note in this context that the equative copula *in* (Written Tibetan *yin*) retained a 'plain factual' meaning in Purik, evidently because it did not contrast with a second equative copula (unlike in many other dialects, where *yin* was thereby epistemicized). The evidence of the copulas thus suggests that evidentiality first emerged in Purik when a form of the full verb *'dug* 'stay' acquired its testimonial meaning.

The testimonial *duk* expresses that the speaker directly witnessed the state indicated but is not familiar with its history. It implies the speaker's inductive inference that the state in reality corresponds to what she perceived and indicated

---

2 Compare Aikhenvald's definition of evidentiality as "a linguistic category whose primary meaning is source of information" (2004: 3) and Tournadre and LaPolla's definition of evidential marking as "representation of source and access to information according to the speaker's perspective and strategy" (2014: 240).
3 While I render forms from Purik and forms mainly reconstructed on the basis of Purik with voiceless final stops, I generally retain the spelling of forms attested in Written Tibetan (WT) and accordingly leave final stops voiced, even though they are likely to have been devoiced before a pausa already in Proto-Tibetan.
4 Perhaps similar phenomena can be observed in the Papuan languages Oksapmin, Foe, and Fasu, with regard to which San Roque and Loughnane note that systems "with opposed participatory(-factual) and visual(-sensory) evidential inflections challenge accepted typologies of evidentiality, which typically do not include participatory or factual categories, but treat participatory experience as something entirely separate from evidence (Willett 1988: 91), or as a secondary or extended meaning of visual, direct, and first-hand categories (Aikhenvald 2004: 186–193)" (2012: 152).
5 Tournadre (1996), Volkart (2000), and Hill (2013) also use the term 'testimonial' for *'dug*.
6 For the term 'epistemicization' see Zemp (2013). We will see that the 'epistemicized factual' function of *yod* is also behind its indicating "old-assimilated knowledge" in Lhasa Tibetan (cf. DeLancey 1986 etc.).

it to represent based on her[7] assumption that she was not deceived. In contrast, the factual *jot* expresses a present state the speaker deductively infers to hold at the moment of speaking from what she knows about its history. A central characteristic of deductive inferences is reflected by the fact that the use of *jot* neither depends on a recent direct testimony nor would be proven wrong by a simple piece of conflicting evidence.

The content of the present overview of the Purik verb system is outlined below. For the wide variety of constructions that employ either an equative or an existential copula, the sections in which they are discussed are indicated in Tab. 1. The derived copulas that can replace the basic copulas in most of the constructions of Tab. 1 are listed in Tab. 2, again together with crossreferences.

Simple Past: (*ma*) V(-*s*) (§2.1)
Simple Negated Generic Prospective: *mi* V (§2.2)
Dynamic Past: V-*(s)e joŋ-s*, V-*(s)e soŋ* (§2.3)
Constructions employing the
– existential copulas *jot* or *duk* (§3, cf. also Tabs. 1 and 2)
– equative copula *in* (§4) (cf. also Tabs. 1 and 2)

More particular evidentials:
– quotative (-)*lo* (§5.1)
– indirect evidential V-*tʰik soŋ(-set)* (§5.2)
– assumptive -*tʃapo* (§5.3)

Postsentential demonstratives: "proximate" *de* and "obviative" *e* (§6)

Tab. 1: The copular constructions of Purik.

Basic meaning	Equative copula	Negated	See. §	Existential copulas	Negated	See. §
Future	V-*tʃ-in*	V-*tʃa men*	4.1	V-*tʃa jot*	V-*tʃa met*	3.1.2
				V-*tʃa duk*	V-*tʃa mi-nduk*	
Progressive	–	–		V-*en-jot*	V-*pa-met*	3.1.3
				V-*en-duk*	V-*pa-mi-nduk*	

---

[7] I am generally using female forms in order to make up for the fact that I almost exclusively worked with male informants. Note that the Purik pronoun for the third person (*kʰo* '(s)he') does not distinguish between genders.

Tab. 1 (continued)

Basic meaning	Equative copula	Negated	See. §	Existential copulas	Negated	See. §
Prospective	–	–		V-et	V-pa-met	3.2.4
				V-(t/n)uk	mi V	3.2.5
Habitual	–	–		V-pa-t	mi V-pa-t	3.2.6
				–	–	
Resultative	V-se in	ma V-pa in	4.2	V-se jot/met	ma V-pa jot	3.1.4
				V-se duk/ mi-nduk	ma V-pa duk	
Inferential	–	–		V-set	–	3.2.3
				V-suk	ma V-suk	3.2.2
Perfective	V(-s)-p-in	ma V(-s)-p-in	4.3	–	–	
				–	–	

Tab. 2: The copulas of Purik.

	Equative	Existential	
	(Plain factual)	(Epistemicized) factual	Testimonial
Present	in, §4 (inferential in-suk, §3.2.2)	jot, §3	duk, §3
Past	in-m-in, §4.4	jot-p-in, §4.4	simple repeated testimony
			jot-suk, §3.2.2 duk-p-in, §4.4
Inferential	in-m-in-suk, §4.4, 3.2.2	jot-p-in-suk, §4.4, 3.2.2	–

9.2 Simple finite verb forms

9.2.1 The Simple Past (ma) V(-s)

The Simple Past facilitates an epistemically neutral description of a past event; it consists of the plain verb root (viz. the past stem of *tʃʰa* 'go', *soŋ* 'went', and *za* 'eat', *zos* 'ate', the only two verbs of Purik for which it differs from the root) and an -s-suffix if the root in question denotes a transitive event. Examples (1)–(3) illustrate the basic principles of the Simple Past; (2) shows its negation by *ma*.

Examples (4)–(6) show that certain contexts regularly trigger a resultative analysis of intransitive verbs viz. an inchoative analysis of a transitive verb, as in (7).⁸

(1) ŋa-a   rdʒet
    I-DAT   forget
    'I forgot!'

(2) kʰo-a   ʃaŋ   ma   kʰor
    (s)he-DAT   consciousness NEG   turn
    '(S)he didn't regain consciousness.'

(3) kʰo-s   kʰunt-i   naŋ-po   ʂṭip-s
    (s)he-ERG   themselves-GEN   house-DEF   tear.down-PST
    'He tore his family's house down.'

(4) ɬtoχs-a
    become.hungry-Q
    'Are you hungry (now)?' (lit. 'Did you become hungry?')

(5) tʰoŋ-a
    be.visible-Q
    'Can you see (it)?' (lit. 'Did it become visible to you?', and in other contexts: 'Did you see it?')

(6) tʃʰarpa   joŋ-s
    rain   come-PST
    'It's started to rain.' (In other contexts: 'It rained.')

(7) baŋ   zer-s
    adhan   say-PST
    'The adhan's started to pray.' (In other contexts: 'The adhan prayed.')

9.2.2 The Simple Negated Generic Prospective *mi* V

When a simple verb stem is preceded by the negating *mi* as in (8)–(11), it is interpreted as conveying a generic prospective notion that may be paraphrased as 'I (would) never V'. Note that this Simple Negated Generic Prospective does not have a simple affirmative equivalent.

---

8 Examples (4) and (5) are regularly used in the resultative sense, while (6) and (7) have been attested in it but more commonly describe past events.

(8) ŋa-s   mi   tʰuŋ
    I-ERG   NEG   drink
    'I don't smoke.' (This may also mean 'I don't drink.' In either context, it may also be translated prospectively as 'I will not smoke/drink if I get the chance to.')

(9) ŋa-a   mi   rgos
    I-DAT   NEG   need
    'I don't (or won't) need that.'

(10) zer-aŋ-wa,   ŋa-s   su-a   mi   zer
     say-TE-hey⁹   I-ERG   who-DAT   NEG   say
     'Tell me, come on! I don't (or won't) tell anyone.'

(11) dj-u-la   ŋa-na   mi   ʒiks
     this-DEF-DAT   I-EMPH   NEG   be.afraid
     '(As far as I'm concerned) I'm not scared of this.' (or: 'I won't be scared of something like this.')

9.2.3 Dynamic Past V-*(s)e joŋ-s/soŋ*

A more vivid description of a past event is rendered by subordinating the *-(s)e*-participle of the verb denoting that event to a basic motion verb. The event is conceptualized as having approached the speaker by *joŋ-s* 'came', as illustrated in (12), and as having proceded into any other direction by *soŋ* 'went', as in (13). The verb *joŋ-s* strongly implies that the speaker was present at and directly witnessed the event (and represented its goal, even if by accident), cf. (12). Since the assertion of a movement normally preconditions the testimony of the moving entity in at least two different locations, *soŋ* tends to similarly imply that the informant directly witnessed the event. However, examples (14)–(17) demonstrate that neither V-*(s)e joŋ-s* nor V-*(s)e soŋ* grammatically indicate direct testimony. In (14), *laŋs-e joŋ-s* 'came rising' is metaphorically extended from the 'real world' to the 'world of living beings'. That the event was not directly witnessed is even

---

9 While both *-aŋ* and *-wa* correspond to what are generally classified as 'clitics', I choose not to distinguish 'clitic boundaries' from other boundaries by means of an equals sign (instead of a hyphen or a mere space), as per the Leipzig Glossing Rules. Instead of just three distinct degrees of bonding (i.e. the one that holds between two words, a clitic and its host, and an affix and its host), I am convinced that any language exhibits a continuum of construction-specific degrees of bonding that may hold between two morphemes.

more evident in (15), where *kʰjor-e soŋ* 'became bent' is metonymically extended into a temporal dimension. Furthermore, (17) exemplifies that both V-*(s)e joŋ-s* and V-*(s)e soŋ* may also be used to describe a motion controlled by the speaker. Both constructions are also commonly used to describe two consecutive events, as illustrated in (17).

(12) *hendaʁ-na ldwat but-e   joŋ-s*
     roof-ABL   DRM   fall-CNJ   come-PST
     'It fell down from the roof at once.'

(13) *tʃʰu-u   bo-se   soŋ*
     water-DEF   be.spilled-CNJ   went
     '(Some of) the water has spilled.'

(14) *kʰo-e   stroq   but,   jaŋ   laŋs-e   joŋ-s*
     (s)he-GEN   soul   fall   again   rise-CNJ   come-PST
     Her/his life was spared, (s)he stood up again.

(15) *jurba-o   kʰjor-e   soŋ*
     canal-DEF   become.bend-CNJ   went
     'The canal has become curved.'

(16) *drul-e   joŋ-s*
     walk-CNJ   come-PST
     '(I) came by foot.'

(17) *ʒiŋ-po   smo-se   joŋ-s*
     field-DEF   plow-CNJ   come-PST
     'I came (here) after having plowed the field.'

9.3 The existential copulas: testimonial *duk* vs. factual *jot*

9.3.1 Full forms

The two existential copulas *duk* and *jot* consistently exhibit the testimonial and factual functions mentioned in §1 to respectively reflect generalized inductive and deductive inferences. It is shown in §3.1.1 that both *duk* and *jot* as well as the suffixes containing them are construed from the perspective of an 'informant' that corresponds to the speaker in a statement, the addressee in a question, and any reported speaker (or thinker). I then consider how *duk* and *jot* are used after adjectives or locational nominals (i.e. (pro)nouns in the dative, locative, or inessive case, see §3.1.1), after the 'prospective' -*tʃa*-infinitive (§3.1.2), the 'progressive' -*en*- (§3.1.3), or the 'conjunctive' -*(s)e*-participle (§3.1.4).

Even though the existential copulas immediately follow all of the nominalizations just mentioned, their negated correspondences are not parallel. This is not surprising, given that the question of what falls under the scope of a negation is expanded when the verb expresses evidential and epistemic notions in addition to temporal and aspectual ones. Hence, while V-*tʃa met/mi-nduk* is the regular negation of the prospective V-*tʃa jot/duk* (where both the affirmative and negative may be paraphrased as 'there is (no) indication for a future V-ing'), *V-*en met/mi-nduk* is ungrammatical, presumably because it would not be clear whether the negation has scope over just the progressive or the event as a whole. Instead, one has to use the more general V-*pa met/mi-nduk* 'there is no V-ing'. Finally, V-*(s)e met/mi-nduk*, is only used with verbs that entail the disappearance of the S- or the O-argument – *nota bene* in order to indicate that the event *took place* (while its negation can again only be expressed by means of the more general -*pa*-infinitive, i.e. *ma* V-*pa jot/duk* 'has not V-ed').

Section 3.1.5 treats a few contexts in which only one or the other of the two existential copulas may be used.

9.3.1.1 After adjectives and locational nominals

The basic syntactic functions of the existential copulas are exemplified in (18)–(20): in (18), *duk/jot* locate an entity/entities (*pulispa* 'policemen') at a certain place (*zamb-e-r-i-ka* 'by the bridge'), in (19), they indicate the existence of an entity (*pene* 'money', here specifying its quantity by *maŋmo* 'a lot') at a certain place (*ŋa-a* 'to me, on me'), and in (20), they attribute a quality (*rgjala* 'good', with respect to *zbri-a* '(at) writing') to an entity ($k^h o$ '(s)he'). These three main functions may be called locational or qualitative existential (18), existential in the narrow sense or quantitative existential (19), and attributive (20), which can be either qualitative or quantitative.

(18) *zamb-e-ri-ka*   *pulispa*   *joŋ-s*   *duk/jot*
      bridge-GEN-this-LOC   police.man   come-PST   EX.T/EX.F
      '(I saw / I know that) there are policemen by the bridge.'

(19) *ŋa-a*   *pene*   *maŋmo*   *duk/jot*
      I-DAT   money   a.lot   EX.T/EX.F
      '(I saw / I know that) I have a lot of money.'

(20) $k^h o$-*a*   *zbri-a*   *rgjala*   *duk/jot*
      (s)he   write-INF   good   EX.T/EX.F
      '(I saw / I know that) (s)he's good at writing.'

In all of (18)–(20), the copula *duk* is used when the speaker recently (typically immediately prior to the utterance) acquired the information conveyed by direct testimony. In contrast, the speaker uses *jot* when she does not base her statement on the currently available direct evidence but simply knows for a fact that the policemen are stationed there in (18), that she has (generally) not been short of money in (19), and when she is well-acquainted with the subject's writing skills in (20).

The choice between factual *jot* and testimonial *duk* in questions is always calculated from the anticipated perspective of the addressee.[10] The interrogator knows that the addressee will have to choose between the same two forms that are available to herself and to every speaker of the language. In (21), the interrogator may therefore appeal to the addressee's knowledge (i.e. what she has experienced enough times for her to be sure that it's a fact) by means of *jot-a* or her direct testimony (here: when she saw the subject writing) by means of *dug-a*.

(21) kʰo-a   zbri-a   rgjala   dug-a/jot-a
     (s)he   write-INF   good   EX.T-Q/EX.F-Q
     'Is (s)he good at writing (from what you saw / from what you know)?'

In the context of reported speech, the choice between factual *jot* and testimonial *duk* is calculated from the perspective of the reported speaker or more generally the source. Thus, in (22) the 'quotative' *-lo* (cf. §5.1) unequivocally indicates that the verbal form reflects the viewpoint of that source. Accordingly, *jod-lo* indicates that the source depicted the information in question as a fact, while *dug-lo* indicates that the source based his/her statement on a direct testimony (only).[11]

(22) kʰo-a   pene   maŋmo   dug-lo/jod-lo
     (s)he-DAT   money   a.lot   EX.T-HS/EX.F-HS
     'I heard that (s)he has a lot of money (at the moment / in general).'

In order to keep the ensuing analysis slim, I do not consistently cover all three utterance types in the remainder of this chapter. However, it must be kept in mind that the choice between *jot* and *duk* as well as the related suffixes always reflects the perspective of the "informant", following Bickel's (2008)

---

[10] Tournadre and Dorje (2003: 94) refer to this phenomenon as the "rule of anticipation".
[11] That the hearsay marker *-lo* regularly leaves the identity of the source unspecified has no bearing on the fact that it specifies that source's access to the reported information. In contrast, personal pronouns are consistently construed from the viewpoint of the current (reporting) speaker, thus *kʰo-a* rather than *ŋa-a* in (22), while coreferential pronouns are generally omitted. Tournadre and Dorje (2003: 215) coin the term "hybrid reported speech" in order to describe essentially the same phenomena in Lhasa Tibetan.

terminology,[12] i.e. the speaker in statements, the addressee in questions, and the source in reported speech.

9.3.1.2 Future V-*tʃa duk/jot*, negated V-*tʃa mi-nduk/met*
Examples (23)–(25) illustrate the use of the existential copulas after the -*tʃa*-infinitive, which indicates a prospective meaning (cf. §4.2.4 in Zemp 2013). By using the negated testimonial *mi-nduk* (cf. its factual equivalent *met*) after the infinitive *tʰjaq-tʃa* in (23), the informant expresses that she will not be able to lift a certain object if the addressee does not help her, and that she reached this verdict after herself trying to lift it. The interrogative factual *jot-a* in (24), on the other hand, appeals to the addressee to consider evidence beyond what is directly attestable to everybody involved (i.e. how her right arm feels or how much it hurts during work rather than, e.g., the size of the pile of wheat that needs to be threshed). Finally, in (25), *jod-lo* indicates that the quoted source had access to information that allowed him[13] to depict the imminent arrival of cars in Kargil as a fact.

(23) tʰjaq-tʃa   mi-nduk,   ŋa-a   ɲan-tʃa   mi-nduk,   gjen-tsa-a   tʰjoq
     lift-INF2   NEG-EX.T   I-DAT   be.able-INF2   NEG-EX.T   up-LIM-DAT   lift\IMP
     '(I) can't lift it, (I) can't do it, lift it up a little higher!'

(24) jaraŋ-a   jaŋ   las   ba-a   ɲan-tʃa   jot-a
     you(hon.)-DAT   again   work   do-INF   be.able-INF2   EX.F-Q
     'Will you be able to do work again?'

(25) ŋa-s   aʁ-i-ka-na   tri-s-p-in   diriŋ   gaɽi   ɬep-tʃa   jod-lo
     I-ERG   Agha-G-LOC-ABL   ask-PST-NR-EQ   today   car   arrive-INF2   EX.F-QUOT
     'I asked the Agha, and (he) said that today cars will get through (to Kargil).'

9.3.1.3 Present (continuous) V-*en-duk/jot*, neg. V-*pa-min-duk/met*
The -*en*-participle indicates an event that is ongoing at the moment to which the superordinate matrix verb relates. If that verb is an existential copula, this corresponds to the moment of speaking. Thus, *zer-en-duk* in (26) expresses that

---

[12] Different scholars have referred to essentially the same phenomenon by means of a number of different terms including "epistemic source" (Hargreaves 2005), "locutor" (Curnow 1997; Aikhenvald 2004), or "source of information" (Tournadre 2008).

[13] Note that the Agha might not be the ultimate, original but only an intermediate source; he probably got the information from his son who had called him on his way back from Kashmir. Irrespective of who it was, *jod-lo* indicates the privileged access of that *ultimate* source of information.

the informant observes the ongoing event at the time of speaking, while *zer-en-jot* in (27) means that she has herself been performing it and wants to continue doing so.

(26) kʰo-s   sawaq-po   ldzap-se   zer-en-duk
     (s)he-ERG   lesson-DEF   repeat-CNJ   say-PROG-EX.T
     '(S)he's repeating (what (s)he's learned in) the lesson.'

(27) ŋa-s   sawaq   zer-en-jot,   tʃi   graʁ-et
     I-ERG   lesson   say-PROG-EX.F   what   chat-CRT
     'I'm teaching (here)! Why are you talking to each other?'

Whereas the negation of the existential copula after the *-tʃa*-participle negates the entire proposition, the *-en*-participle cannot be subordinated to a negated existential copula and must instead be replaced by the *-pa*-infinitive. This restriction presumably occurs because it would otherwise not be clear whether the negation should have scope over the entire proposition or just the notion of 'ongoingness'. The negation of the *-pa*-infinitive (i.e. *zer-ba min-duk/met* 'lit. There is no saying.') is more general and thus better suited for that purpose.

9.3.1.4 Resultative V-*se duk/jot* (or V-*se min-duk/met*), neg. *ma* V-*pa duk/jot*

After the *-(s)e*-participle the affirmative *duk* in (28) and (30) and *jot* in (29) and (31) express the same testimonial and factual notions as elsewhere; note that *jot* relates to things that tend not to be directly observable in an objective way.

(28) lam-po   djaŋ-p-e-ka   kan-e   duk
     way-DEF   wall-DEF-G-LOC   rest-CNJ   EX.T
     'The (elevated) road is held up by the wall.'

(29) de   spera-o   tʃʰa-kʰan-pw-e-ka   kan-e   jot
     that   word-DEF   go-NLZR-DEF-G-LOC   depend-CNJ   EX
     'That depends on who goes (with me).'

(30) nor-un   ril   dams-e   duk,   kʰuks-e   duk
     sheep-PL   DRM   gather-CNJ   EX.T   be.under.control-CNJ   EX.T
     'The sheep are standing closely together, (they are) under control.'

(31) di   bomo   ŋa-a   kʰuks-e   jot
     this   girl   I-DAT   be.under.control-CNJ   EX.F
     'This girl is devoted to me.'

When the event denoted by the *-(s)e*-participle involves the disappearance or disintegration of the entity undergoing it, the (testimonial or factual) existential copula following it has to be negated, as illustrated in (32)–(34).[14] A participle like *ʃi-se* 'having died' may be used with either the negated or the affirmative existential copula depending on whether the informant wants to focus on the soul (as in example 33) or on the body (as in example 32) of the dead person or animal. It is no coincidence that the dead body that is referred to with an affirmative copula consecutively falls prey to the crows, who poke out its eyes until they are no more, as the negated copula in the second part of (32) indicates.

(32) *are-ka   bil-ek   ʃi-se   duk,   pʰoroq   saq   joŋ-se*
     that-LOC   cat-INDF   die-CNJ   EX.T   crow   all   come-CNJ
     mig-un   gaŋma   toχ-se   mi-nduk
     eye-PL   all   poke-CNJ   NEG-EX.T
     'There is a dead cat over there, the crows have come and poked its eyes out completely.'

(33) *uks   mi-nduk   dj-ul-la,   dj-u   ʃi-se   mi-nduk*
     breath   NEG-EX.T   this-DEF-DAT   this-DEF   die-CNJ   NEG-EX.T
     'There is no life in this; it's dead.'

(34) *ŋ-ji   mi   ʃi   zer-s   ha   mi   ʃi*
     I-GEN   man   die   say-PST   ...   man   die
     'My husband died, she said.' 'Huh?' 'My husband died.'
     mi   ʃi   zer-s   nam   ʃi   gundea   ʃi
     man   die   say-PST   when   die   yesterday   die
     'My husband died, she said.' 'When did he die?' 'Yesterday.'
     ni   dare   kap-se   met
     so?   now   bury-CNJ   NEG;EX.T
     'And now?' 'He's buried (and gone).'

9.3.1.5 Non-finite contexts

In conditional clauses and nominalizations, only the factual *jot* (but not *duk*) can serve as a predicate, since these contexts depend on an unmarked, epistemically neutral proposition.[15] On the other hand, there is also one typical context in which only testimonial *duk* is possible, namely indirect questions seeking knowledge that can only be acquired by means of a direct testimony.

---

14 That the (disintegrating) entity triggering the negation of the existential copula is the O-argument of a transitive clause such as (33) but the S-argument of an intransitive clause such as (32) or (34) may be considered as a type of "syntactic ergativity" in the sense of Dixon (1994).
15 This was noted for Lhasa Tibetan by Chang and Chang (1984: 607–608) and DeLancey (1990: 298, 315–316).

The epistemically neutral factual meaning of *jot* is retained before the conditional marker *-na*, as shown in (36) – a construction that depends on an epistemically neutral proposition. The plain factual function also adheres to *jot* when it is nominalized, e.g., by the relativizer *-kʰan*, or by the participial *-en* indicating simultaneity, as in (36), etc. In example (37) the direct evidential *-duk* of the first clause indicates that the informant bases her statement on direct testimony, but the existential copula to which the assumptive inferential *-tʃapo* is suffixed must be *jot*, again due to its plain factual reference.

(35) jaŋ   stoŋ   tʃik   ɲet-tʃa   jot-na   d-o   taŋ-ma   rgo-ʃ-in
     again   1,000   one   find-INF2   EX.F-CND   that-DEF   give-INF   need-INF2-EQ
     'If (you) can afford another 1000, (you) should give that.'

(36) qaqaqaqa   od-o   tʰul   skroχ-se   in,
     qaqaqaqa   that.very-DEF   egg   churn-CNJ   EQ
     alta-a   tʰul   taŋ-tʃa   jot-en-tʃik
     later-DAT   egg   give-INF2   EX.F-PROG-INDEF
     '"Qaqaqaqa!", that's when (the hen is) "churning" its egg, when it's about to lay an egg.'

(37) e   beto   zems-e   dul-en-duk,   skje-tʃa   jot-tʃapo
     that   cow   avoid-CNJ   walk-PROG-EX.T   give.birth-INF2   EX.F-ASSUM
     'That cow walks hesitantly; perhaps it is about to give birth.'

There are also contexts in Purik in which only the testimonial existential copula *duk* (but not *jot*) may be used. Examples (38) and (39) illustrate a type of subordinated indirect questions demanding information to be acquired by direct testimony. Naturally, only *duk* is suited for this function.

(38) ras-po   ɲuk,   ɬjaχmo   dug-a   ŋtsoqpo   ɬto-s
     cloth-DEF   cow   good   EX.T-Q   bad   look\IMP-IMP
     'Feel the cloth! Look whether it's good or bad!'

(39) kʰunt-es   tʃi   b-en-dug-a   ɬto-s
     they-ERG   what   do-PROG-EX.T-Q   look\IMP-IMP
     'Look what they're doing!'

9.3.2 Suffixed forms

9.3.2.1 V-z-duk

I have come across very few instances of V-*z-duk*. The head of this construction is the copula rather then the preceding verb. As a consequence, V-*z-duk* in (40) and (41) *attests a present state* resulting from a past event. That V-*z-duk* thereby fades out the event that led to the directly attested state is clearly notable in case of the transitive *taŋ-z-duk* in (40) (which is less accusing than either *taŋ-suk* '(you) have apparently put' or *taŋ-se duk* '(you) have put it the way it is now', cf. §3.1.4).

(40) kot̪-i   goŋṣtsa-o   ldabldab-a   taŋ-z-duk,   pʰjarpʰjar-la
     coat-GEN   lap-DEF   hanging-DAT   give-STAT-EX.T hanging.down-DAT
     taŋ-z-duk,   zom-ba-mi-nduk,   osmet-tʃik   tʃʰ-en-duk
     give-STAT-EX.T   suit-INF-NEG-EX.T   bad-INDF   go-PROG-EX.T
     'The lap of the coat is hanging down, it doesn't suit (you), it looks awkward.'

(41) di   kor-e-aŋ-na   tʃa   mana   gaŋ-z-duk,   pʰet-tʃik   pʰri-s
     this   cup-G-INE-MPH   tea   very   be.full-STAT-EX.T half-INDF   reduce-IMP
     'But this cup is so full of tea, reduce it by the half!'

9.3.2.2 Inferential V-*suk*

In the V-*suk* construction the main verb and not the copula is the head. A few examples suffice to illustrate use of this frequently encountered construction.[16] Both *soŋ-suk* and *pʰoχ-suk* in (42) indicate that a past event is inferred on the basis of its directly attested result; *ʃes-en-duk* also points to the fact that the speaker is actually *looking* at the apricots. Unlike the conjunctive *-(s)e*-suffix, which lacks the *-s-* after verbs ending in *-r*, *-l*, *-n*, and *-t*, the inferential *-suk* never drops the *-s* and is instead often affricized after the first three of these finals, as exemplified by *mel-tsʰuk* in (43). In (44), the interrogative *ran-sug-a ~ [rantsʰuga]* is followed by a negated question tag *mi-nduk*. The proper negation of V-*suk*, however, is facilitated by a preceding *ma*, as illustrated in (45).

(42) tʃuli   sarasire   soŋ-suk,   ot   pʰoχ-suk   tʃuli   karpo
     apricot   reddish   went-INFR   light   lit-INFR   apricot   white
     ʃes-en-duk
     estimate-PROG-EX.T
     'The apricots have become reddish, the light hit them (they have come to shine); the apricots look bright.'

(43) kʰ-i   puksmo   mel-tsʰuk,   jaŋ   dorm-ek   kʰjoŋ-tʃa-o
     you-GEN   knee   wear.off-INFR   again   pants-INDF   bring-INF2-DEF
     'The knees (of your pants) is worn off; you'll have to get new pants.'

---

16 While V-*z-duk* primarily makes a statement about a present state, V-*suk* primarily relates to a past event.

(44) madi   ol-j-aŋ   soŋ-set   tʃʰu   taŋ-ma   ran-sug-a
     Mehdi   meadow-G-INE   went-RES   water   give-INF   be.time-INFR-Q
     mi-nduk   ɬta-a
     NEG-EX.T   look-INF
     'Mehdi's gone to the meadow to see whether the time to water has come or not.'

(45) bjama   na   semen-po   ma   gres-suk
     sand   and   cement-DEF   neg   become.mixed-INFR
     'The sand and the cement haven't become mixed (properly).'

Non-resultative inferential *in-suk*

When suffixed to the equative copula *in*, as in (46)–(49), *-suk* indicates a general inference of an equation on the basis of information just acquired or just understood. Note that *in-suk* is used after an adjective in (48) and after the conjunctive *-se*-participle in (49) and thereby relates to the intrinsic (here: irreversible) properties of an entity.

(46) kʰo   spera   kʰjen-kʰan   in-suk
     (s)he   word   have.a.presentiment-NMLZ   EQ-INFR
     '(S)he appears to be someone who is able to tell what people are about to say.'

(47) smiŋ   in-suk
     smiŋ   EQ-INFR
     'It appears that it's the *smiŋ* (name of a mountain) (I don't have any doubts anymore now that we have come closer).'

(48) dj-u   ṣniŋma   in-suk
     this-DEF   old   EQ-INFR
     'This (aereal photography of Kargil) appears to be old.'

(49) pʰe   kʰimo   taŋ-se   in-suk   iks-en-duk   zer   kʰo-a
     flour   a.lot   give-CNJ   EQ-INFR   choke-PROG-EX.T   say   (s)he-DAT
     'She's apparently put in too much flour. Tell her that it's difficult to swallow!'

The suffix *-suk* expresses the same general inferential notion after complex forms ending in the copula *in*, such as V-(s-)p-in-suk in (50) or (51), jot-p-in-suk in (52), V-tʃ-in-suk in (53), or its negation V-tʃa men-suk in (54). Furthermore, *-suk* serves the same function after the affirmative 'habitual' V-pa-t in (55), its negation in (56), or its past form (ending in the equative copula again) V-pa-t-p-in illustrated in (57).

(50) *kʰje-s   ʁalat   sam-b-in-suk*
     you-ERG   wrong   think-INF-EQ-INFR
     'You appear to have thought wrong.'

(51) *dare   ʂkut   ŋon-et,   kʰo-s   ʂku-s-p-in-suk*
     now   theft   become.known-FCT   (s)he-ERG   steal-PST-INF-EQ-INFR
     'Now the theft is manifest: it was she who stole (it).'

(52) *bapʰro-a   kʰjer-tʃ-in-suk*
     covering-DAT   take.away-INF1-EQ-INFR
     '(The cows) are taken to their insemination (I guess).'

(53) *kʰjeraŋ   tʰoŋ-ma-na   jaaŋ   ba-tʃa   men-suk*
     you   be-visible-INF-CND   again\EMPH   do-INF2   NEG;EQ-INFR
     'Now that (she)'s seen you, she's not going to do it again, it appears. (The one year old Jabin had made a funny noise before that.)'

(54) *ŋat-i   spera   ma   go-na-ŋ   tʃʰaχtsik   tʃʰut-pa-t-suk*
     we.PL-GEN   word   NEG   hear-CND-TE   a.little   understand-INF-FCT-INFR
     'Even if she (the one year old Jabin) doesn't hear our words, she understands a little, it appears.'

(55) *do-o   mi   zer-ba-t-suk*
     that-PEF   NEG   say-INF-FCT-INFR
     '(I now realize or think that) (we) don't say that.'

(56) *ŋa-s   sam-et   kʰo-e   tʰu-j-aŋ   tug   joŋ-ma-t-suk*
     I-ERG   think-FCT   (s)he-GEN   spit-G-INE   poison   come-INF-FCT-INFR
     'I think that there is even poison in their (i.e. the *ɬakotse's*) spit. (Now that I think about it!)'

(57) *snas-i   namz-e-aŋ   kol-ba-t-p-in-suk*
     I-ERG   think-FCT   use-INF-FCT-INF-EQ-INFR
     'It appears to have been used in the past.'

The past-testimonial existential copula *jot-suk*

As illustrated in (58) and (59), *jot-suk* indicates a directly attested past state (rather than an inferred present state, as one might expect from merely adding up its components). In full analogy to *jot*, its suffixed forms V-*et* and V-*set* through the addition of -*suk* respectively indicate an event ongoing at the time it was witnessed in the past and an event completed by the time its result was attested in the past, as shown in (60) and (61).

(58) rgjamtsʰo-u ŋa tra-se   soŋ,   tʃʰu-u   di-s   jot-suk
     river-DEF   I   wade-CNJ   went   water-DEF this-ERG EX-INFR
     'I waded through the river, the water came upto here (pointing to the chest).'

(59) kʰo-s   paχspa   ɲe-n-jot-suk   gundea   di-ka,
     (s)he-ERG skin   rub-PROG-EX.F-INFR   yesterday   this-LOC
     diriŋ   kʰo-a   dul-e   in-suk
     today   (s)he-DAT   become.soft-CNJ   EQ-INFR
     '(S)he was rubbing leather here yesterday, today, it appears to have become soft.'

(60) ʒiksmo   tʃig-i-ka,   jaŋ   rgjab-a   ɬte-en,   jaŋ   joŋ-et-suk,
     fear   one-G-LOC   again   back-DAT   look-PROG   again   come-CRT-INFR
     'Very much in fear, he kept looking back, came again (towards us),
     jaŋ   rgjab-a   ɬte-en   joŋ-et-suk,   kʰo   rgjab-a   ɬte-en
     again   back-DAT   look-PROG come-CRT-INFR   he   back-DAT   look-PROG
     came, while looking back again, looking back,
     ʒik-se   rgjab-a   ɬte-en   joŋ-suk-pa
     be.afraid-CNJ back-DAT   look-PROG   come-INFR-FOC
     while fear made him look back (again and again), he came (towards us).'

(61) kʰo-s   ŋ-ji   naŋ-po-a-aŋ   tʃu   ʂtat-set-suk   ma   ɬta-a
     (s)he-ERG I-GEN   house-DEF-DAT-too   water   put.on-RES-INFR   NEG   look-INF
     'He had accidently (lit. without looking) flooded my house, too.'

9.3.2.3 Factual resultative V-*set*

The factual resultative V-*set* (< V-*s-yod*) factually indicates both the past event that has led to a currently valid result as well as that resultant state. This peculiar double focus results from the fact that the construction originally had a 'perfect' meaning, and that this meaning was not lost when the construction acquired a 'past' meaning while its head shifted from the copula to the verb. Examples (62)–(65) illustrate that the familiarity the use of V-*set* requires may not only arise when the informant actually instigated has been the event in question, as in (62) and (63), but also when she repeatedly or continuously experienced it, as in (64), or when she was observing it, as in (65). Furthermore, in (44) above, V-*set* is used because the informant is aware of what the subject, his brother, is currently (supposed to be) doing.[17]

---

[17] Example (44) neatly reflects the deductive inference *jot* indicates through the opposition by *duk*: Even if the brother of the informant turned out to be on a small detour from his actual mission, the informant would still be generally agreed by speakers of Purik to have said the truth.

(62) ṣta-o   ṣtat-e   joŋ-set
    horse-DEF hand.over-CNJ   come-RES
    'I have come to bring the horse (back).'

(63) marpo   zaŋsbw-i-aŋ   taŋ-se   ʒu-set   ŋa-s
    red   copper.pot-G-INE   give-CNJ   melt-RES   I-ERG
    'I've melted (it) in a red copper pot.'

(64) laqp-i-ka   tsʰerma   zuk-set
    hand-G-LOC   thorn   sting-RES
    'Thorns have pricked (my) hand. (I felt when it happened during work.)'

(65) tʃʰu-u   χol-set
    water-DEF   boil-RES
    'The water's boiling. (I've had an eye on it.)'

Patronizing V-*set-in*

The factual resultative V-*set* combines with the adversatively used simultaneous participle *-en-/-in-* (cf. Zemp 2013: §4.2.2) and a suspended intonation in a construction with a 'patronizing' meaning. As illustrated in (66) and (67), with V-*set-in* the speaker expresses that the addressee should already know something. The speaker is in the position to make such a claim because she witnessed how the addressee acquired the knowledge in question. The composite meaning of the suspended V-*set-in* may be paraphrased as 'While I know that V has taken place, you seem to have forgotten about it.' If the predicate involves the disappearance of the entity in the absolutive case, the same patronizing notion is expressed by a conjunctive participle and a negated factual existential copula, as in (68) and (69).

(66) kʰo   joŋ-set-in
    (s)he   come-RES-PROG
    '(S)he's been here already for some time (and you know that).'

(67) kʰjes   kʰur-set-in,   tsʰat-aŋ,   ɲis-na   tʃi   ba-tʃ-in
    you-ERG   carry-RES-PROG   be.ok-TE   two-with   what   do-INF2-EQ
    'You carry (the camera) with you! Isn't that enough? What are you gonna do with two (cameras)?'

(68) tʃi   soŋ-wa,   kemra-o   ṣku-s   kʰjer-e   met-in
    what   went-hey   camera-DEF   steal-CNJ   take.away-CNJ   EX;NEG-PROG
    'What's wrong (with you)? (You know that) someone's stolen the camera.'

(69) naam-na   soŋ-se   met-in   kʰo
    when\EMPH-ABL   went-CNJ   EX;NEG-PROG   (s)he
    'Oh (s)he's been gone for a long time! You know that!'

9.3.2.4 Prospective certaintive V-*et*

By using V-*et* (< V-*yod*), the informant expresses having recognized the premises under which a future event may be depicted as guaranteed. In all the contexts in which Purik V-*et* is attested, it indicates the informant's certainty that an event will take place.

The 'certaintive' suffix takes the form -*et* (pronounced *[-ət]*) after any root-final consonant (e.g. *kʰjer-et* from *kʰjer* 'take away', *kʰṣel-et* from *kʰṣel* 'be ashamed', *bos-et* from *bos* 'call (of an animal)', *ɬtsam-et* from *ɬtsam* 'make warm', *len-et* from *len* 'take', *straŋ-et* ~ *[strãət]* from *straŋ* 'straighten', etc.). This suffix voices final labials and velars (e.g. *hjab-et* from *hjap* 'fan', *ɬug-et* from *ɬuk* 'pour', etc.) but not dental stops (e.g. *zgrat-et* from *zgrat* 'lean against', etc.), and both voices and fricatizes uvular stops (e.g. *ʒaq* 'put, keep, leave' : *ʒaʁ-et*, etc.). Tab. 3 illustrates the variants of -*et* after root-final vowels.

Tab. 3: The certaintive verb forms (V-*et*) of roots ending in vowels.

Root final	Factual ending	Verb root	Factual form
-*a*	-0-*et* [ɛt]	*ba* 'do'	*b-et* [bɛt]
		ṣŋa 'harvest'	*ṣŋ-et* [ṣŋj ɛt] ~ [ṣɲɛt]
-*e*	-0-*et* [ɛt]	*ɲe* 'rub'	*ɲe-t* [ɲet]
-*o*	-0-*et* [-øət] ~ [-wɛt]	*tʃo* 'make'	*tʃo-et* [tʃøət] ~ [tʃwɛt]
-*u*	-*u*-*it* [-yit] ~ [-wit]	*ŋu* 'cry'	*ŋu-it* [ŋyit] ~ [ŋwit]
-*i*	-*i*-*t*	*ṣtsi* 'count'	*ṣtsi-t*

Because their analysis has proven challenging, it is appropriate to adduce a large number of examples to illustrate the functions of V-*et*. Its different uses can all be accommodated by a 'certaintive prospective' meaning. This characterization works

i) in those contexts in which the informant plans to instigate an action in the future (and if she is already performing it, she must be conceived of as having its future achievement in mind), cf. (70)–(73)
ii) where she asserts a generic event and thereby expresses that under certain circumstances, an event will definitely take place (because it always takes place under these circumstances), cf. (74)–(80)
iii) in those contexts which I mistakenly analyzed as present continuous "endopathic sensations" (Zemp 2013, following the terminology of Tournadre 1996: 226), but which either involve a prediction based on present information to which the informant has privileged access, cf. (86)–(87), or describe a generic event (i.e. a sensation the informant always experiences under certain circumstances), cf. (89)–(94).
iv) for peculiar uses of *zer-et* 'she said/says/will say', (94), (95) and (96)
v) for strong warnings that imply that an event will take place if it is not immediately inhibited, cf. (97)–(99).

The volitional use of V-*et* illustrated in (70)–(73) is typical for 'conjunct'[18] forms in the world's languages. It may be characterized as involving deductive reasoning along the following lines: 'Since what I want to do is (eventually) done, and since I want to do V, V will be done.' In both (70) and (71), *tʃʰ-et* describes an action the informant is already performing or is about to perform or resume (after talking). Similarly, *joŋ-ed-lo* in (71) indicates that the subject was herself reported as having expressed her intention to come; and the first half of the sentence suggests that the person in question is already on her way. A prospective analysis forces us to view the informant in all of these examples as having the *achievement* of the event in mind. This analysis neatly captures the certaintive verb forms used in (72) and (73), both of which relate to the informant's future actions.

(70) ga-r   tʃʰ-et
     while-LOC   go-CRT
     'Where are you going?'

(71) ŋa   kʰo-a   su-se   tʃʰ-et,   kʰo   joŋ-ed-lo
     I   (s)he-DAT   go.to.receive-CNJ   go-CRT   (s)he go-CRT-HS
     'I'm going to receive her/him, (s)he's coming, I hear.'

(72) kʰir-i   in-na   na   bor,   ŋa-s   taŋ-et
     you-GEN   EQ-CND   oath   put   I-ERG   give-CRT
     'Swear that it's yours and I'll give it to you.'

(73) ɲiska-s   zbraχ-se   kus   tab-et
     both-ERG   join-CNJ   call   cast-CRT
     '(We will) both call jointly.'

The factual ending -*et* is also very commonly used to describe what I have called 'generic events', which means that it depicts an event as always taking place whenever certain conditions apply, as illustrated in (74)–(80). (Note that in (76) and (78)–(80), condition is actually explicitly mentioned.) The informant may depict such a causality as based on what she knows about the natural world or the customs of a group of people.

---

18 Even if the terms "conjunct" and "disjunct" (see. Hale 1980) are inadequate to describe Purik *jot* and *duk* (etc.), it appears – as Hargreaves (2005) claimed for conjunct forms in Kathmandu Newar – that Purik V-*et* in certain contexts expresses the informant's "privileged access" to some information.

(74) lo   kʰatʃig-a   joŋ-et,   lo   kʰatʃig-a   joŋ-ma-ŋ   met
     year   some-DAT   come-CRT   year   some-DAT   come-INF-too NEG.EX
     'Some years it does (snow here), some years it doesn't.'

(75) bo   ʒbʒi-a   man   tʃʰ-et
     dry.measure   four-DAT   dry.measure   go-CRT
     'Four *bo* equal one *man*.'

(76) ɲoskar   tʰaq-pa-na   mar   biŋ-et
     rape   grind-INF-CND   oil   come.out-CRT
     'When you grind rape(seed), oil comes out.'

(77) pʰrik   ma   skul-ba   pʰur-et
     DRM   NEG   move-INF   fly-CRT
     '(It, a certain bird) can fly without moving (its wings at all).'

(78) kʰs̩u   ma   kʰs̩u-na   kiʃik   tab-et
     wash   NEG   wash-CND   flea   cast-CRT
     'If (you) don't wash (yourself), (you) will have fleas.'

(79) ʒbʒi   na   pʰet-i-ka   baŋ   zer-et
     four   and   half-G-LOC   adhan   say-CRT
     'At half past four the *adhan* (prayer) is called.'

(80) tozar   za-tsa-na   nor   gaŋma   kug-et
     lunch   eat-LIM-CND   sheep   all   gather-CRT
     'He controls all his sheep while he eats lunch (a Kashmiri goat-herder).'

The form *ɬtoχs-et* '(I'm) hungry' illustrates why I mistook V-*et* as describing ongoing endopathic sensations. Only when it is preceded by *tʃi* 'what' in *tʃi ɬtoχs-et* 'What do you feel like eating?' does its prospective construal becomes manifest.

When V-*et* is used in a question about a future event that lies outside of the addressee's control, it often relates to that addressee's privileged access to the event. In (81)–(84), the addressee is asked to base his judgment on information that is available to him only. In (81) only the addressee is in the position to judge whether the dirt is coming off the clothes he is in the middle of washing. Similarly, the addressee is asked to weigh his ability to see despite the encroaching darkness in (82) (cf. also the haplologized negated form *tʰoŋ-m-ét*, which is more common than the full form *tʰoŋ-ma-met*). In (83), the addressee is asked to judge his ability to work in view of a certain task, and in (84), finally, his financial security.

(81) guntʃa   daʁ-et-a
    cloth   become.clean-CRT-Q
    'Does the dirt come off (the clothes you're in the middle of washing)?'

(82) kʰjeraŋ-a   lam-po   tʰoŋ-et-a,   ŋa-a   tʃaŋ
    you-DAT   way-DEF   be.visible-CRT-Q   me-DAT anything
    tʰoŋ-m-ét
    be.visible-INF-NEG;EX
    '(At night) Can you see the path? (Will you be able to see in time where the path is taking us?) I can't see anything!'

(83) kʰjeraŋ-a   di   las-po   lam-et-a   met
    you-DAT   this   work-DEF   feel.like-CRT-Q   NEG;EX
    'Do (or will) you have the energy to do this (or not)?'

(84) ane   pʰru   tsoq   son-et-a   kʰjeraŋ-a,   lokʰor-i
    wife   child all   be.alive-CRT-Q   you-DAT   one.year-GEN
    bos   tʃʰ-et-a
    livelihood   go-CRT-Q
    'Are you able to make a living for your wife and your kids? Will you get them through?'

That V-*et* may relate to the informant's privileged access to information is much less evident in statements. In (85), the speaker by using *ɲy-it-ta* appears to express that she – unlike the addressee – is able to recognize when her own baby is about to cry even though it cannot yet be heard. Two more uses of V-*et* may be taken as either expressing the informant's privileged access or a generic notion. In (86), the speaker appears to be predicting how other people will react to the addressee's behavior on the basis of how she herself reacts to it. With the form *pʰoʁ-et* in (87), the informant makes a safe prediction (or draws a conclusion) based on what she knows about the world, how she experienced the climate outside on the same day prior to the utterance, and how she herself feels.

(85) kʰo   tsʰups-wa,   ɲy-it-ta
    (s)he   sulk-hey   cry-CRT-REC
    '(S)he's about to cry; well, now, (s)he's crying (you'll hear in a second).'

(86) kʰje-s   has   maŋmo   ma   toŋ,   mi-in   stroʁ-et
    you-ERG   sweet.talk   a.lot   NEG   give\IMP   man-PL   scare.away-CRT
    'Don't talk too sweet! People will be scared away. (It scares *me* away!)'

(87) straŋ-a   tʃʰ-et,   silmo-a   łuŋ   pʰoʁ-et
    porch-DAT   go-CRT   cool-DAT   wind   hit-CRT
    'I'm going out on the porch, into the cool, to get some fresh air.'

The other uses of V-*et* that I mistook for "endopathic sensations" all describe sensations that the speaker always perceives under certain cirumstances, cf. (88)–(92). (Note that *ʒiks-ed-lo* in (90) expresses that the *reported speaker* is expected to be frightened whenever he is confronted with the cause of his fear.) In (91), the addressee is asked whether he doesn't get bored *from time to time* rather than whether he is bored at the moment of speaking. Finally, *tʃʰes-pa-met-a* and *tʃʰes-et* in (92) both describe a feeling of trust that is not restricted to the moment of speaking but should hold generally.

(88) ŋa   sɲiŋ   dar-et,   zer-ba   ɲan-ma-met
     I   heart   shiver-CRT   say-INF   be.able-INF-NEG;EX
     'I'm frightened, nervous (i.e. talking to a woman), I can't say (that I like her).'

(89) ŋj-i   sɲiŋ   rduŋ-ed-ou,   ʒiks-et
     I-GEN   heart   beat-CRT-hey   be.afraid-FCT
     'My heart's beating! I'm scared! (I'm afraid of hights!)'

(90) kʰo   ʒiks-ed-lo
     (s)he   be.afraid- CRT-QUOT
     '(S)he said that (s)he's scared.'

(91) kʰjeraŋ   sun-ma-met-a
     you   be.bored-INF-NEG;EX-INT
     'Don't you feel bored (sometimes)?'

(92) jaraŋ   ŋj-i-ka   tʃʰes-pa-met-a,   ŋa   jar-i-ka   tʃʰes-et
     you(hon.)   me-G-LOC   trust-INF-NEG;EX-Q   I   you(hon.)-G-LOC   trust-CRT
     'Don't you trust me? I trust you.'

The question-and-answer pair given in (93) and (94) exemplifies a use of V-*et* that is likely to be restricted to a semantically neutral *verbum dicendi* such as *zer* 'say'. The certaintive V-*et* is used instead of a past form, because the speaker can be expected to utter the same thing if asked again.

(93) kʰo-s   tʃʰa-a-met   zer-et
     (s)he- ERG   go-INF-NEG;EX   say-CRT
     '(S)he said (and will still say) that (s)he won't go.'

(94) odo-o   zer-et-a
     that.very-ERG   say-CRT-Q
     'Did (s)he say that?'

Finally, the deductive meaning of V-*et* facilitates its use in urgent appeals to take immediate action against an event, as illustrated by (95)–(98). In these examples, the speaker predicts that an event is certain to take place. Since the addressee, however, is in all three cases able to tell that the impending event would be harmful, the addressee infers that he is urged to take immediate action against it. Essentially the same notion of an impending event is also expressed by the subordinated interrogative tʃʰ-et-a in (98).[19]

(95) zbrul-is   so   tab-et
     snake-ERG   tooth   cast-CRT
     '(Watch out!) The snake is going to bite (you)! (Said when it's already opened its mouth.)'

(96) o   marius   kaŋma   tʃʰu-jaŋ   tʃʰ-et
     hey   Marius   foot   water-INE   go-CRT
     '(Watch out) Marius! (You're) about to put your foot into the water (i.e. a puddle)!'

(97) ŋj-i   laqpa   tʃaʁ-et
     me-GEN   hand   break-CRT
     '(You're) breaking my hand!'

(98) dj-u   goloʁa   tʃʰ-et-a   sam-se   ŋj-i   tsʰe   biŋ
     this-DEF   falling.down   go-CRT-Q   this-CNJ   me-GEN   life   go.out
     'Thinking that this was about to fall down, I was scared to death.'

9.3.2.5 Prospective potential V-(t/n)uk

The allomorphs of the potential prospective ending V-(t/n)uk after vowels and alveolar consonants are given in Tab. 4.

Tab. 4: The allomorphs of the potential prospective ending -(t/n)uk.

Stemfinal vowel		*-uk	Alveolar stemfinal		*-uk	Other stemfinal		*-duk
–a	>	–o	–r	>	–r –uk	–p	>	–p –tuk
–e	>	–e	–l	>	–l –uk	–k	>	–k –tuk
–o	>	–o	–t	>	–t –uk	–q	>	–q/χ –tuk
–i	>	–i	–n	>	–n –uk	–m	>	–m –nuk
–u	>	–u	–s	>	–s –uk	–ŋ	>	–ŋ –nuk

---

[19] A much less urgent warning may be expressed by means of V-(t/n)uk, cf. §3.2.5 immediately below.

The potential prospective ending V-*(t/n)uk* merely considers possible future events. As in (100), this construction can be used to express a much less urgent warning than with V-*et* (cf. examples (95) – (97)). The most frequent use of V-*(t/n)uk* is for events outside of the informant's control, as in (101) and (102) (where the additional *-hii*-suffix emphasizes the speaker's wondering about the future). Similarly, in (101)–(104), the speaker asks the addressee to take a guess about what a future event might look like by evaluating the present indication for it. The use of V-*(t/n)uk* may even express that the informant is only considering future actions even if she would herself control them, as in (106) and (107), but it may also imply lack of control, as in (108).

(99) *wa,   baɬaŋ-po-a   tsuru   ma   ɬtsoŋ,   ritʃo   taŋ-nug-hii*
hey   COW-DEF-DAT provocation NEG   raise\IMP horn   give-POT-DUB
'Don't provoke the cow! She might stab you with her horns!'

(100) *jaa   stor-uk   jaa   mi   tʃig-is   kʰjer-uk,   de-i*
either   be.lost-POT   or   man   one-ERG   take.away-POT   that-GEN
ŋa-s   gra   len-tʃ-in
me-ERG   compensation   take-INF2-EQ
'(I don't care) whether (you) lose it or whether someone steals it, I will want the same back.'

(101) *lip   pʰjaχ-se   kʰjer-ug-hii*
DRM   sweep-CNJ   take.away-POT-WND
'Won't someone steal it (if you don't watch it)?'

(102) *dj-uw-a   tsam   ri-ik*
this-DEF-DAT   how.much   be.worth-POT
'How much will this be worth (i.e. how much will actually be paid for it)?'

(103) *ldan-ma   ʒaχm-ek   tsam-ts-ik   tʃʰo-ok*
become.done-INF   day-INDF   how.much-LIM-INDF   go-POT
'How many days will it take for it to be done?'

(104) *di   tʰintʃas-po   naŋ-po   gaŋma-a   kʰjet-tug-a*
this   carpet-DEF   house-DEF   all-DAT   be.sufficient-POT-Q
'Will this carpet be big enough for the whole room?'

(105) *sɲiŋ-a   doχs-et,   samba   maŋmo   joŋ-et,   tʃi*
heart-DAT   be.irritated-CRT   thought   a.lot   come-CRT   what
bo-ok   zer-e
do-POT   say-CNJ
'(I) have sorrows, (I'm) thinking a lot about what I should do.'

(106) jaraŋ-a   zaruri   jot-na   ŋa-s   jaraŋ-a   ṣmul
      you(hon.)-DAT   important   EX-CND   me-ERG   you(hon.)-DAT   rupee
      stoŋ   sum   ski-se   taŋ-nuk
      1000   three   borrow-CNJ   give-POT
      'If it's important to you I might lend you 3000 rupees.'

(107) ŋa-s   kʰo-a   rjaq   zdam-nuk
      me-ERG   (s)he-DAT   drm   pull.together-POT
      'I might hug her (just like that).'

(108) kʰjaŋ-a   kʰo-ika   rduŋ-ma   pʰot-ug-a
      you-DAT   (s)he-LOC   beat-INF   be.capable-POT-Q
      'Would you be capable of hitting her/him?'

Example (109) illustrates an interrogative V-*(t/n)ug-a* together with its question tag *mi* V, that is, with what appears to be construed as its closest negated correspondence. Example (110) shows that a negative *mi* V may similarly be followed by an interrogative V-*(t/n)ug-a* (i.e. in reversed order). The Simple Negated Generic Prospective *mi* V is discussed in §1.2.

(109) kargilw-a   tʃʰ-og-a   mi   tʃʰa   sam,   tʰetʰom   soŋ
      Kargilo-DAT   go-POT-Q   neg   go   think   doubt   went
      'I'm not sure whether I should go to Kargilo.'

(110) ga-r   duk-tuk-gii,   braŋsa   mi   tʰop,   tʰop-tug-a
      which-TERM   stay-POT-DMND   hotel   NEG   find   find-POT-Q
      'Where will (we) stay? (We) won't find a place to stay over night, will (we)?'

9.3.2.6 Habitual V-*pa-t*

The habitual V-*pa-t* (< *V-*pa-yod*) illustrated twice in (111) lacks a testimonial equivalent. This is not surprising, since the repeated occurrence of an event cannot be asserted by means of the single (and simple) testimony *duk* indicates. That it can be inferred from a missing piece of evidence (often an idea), however, is demonstrated by (55) and (56), where V-*pa-t* is followed by the inferential -*suk*. The negation of V-*pa-t* is indicated by a preceding *mi*, as shown in (112).

(111) nor-i   paχsp-e-ka   joŋ-ma-t,   saqti   bun-ma-t,   rumbu-i
      sheep-GEN   skin-G-LOC   come-INF-FCT   firm   itch-INF-FCT   tick-GEN
      so-s
      tooth-ERG
      '(Ticks) may be in the sheep's furs; the bite of a tick (normally) itches heavily.'

(112) kʰo   mana   mi   kʰṣel-ba-t
       (s)he   very   neg   become.ashamed-INF-FCT
       '(S)he's never ashamed (i.e. in situations in which others might well be).'

9.4 The equative copula *in* (*yin*)

Unlike in most other spoken varieties of Tibetan, in Purik the equative copula *in* (WT *yin*) is not opposed to a second basic equative copula. Examples (113)–(115) illustrate the use of the plain factual equative copula *in* after nouns and pronouns. In (116), *in* attributes a property to an entity and thereby contrasts with the existential copulas by relating to intrinsic and unchangeable qualities of an entity.

(113) dj-u   tʃi   in
       this-DEF   very   EQ
       'What's this?'

(114) ŋa   kʰo-e   ata   in
       I   (s)he-GEN   father   EQ
       'I'm her/his father.'

(115) e-u   jar-i   in-a
       the.other-DEF   you(hon.)-GEN   EQ-Q
       'Is that other one yours?'

(116) di   sman-po   rgjala   in   jaraŋ-a
       this   medicine-DEF   food   EQ   you(hon.)-DAT
       'This medicine is good for you.'

The equative *in* may also contrast with the existential copulas after certain nominalizations. However, while the *-tʃa*-participle remains clearly distinct when it occurs before the existential copulas (cf. §3.1.2), it fuses with the equative copula to yield the form V-*tʃ-in*, discussed in §4.1. On the other hand, unlike the existential copulas (cf. §3.1.3), equative *in* cannot occur with the *-en*-participle, evidently because the intrinsic notion of *in* is incompatible with the progressive notion of *-en-*. After the adjectival *-(s)e*-participle, *in* also relates to intrinsic properties of the entity under focus, see §4.2. Finally, suffixed to the subordinating *-pa*-infinitive, *in* is used to form both the Remote Past V-*(s-)p-in* and the past forms of all copulas, as discussed in §4.3 and §4.4 respectively.

9.4.1 Factual prospective V-tʃ-in

The factual prospective marker V-tʃ-in asserts events that – at least according to the speaker's world-view – always take place (in a certain way), see for instance (117). Given that it incorporates the prospective participle, V-tʃ-in might be more adequately translated by 'will (always) V'. Only the prospective reading is possible when V-tʃ-in confidently predicts a particular event (rather than that the statement is based on evidence or knowledge, as the existential copulas would indicate), as in (118). The negation of a simple V-tʃ-in is V-tʃa men, but there are two different ways in which the complex V-pa rgo-ʃ-in 'needs to V, will need to V' may be negated depending on the scope of the negation, cf. (119) and (120).

(117) rdo-e-ka　　ɬtʃaχs-po　rgjab-a-na　　tsaʁa　joŋ-tʃ-in,
　　　 stone-G-LOC iron-DEF　throw-INF-CND spark　come-INF2-EQ
　　　 tsaʁ-i-ka　　me　　gjur-tʃ-in
　　　 spark-G-LOC fire　become-INF2-EQ
　　　 'When (you) hit the iron against a rock, there are sparks. And from these sparks fire originates.'

(118) kʰjeraŋ　kʰo-i-ka　　　non-tʃ-in
　　　 you　　 (s)he-G-LOC　catch.up-INF2-EQ
　　　 'You will catch up with him. (I believe in you!)'

(119) ɬaṣtsi　kʰur-e　　　jot-na　　tri　　joŋ-tʃ-in,　　zer-ba
　　　 musk　 carry-CNJ　EX.F-CND smell come-INF2-EQ say-INF
　　　 rgo-ʃa　　men
　　　 need-INF2 NEG;EQ
　　　 'If you have musk on you, people will smell it, (so) you don't need to tell!'

(120) ʒan-mi-i-ka　　　rdjaŋ-ma　mi　 kal-ba　　　rgo-ʃ-in
　　　 other-man-G-LOC trust-INF　NEG put.on-INF need-INF2-EQ
　　　 '(You) must not trust other people.'

9.4.2 Intrinsic resultative V-se in

When used after the adjectival -(s)e-participle, the equative in again contrasts with the existential copulas (cf. §3.1.4) and again relates only to the intrinsic properties of the entity in focus. In (121), in indicates that struŋ-se 'driving' is not about a temporary state of the subject but about her *ability* to drive, which, she maintains even when she is not currently driving. By highlighting the intrinsic and unchangeable features of the adjectival participle, the equative copula in in (122) expresses the strictly polar question whether the job has been carried out or not (while the existential copulas would relate to the availability of the result of the job at the moment of speaking).

(121) kʰo-s tʃoq struŋ-se in
      (s)he-ERG moment drive-CNJ EQ
      'He's just started driving (a short while ago)!'

(122) tsʰonm-ek kʰjoŋ-se in-a
      vegetable-INDF bring-CNJ EQ-Q
      'Did (you) *buy/bring* some vegetables?'

9.4.3 Remote Past V-*(s-)-p-in*

In contrast to the resultatively analyzable Simple Past, the Remote Past V*(-s)-p-in* never allows for a resultative analysis. It signals that the event was completed (well) prior to the moment of speaking, cf. (123)–(126).

(123) aʁabbas su-s ɬtan-s-p-in kʰjaŋ tʃoq
      Agha.Abbas who-ERG show-PST-INF-EQ you moment
      joŋ-se-na
      come-CNJ-EMPH
      'Who introduced you to (lit. who showed you) Agha Abbas when you had just arrived here?'

(124) ŋa-s rdam ma rdam-s-p-in, kʰjer-es taŋ-s-p-in
      I-ERG choose NEG choose-PST-INF-EQ you-ERG give-PST-INF-EQ
      'I didn't choose; you gave (it to me).'

(125) kʰo-s na bo-s-p-in, de las-po mi ba zer-e
      (s)he-ERG oath put-PST-INF-EQ that work-DEF NEG do say-CNJ
      'He's sworn that he would never do that.'

(126) kʰjeraŋ ga-r skje-p-in
      you which-TERM be-born-INF-EQ
      'Where were you born?'

9.4.4 Past forms of the copulas: *in-m-in, jot-p-in, duk-p-in*

Past forms may be built from all three basic copulas by subordinating their *-pa-* infinitives to the equative copula *in*, yielding *in-m-in*, *jot-p-in*, and *duk-p-in*. Past equative *in-m-in* is predominantly used in hypothetical protases, as in (127) (while the predicate of the main clause commonly precedes *-pa*). Second, *jot-p-in* factually describes a state that held during a past period of time, cf. (128). Finally, *duk-p-in* competes with *jot-suk* (cf. §3.2.2) in indicating the direct testimony of a past state. In contrast to *jot-suk*, which is used when the informant bases her statement on a single testimony of a past state, *duk-p-in* implies repeated testimony of a state that went on during a past period of time, as exemplified in (129). (For the use of the inferential *-suk* after *jot-p-in*, cf. example 52.)

(127) ŋa kʰjeraŋ in-m-in-na baŋ taŋ-nuk-pa
I you EQ-INF-EQ-CND running give-POT-FOC
'If I were (i.e. had been) you, I would have run.'

(128) ri-a rawaq-po na ru-u ɲambo jot-p-in,
mountain-DAT goat-DEF and kid-DEF together EX-INF-EQ
dare ru-u min-duk, bar be-se gar soŋ
now kid-DEF NEG-EX.T space open-CNJ where WENT
'In the mountain the goat and the kid were together, now the kid is gone; where did it go, separated from its mother?'

(129) kʰo gundea hati-a duk-p-in
(s)he yesterdday store-DAT EX.T-INF-EQ
'(S)he was in the store yesterday. (I saw her there more than once but don't have any more information on whether (s)he was there all the time.)'

9.5 Remaining evidentials

I briefly discuss three constructions that more closely correspond to evidentials in the sense of Aikhenvald (2004), namely 'quotative' *(-)lo* in §5.1, 'indirect evidential' V-*tʰik soŋ-set* in §5.2, and 'assumptive' *-tʃapo* in §5.3.

9.5.1 Quotative -lo

The only marker of Purik that directly indicates the source of the conveyed information is the quotative *-lo*, which can be found in examples (22), (25), (72), and (92) above. Two examples suffice to illustrate the fact (already mentioned in §3.1.1) that the existential copula preceding *-lo* is always construed from the viewpoint of the informant, cf. (130) and (131); *(-)lo* is not only used as a suffix but also as a finite predicate meaning 'said' as in (132)–(134).[20]

---

[20] For a thorough discussion of that "transcategorial" (see Robert 2004) morpheme, see Zemp (2013: §4.5.6).

(130) zbrul-is   sɲaxs   ba-na   bi   pʰut-iin   bi
      snake-ERG   magic   do-CND   bird take.down-PROG\EMPH   bird
      saʁ-i   ʃoqpa   sul   but-e   soŋ-se   zbrul-i
      all-GEN   wing   DRM   fall.down-CNJ   went-CNJ   snake-GEN
      kʰ-e-aŋ   tʃʰ-en-dug-lo
      mouth-G-INE   go-PROG-EX.T-QUOT
      'When the snake uses its magic, by pulling the birds down (steadily), all the birds will lose their wings at once and fall into the snakes mouth, it is said.'

(131) kʰoŋ   kʰunt-i   las   jod-lo
      they   they-GEN   work   EX.T-QUOT
      'They have (their own) work (they say).'

(132) tʃi   lo
      what   QUOT
      'What did (you/(s)he) say?'

(133) su-s   lo
      who-ERG   QUOT
      'Said who? Who said that?'

(134) tʃaŋ   ma   lo
      at.all NEG   QUOT
      '(She/I) didn't say anything.'

9.5.2 Indirect evidential V-tʰik soŋ(-set)

Purik also has a construction best described as an 'indirect evidential'. A speaker may use V-tʰik soŋ-set (or V-tʰik soŋ) if she infers a resultative event based on some noise (135), or less specific evidence (136).

(135) kʰo-e   haʈi-i   zgo-u   tʃuk-tʰik   soŋ-set,   skad
      (s)he-GEN   store-GEN   door-DEF   close-guess   went-RES   sound
      joŋ-s-de,   zgo   tʃuk-p-i
      come-PST-PD   door   close-INF-GEN
      '(I think) he's closed (the door to) his store; I heard the noise (you heard it, too, didn't you?) of a closing door.'

(136) de   ʈipi-u   baa-s   kʰur-tʰik   soŋ-set
      that   hat-DEF   father(hon.)-ERG   carry-guess   went-RES
      'Father probably took that hat with him. (He sometimes wears a hat.)'

9.5.3 Assumptive -*tʃapo*

The use of the assumptive suffix -*tʃapo* is illustrated in (137)–(139) (as well as example 37). It is also attested in the neighboring Balti; Read (1934: 34) lists it as an adverb meaning 'perhaps'. In Purik, it may safely be treated as a suffix, and it consistently indicates a guess made on the basis of directly attested evidence.

(137) *marius-is   kʰur-po   traχ-s,   kʰo   tʃʰa-tʃ-in-tʃapo*
      Marius-ERG load-DEF tie-PST (s)he go-INF2-EQ-ASSUM
      'Marius has tied the load (onto his back), he's perhaps ready to go.'

(138) *kʰo-a   tsʰat   soŋ-tʃapo,   ɬuŋ   hjab-en-duk*
      (s)he-DAT heat   went-ASSUM   air   fan-PROG-EX.T
      'He's perhaps feeling the heat; he's fanning (the air).'

(139) *kʰo   kʰun-en-duk,   kʰo-a   zermo   joŋ-et-tʃapo,*
      (s)he   moan-PROG-EX.T   (s)he-DAT   pain   come-EX-ASSUM
      rdoŋraŋ-po   ʒik-se   duk
      face.color-DEF become.bad   EX.T
      'He's moaning; perhaps, he has pain; the color of his face is really bad.'

9.6 Sentence-final demonstratives

The last markers that deserve to be mentioned in this overview of evidentiality in Purik are the two sentence-final demonstratives *de* and *e*. Just like *duk* and *jot*, both the 'pro- and the postverbal' *de* and *e* make an indication about the speaker's access to information. However, while *duk* and *jot* as well as evidentials in Aikhenvald's (2004) narrower sense are primarily grounded in the situation of the event indicated, the sentence-final demonstratives are – just like ad- and pronominal demonstratives – primarily grounded in the situation of the current speech act.[21] When used proverbally, i.e. as the sentence predicate, *de* and *e* indicate the existence of an entity or a property. While *de* conveys old information, *e* conveys information yet to be identified by the addressee. When used postverbally, i.e. suffixed to the predicate of a sentence, *de* and *e* respectively express whether the information conveyed by the entire sentence is old or has yet to be identified by the addressee.

In the proverbal position, *de* and *e* contrast with *duk* and *jot* in indicating the existence of an entity or a property. As illustrated in (140)–(142), the 'proximate'

---

[21] The event-grounding of *past* evidentials (indicating, e.g., whether a past event was directly witnessed) more strikingly contrasts with the speech-act grounding of *de* and *e*.

de points to an entity or property before the speaker and addressee and which they had previously identified. In contrast, the 'obviative' *e* in (143)–(145) points to an entity or property that warrants the addressee's attention. The short dialogue (146) illustrates that the proverbal *e* may also be used in a question appealing to the addressee to show an object, whereas *de* is be used by that addressee in order to show the object in question.

(140) *kulik-po di-ka pʰjal-la de*
key-DEF this-LOC hanging-DAT PD
'The key's hanging here (where it's supposed to be).'

(141) *ŋa kʰatʃul-la de*
I Kashmir-DAT PD
'I was in Kashmir here (in this picture).'

(142) *bi-a-na taŋtaŋ tʃʰa-tʃ-in dare dj-u tsʰettsʰet de*
fall.out-INF-CND bleak go-INF2-EQ now this-DEF bristly PD
'When (the hair) falls out, (the head) will become bald; now, it is bristly (as you know, look).'

(143) *tʃuli ma za-a jot, are-ka e*
apricot neg eat-INF EX.F that.distal-LOC OD
'(We) haven't eaten (all) the apricots, they're over there.'

(144) *saspol e*
Saspol OD
'That's Saspol over there!'

(145) *sŋuntʃoqtʃoq e*
deep.green OD
'Look, how green it is over there!'

(146) A: *ŋj-i ʃite-a pʰuṭw-ig jot*
I-GEN side-DAT photo-INDF EX.F
'I have a photo with me.'

B: *ga-r e*
which-TERM OD
'Where is it?'

A: *di-ka de*
this-LOC PD
'Here it is.'

When used postverbally, *de* and *e* point to more complex information viz. the one conveyed in the sentence to which they are suffixed. As illustrated in (147)–(149), which all occurred within a story, postverbal *-de* implies that the preceding sentence represents information that should be clear to the addressee because it is crucial for the continuation of the story. In contrast, *-e* in (150)–(152) implies that the preceding sentence represents new information the addressee may know by looking where the speaker is looking.

(147) ʃi   ma   ʃi-a   jot-de
      die   NEG   die-INF   EX-PD
      'Of course, (she) hadn't died (but only pretended to be dead), you see.'

(148) ta   ɲis-po   kʰaŋma-a   jot-de
      now   two-DEF   home-DAT   EX-PD
      'Now, the two where at home, you see.'

(149) ʈtʃar-s-pa,   zug-a   ʒaq-pa-na   di-ka,   ser   tʃʰaqtsek
      weigh-PST-INF   like.this-DAT   put-INF-CND   this-LOC   gold   a.little
      guz-de
      spill-PD
      'When she was done weighing (the gold), because she had put (some glue) here like this, a little bit of gold stuck (to the scales), you see.'

(150) are   jul-po   ɖonmo   in-sug-e,   zbjarpa   warpa
      that   village-DEF   warm   EQ-INFR-OD   willow   and.the.like
      dug-e
      EX.T-OD
      'That village over there appears to have a warm climate; there are willows and all, look!'

(151) kʰo   ɬeb-e
      (s)he   arrive-OD
      '(S)he's arrived, look! (There (s)he is!)'

(152) are-ka-na   pʰru-ik   but-e   joŋ-z-ei
      that-LOC-ABL   child-INDF   fall-CNJ   come-PST-OD
      'A child fell down over there, look!'

9.7 Concluding remarks

In Purik the equative copula *in* (Written Tibetan *yin*) is not contrasted with a second equative copula as it is in many other Tibetan varieties. The existential copula *jot* (WT *yod*) has a plain factual meaning in those constructions (conditional clauses and nominalizations) in which it does not contrast with *duk* (WT *'dug*). In those constructions in which *jot* and *duk* contrast, *duk* indicates that something was directly attested by the speaker and *jot* indicates that the speaker simply knows something, and that her knowledge does not depend on recent direct testimony. Many evidential constructions are formed from *jot* and *duk*, and they are all broadly in keeping with these meanings. The constructions V-*(s)e soŋ* and V-*(s)e joŋ-s* may imply the speaker's presence when an event happened. Purik has other more marginal evidential formations, which are also outlined above.

Abbreviations

ABL ablative, ASS associative, ASSUM assumptive, AUG augmentative, CAUS causative, CMPL completive, CND conditional, CNJ conjunctive, RT certaintive, DAT dative, DEF definite article, DMND demanding, DRM dramatizer, DST distal, DUB dubitative, EMPH emphatic marker, EQ equative copula, ERG ergative, EX.F factual existential copula, EX.T testimonial existential copula, FCT factual verb ending, FOC focus marker, G(EN) genitive, IMP imperative, INE inessive, INF infinitive (-*pa*), INF2 prospective infinitive (-*tʃa*), INFR inferential, INT interrogative, LIM limitive, LOC locative, NEG negation, NLZR nominalizer (-*kʰan*), OD obviative sentence-final demonstrative, PD proximate sentence-final demonstrative, PE plural excluding the addressee, PL plural, POT potential, PROG progressive, PST past tense, REC recapitulating, STAT stative, TE topic extending, TERM terminative (case), WND wondering.

References

Aikhenvald, Alexandra. 2004. *Evidentiality*. Oxford: Oxford University Press.
Bailey, T. Grahame. 1920. *Linguistic Studies from the Himalayas* (Asiatic Society Monographs 18). London: Royal Asiatic Society.
Bickel, Balthasar. 2008. Verb agreement and epistemic marking: A typological journey from the Himalayas to the Caucasus. In B. Huber, M. Volkart & P. Widmer (eds.), *Chomolangma, Demawend und Kasbek, Festschrift für Roland Bielmeier*, 1–14. Saale: International Institute for Tibetan and Buddhist Studies.
Chang, Betty & Kun Chang. 1984. The certainty hierarchy among Spoken Tibetan verbs of being. *Bulletin of the Institute of History and Philology. Academia Sinica* 55(4). 603–634.
Curnow, Timothy. 1997. *A Grammar of Awa Pit*. Ph.D. dissertation. Canberra: Australian National University.
DeLancey, Scott. 1986. Evidentiality and volitionality in Tibetan. In Wallace Chafe & Johanna Nichols (eds.), *Evidentiality: The Linguistic Coding of Epistemology*, 203–213. Norwood, NJ: Ablex Publishing Corporation.

DeLancey, Scott. 1990. Ergativity and the cognitive model of event structure in Lhasa Tibetan. *Cognitive Linguistics* 1(3). 289–321.
Dixon, Robert M. W. 1994. *Ergativity*. Cambridge: Cambridge University Press.
Hale, Austin. 1980. Person markers: Finite conjunct and disjunct verb forms in Newari. *Papers in South-East Asian Linguistics* 7. 95–106.
Hargreaves, David. 2005. Agency and intentional action in Kathmandu Newar. *Himalayan Linguistics* 5: 1–48.
Hill, Nathan. 2013. *ḥdug* as a testimonial marker in Classical and Old Tibetan. *Himalayan Linguistics* 12(1). 1–16.
Konow, Sten. 1909. Purik. In Sir George Abraham Grierson (ed.), *Linguistic Survey of India, Vol. III, Part I. Tibeto-Burman Family: Himalayan Dialects, North Assam Group*, 42–50. Delhi: Motilal Banarsidass.
Purig, Rinchan. 2007. *Purig skad = The Purig language*. Karachi: Purig Shazdeychan Foundation.
Rangan, K. 1979. *A Grammar of Purki, a Language of the Tibeto-Burman family, Spoken in Ladakh District, Kashmir* (Grammar Series 5). Mysore: Central Institute of Indian Languages.
Read, A.F.C. 1934. *Balti Grammar* (J. G. Forlong Fund, Vol. XV). London: Royal Asiatic Society.
Robert, Stéphane. 2004. The challenge of polygrammaticalization for linguistic theory: fractal grammar and transcategorial functioning. In Zygmunt Frajzyngier, Adam Hodges & David S. Rood (eds.), *Linguistic Diversity and Language Theories* (Studies in Language Companion Series 72), 119–142. Amsterdam and Philadelphia: Benjamins.
San Roque, Lila, and Robyn Loughnane. 2012. The New Guinea Highlands evidentiality area. *Linguistic Typology* 16(1). 111–167.
Sharma, D.D. 2004. *Tribal Languages of Ladakh, Part III. A descriptive Grammar of Purik and Balti* (Studies in Tibeto-Himalayan Languages 4). New Delhi: Mittal.
Tournadre, Nicolas. 1996. *L'ergativité en tibétain. Approche morphosyntaxique de la langue parlée* (Bibliothèque de l'information grammaticale). Louvain: Peeters.
Tournadre, Nicolas. 2008. Arguments against the concept of 'conjunct'/'disjunct' in Tibetan. In B. Huber, M. Volkart & P. Widmer (eds.), *Chomolangma, Demawend und Kasbek, Festschrift für Roland Bielmeier*, 281–308. Saale: International Institute for Tibetan and Buddhist Studies.
Tournadre, Nicolas & Sangda Dorje. 2003. *Manual of Standard Tibetan. Language and Civilization*. Ithaca: Snow Lion.
Tournadre, Nicolas & Randy LaPolla. 2014. Towards a new approach to evidentiality. *Linguistics of the Tibeto-Burman Area* 37(2): 240–263.
Volkart, Marianne. 2000. The meaning of the auxiliary *'dug* in the aspect systems of some Central Tibetan dialects. *Linguistics of the Tibeto-Burman Area* 23(2). 127–153.
Willett, Thomas. 1988. A cross-linguistic survey of the grammaticalization of evidentiality. *Studies in Language* 12(1). 51–97.
Zeisler, Bettina. 2004. *Relative Tense and Aspectual Values in Tibetan Languages: A Comparative Study*. Berlin; New York: Mouton de Gruyter.
Zemp, Marius. 2013. *A Historical Grammar of Purik Tibetan*. PhD-thesis at the University of Bern.

Juha Yliniemi
10 Copulas in Denjongke or Sikkimese Bhutia

བཀའ་འགྱུར་ བསྟན་འགྱུར་ནང་ ཨིན་ཨིན་ སྨྲ་སྨྲ་ ལབ་མ་ཁན་ བོན་བོ་ སྨྲ་དོ། ཨོ་འདི་ བྱིས་སྟེ་ཀི་ ང་ དཔྱ་ འབྲས་ལྗོངས་ སྐད་ལས་ བཤད་པོ་ བྱིས་ བར་ ཅེན་ སྐད་ཀྱི་ ཆེ་བ་ བོན་ཤད་ སྨྲད།

'In Kangyur and Tengjur [ĩ: ĩ:] and [bɛʔ bɛʔ] occur frequently. Therefore, if I now explain them in the Denjongke language, the greatness of the language becomes evident.'
–Khenchen Lha Tshering Rinpoche

10.1 Introduction

Tibetic languages are known for their evidentially rich copula systems (e.g. Bielmeier 2000; Garrett 2001; Hongladarom 2007; Gawne 2013). This contribution presents the first detailed description of the copulas of Denjongke, or Sikkimese Bhutia (India). Although the copulas in Denjongke are also used as auxiliaries following the verbal complex, the treatment in this study focuses on pure copula uses, i.e. basic copulas and constructions where two basic copulas are combined either directly (combinatory copulas) or with nominalization (nominalized copulas).

I begin with some background information on the language, its speakers (§2) and the present study (§3). Section 4 introduces the basic copulas (§4.1), describes the differences between equative and existential copulas (§4.2) and briefly illustrates the uses of the interrogative copula (§4.3). Section 5 focusses on the evidential distinctions in copulas. After an overview (§5.1) and a short comparison with two related languages (§5.2), evidential phenomena related to each of the declarative basic copulas (§5.3–§5.5) and the reportative copula substitute (§5.6) are described in detail. Section 6 describes complex copula

---

Note: I am especially grateful to Nathan W. Hill for giving detailed feedback on two versions of this chapter. I would also like to thank the following scholars (in alphabetical order) for their feedback on various versions of this study: Alexandra Aikhenvald, Erik Andvik, Ellen Bartee, Scott DeLancey, Lauren Gawne, Fred Karlsson, Ken Manson, Matti Miestamo, Hella Olbertz, Kaius Sinnemäki and an anonymous reviewer. I would also like to express by gratitude to Yeshe Rinzing Bhutia, who provided the written Denjongke forms for many of the example sentences, and to Sonam Gyatso Dokhangba, who reviewed most of the example sentences. The remaining errors and inadequacies are naturally mine.

constructions, i.e. combinatory copulas, which directly combine two copulas (§6.1), and nominalized copulas, which combine two copulas through nominalization (§6.2). The conclusion presents a table summarizing all copula uses, with references to examples, and a note on grammaticalization of evidentiality in Tibetic language (§7).

10.2 Background

Denjongke is a Tibetic (Tournadre 2008: 283) language, spoken in the formerly independent kingdom of Sikkim, which is now a state of India. One of the most closely related languages within the Tibetic family is Dzongkha, the official language of Bhutan. The Census of India 2001 lists 41,825 speakers for Denjongke, whereas a few Denjongke language teachers have given estimates of some 25–30,000 speakers at present. The exact number of speakers is difficult to determine because many young ethnic Denjongpas either do not speak the language or have a very limited knowledge of it. Moreover, many Lepchas living close to Denjongpas are reported to speak Denjongke. Denjongke grammar has been described by Sandberg (1888, 1895). Walsh (1905), Grierson ([1909] 1967) and Shafer (1974) also provide some lexical data and historical-comparative observations on Denjongke phonology. Sandberg (1895: 44/45) gives a brief list of sentences illustrating Denjongke copulas (which he calls "substantive verbs"), but his description is not very detailed. References to Sandberg (1895), when relevant, are given later in this chapter.

The most common endonym of the language is Lhoke[1] 'southern language', while Denjongke[2] is a pan-Tibetan term better understood by other Tibetan-related communities. In India, the language is widely known as (Sikkimese) Bhutia, and in the Ethnologue (Lewis et al. 2013) as Sikkimese. The dialects of the Northern villages of Lachen and Lachung are called by the names of these villages.

---

[1] Written Tibetan *lho-skad*. The Lhomis, a Tibetic language speaking group in Nepal, also call their language *lho-ket* 'southern language' (Vesalainen 2014).
[2] འབྲས་ལྗོངས་སྐད *'bras-ljongs-skad* [dɛndzoŋkɛʔ] is traditionally translated as 'language of the valley of rice', but one of the developers of the written language, པདྨ་རིག་འཛིན་ སྟག་ཆུང་དར་པོ *Pema Rinzing Takchungdarpo*, maintains that the meaning is rather 'language of the valley of fruit'.

Until the annexation by India in 1975, Denjongke was exclusively an oral language while Classical Tibetan was used for writing (Dewan 2012: 171, 418). Under Indian rule, Denjongke, along with other minority languages of Sikkim, was introduced as an elective subject at schools. For this purpose a literary form of the language was needed. Through the efforts of རྫོང་ཁུན་ཆེརིང་བྷུ་ཊི་ཡ་ *Norden Tshering Bhutia* the Tibetan script with modifications[3] was adopted for writing the language. Schoolbooks were produced, most often by translating from existing Tibetan materials, first by དཔལ་ལྡན་ལ་ཆུང་པ་ Palden Lachungpa and then extensively by པདྨ་རིག་འཛིན་སྟག་ཆུང་དཀར་པོ་ Pema Rinzing Takchungdarpo. More recently, other types of literature have appeared. In 1996 བྷའི་ཅུང་ཚིས་བཅུད་དཀར་པོ་ Bhaichung Tsichudarpo (now retired Text Book Officer of the Government of Sikkim) published the first Denjongke novel called རེ་རྩེ *richhi* 'hope', and several authors have produced, among other things, poetry, proverbs and plays. At present, there are some 30 authors who have produced Denjongke literature (Pema Rinzing Takchungdarpo, personal communication, Autumn 2013). A daily Denjongke radio programme has been broadcast since the 1960s, first from Kurseong (West Bengal) and later from Gangtok All India Radio station. Dictionaries have been produced by N. T. Bhutia and Takchungdarpo (2001), P. Bhutia (2004), Lama (2013), Takchungdarpo (2013) and Phenasa (2013).

Despite literary development, due to heavy influence of Nepali and to some extent English, Denjongke is an endangered language.[4] One factor expediting language loss among children and young people is that children who attend school often do not live with their parents, where they could stay in contact with the language community, but instead stay in 'hostels' near their schools, where they lose contact with the speakers of their mother-tongue.

Another factor contributing to language loss that I have heard some speakers of the language themselves comment on is the reluctance of many younger

---

3 The most important Denjongke innovation to the Tibetan writing system is the application of the tsha-lag (as ཿ in ཇ) to letters with which it cannot occur in classical Tibetan. One reason for this innovation was that some of the historical labial-palatal sequences, for instance /pj/ and /mj/, which in Lhasa Tibetan have merged into /tɕ/ and /ɲ/ respectively, are in Denjongke pronounced as sequences /pj/ /mj/ and written པྱ and མྱ. Another reason was the need to introduce spellings for frequently heard foreign loan words like proper names which have such consonantal sequences that appear the Tibetan writing but have since developed into retroflexes in the inherited lexicon of Denjongke. For instance /kr/, as in Khrishna, and /pr/, as in Pradhan, are now written as ཀྲ and པྲ respectively because ཀྲ and པྲ without a tsha-lag are pronounced as a retroflex /ʈ/. Another innovation in Denjongke writing is word-breaks, as exemplified in the example sentences. Some words are spelled in various ways by different authors, and sometimes by the same author, e.g. ལེགས་, ལེས་ and ལེམ་ for *lěm* 'good'.
4 Turin (2012) calls the language "severely endangered" and van Driem (2007: 312) even "moribund".

speakers to speak the language because they feel they cannot use the honorific forms properly. Instead of taking the risk of being rebuked by elders, the young people often save face by not speaking Denjongke. At present, the language is still actively spoken in various communities across Sikkim, but most speakers, excluding some older ones living in tight-knit Denjongpa communities in the countryside, are bilingual in Nepali.

10.3 Data

The language data used in this study are derived from both oral and written sources. The audio-recorded spoken data, which consist both of naturally occurring transcribed texts and elicitation, were gathered through original fieldwork in Sikkim and adjacent areas over a period of about two and a half years (2012–2014). For the most part, elicited utterances were not translations of sentences from another language. Rather, the consultants volunteered illustrative example sentences of a particular copula or responded to a suggested context. Elicited sentences were cross-checked with other consultants. Elicitation was carried out in English, Nepali and Denjongke.

The source of the examples sentences, including the identity of the speaker and information on whether the example was naturally occurring or elicited, is indicated after the free translation. Elicited sentences that have been cross-checked with several consultants have no source-marking. The language consultants who spoke the example sentences are listed in Tab. 1. Unfortunately only one woman was available as a consultant.

Tab. 1: Denjongke consultants from whom spoken data was obtained.

Initials	Gender	Age	Place of origin
DB	M	60+	Tashiding, West Sikkim
NB	M	20+	Tashiding, West Sikkim
PT	M	30+	Tashiding, West Sikkim
RM	F	50+	Tashiding, West Sikkim
RS	M	50+	Tashiding, West Sikkim
TB	M	40+	Ralang, West Sikkim
KN	M	20+	Lingtam, Upper Martam, East Sikkim
PD	M	30+	Lindgum, Ranka, East Sikkim
KT	M	60+	Bermeok, South Sikkim
YR	M	40+	Kewsing, South Sikkim
SG	M	50+	Barphung Lingdam, South Sikkim

The written sources used as data are: 1) the first Denjongke novel called རེ་རྩེ་ *richhi* 'hope', written by བྷའི་ཅུང་ཚེས་བཅུ་དར་པོ་ *bha'i-cung tshes-bcu-dar-po*, published in 1996 (see Tsichudarpo 1996), 2) a collection of folk-stories and moral teachings རྣ་གསུང་ དང་གཏམ་བཤད *rna-gsung dang gtam-bhad* compiled by ཀར་མ་ བློ་བཟང་ བྷོ་ཏི་ཡ *kar-ma blo-bzang bho-ṭi-ya* (see K. L. Bhutia 2013) and 3) a treatise on Denjongpa marriage customs སྦར་ཕུང་ ལིང་དམ་ འགྲོ་ལིས *sbar-phung ling-dam 'gro-lis* by བསོད་ནམས་ རྒྱ་མཚོ་ རྡོ་ཁང་བོ་ *bsod-nams rgya-mtsho rdo-khang-bo* (see Dokhangba 2001). These written sources include dialogues in the colloquial language and give written expression to spoken language morphemes that do not usually appear in writing, such as the attention marker = ɡo and the clause-final discourse marker = ɲa, the meaning of which remains to be explored. The Tibetan script for literary examples has been adopted from their original sources, which bear some inconsistencies as a testimony to the not fully standardized writing system. For spoken examples, ཡེ་ཤེས་ རིག་འཛིན་ བྷོ་ཊི་ཡ *Yeshe Rinzing Bhutia*, kindly provided the Denjongke script for most of the examples. Page references to literary examples are given at the end of the example after the translation.

The phonemic transcription below attempts to follow spoken pronunciation, not reading or spelling style pronunciation (for a discussion on the differences see Sprigg 1991), e.g. the progressive marker བཞིན་ *bzhin* is transcribed, following spoken pronunciation in Tashiding (village in West Sikkim), as zɛ̃ː despite zin being the reading pronunciation. Word-final glottal stops, which are systematically marked in the transcription, are pronounced utterance-finally as [ʔ] but utterance-medially usually as lengthening on the vowel. The phonetic/phonemic symbols are from the IPA except for /g/ representing IPA [ɡ] and /a/ representing IPA [ɐ].[5] When an example sentence re-occurs within the text, I have given it as a new number. The earlier occurrence is given in square brackets within the body of the text, e.g. (40) [10].

---

[5] Two notes on phonology are in order. First, according to my acoustic study, Denjongke has only a two-way height contrast /i/, /ɛ/ among short front unrounded vowels and a three-way contrast among long vowels /iː/, /eː/, /ɛː/. The short mid vowel is symbolized as /ɛ/ rather than /e/ because its F1 value corresponds to /ɛː/ rather the /eː/, which occasionally has overlapping F1 values with /i/. Second, Denjongke has a four-way distinction in plosives and affricates, e.g. /p/ voiceless unaspirated, /pʰ/ voiceless unaspirated, /b/ voiced and /p'/ voiceless lightly and inconsistently aspirated followed by breathy voice. In the transcription, the inverted apostrophe ', as in /p'jɐ/ 'do' in example (2), stands for the historically voiced plosives and affricates which are in written Tibetan written with simple characters without pre- or superscripts.

10.4 Copulas

This section gives an overview of Denjongke copula construction (§4.1) and illustrates the equative and existential uses of the copulas, with an emphasis on the past equative uses of *du?*, which are surprising considering the basically existential character of *du?* (§4.2). Lastly, I exemplify the uses of the interrogative copula (§4.3).

10.4.1 Overview of the basic copulas

Copulas are words that have little independent meaning apart from linking two arguments. In other words, copulas "have relational rather than referential meaning" (Dixon 2010: 159). In Denjongke, copulas can be defined as those verbs which can link a nominal argument to an adjectival argument. This definition includes both equative copulas and existential copulas. Equative copulas can link together two non-case-marked noun phrases or an non-case-marked noun-phrase to an adjective phrase. Existential copulas, in addition to linking an non-case-marked noun phrase to an adjective phrase, can occur with one argument (pure existential use) or link an non-case-marked noun phrase to a case-marked noun phrase (locative and possessive uses). The Denjongke copulas are not totally devoid of lexical meaning, because they encode evidential distinctions, as described in §5.

Denjongke has five basic copula verbs, four of which are used in declarative sentences and one in questions (see Table 2). The basic copulas are divided into equative and existential. Furthermore, the declarative copulas are evidentially divided into personal, sensorial and neutral. The five basic copulas are the personal equative *í:* (neg.*mḛ̀:*), the personal existential *jə̀?* (neg. *mè?*), the sensorial existential *du?* (neg. *mìndu?*), which can also be used, perhaps surprisingly, for past equation/identification, the evidentially neutral *bɛ?* (neg. *mə̀mbɛ?*), which is basically equative but also has some existential-like uses, and the interrogative *bo/mo* (neg. *mə̀mbo*). In addition, Denjongke has a reportative marker = *lo*, which can function as a copula substitute for equative copulas but not for existential copulas.

The declarative basic copulas can also be combined into two types of complex copula structures. Firstly, two copulas can be directly combined to form two combinatory copulas *ímbɛ?* and *indu?*. Secondly, two copulas may be combined with the help of the nominalizers *-po/bo* and *-kʰɛn~kʰɛ̃:* to form several nominalized constructions, e.g. *ím-bo bɛ?*, *jə̀-kʰɛn bɛ?*.

Table 2 summarises the main features of the five basic copulas and their negatives. The equative vs. existential divide does not entirely hold for both *du?*

and *bɛʔ*; *duʔ* can occur in past equative constructions and *bɛʔ* can occur in some existential type of constructions (hence the dotted line). Summarizing tables of nominalized constructions and all copulas are given in §6.2 and §7 respectively.

Tab. 2: The five basic copulas and their negatives.

		Declarative			Interrogative
		Personal	Sensorial	Neutral	
Equative (pos./neg.)	Present	ཨིན་/མན་ ĩː/mẽ̀,		སྱུད་/མན་སྱུད་ bɛʔ/mɛ̀mbɛʔ	བོ་ (མོ་)/མན་བོ་ bo (mo)/ mɛ̀mbo
	Past		འདུག་/མིན་འདུག་ duʔ/mìnduʔ		
Existential (pos./neg.)		ཡོད་/མེད་ jòʔ/mèʔ			

10.4.2 Equative and existential (ELPA) copulas

The equative copulas *ĩː* and *bɛʔ* either equate two arguments (cf. (1, 3)) or identify the first argument as a member of a category (cf. (2)). Dryer (2007: 233) calls similar comparative categories "referential" and "non-referential" respectively, whereas Pustet (2003: 29) calls them "identificational" and "ascriptive" respectively. The first argument in equative sentences is an unmarked noun phrase (cf. (1)) or a non-finite clause (cf. (2)).

(1) རྨི་ལམ་[6] ལབ་མཁན་ རྨི་ལམ་རང་ སྱུད།
 ɲílam làp-kʰɛ̃ː ɲílam-rã̀ː bɛʔ
 dream say-NMLZ dream-EMPH COP.EQU.NE
 'A dream is (just) a dream.' (Richhi 116)

(2) གཅིག་གིས་ གཞན་པོ་ ཕན་པོ་ བྱས་པད་ དགེ་བའི་ གཡོག་ ཨིན།
 tɕiː=ki[7] *ʑen=lo pʰempo pʲja-ɕɛʔ gɛwø: jóʔ ĩː*
 one=ERG other=DAT help do-INF merit.GEN work COP.EQU.PER
 'Helping one another is a meritorious act.' (Richhi 5)

---

6 This word may also be spelled གཉིད་ལམ་ *gnid-lam*, which reflects the pronunciation better.
7 All case markers are here analysed as clitics, because of their phrasal, phonologically non-prominent and transcategorial character (see Tournadre 2010 for the transcategoriality of Classical Tibetan cases).

The second argument in equative clauses is an unmarked noun phrase (cf. (1–3)), a personal pronoun in the genitive (cf. (4+5)), an adjective phrase (cf. (6+7)), or very rarely a noun phrase marked with a spatial case (cf. (8)).

(3) མོ་རའི་མོ་བྱུད་ཨིན།
    mù   ɲè: mòby?   ĩ́:
    she   my   wife   COP.EQU.PER
    'She is my wife.'

(4) འདི་ རའི་ ཨིན།
    di   ɲè: ĩ́:
    this my   COP.EQU.PER
    'This is mine.'

(5) གུན་ཅི་གིས་ ཡི་གེའི་ ཁ་བྱང་ བལྟ་སྟེ་
    kantɕʰi=ki   jìgi: kʰatɕã: ta-ti
    younger.sister(NEP)=ERG   letter.GEN   address   look-NF
    'Kanchi looks at the address in the letter and says it is elder sister

    ཨའི་ ཆོས་སྐྱིད་ཀྱི་ བྱུད་ སེ་ ལབ་བཞིན་
    ái   tɕʰøki=ki   bɛʔ   sé: làp-zɛ̃́:
    elder.sister Choki=GEN   COP.EQU.NE   QUOT   say-PROG
    Chöki's...' (Richhi 139)

(6) རའི་ བོ་ཙོ་ ཐམས་ཅད་ལས་ འཛིགས་དྲགས་ ཨིན་, ལེགས་ ཨིན།
    ɲè: p'otso   tʰamtɕɛ=lɛ   dzikṭa?   ĩ́:,   lɛ̀m   ĩ́:
    I.GEN   child   all=ABL   excellent   COP   good   COP.EQU.PER
    'My child is the best of all, a good one.' (RM, story of my son)

(7) འཛམ་གླིང་ འདིའི་ གནས་སྟངས་ མནི་སུ་རང་ ཡ་མཚན་དྲགས་ བྱུད།
    dzamliŋ   di: né:tã: né:murã: jàmtsʰit̯'aʔ   bɛʔ
    world   this.GEN   condition   really   amazing   COP.EQU.NE
    'The condition of this world is really amazing.' (Ricchi 136)

(8) རའི་ ཕ་ཡུལ་ སི་ཉེ་ཡོ་ ཨིན།
    ɲè: pʰay: síɲɛ=lo   ĩ́:
    I.GEN   fatherland   Sinye=DAT   COP.EQU.PER
    'My native place is Sinye.' (DB, life-story)

The existential copulas *jð?* and *du?*, on the other hand, occur in existential (cf. (9+10)), locative (cf. (11+12)), possessive (cf. (13+14)) and attributive sentences (cf. (15+16)), hence the term ELPA verbs (Caplow 2000). The semantic difference between the existentials *jð?* and *du?* is described in §5.

(9) ངམ་ ཡོད་ཀ?
    ŋám   jø̀:-ka?
    sugar COP.EX.PER -PQ
    'Is there sugar?'

(10) ངམ་ འདུག་ཀ?
     ŋám   du-ka?
     sugar COP.EX.SEN –PQ
     'Is there sugar?'

(11) ད་ལྟ་ བྷའི་ལཿ སྨན་ཁང་ན་ ཡོད་ཀ?
     t'ata   bhaila: méŋkʰã:=na   jø̀:-ka
     now   Bhaila   hospital=LOC COP.EX.PER-PQ
     'Is Bhaila now in hospital?' (Richhi 24)

(12) ཁོང་གི་ ཁྱིམ་ན་ དེབ་ཚུ་ གེས་པོ་ འདུག
     kʰõ:=gi   kʰim=na   t'ɛp-tsu   kɛ:p(o) du?
     he.HON=GEN house=LOC   book-PL   many   COP.EX.SEN
     'There are a lot of books at his house (I just saw).' (YR, elicitation)

(13) ཚ་རོགས་ཀྱི་/ཚ་རོགས་ལོ་ བོ་ཙོ་ ག་ཙོད་ ཡོད་པོ?
     tɕʰɛro=ki/tɕʰɛro=lo   p'otso   k'adzø?   jø̀-po
     friend=GEN/friend=DAT child   how.many COP.EX.PER-NMLZ
     'How many children does the friend (=you) have?'

(14) ཨོ་འདི་ ཁོང་གི་ འདུག
     ódi   kʰoŋ=gi   du?
     that   he= GEN   COP.EX.SEN
     'It is his.'

Both the existentials *jø̀?/du?* (cf. (15+16)) and the equatives *ı̃́:/bɛ?* (cf. (17+18)) are used in adjectival predication, similarly to Lhasa Tibetan (Chang and Chang 1984: 614–616, Tournadre and Dorje 2003: 120–122).

(15) ཁུའི་གི་ བ་ཀེག་ འདི་ ལེབ་ཏི་ མ་ལག་ ཡོད།
     kʰui=ki   baik=di   lèpti   màla?   jø̀?
     his=GEN   bike=DEMPH   very   fast   COP.EX.PER
     'His (motor)bike is very fast.' (NB, elicitation)

(16) ལྷོག་པར་གྱི་ སྙིང་པོ་ལེབ་ཏི་ལེམ་ འདུག
     ló?par=ki   ɲiŋpo   lèpti   lèm   du?
     X-ray=GEN   essence   very   good   COP.EX.SEN
     'The results of the X-ray look very good.' (Richhi 29)

(17) ཨོ་འདི་ ལེབ་སྟི་ ལེམ་ སྦད།
    ódi   lɛ̀pti   lɛ̀m   bɛʔ
    that   very   good   COP.EQU.NE
    'That is very good.'

(18) ཨོ་འདི་ ཧ་གོ་ དགོས་པོ་ གལ་ཆེན་ ཨིན།
    ódi   háko   goː-po   kʼɛːtɕʰíː   íː
    that   understand need.to-NMLZ important   COP.EQU.PER
    'It is important to understand that.' (Richhi 7)

The somewhat ambiguous position of *bɛʔ* in the equative vs. existential dichotomy is illustrated in (cf. (19+20)) where *bɛʔ* appears in quantified locative and quantified existential uses respectively. In (19+20), *bɛʔ* cannot be used without the quantifier. In the short exchange in (20), person A uses *bɛʔ* with a quantifier. In B's reply, however, the quantifier is lacking and hence the copula is changed to *jɔ̀ʔ*.

(19) ཞིང་ འདིན་ རྡོ་ གྱིས་པོ་ སྦད།
    ɕìŋ=di=na   do   kɛːp(o)   bɛʔ
    field=DEMPH=LOC   stone   much   COP.EQU.NE
    'There are a lot of stones in the field.'

(20) a. དུས་ཚོད་ གྱིས་པོ་ སྦད་ ད་རུང་ བུ་སྲིང་ལགས།⁸
       tʼytsʰø̀ʔ   kɛːpo   bɛʔ   tʼaruŋ   pʼusim=la
       time   much   COP.EQU.NE   still   little.sister=HON
       'There's still a lot of time, sister.'

    b. ཨ་རྫི! ཨ་རྒྱ་ དུས་ཚོད་ ཡོད་ གསུང་སྟི་ཏོ
       ádzi   ágja   tʼytsʰø̀ʔ   jɔ̀ʔ   súŋ-ti=to
       darn   big.brother   time   COP.EX.PER   say-NF=CEMPH
       'Darn! Brother, it's maybe not a good idea to say that there

       མི་སྟིག་ལོ།
       min-ɖik=lo
       NEG-be.suitable=REP?⁹
       is time.' (Richhi 56)

---

8 One educated consultant from Barfung Lingdam, South Sikkim, found the use of སྦད་ *bɛʔ* here inappropriate and preferred the use of འདུག་ *duʔ*.
9 It is as yet unclear whether=*lo* here is an extended use of the reportative or a loan of the Napali tag question *la*.

An anonymous reviewer noted that *kɛːp(o)* 'much, many' in (19) and (20a) could possibly be analysed as a noun phrase, giving (19) the translation 'In the field stones are many' (cf. 'In this place he is the boss.'). This analysis would align (19) and (20a) with typical equative uses. However, if (19) and (20a) were equative clauses, one would expect that the other equative copula *ĩː* could replace *bɛʔ* if the context were appropriate. I have not yet come across naturally occurring examples of *ĩː* occurring in quantified clauses similar to (19) and (20a). When asking for acceptability judgments on whether *ĩː* could be used instead of *bɛʔ* in (19) and (21a) the results were mixed. Consultant YR accepted the use of *ĩː* in a sentence such as (19) ((21a) was not asked), whereas consultant KT denied the acceptability of replacing *ĩː* for *bɛʔ* in (19) or (21a). The issue is left open for further research.

I will lastly exemplify the past equative uses of *duʔ*, which are somewhat surprising because *duʔ* functions otherwise as an existential copula. Examples (21–22) show that *duʔ* is used for past identification, as in (21), but not for present identification, as in (22), where *bɛʔ* or *ĩː* would be used instead.

(21) ང་སློབ་ཕྲུག་ ཨིན་པོའི་ སྐབ་ལོ་ བྷན་ད་རི་ འདི་ ང་ཚའི་
     ŋà lópt^huʔ   ím-bøː   kap=lo   bhandari=di   ŋàtɕi
     I   student   COP-NMLZ.GEN   time=DAT   Bhandari=DEMPH   our
     'When I was a student Bhandari was

     གཙོ་ཆེ་ བློན་པོ་ འདུག་གོ།
     tsotɕ^hi   lǿmpu   duː=ɕo.
     prime   minister   COP.EX.SEN=ATT
     our Chief Minister.' (KT, elicited)

(22) *ད་རེས་ འབྲས་ལྗོངས་གི་ གཙོ་ཆེ་ བློན་པོ་ པ་བན་ ཚམ་གླིང་ འདུག་གོ།
     *tʼa   ɖendzõː=gi   tsotɕ^hi   lǿmpu   pawan   tsamliŋ   duː=ɕo
     now   Sikkim=GEN   prime   minister   Pawan   Chamling   COP.EX.SEN =ATT

In (21), the proposition is based on an experience in the speaker's lifetime, but in (23) the speaker bases their statement on secondary sources on history.

(23) སྔོན་ལས་ རྒྱ་གར་གི་ གཙོ་ཆེ་ བློན་པོ་ ནེ་རུ་ འདུག་གོ།
     ɲénlɛ   gjagar=gi   tsotɕ^hi   lǿmpu   nɛhru   duʔ
     earlier India=GEN   prime   minister   Nehru   COP.EX.SEN
     'Earlier India's Prime Minister was Nehru.'

In (24) and (26), *duʔ* is again used for past identification whereas the equivalent sentences (25) and (27), when used for present identification, are not allowed (*bɛʔ* and *ĩː* are used instead). Example (24) is said of a person who changed their name.

(24) ཞོན་ལས་ ཁོང་གི་ མིང་ འདི་ ཚེ་རིང་ འདུག
    ɲènlɛ   kʰõ:=gi   mìŋ=di   tsʰeriŋ   du?
    earlier his=GEN name=DEMPH Tshering COP.EX.SEN
    'Earlier his name was Tshering.'

(25) *ཁོང་གི་ མིང་ འདི་ ཚེ་རིང་ འདུག
    *kʰõ:=gi   mìŋ=di   tsʰeriŋ   du?
    his=GEN name=DEMPH Tshering COP.EX.SEN
    *'His name is Tshering.'

(26) ཨོ་འདི་ སྐབས་ འདི་ འཁོར་ལོ་ འདི་ ཚེ་རིང་གི་ འདུག
    ódi   gã:=di   kʰorlo=di   tsʰeriŋ=gi   du?
    that time=DEMPH car=DEMPH Tshering=GEN COP.EX.SEN
    'At that time, this car was Tshering's.'

(27) *འདི་ འཁོར་ལོ་ འདི་ ཚེ་རིང་གི་ འདུག
    *di   kʰorlo=di   tsʰeriŋ=gi   du?
    this car=DEMPH Tshering=GEN COP.EX.SEN
    *'This car is Tshering's.'

Equative uses of *du?* are also noted by Sandberg, whose examples, however, have present tense English translations and are said to be used "by the more Tibetanized folk" (1895: 44). For an example, see (28), in which the phonological representation is edited from the original. Thus far, I have not come accross present uses of *du?* such as the one in (28), hence the initial question mark.

(28) ?ཨོ་འདི་ བུམ་ འདི་ ངའི་ མོ་བྱུད་ འདུག
    ?ódi   pʻum   di   ɲè: mòbi   du?
    that girl demph my wife COP
    ?'That girl is my wife.' (Sandberg 1895: 44)

The equative uses of *du?* in (21–28) illustrate the fact that *du?* is not a strictly existential copula. The reason for this behaviour of *du?* is as yet unclear.

10.4.3 The equative interrogative *bo/mèm-bo*

The equative interrogative copula *bo* (*mo* in some speech varieties) occurs in equative questions with question words, as in (29) and (30), but not with existential/locative questions (31) or equative question without a question word (32).[10]

---

[10] There seems to be some dialectal variaton in acceptance of *bo* without a question word. Consultant KT did not consider (32a) felicitous, whereas consultant RS accepted the construction.

(29) འདི་གན་པོ?
    di   kʻan   bo
    this what COP.EQU.Q
    'What is this?'

(30) འདི་ག་པོ?
    di   ka   bo
    this who COP.EQU.Q
    'Who is he?'

(31) a. *ཁུ་གན་པོ?
      *kʰu   kʻana   bo
      he   where COP.EQU.Q

   b. ཁུ་གན་ཡོདཔོ/འདུགཀོ?
      kʰu   kʻana   jə̀-po/du-ko
      he   where COP.EX.PER-NMLZ/COP.EX.SEN-NMLZ
      'Where is he?'

(32) a. *ཆོད་སློབ་ཕྲུག་པོ?
      *tɕʰø?   lóptʻu   bo
      you   student COP.EQU.Q

   b. *ཆོད་སློབ་ཕྲུག་སྲེད་ག?
      tɕʰø?   lóptʻu   bɛ-ka
      you   student COP.EQU.NE-PQ
      'Are you a student?'

In both (29) and (30), the declarative copula *bɛ?* may replace the interrogative *bo*, as in *di kʻan bɛ?* 'What is this?' and *di ka bɛ?* 'Who is this?'. The question words *kʻan* 'what' and *ka* 'who' reveal these clauses to be questions even in the absence of the interrogative copula.

With an attributive question word, as shown in (33), *bo* is used in variation with *jə̀-po*.[11]

(33) ཁུ་གཏེམ་པོ/ཡོདཔོ?
    kʰu   kʻatɛm   bo/jə̀-po
    he how/what.kind COP.EQU.Q/COP.EX.PER-NMLZ
    'What kind of man is he?'

---

11 Similarly to declaratives, attribution is a common playground for both equative and existential copulas.

The final example (34) illustrates the use of the negative interrogative copula, which occurs without a question word. The speaker in (34) is talking with his friends about a third person they met many years ago. Suddenly, the speaker sees someone who looks like the person they are talking about and asks his friend:

(34) ཨོ་འདི་ མི་ ཨོ་འདི་རང་ མནམ་བོ།
 ódi   mí   ódi-rã: mèm-bo?
 that   man   that.one-EMPH   NEG-COP.EQU.Q
 'Isn't that the person (we met)?' (TB, elicited)

The negative *mèmbo*, in contrast to positive *bo*, may also occur in locational clauses, see (87) in §10.6.1.

10.5 Evidentiality

This section gives an overview of the evidential phenomena expressed by the copulas (§5.1), briefly compares the Denjongke copula system to those of Dzongkha and Standard Tibetan (§5.2) and then discusses in more detail the basic copulas (§5.3–§5.5) and the reportative as a copula substitute (§5.6).

10.5.1 Overview

Aikhenvald (2004) defines evidentiality as coding "information source". In Denjongke, however, the copulas are better characterized simply as expressing different *types of knowledge*.[12] Consequently, the term evidentiality here applies to the three types of knowledge that Denjongke speakers may claim to have concerning an event or entity. The types of knowledge are personal, sensorial and neutral. The category name 'personal' is adopted from Hill's (2012: 391) discussion of Lhasa Tibetan, although in Denjongke, as will be shown below, personal copulas function somewhat differently from Lhasa/Standard Tibetan (Tournadre and Dorje 2013). Other characterizations for the related but not necessarily identical categories in Tibetic languages are "old knowledge" (Huber 2000), "assimilated knowledge" (van Driem 1998: 127), "strong empathy" (Häsler 1999: 151), "ego" (Garrett 2001, Gawne 2013), "egophoric" (Tournadre 2008) and "self" (Bartee 2007: 137).

The term "sensorial", earlier used by Tournadre and Jiatso (2001: 78), was chosen as a category name, because it is the shortest way to refer to sensory

---

[12] Gawne (2013: 152) prefers the term "modality" to "evidentility" as a cover term for copula distinctions in Yolmo.

experiences. Alternative terms are "sensory evidential" (Hill 2012: 389), "testimonial" (Tournadre and Dorje 2003: 110) and "perceptual" (Gawne 2013: 163).

The personal copulas *î:* and *jə̂?* express the speaker's personal knowledge. The knowledge is considered personal either because the speaker already possesses it (in contrast to recently acquired knowledge marked by sensorial copulas) or because the referent of the proposition is present at the time of speaking (in contrast to neutral copulas, which are used for spatiotemporal backgrounding). Moreover, in nominalized expressions ending in *î:*, 'personalness' may be realized as the speaker's emotional involvement (see §6.2.2). In addition, *î:* is associated with performing a type of speech act of identification, whereas *bɛ?* focusses on the consequences of identification (see §5.5). It is worth noting that the personal copulas in Denjongke are less grammaticalized (i.e. more semantically oriented) than their cognates in Lhasa/Standard Tibetan, as discussed later in this section.

In contrast to the personal copulas *î:* and *jə̂?*, which are based on the speaker's already existing knowledge, the basically existential copula *du?* refers to a specific event where the knowledge was sensorially acquired (similarly Gawne's [2013: 164] perceptual for Yolmo). When used for present occurrences, *du?* has overtones of newness (contra oldness implied by *jə̂?*). When used as an auxiliary, *du?* has overtones of momentariness (contra continuation implied by *jə̂?*), see §5.4.

The neutral, basically equative copula *bɛ?*, on the other hand, does not refer to a sensory experience as *du?*, and lacks the cognitive assimilation and spatiotemporal proximity implied by *î:* and *jə̂?*. Even when having either old personal or recent sensorial knowledge about an event, the speaker may for contextual reasons background these sources of knowledge and instead use the neutral *bɛ?*.[13] When *bɛ?* syntactically overlaps with the sensorial *du?*, the use of *bɛ?* signifies that the proposition is generally asserted without reference to a specific sensory experience. It can be used, for instance, when the speaker and the addressee share the same visual experience at the moment of speech, and, therefore, it would be redundant for the speaker to use an evidential to make explicit how the information was received.

10.5.2 Comparison with Dzongkha and Standard Tibetan

A notable difference between the Denjongke copula system and that of Dzongkha (see Tab. 3 below), a closely related language, is that Denjongke lacks an equative copula for (newly acquired) sensorial knowledge. Whereas Dzongkha has both

---

13 See Hill (2013) for the contextual semantics of Lhasa Tibetan evidentials.

ཨིན་ *'ing* (a cognate of Written Tibetan ཨིན་ *yin*, similarly to Denjongke *í:*) for old information and ཨིནམས་ *'immä* for newly acquired information (van Driem 1998: 127), Denjongke has only one equative copula ཨིན་ *í:*, which marks old information and spatiotemporal proximity.

Tab. 3: Dzongkha copulas (adapted from van Driem 1998).

	Assimilated (old)	Aqcuired (new)
Equative	ཨིན་ *'ing*	ཨིནམས་ *'immä*
Existential	ཡོད་ *jö*	འདུག་ *du:*

The lack of an equative copula for newly acquired knowledge in Denjongke seems to cause a difference in the semantics between Denjongke *í:* and its cognate in Dzongkha. The meaning of Dzongkha *'ing* as assimilated/old knowledge is affected by its opposition to the newly acquired knowledge marker. The meaning of Denjongke *í:*, on the other hand, focusses on spatiotemporal proximity (rather than oldness of information) because it is paradigmatically contrasted, not with a copula expressing sensorial, newly acquired knowledge, but with the neutral copula *bɛʔ*, which implies spatiotemporal backgrounding.

An important fact about Denjongke "personal evidential" is that it is not as much restricted by the concept of grammatical person as the related category "ego(phoric)" in "Standard Tibetan" (Garrett 2001; Tournadre and Dorje 2003). According to Garrett, ego(phoric) copula constructions are "rather free, allowing the overt or implied first-person to be a grammatical subject, object, possessor of a subject or object, or even a possessor of a possessor. Nevertheless, *all ego sentences share a first-person restriction of some kind*" (2001: 103, emphasis mine). Garrett further notes that in some uses of *yin* [jĩn], such as in (35), the 1st person may be syntactically absent. In these cases, however, the referent has to be "closely related to the speaker, e.g. his son" (2001: 141/142). (The example is edited from the original.)

(35) Standard Tibetan
 ?ཁོ་ དགེ་རྒན་ ཡིན།
 ?kho dge.rgan yin
 he teacher COP
 '?He is a teacher.'
 'He (my son) is a teacher.'

(36) Denjongke
 ཁོང་ སློབ་དཔོན་ ཨིན།
 kʰõ: lópõ: í:
 he.HON teacher COP.EQU.PER
 'He is a teacher.'

The difference between Standard Tibetan (35) and Denjongke (36) is that in Denjongke the personal copula î: (cognate of ཡིན་ yin) is freely used without any requirement for the referent to be closely related to the speaker. A similar difference between the Standard Tibetan "egophoric" and the cognate Yolmo "ego" forms has been noted by Gawne, who comments that Yolmo "ego copulas do not relate to the subject of the sentence, or the relationship of the speaker to the subject, but instead express the speaker's knowledge" (2013: 192). Similarly to Yolmo, Denjongke personal copulas refer to the speaker's personal knowledge rather than the speaker's involvement in the event or relationship to the subject.[14] A possible difference between Denjongke and Yolmo, however, is that in a sentence such as (36) the "personal" evidentiality of î:, owing to the contrast with the spatiotemporally backgrounding equative bɛʔ, appears to focus more on the spatiotemporal closeness of the referent (i.e. the person introduced is present) than on the speaker's already existing knowledge. Some other Tibetic languages, which do not share the 1st person restriction of Standard Tibetan with reference to the cognate of the 'egophoric' yin, are Balti, Purik and Lower Ladakhi (Bielmeier 2000).

Sometimes the syntactically motivated terms 'disjunct' (equivalents of bɛʔ/duʔ) and 'conjunct' (equivalents of î:/jə̀ʔ), originating from Hale (1971, 1980), have been used in describing Tibetic copulas (e.g. DeLancey 1990, 1992). However, if applied to Denjongke, these syntactic terms referring to co-reference fail to facilitate an insightful analysis, because the real factors behind copula choice are semantic and pragmatic rather than syntactic. For a thorough criticism of the concepts 'disjunct' and 'conjunct', see Tournadre (2008).

Although this chapter focusses on the semantic distinctions expressed by the copulas, two additional morphemes, which code (epistemic) types of knowledge, deserve brief mention. The first is the dubitative marker -ṭo 'probably, maybe', which attaches directly to the verb stem. Within the copulas, -ṭo only occurs with the personal copulas jə̀ʔ and î: but not with sensorial duʔ or neutral bɛʔ, e.g. jə̀-ṭo (neg. mè:-ṭo) 'there probably is' ('there probably is not') and ı̂n-ṭo (neg. mɛ̃̀:-ṭo) 'it probably is' ('it probably is not'). Among other Tibetic languages, a cognate of -ṭo is found, for instance, in Lhasa Tibetan (Denwood 1999: 131) and Yolmo (Gawne 2013: 159). The second morpheme is the apparent marker ḍa 'it seems', which attaches to the nominalized forms of the personal copulas, as in jə̀-po ḍa (neg. me:-po ḍa) 'there seems to be' ('there seems not to be') and ı̂m-bo ḍa (neg. mɛ̃̀:-po ḍa) 'it seems to be' ('it seems not to be'). A cognate of Denjongke ḍa is found in Lhasa Tibetan (e.g. Denwood 1999: 127).

The next sections illustrate the use of each of the basic copulas.

---

[14] However, spatiotemporal proximity of the referent (see §5.5) and the speaker's emotional involvement (see §6.2.2) may be viewed as a weak type of speaker-involvement in Denjongke.

10.5.3 Personal copulas

The personal knowledge expressed by the personal copulas may mean that 1) the proposition in question is evidentially based on their old, existing knowledge, 2) that the referent of the proposition (who does not have to be the first person) is spatiotemporally proximate or 3) the speaker is emotionally involved in the event. The last sense has been attested only with *î:* as the final copula of nominalized constructions. The first two senses are expressed by both personal copulas *î:* and *jə̂ʔ*. There is, however, a difference in that *î:* seems to focus on spatiotemporal proximity, whereas *jə̂ʔ* expresses more clearly both old knowledge and spatiotemporal proximity. The reason for this difference between *î:* and *jə̂ʔ* seems to be that the semantics of the personal copulas are affected by the other copulas they evidentially contrast with.

Because *jə̂ʔ* in its ELPA-functions contrasts with both the sensorial *duʔ* and the neutral nominalized copula construction *jə̂-po bɛʔ/jɛ̀bbɛ*, it has developed semantics in opposition to both of these contrastive copulas. The focus on the speaker's old, already existing (and hence personal) knowledge arises from the opposition to *duʔ*, which makes reference to a specific, usually recent knowledge-acquiring event. The sense of spatiotemporal proximity ('here and now'), on the other hand, arises from the contrast with the neutral nominalized construction *jə̂-po bɛʔ/jɛ̀bbɛ*, which is used for spatiotemporal backgrounding ('there and then', similarly to mere *bɛʔ*).

The equative personal copula *î:*, in contrast, lacks a contrastive sensorial equative (the marginal combinatory sensorial equative *índuʔ*, see §6.1, does not contrast with *î:* in most contexts) and therefore the semantics of *î:*, focussing on spatiotemporal proximity, are mainly affected by its contrast with the neutral, spatiotemporally backgrounding *bɛʔ*. Nevertheless, as shown in §5.3.1, a case can be made for *î:* also making reference to the speaker's already existing knowledge. In addition to the above three senses, *î:* is associated with a type of speech act of identification, as is shown in §5.5.

10.5.3.1 Personal equative ཨིན་ *î:*

In equation, the personal *î:* contrasts frequently with the neutral *bɛʔ* (§5.5) and marginally with the sensorial *índuʔ* (§6.1). In attributive sentences, *î:* contrasts with the neutral *bɛʔ*, the personal *jə̂ʔ* (§5.3.2) and the sensorial *duʔ* (§5.4).

In equative sentences such as (37–38), it is usually not obvious that *î:* would mark older knowledge than *bɛʔ*, because both sentences could be used as soon as the knowledge is gained. The difference is rather characterized in terms of the presence or absence of the referent, the referent being present in (37) and absent in (38) (see also §5.5).

(37) ཁོང་གི་ མིང་ ཚེ་རིང་ ཨིན། $k^hõ:=gi$ $mìŋ$ $ts^heriŋ$ $ĩ:$

(38) ཁོང་གི་ མིང་ ཚེ་རིང་ བེད། $k^hõ:=gi$ $mìŋ$ $ts^heriŋ$ $bɛʔ$
                             he.HON=GEN   name   Tshering   COP.EQU
                             'His name is Tshering.'

In attributive sentences such as (39–40), however, the difference of $ĩ:$ and $bɛʔ$ with reference to integration of knowledge becomes clearer.

(39) ཁུ་ རྒྱགས་ནས་ ཨིན།
     k^hu $gjanam$ $ĩ:$
     he   fat   COP.EQU.PER
     'He is (a) fat (one).'

(40) ཁུ་ རྒྱགས་ནས་ བེད།
     k^hu $gjanam$ $bɛʔ$
     he   fat   COP.EQU.NE
     'He is fat.'

Consultant KN commented that in order to say (39) of a person who is present, the referent has to be the speaker's earlier acquaintance, whereas (40) could be said when seeing the referent for the first time.[15]

The semantic difference between personal $ĩ:$ and neutral $bɛʔ$ is also seen when the copula is followed by the (clausal) attention marker $=ço$, which may mark a proposition as attention-worthy either to the speaker or to the addressee. When used with the personal copula $ĩ:$, which marks integrated knowledge, $=ço$ marks the information in the proposition as attention-worthy to the addressee, not to the speaker. For an example, see (41).

(41) ང་ ཁོང་གི་ བུ་ ཨིན་ཤོ།
     $ŋà$ $k^hõ:=gi$ $p\text{'}u$ $ĩ:=ço$
     I   he.HON=GEN   son   COP.EQU.PER = ATT
     'I'm actually his son (which you don't seem to know).' (PT, elicited)

---

15 The difference in choosing $bɛʔ$ rather than $duʔ$ is addressed in §5.5.

In (41), Person A and B are talking about a certain man. The man who is the topic of the discussion is actually A's father. In the course of the conversation, A has reason to believe that B is not aware of this fact. To counter this false assumption, A uses the attention marker to communicate to the addressee that he (the speaker) knows that what he is saying is probably unexpected and newsworthy, and hence attention-worthy, to the addressee.

With *bɛʔ*, on the other hand, *=ɕo* may mark the proposition as attention-worthy either to the speaker (cf. (42)) or to the addressee (cf. (43)).

(42) ཨུ་ !ཨོ་ཉི་ལགས་ཚུ་ སྦད་གོ།
 já:,   óɲi=la:-tsu   bɛ=ɕo
 O   child=HON-PL   COP.EQU.NE=ATT
 'O, it's the children.' (Richi 25)

(43) ལབ་མཁན་ དོན་དག་ འདི་ འོད་འདི་ སྦད་གོ།
 làp-kʰɛ̂:   tʼønda=di   ódi   bɛ=ɕo
 say-NMLZ   meaning=DEMPH   that   COP.EQU.NE=ATT
 'The meaning of the (afore)said is this.' (JF, folk-story of the golden axe)

The proposition in (42) is accompanied by an exclamation to underline the noteworthy character of the information about the comers' identity to the speaker. In (43), in contrast, the speaker marks the main teaching of a moral story newsworthy to the addressee by using *=ɕo*. The fact that with *ǐ:=ɕo* attention-worthiness is addressee-oriented but with *bɛ=ɕo* either speaker or addressee-oriented suggests that *ǐ:* is a marker of old, already existing knowledge, whereas *bɛʔ* is neutral with respect to when and how the information was acquired.

The copula *ǐ:*(as also *bɛʔ*) co-occurs with any of the first, second or third person pronouns, see (44), showing that the 'personal' semantics of *ǐ:* have not been grammaticalized into a syntactic requirement for the first person to appear with *ǐ:* or into a semantic requirement for the referent to be closely related to the speaker (contra Lhasa Tibetan, see Garrett 2001: 141/142). The semantic difference of using *ǐ:* and *bɛʔ* is discussed in §5.5.

(44) ཁོ་/ལྱུན་རྒྱས་/ང་ སྨན་པོ་ ཨིན་/སྦད།
 kʰö:/ḷeŋge:/ŋà   mémpo   ǐ:/bɛʔ
 he.HON/you.HON/I   doctor   COP.EQU.PER/COP.EQU.NE
 'He is a doctor./ You are a doctor./ I am a doctor.'

Prototypically equative copulas describe situations that exist in the present, but in appropriate contexts, they may convey past meanings. This is exemplified in (45) where the adverbial སྔོན་ལས་ *ɲénlɛ* 'earlier' enforces a past interpretation of the sentence with *ǐ:*.

(45) ང་འདི་སྔོན་ལས་གན་འདེ་ཏུ་མ་གོ་མཁན་མི་གཅིག་ཨིན།
    ŋà=di   ɲénlɛ   k'andɛ   hamago-kʰɛ̃:
    I=DEMPH   earlier   anything   NEG.understand-NMLZ
    mí   tɕi?   ĩ:
    person   one   COP.EQU.PER
    'Earlier I was a man who didn't understand anything.' (KT, life-story)

When used with an adjectival argument, as in (46) [18] and (47) [6], the use of the equative copula ĩ: implies that the adjective expresses a defining or identifying characteristic of the nominal it is linked with.

(46) ཨོ་འདི་ཧ་གོ་དགོས་པོ་གལ་ཆེན་ཨིན།
    ódi   háko   go:-po   k'ɛ:tɕʰĩ: ĩ:
    that   understand   need.to-NMLZ   important   COP.EQU.PER
    'It is important to understand that.' (Richhi 7)

(47) དའི་བོ་ཙོ་ཐམས་ཅད་ལས་འཛིགས་དྲགས་ཨིན། ལེགས་ཨིན།
    ɲè: p'otso   tʰamtɕɛ=lɛ   dzikta?   ĩ:,   lɛ̀m   ĩ:
    I.GEN   child   all=ABL   excellent   COP.EQU.PER   good   COP.EQU.PER
    'My child is the most excellent one (lit. excellent from all), a good one.'
    (RM, story of my son)

More examples of ĩ: are found in §5.5, where ĩ: is contrasted with bɛ? and the other copulas. The use of ĩ: as the final copula of nominalized constructions is addressed in §6.2.2.

10.5.3.2 Personal existential copula ཡོད་ jø?

Similarly to ĩ:, the personal existential copula jø?[16] codes the speaker's already existing knowledge (contra sensorially acquired knowledge marked by du?) and spatiotemporal proximity (contra spatiotemporally backrounding nominalized copulas, e.g. jø-po bɛ?/jɛ̀bbɛ?). The use of jø? usually also entails that the situation depicted in the sentence continues to exist at the moment of speech (contra du? which reports an observation at a particular moment). jø? can only mark those experiences about which it is possible to acquire personal knowledge over time (e.g. what a friend's character is like), whereas the other existential copula du? will be used for coding momentary experiences (e.g. what a friend is wearing today). It seems impossible to gain personal knowledge of distant

---

16 The copula jø? is pronounced by most children and young adults as jɛ?, without rounding in the vowel. Rounding in front vowels, in general, seems to be disappearing.

historical events. Therefore historical events are reported with non-personal forms, see (68). If speakers need to distance themselves from the intimate knowledge and present actuality of the proposition implied by the use of *jə̀ʔ*, they use the nominalized constructions *jə̀-po bɛʔ/jɛbbɛʔ* and *jə̀-kʰɛn bɛʔ*, which are discussed in §6.2.1.

The type of knowledge coded by *jə̀ʔ* is illustrated by (48) [15].

(48) ཁྱིའི་ བ་ཅིག་ འདི་ ལེབ་ཏི་ མ་ལག་ ཡོད།
    kʰui=ki   baik=di   lɛ̀pti   màla?   jə̀ʔ
    his=GEN   bike=DEMPH very fast   COP.EX.PER
    'His motorbike is very fast.' (NB, elicited)

The condition of the motorbike in (48) is part of the already existing knowledge of the speaker, who knows the bike and its owner. When commenting on an unknown biker who just passes by fast, the immediate sensory evidential *duʔ* would be chosen. In Kyirong Tibetan, a sentence equivalent to (48) and a cognate of *jə̀ʔ* as copula implies that the speaker has had a "personal experience" of the speed of the bike by riding it (Huber 2002: 138). In Denjongke, however, riding the bike oneself is not required for a sentence such as (48). It is enough just to know the condition of the bike, for one reason or another, very well. In other words, *jə̀ʔ* refers merely to the knowledge state of the speaker, not to any specific type of personal involvement.

Example (49), taken from Bhaichung Tsichudarpo's novel *Ricchi*, shows how the author of a novel may use personal forms by virtue of having personal knowledge because he has created the characters and the storyline.[17]

(49) ནུབ་ འབྲས་ལྗོངས་ཀྱི་ བཙོམ་ སྦུ་རེ་ སྨན་ཁང་ན་ སྨན་པོ་ གསྐར་མ་ ཡོད།
    nùp   ɖendzǿ:=gi   sòmbarɛ   méŋkʰã:=na   mémpo   karma   jə̀ʔ
    west Sikkim=GEN   Sombare hospital=LOC doctor Karma   COP.EX.PER
    'It is in West Sikkim's Sombare hospital that doctor Karma is.' (Richhi 161)

The exact semantic interpretation of *jə̀ʔ* is dependent on the context. This is illustrated in (50), in which *jə̀ʔ* may convey either personal knowledge gained through metaphorical proximity to the referent (friendship) or personal knowledge gained by literal proximity (being in the referent's presence).

---

17 The novel *Richhi* also quite systematically uses the personal auxiliary construction verb+*po ĩ:* rather than the neutral verb+*po bɛʔ* for third person referents' past actions within the author's omniscient narration.

(50) Bill Gates ཨོ་ འདུལ་ གེཔོ་ ཡོད།
 bil geits=lo ɲỳ: kɛ:p jø̀?
 Bill Gates=LOC money a.lot COP.EX.PER
 'Bill Gates has a lot of money (as I have come to know personally either because Gates is close to me metaphorically [i.e. a friend] or close to me literally [i.e. present now]).' (KT elicited)

Example (50) implies either that the speaker is Bill Gate's friend and so personally knows about his wealth (contra sensorial du?) or that Bill Gates is present at the time of speaking (contra neutral jèbbɛ?).

The copula jø̀? is not a typical choice for a simple, second person attributive sentence, perhaps because it would seem arrogant to claim ingrained personal knowledge about another person's qualities to their face, see (51).

(51) ཁུ་/ང་/?ཆོད་ རྒྱགས་ནམ་ ཡོད།
 kʰu/ŋè/?tɕʰø gjanam jø̀?
 he/I/?you fat COP.EX.PER
 'He is fat. / I am fat. / ?You are fat.'

According to van Driem (1998: 136), second person attributive sentences with the Dzongkha copula ཡོད jø (cognate of Denjongke jø̀?) are not allowed. Instead, འདུག་ du: (cognate of Denjongke du?) has to be used. Van Driem (1998: 136) states that in attributive sentences "knowledge about the second person referent is by definition objective" (and hence not personal). In Denjongke, however, the second person version of (51) is acceptable at least in the special case when the speaker tries to convince the addressee who is reluctant to believe the proposition. In these cases, the copula jø̀? may be followed by the attention marker =ɕo to emphasize the addressee's counterexpectation and, hence, the newsworthiness of the claim for the addressee. All the other copulas, in different contexts, can more freely link the second person with an adjectival attribute. This is shown in (52). For semantic differences between the copulas in (52), see the discussion under example (81).

(52) ཆོད་ རྒྱགས་ནམ་ ཨིན་ / འདུག / བེད།
 tɕʰø? gjanam ĩ:/du?/bɛ?
 you fat COP.EQU.PER/COP.EX.SEN/COP.EQU.NE
 'You are a fat one.'/ '(I see) you are fat.'/ 'You are fat.'

It is a well-known phenomenon in Tibetan languages that when forming questions speakers do not evidentially base their copula choice on their own knowledge but on the anticipated knowledge of the addressee (cf. Tournadre's [2008: 296, 300] "rule of anticipation" in Standard Tibetan, see also Hyslop [2014] for the same in non-Tibetan Kurtöp). For Denjongke, this is illustrated in the question and answer pairs (53) [9] and (54) [partly 13], where the use of the personal copula in the question does not reflect the speaker's own knowledge state but her estimation of the addressee's knowledge state.

(53) a. ངམ་ ཡོད་ཀ?
   ŋám jɤ̀:-ka?
   sugar COP.EX.PER-PQ
   'Is there sugar?'

 b. ཡོད།
   jɤ̀?
   COP.EX.PER
   'Yes, there is.'

(54) a. ཚོགས་ཀྱི/ཚོགས་ལོ་ བོཙོ་ གཙོད་ ཡོད་པོ?
   tɕʰεro=ki/tɕʰεro=lo p'otso k'adzɤ? jɤ̀-po
   friend=GEN/friend=DAT child how.many COP.EX.PER-NMLZ
   'How many children does the friend (=you) have?'

 b. ངའི་(ཀྱི)/ངའོ་ བུམ་ གསུམ་ ཡོད།
   ɲὲ:(=ki)/ŋὲ=lo p'um súm jɤ̀?
   I.GEN(=GEN)/I=DAT daughter three COP.EX.PER
   'I have three daughters.'

In (53a) and (54a), the use of the personal copula *jɤ̀?* suggests that the speaker deems the addressee as someone who has personal knowledge of the questioned fact. It would be an interesting line of research to find out what copula is used in the answer if the copula in the question does not correctly reflect the addressee's knowledge state. De Villiers et al. observed that "Tibetan children are not led by the evidential posed in a question, but base their answers on their own judgment of the scenario" (2009: 44).

More examples of *jɤ̀?* are provided in next sections §5.4 and §5.5, where its use is contrasted with *du?* and *bε?* respectively.

10.5.4 Sensorial copula འདུག་ *du?*

The use of the sensorial copula *du?* indicates that the proposition is evidentially based on a specific, most often recent or current event that the speaker has sensorially (not necessarily visually) attested. Information expressed through the personal evidentials is also first acquired sensorially, but later with time and/or repeated exposure the knowledge becomes so assimilated that no reference to a specific event needs to be made (similarly Gawne [2013: 203] on Yolmo). Whereas *jø?* conveys that the speaker's knowledge state has existed before ('I already know'), *du?* implies that the knowledge was recently acquired ('I came to know'). The neutral *bɛ?*, on the other hand, marks a proposition non-committed as to the type of knowledge. *bɛ?* is used when the speaker and the addressee share a sensorial experience, whereas *du?* is primarily used when the addressee does not share the sensorial experience with the speaker, as discussed under (63), (79) and (80).

Because *du?* often refers to a recent event where knowledge was acquired, it can gain overtones of 'newness' or 'mirativity' (DeLancey 1997). The overtones of newness in the cognates of this copula in other Tibetic languages have been reported, among others, by Bielmeier (2000: 104), Denwood (1999: 123), Hongladarom (2007: 29) and Huber (2002: 139). It should be noted, however, that 'newness' does not necessarily entail 'unexpectedness' or 'surprise' (Zeisler 2000: 40). Hill (2012) argues for the basic meaning of *du?* in Standard Tibetan being sensorial rather than mirative. Although the use of *du?* in Denjongke often implies recently acquired knowledge, Denjongke has a separate attention marker =*ɕo* that can be attached even to the sensory evidential *du?* (*duː=ɕo*) to emphasize the attention-worthiness (caused by surprise, counterexpectation, sudden realization etc.) of the information either to the speaker or to the addressee (see examples (61), (68)).[18] Although *du?* may have some undercurrents of newness, the Denjongke language system does not appear to grammaticalize any 'surprise' value with *du?*.

The implied momentariness of *du?*, in contrast to the permanence suggested by *jø?*, is especially seen when the two copulas are used as auxiliaries. In auxiliary uses with the progressive *zɛ̃ː*, both *kʰu jó? pʼja-zɛ̃ː du?* 'He was working' and *kʰu jó? pʼja-zɛ̃ː jø?* 'He is working' could be said in a situation where the speaker does not see the man working at the moment of speech. Choosing the option with *du?* implies that the speaker recently saw the referent working, but is agnostic as to whether the referent is still working at the moment of speech (hence the past translation). The option with *jø?*, however, implies the speaker's personal knowledge that the action still continues at the time of speech (hence the present translation).

Examples (55–68) illustrate the evidential semantics of *du?*. First, consider (55) [10], a question where the speaker has to make an estimate of the addressees' state of knowledge.

---

18 For more on Denjongke attention marker =*ɕo*, see Yliniemi (2016).

(55) རང་འདུག་ག?
 ŋám du-ka?
 sugar COP.EX.SEN-PQ
 'Is there (any) sugar?'

In (55), the speaker assumes that the addressee is not in personal possession of the knowledge asked for, i.e. that the addressee may have to look around right then to find out whether there is sugar. In (53) above, on the other hand, where the copula jø? is used instead of du? in the otherwise identical sentence, the speaker assumes that the addressee already has assimilated knowledge on the availability of sugar and can answer the question without searching.

In light of what was said above, example (56) seems at first sight anomalous.

(56) a. ཆོད་ནོ་ བྱང་པོ་ལོ། འདུག་ག?
 tɕʰø: nò: bjã:-bo=lo   du-ka
 you   cow disappear-NMLZ=REP COP.EX.SEN-PQ
 'Your cow is said to have disappeared, is it (here)?'

b. འདུག་གེ་ཤོ།
 du-kɛ=ɕo
 COP.EX.SEN-IN=ATT
 'Why, it is indeed.' (TB, elicited)

In (56), the first speaker has found a cow that he brings to the second speaker. When making an estimate of the addressee's state of knowledge, speaker A in (56) would perhaps be expected to use the personal copula, because the addressee is supposed to have personal, integrated knowledge about his cows. The focus here, however, seems to fall on the specific sensory experience of identifying the cow, not on the existing knowledge state. The attention marker =ɕo in B's answer expresses the speaker's surprise, indicated by the old-fashioned exclamation 'why' in the translation.

The contrast of du? and jø? is further illustrated in (57–59). The question in (57) is formulated in a way that eliminates the possibility of echoing in the answer the same copula that was used in the question.

(57) ཚྭ་ ཐོབ་ག?
 tsʰa tʰop-ka?
 salt find-PQ
 'Is there (any) salt?'

(58) མེད།
 mè?
 NEG.COP.EX.PER
 'No, there isn't.'

(59) སེན་འདུག
    mìndu?
    NEG.COP.EX.SEN
    'No, there isn't.'

To a customer's question (57) the shopkeeper may answer (58) if he knows from before that there is no salt (*mè?* is the negative of *jø̀?*), or (59), if he is not sure from the outset but finds out whether there is salt by looking around (*mìndu?* is the negative of *du?*).[19]

In the above examples, *du?* refers to the speaker's sensory experience at the time of speaking or just prior to speaking. Examples (60–61), on the other hand, illustrate the uses of *du?* in which the sensory experience happened in more distant past.

(60) ཁོང་གཉིས་པོ་མོའི་ཁྱིམ་ན་སླེབས་པའི་སྐབས་མོ་ཁྱིམ་ན་
    kʰõ: ɲì:po mù=i kʰim=na lɛp-ø: gã: mù kʰim=na
    they two   she=GEN house=LOC reach-NMLZ.GEN time she house=LOC
    'When the two of them reached the house, she wasn't

སེན་འདུག
    min-du?
    NEG-COP.EX.SEN
    at home.' (Richhi 96)

At the time of arriving at their friend's house, the protagonists in (60) sensorially attested that she was not at home. This use of *mìndu?* can either be seen as a case of the author of this literary work taking the viewpoint of the characters or, as Zeisler (2000: 50) suggests, as the author looking at the scene as if from a window as an observer.

Now consider (61), another example of a past use of *du?*, and a rare instance of *du?* being used of the first person (see for instance Denwood 1999: 123 for similar examples from Lhasa Tibetan).

---

19 By using the intensifier *-kɛ* in *mìndu-kɛ*, the speaker can add engagement in his involvement in the situation. Whereas *mìndu?* could be said after just looking around, *mìndu-kɛ* would be appropriate after spending some time moving objects while searching. In addition to personal involvement, the intensifier *-kɛ* may imply certainty. For instance, according to some of my consultants *du-kɛ* is considered to carry more certainty than mere *du?* when reporting sensory experience. In this respect, it is similar to *-kɛ́/-gɛ́:* in Kyirong Tibetan, which is reported to mark increased assertiveness (Huber 2002: 136).

(61) མདང་རས་ གཉིད་ལམ་ གཅིག་ མཐོང་ཅེ། གཉིད་ལམ་ན་ ང་ སྨན་ཁང་ན་
dã: ŋà: ɲílam tɕi? tʰõ:-tɕɛ ɲílam=na   ŋà   méŋkʰa=na
yesterday I   dream one   see-PFV   dream=LOC I   hospital=LOC
'Yesterday I saw a dream. In the dream I was

འདུག་གོ།
du:=ɕo
COP.EX.SEN=ATT

in the hospital!' (YR, elicited)

Usually information about oneself is by definition personal, and hence marked by ĩ: and jø?, but here the speaker has observed himself in a dream. When waking up from a dream, the dreamer gets an outsider's perspective into her own life. Therefore, the sensorial evidential du? can be used when talking about oneself. The copula is here followed by the attention marker =ɕo, which indicates that the information was, and perhaps still is at the moment of speaking, surprising to the speaker.

In (62), the speaker is helping another person to sit inside a car. The choice of du? as copula indicates either that the speaker does not expect his addressees to have definite knowledge about the whereabouts of the pillow or that he is speaking to himself.

(62) ག་ལུས་ ག་ལུས་ འཛུལ་, འདི་ཁར་ རྒྱབ་ ཨེད་, གོ་ལོ་ ང་བོ་ འཛོལ་ ག་ན་
k'aly? k'aly   dzy: dikʰa: gjap ɛ?,   kolo,   ŋa:bø: k'ana
slowly slowly enter   here   back press   EXCLAM pillow   where

འདུག།
du?
COP.EX.SEN

'Come in slowly. Lean your back here. Hey, where is the pillow?' (Richhi 21)

In (63) [16], a doctor is examining a patient's X-ray pictures and comments on them:

(63) ལོག་པར་གྱི་ སྙིང་པོ་ ལེབ་ཏི་ ལེམ་ འདུག།
ló?par=ki   ɲiŋpo   lèpti   lèm   du?
X-ray=GEN   essence very   good COP.EX.SEN
'The results of the X-ray look very good.' (Richhi 29)

In (63) the doctor who looks at the X-ray pictures uses du? probably either because the addressee cannot see what the doctor sees or cannot intepret what he sees as the doctor can. The sensorial du? is mainly used when the addressee does not share the same sensorial experience as the speaker. If the speaker and the addressee both see the same thing bɛ? is more likely used.

Although information coded by *du?* is most often visual, it can also mark knowledge as deriving from the other senses, hearing (cf. (64)), tasting (cf. (65)), smelling (cf. (66)) or touching (cf. (67)).

(64) པང་ཁར་ཨ་ལུས་འདུག
 paŋkʰa: ály: du?
 outside cat COP.EX.SEN
 'There's a cat outside (as I heard it meowing).'

(65) འདི་གསོལ་ཐུགས་ཞིམ་པོ་འདུག
 di sø:tym ɕìmpu du?
 this curry delicious COP.EX.SEN
 'This curry is delicious (as I can taste).'

(66) འདི་གསོལ་ཐུགས་ཀྱི་དྲི་མ་ཞིམ་པོ་འདུག
 di sø:tym=ki t'im ɕìmpu du?
 this curry=GEN smell delicious COP.EX.SEN
 'This curry smells delicious.'

(67) འདི་གི་འདི་རྣོན་རྒགས་འདུག
 di k'i=di   nøʈa? du?
 this big.knife=DEMPH sharp COP.EX.SEN
 'This (big) knife is sharp (as I can feel).' (PD)

Example (68) presents a problem for anchoring *du?* to the speaker's specific sensory experience. The information has been heard from other people or read from books.

(68) ཨ་ཀུ་གིས་མ་གསན་པོ? རྡང་པོའི་རྒན་པོ་ཚུ་གིས་
 áku=ki   ma-sém-bo   t'ã:py: gempo-tsu=ki
 uncle=ERG NEG-hear-NMLZ of.old old.man-PL=ERG
 'Hasn't the uncle heard? The elders of old (used to say):

"ཕོ་ཙོ་ད་མོ་བྱུད་ལེན་ཆེ? ཨི་ནེ་ གཡུང་ བརྡུང་"
 p'otso t'a mòby? lèn-ɕɛ? ĩ:-nɛ   k'atɕuŋ   duŋ
 child now wife take-INF COP.EQU.PER-COND metal.ornament hit
 "If (your) child is to take a wife, make a kachung-plate."

དེ་ གཡུང་ ལབ་སྟེ་ གཉེན་ གྱི་ རྟགས་ བུ་མོ་གིས་ བཏགས་པད་
 tɛ k'atɕuŋ   làpti ɲén=gi   ta? p'umu=ki ta:-ɕɛ?
 so metal.ornament called wedding=GEN sign girl=ERG wear-INF
 So there is indeed an old tradition stating that "kachung" is the sign of

ཅིག་ དར་ཕུའི་ ལུང་བསྟན་ ཅིག་ འདུག་གོ།
tɕi?   t'ǎ:py: lùŋtɛn   tɕi?   du:=ɕo
one   of.old   tradition one   COP.EX.SEN=ATT

marriage worn by a girl.' (sbar-phung ling-dam 'gro-lis 89)

Although the speaker of (68) probably has known the information for a long time, he cannot use the personal *jə̀?* here because that would imply that he was present himself at the time when the tradition was formed. Because it is not possible to gain personal knowledge of such a historically oriented word as 'tradition', the speaker uses sensorial *du?*, which makes reference to the event(s) in which he has gained the information. An alternative for using *du?* would be to background the handing down of information by using one of the evidentially neutral nominalized construction *jə̀-po bɛ/jɛbbɛ?* or *jə̀-kʰɛn bɛ?*, the first of which is used analogously to (68) in (96).

10.5.5 Equative neutral སྦད་ *bɛ?* in comparison with other copulas

The equative neutral copula *bɛ?*[20] is semantically somewhat similar to Lhasa Tibetan རེད་ red. It also resembles in form the Shigatse evidentially neutral copula *pìè* (Haller 2000: 186), the Lhomi copula *bet*[21] (neg. *mem-pet*, Vesalainen 2014) and the last syllable of the Kyirong Tibetan (Lende) copula *jìmbɛ:* which codes recently acquired generally valid facts (Huber 2000: 157). Moreover, *[bɛ(?)]* is found instead of *[re?]* /red/ in some Tsang Tibetan varieties (Tournadre and Jiatso 2001: 82). According to Bielmeier (2000: 121), the Shigatse *pìè* and Lhomi *bet* derive from Written Tibetan བྱེད་ *byed* 'make'. The same may be true of Denjongke *bɛ?*.

bɛ? is basically an equative copula which, however, syntactically overlaps with the existential copulas *jə̀?* and *du?*, not only in adjectival predication but also in quantified existentials and quantified locatives. *bɛ?* is evidentially non-committed unlike the sensorial *du?* and the personal copulas *jə̀?* and *ĩ:*. Therefore *bɛ?* can be used in many contexts as a matter-of-fact generally asserting variant of the other copulas.

---

20 I have heard some older speakers in Barapathing, East Sikkim, use the form *mɛ?* instead of *bɛ?*. Similar ambivalence is seen in Grierson (1967 [1909]: 121), who lists "*bä, pä* and *mä*" as copula options (in addition to "*in* or *yin*"). The story of the prodigal son accompanying Grierson's description (gotten through David MacDonald) has the written form སྨད་ *smad* and the pronunciation given as "*mä*" (Grierson (1967 [1909]: 123, 125).

21 Lhomi allows for word-final plosive /t/ to be realized. In Denjongke, the dental plosive is reflected in writing སྦད་ *sbad*, but the spoken realization of the final plosive is a glottal stop or a lengthened vowel.

10 Copulas in Denjongke or Sikkimese Bhutia — 327

Probably the most difficult task in analyzing Denjongke copulas is to identify exactly what is the difference between equative sentences which differ only in the choice of copula *ǐː* vs. *bɛʔ*. Two things, however, can be said. First, *ǐː* seems to perform a type of speech act of identifying whereas *bɛʔ* takes the identification for granted and leaves room for the implications of this identification. For example, consider the two questions-answer pairs in (69) and (70), which were volunteered by one of my consultants, when I was trying to tease out the difference between *ǐː* and *bɛʔ*.

(69) a. སྨན་རྒྱས་ག་པོ?
    lɛŋgɛː   ka   bo
    you.HON   what   COP.EQU.Q
    'Who are you?'

  b. ང་ཨམ་རྗེ་ཨིན།
    ŋà   ámdzi   ǐː
    I   doctor   COP.EQU.PER
    'I'm a doctor.'

(70) a. སྨན་རྒྱས་གན་བྱས་མཁན་པོ?
    lɛŋgɛː   kʻan   pʻja-kʰɛn   bo
    you.HON   what   do-NMLZ   COP.EQU.Q
    'What do you do (for living)?'

  b. ང་ཨམ་རྗེ་སྡུད།
    ŋà   ámdzi   bɛʔ
    I   doctor   COP.EQU.NE
    'I'm a doctor.' (TB)

In (69) and (70), *ǐː* is used in the answer to the question concerning identity (69), and *bɛʔ* is used when the question relates to doing (70). This implies that *ǐː* is more concerned with the act of identifying itself, as if performing a type of speech act of identifying, whereas *bɛʔ* takes some distance from identifying and so suggests focussing on the implications of this identification (e.g. activities of a doctor). These are, however, not fixed rules; in another instance, the same consultant gave the sentence *ŋà ámdzi bɛʔ* as an answer to the question in (69).

The possibility of choosing between *ǐː* and *bɛʔ* to convey different evidential nuances about the same situation shows, similarly to Lhasa Tibetan (Hill 2013: 50), that there is no strict epistemological hierarchy among the copulas within which the speaker would have to choose the one considered to carry the highest degree of certainty.

When bringing up this same topic of *ǐː* vs. *bɛʔ* with two other consultants, they volunteered comparative sentence pairs (71+72) and (73+74) respectively (*mɛ̂ː* and *mɛ̀mbɛʔ* are the negations of *ǐː* and *bɛʔ* respectively).

(71) རང་ཚོ་ སློབ་ཕྲུག་ ཨིན།
    ŋàtɕaʔ   lóptʰuʔ   íː
    we   student   COP.EQU.PER
    'We are students.'(NB)

(72) རང་ཚོ་ སློབ་ཕྲུག་ བེད། རང་ཚོ་ འདྲེས་ བྱོས་ མི་ལེགས།
    ŋàtɕaʔ   lóptʰuʔ bɛʔ   ŋàtɕaʔ dɛm   p`ja mì-lɛʔ
    we   student COP.EQU.NE we   such do   NEG-be.good
    'We are students. We mustn't do like that.' (NB)

(73) ང་ སློབ་ཕྲུག་ མེན།
    ŋà   lóptʰuʔ   mɛ̃ː
    I   student   NEG.COP.EQU.PER
    'I am not a student.' (YR)

(74) a. ཁྱོད་ འདི་ སློག་ཅིག
      tɕʰøʔ   di   ɖok-tɕʰ(i)
      you   this   read-IMP
      'You, read this!'

    b. ང་ སློབ་ཕྲུག་ མན་སྦད། ང་ དབྱིན་ཇི་ སློག་ མི་ཤེས།
      ŋà   lóptʰuʔ   mèm-bɛʔ   ŋà   índʑi   ɖok   mì-ɕeː
      I   student   NEG-COP.EQU.NE I   English read NEG-know
      'I'm not student. I can't read English.' (YR)

Again, in both (71) and (73) *íː* is used for simple identification of people, whereas in the use of *bɛʔ* in both (72) and (74) it is the implications of identification that are in focus. Example (72) is concerned with responsibilities of students (they should behave in a certain way) and in (74) the central question is abilities of a student (they can read English). Whereas *íː* in (71) and (73) identifies certain people by their occupational status (or lack of it), the use of *bɛʔ* in (72) and (74) focusses on responsibilities and abilities of students in general.

The second thing that can be said about the difference between *íː* and *bɛʔ* is that *íː* is associated with spatiotemporal proximity, with the 'here and now', whereas *bɛʔ* is associated with spatiotemporal distancing, 'there and then'. A conditioning factor in choosing between *íː* and *bɛʔ* is the presence or absence of the referent in the clause. Consultant PT from Tashiding preferred the identifying, equative copula *íː* when the person referred to was present, whereas *bɛʔ* was preferred when the referent was absent. This observation is illustrated in examples (75–77) below:

(75) a. ཁུ་ རྒྱགས་ནམ་ ཨིན།
      kʰu   gjanam   íː
      he   fat   COP.EQU.PER
      'He's (a) fat (one).' (referent present)

b. ཁུ་རྒྱགས་ནམ་སླད།
   kʰu   gjanam   bɛʔ
   he   fat   COP.EQU.NE
   'He is fat.' (referent absent)

(76) a. ཁོང་ཕྱི་རྒྱལ་པོ་ཨིན།
     kʰõ: tɕʰigɛːbo   ĩ:
     he.HON   foreigner   COP.EQU.PER
     'He's a foreigner.' (referent present)

b. ཁོང་ཕྱི་རྒྱལ་པོ་སླད།
   kʰõ: tɕʰigɛːbo   bɛʔ
   he.HON   foreigner   COP.EQU.NE
   'He's a foreigner.' (referent in photo)

(77) a. འདི་ཁོང་གི་ཁྱིམ་ཨིན།
     di   kʰõŋ=gi   kʰim   ĩ:
     this he.HON=GEN house COP.EQU.PER
     'This is his house.' (owner present)

b. འདི་ཁོང་གི་ཁྱིམ་སླད།
   di   kʰõː=gi   kʰim   bɛʔ
   this he.HON=GEN house COP.EQU.NE
   'This is his house.' (owner absent)

Consultant YR, when given the task of describing the difference between the sentences *kʰõ: ámdʑi ĩ:* and *kʰõ: ámdʑi bɛʔ* 'he is a doctor', first commented that in the first sentence the person is alive and in the second one dead, thus just bringing the presence vs. absence distinction to another level and adding temporal distance to spatial distance. Similarly, Chang and Chang (1984: 609) provide an example from Lhasa Tibetan where a boy says about his dead father དའི་རའི་ང་པ་རེད་ *tʰa ti ŋɛː pápá rèː* 'Now, this is my father'. As the copula *jìː* would be usually used if the father were alive, Chang and Chang see the choice of *rèː* as copula to indicate "emotional distance". Their analysis appears similar to Häsler's (1999: 151) description of Derge Tibetan *jĩː* as marking "strong empathy" and *rèː* marking "weak empathy" and Kretschmar's (1986: 65) "die innere Regung des Sprechers" (the speaker's inner emotion). It should be noted that the above observations on the difference between *ĩ:* and *bɛʔ* are tentative in nature and need to be followed by a more rigorous study of naturally occurring examples.

Earlier in (53) and (55), I showed that in questions Denjongke speakers make estimates about their addressee's state of knowledge. In questions relating to identity, however, copula choice may also be conditioned by whether the questioner wants to present themselves as someone who already knows or at least has a hypothesis of the answer (í:), or as someone who does not know the answer (bɛʔ). For an example, consider (78).²²

(78) a. ཆོད་སློབ་ཕྲུག་སྲེད་ག?
     tɕʰø? lóptʰuʔ bɛ-ga
     you   student   COP.EQU.NE-Q
     'Are you a student?'

   b. ཆོད་སློབ་ཕྲུག་ཨིན་ག?
     tɕʰø? lóptʰuʔ íŋ-ga
     you   student   COP.EQU.PER-Q
     'You are a student, aren't you?'

In swiftly transitory attributive situations, as shown in (79), jø̀ʔ cannot be used because it suggests that the information in the sentence is old and ingrained. Then, the choice of copulas is narrowed down to duʔ and bɛʔ.

(79) a. འདི་གོས་ལག་ཚུ་རྙིག་ག་སྲེད།
     di   kʼola-tsu   tʼika   bɛʔ
     this clothing-PL dirty COP.EQU.NE
     'These clothes are dirty.'

   b. འདི་གོས་ལག་ཚུ་རྙིག་ག་འདུག།
     di   kʼola-tsu   tʼika   duʔ
     this clothing-PL dirty COP.EX.SEN
     'These clothes are dirty (I see).'

One of the contexts where someone would say (79a) instead of (79b) is when the experience of seeing the clothes, and hence the acquired knowledge, is mutual between the speaker and the addressee. In these cases, there is no need to underpin one's assertion with an evidential.

The last two examples (80) and (81) summarize the evidential differences between the basic declarative copulas by contrasting bɛʔ with other copulas in locative and attributive use respectively.

(80) a. ཞིང་འདིན་ནང་རྡོ་གནས་པོ་ཡོད། ɕiŋ=di=na do kɛ:p(o) jø̀ʔ
   b. ཞིང་འདིན་ནང་རྡོ་གནས་པོ་འདུག། ɕiŋ=di=na do kɛ:p(o) duʔ
   c. ཞིང་འདིན་ནང་རྡོ་གནས་པོ་སྲེད། ɕiŋ=di=na do kɛ:p(o) bɛʔ
     field=DEMPH=LOC stone much COP
     'There are a lot of stones in the field.'

Whereas (80a) could be said by the owner of a field, who has old, personal knowledge about his field, (80b) would be said by someone who has just seen

---

22 There are also other ways to form questions which are not treated here.

the field for the first time (or after a very long time) as a comment to someone else who does or did not share the same experience. Example (80c), in contrast, featuring the general neutral copula *bɛʔ*, can be said by someone who has never seen the field before to an accompanying friend who also sees the field. In this case, the sensory evidential *duʔ* is not needed, because the knowledge is mutual (they both see the field). Furthermore, (80c) could also be said in a situation where the speaker has knowledge about the field from before (old knowledge) but wants to, for some reason, distance himself from the epistemically more committed copula *jə̀ʔ*, which would imply personalness of knowledge.

The attributive use of *bɛʔ* in contrast with the other copulas is illustrated with the adjective *gjanam* 'fat, sturdy' in (81) below.

(81) a. ཁུ་རྒྱགས་ནམ་ཨིན། *kʰu gjanam ĩ́ː* 'He is a fat one (as I know).'
b. ཁུ་རྒྱགས་ནམ་ཡོད། *kʰu gjanam jə̀ʔ* 'He is fat (as I know).'
c. ཁུ་རྒྱགས་ནམ་འདུག *kʰu gjanam duʔ* 'He is fat (as I just saw).'
d. ཁུ་རྒྱགས་ནམ་སྦད། *kʰu gjanam bɛʔ* 'He is fat (as I generally assert).'

The first sentence with *ĩ́ː* (81a) identifies the referent as a member in the class of "fat ones". The copula *duʔ* in (81c) is used when (or shortly after) meeting the person described for the first time (or after a long time). Whereas *duʔ* codes knowledge acquired by momentary recent observation, the use of *jə̀ʔ* in (81b) suggests that the statement is based on the speaker's pre-existing knowledge. The copula *bɛʔ* in (81d), on the other hand, is neutral in these respects, implying neither the personalness of *jə̀ʔ* nor the immediacy and sensorialness of *duʔ*. With *bɛʔ*, the emphasis seems to fall on the information expressed in the sentence rather than on the type of knowledge the speaker purports to have.

10.5.6 Reportative marker =*lo* as copula substitute

The reportative marker =*lo* may be used as a substitute for equative copulas,[23] as shown in (82), but in existential reportative clauses the copula is obligatorily present, as shown in (83) and (84).

(82) ཁུ་ཨམ་རྫི་ལོ།
kʰu ámdzi=lo
he doctor=REP
'He's reportedly a doctor. / He's a doctor, I hear.' (YR)

---

[23] Some of the other Tibetic languages that employ =*lo* as a reportative/hearsay marker are Classical Tibetan (Jäschke 1888: 551–552), Dzongkha (van Driem 1998: 405–406), Lamjung Yolmo (Gawne 2013:323), Lhomi (Vesalainen 2014: 131) and Kyirong Tibetan (Huber 2002: 107).

(83) ཨོན་ ཚ་ ཡོད་ལོ་/འདུག་ལོ།
    óna   tsʰa   jø̀:=lo/du:=lo²⁴
    there salt   COP.EX.PER=REP/COP.EX.SEN=REP
    'There's reportedly salt in there.'

(84) *ཨོན་ ཚ་ ལོ།
    *óna   tsʰa=lo
    there salt= REP

The use of the reportative marker =lo with the existential copulas jø̀? and du? shifts the evidential anchoring of the copula from the speaker to the person who is the source of information. In other words, "evidential information is retained from the the original utterance" (Gawne 2013: 135, see also Tournadre 2008: 295/296). The shifting of evidential anchoring is illustrated in (85–86).

(85) a. ཁུ་ སྒང་ཏོག་ན་ འདུག
        kʰu   gã:to:=na   du?
        he   Gangtok=LOC COP.EX.SEN
        'He's in Gangtok (I saw him).'

    b. ཁུ་ སྒང་ཏོག་ན་ འདུག་ལོ།
        kʰu   gã:to:=na   du:=lo
        he   Gangtok=LOC COP.EX.SEN=REP
        'He's reported to be in Gangtok (they said they saw him).'

(86) a. ཁུ་ སྒང་ཏོག་ན་ ཡོད།
        kʰu   gã:to:=na   jø̀?
        he   Gangtok=LOC COP.EX.PER
        'He's in Gangtok (I know it well).'

    b. ཁུ་ སྒང་ཏོག་ན་ ཡོད་ལོ།
        kʰu   gã:to:=na   jø̀:=lo
        he   Gangtok=LOC COP.EX.PER=REP
        'He's reported to be in Gangtok (They know it well).'

Whereas in (85a) it is the speaker himself who saw the person under discussion, in (85b) the copula du? reports someone else's sensory experience. Similarly, in (86a) the copula jø̀? implies the speaker's personal, pre-existing knowledge, whereas (86b) reports a situation where the speaker has been persuaded that the source of his information has personal knowledge. By using du? the speaker just

---

24 For the difference between jø̀:lo and du:lo see examples (85–86).

claims that at a past point the person in question has been seen to be in Gangtok but that there is no guarantee of the person still being there. The copula *jø?*, on the other hand, indicates more intimate knowledge, possibly based on personal involvement, and includes the claim that the person referred to is still in Gangtok at the time of speech. The personal involvement could, for instance, take the form of the speaker having ordered the person in question to go to Gangtok for a few days and having seen him leave in the morning.

The discussion so far has focussed on the lone occurrances of the basic copulas *ĩ:, jø?, du?, bɛ?* and *bo* and the copula substitute =*lo*. The following section addresses the complex copula constructions.

10.6 Complex copulas: combinatory copulas and nominalized copulas

In addition to the basic copulas, Denjongke employs a number of complex copulas in which two basic copulas are combined together, either directly (combinatory copulas) or with the help of nominalization (nominalized copulas). These complex forms fill communicative gaps in the copula system, i.e. they help Denjongke speakers express evidential nuances that cannot be expressed by the mere basic copulas and avoid unwanted meanings that are implied by the basic copulas. I first describe the two combinatory copulas (§6.1) and then the several nominalized copulas (§6.2).

10.6.1 Combinatory copulas ཨིན་སྲུད་ *ímbɛ?* and ཨིན་དུག *indu?*

The basic copulas may be directly combined to form the concurring/agreeing equative *ímbɛ?* and the sensorial equative *indu?* (which occurs quite rarely). The copula *ímbɛ?*, which resembles in form the Dzongkha ཨིན་པས་ *'immä*, marks the speaker's agreement with what the addressee has just said. In the same vein, Dzongkha ཨིན་པས་ *'immä* can be used to "politely punctuate someone else's narrative" (van Driem 1998: 127). In examples (87) and (88), the speaker concurs with someone else's statement.

(87) a.   ཨ་རྒྱ་ཡང་དམག་མིའི་ནང་རང་མན་བོ?
       ágja=jãː   *máːmiː=na=rãː*   *mɛ̀mbo?*
       big.brother=also   army.GEN=LOC=EMPH   NEG.COP.EQU.Q
       'Isn't the brother also in the army?'

b. དམག་མིའིན་ ཨིན་སུང་།
   má:mi:=na   ímbɛ?
   army.GEN=LOC   COP.CONCUR
   'Yes, he is indeed in the army.' (Richhi 56)

(88) ཨིན་སུང་། ཁམ་ རང་གིས་ ལབ་པོ་ བདེན་ སྦད།
ímbɛ?,   raŋ=gi   làp-o   dɛn   bɛ?
COP.CONCUR   you=ERG   say-NMLZ   true   COP.EQU.NE
'It is indeed so. What you say is true.' (rna-gsung dang gtam-bshad 39)

It is noteworthy that in (87) both the negated question *mèm-bo* and the concurring *ímbɛ?* take a locative argument, a construction not attested with the lone copula *bɛ?*.[25]

Now consider (89), which is an example of the sensorial equative *índu?*.

(89) པ་སྦུན་ ཙམ་གླིང་ འདི་ རང་འི་ བློན་པོ་ གཙོ་བོ་ ཅིག་ཀུ་
pawan   tsamliŋ=di   ŋàtɕi   lømpu   tsou   tɕiku
Pawan   Chamling=DEMPH   our   minister   main   only

མན་བར་
mèmba:
NEG.COP.EQU.NE.SUP
'Pawan Chamling is not only our Prime Minister,

མི་ ཡིག་རིགས་ མཁས་དགས་ ཅིག་ ཨིན་འདུག
mí   jìgri   kʰɛːta?   tɕi?   índu?
person   literature   skillful   one   COP.EQU.SEN
but he is also a skillfull literary figure.' (KT, elicited)

The copula *índu?* combines some of the meanings of both copulas *î:* and *du?*. Whereas *î:* marks the equative function (Mr. PC is identified as a skilful writer), *du?* implies that there was a past personal sensory experience where this knowledge was gained, for instance, in the case of my consultant, experience of reading Mr. PC's writings.[26] The difference between *índu?* and the equative use of *du?* is that *índu?* is used for present identification (based on past sensorial experience) and *du?* for past identification.

Apart from *ímbɛ?* and *índu?*, no other combinations of basic copulas (e.g. **bɛdu?*, **dubɛ?*, **bɛî:*) were acceptable to my consultants.

---

[25] *bɛ?*, however, appears in quantified locatives and existentials, see (19–20).
[26] My consultant's attempt to translate *índu?* in (89) into Nepali was हो रहेछ *ho rahecha*.

10.6.2 Nominalized copula constructions

The dichotomy between î: and bɛʔ within equative copulas, and jøʔ and duʔ within existential copulas, is neutralized in nominalized constructions so that only î: and jøʔ occur nominalized with the nominalizers -po/bo and -kʰɛn ~kʰɛ̃:.[27] Therefore, the morpheme glosses of nominalized copulas below do not have information on evidentiality, e.g. ím-bo is glossed as COP.EQU-NMLZ (not as COP. EQU.PER-NMLZ). The evidential value of a nominalized construction is based on the last copula, e.g. bɛʔ in the construction ím-bo bɛʔ and î: in the construction jø̀:-po î:. The nominalized part of the construction only marks the equative vs. existential dichotomy, e.g. ím-bo in ím-bo bɛʔ marks the construction as equative and jø̀:-po in jø̀:-po î: marks the construction as existential.

The nominalized equative expressions are ím-bo bɛʔ (neg. mɛ̃̀:-bo bɛʔ), ím-bo î: (neg. mɛ̃̀:-bo î:), íŋ-kʰɛn bɛʔ (neg. mɛ̃̀:-kʰɛn bɛʔ) and íŋ-kʰɛ̃: î: (neg. mɛ̃̀:-kʰɛ̃: î:). The existential expressions are jø̀:-po bɛʔ (neg. mè:-po bɛʔ), jø̀:-po î: (neg. mè:-po î:), jø̀:-kʰɛn bɛʔ (neg. mè:-kʰɛn bɛʔ) and jø̀:-kʰɛ̃: î: (neg. mè:-kʰɛ̃: î:). Table 4 gives a summary of the different nominalized forms.

Tab. 4: Nominalized copula constructions.

Equat./Exist.	Evidentiality	Nominalised construction
Equative	Personal	ཨིན་པོ་ཨིན་ ím-bo î: (neg. མན་པོ་ཨིན་ mɛ̃̀:-bo î:)
		ཨིན་མཁན་ཨིན་ íŋ-kʰɛ̃: î: (neg. མན་མཁན་ཨིན་ mɛ̃̀:-kʰɛ̃: î:)
	Neutral (possibly assertive)	ཨིན་པོ་སྲད་ ím-bo bɛʔ (neg. མན་པོ་སྲད་ mɛ̃̀:-bo bɛʔ)
		ཨིན་མཁན་སྲད་ íŋ-kʰɛn bɛʔ (neg. མན་མཁན་སྲད་ mɛ̃̀:-kʰɛn bɛʔ)
Existential	Personal	ཡོད་པོ་ཨིན་ jø̀:-po î: (neg. མེད་པོ་ཨིན་ mè:po î:)
		ཡོད་མཁན་ཨིན་ jø̀:-kʰɛ̃: î: (neg. མེད་མཁན་ཨིན་ mè:kʰɛ̃: î:)
	Neutral	ཡོད་པོ་སྲད་ jø̀:-po bɛʔ (neg. མེད་པོ་སྲད་ mè:-po bɛʔ)
		ཡོད་པ་སྲད་ jèbbeʔ/jøbbeʔ (neg. མེད་པ་སྲད་ mèbbeʔ)
		ཡོད་མཁན་སྲད་ jø̀:-kʰɛn bɛʔ (neg. མེད་མཁན་སྲད་ mè:-kʰɛn bɛʔ)

Most frequently, the nominalized constructions end in the neutral copula bɛʔ. Constructions ending in the neutral copula bɛʔ are used by Denjongke speakers to dissociate themselves from the evidential values of î:, jøʔ and duʔ. I first give

---

[27] Garrett (2001: 105) considers these type of contexts, where only ego evidentials (the equivalents of î: and jøʔ) can appear, as evidence for his view that ego evidentiality is not coded lexically in the copulas, but is a "pragmatic property" caused by the absence of other, overt evidentials such as འདུག་ ʼdug.

examples of neutral constructions ending in *bɛʔ* (§6.2.1) and after that personal constructions ending in *î:* (§6.2.2).

10.6.2.1 Evidentially neutral constructions (ending in *bɛʔ*)

Nominalized copula constructions ending in *bɛʔ* are evidentially neutral. Examples (90–93) exemplify equative and (94–100) existential uses. The neutral equative constructions *îm-bo bɛʔ* and *íŋ-kʰɛn bɛʔ* have both present and past uses. Example (90) shows that *îm-bo bɛʔ* may be used, similarly to *imbɛʔ* (see §5), as a concurring expression. Here, however, the speaker does not concur with another speaker who is present (as in the examples of *imbɛʔ*), but she agrees in her mind with something she is thinking about (her parents advice).

(90) མོའི་ སེམས་ན་ འདེ་ མནོ་ཤད་ ཨིན་ མནེ་མུ་རང་ ཨིན་པོ་
    mu=i   *sém=na*   *deː*   *nóː-ɕɛ*   *î:*   *nɛ́ːmurã̃ː*   *îm-bo*
    she=GEN   mind=LOC   thus   think-INF   COP   really   COP.EQU-NMLZ

    བད།
    bɛʔ
    COP
    'She thinks in her mind that it surely is like that.' (Richhi 119)

Similarly to (90), *íŋ-kʰɛn bɛʔ* in (91) signifies concurrence within one's own thoughts. In (91), the omniscient narrator has taken the perspective of the novel's characters that are admiringly looking at a young couple leading a ceremony.

(91) མི་ཚོགས་ གེས་པོ་ལོ་ སྟམས་ སྟོན་དི་ མི་ཚུའི་ འདོད་ཡིད་
    mítsʰoʔ   *kɛːpo=lo*   *tɛm*   *tøn-di*   *mí-tsu=i*   *døːjiʔ*
    crowd   a.lot=DAT   show   show-NF   human-PL=GEN   desires
    '(They were) able to capture people's deepest desires while acting in front

    འཕྱོག་ ཚུགས་མཁན། ཨིན་ ཨིན་མཁན་ བད, ད་ཏ་
    pʰjok   *tsʰuː-kʰɛ̃ː*   *î:*   *íŋ-kʰɛn*   *bɛʔ*,   *tʼata*
    snatch   can-NMLZ   COP.EQU.PER   COP.EQU-NMLZ   COP.EQU.NE   now
    of a great crowd. Indeed, all the arrangement so far had been

    ཟངས་གི་ གོ་སྒྲིགས་ ཐམས་ཅད་ ཁོང་ གཉིས་པོའི་ འགོ་འཛིན་
    sã̃ː=gi   *kʼoɖiʔ*   *tʰamtɕɛʔ*   *kʰõː*   *ɲíː-pø*   *gokʰḭː=na*
    until=GEN   arrangement   all   they   two-NMLZ.GEN   leading=LOC
    (successfully) fulfilled under their leadership.'

    སྒྲུབ་ ཡོད་པོ།
    ɖup   *jø̃-po*.
    fulfil   COP.EX-NMLZ
    (Richhi 82)

The nominalized constructions in (90) and (91) add assertive force to the statements, as suggested by the English expression 'surely' and 'indeed' respectively. Consultant YR commented that the constructions *íŋ-kʰɛn bɛʔ* and *ím-bo bɛʔ* are used in debates to make assertions that are true contemporaneously with the speech act.

In addition to present assertive uses, *ím-bo bɛʔ* and *íŋ-kʰɛn bɛʔ* are compatible with past events or states. In (92+93), *ím-bo bɛʔ* and *íŋ-kʰɛn bɛʔ* appear to be used quite interchangeably.

(92) ཁུ་སྔོན་ལས་ངའི་གྲོགས་ཀུ་ཨིན་པོ་སྲད།
    kʰu   ɲénlɛ   ɲèː   tʻoku   ím-bo   bɛʔ
    he   before   my   friend   COP.EQU-NMLZ COP.EQU.NE
    'He was my friend before.' (KT, elicited)

(93) ཁུ་ངའི་གྲོགས་ཀུ་ཨིན་མཁན་སྲད།
    kʰu   ɲèː   tʻoku   íŋ-kʰɛn   bɛʔ
    he   my   friend COP.EQU-NMLZ COP.EQU.NE
    'He was my friend.' (PT, elicited)

Examples (94–100) illustrate neutral existential constructions. Examples (94) and (95) are taken from two folk-stories where the speaker does not want to give the impression, by using the lone copula *jø̀ʔ*, that he was personally involved in the events of the story, or by using the the sensorial *duʔ*, that the event was recently sensorially attested by someone. Therefore, the neutral nominalized copula construction is chosen.

(94) ཁོང་ཚོའི་ནོར་འབྲོག་ན་སེམས་ཅན་པ་གླང་ར་དང་ལུག
    kʰõː-tsyː   nòːɖoʔ=na   sémtɕẽː pʻa   lã̀ː   rà   dã̀ː   lùʔ
    they-PL.GEN   cattle=LOC animal   cow   bull goat and   sheep
    'In their cattle, they had a lot of animals such as cows, bulls, goats and

    ལ་སོགས་གྲེས་པོ་ཡོད་པོ་སྲད།
    làsoː   kɛːp   jø̀ː-po   bɛʔ
    etc   a.lot   COP.EX-NMLZ COP.EQU.NE
    sheep etc.' (rna-gsung dang gtam-bshad 1)

(95) དང་པོ་ཅིག་ཀ་གྲོང་གཅིག་ན་མི་གཅིག་ཡོད་མཁན་སྲད།
    tʻã̀ːpu   tɕika   kʻjõ̀ː   tɕi=na   mí   tɕiʔ   jø̀ː-kʰɛn   bɛʔ
    long.ago once   village one=LOC man one   COP.EX-NMLZ COP.EQU.NE
    'Once long ago there was a man in one village.' (TB, story of two bulls)

The construction *jø̀ː-po bɛʔ*, which allows the existential meaning to be taken from *jø̀ʔ* and the evidential meaning taken from *bɛʔ*, is so common that in spoken language this evidentially neutral existential form (vs. existentials jø? and du? which are evidentially loaded) has merged into jøbbɛ?/jɛ̀bbɛ? (neg. mɛ̀bbɛ?).The Standard/Lhasa Tibetan (close to) pragmatic equivalent to jøbbɛ?/jɛ̀bbɛ? is jò:re:, which is etymologically a nominalized construction as suggested by one of the alternative written forms yod.pa.red (Denwood 1999: 119, Hill 2010).[28] In Denwood's analysis of Lhasa Tibetan, jò:re: "implies no such first hand knowledge [as jø: and du:], though it does not specifically rule it out" (1999: 122). The same can be said of jø-po bɛ? (or jøbbɛ?/jɛ̀bbɛ?) in Denjongke. The neutral evidential value of the construction is derived from the last copula bɛ?.

In addition to being used for past events jø-po bɛ? and jø:-kʰɛn bɛ? are also used for present events.[29] In these cases, using the simple copula jø? is not desirable, because the information in the sentence is presented as uncontested, general knowledge. The following three examples exemplify the present uses of jø:-po bɛ? (96), jø-kʰɛn bɛ? (97) and jɛ̀bbɛ? (98), the colloquial equivalent of jø:-po bɛ?.

(96) དུས་ད་རིང་ཡང་ང་ཚོག་མི་ཚུའི་ཀྲང་པའི་ཞབས་ལོ་ཉེག་ཇོང་
     t´y: t´ariŋ=jã: ŋàtɕa? mí-tsy: kã:pø: thi:-lo   ɲèkjõ:
     period today=too we   human-PL.GEN foot.GEN heel.DAT notch
     'Even at present time there is a tradition saing that the fact that

ཡོད་པོ་འདི་དུས་ཇོ་འདིའི་སྐབས་འདྲེ་མོས་
jø-po=di   t´y: ódi: kap   dɛmø:
COP.EX-NMLZ=DEMPH period that.GEN time demoness.ERG
there is a notch in the heel of the human foot is a mark of the demoness

ཕོག་སྟེ་ཟ་བའི་བཞུགས་ཨིན་སེ་ལབ་པའི་ལུགས་སོལ་
pok-ti   sà-sa-wø: ɕý: ǐ:-se   làpø: lùksø:
pluck-NF at-eat-NMLZ.GEN trace COP.EQU.PER-QUO say.GEN tradition
at that time having plucked and eaten (that place).'

---

28 In Lhasa Tibetan, however, there is a current distinction between the historically nominalized form jò:re: and the synchronically nominalized construction jø-bo-re: (Denwood 1999: 119).
29 This is in line with the observation of Goldstein, et al. (1991: 58) on modern literary Tibetan that the nominalizer-copula sequence པ་རེད་ -pa-red (cf. Denjongke ཡོད་སྡུད་ -po bɛ?) following a verb may get either past or present habitual meaning.

ཡོད་པོ་སླད།
jø̀-po   bɛ?
COP.EX-NMLZ   COP.EQU.NE
(rna-gsung dang gtam-bshad 19–20)

(97) ང་ཅིའི་ལེའུ་འོ་འདྲས་གོས་པོ་ཡོད་མཁན་སླད།
ŋàtɕi   lìu   ódɛm   kɛ:po   jø̀-kʰɛn   bɛ?
our   phase   like.that many   COP.EX-NMLZ   COP.EQU.NE
'We have many such phases.' (SG, story of marriage customs)

Example (96) is the last line of a folkstory which purports to give the origin of a current fact, and (97) is a summary statement at the end of an exposition on the various phases involved in getting married among the Denjongpa. The information in both examples is presented as uncontested, general knowledge.

The example of *jèb-bɛ?* (98) comes from my discussion with one consultant.

(98) ཨོན་དགོན་པོ་གཅིག་ཡོད་བསླད།
óna   gjømpo   tɕi?   jèbbɛ?
there monastery   on   COP.EX.NE
'There's a monastery there.' (KN, discussion)

In the context of (98), the consultant KN is telling about his father, who is an overseer of a small monastery. When I asked where the monastery is located, KN continued with a description of the location and ended in (98). The copula *jèbbɛ?* here marks generally known, uncontested knowledge. It is the location of the monastery that is the topic of the discussion, not whether or not there is a monastery somewhere. Had the original question been whether or not there is a monastery somewhere (potentially contested knowledge), the speaker would have more likely used the personal evidential *jø̀?* rather than the neutral *jèbbɛ?*.

Examples (99) [50] and (100) illustrate the difference between *jø̀?* and *jèbbɛ?*.

(99)   Bill Gates ལོ་དངུལ་གོས་པོ་ཡོད།
       bil   gɛits=lo   ɲỳ: kɛ:p   jø̀?
       Bill   Gates=LOC   money   a.lot   COP.EX.PER
       'Bill Gates has a lot of money (as I have come to know personally).' (KT elicited)

(100) Bill Gates ལོ་དངུལ་གོས་པོ་ཡོད་སླད།
       bil   gɛits=lo   ɲỳ: kɛ:p   jèb-bɛ?
       Bill   Gates=LOC   money   a.lot   COP.EX.NMLZ-COP.EQU.NE
       'Bill Gates has a lot of money (as is generally known).' (KT, elicited)

Example (99) expresses the speaker's personal knowledge by implying either that the speaker is Bill Gate's friend or that Bill Gates is present at the time of speaking. In the latter case, the difference between *jø?* and *jɛ̀bbɛ?* is similar to the difference between *í:* and *bɛ?* in (75–77). Example (100), on the other hand, is a general statement where the connection to a specific sensory event (contra *du?*, which refers to a specific instance of finding out) and personal knowledge (contra *jø?*) are backgrounded by using the neutral *jɛ̀bbɛ?*.

10.6.2.2 Personal constructions (ending in *í:*)

The following examples illustrate constructions ending in the personal copula *í:*. Thus far, I have found no examples of nominalized constructions ending in *í:* in naturally occurring texts, either spoken or written. Therefore, all of the examples below are elicited. A fuller description of personal nominalized copulas would require natural examples from an extensive corpus. Equative forms are given first (cf. (101–109)) and existentials afterwards (cf. (110+111)).

(101) ཁུ་ རའི་ གཉེན་མཚན་ ཨིན་མཁན་ ཨིན། ཨིན་རུང་ ཁུ་ རབོ་
kʰu ɲè: ɲéntsʰɛ̀: iŋ-kʰɛ̀: í:. í:ruŋ kʰu ŋà:=lo
he my relative COP.EQU-NMLZ COP.EQU.PER still he I=DAT
'He is (supposed to be) my relative. Still, he doesn't look

ལོགཏ་ མི་ཀྱབས་ བྱད།
lòkta mi-kja(p) bɛ?
care NEG-do COP.EQU.NE
after me.' (KT, elicited)

In (101), by using the nominalized construction *iŋ-kʰɛ̀: í:* rather just *í:*, the speaker appears to underline the fact that the referent is the speaker's relative and thus give rise to the idea of a relative's obligations (which have been neglected). Using *iŋ-kʰɛ̀: í:* seems to add some force to the proposition ('he is supposed to be') compared to the lone *í:*, which just identifies the referent as a relative. The speaker also shows his personal emotional involvement (he is disappointed) by using the personal *í:* rather than the neutral *bɛ?*. In (101), the latter clause, which uses the neutral copula *bɛ?* as auxiliary, does not imply the speaker's emotional involvement but rather just explains the reason for the speaker's disappointment. In expressing present feelings of the speaker, the Denjongke *í:* appears to bear resemblance to its cognate in Drokpa Tibetan, which is described as marking personal engagement ("personliche Engagement") and inner (e)motion ("innere Regung") (Kretschmar 1986: 65).

Now consider (102) and (103) where personal and neutral equatives are contrasted. Nominalized constructions are used because the sentences refer to the past.

(102) ཁུ་སྔོན་ལས་ངའི་གྲོགས་ཀུ་ཨིན་པོ་ཨིན།
   kʰu ɲénlɛ ɲè: tʼoku ím-bo   î:
   he before my friend COP.EQU-NMLZ COP.EQU.PER
   'He was my friend before.' (KT, elicited)

(103) ཁུ་སྔོན་ལས་ངའི་གྲོགས་ཀུ་ཨིན་པོ་བྱད།
   kʰu ɲénlɛ ɲè: tʼoku ím-bo   bɛʔ
   he before my friend COP.EQU-NMLZ COP.EQU.NE
   'He was my friend before.' (KT, elicited)

Consultant KT commented that the difference between (102) and (103) is that in (102) the speaker expresses that she is presently experiencing sadness about a broken relationship whereas (103) is a purely factual statement with no emotional overtones. Another consultant YR (from Kewsing), according to whom *íŋ-kʰɛ̂: î:* and *íŋ-kʰɛn bɛʔ* could also be used in (102) and (103) instead of *ím-bo î:* and *ím-bo bɛʔ* respectively, commented that (103) is a neutral statement that does not presuppose any continuation of the discourse. The addressee of (102), on the other hand, is expecting the speaker to continue by giving the reason for his emotional involvement implied by the personal *î:* at the end. YR also noted that (102) could be said on the basis of the referent being present at the time of speech. The justification for using *ím-bo î:* or *íŋ-kʰɛ̂: î:* in (102) could thus be either emotional involvement of the speaker or the presence of the referent.

Consultant PT, commenting on sentences (104+105),

(104) ཁུ་ངའི་གྲོགས་ཀུ་ཨིན་མཁས་ཨིན།
   kʰu ɲè: tʼoku íŋ-kʰɛ̂:   î:[30]
   he my friend COP.EQU-NMLZ COP.EQU.PER
   'He was my friend.' (PT, elicited)

(105) ཁུ་ངའི་གྲོགས་ཀུ་ཨིན་མཁན་བྱད།
   kʰu ɲè: tʼoku íŋ-kʰɛn   bɛʔ
   he my friend COP.EQU-NMLZ COP.EQU.NE
   'He was my friend.' (PT, elicited)

said that whereas in (105) the relationship is totally over, the personal evidential in (104) suggests that there is some continuation of the relationship in the form of perhaps seeing now and then. Thus, the use of the personal evidential seems

---

30 PT said that using *ím-bo î:* and *ím-bo bɛʔ* in (104) would have about the same meaning as *íŋ-kʰɛ̂: î:* and *íŋ-kʰɛn bɛʔ* respectively but that the former constructions are not actively used in his speech variety.

to suggest some type of present personal relevance, or spatiotemporal foregrounding, for the speaker.

The speaker's current emotion is again the driving force in the use of the personal copula in (106). This time the emotion is confusion. The speaker's established belief is challenged by some new information. The use of the personal construction *ím-bo ĩ́:* (according to some consultants also *iŋ-kʰɛ̃: ĩ́:* could be used here), implying emotional involvement (here confusion), calls for an explanation that is given in the following sentence.

(106) མི་འདི་སྔོནམ་ཨམརྗི་ཨིནམོ་ཨིན།
     mí=di   ɲéma   ámdzi   ím-bo   ĩ́:
     man= DEMPH before doctor COP.EQU-NMLZ COP.EQU.PER
     'Earlier this man was a doctor,

     དཔྱོ་ཏོ་འཁོརལོ་སྐུལམཁན་ཐོནཚཀེགོ།
     tʼato=to   kʰorlo ky:kʰɛ̃: tʰøn-tsʰakɛ=ɕo.³¹
     now=CEMPH wheel   driver become-PRF=ATT
     but now he has become a driver! (I'm confused)' (KN, elicited)

In the speech of PT from Tashiding (West Sikkim), both *ĩ́:* and *ím-bo ĩ́:* can be used in the present meaning, as shown in (107+108).

(107) ཁོང་ངའི་ཡབ་ཨིན།
     kʰõ: ɲè: jà:p   ĩ́:
     he.HON my   father.HON COP.EQU.PER
     'He is my father.' (PT, elicited)

(108) ཁོང་ངའི་ཡབ་ཨིནམོ་ཨིན།
     kʰõ: ɲè: jà:p   ím-bo   ĩ́:
     he.HON my   father.HON COP.EQU-NMLZ COP.EQU.PER
     'He is my father.' (PT, elicited)

---

31 By using the perfect form *-tsʰa:* as in *kʰu òn-tsʰa:* 'He has come' the speaker implies having seen the referent's act of coming. On the other hand, by using the forms *-tsʰa-kɛ, and -tsʰa-du and -tsʰa-du-kɛ*, as in *kʰu òn-tsʰakɛ* 'He has come' the speaker implies that she has got the information about the referent's coming after the fact, for instance by seeing the referent, who had already come. Thus far, I have not been able to find out the semantic difference between *-tsʰa-kɛ, -tsʰa-du* and *-tsʰa-du-kɛ*.

When inquiring about the difference between (107) and (108), PT's answer was that the latter one (with ím-bo î:) was "more calm", "more polite", "nicer" and "making the listener feel good". Another consultant (YR), on the other hand, claimed that only (107) and not (108) could be used when the father is present.

As pointed above, existential copulas have a clear motivation for forming nominalized evidentially neutral constructions, because both of the existentials jø? and du? are by themselves evidentially loaded. Among the equative copulas î: and bɛ?, however, it is more challenging to describe the exact difference between the sentences in (109).

(109) a. ངའི་ཨ་པོ་འདི་ཨམ་རྗེ་ཨིན།   ɲè: ápo=di ámdʑi î:
      b. ངའི་ཨ་པོ་འདི་ཨམ་རྗེ་སྦད།   ɲè: ápo=di ámdʑi bɛ?
      c. ངའི་ཨ་པོ་འདི་ཨམ་རྗེ་ཨིན་པོ་སྦད།   ɲè: ápo=di ámdʑi ím-bo bɛ?
      d. ངའི་ཨ་པོ་འདི་ཨམ་རྗེ་ཨིན་མཁན་སྦད།   ɲè: ápo=di ámdʑi íŋ-kʰɛn bɛ?
      e. ངའི་ཨ་པོ་འདི་ཨམ་རྗེ་ཨིན་པོ་ཨིན།   ɲè: ápo=di ámdʑi ím-bo î:
      f. ངའི་ཨ་པོ་འདི་ཨམ་རྗེ་ཨིན་མཁན་ཨིན།   ɲè: ápo=di ámdʑi íŋ-kʰɛ̂: î:
        my father=DEMPH doctor COP
        'My father is/was a doctor.'

Some things, however, can be said. All the forms in (109) can be used for both past and present events/states, although with î:, and perhaps also with bɛ?, a past interpretation usually requires a past adverbial. The difference between the personal forms ending in î: (a, e, f) and the neutral forms ending in bɛ? (b, c, d) as already discussed in §5.5, is that the personal forms are concerned with the act of identification whereas the neutral forms leave more room for the consequences of the identification. In existential constructions the nominalizers -po and -kʰen appear to be used quite interchangably, but with equatives, -po and -kʰen seem to have more specialized uses, at least for some speakers. For instance, PT from Tashiding can use (e) for a living person, whereas (f) would be preferred when speaking about a dead person. PT's characterization of the difference between sentences analogous to (a) and (e) was already given with example (107–108). Furthermore, it has been shown above that (109c) and (109d) may add assertive force to a statement and that (109e) and (109f) may express the speaker's emotional involvement.

At present, my hypothesis is that the speaker of sentences such as (109) will choose ím-bo bɛ? (c) instead of bɛ? (b) when she wants to emphasize the equative function of î: (which is backgrounded by bɛ?) in contexts where the lone î: is undesirable either because of its personal evidentiality or because of its preference for deictic anchoring in the here and now. The nominalized copula constructions have a reduced anchoring to the present compared to lone copulas, lending themselves both to present and past uses (analogously to stative verbs).³²

Lastly, I give two examples (110+111) of the personal existential constructions, where existentiality is expressed by the nominalized copula jð-po/jð-kʰɛn and the personal evidential value by î:.

(110) ང་ཨོན་ཡོད་པོའི་དུས་ཚོད་ལོ་ཁུ་ཡང་ཡོད་པོ་
ŋà   óna   jð-pø: t'ytsʰø=lo   kʰu=jã: jð-po
I   there COP.EX-NMLZ.GEN time=DAT   he=too   COP.EX-NMLZ
ཨིན།
î:
COP.EQU.PER

'At the time I was there, he was (there) too.' (YR, elicited)

In (110) the speaker uses the nominalized constructions jð-po rather than the mere copula jð? because jð? typically implies that the described situation persists at the moment of speech. The event referred to in (110), however, happened in the past and the speaker does not want to imply its present actuality. On the other hand, the personal copula î: rather than the neutral bɛ? is chosen as the final auxiliary, because the speaker was personally present at the referred time.

Example (111) is another instance of a personal existential construction. Here jð:-kʰɛ̃: î:=ɕo could be used in place of jð-po î:=ɕo.

(111) ཨེ་དེབ་འདི་ངའི་ཁར་ཡོད་པོ་ཨིན་གོ
ɛ: t'ep   di   to   ɲè:-tsa: jð-po   î:=ɕo³³
o   book   DEMPH CEMPH   with.me   COP.EX-NMLZ   COP.EQU.PER=ATT

'O, I would have had he book (all along), you know.' (KN, elicited)

In (111), person A has been trying to get hold of a certain book by asking for it from among his various friends. After finally managing to obtain the book, he meets person B who has not heard about A's need for the book. After A tells B about his search and finding the book, B answers (111). The nominalized jð-po is used instead of mere jð? because the speaker makes reference to a past point of time. He had the book when his friend was looking for it. Using mere jð? (or jð:=ɕo) would put the emphasis on having the book presently ('I have the book'), whereas the nominalized form enables one to convey the past-oriented meaning equivalent to English 'I would have had the

---

32 For eventive/dynamic verbs, the nominalizer -po/bo has in effect become a past tense marker, e.g. sà-bo î: > sà-u î: 'ate', but for stative verbs the nominalized form can be used in the present meaning, e.g. ga-bo î: > ga-u î: 'love'. Therefore the copulas side with stative verbs in letting the context be the final arbiter with reference to present vs. past meaning.

33 As already shown in (41), with the personal copula î: the attention-worthiness marked by =ɕo is addressee-oriented.

book (if you had asked me)'. The personal final copula í: in (111) most likely signifies the fact that the speaker had the personal experience (and thus personal knowledge) of possessing the book at the time when the addressee was looking for it.

10.7 Conclusion

Denjongke has five basic copulas and several structurally more complex forms in which two copulas are combined together either directly (combinatory copulas) or with nominalization (nominalized copulas). The complex forms fill communicative gaps in the basic copula system. This chapter also described the use of the reportative as an equative copula substitute. All the declarative copula forms discussed in this study, with references to examples, are presented in Tab. 5. The interrogative examples are (29–34) and (87).

Tab. 5: The main features of Denjongke declarative copula constructions.

Eq./Ex.	Evidentiality	Copula combinations	Examples
Equat.	Personal	ཨིན་ í:	2–4, 6, 8, 18, 36/37, 39, 41, 44–47, 52, 69, 71, 73, 75–77, 78, 81, 107, 109
		ཨིན་པོ་ཨིན་ ím-bo í:	102, 106, 108, 109
		ཨིན་མཁན་ཨིན་ íŋ-kʰɛ̃: í:	101, 104, 109
	Neutral	སུང་ bɛʔ	1, 5, 7, 17, 19/20, 38, 40, 42, 43/44, 52, 70, 72, 74–81, 109
		ཨིན་པོ་སུང་ ím-bo bɛʔ	90, 92, 103, 109
		ཨིན་མཁན་སུང་ íŋ-kʰɛn bɛʔ	91, 93, 105, 109
		ཨིན་སུང་ ím-bɛʔ (concurring)	87/88
	Sensorial	ཨིན་འདུག ín-duʔ	89
	Reportative	ལོ་ =lo	82
Exist.	Personal	ཡོད་ jə̀ʔ	9, 11, 13, 15, 20, 48–51, 53/54, 80/81, 86, 99
		ཡོད་པོ་ཨིན་ jə̀:-po í:	110/111
		ཡོད་མཁན་ཨིན་ jə̀:-kʰɛ̃: í:	111
		ཡོད་ལོ་ jə̀:=lo	83, 86
	Neutral	ཡོད་པོ་སུང་ jə̀:-po bɛʔ	94, 96, 98, 100
		ཡོད་བ་སུང་ jèbbɛʔ/jə̀bbɛʔ	
		ཡོད་མཁན་སུང་ jə̀:-kʰɛn bɛʔ	95, 97
	Sensorial	འདུག duʔ	10, 12, 14, 16, 21, 23/24, 26, 52, 55/56, 59–68, 79–81, 85
	Reportative	འདུག་ལོ་ du:=lo	83, 85

An evidentially interesting feature in the present study is the behavior of personal evidentials, which were shown to be more semantically oriented than the category "egophoric" in Standard Tibetan (Tournadre and Dorje 2003). The Tibetic languages form a grammaticalization cline where the personal/ego(phoric)/self forms become gradually more strongly associated with the first person. At times, this process of grammaticalization may be noticed language-internally. Hongladarom (2007: 22) reports that in Rgyalthang Tibetan (a variety of Kham) folkstories and songs use "egophoric/self" forms in contexts where in everyday speech one expects a non-egophoric form. This suggests that Rgyalthang folkstories preserve an earlier form of the language, in which the current "egophoric/self" forms (somewhat corresponding to "personal" in Denjongke) are less restricted by the syntactic category of person than in the present spoken Rgyalthang.

The most grammaticalized end seems to be occupied by Standard Tibetan, which has developed a syntactic requirement for the presence of the first person in association with the egophorics (corresponding to 'personal' here) (Tournadre 2008: 296). Exceptions are only allowed if the referent is closely related to the speaker, see (35). Shigatse and Themchen Tibetan (Haller 2000: 187), on the other hand, appear not to have a syntactic restriction but have instead a semantic restriction: the speaker has to be quite specifically involved in the event. Denjongke (together with Yolmo, see Gawne 2013: 191–193) represents a yet less grammaticalized stage. The use of *î:* as copula is not syntactically restricted to the first person, the referent in the clause does not need to have an especially close relationship to the speaker, and the speaker's involvement may be non-existent or very weak.

Abbreviations

ABL ablative, ATT attention, CEMPH contrastive emphatic, COND conditional, CONCUR concurring, COP copula, DAT dative-locative, DEF definite, DEMPH deictic emphatic, EGO ego(phoric), EMPH emphatic, ERG ergative, EX existential, EXPER experiental, EXCLAM exclamative, GEN genitive, HON honorific, EQU equative, IMP imperative, IN intensifier, INF infinitive, LOC locative, NE neutral, NEG negative, NF non-final, NMLZ nominalizer, PER personal, PFV perfective, PL plural, PRF perfect, PQ polar question, PROG progressive, PST past, Q question, QUO quotative, REP reportative, SEN sensorial, SUP supine.

References

Aikhenvald, Alexandra. 2004. *Evidentiality*. Oxford: Oxford University Press.
Bartee, Ellen. 2007. *A Grammar of Dongwang Tibetan*. Santa Barbara: University of California PhD dissertation.
Bielmeier, Roland. 2000. Syntactic, semantic, and pragmatic-epistemic functions of auxiliaries in Western Tibetan. *Linguistics of the Tibeto-Burman Area* 23(2). 79–125.
Bhutia, Karma Lobsang. 2013. རྫ་གསུང་དང་གཏམ་དཔེ [English title: Sikkimese Bhutia oral stories and moral dialects]. Gangtok: Bhutia Kayrab Yargay Tsogpo.
Bhutia, Norden Tshering & Pema Rinzing Takchungdarpo. 2001. *Bhutia-English dictionary*. Gangtok: Kwality Stores.
Bhutia, Pintso. 2004. *Bhutia English dictionary*. Gangtok: Pintso Bhutia.
Caplow, Nancy. J. 2000. The epistemic marking system of émigré Dokpa Tibetan. Unpublished manuscript.
Chang, Kun & Betty Shefts Chang. 1984. The certainty hierarchy among Spoken Tibetan verbs of being. *Bulletin of the Institute of History and Philology, Academia Sinica* 55 (4). 603–635.
DeLancey, Scott. 1990. Ergativity and the cognitive model of event structure in Lhasa Tibetan. *Cognitive Linguistics* 1(3). 289–321.
DeLancey, Scott. 1992. The historical origin of the conjunct-disjunct pattern in Tibeto-Burman. *Acta Linguistica Hafniensia* 25. 289–321.
DeLancey, Scott. 1997. Mirativity: the grammatical marking of unexpected information. *Linguistic Typology* 1. 33–52.
Denwood, Philip. 1999. *Tibetan*. Amsterdam: John Benjamins.
Dewan, Dick B. 2012. *Education in Sikkim: an historical retrospect, pre-merger and post-merger period*. Pedong (Kalimpong): Tender Buds' Academy.
Dixon, R. M. W. 2010. *Basic linguistic theory, Volume 2: grammatical topics*. Oxford: Oxford University Press.
Dokhangba, Sonam Gyatso. སྦྲགས་སྦྱོར་ཡིད་དགའ་འགྲོ་ཡིས [English title: Sikkimese marriage custom and rites]. Siliguri: Amit Offset Press.
van Driem, George. 1998. *Dzongkha* (Languages of the Greater Himalayan Region 1). Leiden: Research School CNWS.
van Driem, George. 2007. Endangered languages of South Asia. In Matthias Brenzinger (ed.), *Language diversity endangered* (Trends in Linguistics 181), 303–341. Berlin: Mouton de Gruyter.
Dryer, Matthew. 2007. Clause types. In Timothy Shopen (ed.), *Language typology and syntactic description 1: Clause Structure*, 224–275. Cambridge: Cambridge University Press.
Garrett, Edward. 2001. *Evidentiality and Assertion in Tibetan*. Los Angeles: University of California PhD dissertation.
Gawne, Lauren. 2013. *Lamjung Yolmo Copulas in Use: Evidentiality, Reported Speech and Questions*. Melbourne: University of Melbourne PhD dissertation.
Goldstein, Melvyn C., Gelek Rimpoche, and Lobsang Phuntshog. 1993 [1991]. *Essentials of Modern Literary Tibetan: A reading course and reference grammar*. New Delhi: Munshiram Manoharlal Publishers.
Grierson, George Abraham. 1967 [1909]. *Linguistic Survey of India* 3(1). Delhi: Moti Lal Banarsi Dass.

Hale, Austin. 1971. *Person Markers: Conjunct and Disjunct Forms* (Topics in Newari Grammar 1). SIL mimeograph.
Hale, Austin. 1980, Person markers: finite conjunct and disjunct forms in Newari. In R. Trail et al. (eds.), *Papers in Southeast Asian Linguistics* 7: 95–106.
Haller, Felix. 2001. Dialekt und *Erzählungen von Shigatse*. (Beiträge zur tibetischen Erzählforschung 13.) Bonn: VGH Wissenschaftsverlag.
Häsler, Katrin Louise. 1999. *A Grammar of the Tibetan Sde.dge* (སྡེ་དགེ). (Bern: University of Bern PhD dissertation.
Hill, Nathan W. 2010. A Note on the Phonetic Evolution of yod-pa-red in Central Tibet. *Linguistics of the Tibeto-Burman Area* 33(1). 93–94.
Hill, Nathan W. 2012. "Mirativity" does not exist: ḥdug in "Lhasa" Tibetan and other suspects. *Linguistic Typology* 16(3). 389–433.
Hill, Nathan W. 2013. Contextual semantics of 'Lhasa' Tibetan evidentials. *SKASE Journal of Theoretical Linguistics* 10(3). 47–54.
Hongladarom, Krisadawan. 2007. Evidentiality in Rgyalthang Tibetan. *Linguistics of the Tibeto-Burman Area* 30(2). 17–44.
Huber, Brigitte. 2000. Preliminary report on evidential categories in Lende Tibetan (Kyirong). *Linguistics of the Tibeto-Burman Area* 23(2). 155–174.
Huber, Brigitte. 2002. *The Lende subdialect of Kyirong Tibetan: a grammatical description with historical annotations*. Bern: University of Bern PhD dissertation.
Hyslop, Gwendolyn. 2014. On the category of speaker expectation of interlocutor knowledge in Kurtöp. *Proceedings of the Fortieth Annual Meeting of the Berkeley Linguistics Society*. 201–214.
Jäschke, Heinrich August. 2007 [1888]. *A Tibetan-English Dictionary: with special reference to the prevailing dialects, to which is added an English-Tibetan vocabulary*. Delhi: Motilal Banarsidass.
Kretschmar, Monika. 1986. *Erzählungen und Dialekt der Drokpas aus Südwest-Tibet* (Beiträge zur tibetischen Erzählforschung 8). Sankt Augustin: VGH Wissenschaftsverlag.
Lama, Dorjee Rinchen. 2013. *English-Bhutia-Hindi-Nepali dictionary*. Gangtok: Kwality Stores.
Lewis, M. Paul, Gary F. Simons & Charles D. Fennig (eds.). 2013. *Ethnologue: Languages of the World (17th edition)*. Dallas, Texas: SIL International. http://www.ethnologue.com (accessed 11 April 2015).
Phenasa, Lopsang Ugen. 2013. New light multilingual dictionary prajna (English-Sherpa-Bhutia [=Denjongke]-Nepali-Tibetan). s.l. s.n.
Pustet, Regina. 2003. *Copulas: Universals in the Categorization of the Lexicon*. Oxford: Oxford University Press.
Sandberg, Graham. 1888. *Manual of the Sikkim Bhutia Language or Dénjong Ké*. Calcutta: Oxford Mission Press.
Sandberg, Graham. 1895. *Manual of the Sikkim Bhutia Language or Dénjong Ké* (second and enlarged edition). London: Archibald Constable & Co.
Shafer, Robert. 1974. *Introduction to Sino-Tibetan*. Wiesbaden: Otto Harrassowitz.
Sprigg, Richard Keith. 1991. The spelling-style pronunciation of Written Tibetan, and the hazards of using citation forms in the phonological analysis of spoken Tibetan. *Linguistics of the Tibeto-Burman Area* 14(2). 93–131.
Takchungdarpo, Pema Rinzing. 2013. *'bras-ljongs-po lho-pa' skad-yig tshig-mdzod* [Denjongke-Denjongke dictionary]. Gangtok: Kwality Stores.

Tournadre, Nicholas. 2008. Arguments against the concept of 'conjunct'/'disjunct' in Tibetan. In Huber, Brigitte, Marianne Volkart, and & Paul Widmer (eds.), *Chomolangma, Demawend und Kasbek, Festschrift für Roland Bielmeier zu seinem 65. Geburtstag* (Beiträge zur Zentralasienforschung 12), 281–308. Saale: International Institute for Tibetan and Buddhist Studies.

Tournadre, Nicholas. 2010. The Classical Tibetan cases and their transcategoriality: from sacred grammar to modern linguistics. *Himalayan Linguistics* 9(2). 87–125.

Tournadre, Nicolas & Sangda Dorje 2003. *Manual of Standard Tibetan*. Ithaca, N.Y.: Snow Lion Publications.

Tournadre, Nicholas & Konchok Jiatso. 2001. Final auxiliary verbs in literary Tibetan and in the dialects. *Linguistics of the Tibeto-Burman Area* 23(3). 49–111.

Tsichudarpo, Bhaichung. 2003 [1996]. རེ་ཚེ་ [Hope]. Gangtok: Kwality.

Turin, Mark. 2011. Results from the Linguistic Survey of Sikkim: mother tongues in education. In McKay, Alex and Anna Balikci-Denjongpa (eds.), *Buddhist Himalaya: Studies in Religion, History and Culture* (Proceedings of the Golden Jubilee Conference of the Namgyal Institute of Tibetology, Gangtok, 2008), Vol II, 127–142.

Vesalainen, Olavi 2014. A *Grammar Sketch of Lhomi*. Unpublished manuscript, 398 p.

Villiers, Jill de, Jay Garfield, Harper Gernet-Girard, Tom Roeper & Margaret Speas. 2009. Evidentials in Tibetan: Acquisition, semantics, and cognitive development. In Stanka Fitneva & Tomoko Matsui (eds.), *Evidentiality: A window into language and cognitive development (New Directions for Child and Adolescent Development* 125), 29–47. San Francisco: Jossey-Bass.

Walsh E. H. C. 1905. A Vocabulary of the *Tromowa Dialect of Tibetan Spoken in the Chumbi Valley (So Far as it Differs from Standard Tibetan): Together with a Corresponding Vocabulary of Sikhimese and of Central (Standard) Tibetan (the Corresponding Sikhimese Words Supplied by Sub-inspector S. W. Laden La, Bengal Police)*. Calcutta: Bengal secretariat Book depot.

Yliniemi, Juha. 2016. Attention marker =ɕo in Denjongke (Sikkimese Bhutia). *Linguistics of the Tibeto-Burman Area* 39(1). 106–161.

Zeisler, Bettina. 2000. Narrative conventions in Tibetan languages: the issue of mirativity. *Linguistics of the Tibeto-Burman Area* 23(2). 39–77.

Gwendolyn Hyslop and Karma Tshering
11 An overview of some epistemic categories in Dzongkha

11.1 Introduction

Tibetic languages are well-know for their complex evidential systems. As the number of descriptions of Tibetic languages grows, so too does the controversy over how to best anlayze the data and theorize over the typological implications. Some of the debate is no doubt due to the fact that "Tibetan" actually comprises several distinct languages and dialects, many of which are still only partially described or entirely undescribed, and that no one analysis can be expected to hold for so many different varieties of speech. This chapter contributes to our understanding of Tibetic languages and their evidential systems by presenting an analysis of evidentiality and related categories in Dzongkha, a Tibetic language of Bhutan. Many of the categories discussed here have been described already in van Driem (1998); we take this as a starting point and build from there.

Background information on Dzongkha and the relevant epistemic contrasts is provided in §2. The next three sections present aspects of the Dzongkha system, with §3 presenting the copulas, §4 discussing progressive aspect, and §5 describing the reported speech marker. The final section offers a conclusion. It will be noted that this chapter does not present all aspects of the grammar which participate in the epistemic system; rather, we focus on the aspects which are best understood.

11.2 Background

11.2.1 Dzongkha

Dzongkha, the national language of Bhutan, is spoken by approximately 160,000 native speakers in western Bhutan (van Driem 1998). However, as a language of government and prestige, Dzongkha is also widely spoken as a second language by people from many different ethnolinguistic groups. In a country with a

---

Note: A version of this contribution was originally presented at the 24th meeting of the Southeast Asian Linguistics Society. We are grateful to the audience there for their comments and questions, especially Nicolas Tournadre and Nathan W. Hill. We also thank Lauren Gawne and two anonymous reviewers for further feedback. Any ultimate errors are our own.

population of greater than 700,000, it is safe to venture that there are more non-native speakers than there are native speakers of Dzongkha.

The analysis presented here is drawn primarily from Dzongkha as it is spoken by native speakers in Wangdi and Thimphu. Data are primarily collected via two sources. First, the first author draws on eight years of observing and participating in conversation and narration amongst native speakers living in Bhutan and abroad. The second author supplements this through native speaker intuition.

Like other Tibetic languages, Dzongkha verbs are inflected for T(ense)A(spect) M(ood)E(videntiality) via suffixes, nominalizations, and auxiliaries. Often, the question of whether a particular construction involves suffixes or auxiliaries is one of diachrony versus synchrony and many of the synchronic suffixes can be shown to be historically derived from auxiliaries, nominalizers, or a combination of both. Synchronically, constructions involving nominalizations are still quite prevalent and a number of copulas, contrasting a wide range of verbal properties, are used in the language.

Examples of an inflected verb, nominalization, and simple copula clause are below,[1] with (1) showing a finite verb marked with the egophoric progressive -*do*, (2) showing an infinitival verb and copula, and (3) showing a copula clause with the equative copula '*ing*. Both finite morphology and copula clauses will be discussed below in greater detail as part of the epistemic system.

(1) *nga jodo*
    nga   jo-do
    1.SG   go-PROG.EGO
    'I am going.'

(2) *nga joni 'ing*
    nga   jo-ni   'ing
    1.SG   go-INF   COP.EQ
    'I will go.'

---

[1] Data are represented in the Roman Dzongkha orthography, developed by George van Driem and Karma Tshering and outlined in van Driem (1998). For the most part, the relationship between symbol and corresponding IPA symbol should be straightforward. There are some exceptions, however; coda -*ng* usually indicates that the previous vowel is nasalized. An apostrophe (') before a sonorant indicates a high toned vowel while one after an obstruent indicates that the obstruent is (often) devoiced and that the following vowel is extra low-toned and breathy. The circumflex (^) indicates a long vowel. Some tonal contrasts are not marked, however; for example, *chim* 'house' and *chim* 'liver' have an identical representation in Roman Dzongkha but differ in terms of tone: *chim* 'liver' has a high/rising tone when compared to *chim* 'house', which has a high falling tone. See Mazaudon and Michailovsky (1988) and van Driem (1998) for further discussion.

(3) *nga Karma 'ing*
    nga   Karma   'ing
    1.SG   Karma   COP.EQ
    'I am Karma.'

11.2.2 Terminology

The terms 'evidentiality', 'mirativity', and 'egophoric' are used in this chapter. All of these terms have evoked substantial debate in the literature but we will not delve much into that discussion. Rather, we will focus on the way in which we use the terms here and how they can be applied to Dzongkha to capture the contrast made in the language. Aikhenvald describes 'evidentiality' as the grammaticalized encoding of information source (2004: 14). We treat three forms as evidentials in Dzongkha; these are the inferential copulas *yönime*, *ongime* and hearsay marker =*lo*.

A related but distinct category is that of mirativity, which marks *unexpected* information. DeLancey defines mirativity as "the status of the proposition with respect to the speaker's overall knowledge structure" (1997). It is worth pointing out that the term 'mirative' has often been used by different authors to refer to different phenomena.[2] Hyslop (2011) defines mirativity as encoding *expectation of knowledge* and we follow that definition here. As we will show below, the Dzongkha mirative encodes that knowledge was newly acquired.

The term 'egophoric' is used to describe a category but that has received less attention in the literature. For our purposes, we can use Tournadre (2008) as a starting point; he describes egophoric as expressing "personal knowledge or intention on the part of the actual speaker" (2008: 295), stating there is a broad scope and narrow scope. The use of 'egophoric' here seems most inline with the broad scope described for Lhasa Tibetan, though it is premature to simply equate the two categories, especially considering that the nature of the Dzongkha category is still somewhat unclear.

It is important to keep in mind that our use of these terms is meant to be somewhat of a shortcut, aiding the reader to better understand the phenomena in Dzongkha; we do not presume to equate, for example, the Dzongkha 'mirative' with what has been described as a mirative for other languages. Rather, we use

---

[2] See also the view espoused in Hill (2012) and the debate that followed in other articles of the same issue.

these terms here because they seem to match most closely to what we believe the Dzongkha forms contrast.

11.2.3 Previous analysis

Van Driem's (1998) Dzongkha grammar provides the most extensive analysis of Dzongkha epistemic categories to date, including a description of the copulas, progressive aspect, and the hearsay marker.

Van Driem (1998: 125) presents *'ing* and *'immä* as equational copulas ("equative forms of the verb 'to be'") and *yö* and *dû* as existential copulas ("correspond(ing) to the existential locative and attributive senses of the English verb 'to be'"). Of the distinction between the equational copulas, van Driem states:

> The difference between *'ing* and *'immä* is an important distinction in Dzongkha which has to do with assimilated versus acquired knowledge. The form *'ing* expresses old, ingrained background knowledge which is or has become a firmly integrated part of one's conception of reality, whereas the form *'immä* expresses knowledge which has been newly acquired. (1998: 127)

Two examples help illustrate this difference:

(4) *'aphi*   *'mi*   *d'i*   *dr'ungnyi*   *'ing*
    that   man   the   clerk   be
    'That man is a clerk.'[3] (van Driem 1998: 128)

(5) *'aphi*   *'mi*   *d'i*   *dr'ungnyi*   *'immä*
    that   man   the   clerk   be
    'That man is a clerk [as I have come to know].'[4] (van Driem 1998: 128)

As a result of these different semantics, *'ing* and *'immä* are not used equally with all persons. *'immä* tends to be used most frequently with third person referents. Use with second person is less common and "exceedingly rare" with first person

> because it is not very usual for a speaker to want to express a recently gained insight into the identity of the person to whom he is speaking, and under normal circumstances a speaker has even less occasion to express a recently acquired insight regarding his own identity. (van Driem 1998: 128).

See van Driem (1998: 125–134) for further discussion.

---

3 We are reproducing data here faithful to its original source but will make reference to any needed corrections. For example, in this particular example, the determiner 'the' would be more accurately written as <di>, without the <'>.
4 The determiner should be written as <di>.

Van Driem initially describes the contrast between *yö* and *dû* as identical to that for *'ing* and *'immä* (1998: 135), though later states that while both *yö* and *dû* can be used with third person referents only *dû* can be used with a second person reference (1998: 136) and *yö* can only be used with first person. He reasons that *dû* is required for second person because "knowledge about a second person referent is by definition objective" and *yö* is required for first person because "knowledge about a first person referent is inherently personal". As we will show below, van Driem 's (1998: 135) initial observation about *yö* and *dû* is correct; that is, like *'ing* and *'immä*, *yö* and *dû* mark new and assimilated knowledge, respectively, and can be used for any referent, given the correct context.

Van Driem (1998) also describes the Dzongkha progressive *-do* and *-dä*, the difference between which, we will see below, is difficult to fully capture. Van Driem describes *-do* to express "an activity which the subject by his or her own observation knows to be going on in the present" (1998: 201) as a "witnessed progressive activity" (1998: 202), and that it "implicitly excludes the observation of the person addressed" (1998: 203). Van Driem also notes, however, that *-do* is also used for "natural phenomena which are objective circumstances in nature" (1998: 203). This last statement seems slightly at odds with the notion of implicitly excluding the addressee's observation.

The suffix *-dä* is diachronically composed of *-do* plus the suffix of 'newly acquired information' *-wa* (-བས་) (1998: 202). This form contrasts with *-do*, in that it is used as follows: The ending *-dowa* (-དོབས་) expresses either (1) an activity which has already begun and which the speaker has only just recently observed or (2) an activity in progress which the speaker witnessed at some time in the recent past but does not observe at the moment of speaking (1998: 202). Van Driem also observes that while *-dä* can be used with temporal adverbs denoting past time, the form *-do* cannot. In past tense readings, *-dä* "resembles a classical aorist to some extent in that the activity is unbounded in time: It is not precluded that the activity is still going on at the moment of the utterance, albeit unobserved by the speaker" (1998: 206). In other words, the speaker does not know if the event is still underway or has completed. Finally, *-dä* is not normally used with first person as this "would imply that the speaker was not there to see whether and when the activity in question ceased" (1998: 208). However, *-dä* can be used with first person in the context of a dream.

11.3 Copulas

Dzongkha has a large set of copulas which are used for equative (equative copulas), attribution, location, and possession (existential copulas) functions yet also participate in the verbal domain through various nominalizations. As such, the copulas also encode epistemic contrasts. Dzongkha has sets of affirmative and negative existential and equative copulas. We will focus on only the affirmative copulas in this chapter.

Note that van Driem (1998) identified four copulas (*yö, dû, 'ing, 'immä*) while we identify eight, some of which are diachronically composed of a copula root plus suffix. Some of these multisyllabic forms are clearly one phonological word (e.g. *yönime*) while others are still two words, phonologically (e.g. *yöp ong*). Despite the phonological differences, they can be identified as separate copulas rather than copulas plus affixes, due to their unique semantics. The copulas discussed in this section are not an exhaustive list of forms; future studies should also examine *yöbi, yöp 'ing, yöpme, yöp 'immä, ongmä, yönime, 'imdre* and possibly others.

11.3.1 Existential copulas

Dzongkha existential copulas are also used for attribution, location, and possession (with a locative or genitive pronoun). We discuss four of these copulas which participate in the larger epistemic system; these are first summarized in Tab. 1.

Tab. 1: Dzongkha existential copulas.

Form	Function	Diachronic source
yö	Non-mirative	WT *yod*
dû	Mirative	WT *'dug*
yönime	Inference	WT *yod.ni.mas* (*-ni.mas* on true verbs encodes inferential future tense)
yöp ong	Speculative	WT *yod.pa.'ong*

The two most common existential copulas are *yö* and *dû*, which are used to contrast new versus old information, as has essentially been described by van Driem (1998), who states "*yö* is used to express assimilated or personal knowledge, whereas *dû* is used to express something about which the speaker has only acquired or objective knowledge" (1998: 135). The form *yö* is used for contexts in which the speaker already possesses the information while *dû* is used for contexts in which the information is newly acquired. For example, the copula *yö* is used, as in (7), in contexts in which the speaker has seen the money or because they are very close with the referent, for example a spouse or other close family member or friend. The mirative copula *dû* is used when the information is new for the speaker. Example (8) could be said in contexts when the speaker has recently learned someone has money. For example, this could be that the referent pulled money out from his pocket in front of her, or if the speaker had heard from someone else that the referent had money. Note that the important distinction between *yö* and *dû* is not the way in which the speaker gained her knowledge. While the mirative *dû* most often is used when the speaker gained her knowledge through direct, visual evidence, it is not limited to these contexts.

(6) *khôna tiru yö*
    khô=na   *tiru*   *yö*
    3.SG.MSC.OBL=LOC   money   COP.EXIS
    'He has money.' (I know, because I have seen it or because I am very close with him)

(7) *khôna tiru dû*
    khô=na   *tiru*   *dû*
    3.SG.MSC.OBL=LOC   money   COP.EXIS.MIR
    'He has money.' (I just discovered this)

Both *yö* and *dû* are also used very commonly in questions. In such cases, the choice between *yö* and *dû* is based on whether or not the speaker expects the interlocutor to have recently acquired the knowledge or have already known it. The question in (9), for example, could be asked to someone the speaker expects to know the referent well, such as a spouse or close friend or family member. On the other hand, (10) would be said if the speaker expected the interlocutor had only recently gained the information, for example if they had just checked someone's wallet and the speaker wanted to know what they had found out.

(8) *khôna tiru yoga*
    khô=na   *tiru*   *yö*   *ga*
    3.SG.MSC.OBL=LOC   money   COP.EXIS   QP
    'Does he have money?' (I assume you already know)

(9) *khôna tiru dûga*
    khô=na   *tiru*   *dû*   *ga*
    3.SG.MSC.OBL=LOC   money   COP.EXIS   QP
    'Does he have money?' (I assume you just found out; you didn't already know)

The other two copulas, used much less frequently, are *yönime*, which is used when the speaker makes an inference based on evidence (visual or otherwise) and *yöp ong*, which is more like speculation or presumption. Consider the examples below:

(10) *khôna tiru yönime*
     khô=na   *tiru*   *yönime*
     3.SG.MSC.OBL=LOC   money   COP.EXIS.IND
     'He has money.' (I am inferring this based on evidence)

The inferential copula *yönime* in (11) is used because the speaker is making an inference based on some evidence; she does not have direct experience. For example, (11) could be said if the speaker had visited someone's home and noted it was filled with nice belongings or that the speaker had a nice car. The speculative *yöp ong*, on the other hand, could not be used in this context. Instead, *yöp ong* is used when the speaker has other reasons for speculating, such as previous knowledge. For example, (12) could be said in the context when you know that someone used to have money and you have seen that they never spend it; therefore, you speculate he still has money. *yönime* is based on evidence you have seen while *yöp ong* is not necessarily linked to evidence.

(11) *khôna tiru yöp ong*
 khô=na tiru yöp ong
 3.SG.MSC.OBL=LOC money COP.EXIS.NMZ come
 'He probably has money.' (I am speculating)

These two forms can also be used in questions, but much less commonly. A question with *yönime*, as in (13), would be asked when the speaker knows the interlocutor has some familiarity with the referent, for example has visited his house or has other means to be able to infer information about him. When using *yöp ongga*, as in (14), however, the speaker does not have any particular reason to expect the interlocutor to have the answer.

(12) *khôna tiru yönimega*
 khô=na tiru yönime ga
 3.SG.MSC.OBL=LOC money COP.EXIS.IND QP
 'Does he have money?' (I assume you have inferred this)

(13) *khôna tiru yöp ongga*
 khô=na tiru yöp ong ga
 3.SG.MSC.OBL=LOC money COP.EXIS.NMZ come QP
 'Would he have money?' (I don't assume you know/I have no particular reason for asking/rhetorical question)

11.3.2 Equative copulas

Similarly, a four-way contrast can be identified among the equative copulas, the primary function of which is to encode equation and proper inclusion. These are summarized in Tab. 2.

Tab. 2: Dzongkha equative copulas.

Form	Function	Diachronic source
'ing	Non-Mirative	WT yin
'immä	Mirative	WT yin.pas
ongnime	Inference	WT 'ong.ni.mas
'ing mong	Speculative	WT yin.pa.'ong

The contrast made by *'ing* versus *'immä* is similar to what was described above for *yö* versus *dû*. The non-mirative *'ing* (used for 'assimilated' or 'old, ingrained background' knowledge in van Driem's [1998: 127] terminology) is used for contexts in which speakers already have information while *'immä* (for 'newly acquired' information according to van Driem [1998: 127] is used when the information is new. An example such as that in (14) could be uttered in contexts where the speaker has already known Karma for some time while (15) would be said if the speaker had only just discovered this person was Karma. It is important to point out that the source of knowledge for (15) is not relevant. Most commonly (15) would be said when the speaker has personal experience meeting Karma or seeing a picture of Karma, but it could also be said when someone else has told the speaker of Karma, or that the realization this person was Karma was made because the speaker recognized Karma's smell as he walked by. Another context in which the mirative equative copula could be used is as follows. Imagine the speaker sees someone in the distance coming toward her but cannot recognize the person. Once the person gets close enough for the speaker to realize who it was, she could say (15).

(14) *kho Karma 'ing*
kho   Karma   'ing
3.SG.MSC   Karma   COP.EQ
'He is Karma.' (I know this; it is not new information)

(15) *kho Karma 'immä*
kho   Karma   'immä
3.SG.MSC   Karma   COP.EQ.MIR
'He is Karma.' (I have just discovered)

There are also inferential and speculative forms of the equational copula, shown in (16) and (17), respectively:

(16) *kho Karma ongnime*
kho   Karma   ongnime
3.SG.MSC   Karma   COP.EQ.IND
'He is Karma.' (I have inferred this)

(17) *kho Karma 'ing mong*
    kho   Karma   'ing mong
    3.SG.MSC Karma   COP.EQ.PRES
    'He is probably Karma.' (I am speculating about this)

Contexts in which (16) could be said are those in which the speaker has some evidence that the referent is Karma and based on that is making an inference that he is Karma. In (17), on the other hand, it is not necessary that the speaker has evidence; she could be presuming or speculating for any number of reasons.

These four equative copulas, like their existential counterparts, can also be used in questions; the latter two are used only rarely. In making questions with these forms, the speaker is making an assumption about the knowledge state of the interlocutor. For example, (18) could be said when the speaker expects the interlocutor to know whether someone is or is not Karma based on previous knowledge which has been established in the person's memory. This situation contrasts sharply with (19), in which the speaker assumes the interlocutor has only recently acquired the knowledge necessary to answer the question.

(18) *kho Karma 'ingna?*
    kho   Karma   'ing   na
    3.SG.MSC Karma   COP.EQ QP
    'Is he Karma?' (I assume you already know)

(19) *kho Karma 'immäga*
    kho   Karma   'immä   ga
    3.SG.MSC Karma   COP.EQ.MIR QP
    'Is he Karma?' (I assume you just found out, you didn't already know)

The inferential and speculative equational copulas are used even more rarely in questions. The inferential could be used, as in (20), if the speaker expects the interlocutor to have formed an opinion about whether or not the referent is Karma based on evidence, for example, if the interlocutor had heard a description or seen picture of the referent. Use of speculative *'ing mong* in a question, as in (21), would be more like a rhetorical question, which the interlocutor had no expectation of the interlocutor's knowledge.

(20) *kho Karma ongnimega*
    kho   Karma   ongnime   ga
    3.SG.MSC Karma   COP.EQ.IND QP
    'Is he Karma?' (I assume you have inferred this)

(21) *kho Karma 'ing mongga*
    kho   Karma   'ing mong   ga
    3.SG.MSC   Karma   COP.EQ.PRES   QP
    'Would he be Karma?' (I don't assume you know/I have no particular reason for asking/rhetorical question)

11.4 Progressive aspect

Progressive aspect in Dzongkha has been described by van Driem (1998) as being composed by one of two forms: *-do* and *-d*ä (still *-dowe* for some dialects). Our analysis of the forms is summarized in Tab. 3.

Tab. 3: Dzongkha progressive aspect suffixes.

Form	Function	Diachronic source
-do	Egophoric	unknown
-dä	Alterphoric	*-do*+ WT *bas*

Canonically, the egophoric *-do* is used when the speaker self-reports or reports on behalf of someone else, while *-dä* is used when the speaker reports on someone else. Consider (22) and (23) for typical examples:

(22) *nga to z'ado*
    nga   to   z'a-do
    1.SG   cooked.rice   eat-PROG.ALT
    'I am eating.'

(23) *kho to z'adä*
    kho   to   z'a-dä
    3.SG   cooked.rice   eat-PROG.ALT
    'He is eating.'

However, if the speaker wants to assert her inclusion, she can use *-do* with third person, as in:

(24) *kho to z'ado*
    kho   to   z'a-do
    3.SG   cooked.rice   eat-PROG.EGO
    'He is eating.'

The suffix -*do* can be used with third person if, for example, the speaker is with the person at the time of the action and the speaker would like to include herself in the action. However, the speaker does not *have* to use -*do* in those contexts; she could equally report on a third person she is with using the alterphoric -*dä*, in which case she is distancing herself somewhat from the action.

The actual difference between -*do* and -*dä* is nuanced and complex and we still struggle to fully understand its meaning. To offer a bit of further insight into the difference between -*do* and -*dä*, we offer the following further observations. The egophoric progressive -*do* tends to be used only in present time and for actions that take place close to the speaker while -*dä* can be used readily in the past time as well as present. -*do* is used for questions when the speaker expects the hearer to be involved in the answer. On the other hand, -*dä* would be used if describing one's actions while watching one's self in a movie. In short, the use of -*dä* implies the speaker is not part of the action while -*do* implies the speaker is including herself. In this way, the Dzongkha egophoric progressive -*do* seems similar to the Kurtöp 'egophoric' -*shang*, wherein Hyslop describes the use as encoding speaker "privileged or exclusive access to knowledge" (2014a: 207); however, unlike the Kurtöp[5] form, it is not clear that the Dzongkha progressive -*do* entails an expectation of the interlocutor's knowledge.

11.5 Hearsay marker

The final morpheme discussed in this study is the evidential clitic =*lo*, which can attach to the right edge of any phrase in order to denote hearsay, or that the speaker received her information by hearing it from someone else. An example is (25):

(25) *Jamyang tsêm tsedolo*
 Jamyang tsêm tse-do=lo
 Jamyang play play-PROG.EGO=HSY
 'Jamyang is playing.' (I know because someone told me)

There are no morpho-semantic restrictions on the distribution of =*lo*; it can attach to any tensed phrase. In all these contexts, the function of =*lo* is to remove the speaker as the source of evidence, pointing to someone else as having orally conveyed the information to the speaker. The epistemic value of the tensed clause

---

5 The exceptionality of the Kurtöp 'egophoric' is discussed in Hyslop (2014).

is then attributed to the source of knowledge and not the speaker. Consider the examples below, in which =*lo* is attached to an egophoric-marked verb (26), and alterphoric-marked verb (27), a mirative copula (28), and a non-mirative copula (29).

(26) *kho to z'adälo*
    kho   to   z'a-dä=lo
    3.SG   cooked.rice   eat-PROG.ALT=HSY
    'He is eating.' (I heard from someone who does not have privileged access to knowledge)

(27) *kho to z'adolo*
    kho   to   z'a-do=lo
    3.SG   cooked.rice   eat-PROG.EGO=HSY
    'He is eating.' (I heard from someone who has privileged access to knowledge)

(28) *khôna tiru yölo*
    khô=na   tiru   yö=lo
    3.SG.MSC.OBL=LOC   money   COP.EXIS=HSY
    'He has money.' (I heard from someone who has old knowledge of this)

(29) *khôna tiru dûlo*
    khô=na   tiru   dû=lo
    3.SG.MSC.OBL=LOC   money   COP.EXIS.MIR=HSY
    'He has money.' (I heard from some one who has just discovered this)

Note that the relevant epistemic contrast is maintained with the addition of =*lo* in each example (26–29); however it is now attributed to the person who conveyed this knowledge to the speaker.[6] In other words, in (26) someone with privileged access to knowledge about the referent told the speaker that that person was eating; in (27) someone who did not have privileged access about the referent told the speaker that that person was eating; in (28) someone with old knowledge about the referent conveyed to the speaker that that person had money; and, finally, in (29), someone who only just discovered that the referent had money told this to the speaker. Simply put, the speaker is passing on a message she heard from someone else.

---

[6] These data, in particular, provide a nice illustration of the 'multiple viewpoints' discussed in Evans (2005).

11.6 Summary and conclusions

In this brief survey of the main epistemic contrasts found in Dzongkha, we have updated the analysis, showing contrasts which can be categorized as evidentiality, mirativity, egophoric and speculation – all part of a larger system concerned with epistemicity at large. The forms which are concerned with source of knowledge, or evidentiality, are *yönime* 'COP.EXIS.IND', *ongnime* and *=lo* 'HSY';. The forms which are concerned with whether or not the knowledge was old or just recently acquired are *dû* 'COP.EXIS.MIR' and *'immä* 'COP.EQ.MIR'; we consider these to be examples of mirativity. Two verbal suffixes contrast whether or not the speaker (or deictic center) has privileged access to the knowledge; as this contrast seems most similar to what has been called 'egophoric' in Tibetan, we adopt that terminology here. Finally, two copulas encode what we characterize as speculation. These forms and their corresponding categories are summarized in Tab. 4.

Tab. 4: A selection of forms involved in evidentiality and related categories in Dzongkha.

Evidential	Mirative	Egophoric	Speculation
yönime	*dû* (vs. *yö*)	*-do*	*yöp ong*
'COP.EXIS.IND'	'COP.EXIS.MIR'	'PROG.EGO'	'COP.EXIS.NMZ' come
ongnime	*'immä* (vs. *'ing*)	*-dä*	*'ing mong*
'COP.EQ.IND'	'COP.EQ.MIR'	'PROG.ALT'	'COP.EQ.PRES'
=lo 'HSY'			

The forms above are present – in fact, obligatory – in finite clauses involving copulas or progressive aspect, including when posing questions. We have not examined other aspects or tenses in this chapter, though our current understanding suggests similar contrasts are made throughout all aspects of the grammar and indeed van Driem (1998) mentions several others. The only exception to this would be that negative statements, imperatives, and non-finite clauses do not mark such epistemic contrasts. In short, these epistemic contrasts are integral to Dzongkha grammar. One cannot speak Dzongkha without taking into consideration the rich range of epistemic contrasts presented here.

Abbreviations

1 1st person, 3 3rd person, ALT alterphoric, COP copula, EGO egophoric, EQ equative, EXIS existential, HSY hearsay evidential, IND indirect evidential, INF infinitive,

LOC locative, MIR mirative, MSC masculine, NMZ nominalizer, OBL oblique, PROG progressive, QP question particle, QUOT quotative, SG singular, WT Written Tibetan

References

Aikhenvald, Alexandra. 2004. *Evidentiality*. Oxford & New York: Oxford University Press.
DeLancey, Scott. 1997. Mirativity: The grammatical marking of unexpected information. *Linguistic Typology* 1. 33–52.
van Driem, George. 1998. *Dzongkha*. Leiden: Research School of Asian, African and Amerindian Studies.
Evans, Nicholas. 2005. View with a view: toward a typology of multiple perspective. *Proceedings of the Annual Meeting of the Berkeley Linguistics Society* 31(5). 93–120.
Gawne, Lauren. This volume. Egophoric evidentiality in Bodish languages. In Lauren Gawne & Nathan W. Hill (eds.). *Evidential Systems of Tibetan Languages,* 61–94. Berlin; Boston: Mouton de Gruyter.
Hill, Nathan W. 2012. 'Mirativity' does not exist: ḥdug in 'Lhasa' Tibetan and other suspects. *Linguistic Typology* 16 (3). 389–433.
Hyslop, Gwendolyn. 2011. Mirativity in Kurtöp. *Journal of South Asian Linguistics* 4(1). 43–60.
Hyslop, Gwendolyn. 2014a. On the category of speaker expectation of interlocutor knowledge in Kurtöp. *Proceedings of the Annual Meeting of the Berkeley Linguistics Society* 40. 201–214.
Hyslop, Gwendolyn. 2014b. "The grammar of knowledge in Kurtöp". In Alexandra Aikhenvald and R. M. W. Dixon (eds.), *The Grammar of Knowledge: A Cross-linguistic Typology,* 108–131. Oxford: Oxford University Press.
Mazaudon, Martine & Boyd Michailovsky. 1988. Lost syllables and tonal contour in Dzongkha. In David Bradley, Eugénie J. A. Henderson, Martine Mazaudon (eds.), *Prosodic Analysis and Asian Linguistics: To Honour R. K. Sprigg*, (Pacific Linguistics Series C 104), 115–36. Canberra: Australia National University.
Tournadre, Nicolas. 2008. Against the concept of 'conjunct'/'disjunct' in Tibetan. In Brigitte Huber, Marianne Volkart, Paul Widmer, and Peter Schwieger (eds.), *Chomolangma, Demawend und Kasbek, Festschrift für Roland Bielmeier*, 281–308. Halle: International Institute for Tibetan and Buddhist Studies GmbH.

Zoe Tribur
12 Observations on factors affecting the distributional properties of evidential markers in Amdo Tibetan

12.1 Introduction

Current work on evidentiality has raised the question of the nature of the interaction between grammatical evidential systems and other areas of semantics, morphosyntax and discourse-pragmatics (Gawne 2013; Tournadre and LaPolla 2014). Like other varieties of Tibetan, Amdo Tibetan is characterized by a highly developed system of markers that occur at the end of a finite clause and express a range of functions collectively referred to as 'evidentiality'. As will be shown here, this system has constructions with functions that do not involve evidence—specifically they encode epistemic modality and factuality—but which must nonetheless be included in analyses of Amdo Tibetan evidentiality because, together with more classically-defined evidential markers, they form a coherent grammatical paradigm. I refer to this grammatical domain as 'epistemic-factual-evidentiality'.

The Amdo Tibetan epistemic-factual-evidential system is morphosyntactically and semantically complex as a result of significant interaction with other domains within the language. Most notably, epistemic-factual-evidentiality is strongly connected to the grammatical category of tense-aspect, but also the inherent lexical aspect of verbs, the aspect of the clause (which may be altered from that of the verb with the addition of Aktionsart markers),[1] and the category of grammatically expressed speaker perspective that I refer to as 'egophoric', following Tournadre (1996: 217–220). I differentiate the egophoric from evidentiality because egophoric distinctions are made in factual clauses.

I have four aims in this chapter. The first is to flesh out the paradigm of post-verbal markers in Amdo Tibetan, of which markers expressing evidence form but a subset. The second is to demonstrate that the Amdo Tibetan evidential system is semantically complex, i.e. individual evidential markers within this paradigm express additional functions, such as tense-aspect. My third aim is to demonstrate

---

[1] While I am aware that the terms 'lexical aspect' and 'Aktionsart' are used interchangeably in the literature, I use the term 'Aktionsart' specifically to refer to the class of post-verbal auxiliaries that alter the lexical aspect of the verb stem.

the extent to which the distribution of individual markers is influenced by factors beyond their epistemic-factual-evidential value, such as discourse-pragmatics, the inherent lexical aspect of the verb stem, and clause level Aktionsart. This chapter does not provide a complete verbal paradigm, but rather provides a general overview of the three sub-categories within the grammatical epistemic-factual-evidential paradigm.

This chapter is organized as follows. Section 12.2 provides background information on Amdo Tibetan. Section 12.3 presents an overview of the Amdo Tibetan verbal system, including summaries of previous analyses. Section 12.4 provides an overview of the morphosyntactic properties of epistemic-factual-evidential post-verbal markers. Section 12.5 presents detailed descriptions of the interaction between grammatical epistemic-factual-evidentiality and tense-aspect in a select sample of temporal-aspectual domains. Section 12.6 discusses the interaction between epistemic-factual-evidential post-verbal markers and the lexical aspect of verbs. Section 12.7 describes non-evidential, i.e. factual post-verbal markers. Section 12.8 briefly introduces epistemic modal post-verbal markers. Section 12.9 discusses the epistemic-factual-evidential paradigm of equative copular clauses. Section 12.10 concludes this study.[2]

12.2 Language background

Amdo, the easternmost region of Tibet, spans most of Qinghai Province as well as prefectures in southern Gansu Province and northeast Sichuan Province. Amdo

---

[2] Data elicited by the author is transcribed phonemically. Unless otherwise noted, I preserve the transcriptions and translations of data excerpted from previously published sources. Consequently, the data included in this study reflect the phonological diversity of Amdo Tibetan dialects. Previously published data that originally appeared in the Tibetan script are transliterated according to the conventions of Wylie (1959). Previously unpublished data was recorded in the field, in various parts of Amdo between 2012 and 2016, and includes elicited examples as well as excerpts from natural discourse. Most of the data included in this study were collected from multiple speakers of varying ages and tribal affiliations in Gcig sgril County, Mgo log Prefecture, Qinghai Province. I have worked most extensively with speakers from two tribal areas, now re-designated as 乡(xiang), or 'village': Khang sar and neighboring Khang rgan. Though the two areas are closely located and have a long history of intermarriage, people from both have told me that they speak in slightly different ways. I have also observed differences in the collection of my data, but as of yet am unable to determine if the variation I have observed is truly dialectal or a product of other social factors, like age, sex or education level. I also include examples from a speaker from Hualong County, Qinghai.

is characterized by a high degree of cultural, religious and linguistic diversity. Outside of linguistic and other academic contexts, 'Amdo Tibetan' (*A mdo skad cha*), refers to the speech of all Tibetan residents of this region. However, for phylolinguistic purposes, the label 'Amdo Tibetan' is here used to refer to the Tibetan topolect[3] with the largest number of speakers and widest geographic distribution in Amdo, although there are other Tibetan varieties spoken in the region (e.g. Cone, see Jacques 2014). Amdo is also home to many speakers of non-Tibetic languages, including languages from the Sinitic branch of Trans-Himalayan as well as from the Mongolic and Turkic language families.

There is striking evidence of phonological and morphosyntactic convergence in all of the languages spoken in Amdo, prompting some scholars to describe the region as a *Sprachbund* (Dwyer 1995; Slater 2003; Janhunen 2012). One such convergence is the presence of an obligatory system of grammatical marking on the verb phrase that expresses evidentiality. Evidential systems have been described for non-Tibetic languages spoken in Amdo, including the region's Mongolic languages, Mangghuer (Slater 2003), Mongghul (Qinggeertai 1991), and Baonan (Chen 1987), the Turkic language, Salar (Dwyer 1998) and the Sinitic creole language, Wutun (Chen 1989).

Amdo Tibetan shares a common orthography, Written Tibetan, with other Tibetan topolects such as Standard Tibetan, also referred to as Lhasa Tibetan.[4] Compared with Standard Tibetan, Amdo Tibetan is phonologically archaic, preserving a large inventory of syllable onsets (de Roerich 1958; Hua 1982; Janhunen

---

[3] I employ the label 'topolect' to refer to a genetic level above that of dialect. Thus Amdo Tibetan is a topolect, and Mgo log Tibetan and Rdo sbis Tibetan are dialects of Amdo Tibetan. Topolect is, in fact, a Latinate translation of the Chinese term 方言 (*fāngyán*), originally used to refer to the major Sinitic branches, such as Yue Chinese and Mandarin chinese, while the terms like 土语 (*tǔyǔ*, 'local language') or 次方言 (*cìfāngyán*, 'minor *fāngyán*') refer to the 'smaller' sub-varieties, or dialects, within topolects. So, Cantonese is a dialect of Yue Chinese and Beijing Mandarin is a dialect of Mandarin Chinese. 'Topolect' avoids some of the cultural baggage that comes with applying the term 'language' to sub-units within linguistic entities such as Chinese. It also neatly side steps the question of mutual intelligibility across genetically related speech varieties, which tends to be the *de facto* (and rather haphazardly applied) yard stick for dividing languages from dialects.

[4] The label 'Standard Tibetan' is used in preference to 'Lhasa Tibetan', as the former encompasses the standardized speech of the international Tibetan community, which differs in minor ways from that of Lhasa, proper (Hill 2013a: 54).

and Kalsang 2014; Janhunen 2012).[5] In keeping with a segmentally more complex syllable inventory, most Amdo Tibetan dialects are toneless.[6]

Intelligibility across Amdo Tibetan dialects is quite high (Green 2012). Nonetheless, there is considerable dialectal variation in phonology as well as morphosyntax. This diversity is reflected in the data presented throughout this chapter. In addition to historically present levels of diversity, Amdo Tibetan is a minority language spoken in a region that is experiencing rapid demographic and social change which has a significant impact on language performance that varies considerably from individual to individual.

12.3 Epistemic-factual-evidentiality as a verbal category in Amdo Tibetan

12.3.1 Summary of existing analyses

Previous research has focused on Amdo Tibetan evidential post-verbal markers, largely excluding the non-evidential members of the finitizing post-verbal marker paradigm. The analysis of evidential post-verbal markers offered here largely corresponds to those presented by earlier authors, with the exception that I argue that they form a paradigm with epistemic-modal and factual post-verbal markers. Other authors have described the evidential system in detail for specific dialects, most notably for the Mdzo dge dialect (Sun 1993), the Chap cha dialect (Ebihara 2009a, 2009b, 2011), and the Them chen dialect (Haller 2000, 2004). In spite of the descriptive overlap, there is some controversy as to where the semantic boundaries of evidentiality lie and what kinds of interactions there are with other grammatical systems, such as modality. Three analyses from three previous descriptions of Amdo evidentiality are provided in Tabs. 1–3, below. Table 2 is translated from German.

---

[5] Amdo Tibetan even reflects the Old Tibetan (7th-10th century) palatalization of bilabials before -e- and -i-, lost in Written Tibetan, e.g. Them chen dialect has /mɲə/ 'Mensch' and /mɲe/ 'Feuer' (Haller 2004: 38) for Written Tibetan *mi* 'person' and *me* 'fire' and Old Tibetan *myi* and *mye* (see Hill 2013b: 67).

[6] The speech of pastoralists living in Rma stod, which is the largest county in Mgo log Prefecture, has developed a phonemic contrast between low and high tones in syllables with nasal onsets as the result of a loss of contrast between voiced and voiceless nasals (Wang 2011). To my knowledge, all other varieties spoken in Mgo log, including Gcigs gril and Pad ma, do not have phonemic tone.

Tab. 1: Sun's (1993) evidential inventory.

Default	Direct evidence	Indirect evidence	Immediate evidence	Quotative
-nə/-Ø	-tʰæ	-zəg	-ʰkə	se

Tab. 2: Haller's (2004: 137) evidential inventory.

	Volitional-evidential	Non-volitional evidential	Non-evidential
Imperfective a	-ɣəjo/-kəjo	-ɣəjokə/-kəjokə	-ɣəjozəç /-kəjozəç
Imperfective b	-a	-ɣə/-kə	-zəç
Perfective Ia	-jo	-jokə	-jozəç
Perfective Ib	-nəjən	-nəre	-nəjənzəç
Perfective II	-a	-tʰa	-zəç
Future	-dʐəjən	-dʐəre	-dʐəjənzəç

Tab. 3: Ebihara's (2011: 68/69) perfective evidential inventory.

Speaker performed	Perceived directly	Inferred or informed by another person
-a	-tʰa	-zək

These three authors differ in the labels they use for the various evidential categories. For example, Sun refers to Ebihara's 'speaker performed' and Haller's 'volitional evidential' as the 'default evidential'. There are other differences, as well: Ebihara's description focuses only on evidential values in perfective aspect. For both Sun and Ebihara, -nərɛt and -nəjən are outside of the evidential system, but Haller includes these two forms in his description. The quotative marker, *se*, is not included by Ebihara and Haller as part of the evidential system, but is included by Sun (1993: 982–986). The most significant difference between these three analyses is the wider distributional pattern Haller describes for the element *zəç*.

In addition to the distributional properties they observe for -*zəç*, Sun and Ebihara also differ from Haller in their functional analysis. Rather than analyzing tense-aspect as part of the inherent semantics of the marker, these authors treat -*zəç* as primarily expressing an evidential distinction which in turn is restricted in the temporal event profiles that it can logically be associated with. The fact that -*zəç*, glossed as 'indirect evidence' in Sun and as 'inferred' in Ebihara, only occurs in perfective clauses is attributed to the nature of the evidential distinction -*zəç* marks, indicating the speaker was unaware of the event's occurrence, a situation most likely encountered in events completed prior to the time of speech. Thus, in the opinion of these two authors, a past connotation of -zəç is not an explicit function of the marker, but rather an epiphenomenon emerging from the logical constraints of its evidential function. In contrast, Haller consciously presents evidential categories on the basis of which forms are found for which tense-aspect categories.

As mentioned, the analyses of Ebihara, Haller and Sun differ in which markers are included in their description of the Amdo Tibetan evidential system. The criteria is based partly on function—whether or not the marker in question can be said to express a function that meets the definition of evidentiality—and partly on paradigmatic properties. Thus, the quotative is included in Sun's analysis on functional grounds because it expresses "another type of indirect information-source: evidence via verbal report" (1993: 982) while it is excluded from the other two analyses, presumably because it does not occur in the same morphosyntactic paradigm as the other evidential markers. As we see in (1+2), the quotative marker may directly follow a verb stem or follow another evidential marker.

(1) ami   lhæmo   tɕo   ma   ndʐo   se
    mom.ERG   lhamo.DAT   2S.ABS   NEG   go.IPFV   QUOT
    'Mom said to Lha-mo: "Don't go!" (I heard).'
    (Sun 1993: 985 [Mdzo dge])

(2) adæ   təb   =sʰoŋ   =zəg   se
    uncle   faint   =AUX   =IE   QUOT
    1. 'Uncle passed out' (I heard from a non-eyewitness).
    2. 'Uncle passed out' (I heard from Uncle himself).
    (Sun 1993: 984 [Mdzo dge])

Quotative =zer (=se in Mdzo dge) can apparently follow any verbal grammatical marker and occur with any tense-aspect value (Sun 1993: 85/6). The quotative is therefore not part of the same morphosyntactic paradigm as the other evidential markers. In contrast to =zer, the markers -nərɛt and -nəjin are distributed in paradigmatic opposition to the other evidential markers. However, -nərɛt and -nəjin are excluded from Sun's evidential paradigm because their function is non-evidential in his analysis (1993: 950/951).

With the exception of Haller (2004), the authors summarized above treat evidential finitizing post-verbal morphemes as a separate class, apart from factual and epistemic modal markers that morphosyntactically occur in the same position. However, given the frequent occurrence with which these non-evidential markers occur, as well as the fact that they form part of the same paradigm as the evidential set of markers, I argue that leaving them out of an analysis of Amdo Tibetan evidentiality results in a partial understanding of the system. Evidential markers are a subset of a highly developed epistemic-factual-evidential system, one which obliges speakers, under certain conditions to express evidence and under others to express epistemic certainty, volition or factuality. The conditions under which speakers choose or are compelled not to express evidence are as important for understanding evidentiality as those conditions under which they are obliged to express evidence.

Amdo Tibetan shares with all Tibetic languages a patterning between declarative and interrogatives sentences according to which the evidential value of the question anticipates the value of the answer;[7] tense-aspect markers and other verbal elements are also similarly anticipated. As this pattern is well known in Tibetic languages it is not discussed further in this chapter.

12.3.2 Grammaticalized epistemic-factual-evidentiality in Amdo Tibetan

While I employ the label 'epistemic-factual-evidentiality' in this contribution, my analysis of the clause final post-verbal morphological paradigm in Amdo Tibetan conforms to the notion of 'Acquired Knowledge' proposed by Cornillie (2009), a broad semantic domain that subsumes both epistemic and evidential grammatical functions. I follow Foley and van Valin (1984) in treating evidentiality as an epistemic sub-category that is distinct from epistemic modality. The term 'evidentiality' adopted in this study follows the definition given in Tournadre and LaPolla, viz. "the [grammatical] representation of source and access to information according to the speaker's perspective and strategy" (2014: 240).

Post-verbal markers form a structural paradigm because they finitize the verb and mark the end of a clause. (These structure of the verb complex are outlined in Tab. 4 in §4.1, below). Examples (3–5) are of clauses that grammatically encode evidence; (6–8) are examples of non-evidential, non-modal (i.e., 'factual') clauses; and the final example (9) is of a clause that is un-marked for evidence, but marked for a high level of probability using an epistemic post-verbal marker.

Egophoric evidence

(3) ŋi   kʰara   tɕʰer   -a
     1S.ERG   candy   carry.PST -EGO
     'Ich nahm die Bonbons weg.' ['I took away the candy.']
     (Haller 2004: 146 [Them chen])

---

[7] Sun refers to this pattern as the "conversational principle of cooperation" (1993: 959). Tournadre and Dorje (2003: 93) describe the same pattern in Standard Tibetan, which they refer to as "the rule of anticipation" (see also Tournadre and LaPolla 2014: 245).

Direct evidence

(4) mərgə   χwetɕʰa   tɕʰəzəç   -a   ɸti   -tʰa
    3S.F.ERG book   what   -DAT   see.PST   -PFV.DE
    'Was für (ein) Buch las sie?' ['What book did she read?']
    (Haller 2004: 146 [Them chen])

Indirect evidence

(5) mərgə   χwetɕʰa   tɕʰəzəç   -a   ɸti   -zəç
    3S.F.ERG book   what   -DAT   see.PST   -PFV.IE
    'Was für (ein) Buch las sie?' ['What book did she read?']
    (Haller 2004: 147 [Them chen])

Non-egophoric factuality

(6) ŋa   kʰu   -nəre
    1S   sick   -FCT.NEGO
    'Ich bin krank (und liege im Bett).' ['I am sick (and lying in bed).']
    (Haller 2004: 145 [Them chen])

Egophoric factuality

(7) tɕʰi   rdzəntə   χwetɕʰa   tɕʰəzəç -a   ɸti   -nəjən
    2S.ERG   usually   book   what   -DAT   see.PST   -EGO.FCT
    'Was für Bücher liest du üblicherweise' ['What books do you usually read?']
    (Haller 2004: 144 [Them chen])

Non-egophoric factuality (future)

(8) mərge   çə   -dzəre
    3S.F   die   -FUT.FCT.NEGO
    'Sie wird sterben.' ['She will die.']
    (Haller 2004: 149 [Them chen])

Probable modality

(9) mo   da   rem.ma   thon   -sa.yod
    3S.F   now   quickly   arrive   -FUT.MOD
    'She will [should] be right back.'
    (Sung and Lha 2005: 213)

Clauses (3–5) illustrate three separate categories of grammatical evidence: egophoric evidence (knowledge of one's own intentions, see Tournadre 1996: 217–220 et passim; Gawne, this volume), direct evidence (knowledge based on directly experiencing or perceiving an event or situation), and indirect evidence (knowledge based on evidence of an event that is generated from the event or situation itself, such as a result, but without directly experiencing or witnessing the event in question). The three evidential categories, which vary in form because evidential markers also express tense-aspect,[8] are possibly more prominent in discourse than either of the two factual (evidentially-neutral) categories or the epistemic-modal categories. Factual post-verbal markers tend to dominate what might be thought of as teaching genres of speech, i.e., storytelling about third persons (especially historical or legendary people), lectures on religious and other scholarly topics and any sort of recounting of generally received truths (see §7). Epistemic-modal post-verbal markers occur in all genres of speech to express a range of speaker stances, ranging from extreme confidence, or even arrogance, about the validity of a statement, to extreme doubt. Expressions of factuality and evidentiality may be employed toward epistemic ends, but epistemic-modal post-verbal markers are, like factual post-verbal markers, evidentially neutral.

According to Chafe, the expression of evidence frequently implies (lack of) reliability (1986: 266). As Shao (2014: i) points out, this is not the case with Amdo Tibetan. For Amdo Tibetan speakers, the evidential value of a clause, i.e. the evidence a speaker has for a given proposition, is distinguishable from the degree of certainty or confidence the speaker feels about the validity of the information she is asserting. Evidential and epistemic modal markers occur in paradigmatic opposition to one another: a speaker may either chose to assert the source of information, or she may choose to assert her degree of confidence about the information's truth-value. Thus, the assertions expressed in (3–5) are equally confident, reliable and certain, even though the information of (3) is based on the speaker's own knowledge of the event as an active participant; (4) presupposes that the information is based on the event in question being directly witnessed, but not participated in; and (5) presupposes that the event was neither witnessed nor participated in and is known only indirectly.

Examples (6–8) illustrate clauses that do not encode evidence, or, are evidentially neutral. As with examples (3–5), they are neutral regarding speaker stance, or confidence about the truthfulness of the assertion. Instead, the information

---

8 Tense-aspect is expressed in other constituents of the clause, including the verb stem, for those verbs with more than one stem form, and in post-verbal aspectual markers (see §4.1, Tab. 4). Nonetheless, in many cases tense-aspect is only expressed by the epistemic-factual-evidential marker of a clause. Examples (3–9) illustrate interactions between epistemic-factual-evidential categories and tense-aspect. Examples (3–4) are of perfective clauses; (6–9) are imperfective (present tense and habitual) clauses; (7–8), both non-evidential, are future clauses. Moreover, as we can see in examples (4), (5), and (6-8), tense-aspect meanings are an inherent part of the semantics of some post-verbal markers. Indeed, in (7) and (8), post-verbal markers are the only indicator of tense-aspect.

expressed in the clauses might be termed 'facts', which are stripped of any evaluative (epistemic-modal) or source-based (evidential) information. I therefore refer to these forms as 'factuals'.

Factual post-verbal markers are employed as a focus construction, used when the speaker wishes to direct focus to a part of a proposition, rather than the preposition as a whole (Sung and Lha 2005: 260/261); this may be the case with (6), which could be uttered by way of explanation as to why one hasn't come to work.[9] They are also used in contexts in which a given proposition is disconnected from any possible kind of evidence, such as recurring events or actions as in (7), which is a habitual clause, or in the case of events or situations which have yet to arise, as in the future-tense clause in (8). Finally, factuals are used to express information that falls into the semantic category of 'general knowledge' or in contexts in which the speaker simply wishes to assert a fact independent of any evidence she might have for it. In particular in future contexts, factuality overlaps with modality as the choice to highlight an event's inevitability inherently connotes a sense of absolute reliability and confidence in the truthfulness of an assertion. In contrast to (9), the construction in (8) is epistemically neutral: it is merely an assertion of a fact the speaker expects will take place in the future. The functions of factual post-verbal markers will be discussed in §7.

If a speaker of Amdo Tibetan wishes to communicate the degree of confidence she feels in the information she is asserting, she will use a modal post-verbal marker, as in (9), and leave off any evidence she may have. I therefore argue that for Amdo Tibetan speakers, evidentiality and epistemic modality are distinct verbal categories, expressed by members of a single grammatical paradigm.

12.4 Amdo Tibetan verb structure

In this section, I briefly discuss the structural properties of post-verbal markers in Amdo Tibetan. Post-verbal markers mark a verb as finite and signal the end of a (verbal) clause. Like other Tibetan topolects, Amdo Tibetan has both verbal and copular clauses. Although this chapter focuses on verbal clauses, some discussion of copula clauses is included at §9.

---

9 I ran this example by a Mgo log consultant, who offered this possible context.

12.4.1 Structural properties of finite verbs in Amdo Tibetan

The templatic structure of finites verbs (excluding imperative clauses) is represented in Tab. 4, below, and illustrated by examples (10–13).

Tab. 4: Amdo Tibetan finite verb structure.

(subject/ agent/ experiencer)	(object)	(Q/neg.)	**VERB**	(neg.)	(Q)	(Aktionsart)	(aspect)	**evidential/ modal/ factual**	(Q)

Table 4 illustrates the complexity of simplex (non-imperative) Amdo Tibetan clauses. Table 4 also shows how the only obligatory constituent of a clause is the finite verb, which in the case of interrogative or declarative clauses, consists of a verb stem and a post-verbal marker that expresses either evidentiality, epistemic modality or factuality. Nonetheless, the verb complex can be quite intricate, containing additional post-verbal morphemes. Examples (10–12) illustrate this complexity.

(10) agent   object   **VERB**   Neg.   Aktion.   **EPST/EVID/FACT**
     khərgi   *ɕa*   *za*   *ma*   *-bʒəx*   *-zəç*
     3s.ERG   meat   **eat.NPST**   NEG.PFV   -COMPL.PFV   **-PFV.IE**
     'He didn't finish eating the meat.' (Speaker heard this information from somebody else or else deduced what happened from seeing the leftover meat.)

(11) Interrogative   **VERB**   **EPST/EVID/FACT**
     ə-   *wɨt*   *-tha*
     Q-   **go.PST**   -PFV.DE
     'Did he leave?' (Speaker expects listener to have witnessed him go.)

(12) subject   **VERB**   (Aktion.)   **EPST/EVID/FACT**
     ɣnam   *wap*   *-tshar*   *=jokə*
     sky   **rain.PST**   -CNC   =PRF.DE
     'It's finished raining (the ground is still wet).'
     (Mgo log)

Clauses (10–12) are all marked with evidential (as opposed to factual or epistemic) post-verbal markers. In addition to evidential post-verbal markers, (10) and (12) also include Aktionsart post-verbal markers, which precede the finitizing evidential markers. To avoid confusion, I refer to Aktionsart post-verbal markers as auxiliaries.

As the template in Tab. 4 makes clear, the internal order of auxiliaries and finitizing post-verbal markers is relatively fixed. The epistemic-factual-evidential post-verbal marker always occurs at the end of the verb complex, signaling the end of the clause. However, the positions of negation and interrogation affixes vary depending on the identities of other post-verbal morphemes. They precede the verb stem unless there is an aspect or Aktionsart auxiliary, in which case they follow the verb stem and precede the auxiliary.

12.4.2 Unmarked and zero-marked categories

As stated above, epistemic-factual-evidential post-verbal markers are obligatory constituents of finite clauses. The exception is imperative clauses, of which Amdo Tibetan has more than one type. Example (13) is an imperative clause and (14) is a hortative clause.

(13) ɕa   zui!
    meat   eat.JUS
    'Eat the meat!'

(14) ta   ɕa   za.
    now   meat   eat.IPFV
    '(Let's) eat the meat.'

Whereas imperative clauses are unmarked for epistemic-factual-evidentiality, when the absence of explicit marking signals the egophoric, its paradigmatic contrasts compel the analysis of zero-suffixation. In most dialects egophoric evidence is marked by a suffix in declarative clause, *-a* or *-Ca* in Them chen, *-a* in Chab cha (Ebihara 2011), *-(N)ə* or zero in Mdzo dge, but it is consistently zero-marked in interrogative and negative clauses. Example (15) is a declarative example from Them chen, (16) is a negative clause from Mdzo dge and (17) is an interrogative clause from the A rig dialect.

(15) ŋi   tɕʰu   kʰa   len   -a.
    1S.ERG   2S.GEN   mouth   hear   -EGO
    'Ich höre auf dich.' ['I'm listening to you.]'
    (Haller 2004:141 [Them chen])

(16) ŋə   ndaŋ   tɕʰaŋ   -zəg   ma-   ntʰoŋ (*-nə).
    1S.ERG   last.night   liquor   -IDF   NEG.PFV-   drink
    'I didn't drink any liquor last night.'
    (Sun 1993: 957 [Mdzo dge])

(17) cçho teruŋ suıluŋ -a   ɯ -soŋ?
     2S   today xining -DAT Q -go.PST
     '你今天去西宁了吗?'['Did you go to Xining today?']
     (Shao 2014: 73 [A rig])

In my Mgo log data, even in declarative clauses the egophoric is zero-marked, as in (18).

(18) (ŋi)   ɕa   za   -Ø.
     (1S.ERG) meat eat.IPFV -EGO
     '(I) eat meat.'
     (Mgo log)

Contrast the translation of (17) with examples of two kinds of imperative clause from the same dialect, (13) and (14), above.

Example (17) could also have a past habitual interpretation, but this would need to be expressed via adverbs or by context. The default interpretation of (18), then, is habitual present. This ambiguity between past and present interpretations for egophoric zero marked clauses is also found in clauses with stative lexical verbs, as in (19) below. As with active clauses, the default interpretation of (19) is that it is true at the time of speech. Stative clauses are discussed in greater detail in §6 below.

(19) ŋi   mgo   -wa   khu   -Ø.
     1S.GEN head -DAT   hurt -EGO
     'My head hurts.' Or, 'my head hurt.'
     (Mgo log)

It appears likely that egophoric evidence was originally unmarked and continues to be so in contexts of negation and interrogation for all dialects, and in all contexts for a minority of dialects. In other words, as the non-egophoric evidential categories (direct and indirect evidence) developed, the egophoric emerged as a distinct coherent evidential category in response. This proposal concerning the emergence of the egophoric in Amdo finds some confirmation in the fact that in subordinate clauses Standard Tibetan neutralizes evidential contrasts in favor of the (formally speaking) egophoric (cf. Chang and Chang 1984: 607/608; DeLancey 1990: 298) and that *yin*, a form cognate to the Standard Tibetan egophoric, prevailed in Classical Tibetan in both subordinate and finite clauses.

12.4.3 Etymological versus semantic compositionality

Epistemic-factual-evidential post-verbal markers include monosyllables as well as polysyllables. It is quite apparent that most polysyllables evolved from etymologically compositional source constructions. Even so, the morphosyntactic properties of many polysyllabic post-verbal markers indicate that they are semantically non-compositional. The following examples (20–28) illustrate some of the differences in form and distributional patterns of these two syntactic categories. Three evidential categories are represented: egophoric (EGO), direct evidence (DE) and indirect evidence (IE).

(20) *tondip   -kə   lika   bʒəx   -soŋ   -tha.*
    Tondrup -ERG   work   quit   -PFV   -PFV.DE
    'Tondrup quit work.' (Speaker either witnessed Tondrup quit, or is a co-worker or some other close associate who has direct knowledge of the fact that Tondrup quit his job.)
    (Mgo log)

(21) *lika   bʒəx   -tha.*
    work   quit   -PFV.DE
    '(He) quit working.' (i.e., the task is unfinished. The subject may resume working on it in the future. Speaker witnessed him stopping.)
    (Mgo log)

(22) (a) *tʃhɯzika   ŋa   khapar   ptɔŋ   =mɛt.*
       why   1S.DAT phone   hit   =NEG.PRF.EGO
       'Why haven't you called me?'
   (b) *jot!   ɲi   khapar   ptɔŋ   =jot.*
       PRF.EGO. 1S.ERG phone   hit   =PRF.EGO
       'I did! I called (you).'
       (Mgo log)

(23) *lika   ma-   bʒəx   -tha.*
    work   NEG.PFV- quit   -PFV.DE
    '(He) didn't quit working (i.e., before finishing).' (Speaker has direct knowledge that the subject either finished the task or was still working on it at the time of speech.)
    (Mgo log)

(24) *ɣnam   wap   -tshar   ə-   jokə.*
    sky   rain.PST   -CNC   Q-   PRF.DE
    'Has it finished raining (on you)?' (A question that might be asked of someone over the phone.)

(25) ɣnam   wap   -tshar   = jokə.
     sky   rain.PST   -CNC   =PRF.DE
     'It has finished raining.' (It's not raining (on me) now.)
     (Mgo log)

(26) ɕa   za   -kə.
     meat   eat.IPFV   -IPFV.DE
     '(He) eats meat.' (Speaker knows this person or has seen them eat meat.)
     (Mgo log)

(27) ɕa   ə-   za   -kə
     meat   Q-   eat.IPFV   -IPFV.DE
     'Does (he) eat meat?' (Addressee should know the person or else be sitting next to them as they eat.)
     (Mgo log)

(28) ɕa   za   -kot
     meat   eat.IPFV   -PROG.EGO
     '(I) am eating the meat.' (cf. example 17)
     (Mgo log)

With the exception of (22), examples (20–28) were elicited from a single speaker of the Mgo log dialect, a male in his late thirties. Examples (22a+b) were excerpted from a recording of a spontaneous, natural dialog between an 18-year old male and a 21-year old female from the same region of Mgo log as the other speaker. *-tha* (past direct evidence), *-kə* (imperfective direct evidence) and *-zəç* (past indirect evidence) are suffixes. They are defined as such because they occur following either a semantic main verb or an Aktionsart/aspectual clitic. They also form morphophonological units with the preceding elements that cannot be interrupted with the interrogative marker *ə-* or negative markers *mə-* or *ma-*. Consequently, interrogation and negation markers must occur before the preceding element, as we see in (22–24). In contrast, *=jot* (perfect egophoric), *=jokə* (perfect direct evidence) and *=mɛt* (negative perfect egophoric) are all cliticising auxiliaries. Like the suffixes, auxiliaries occur after the semantic main verb or any other tense-aspect markers, as in (22), (24) and (25). However, they do not form a single morphosyntactic unit with the preceding element. They may follow the interrogative marker, as in (22).

This small, closed class of auxiliaries (*=jot, =jokə,* and *=mɛt*) may be considered verbs because they also occur as lexical verbs—copulas—and also occur alone, as the sole overt constituent of an entire clause, as we see with *jot* in (22b). There is a separate set of negative evidential auxiliaries for perfect egophoric (PRF. EGO), and perfect direct evidence (PRF.DE). So, in (22a) *=mɛt* expresses perfect aspect, egophoric evidence and negation.

Several evidential markers are multisyllabic, with forms that are transparently derived from morphologically complex constructions but which synchronically behave as single syntactic units. These apparently morphologically compositional forms are semantically non-compositional and so may be considered single, unitary morphosyntactic forms. Note that in (24+25) =*jokə* contains the element *kə*, which occurs alone as the imperfective direct evidence suffix in (26+27). Typically, multisyllabic evidential markers have etymological roots that can be traced to a combination of suffix and clitic. There is ample evidence that *jokə* and the perfect *jot* egophoric marker are etymologically related, including the fact that the IPF.IE marker may be pronounced /jotkə/ in slow, careful speech and that both markers may also function as locative or possessive copulas. Whether the resulting marker has properties of a clitic or a suffix depends on which element is in the first position within the morpheme. In the case of =*jokə*, the first element is =*jo*, or =*jot*, which is a clitic. =*jokə* not only can occur in isolation, as a stand-alone clause as *jot* does in (22b), but it may also occur as a copular verb. Another example of an etymologically complex, but semantically non-compositional evidential marker is the factual suffix -*nərɛt*, presented in (29).

(29) *xaxa   -gə   ɕa   za   -nərɛt.*
     muslim   -ERG   meat   eat.IPFV -FCT.NEGO
     'Muslims eat meat.' (It is well known.)
     (Mgo log)

The TAME (tense-aspect-mode-evidential) value of a clause may be compositional, emerging from the structural and semantic relationships between the lexical verb stem and all post-verbal markers. This is illustrated by example (10), a negative past tense clause in which the past tense is conveyed through past forms of the following grammatical markers, including the negative marker *ma-*.

The negative past tense construction consists of a non-past verb stem and the past tense negative prefix. The presence of a completive Aktionsart marker -*bʒəx*, which is also inflected for past tense, attracts the semantic as well as morphosyntactic scope of both negation and indirect evidentiality. Example (10) implies that the agent ate part of an available quantity of meat, but stopped before consuming all of it. Thus the scope of negation does not extend to the entire act of eating. The completive marker also implies that the part of the eating event that the speaker is representing as indirect knowledge is the termination point. The speaker may or may not have directly witnessed the agent eating at an earlier stage of the event, but she was not around to witness the agent finishing their meal. The speaker then witnessed the aftereffect, i.e., saw the leftover meat giving her strong evidence to support the assertion that the event in question was not performed to completion. While -*zaç* also encodes past tense, this feature is largely redundant in (10), because multiple other elements in the clause also provide information about tense-aspect. The primary function of -zəç in this clause is an evidential one, making it clear that speaker only knows of the uncompleted act indirectly, through other sources of information than her own volitional participation or direct experience.

The next section summarizes the ways in which epistemic-factual-evidential post-verbal markers also express tense-aspect.

12.5 Epistemic-factual-evidentiality and tense-aspect

Rather than providing an exhaustive treatment, the current section illustrates the range of the interactions and morphological overlap between tense-aspect and epistemic-factual-evidentiality by providing select examples from a limited sample of temporal-aspectual domains. Because factual and epistemic post-verbal markers are given their own sections, this section focuses primarily on the temporal-aspectual interactions of evidential post-verbal markers.

The temporal-aspectual interpretations of epistemic-factual-evidential markers are part of their inherent semantic properties, even though other elements in a clause may also express tense-aspect. The importance of epistemic-factual-evidential post-verbal markers in marking tense-aspect is especially apparent in cases where the lexical verb does not have distinct stems for past and non-past tense and where there are no other post-verbal markers or any adverbial indicators of time, as in (30).

(30) çɨ   -zəç.
     die   -PFV.IE
     '[He] died.' (Speaker inferred this information from evidence after the fact or learned it secondhand, through hearsay or a news report. Also, the subject may not, in fact, be dead.)
     (Mgo log)

The lexical verb in (30), 'die', has only one stem form and is thus neutral for tense. The past interpretation of the clause is therefore entirely due to the presence of -zəç, which also marks the clause as information that the speaker knows from indirect evidence.

In contrast, the tense-aspect functions of epistemic-factual-evidential post-verbal markers may not be apparent in clauses that include verb stems that are inflected for tense (examples (31–33)).

(31) ɕa   zu   -Ø.
     meat   eat.PFV   -EGO
     '(I) ate the meat.'
     (Mgo log)

(32) *khərgi ɕa   zu   -tha.*
     3S.ERG meat eat.PFV -PFV.DE
     'He ate the meat.' (I know this because I watched him eat it.)
     (Mgo log)

(33) *ɕa   zu   -zəç.*
     meat eat.PFV -PFV.IE
     '(He) ate the meat.' (I infer this from the meat being gone.)
     (Mgo log)

In (31), the zero marker indicates that the event is a form of egophoric (EGO), or self, knowledge for the speaker.[10] The speaker knows of this event because she intended for it to happen and caused it to occur. In contrast, (32) is marked with -*tha*, indicating knowledge that was gained through direct sensory experience (DE) as the event unfolded. The clause in (33) is marked as indirect evidence (IE) by the suffix -*zəç*, meaning that the speaker knows of this event through indirect evidence, either through learning about it from someone else or from directly seeing the after-effect. In addition to expressing evidentiality, all three forms also express functions associated with other grammatical categories. In all three clauses the final element conveys tense and also, at least in the case of (31) and (33), helps identify the agent.

12.5.1 Perfective clauses

The greatest range of grammatically expressed evidential categories is found in past tense clauses. Depending on the type of construction, past tense predicates are obligatorily marked egophoric (EGO), direct evidence (DE), indirect evidence (IE), or as evidentially-neutral, i.e., either factual (FCT) or epistemic. Factual-marked past tense clauses are further sub-categorized as egophoric factual (FCT.EGO) and non-egophoric factual (FCT.NEGO). The relative richness of evidential distinctions in the past tense, as opposed to present or future tenses is

---

10 In (31), the zero marker is labeled 'EGO,' because it occurs with both perfective and imperfective verb stems but its presence on imperfective verb stems is incompatible with a future interpretation. The presence of a zero marker on an imperfective stem therefore expresses egophoric evidentiality (and implies an *origo* subject, see Note 15 below).

not surprising when we consider that "a significant number of languages distinguish evidentiality only in the past" (Aikhenvald 2004: 8).[11]

Time is inextricably tied up in human perceptions of situations, and thus in subtle ways time is also a factor in evidence for situations. The role of time in distinguishing types of evidence is most apparent in certain contexts in which the evidential distinctions between the two perfective non-egophoric evidential markers, direct evidence -*tha* (PFV.DE), and indirect evidence -*zəç* (PFV.IE), become irrelevant or difficult to maintain. In particular, certain aspects of weather events, such the initiation of rainfall, seem to pose problems for distinguishing between direct and indirect evidence (egophoric evidence is not possible). In such cases, consultants seem to feel that the primary difference between -*tha* and -*zəç* comes down to temporal distance, with the former implying a more recent past event than the latter.

(34) ɣnam   wap   -bʒəx   -taŋ   -tha.
     sky   fall.PST -COMPL -PFV   -PFV.DE
     'It just started to rain.' Or, 'it already started to rain.'
     (Mgo log)

(35) ɣnam   wap   -bʒəx   -taŋ   -zəç.
     sky   fall.PST -COMPL -PFV   -PFV.IE
     'It started raining awhile ago.' Or, '(I didn't realize that) it started raining!'
     (Mgo log)

Examples (34+35) were produced by two female speakers of the Mgo log dialect, aged 21 and 23.[12] The two feel that both clauses could be uttered under different conditions. The clause in example (34) might be uttered as a general exclamation shortly after it has started to rain, by someone who is either outside at the time, or somewhere where they were able to perceive the rainfall happening. A second scenario involves answering a question (maybe over the phone) about whether or not it has rained yet. The use of the perfective marker -*taŋ* in this case gives a sense of 'already'. As for (35), the first scenario involves the speaker having

---

11 Within Trans-Himalayan languages with grammaticalized evidentiality, Bunan (West-Himalayish) restricts evidential marking to the past tense and, to a limited extent, the future tense (Widmer 2014: 478).
12 Prior to this, the 21 year old, who is a primary consultant for me, defined -*tha* as being used for situations that are 'personally witnessed' (亲眼看到的) and -*zəç* as being used for situations that are not personally witnessed. I've found most of my consultants are at least aware of the evidential functions of these two morphemes, although they may not be consciously aware of such functions for other morphemes.

direct experience of the rain, like the speaker of (34), but a certain amount of time has passed since the initiation of the rainfall. The second scenario involves the speaker stepping outside into unexpected rainfall—she wasn't aware of the rain when it started, but knows that it started to rain because it is raining now.

The primary difference between (34) and (35) is that the event of rain starting to fall is more recent. In both cases, the rain is still on-going at the time of speech. The connection between the recent past and direct evidence and the distant past and indirect evidence may have to do with memory: the longer ago in the past a situation occurred, the less likely we are to have memories of the actual situation itself and the more likely we are to know about it through indirect evidence, such as resulting states or hearing other people talk about it. While the initiation of a weather event such as rain is vivid when it takes place, it may soon be forgotten and our knowledge of the situation may be based more solidly on the fact that it is raining now. In this particular context, the decision between these two evidential markers is based more on time, rather than evidence.

12.5.2 Perfect clauses

Perfect clauses in Amdo Tibetan distinguish between three evidential categories: egophoric evidence, direct evidence and indirect evidence. Perfect clauses may also be factually or epistemically marked, but the current section focuses on the first three. It appears that the forms and functions of perfect clauses vary little, if at all, across Amdo Tibetan dialects. Table 5 presents an inventory of perfect markers, as described in Haller's grammar of the Them chen dialect (2004: 142). English translations of his original labels are given in parentheses below my own labels.

Tab. 5: Perfect Evidential post-verbal markers in Them chen (Haller 2004: 142).

	Egophoric (volitional, evidential)	Direct Evidence (non-volitional, evidential)	Indirect Evidence (non-evidential)
Assertive	-jo	-jokə	-jozəç
Negative	-me	-mekə	-mezəç
Interrogative	-əjo	-əjokə	

Haller does not include a form for negative interrogative clauses. However, when I pressed one of my Mgo log consultants to do so, he produced (36), below, which he then interpreted as a question one might ask over the phone after hearing from the other person that the dog had gotten onto the dinner table while the friend was in the kitchen. Nonetheless, it seems safe to assume that such forms as (36) are rare in natural discourse.

(36) zama   zu   -ə   =jotzəç?
     food   eat.PFV   -Q   =PRF.IE
     'Did (he) eat the food?' (Lit. 'Has he eaten the food?')
     (Mgo log)

Haller refers to this construction as a sub-type of perfective clauses: "Perfektiv Ia [perfective 1a]" (2004: 142). Sung and Lha refer to it as "durative past and continuous aspect" (2005: 208). Sun (1993) and Norbu et al. (2000) both include examples of this construction in their data but do not directly address it. Ebihara does not mention it, at all. To my knowledge, Shao is the only author to use the label "完成体 [perfect aspect]" (2014: 49, 60).[13] I follow Shao's terminology because this construction conforms to Comrie's definitions of the "perfect of result" (1976: 56–58). According to consultants, it is also often used for recent events, which also meets Comrie's definition of "perfect of recent past" (1976: 60/61). Amdo Tibetan speakers thus use the clause types given in Tab. 5 and example (36) to express that an event either recently took place or began (the difference in interpretation is due to the inherent aspect of the verb root—see §5) and "the resulting state is continued to the time of speech" (Sung and Lha 2005: 208/209).[14]

This function is common to all the forms given in Tab. 5. The forms in the three columns therefore differ only in terms of their evidential values. This distinction is further illustrated by examples (37–39).

(37) nga   -e,   nga   yu'u   -na   zog   rdzi   yed   =yod.
     1S   -PART,   1S   home   -DAT   livestock   herd   do   =PRF.EGO
     'I'm a herdsman in my native region.' (Lit. 'As for me, I've herded livestock at home.')
     (Norbu et al. 2000: 122)

---

13 On p. 49 Shao applies this label to egophoric V-jo: and factual V-jo-nɯ-re:. On p. 60, he applies it to indirect evidence -jo-zɯk and two forms that he refers to as direct evidence (亲知), -jo-kɯ₂, which conforms to Haller's direct perfect, -jokə, and -jo-tha, a form that I have (rarely) encountered in natural discourse, but which I have not seen in any linguistic accounts of Amdo Tibetan or any other Tibetan topolect.

14 My impression of the discourse-level distribution of perfect clauses is that they seem quite common in conversation but quite rare in other genres. For example, in the three narrative texts included in Haller (2004: 166-206) the perfect construction occurs just once, as a in a quoted exchange between two characters. Haller 2004: 168, line 46 (bolded for emphasis): [...]"ama! ta ndə, ndəɲiɣa ɣɲəl-əjola?"[...] 'Mother! Now these, these two have fallen asleep?'

(38) mərge   tɕʰampa   hoχ   =jokə.
     3S.F.DAT head.cold   strike.PST   =PRF.DE
     'Sie ist erkältet.' ['She has a cold.']
     (Haller 2004: 144 [Them chen])

(39) tɕʰo   ɸti   -na,   ŋa   rgi   =jokə.
     2S.DAT see.PST   -COND   1S   grow   =PRF.DE
     'Ich sehe älter aus als du.' (Der Sprecher stellt den Vergleich anhand eines Fotos an, das beide zeigt.'
     ['Compared to you, I (look) older.' (The speaker is talking about a picture of speaker and interlocutor).]
     (Haller 2004: 143 [Them chen])

Example (37) is an egophoric perfect clause uttered in the context of a dialog about work. The action of herding livestock is a volitional, controlled event for the speaker, so she naturally uses the egophoric form. The English translation provided by Norbu et al. is in the present tense. To paraphrase Sung and Lha (2005: 208/209), the use of the perfect in such situations has the effect of emphasizing the continuous effect of the event discussed. The dialog from which (37) was extracted presumably occurred outside of the speaker's homeland. She was thus not currently engaged in herding, but nevertheless continued to identify as a herder and expected to resume this work in the near future. Her use of the perfect expresses the nuance of a past event that continues to be relevant at the time of speech.

Example (40) includes a third person subject and a predicate marked as indirect evidence.

(40) ɣdzonma   bdzaχ   =jozəç.
     Drolma   be.full   =PRF.IE
     'Drolma ist offenbar satt.' (Ihr Teller ist noch halbvoll).
     ['Drolma is apparently full.' (Her plate is still half-full).']
     (Haller 2004: 144 [Them chen])

Satiety is typically not an externally observable phenomenon. In (40) the speaker infers that Drolma is full by observing the unfinished food on her plate and reasoning that Drolma hasn't finished the food because she is full. The word *bdzaχ* 'full' is a stative verb, so the speaker could have chosen to use a present tense construction (the German translation Haller provides is present tense). By using the perfect, instead, the speaker emphasizes the fact that the condition of Drolma's being full began prior to the time of speech (and the act of her leaving her plate half full) but continues to be in effect at the time of speech.

The primary distinction between direct and indirect evidence in perfect clauses is determined by an intersection between the time in which the event occurred and when the speaker became aware of it. If the speaker experienced the event in question as it unfolded, then the direct evidence perfect marker *=jokə* is used. In such cases, the decision to use the direct evidence perfect construction instead of a direct evidence past construction comes down to a temporal-aspectual distinction, and not an evidential distinction. In contrast, the indirect evidence perfect construction is used in cases in which the speaker was not aware of an action, event or situation at the time in which happened or, in the case of states like (40) began. The speaker infers that the event took place in the past because she perceives the resulting state. In other words, the aspectual value of clauses such as (40), above, and (41), below, is determined by the evidential value; the resulting state provides the evidence by which the speaker infers that an event took place.

(41) ɣdʐonma -yə χwetɕʰa -te ɸti =jozəç.
Drolma -ERG book -DEF.DAT see.PFV =PRF.IE
'Drolma hat das Buch offenbar gelesen.' (Sie kennt dessen Inhalt.)
['Drolma has apparently read the book.' (She knows its contents.)]
(Haller 2004: 143 [Them chen])

Kelsang Norbu (personal communication, August 2013) confirms that the perfect indirect evidence marker *=jozəç* typically occurs in clauses that not do not contain *origo* arguments.[15] Given that perfective events involving one's self are prototypically known either through perception of the planning/volitional stage or else perception of the on-going stage of the event, this is not surprising. Nonetheless, there are contexts in which information about oneself is learned indirectly. In such cases, Amdo Tibetan speakers make use of indirect evidential markers to express this nuance, as in (42).

(42) ŋa tɕhoŋ -tu ɦgokm̥an maŋazɯk nthoŋ =jozɯk.
1s small -when medicine many drink.PFV =PRF.IE
tawar -tɯ ŋa tɕaŋ khu -dʐɯ-me-kɯ₂
now -DET 1s never be.ill -FUT.EGO
'我小时候喝过很多预防病的要，现在从不得病.'
['I took a lot of preventative medicine when I was younger, so now I never get sick.']
(Shao 2014: 127 [A rig])

---

[15] I use the term 'origo' to refer to the morphosyntactic pattern that aligns the epistemic-factual-evidential value of first person subjects in declarative clauses with that of second person subjects in interrogative clauses. This pattern has been previously referred as 'conjunct-disjunct', first used by Hale (1980) in his description of Newari, another Trans-Himalayan language.

According to Shao in (42) "句末附加拟测示证记成立，表示说话者记忆不深，他是根据自己现在从不的病而得出的判断，说话者叙述一件与自己相关的，遥远的过去的事，在此过程中，阿柔话是将其作为非亲见的一件事来处理的 [the verb ending in the first clause expresses that the speaker's memory of the event is unclear]" (2014: 127). The speaker infers that he took a lot of preventative medicine as a child, based on the fact that "now I never get sick", rather than a specific recollection of having done so. This particular function of indirect evidence in first person clauses—stressing that information about one's self was inferred—seems especially pertinent to the complex temporal-aspectual contexts in which the perfect function is used: while the event in question has already reached a terminal end point by the time of speech, the resulting state is still on-going. The use of the indirect evidential form =*jozəç* makes it clear that the speaker was not aware of or in control of the event as it occurred, but infers it happened from encountering the on-going result. While clauses like (42) do occur, most clauses with =*jozəç* that are found in the data I had access do not involve *origo* arguments.

12.5.3 Imperfective clauses

In imperfective non-future clauses, only two evidential values are distinguished: egophoric, and non-egophoric. Factual and modal values are also distinguished in imperfective clauses. The current section discusses two constructions that express imperfectivity. The first construction, which I refer to simply as the 'imperfective construction,' expresses habituality when it occurs with non-stative verbs (stative verbs are discussed in §6). The second construction expresses progressive aspect, so I refer to it as the 'progressive construction.'

12.5.3.1 The imperfect construction (habitual aspect)

Only two evidential categories are distinguished in habitual aspect clauses: egophoric and direct evidence. Egophoric habitual aspect appears to be zero-marked in all dialects. Habitual direct evidence is marked by -*kə*. When either of these markers occur immediately after the stem of an active verb, then the resulting clause is habitual. Example (26) above is of a direct evidential habitual present clause. Although the default interpretation of example (26) is habitual present, it may also be understood as habitual past, depending on the presence of past tense-associated adverbs. The habitual aspect interpretation is specified by the active lexical aspect of the verb 'eat', otherwise the imperfective direct evidence marker expresses -*kə* present tense. It is assumed that the speaker has some sort of direct evidence that the agent of (26) is a meat eater. If she doesn't have evidence of this fact, then she might choose instead to use the non-egophoric factual marker -nəre.

12.5.3.2 Progressive aspect

There are two progressive aspect constructions, both of which can occur in past as well as present tense constructions, although in the absence of overt references to a past time, the default interpretation for both is progressive present. For space considerations, only the first progressive construction will be discussed here.[16] This construction consists of the form -kot, which is then followed by either egophoric zero or the direct evidence imperfective marker -kə.[17]

Depending on the dialect, there appear to be only two evidential distinctions marked in progressive aspect: egophoric and direct evidence. This restriction may be due to the function of the progressive aspect, which (with rare exceptions—see §6.3) is typically confined to activities and is used to express that an activity is ongoing relative to a specific point in time, either the time of speech or some other temporal reference point. If the temporal reference point is the time of speech, then the speaker is expressing knowledge of an action as it takes place, entailing that she is either performing the action herself or is witnessing it unfold. Likewise, if the temporal reference point is some other time, knowledge of an action as it unfolds entails a more direct experience of the event than simply deducing it took place.

Examples (43+44) illustrate the progressive aspect construction. The first progressive construction is typically used with action verbs, which tend to be

---

16 The second progressive construction, consisting of the etymological element ndəç 'sit', varies somewhat in its morphology from dialect to dialect and may, in fact, not be found in every dialect. Sung and Lha (2005: 370–371) refer to a form -'dug.gi as a perfective progressive marker, indicating that an action began prior to the time of speech and is still on-going. Haller (2004: 154) also describes a version this construction in Them chen. In Mgo log, the construction is realized as -ndəçjot for the (rarely used, apparently) egophoric form, -ndəçjokə for the more common non-egophoric form, and -ndəçjonəre for the factual non-egophoric form.

17 One Mgo log consultant, who has spent considerable time in other regions of Amdo, says clauses such as ɲe mbot kozəç (fire burn PRG.IE) 'Apparently a fire was burning' occur occasionally in the context of someone repeating a reported event they heard from someone else (which would entail a past tense interpretation). His relatives, present in the room at the time, backed him up, but other of my Mgo log consultants found the form -kozəç, or indeed the element zəç in any non-past context unacceptable.

controllable, therefore the distribution of egophoric versus direct evidence forms is largely predictable based on clause volition.

(43) ŋi   ʃafa   -ɣɨ   thoxwa   pɕi   -kot   -Ø.
     1S.ERG   sofa   -GEN   top   wipe.NPST   -PROG   -EGO
     'I'm wiping down the sofa.'
     (Mgo log)

(44) ʃafa   -ɣɨ   thoxwa   pɕi   -ko-kə
     sofa   -GEN   top   wipe.NPST   -PROG-IPFV.DE
     '[You are] wiping down the sofa.'
     (Mgo log)

Haller (2004: 138), Sung and Lha (2005: 127), and Shao (2014) all decompose the progressive construction into a multi-morphemic constituency. Shao (2014: 41/42) provides the most in-depth explanation of this morphologically compositional analysis. Unlike Haller's (2004), Sung and Lha's (2005) and my own data, in which the forms -ko and -kokə predominate, Shao's data seem to indicate that his A rig consultants always produced the progressive construction as -kɯjokɯ, as in (45).

(45) ptʂwaɕhi   -kɯ   ŋa: tɕha   hku   -kɯ$_1$ -jo   -kɯ$_2$.
     Tashi   -ERG   1S.DAT tea   boil   -PROG   -AUX   -MIR
     '扎西正在给我煮茶' ['Tashi is boiling tea for me.']
     (Shao 2014: 41 [A rig])

Shao analyzes the direct evidence progressive construction, illustrated in (46), as composed of three morphemes: /kɯ$_1$+jo+kɯ$_2$/, in which /kɯ$_1$/ is "小品词 [a particle]" (2014: 42) that Shao glosses "PROG", the second marker is glossed as 'AUX', and the third marker /kɯ$_2$/ expresses "亲见示证标记和新知标记 [direct evidence and mirativity]" (2014: 42). The first /kɯ/ morpheme would have to be analyzed as not having an evidential meaning because otherwise the only logical meaning it could have in example (44) would be direct evidence and then its appearance in the egophoric first progressive construction would be difficult to account for. Many Amdo Tibetan speakers, including most of my Mgo log consultants, produce versions of either form that correspond to Shao's decomposed analysis when asked to speak slowly or more clearly. However, since the element kə (or /kɯ$_1$/, in Shao's transcription of the A rig dialect) expresses direct evidence when it occurs alone after a finite verb, I think that synchronically the first progressive construction is not semantically analyzable.

12.5.4 Diverging functions of -zəç?

Haller (2004), Sung and Lha (2005), and Shao (2014) all analyze *zəç* as a structurally independent element that has one function, expressing indirect evidentiality, regardless of tense or aspect. In forms such as *-yəjozəç*, which Haller labels 'imperfective non-evidential', the element *zəç* contributes the evidential value while the other two elements, *yə* and *jo*, contribute the imperfective reading. However, as was shown in §2.3, the presence of *-zəç* in isolation without any other grammatical markers is sufficient enough to coerce a past interpretation of an active clause. It is also sufficient to coerce a perfective change of state interpretation in non-copular stative clauses (§6, below).

In certain contexts, *-zəç* effectively contrasts with both *-yəjozəç* and *-Ø*, as in (46), (47) and (48). All three clauses consist of 'be.ill', a lexical verb that does not have distinct perfective and imperfective stems. Note also that (48) is ambiguous with regard to tense.

(46) khərgə mgo -wa khu -zəç.
3S.ABS head -DAT be.ill -PFV.IE
'He got a headache (but is fine, now).' (There are a bunch of empty beer bottles on the ground and the speaker did not see his friend in school that day, so the friend must have given himself a hangover.)
(Mgo log)

(47) ɣdzonma kʰu -yəjozəç.
drolma be.ill -PROG.IE
'Apparently Drolma is ill.' (She has not come to school.)
(Haller 2000b: 186 [Them chen])

(48) ɲi mgo -wa na -Ø.
1S.GEN head -DAT hurt -EGO
'My head hurt.' Possible, but less likely, 'My head hurts.'
(Mgo log)

Forms such as *-yəjozəç* are obviously etymologically compositional—and often recognized by speakers as such—and there is a transparent connection between the element *zəç* in as it occurs in (47) and *-zəç* as it occurs in (46). Nonetheless, *-yəjozəç* and *-zəç* display complementary patterns of distribution and thus appear to be developing as separate, albeit related, morphemes with distinct, non-compositional functions.

12.5.5 Use of evidential post-verbal markers to express epistemic functions

Evidential markers are sometimes employed to express a speaker's attitude toward an event (see also §9). One such use is highlighted in example (30) above. In certain genres of narrative discourse, the use of the past indirect evidential is used to imply that a given event didn't really take place. According to one consultant, the phrase in (30) occurs frequently in legendary or fictional storytelling to hint that the subject is very likely not dead, or, in religious tales, will be reborn later on. This contrasts with the clauses in (49), below, in which the use of the perfective aspect marker *soŋ* implies finality and thus the end of the character as a participant in the story, and (49), also below, in which the use of the suffix *-tha* explicates direct experience (and therefore confirmation) of the character's death.

(49) çɨ   -soŋ   -zəç.
     die   -PFV   -PFV.IE
     '(He) (definitely) died.' (Speaker learned this information secondhand, or from encountering the body.)
     (Mgo log)

(50) çɨ   -tha.
     die   -PFV.IE
     '(He) died.' (Speaker watched or heard him die.)
     (Mgo log)

For both (49) and (50), one of the possible routes by which the speaker could have learned of the subject's death is a verbal report. This possibility seems to be largely due to the nature of the event in question, where indirect evidence of someone's death may take the form of other people's reactions to that death. My consultants tell me that the clause in (50) is also quite shocking, or rude, and should preferably never be said of a human being, and should definitely never be said to bereaved people.

12.6 Evidentiality and lexical aspect

Lexical aspect refers to the situation type that a particular predicate encodes. Verb roots have lexical aspect as part of their inherent semantics, which also include semantic elements that are not traditionally considered to be a part of lexical aspect, such as controllability.[18] Inherent aspect is a semantic property of verb roots; lexical aspect is a semantic property of predicates and thus includes semantic contributions from verbal suffixes, including epistemic-factual-evidential morphemes.

While the imperfective function (ongoing in the present, i.e., time of speech) of perfect clauses is unvarying, the perfective interpretation of a given clause is determined by the lexical aspect of the verb root or, when Aktionsart markers such as conclusive -bʒəx occur, by Aktionsart. Perfect clauses are either interpreted as perfective, meaning the encoded proposition is understood as having ended at the time of speech, or else as inceptive, meaning the encoded proposition, having been initiated in the past, is still on-going at the time of speech. Perfect clauses are interpreted as inceptive or perfective depending on whether or not the predicate is durative or dynamic, following Vendler's (1957) classification of situation types. Durative predicates in perfect clauses have an inceptive interpretation and dynamic predicates have a perfective interpretation. Durative predicates are those which, according to Comrie (1976: 41), last for a period of time and that lack any discernible internal stages or phases into which it can be further broken down.

Stative predicates, such as 'full' in example (40) above, are durative and thus trigger an inceptive interpretation when they occur in perfect and perfective clauses. The same is true of processes, such as 'sleep', in (51+52), below. Apart from states and processes, all other predicates are dynamic in a perfect context.

(51) ɣnət   sʰuŋ   -kʰa   ji,   tə   ji   -nu...
     asleep go.PFV   -NMLZ   do,   DET   do   -SUB
     '(Sie) täuschten vor, eingeschlafen zu sein.'
     ['(They) pretended to go to sleep...']
     (Haller 2004: 168/169, l. 45 [Them chen])

---

18 As Sun (1993) and Haller (2004) have described for Amdo Tibetan, and DeLancey (1985) and others have described for Standard Tibetan, controllability is also an important semantic feature of the inherent aspect of verb roots. My use of inherent aspect is distinguished here from lexical aspect, which follows Comrie's (1976) use of the latter term. As has been described in detail by the preceding authors, the inherent aspectual feature of verb roots, +/- controllable, interacts with the predicate-level feature of +/- volitional that in turn interacts with the evidential value of a given clause. Volition and controllability do not interact with tense-aspect, but do interact with lexical aspect, including the functions expressed by Aktionsart markers.

(52) ama!   ta   ndə,   ndə   ɲiya   ɣɲəl   -ə   =jol   -a?
    mother! now   DET,   DET   two   sleep -Q   =PRF.EGO -COMPL
    'Mutter! Ob diese beiden nun wohl eingeschlafen sind?'
    ['Mother! Now have these two fallen asleep?']
    (Haller 2004: 168/169, l. 46 [Them chen])

Examples (51) and (52) are both excerpted from a quoted speech that occurs in Narrative 1 "Wie der König die dämonische Königin bezwang [How the king defeated the demon queen]" (2004: 166–189). The verb root, ɣɲət, meaning 'sleep', is the same in both (51) and (52). The two clauses occur following a scene in which the queen and her daughter have plied the king and a companion with alcohol as part of a scheme. On drinking the alcohol, the two men stumbled around and collapsed. In (51), they pretended to fall asleep and in (52), the daughter asks the mother if they are now sleeping.

Haller does not explain the use of the egophoric marker in (52), but it might have to do with emphasizing the certainty with which the daughter expects her mother to have about the situation. It may also be related to the use of the emphatic question particle -a. Regardless of the evidential value, (51) clearly expresses an inceptive interpretation of 'sleep': 'have fallen asleep', as opposed to 'have slept'. As the following clauses in the narrative make clear, the men are (the other characters assume) still sleeping. The temporal-aspectual composition of (52) is thus one in which the initial point of sleeping (i.e., falling asleep) has ended but the process of sleeping is on-going at the time the daughter asks (52).

12.6.1 Imperfective stative clauses

Amdo Tibetan expresses predicate adjectives with a special class of stative verbs. Generally speaking, pragmatically unmarked stative clauses are always imperfective, regardless of whether the condition described in the clause was true in the past or is true now. Moreover, most (but not all) stative clauses are marked as direct evidence (IPFV.DE) -kə, regardless of the identity of the subject or how the speaker knows the information. As Sun, observes, volition is the critical determiner of the evidential value of first-person clauses (1993: 960); information expressed about the speaker or elicited from the listener is coded as imperfective direct evidence for the same reason as the information about third persons is: the speaker does not have access to the planning of the propositions in questions, so they are marked as direct evidence. The use of -kə is illustrated in examples (53–58), below.

(53) bod.yig   slob   -kha   mi-   dka'   -gi.
    written.tibetan   study   -NMLZ   NEG.IPFV-   difficult   -IPFV.DE
    'It isn't difficult to learn how to write the Tibetan Alphabet.'
    (Sung and Lha 2005: 347)

(54) ŋa   tsho   -kə.
    1S   fat   -IPFV.DE
    'I am fat.'
    [Mgo log]

(55) ɖa   ʃɪgɨ   ʃa   -kə.
    sound   very   good   -IPFV.DE
    '(His/your/my) pronunciation is/was good.'
    (Rep kong)

(56) ŋi   ɖa   mi-   ʃa   -kə.
    1S.GEN   sound   NEG.IPFV-   good   -IPFV.DE
    'My pronunciation is/was not good.'
    (Rep kong)

(57) ta   ŋi   ho   -wa   xtok   -kə.
    NOW   1S.GEN   stomach   -DAT   hungry   -IPFV.DE
    'I'm hungry now.'
    (Mgo log)

(58) ҫchu   ho   -wa   ə-   xtok   -kə.
    2S.GEN   stomach   -DAT   Q-   hungry   -IPFV.DE
    'Were/are you hungry?'
    (Mgo log)

All of the above examples, including the negative clauses in (53) and (56) and the interrogative clause in (58), are marked 'imperfective indirect evidence'. The identity of the subject and time of the proposition must either be explicitly stated in the clause, as 'now' is expressed in (57), 'I' in (56) and (57), and 'you' in (58), or else recovered from context. The stative verb 'be.hungry' in (57+58) is an example of Tournadre and LaPolla's (2014: 242 et passim) class of 'endopathic' verbs and Sun's class 'internal physiological process' verbs.

The same patterns observed for predicative adjectives are also found in comparative adjectival clauses as in (59), below. In this example Haller's 'non-volitional evidential' -yə corresponds to my 'imperfective direct evidence' -kə.

(59) tṣwaɕe   ɸti   -na   ṣtamdẓən   ŋan   -yə.
     Tashi.DAT see.PST -COND   Tamdrin   capable -NVOL.EVID
     'Tamdrin ist fähiger als Tashi.' [Tamdrin is more capable than Tashi.']
     (Haller 2004: 121) [Them chen],

The use of the imperfective direct evidence marker in the examples above, including those with *origo*, can be explained in terms of volition: stative verbs are inherently, or lexically, imperfective, meaning their beginnings and ends are unknown and irrelevant, thus volition, a semantic property associated with perfective events,[19] which have a beginning that might be volitionally initiated or not, are not part of the semantic profile of these verbs.

12.6.2 Employing aspectual distinctions to express evidential functions

In the Mgo log dialect, the progressive construction described in §5 also occurs with a restricted semantic class of stative verbs, namely verbs that express internal emotional states that meet two conditions: they are not controllable and they are not perceptible to other people. In examples (60+61) below, the semantic difference between the marker -*kə* and the progressive construction is apparently not based on tense-aspect, but rather evidential. Examples (60+61) are of acceptable clauses. Examples (62+63) are of unacceptable clauses.

(60) ŋa   sem   rdik   -kə.
     1s   mind   suffer -IPFV.DE
     'I am sad.'
     (Mgo log)

(61) khərgə sem   rdik   -ko-kə.
     3s   mind   suffer -PROG-DE
     'She is sad.'
     (Mgo log)

(62) *ŋa   sem   rdik   -ko-kə.
     1s   mind   suffer -PROG-DE
     'I am sad.'
     (Mgo log)

---

[19] Ebihara (2009b) describes how volition is the primary semantic determiner of the distribution of the two perfective aspect markers, -*taŋ* (volitional) and -*soŋ* (non-volitional) in the Chap cha dialect.

(63) *khərgə   sem   rdik   -kə.
    3s   mind   suffer -IPFV.DE
    'She is sad.'
    (Mgo log)

The clause in (60) and the clause in (61) both have present tense interpretations. The emotion of sadness is uncontrollable and therefore the clauses in which it occurs are non-volitional, so even though the subject in (60) is a first person, the clause is still marked as direct evidence, since the speaker perceives, but does not control or intend, their emotional state. It might seem that the same principles would operate for judging the emotional state of someone else and thus we the clause in (61) would also be marked the simple imperfective direct evidence marker -kə, but example (63) shows that this is not the case. Four Mgo log consultants, including speakers from Khang rgan and speakers from Khang sar, all rejected (63) with the explanation that, in the words of one young woman, "你怎么知道她在心里想什么? [How do you know what the other person feels?]."

While (63) was rejected on evidential grounds, i.e., that the speaker lacks the necessary evidence to make this kind of claim about someone else, (62) was rejected on aspectual grounds: the clause in (62) sounds like sadness is some kind of activity that the speaker is currently (passively?) being engaged in. One speaker, a different young woman, said it sounded like "你正在进行难过的过程[you are in the middle of the process of being sad]."

No one has yet been able to offer me an explanation of why this progressive sense is absent from clause (61). Discussion of the verb 'be sad' is absent from any of the other sources on Amdo Tibetan I have consulted for this study, nor have I had the chance yet to investigate the matter with speakers of other dialects. Therefore it is too soon to say whether or not the use of the progressive aspect marker for present tense expressions of sadness for non-*origo* is a dialectal feature. Nonetheless, one explanation for why the progressive marker is used here might lie in the strict past interpretation Mgo log speakers have for the element *zəç*, which is rejected in present imperfective and future clauses. Because *zəç* is inherently past tense, Mgo log speakers may have innovated an indirect evidence function for the direct evidence progressive marker in this particular semantic context. Note that neither the simple imperfective construction nor the progressive construction (when used in other contexts) express indirect evidence.

12.6.3 Volitional stative clauses

Most predicative adjectives function like examples (53–58) in §6.2 above, i.e. obligatorily marked as imperfective direct evidence (IPFV.DE). However, there are a handful of stative verbs that can occur with or without -kə. Such states are controllable, meaning that instances of their occurrence can either be volitional or non-volitional. The occurrence of -kə marks the clause as non-volitional, meaning that the speaker (or addressee, in the case of interrogative clauses) did not willingly bring about the expressed state. One such controllable state verb is *chog*, meaning 'to be allowed or acceptable' (or 'ok', as it is glossed below). As we see in (64+65) below, this verb occurs as a bare verb stem as well as with the imperfective direct evidence suffix.

(64) glu   blang   -na   mi-   chog   -gi.
     song   sing.PST   -COND   NEG.IPFV-   ok   -IPFV.DE
     'Singing is not allowed.'
     (Sung and Lha 2005: 171)

(65) khyo   song   -na   e-   chog   Ø?
     2S   go.PST   -COND   Q-   ok   EGO
     'Is it OK for you to go?'
     (Sung and Lha 2005: 171)

Example (65) is an interrogative clause that is un-marked, meaning it is egophoric. According to Sung and Lha (2005: 81/82), the difference between the two clauses in (64) and (65) is that (64) is coded for the 'objective perspective' and (64) for the 'subjective perspective'. The labels 'subjective' and 'objective' respectively correspond to the labels 'egophoric' and 'non-egophoric' used here. Example (64) expresses a situation that the speaker finds to be true, namely that there is a rule against singing. In contrast, (65) elicits an opinion or decision from the interlocutor, which means that this statement is volitional, as the formation of opinions and decisions involves a process of foreknowledge and planning on the part of the subject, in this case the interlocutor.

For some stative verbs, the choice to mark a clause as egophoric versus direct evidence can have implications for the semantics of the verb stem beyond tense-aspect, as is shown in (66+67), below. Both clauses were produced by a speaker of the Mgo log dialect who came up with them when asked to illustrate the functional distinctions between egophoric (i.e., unmarked) and direct evidence marking in stative clauses.

(66) ŋa   oma   yga   -kə.
     1S.DAT   milk   like   -IPFV.DE
     'I like milk.'
     (Mgo log)

(67) ŋa   çcho   yga   -Ø.
    1S.DAT   2S   like   -EGO
    'I love you.'
    (Mgo log)

There is no reason to think that the inherent semantics of 'like' differs between the two clauses, but the use of egophoric marking in (67) highlights the volition of the proposition, which translates as a semantically stronger, or more agentive, sense of 'like', in other words, 'love'.

In Amdo Tibetan, genitive participants frequently trigger egophoric marking in first-person declarative clauses and second-person interrogative clauses because such participants are volitional instigators of the proposition. Conversely, the use of the egophoric in the stative clause in (67) highlights the agent-like, volitional participation of the subjects. For (65), this means that the speaker assumes that the interlocutor has the authority to decide whether or not she will go. For (67), it emphasizes the ardor of the speaker's affections. In Amdo Tibetan the use of egophoric as opposed to direct evidence in stative clauses may therefore represent a strategy to emphasize the volitional participation of first person subjects.

12.6.4 Perfective stative clauses

The stative clauses described in the previous section can occur in perfective clauses. Perfective states are the result of a change of state. In the Mgo log dialect, stative clauses may be overtly marked perfective, but only with the indirect evidence (PFV.IE) marker -zəç or the direct evidence (PFV.DE) marker -tha. However, the perfective direct evidence marker may only occur on volitional clauses, meaning its distribution is restricted to controllable stative verbs, i.e., those which can also be egophorically marked.

(68) kʰəga   haba=a   htçʰek   =taŋ   =tʰa.
    3S   dog=DAT   be.scared   =PFV   =PFV.DE
    'He was scared of the dog.'
    (Ebihara 2009b: 109 [Chap cha])

(69) ŋa   ko   -tha.
    1S   understand   -PFV.DE
    'I understand (now).' (Speaker didn't understand before.)
    (Mgo log)

Example (68) is marked with both the perfective aspect marker *-taŋ* and the perfective direct evidence marker *-tha*. Ebihara explains that "emotions and feeling are interpreted as coming to the experiencer" (2009b: 109). The subject of (68) underwent a change of state, becoming afraid. Likewise, example (69) expresses that the subject did not originally understand or know something, but does now. Moreover, the fact that the clause in (69) is marked with direct evidence indicates that the speaker's knowledge was achieved through means beyond her control. Since this is a stereotypical way to respond to directions or other kinds of instructions, the source of information is the addressee of clauses such as (69). Ebihara does not mention whether the state of being afraid is still true for the time of speech, but for example (69), the state of understanding is still true, thus stative clauses marked as perfective direct evidence appear to have an inchoative aspect.

Non-controllable stative verbs, which include all states not related to internal emotional or cognitive processes, only occur in perfective clauses that are marked for indirect evidence. Like perfectively marked controllable stative clauses, such clauses have an inchoative interpretation. In example (70), below, the use of *-zəç* does not indicate that the condition of 'being many' no longer obtains at the time of speech. In fact, it is probable that the utterance is marked in response to learning that there are now many houses in Gcig sgril. The structure of the clause conveys no information about whether or not the condition still holds.

(70) çtʃikrd̩il   -yə   khoŋwa   maŋ   -zəç!
      gcig.sgril   -GEN   house   many   -PFV.IE
      'Gcig sgril has a lot of houses these days!' Lit.,
      'Gcig sgril's houses have become many!'
      (Mgo log)

Interestingly enough, in clauses like (70) the speaker may actually be an eyewitness to the state in question. My consultant uttered (70) to describe his impression of his hometown after returning after an absence of almost 10 years. He knew the houses were many because he saw that it was so, but he was not present to witness the proliferation of houses. The event or situation that precipitated the witnessed state was therefore un-witnessed, and is only indirectly known through seeing the result of that event. However, it is not the change event that matters, as such a proposition would be expressed by an action event verb. Rather, what matters is the previously unknown state resulting from the change in question, hence the use of a stative verb. The consultant indicated that the use of perfective *-zəç* in contrast to imperfective *-kə* highlights the fact that the observed condition was not previously true. It also expresses that the situation is new information for the speaker. The use *-zəç* in a stative clause thus affects the lexical aspect of the verb, but the primary function of the marker is to express that the information encoded in the clause is new to the speaker.

The perfective direct evidence marker -*tha* is ungrammatical in stative clauses according to my consultant, hence the clause in (71) is ungrammatical.

(71) *ɕtʃikrḍil -yə khoŋwa maŋ -tha!
gcigs.gril -GEN house many -PFV.DE
'Gcig sgril's houses have become many!'
(Mgo log)

Presumably, this is because stative clauses are inherently imperfective. The result of a witnessed change of state is also, presumably, witnessed and therefore is marked with the imperfective direct evidence marker. If the speaker wishes to highlight the change event, they will use an active verb such as *joŋ*, 'come' or *ɽʉr*, 'become'. These verbs then take the same kinds of TAME markers with the same interpretations as other active verbs.

The primary function of perfective marking on stative verbs appears to be expressing volition in the case of the egophoric marker and new information in the case of the perfective direct and indirect evidence markers.

12.7 Factual clauses

I argue that evidential post-verbal markers fit into an overarching grammatical category of epistemic-factual-evidential modality from which speakers select markers that highlight either the evidential basis of an assertion or the speaker's stance on the truthfulness of the assertion, or else side-steps both considerations. Support for this claim is partly provided by the functional and distributional properties of the two factual post-verbal markers discussed in the current section. The term 'factual' is used for two markers both of which I argue express neutral evidentiality (Aikhenvald 2004: 25). I refer to the form -*nəjin*[20] as the egophoric factual, and the form -*nərɛt* as the non-egophoric factual.

Elsewhere in the literature there is a lack of consensus as to the functions and distributional properties of these markers. For Sung and Lha, both -*nərɛt* and -*nəjən* express general knowledge, or previous knowledge for which evidence

---

20 -*nərɛt* and -*nəjin* reflect Mgo log pronunciations. Respectively, they correspond to the WT spellings of -*ni.red* and -*ni.yin*. Other dialects vary slightly in their pronunciation of these two forms. Note that the egophoric factual -*nəjin* also has an allomorphic form, -*ni* (Written Tibetan -*nas*), or sometimes -*nə* (Written Tibetan -*ni*).

is unnecessary. Sung and Lha argue that both factual forms serve a focus function and thus their distribution relative to evidential markers is determined by discourse-pragmatic functions. Ebihara (2009a and b) excludes both markers from her analysis of Amdo Tibetan evidentiality. Sun refers to both forms as "the non-committal declarative" and says that the egophoric and non-egophoric forms primarily express differences in epistemiological certainty, with the egophoric form emphasizing "that the reported situation is well known to the speaker" (1993: 951). Haller includes them in the evidential category (as we will see, in some contexts, the distribution of these markers is sensitive to evidential functions), using the label "volitional evidentiell [volitional evidential]" for *-nəjin*, and "nicht-volitional evidentiell [non-volitional evidential]" for *-nərɛt* (2004: 144/145). Shao briefly describes them as "则用于一般的陈述，它并不表明信息一定是非亲见的或亲见的 [generic declaratives, used without making any commitment to whether or not the speaker has any evidence for the assertion]"(2014: 146). Shao also asserts that they are counterparts to the future forms /dʐɯ-re/ and /dʐɯ-jɯn/ (2014: 166/167).

In this section I attempt to provide a brief description of both the egophoric factual and the non-egophoric factual, elucidate the ways in which they are distinct, and describe some of their discourse-pragmatic functions in relation to the rest of the epistemic-factual-evidential post-verbal marker paradigm. Example (72) is a non-evidential transitive clause with third person arguments.

(72) *tʂaɕhi   -gə   htæ   ɲu   -nəre.*
     bkrashis -ERG   horse buy.PST -FCT.NEGO
     'Bkrashis bought a horse.'
     (Sun 1993: 949 [Mdzo dge])

The factual construction is constrained to a set of contexts, described below, otherwise the use of factual post-verbal markers is disfavored in preference to evidential or epistemic ones. Sun describes (72) as "made in a matter-of-fact tone, with the information-source left unexpressed" (1993: 950) and explains that the factual, which he considers 'non-evidential' "is found mainly in generic statements, proverbial sayings, and stories, but is ill-suited for informative reports" (1993: 951). Sun goes on to report that his consultant claims that such an utterance as (72) would likely be met with an inquiry as to how the speaker knows about the situation. Nonetheless, factuals do occur frequently in conversations.

12.7.1 Tense-aspect of factual post-verbal markers

As with the evidential post-verbal markers, factual post-verbal markers interact with tense-aspect. With the exception of Sun (1993), previous accounts of factual post-verbal markers tend to describe them as perfective. The two factual markers express perfective aspect, in the sense that the events and situations that either occurred in the past or that occur repeatedly but which, were they treated as single instances, would be perfective (Comrie 1976: 69/70). This underlying perfective function means that both factual forms are incompatible with stative verbs.

According to Sung and Lha, factual post-verbal markers ("focused past") occur within the context of clauses that encode "previously completed events" with the exception of certain modal verbs like 'should' (2005: 260–261). Likewise, although he does not explicitly label them as such, Haller only gives examples of factual clauses in the past tense. Norbu et al. (2000) do no mention factuals except to briefly describe the form of the egophoric factual, -*nas*, which they describe as a second person interrogative for past tense clauses (2000: 215). In contrast, according to Sun, who refers to the two factual post-verbal markers as "the unmodalized declarative construction", they occur with both past and non-past verb stems (1993: 950–951); Sun's explanation accords with my findings. This distributional property is illustrated with the non-egophoric factual in (73–75).

(73) *zu   -nərɛt.*
     eat.PST -FCT.NEGO
     '(You/he) ate'
     (Mgo log)

(74) *za   -nərɛt.*
     eat.NPST -FCT.NEGO
     '(You/he) regularly eats (something).'
     (Mgo log)

(75) *xaxa   -gə   ɕa   za   -nərɛt.*
     Muslim -ERG meat eat.IPFV -FCT.NEGO
     'Muslims eat meat.' (This is a well-known fact.)
     (Mgo log)

In the examples above, tense-aspect is expressed by the verb stem rather than the post-verbal marker. These examples suggest that, like egophoric clauses which also contain 'eat' (see §2–4), the non-egophoric factual is neutral for tense-aspect. Like the egophoric evidential marker, when the factual occurs with a non-past verb stem, the resulting clause can have a habitual interpretation, as in (75), but such clauses can also have a non-habitual interpretation, as in (74), which is not true of the egophoric evidential.

The temporal properties of factuals are further differentiated from the zero-marked egophoric evidential in that both factuals are incompatible with future clauses[21] and can only occur with perfective aspectual post-verbal markers, as in (76+77), below.

(76) ŋi ȷ̊tɕʰəç -i, ɸɕən -taŋ -nəre.
    1S.ERG be.wrong -NF, give.PST -PFV.TRANS -FCT.NEGO
    'Ich habe (es) irrtümlich weggegeben!' ['I have given (it) up by mistake!']
    (Haller 2004: 137 [Them chen])

(77) ...ta həyə ptṣwi -sʰuŋ -nəre.
    ...now away escape -PFV -FCT.NEGO
    'und er floh nun.' ['...then he fled.']
    (Haller 2004: 160 [Them chen])

The factual construction in (76) appears to highlight that the act of giving was committed in error. However, the same construction in (77), uttered as part of a narrative of historical or legendary events, is used to express that the situation is general knowledge, or is knowledge for which the speaker has no evidence, or need not express any evidence.

When the factual post-verbal markers occur with verb stems that are not marked for tense, the resulting clause can have either a perfective or imperfective interpretation.

(78) 'di ngas thengs dang.bor yi.ge bskur -ni.yin.
    this 1S.ERG incident first.DAT letter send -FCT.EGO
    'This is my first time sending a letter.'
    (Sung and Lha 2005: 261)

(79) ... tə-yi juŋ -ni.
    here come -FCT.EGO
    '...und so hierher gekommen sei.' ['...they came here.']
    (Haller 2004: 178/179, l. 135)

Both of the clauses above are marked for egophoric factuality. Clause (78) is interpreted as present and (79) is interpreted as past. The different temporal values are determined by the discourse context in which the utterances occur. Example (78) describes an event that is happening as it is being communicated. Rather than

---

[21] According to Sun, when the factual post-verbal markers occur with non-past verb stems, the resulting clause has a habitual present or future interpretation (1993: 951). With the caveat that I have not systematically investigated the matter, in my experience I have yet to encounter a factual clause with a future interpretation.

indicating past tense, -*ni.yin* in this clause indicates a perspective on an event that is complete and unitary, or in other words, perfective, even if it is on-going or has yet to happen. The interlocutor is present as the event unfolds and has been engaged with the speaker in a conversation about the letter, thus the event of sending the letter is obvious to both parties. By using the factual egophoric, the speaker of (78) shifts the focus from the situation as a whole to the fact that it is his first time to engage in such an event. In contrast, the clause in (79) was uttered as part of a narrative of a legend and occurred in the context of a long description of situations that took place in the past, as made clear by the use of past tense verbs stems, where applicable, and other grammatical and lexical indicators of past tense.

The factual construction can also combine with the progressive aspect marker -*ko* described in §5. This is illustrated in example (80), below.

(80) *kwəndʑi   zo   -ko   -nə.*
    clothes   sew   -PROG -FCT.EGO
    '(I'm) mending a shirt.'
    (Mgo log)

Example (80) was given as a response to the question, 'What are you doing?' (*tɕhu tɕhizək jekot?*), which appears to be a typical context in which this construction occurs. It thus appears to be another example of narrow focus, which emphasizes a sub-constituent within a proposition, for example an argument, time or place.

It appears, then, that the factual construction can be used for any statement about situations that either are true at the time of the utterance or were true in the past.

As stated above, the primary functions of both forms of the factual construction are to express focus and to avoid expressing evidence. Before discussing the latter function, I first describe the use of the factual to express narrow focus as a strategy for drawing attention to a sub-part of an asserted situation. I also discuss the distinct functions of egophoric factual and non-egophoric factual forms.

12.7.2 Narrow focus

According to Sung and Lha, both egophoric and non-egophoric forms indicate narrow focus, which is perhaps the most common function of either form in conservational discourse. When employed to express narrow focus, the egophoric factual commonly shows up in past interrogative clauses with second person arguments and in the responses to such questions. This distribution is illustrated in (81+82).

(81) *khyo.gnyi.ga   nam   thon   -nas?*
     2S.DU   when   arrive   -FCT.EGO
     'When did you two arrive?'
     (Sung and Lha 2005: 207)

(82) *ngi.gnyi.ga   da.so.ma   thon   -nas.*
     1S.DU   just.now   arrive   -FCT.EGO
     'We two just arrived.'
     (Sung and Lha 2005: 207)

The question in (81) presupposes that the interlocutors have arrived and also that the fact of their arrival itself is, in itself, not important information. What is important is the time of their arrival.

In certain high frequency (i.e., highly predictable) contexts, the factual egophoric also functions as an interrogative marker, obviating the need for the interrogative *ə=*, as in (83).

(83) *zama   zu   -ni?*
     food   eat.PFV   -FCT.EGO
     'Did you eat?'
     (Mgo log)

The utterance in (83) is a standard greeting to an acquaintance and is typically received with an equally formulaic response, *zu, zu*—'I ate, I ate,'—or, simply, *ja, ja*—'sure.' In (83), the event of eating is presumed and taken for granted, such that the entire clause represents general knowledge for both speaker and interlocutor, who are merely going through the motions of requesting and exchanging information for ritualistic, social reasons that have almost nothing to do with the content spoken. I have yet to come across the morphologically more complex *-nəjən* in this context.

When used to express narrow focus, the egophoric factual is not always confined to *origo* clauses. Example (84) was uttered by an Amdo Tibetan speaker from Hualong Hui Autonomous County, in Qinghai, in the midst of a conversation about a third person, the subject of (84), and her studies in the UK. As with (83), the use of *-ni* implies a question.

(84) *iŋlan   nam   joŋ   -ni*
     England   when   come   -FCT.EGO
     'When did (she) come (go) to England?'
     (Hualong)

According to Sung and Lha, the non-egophoric factual also occurs in narrow focus questions, as in (85), below (2005: 261). Note, that unlike (83), the clause is overtly marked as a question, via the interrogative form of the non-egophoric factual -ni.e.red.

(85) ʼdi   khi.dge   -s   thengs dang.bo a.mdo -ʼa
     this   3s   -ERG   time   first   Amdo   -DAT
     yul.bskor ye   -ni.e.red
     travel   do   -FCT.?NEGO
     'Is this his first time traveling in Amdo?'
     (Sung and Lha 2005: 261)

Additional examples of the distributional differences between egophoric and non-egophoric are provided in (86+87).

(86) tɕʰi   rdzəntə   χwetɕʰa   tɕʰəzəç   -a   ɸti   -nəjan
     2S.ERG   usually   book   what   -DAT see.PST   -FCT.EGO
     'Was für Bücher liest du üblicherweise?' ['What books do you usually read?']
     (Haller 2004: 144 [Them chen])

(87) mərgə   rdzəntə   χwetɕʰa   tɕʰəzəç   -a   ɸti   -nəre
     3S.F.ERG usually   book   what   -DAT see.PST   -FCT.NEGO
     'Was für Bücher liest sie üblicherweise?' ['What books does she usually read?']
     (Haller 2004: 144 [Them chen])

Both clauses in (86+87) highlight not the action of reading books, but what books are read. This information is foregrounded against the rest of the situation. The primary difference between the two post-verbal markers is due to the (speaker's perception of) volition of the agent. The agent in (86) is volitional because it is a second person (*origo*) agent in an interrogative clause with a controllable verb 'read'. Example (86) is therefore marked with the form *-nəjan*. The clause in (87) is non-volitional (meaning the speaker was not an intentional participant of the situation), because it has a third-person agent. Similarly, in Haller's analysis clauses with non-controllable verbs occur with the non-egophoric factual, regardless of whether the subject or agent is an *origo*. This distributional property is illustrated in example (88), below.

(88) ŋa   kʰu   -nəre
     1S   be.ill -FCT.NEGO
     'Ich bin Krank (und liege im Bett).' ['I am sick (and am lying in bed).']
     (Haller 2004: 144 [Them chen])

Sung and Lha offer insight into the connection between volition and egophoric marking: the egophoric factual (i.e., "subjective focus" marker, in their words) occurs in clauses that represent subjective, or egophoric, information for the speaker/addressee, while the non-egophoric occurs elsewhere.

Semantic controllable verbs take the egophoric marker in factual clauses when the agent is *origo* and the non-egophoric marker when the agent is a third person agent. Example (89), is an egophorically-marked, narrow focus clause. Because the verb is controllable and the speaker of the declarative clause is also the agent, making this a volitional clause, the egophoric marker is used.

(89) ŋi   kormo   bʑin   -nə
     1S.ERG money   give.PST -FCT.EGO
     'I'm the one who paid.'
     (Mgo log)

According to the consultant who produced (89), the most obvious context for this clause produced would be as an answer to the question, 'Who paid the bill?' (谁付的钱?). The use of a factual marker here, as opposed to an evidential marker, narrows the focus to a sub-element within the clause, in this case the identity of the agent. The answer to the question is framed in such a way as to emphasize the agent, rather than the entire act of paying, since the question itself pre-supposes that the act has taken place.

The use of the egophoric factual marker emphasizes the intention and control of the agent over the act of paying. It would be inappropriate to use the non-egophoric factual in this clause with a non-*origo* agent because paying bills is always construed as a controllable act. Conversely, using the egophoric factual with a non-controllable verb like 'be sick' is also odd, although my consultants don't seem to feel that the resulting clause means that the speaker intended to be sick, so much as they feel that it sounds like the speaker is boasting about their condition.

The exception to the alignment between the egophoric and the semantic property of volition in factual clauses is certain high frequency constructions such as (86) and (88) in which the egophoric factual form -*nəjan*, or its contractions -*ni* or -*na* implies a question. In high frequency questions, especially those that are intended to elicit formulaic responses, the egophoric factual is used in preference to the non-egophoric.

12.7.3 Neutral evidence

As stated above, Haller regards the two factual forms as encoding that a speaker has evidence for an assertion, while Sun, Shao and Sung and Lha regard them as being evidentially neutral, meaning they imply neither the presence nor absence of evidence. The egophoric vs. non-egophoric distinction marked in the factual can be analyzed as a distinction between subjective (egophoric) self-knowledge and objective (non-egophoric) knowledge. Such an analysis is in keeping with Haller (2004) as well as Sung and Lha (2005). However, in certain contexts, it is clear that epistemic, as opposed to evidential, concerns are paramount. In particular, in non-*origo* clauses, the choice of egophoric over non-egophoric factuals comes down to factors like the speaker's certainty (see Sun 1993: 951).[22]

There are thus reasons for analyzing the two factual markers as non-evidential, not least the fact that speakers themselves often describe these forms as expressing general knowledge or common sense. In certain speech genres, factual post-verbal markers, in particular the non-egophoric factual, outnumber evidential or epistemic post-verbal markers. According to Sun factuals rarely occur in conversation, but in my experience factual clauses occur in almost every extended conversation, although less frequently than evidential clauses. Factuals are, however, more dominant in some speech genres than others, occurring frequently in accounts of historical events, Buddhist teachings, classroom lectures, and other genres of monolog. For example, all three of the narratives recorded in Haller (2004: 176) favor non-egophoric factual to evidential post-verbal markers outside of direct speech. This distributional pattern is illustrated in (90). This is a complex sentence, containing four non-finite clauses including one that has an embedded direct quote of an imperative clause.

(90) tə,   wapkə   raŋ   -ɣə   sa   -na.ndol -nu,
     then,   at.all   self   -ERG   eat   -want   -CON
     wapkə   n̪tʰuŋ   -na.ndol -nu,   tɕʰəzəç,   jo   -na,
     not.even drink   -want   -CON,   something,   have   -if,
     wapkə   "ta   ndi   naŋa   ta   wop!"   bzi
     at.all   "now   this   inside   now   fall.IMP" say.PST
     -taŋ   -na,   ta   wap   -ɲdzoχ   -nəre!
     -PFV   -if,   now   fall.PST -COMPL.IPFV[23] -FCT.NEGO

---

[22] It would seem that in some contexts (most notably, narrow focus), however, the distinction between subjective and objective knowledge is unimportant, hence the "creep" of the egophoric form into third person volitional clauses like (89), above.

[23] This clause contains what is likely the completive Aktionsart marker -bʒəχ, here in the imperfective form, which is combined with a past tense stem for the verb 'fall.' Its function is also not addressed by Haller, who notes that this element, which he also identifies as identical to the lexical verb 'put,' always follows the perfecvtive stem in alternation with the imperative stem form zoχ (2004: 152/153). Note that in the Mgo log data, the tense-aspect form of this element always corresponds to that of the lexical verb stem, which it directly follows. The explanation for the combination of non-past lexical verb stem and past Aktionsart post-verbal marker in (89) is unclear to me. It may be a dialectal feature of Them chen or it may represent an irrealis or conditional construction.

'Wenn es jenes, etwas, gibt, das man gerne essen (oder) trinken möchte, und man, 'Fall nun hier hinein!' gesagt hat, ist (es in diese Tasse) schon hineingefallen!'
['So, if there is anything at all that one wanted to eat, anything at all that one wanted to drink, if there is anything at all, if one said, "So, fall inside here now!", then it would fall into the bowl!']
(Haller 2004: 152 [Them chen])

As we can see from (90), narrative Amdo Tibetan texts are characterized by long multi-predicate clause chains. Epistemic-factual-evidential post-verbal markers signaling, as they do, the end of a clause, are thus relatively rare compared to the quantity of non-finite clauses in a given text. Example (90), excerpted from a well known legendary account of an historical event, also demonstrates a factual clause that is not expressing narrow focus. Its assertion is about a situation that was true in the distant past. The speaker is not expected to have experienced the situation first-hand, nor to know anyone else who did. It is also likely that in the typical scenario in which this particular narrative would be told, the audience would include people already familiar with the story. Thus, the assertion in (90) represents general or common knowledge.

My primary Mgo log consultants feel that speakers typically have two reasons for choosing a neutral evidential form: the first is to express that the speaker has no evidence for the situation, but that she still believes what she is saying. Secondly, the speaker has known about a situation for a long time and chooses not to express how she knows about it because she knows it through various means. In either scenario, the use of a factual might also carry certain epistemic implications. Depending on the context, the speaker might be emphasizing the truthfulness of her assertion or she might be (humbly or cautiously) distancing herself as the source of information.

12.7.4 Future factuals

As with non-future factual clauses, the future factual construction distinguishes between egophoric and non-egophoric factuality, respectively -*dzəjən* (or -*dzi*) and -*dzəre*. Example (91) is a case of an egophoric future factual clause.

(91) *ngas   ka.ra   tsi.ge.zig   'debs   -rgyu.yin*
     1S.ERG   sugar   some   add.IPFV   -FUT.FCT.EGO
     'I will add a little sugar.'
     (Sung and Lha 2005: 223)

(92) khaŋ   mbap   -rdʐure
     snow   fall.NPST   -FUT.NEGO
     'It will snow.'
     (Mgo log)

Example (91) is marked with the egophoric future factual because the clause is volitional: the subject, who is the speaker, intends for the action of adding sugar to take place. Clauses such as (91) and (92) are the default way to express that a situation will be true in the future, so it might seem redundant to also label these forms as factual. However, there are multiple other ways to express future situations, in particular using epistemics as discussed below.

12.7.5 Other discourse functions of the factual: polite offers of help in Mgo log

There is one particular verbal construction in the Mgo log dialect (and probably others) that makes use of the element *re*, which occurs in all of the non-egophoric factual constructions. For this reason I refer to it as the non-egophoric intentional future. I have only encountered the interrogative form and, when asked outright, my consultants reject declarative forms. The function of the non-egophoric intentional future is to ask, in an indirect way, whether or not someone wants the speaker to perform a certain action. One consultant, an 18 year-old girl, provided the following examples as two ways for a host (usually a woman) to ask a guest essentially the same thing. Example (93) is the more direct way to ask if the person wants tea, and is not marked for tense-aspect or epistemic-factual-evidentiality. Example (94) is the more indirect way, not only for its use of a non-egophoric factual marker, which removes the volitional intent of the action from the scope of both speaker and listener, but also because it highlights not the drinking of tea, but the pouring of it. Example (94) thus provides multiple levels of distance from the host's intentions, giving the host room to say no without directly refusing the guest.

(93) tɕa   ə-   nthoŋ
     tea   Q-   drink
     'Are you going to drink?'
     (Mgo log)

(94) tɕa   blik   -ə-   re
     tea   pour   -Q-   FCT.NEGO
     'Should some tea be poured?'
     (Mgo log)

If the guest wishes to refuse the invitation in (93), he must do so by directly saying, 'I'm not drinking tea'. If he wishes to refuse the invitation in (94), however, he can simply respond by saying '*ma-re*', 'No'. The use of a factual in this instance provides a socially acceptable way for a guest to refuse a host. A guest in an Amdo Tibetan home typically consumes whatever food or drink the host offers. The less formal the relationship is, the less this rule applies. The verbal acts surrounding the offering and accepting of refreshments serve to reinforce this exchange between host and guest in more formal circumstances and to reduce the sense of obligation in less formal circumstances.

12.8 Epistemic modals

Unlike factuals, which assert that a situation is a fact, or evidentials, which assert the evidence one has about a situation, the Amdo Tibetan epistemic modal post-verbal markers express a speaker's degree of certainty about a given proposition. Modals are therefore used when a speaker either feels unsure about the provenance or truthfulness of the information that she is expressing, or else feels that it is more pertinent to assert her certainty that what she says is true rather than assert how she knows it. There appear to be a large number of modal post-verbal markers, but a complete tally and description of their various functions will have to await a more in-depth analysis than can be provided here. In the current section, I simply present a brief descriptions of a few epistemic modals.

As with evidential post-verbal markers (and to a greater extent than factual post-verbal markers), tense-aspect is an inherent component of the semantics of modal post-verbal markers. Also like evidential post-verbal markers, the temporal-aspectual senses of modal post-verbal markers appear to be non-compositional with regards to their etymological components. Example (95) is a past tense clause and examples (96) and (97) are future tense clause.

(95) nam   wap   -sare
     sky   rain.PST -PST.MOD
     'It probably rained.'
     (Mgo log[24])

---

[24] Not all of the Amdo Tibetan speakers who have helped me over the years recognize the constructions in (95–96). Two of my young female consultants, for example, understand these clauses to mean, literally, 'I have a place to rain' (which is, of course, just nonsense) for (96), and 'This is a place where it rains' for (95). These two speakers are from a different clan than my main Mgo log consultants and members of both clans with whom I have worked have said that they feel that slight differences exist between the two groups' speech.

(96) *nam   mbap   -sajot*
     sky   rain.NPST   -IMD.FUT.MOD
     'It's probably going to rain (any minute).'
     (Mgo log)

(97) *saŋɲin   khaŋ   mbap   khare*
     tomorrow snow   rain.NPST   -FUT.MOD
     'It's probably going to snow tomorrow.'
     (Mgo log)

Example (95) is of a past tense clause expressing a situation for which the speaker has no evidence, but which she feel moderately confident took place. Example (96) is of an immediate future tense clause, deduced from experience and logic, but nonetheless slightly less certain than a similar clause marked with the future factual. Example (97) is a future tense clause, predicting an event that will happen after a longer period of time than that in (96). According to the person who uttered (96), this assertion is less confident or certain than that of a propositionally similar, evidentially marked clause in (23) (see §4.2.2). It appears that the use of evidential post-verbal markers in non-future clauses by default express that the speaker is more certain or confident of an assertion than any modal post-verbal marker.

With regards to their compositionality, both modal post-verbal markers in (95+96) contain the element *sa*, along with etymological elements that recognizable occur in other post-verbal markers, so it is tempting to analyze the element *sa* as providing the modal function to both clauses. However, there is no synchronically transparent reason to analyze the element *jot* in (96) as expressing a future or imperfective sense, nor is there any such reason for analyzing the element *re* in (97) as providing a perfective sense. However, the use of a factual post-verbal marker may, in some contexts, imply an even greater certainty or confidence than the use of an evidential post-verbal marker. In other contexts, however, as noted above in §6, factual post-verbal markers may simply imply lack of evidence or the irrelevance of evidence.

Both (96) and (97), along with a future factual construction, could be used to express an event that the speaker thinks will happen shortly after the time of speech, but (96) emphasizes the immediateness of the anticipated event. Of the three above future clauses, two consultants ranked (96) as the most likely to become true, followed by (96). Example (96) was judged to be "uncertain" (不确定性). The greater certainty of (96) over (97) might have something to do with time. Because (96) explicitly encodes that a situation is anticipated to happen immediately, its falsifiability is also more immediate than for (97), which merely holds that an event is expected to take place sometime after the time of speech.

12.9 Epistemic-factual-evidential distinctions in copular clauses

My argument in this contribution has been that grammatical evidentiality in Amdo Tibetan is part of a larger paradigm, which includes epistemic and factual markers. The contrast among grammaticalized evidence, epistemic stance and factuality is perhaps clearest in equative copular clauses, which do not express tense-aspect distinctions, and thus present a slightly less complex paradigm. However, equative copular clauses do not distinguish as many categories as are distinguished in verbal clauses. I have not conducted extensive research on Amdo Tibetan copular clauses, but the system appears to correspond closely to the Standard Tibetan system. The largest number of distinctions appears to be made within the epistemic category. Examples (98–102), below, illustrate egophoric factual, non-egophoric factual, evidential (EVID) and two epistemic markers in equative copular clauses.

(98) ŋa   rgəgen   jin
      1S   teacher COP.EGO
      'I'm a teacher.'
      (Mgo log)

(99) khərgə ʂkima   -ziç   re
      3S   thief   -IDF   COP.NEGO
      'He's a thief.'
      (Mgo log)

(100) khərgə ʂkima   ziç   jinzəç
      3S   thief   -IDF   COP.EVID
      'He's a thief.' (Speaker has evidence to back this accusation.)
      (Mgo log)

(101) khərgə ʂkima   ziç   jinkhare
      1S   thief   -IDF   COP.MOD$_1$
      'He might be a thief.'
      (Mgo log)

(102) tə   blama X   -kə   khoŋwa   jindzịreko
      DEF   lama X   -GEN   house   COP.MOD$_2$[25]
      'It is most likely Lama X's[26] house.'
      (Mgo log)

The egophoric equative copula (COP.EGO) occurs primarily with clauses that have either *origo* subjects, and less commonly (and under pragmatically marked circumstances) with *origo* genitive arguments. The non-egophoric equative copula (COP.NEGO) occurs with every other type of subject, and occurs regardless of whether or not the speaker has direct, indirect or no evidence for the assertion. Hence, the clause in (99) might be about the speaker's own brother, a character in a movie she saw, or somebody she heard about from a friend. The copula *re*, therefore, appears to be evidentially neutral, as is the copula *jin*. Both forms merely express a fact, without entailing any evidence. The only difference is that *jin* clauses must be about the *origo*, while *re* clauses must be about a non-*origo*.

Clauses (99–102) encode essentially identical propositions. The primary difference between them is essentially their respective epistemic-factual-evidential values. As stated, the clause in (99) is factual, and does not indicate how the speaker knows the subject is a thief, nor does it indicate her degree of confidence about her assertion.

The clause in (100) indicates that the speaker is basing her accusation on evidence of some sort. I mark the copula in (100) as COP.EVID because it is not clear whether her evidence is direct or indirect. The consultant who produced the clauses in (99), (100) and (101) explained that she felt like the evidence for (101) was probably indirect, since if one were to directly witness a person stealing something, one would probably just say so and then use the clause in (106). On the other hand, the consultant also explained that the clause in (99) might be used for someone who steals a lot and so, rather than using a verbal clause to describe a singular act of theft, directly witnessed or not, the speaker has chosen to use an equative construction to express an integral, time-stable trait of the subject. She felt another reason to use the evidential form in (100) is to emphasize the claim being made: the speaker is positive that the subject is a thief because

---

25 The form *jindzịreko* is actually a multimorphemic construction consisting of the modal equative copula *jindzịre* and modal particle -*ko*, which I've only encountered in Mgo log. Note that while *jindzịre* appears to contain the non-egophoric future factual -*dzịre*, it actually does not. In Mgo log, the non-egophoric future is pronounced -*dzure*. My consultants are especially clear on pronouncing the two forms differently.

26 As I have not asked the famous lama in question for permission to use his name in this study, I am omitting it from this data.

she has evidence that this so ("他肯定是个小偷*ze* [(She) says, he is definitely a thief."]). The evidential copula is used to express the speaker's total commitment to the truthfulness of what she is saying. Thus, the clause in (100) might be uttered under two different pragmatic contexts. One context is to express that the speaker does not have direct evidence to support her assertion, but has indirect evidence. The second context is to emphasize that the speaker has evidence to support her assertion, and is not merely repeating information she heard elsewhere or making groundless accusations.

In contrast with (100), the clause in (101), which is epistemically marked, expresses the speaker's lack of total commitment to the assertion. The clause in (102) also expresses that the speaker is not completely committed to the truthfulness of her assertion, but is slightly more certain of what she is saying than the speaker of (101).

As the examples presented in this section indicate, independently of tense-aspect, evidentiality, factuality and epistemic modality form a larger grammatical category that operates as a morphosyntactic paradigm.

12.10 Conclusion

Evidential markers in Amdo Tibetan are semantically complex: they express tense-aspect and also function as finitizing markers, expressing the end of a clause. Their distribution is influenced by many factors unrelated to evidence, including tense-aspect, the semantic features of controllability and volition, and also the lexical aspect of a clause. Moreover, the evidential value of a given marker may vary depending on these factors, as we saw in the case of the progressive aspect marker *-ko(t)* being employed to express direct evidence in verbs expressing internal emotional states in clauses with non-*origo* subjects (§6.3). Finally, evidential markers form part of a larger paradigm together with markers that express epistemic modality and factuality (i.e., are epistemically and evidentially neutral).

Abbreviations

ABS absolutive, AUX auxiliary, COMPL completive Aktionsart, CNC conclusive Aktionsart, CON connective, COND conditional, COP copula, DAT dative, DE direct evidential, DET determiner, DU dual, EGO egophoric, EMPH emphatic, ERG ergative, EVID evidential, EXT existential copula, FCT factive, FUT future, GEN genitive, IDF indefinite, IE indirect evidential, IMP imperative, IMD immediate,

INS instrumental, IPFV imperfective, JUS jussive, LOC locative, MIR mirative, MOD modal, NEG negative, NEGO non-egophoric, NF non-finite, NMLZ nominalizer, NPST non-past, NVOL non-volitional, PART particle, PRF perfect, PFV perfective, PROG progressive, PST past, Q interrogative, TRANS transitive action perfectivity marker.

References

Aikhenvald, Alexandra Y. 2004. *Evidentiality*. Oxford: Oxford University Press.
Chafe, Wallace. 1986. *Evidentiality in English conversation and academic writing*. In Wallace L. Chafe and Johanna Nichols (eds.), *Evidentiality: the linguistic coding of epistemology*, 261–272. Norwood, N. J.: Ablex Pub. Corp.
Chang, Kun & Betty Chang. 1984. The certainty hierarchy among Spoken Tibetan verbs of being. *Bulletin of the Institute of History and Philology, Academia Sinica* 55. 603–635.
Chen, Naixiong (陈乃雄). 1987. *Baoanyu he Mengguyu* 保安语和蒙古语 [The Baonan Language and the Mongolian Language]. Hohhot: 内蒙古人民出版社 Neimenggu Renmin Chubanshe.
Chen, Naixiong (陈乃雄). 1989. Wutun hua de dong ci xing tai 五屯话的动词形态 [Verb forms of Wutun speech]. *Minzu Yuwen*《民族语文》[Minority Languages of China] 6. 26–37.
Caplow, Nancy. 2000. *The epistemic marking system of émigré Dokpa Tibetan*. Santa Barbara: University of California.
Comrie, Bernard. 1976. *Aspect: An introduction to the study of verbal aspect and related problems*. Cambridge: Cambridge University Press.
Cornillie, Bert. 2009. Evidentiality and epistemic modality: on the close relationship between two different categories. *Functions of language* 16(1). 44–62.
DeLancey, Scott. 1984. Notes on agentivity and causation. *Studies in Language* 8(4). 181–213.
DeLancey, Scott. 1985. Lhasa Tibetan evidentials and the semantics of causation. *Proceedings of the Annual Meeting of the Berkeley Linguistics Society* 11. 65–72.
DeLancey, Scott. 1990. Ergativity and the cognitive model of event structure in Lhasa Tibetan. *Cognitive Linguistics* 1(3). 289–321.
DeLancey, Scott. 1991. The origins of verb serialization in Modern Tibetan. *Studies in Language* 15(3). 1–23.
DeLancey, Scott. 1992. The historical status of the conjunct/disjunct pattern in Tibeto-Burman. *Acta Linguistica Hafniensia* 25. 39–62.
Dwyer, Arienne. 1995. From the Northwest China Sprachbund: Xúnhuà Chinese dialect data. *Yuen Ren Society treasury of Chinese dialect data* 1(2). 143–182.
Dwyer, Arienne M. 1998. The Turkic stratigraphy of Salar: An Oghuz in Chagatay clothes? *Turkic Languages* 2(1). 49–83.
Ebihara, Shiho. 2009a. Morphophonological alternation of suffixes, clitics and stems in Amdo Tibetan. 国立民族学博物館研究報告*National museum of ethnology research report* 33(4). 639–660.
Ebihara, Shiho. 2009b. Verbs concerning 'intentionality' and 'directionality' in Amdo Tibetan. In Nagano, Yasuhiko (ed.), *Linguistic substratum in Tibet: New perspective towards historical methodology (No. 16102001) report Vol.3*, 101–114. Suita: National Museum of Ethnology.

Ebihara, Shiho. 2011. Amdo Tibetan. *Tokyo University of Foreign Studies grammatical sketches from the field*. 41–78.

Foley, William & R. van Valin. 1984. *Functional syntax and universal grammar*. Cambridge: Cambridge University Press.

Garrett, Edward J. 2001. *Evidentiality and assertion in Tibetan*. Los Angeles: University of California dissertation.

Gawne, Lauren. 2013. *Lamjung Yolmo copulas in use: Evidentiality, reported speech and questions*. Melbourne: The University of Melbourne dissertation.

Gawne, Lauren. this volume. Egophoric evidentiality in Bodish languages. In Lauren Gawne & Nathan W. Hill (eds.) *Evidentiality in Tibetan languages*, 61–94. Berlin; Boston: Mouton de Gruyter.

Goldstein, Melvyn (ed). 2001. *The new Tibetan-English dictionary of Modern Tibetan*. Berkeley: University of California Press.

Green, Jeffrey R. 2012. Amdo Tibetan media intelligibility. *SIL International Electronic Survey Report* 2012–019.

de Haan, Ferdinand. 2005. Encoding speaker perspective: evidentials. *Linguistic diversity and language theories* 72: 379–397.

Hale, Austin. 1980. Person markers: Finite conjunct and disjunct verb forms in Newari. *Papers in South-East Asian linguistics* 7. 95–106.

Haller, Felix. 2000. Verbal categories of Shigatse Tibetan and Them chen Tibetan. *Linguistics of the Tibeto-Burman Area* 23(4). 175–191.

Haller, Felix. 2004. *Dialekt und Erzählungen von Them chen: sprachwissenschaftliche Beschreibung eines Nomadendialektes aus Nord-Amdo*. Bonn: VGH Wissenschaftsverlag.

Hargreaves, David. 2005. Agency and intentional action in Kathmandu Newar. *Himalayan Linguistics* 5. 1–48.

Hill, Nathan W. 2013a. Contextual semantics of 'Lhasa' Tibetan evidentials. *SKASE Journal of Theoretical Linguistics* 10(5). 47–54.

Hill, Nathan W. 2013b. Old Chinese *sm- and the Old Tibetan word for 'fire'. *Cahiers de Linguistique Asie Orientale* 42(1). 60–71.

Hongladarom, Krisadawan. 1996. On the emergence of epistemic meanings: a study of Tibetan deitic motion verbs. *Mon-Khmer studies* 25. 15–28.

Hua, Kan (华侃). 1982. Anduo fangyan fufuyin shengmu he fuyin yunwei de yanbian qingkuang 安多方言复辅音声母和辅音韵尾的演变情况 [Changes in consonant cluster onsets and consonant codas of Amdo dialects]. *Xibei minzudaxue xuebao: zhexue shekui ke xueban* 《西北民族大学学报：哲学社会科学版》 [Northwest Nationalities University School Press: Philosophical social studies report] 1. 26–34.

Jacques, Guillaume. 2014. A phonological profile of Cone. In Jackson T. S. Sun (ed.), *Phonological profiles of little-studied Tibetic varieties*, 269–375. Taipei: Academia Sinica.

Janhunen, Juha. 2012. On the hierarchy of structural convergence in the Amdo *Sprachbund*. In Pirkko Suihkonen, Bernard Comrie & Valery Solovyev (eds.), *Argument structure and grammatical relations: A crosslinguistic typology*, 126–177. Amsterdam: John Benjamins.

Janhunen, Juha & Kalsang Norbu. 2014. Aspects of Amdo Tibetan segmental phonology. *Studia Orientalia Electronica* 85. 249–276.

Norbu, Kelsang, Karl Peet, dPal ldan bKra shis & Kevin Stuart. 2000. *Modern Oral Amdo Tibetan: A language primer*. Lewiston, New York & Lampeter, Wales: Edwin Mellen Press.

Qinggeertai. 1991. *Tuzu yu he menggu yu* 土族语和蒙古语 [The Tu language and the Mongolian language]. Hohhot: 内蒙古人民出版社 Neimengu remin chubanshes.
de Roerich, Georges. 1958. *Le parler de l'Amdo. Etude de une dialect archaique du Tibet*. Rome: Istituto italiano per il Medio ed Estremo Oriente.
Shao, Mingyuan (邵明园). 2014. Anduo zangyu arou hua de shizheng fanchou 安多藏语阿柔话的示证范畴 [Evidentiality in A-rig Dialect of Amdo Tibetan]. Nankai: Nankai University dissertation.
Slater, Keith W. 2003. *A Grammar of Mangghuer: A Mongolic Language of China's Qinghai-Gansu Sprachbund*. London & New York: Routledge Curzon.
Sun, Jackson T.-S. 1993. Evidentials in Amdo Tibetan. *Bulletin of the Institute of History and Philology, Academia Sinica* 63(4). 944–1001.
Sung, Kuo-Ming & Lha Byams Rgyal. 2005. *Colloquial Amdo Tibetan: A Complete Course for Adult English Speakers*. Xining: Krung go'i bod rig pa dpe skrun khang.
Tai, James. 2003. Cognitive relativism: Resultative construction in Chinese. *Language and linguistics* 4(2). 301–316.
Tournadre, Nicolas. 1996. *L'ergativé en tibétain modern, approche morphosyntaxique de la langue parlée*. Leuven: Peeters.
Tournadre, Nicolas. 2008. Arguments against the concept of 'conjunct'/'disjunct' in Tibetan. In Brigitte Huber, Marianne Volkart & Paul Widmer (eds.), *Chomolangma, Demawend und Kasbek: Festschrift für Roland Bielmeier zu seinem 65. Geburtstag*, 281–308. Halle (Saale): International Institute for Tibetan and Buddhist Studies.
Tournadre, Nicolas. 2014. The Tibetic languages and their classification. In Tom Owen-Smith & Nathan W. Hill (eds.), *Trans-Himalayan linguistics, historical and descriptive linguistics of the Himalayan area*, 105–130. Berlin & New York: Mouton de Gruyter.
Tournadre, Nicholas & Randy J. LaPolla. 2014. Towards a new approach to evidentiality: Issues and directions for research. *Linguistics of the Tibeto-Burman Area* 37(4). 240–263.
Tournadre, Nicolas & Sangda Dorje. 2003. *Manual of Standard Tibetan: Language and Civilization: Introduction to Standard Tibetan (spoken and Written) Followed by an Appendix on Classical Literary Tibetan*. Ithaca: Snow Lion Publications.
Vendler, Zeno. 1957. Verbs and times. *The philosophical Review* Apr 1. 143–160.
Vokurková, Zuzana. 2008. *Epistemic modalities in spoke Standard Tibetan*. Charles University, Prague, and University of Paris 8 dissertation.
Wang, Shuangcheng. 2011. 玛多藏语的声调 Maduo Zangyu de shengdiao [Tones in Maduo Tibetan]. *Minzu Yuwen* 《民族语文》 [Minority Languages of China] 3. 26–32.
Widmer, Manuel. 2014. *A descriptive grammar of Bunan*. Bern: University of Bern dissertation.
Wylie, Turrell. 1959. A standard system of Tibetan transcription. *Harvard Journal of Asiatic studies*. 261–267.

Hiroyuki Suzuki
13 The evidential system of Zhollam Tibetan

13.1 Introduction

Zhollam [*zhol lam*][1] Tibetan (a.k.a. Gagatang Tibetan) belongs to the Melung [*'ba' lung*] subgroup of the Sems-kyi-nyila [*sems kyi nyi zla*] group of Khams [*khams*] Tibetan[2] and is spoken in Gagatang 嘎嘎塘 administrative village, Pantiange 攀天阁 Township, Weixi 维西 County, Diqing 迪庆 [*bde chen*] Prefecture, Yunnan 云南, PRC. I estimate that there are fewer than 1,000 speakers of Zhollam, mainly living in the three hamlets of Gaga 嘎嘎, Shaoluo 勺洛, and Mulu 木鲁. Most are bilingual in Zhollam Tibetan and the Weixi dialect of Chinese. The use of Tibetan by the younger generation is decreasing and it is likely that Zhollam Tibetan will become endangered in the next generation.

This contribution aims to provide a brief description of the overall system of evidential categories in Zhollam Tibetan. Suzuki (2012a) previously described the usage of /⁻ŋɔŋ/ (WrT *snang*) to express evidential meanings. That publication also elucidated that the egophoric in Zhollam Tibetan is an "egophoric vs. non-egophoric" type[3] (Gawne, this volume). Nonetheless, the previous study's lexical focus makes it insufficient for gaining an overview of the evidential system of this dialect. As evidential systems vary greatly, even across a small geographic region, within this contribution I use "Zhollam Tibetan" to designate only the variety spoken in Shaoluo Hamlet,

---

[1] In this publication, Written Tibetan (WrT) forms are in italics and romanised based on the system of René de Nebesky-Wojkowitz (1956: xv).
[2] The dialectal classification in this study basically follows Suzuki (2009). For linguistic features distinguishing the Melung subgroup from the others, see Suzuki (2013).
[3] The definition of the term 'Tibetic' follows Tournadre (2014).

Note: An earlier version of this chapter was presented at the 24th Annual Meeting of the Southeast Asian Linguistics Society (Yangon, 2014). Many thanks are owed to my collaborator He Qun and her mother He Chunzhi. I should also like to thank Nathan W. Hill, Nicolas Tournadre, and Lauren Gawne for their insightful comments. I am also grateful to Gerald Roche and Ellen Bartee for ameliorating my English. Field research was conducted in Weixi, Shangri-La, and Kunming, funded by three Grants-in-Aid for Scientific Research from the Japan Society for the Promotion of Science [JSPS]: "Dialectological Study of the Tibetan Minority Languages in the Tibetan Cultural Area in West Sichuan" (headed by the present author), "International Field Survey of the rGyalrongic Languages" (headed by Yasuhiko Nagano, No. 21251007), and "Study on the Dialectal Development of Tibetan Spoken in Yunnan, China, through a Description of the Linguistic Diversity" (headed by the present author, No. 25770167).

DOI 10.1515/9783110473742-013

from where data for this study were collected. The description given here relies on examples from natural conversation, supplemented with elicited data.

This contribution provides a description of the Zhollam Tibetan evidential system, classifying the relevant verbs into three groups: copulative, existential, and general verbs. An exhaustive description of the epistemic meaning of these verbs, such as Vokurková's for Lhasa Tibetan (2008), is not feasible at this time.[4]

13.1.1 Overview of terminology and the Zhollam evidential

Tournadre and LaPolla define evidential marking as "the representation of source and access to information according to the speaker's perspective and strategy" (2014: 241). Following this definition, the evidential system of Zhollam Tibetan can be divided into two major features: egophoric and non-egophoric, both of which include subsidiary features regarding source and access to information. These two categories vary depending on the nature of verbs. From the viewpoint of a syntactic description of evidentiality, the verbs of Zhollam Tibetan can be classified into three categories: copulative, existential,[5] and general verbs. Morphologically, the egophoric is expressed in each of the verb categories; in addition, other specific source and access to information are reflected in the existential and general verbs only. For general verbs, evidentiality is expressed with verbal suffixes, some of which have arisen from copulative and existential verbs.

This essay adopts the terms 'egophoric' versus 'non-egophoric' as discussed in section 13.2. Based on Tournadre and LaPolla (2014: 243), 'egophoric' functions to indicate personal knowledge. And although Suzuki (2012) uses "self-oriented" instead of "egophoric", here I prefer to adhere to the terminology of Tournadre (2008). There are different terms used for "egophoric" (Tournadre 2008), and its counterpart (e.g. *self-person* vs. *other-person*;[6] egophoric vs. *alterophoric*[7]), but Zhollam Tibetan is not "A vs. B" type but "A vs. non-A" type, and "A" should be *self-oriented* i.e. *egophoric* (see §2 for details).

---

[4] The description in §2.1 is an extract from Suzuki (2012: 3–6), and that in §3.1 is based on Suzuki (2012: 6–10).
[5] Suzuki (2012) uses the term 'predicative verb' for copulative and existential verbs because their grammatical behaviour coincides and differs from other general verbs. They can serve either as a main verb or as an auxiliary verb. This term is, in fact, quite similar to another term 'copula', which is hereafter avoided because of its indifference to the distinction between the 'copulative' and the 'existential'. This study separates these two verb categories, because their evidential strategies differ. Following this treatment, the gloss of copulative verbs is not COP but CPV.
[6] The terminology used in Sun (1993: 955).
[7] The terminology used in Post (2013).

Access to information in Zhollam is sensitive to visual perception. There are several verbal suffixes which indicate access to information, which distinguish visual perception from non-visual perceptions as direct sensory information. In addition, supposition, hearsay, etc., also belong to the evidential system in Zhollam.

13.1.2 A note on the phonetic transcription

In order to give detailed phonetic forms, which is indispensable to dialectology, this contribution employs the conventions of "pandialectal phonetic description" (Tournadre and Suzuki forthcoming), which includes several specific phonetic symbols defined by Zhu (2010) in addition to the symbols of the International Phonetic Alphabet. The tones, which the author has previously analysed as part of a word-tone system (Suzuki 2011), are noted as follows:

¯: high-level   ´: rising   `: falling   ˆ: rising-falling/mid-level.

Tones in square brackets, using 5-grade-Chao numbers, are employed in order to describe a detailed tonal realisation.

13.2 Copulative verbs

13.2.1 Description

The basic evidential distinction in the Zhollam system is *egophoric* (CPV1) versus *non-egophoric* (CPV2). Zhollam makes this distinction with the two declarative verb stems /´jĩ/[8] (and its negative counterpart /´mẽ/) for egophoric and /¯ŋɔŋ/ for non-egophoric.

Tab. 1: Copulative verbs.

		Egophoric	Non-egophoric
declarative	positive	´jĩ	¯ŋɔŋ
	negative	´mẽ	´mi-ŋɔŋ
interrogative	positive	ʔa-jĩ / ´jĩ ´jẽ[9]	¯ŋɔŋ ´mẽ
	negative	non-attested	

---

[8] This form is sometimes pronounced as [zɿ:²⁴, zʅi:²⁴].
[9] The difference between the two forms is not yet evident. Based on the usage in conversations, the latter form does not mean a tag question. The tag question marker in Zhollam Tibetan is /´ʔa ŋɔŋ/ or /´ʔa ŋə/.

One could construct interrogative negative sentences theoretically (e.g. *ˇʔa ˊmẽ), but the native speakers reject such formulations.

In the following, I give examples of the declarative usage with different person subjects:[10]

(1) a ˊŋA-∅ ˊpiː-∅ ˊjĩ / *ˉŋɔŋ
       1-ABS Tibetan-ABS CPV1 / *CPV2
       'I am Tibetan.'
    b ˉtɕʰɵʔ-∅ ˊpiː-∅ ˊjĩ / *ˉŋɔŋ
       2-ABS Tibetan-ABS CPV1 / *CPV2
       'You are Tibetan.'
    c ˋmA-∅-de ˉpʰɑː-∅ ˊjĩ / ˉŋɔŋ
       this-ABS-TOP pig-ABS CPV1 / CPV2
       'This is a pig.'

Based on the judgement of speakers, the use of /ˉŋɔŋ/ in any of the examples shown in (1) is ungrammatical as it is only permitted in clauses with a 3rd person subject, as expected of a non-egophoric form. Note that Zhollam Tibetan normally uses an egophoric form for a 2nd person subject in declarative sentences, which is not the case in the egophoric systems seen in other Tibetic languages (cf. Tournadre 2008). However, there is a certain overlap with /ˊjĩ/, which can also be used in clauses with a 3rd person subject as in (1c). The semantic difference between these two verbs is related to the speaker's attitude toward the proposition. The egophoric option /ˊjĩ/ is especially used for an expression in which the subject is directly related to speakers and addressees, which corresponds to the 'broad egophoric' mentioned in Tournadre (2008: 296) and Gawne (this volume), whereas the non-egophoric counterpart /ˉŋɔŋ/ is used for an expression lacking ego knowledge:

(2) a ˉkʰɣ-∅ ˊpiː-∅ ˉŋɔŋ
       3-ABS Tibetan-ABS CPV2
       'S/He is Tibetan.' (situation: introducing a person)
    b ˉkʰɣ-∅ ˊpiː-∅ ˊjĩ
       3-ABS Tibetan-ABS CPV1
       'S/He is Tibetan (situation: after an introduction of (2a), the speaker of (2b) is aware that: "we are the same ethnic group").'

---

[10] I do not indicate zero marked locatives in the glossing.

Example (2a) is an objective statement of common knowledge, whereas (2b) expresses a certain relation with the speaker, i.e. it is an egophoric enunciation, which may include an inferential meaning.[11] This distinction also applies to sentence (1c), in which, if the speaker wanted to convey more about the pig relative to the speaker, (for example, "it is mine" or "of my family"), /ˊjĩ/ is also acceptable. Note that Zhollam Tibetan has only one *non-egophoric* form and no other choices in an equational statement.

The negative counterpart of /ˊjĩ/ is /ˊmẽ/ and of /ˉŋɔŋ/ is /ˊmi-ŋɔŋ/.

(3) acceptability: negation
    a ˆŋA-Ø   ˋliː biː mə-Ø   ˊmẽ / *ˊmi-ŋɔŋ
       1-ABS   farmer-ABS   CPV1.NEG / *NEG-CPV2
       'I am not a farmer.'
    b ˉtɕʰɯʔ-Ø   ˆpiː-Ø   ˊmẽ / *ˊmi-ŋɔŋ
       2-ABS   Tibetan-ABS   CPV1.NEG / *NEG-CPV2
       'You are not Tibetan.'
    c ˉkʰγ-Ø   ˊsẽ zɯ mə-Ø   ˊmẽ / ˊmi-ŋɔŋ
       3-ABS   cook-ABS   CPV1.NEG / NEG-CPV2
       'S/He is not a cook.'

As shown in (3c), when the subject is 3rd person, /ˊmẽ/ and /ˊmi-ŋɔŋ/ are interchangeable just as they were in (1c) and (2). The examples in (4) show how a speaker can express different nuances about the same fact. In (4a) the speaker uses a non-egophoric negative in the first clause, then an egophoric declarative in the second clause, but in (4b) the speaker uses egophoric forms for both clauses.

(4) a ˆmA-Ø-de   ˋkʰγ-kʰɔŋ   ˊmi-ŋɔŋ   ˆŋa-kʰɔŋ   ˊjĩ
       3-ABS-TOP   3-GEN   NEG-CPV2   1-GEN   CPV1
       'This is not his/hers but mine.'
    b ˆmA-Ø-de   ˆŋA-kʰɔŋ   ˊjĩ   ˋkʰγ-kʰɔŋ   ˊmẽ
       2-ABS-TOP   1-GEN   CPV1   3-GEN   CPV1.NEG
       'This is mine and not his/hers.'

The following yes-no questions in (5) shows a restriction of the interrogative prefix /ˉʔa-/, which can precede almost all verbs, but not /ˉŋɔŋ/. This behaviour of /ˉŋɔŋ/ in interrogative phrases when it functions as an equational copula

---

[11] Based on the present data of Zhollam Tibetan, it appears that the use of the egophoric copulative verb (CPV1) requires involvement or close relationship of ego forms. However, when conducting field research, I have never noticed any difference between the two concepts "being related/personally involved" and "personal knowledge". Cf. §2.2.

means /ˉɲɔŋ/ is not a typical verb. The egophoric form is used for the 2nd person subject in interrogative sentences. This is generally called "anticipation usage", since the addressee will presumably use the egophoric in his answer (Tournadre and LaPolla 2014; Tournadre, this volume).

(5) acceptability: interrogative
 a ˉtɕʰɤʔ-Ø   ˉli su-Ø   ˀa-jĩ / *ˇʔa-ɲɔŋ
   1-ABS   Lisu   Q-CPV1 / *Q-CPV2
   'Are you Lisu?'
 b ˇmʌ-Ø-de   ˉpʰɑː-Ø   ˀʔa-jĩ / *ˇʔa-ɲɔŋ
   this-ABS-TOP pig-ABS   ?Q-CPV1 / *Q-CPV2
   'Is this a pig?'

Adding /ˊʔa-/, the speaker always uses /ˊjĩ/. */ˇʔa-ɲɔŋ/ cannot be used parallel to the declarative expression; it is completely rejected by native speakers. This means that the verbal morphosyntactic construction differs with respect to /ˊjĩ/ and /ˉɲɔŋ/. As shown in (5), the prefix /ˀa-/ cannot make an interrogative sentence with /ˉɲɔŋ/, but there is another way to form an interrogative phrase, namely to add a suffix /ˊjɛ̃/[12] (following /ˊjĩ/) or /ˊmɛ̃/[13] (following /ˉɲɔŋ/):

(6) acceptability: interrogative
 a ˉtɕʰɤʔ-Ø   ˊʂɣː lɔŋ wa-Ø   ˊjĩ   ˊjɛ̃
   1-ABS   person from Zhollam-ABS CPV1 Q
   'Are you from Zhollam?'
 b ˇmʌ-Ø-de   ˉpʰɑː-Ø   ˉɲɔŋ   ˊmɛ̃
   this-ABS-TOP pig-ABS   CPV2   Q
   'Is this a pig?'

In sentence (6a), /ˉɲɔŋ/ can also be used, but the meaning changes a little. It seeks to confirm the speaker's knowledge:

(7) ˉtɕʰɤʔ-Ø   ˊʂɣː lɔŋ wa-Ø   ˉɲɔŋ   ˊmɛ̃
   1-ABS   person from Zhollam-ABS CPV2   Q
   'You are from Zhollam, aren't you?'

The answer to questions (6) can be formed only with /ˊjĩ/ (negative /ˊmɛ̃/) and /ˉɲɔŋ/ (negative /ˊmi-ɲɔŋ/) respectively. So as an answer to (7), /ˊjĩ/ must be used.

---

[12] This form is pronounced not only as [jɛ̃²⁴], but also as [je²⁴ ɦã⁵⁵].
[13] This form is pronounced not only as [mɛ̃²⁴, mjɛ̃²⁴], but also as [me²⁴ ɦã⁵⁵].

There is one example in which only /ˉn̥ɔŋ/ is used for the 1st person subject:

(8) ˊŋA-Ø   ˋkwɔː-Ø   *ˊjĩ / ˉn̥ɔŋ
    1-ABS   who-ABS   *CPV1 / CPV2
    'Who am I?'

(8) is acceptable only if the speaker has lost her memory, because of which the non-egophoric copulative verb is selected. A loss of memory designates inaccessibility to ego knowledge, hence this situation triggers the use of the non-egophoric marker/morpheme.

To summarise the evidential distinctions of the copulative verbs, /ˊjĩ/ and /ˊmẽ/ are egophoric, whereas /ˉn̥ɔŋ/ is not.

13.2.2 Typological remarks

The copulative verbs in Zhollam Tibetan show a morphological distinction reflecting an egophoric value. Other evidential categories such as visual perception and inferential expression are generally not specified in utterances with copulative verbs. My analysis is that the use of an *egophoric* form is prominent, whereas *non-egophoric* is not, which means that the speaker cannot select *non-egophoric* features with a specific intention. Therefore, we can call the system of Zhollam "A vs. non-A" type. This analysis implies that two or more features (e.g. *self* vs. *other*) within the egophoric are unnecessary in Zhollam.

The egophoric of copulative verbs in Zhollam Tibetan seems to be similar to many Tibetic languages described in Tournadre and Konchok Jiatso (2001), however, Gawne (this volume) claims that it is not identical in each Tibetic language. Compared with the system of copulative verbs in Lhasa Tibetan (Tournadre and Sangda Dorje 2009: 410/411) as well as Lhoke (Drenjongke) (Gawne, this volume), Zhollam Tibetan has *only one* non-egophoric form and no other choices such as factual or inferential.

Another point is the difference between "being related/personally involved" and "personal knowledge". Some Tibetic languages like Lhasa Tibetan require involvement/close relationship of ego forms but in other languages such as Yolmo (see Gawne 2013: 192/193) the "ego forms" refer only to personal knowledge, not involvement or relationship. At present, I cannot definitely claim to which category Zhollam belongs, however, my field data leads me to assume it would be closer to Lhasa Tibetan (cf. examples (2b), (4b)).

The usage of /ˉn̥ɔŋ/ (WrT *snang*) as a copulative verb stem is unique to the Melung subgroup to which Zhollam Tibetan belongs. It is not attested to in other Tibetan languages and dialects (Suzuki 2014). The use of *snang* as a copulative verb is derived from its existential use (Suzuki 2012). In many Tibetic languages and dialects, the descendent of WrT *red* is used where Zhollam uses the descendent of *snang*; however, Zhollam Tibetan does have the form corresponding to WrT *red*, i.e. /ˊɦəˤ:/, employed as an adjective 'alright'. See example (21).

13.3 Existential verbs

13.3.1 Description

Existential expressions are constructed by using either an existential verb or a main verb which means 'stay,' 'rest,' etc.[14] A list of existential verb stems in Zhollam Tibetan follows:

Tab. 2: Existential verbs.[15]

declarative	possessive	existential-locational	
		animate	inanimate
egophoric	ˆjɵʔ	V[16]	unavailable
non-egophoric	ˆjɵʔ-ŋɔŋ	ˉŋɔŋ / ˆjɵʔ-ŋɔŋ / V[17]	ˉŋɔŋ
negative			
egophoric	ˆn̪eʔ-ŋɔŋ	NEG-V-EVD[18]	unavailable
non-egophoric	ˆn̪eʔ-ŋɔŋ	ˆn̪eʔ-ŋɔŋ	ˆmA-ŋɔŋ
interrogative			
egophoric	ʔa-jɵʔ	ʔa-V	unavailable
non-egophoric	ʔa-ŋɔŋ	ʔa-ŋɔŋ	ʔa-ŋɔŋ

The egophoric existential-locational uses main verbs such as /ˊʂo:/ and /ˊɦde:/ 'stay.' The main verbs are employed when one expresses the existence of human beings or living things (high animacy[19]). The existential verb /ˆjɵʔ/ can take a

---

[14] The difference between the existential verbs and the main verbs is based on the verb phrase morphology. The latter basically has no limitation and thus can take any suffix (cf. §3).
[15] Negative interrogatives forms are not attested even in the data from elicitation. Informants instead use Chinese expressions.
[16] V in Tab. 2 includes the following general verbs: /ˊʂo:/, /ˊɦde:/, /ˊʂo: ɦde:/, and /ˊʂo: ɦdu?/. All of these originally meant 'stay' or 'rest' and are now quite grammaticalised. They can take verbal suffixes as well as auxiliaries. The WrT etymon for each verb is *bzhugs*, *sdod*, and *bzhugs sdod* respectively.
[17] The differences between these three verbs is illustrated in (9).
[18] See §4 for a detailed description of EVD.
[19] The animacy hierarchy is highly related to evidential marking in the dialects from the southern Khams area (cf. Bartee 2011).

suffix /-ɳɔŋ/, and /ˆjʉʔ-ɳɔŋ/ creates a non-egophoric possessive, especially based on the speaker's visual experience, which is distinguished from other sensory access to information in Zhollam (cf. §4).[20]

A summary of each of the declarative existential sentences with a monotransitive clause follows:

(9) a possessive egophoric
 ˉtsʰə-Ø   ˆjʉʔ
 dog-ABS   EXV1
 '(I) have a dog.'
 b possessive non-egophoric or existential-locational non-egophoric
 ˉtsʰə-Ø   ˆjʉʔ-ɳɔŋ
 dog-ABS   EXV1-EVD
 (1) '(S/He) has a dog.' (acceptable regardless of visual experience)
 (2) 'The dog is here.' (visual experience, e.g. I have just seen)
 c existential-locational non-egophoric
 ˉtsʰə-Ø   ˉɳɔŋ
 dog-ABS   EXV2
 (1) 'There is a dog.'
 (2) 'The dog is (in the kennel).' (acceptable regardless of visual experience)
 d existential-locational non-egophoric animate
 ˉtsʰə-Ø   ʹsoː ʰduʔ
 dog-ABS   stay
 'The dog is/stays (here/in the kennel).'

The following elicited examples illustrate the two existential verbs /ˉɳɔŋ/ and /ˆjʉʔ/ in declarative clauses:

(10) a ʹŋA-Ø   ˉpʰaː-Ø   ˆjʉʔ / *ˉɳɔŋ
 1-ABS   pig-ABS   EXV1 / *EXV2
 'I have a pig.' (possessive)
 b ˉtoː   ˉpʰaː-Ø   *ˆjʉʔ / ˉɳɔŋ
 there   pig-ABS   *EXV1 / EXV2
 'There is a pig.' (existential) (situation: introducing to the addressee the speaker's pigsty[21])

---

[20] It is common for visual experience to be distinguished from other sensory experiences in the dialects spoken in the southern area of Khams, such as Deirong, Xiangcheng, Daocheng, Muli (Sichuan), and the whole of Diqing Prefecture (Yunnan) (cf. Bartee 2007).
[21] Sentence (10b) does not include a mirative reading. It is uttered only when the speaker has visual access to the fact.

c ˊɳA-Ø   ˈlɔŋ bA tʂʰʉ-nɔ̃   *ˆjʉʔ / ˉɳɔŋ
   fish-ABS   river-INE   *EXV1 / EXV2

'The fish is in the river.' (locational) (situation: answer to the question "where are there fish?")

Clauses which express non-egophoric possession, egophoric speaker's existentiality, and all clauses uttered regarding an addressee differ from the constructions presented above. Clauses with non-egophoric possessors are expressed with /ˆjʉʔ-ɳɔŋ/, i.e. /ˆjʉʔ/ followed by the evidential suffix /-ɳɔŋ/, as:

(11) possessive: declarative
   a ˊŋA-Ø   ˉpʰɑː-Ø   ˆjʉʔ
      1-ABS   pig-ABS   EXV1
      'I have a pig.'
   b ˉkʰɣ-Ø   ˉpʰɑː-Ø   ˆjʉʔ-ɳɔŋ
      3-ABS   pig-ABS   EXV1-EVD
      'S/He has a pig.'

It is possible that /ˉɳɔŋ/ in (10c) is an elliptical form of the combination of a verb plus /ˉɳɔŋ/. The omitted word may be /ˆjʉʔ/, for in (11b) /ˆjʉʔ-ɳɔŋ/ can alternate with /ˉɳɔŋ/. /ˆjʉʔ-ɳɔŋ/ in (11b) means that the speaker has just seen a pig there. To the contrary, /ˉɳɔŋ/ itself as an existential cannot take any suffixes.

The form /ˆjʉʔ-ɳɔŋ/ is also used as an existential verb for the 3rd person when the addressee visually perceives a situation, as:

(12) existential: declarative
   a ˉtoː   ˉpʰɑː-Ø   ˉɳɔŋ
      there   pig-ABS   EXV2
      'There is a pig.' (existential) (=10b) (situation: introducing the speaker's pigsty to the addressee)
   b ˋna KA   ˊmə ⁿdo   ˉtsəː-Ø   ˆjʉʔ-ɳɔŋ
      there   person   one-ABS   EXV1-EVD
      'Here is one person.' (existential) (situation: from a window the speaker saw a person in the room)

The existence and location of the speaker are expressed by several verbs (V in Tab. 2), i.e. /ˊʂoː/, /ˈʱdeː/, /ˊʂoː ʱdeː/, or /ˊʂoː ʱduʔ/ 'stay, rest', can be used instead of an existential verb. It is still unclear whether they have different meanings from each other.

(13) ˊŋA-Ø   ˉtɕʰoŋ   ˊʂoː-dA-jĭ
     1-ABS   home   stay-PRS-CPV1
     'I am home.' (situation: answer in a telephone conversation)

These verbs are used for a non-egophoric argument if one hopes to emphasise the existence of an animate being, especially a human being (see (14a)). In addition, /ˈʂoː ɦduʔ/ can be followed by /-ŋɔŋ/ as an evidential suffix, as in (14b) (see §4.2). The addition of /-ŋɔŋ/ will indicate the speaker's visual experience of the existence. The verb /ˆɦdeː/ mainly appears in narratives (cf. (14c)).

(14) existential, human being: declarative
   a ʔA bA-Ø   ˉtɕʰoŋ   ˈʂoː ɦduʔ / ˈʂoː-dA-jĭ
       daddy-ABS   home   stay / stay-PRS-CPV
       'Daddy is home.'
   b ʔA bA-Ø   ˉtɕʰoŋ   ˈʂoː ɦduʔ-ŋɔŋ
       daddy-ABS   home   stay-EVD
       'I have seen that daddy is home.'
   c ʔA n̪i   ˉtsəː-Ø   ˆɦdeː
       grandfather   one-ABS   stay
       'There was a grandfather.'
       (from the story *Dog and Cat*)

In the following section, I describe negative clauses. The negative counterpart of /ˈjʉʔ/ is /ˈn̪eʔ/, which also can be followed by /-ŋɔŋ/ when conveying access to information by visual perception. In fact, /ˆn̪eʔ/ is often followed by /-ŋɔŋ/, because the speaker might know that something no longer exists after witnessing its disappearance or departure. The use of /ˈŋɔŋ/ alone is rarely found. The negated verb form appears in elicitations, it is thus grammatically acceptable. Its form is /ˆmA-ŋɔŋ/.

(15) acceptability check: negation
   a ˈŋA-Ø   ˉpʰɑː-Ø   ˆn̪eʔ-ŋɔŋ / *ˆmA-ŋɔŋ
       1-ABS   pig-ABS   EXV1.NEG-EVD / *NEG-EXV2
       'I do not have a pig.' (possessive) (with visual evidence that the speaker does not possess it)
   b ˉtoː   ˉpʰɑː-Ø   ˆn̪eʔ-ŋɔŋ / ˆmA-ŋɔŋ
       there   pig-ABS   EXV1.NEG-EVD / NEG-EXV2
       'There are no pigs.' (existential) (situation: the speaker looked at the pigsty and confirmed this fact)

As with the copulative verbs, the addition of the prefix /ˈʔa-/, or one of the suffixes /ˈjɛ̃/ or /ˈmɛ̃/, can form an interrogative phrase.[22] Note that /ˈʔa-/ is usually employed in front of /ˉŋɔŋ/ or /ˆjʉʔ-ŋɔŋ/. If the interrogative suffix /ˈmɛ̃/ is added to /ˆjʉʔ-ŋɔŋ/

---

[22] The option of the interrogative affixes depends neither on preference of a speaker nor on pragmatics, but it is concerned with grammatical acceptability. Further investigation is needed.

and /ˆn̻e̠ʔ-n̥ɔŋ/, the interrogative phrase reflects the speaker's attitude of having some doubt as to the truth of the statement, as in (16):

(16) interrogative forms
    a ˉto: ˉpʰɑ:-Ø   ˀA-n̥ɔŋ
       there   pig-ABS   Q-CPV2
       'Is there a pig?' (existential)
    b ˉtɕʰʉʔ-Ø   ˉtɕʰi̠-Ø   ˀa-jʉʔ-n̥ɔŋ
       2-ABS   house-ABS   Q-EXV1-EVD
       'Do you have a house?' (possessive)
    c ˉtɕʰʉʔ-Ø   ˉpʰɑ:-Ø   ˆjʉʔ   ˆjɛ̃
       2-ABS   house-ABS   EXV1-EVD Q
       'Do you have a pig?' (possessive)
    d ˉtɕʰʉʔ-Ø   ˉpʰɑ:-Ø   ˆjʉʔ-n̥ɔŋ ˊmɛ̃
       2-ABS   house-ABS   EXV1-EVD Q
       'Do you really have a house?' (though you live in a city)

13.3.2 Typological remarks

Existential verbs function to express possessive, existential, and locational meanings in Tibetic languages. Huang (2013) provides a more general description of these forms in Tibeto-Burman languages. Suzuki (2014) describes variation of existential expressions in various varieties of the Tibetic languages spoken in the eastern Tibetan cultural area. In these varieties, differences in access to information correlate with differences in linguistic forms expressing existentiality.

The existential verbs in Zhollam Tibetan reflect the differences between possession and existential-locational as well as between egophoric and non-egophoric. Epistemic difference (older vs. novel knowledge) is evidently not marked in Zhollam. The existential expression is sensitive to animacy, basically divided into animate and inanimate; however, humans are distinguished from other animates, a distinction well attested cross-linguistically. The existence of an animate thing can be presented by one of three expressions: an existential verb itself, a possessive verb + a suffix of visual perception /ˆjʉʔ-n̥ɔŋ/, and a main verb 'stay' as /ˊʂo:/, in which the last is principally used for a person. As we will see in section 4, the main verbs can take various auxiliaries and suffixes depending on evidentiality, hence utterances concerning the existence of a person allows us to express various types of source and access to information.

The egophoric of existential verbs in Zhollam Tibetan is clear in declarative and interrogative clauses. In addition, Zhollam Tibetan has a frame that distinguishes the possessive from the existential-locational. This evidential system is not similar to those of the Tibetic languages described in Tournadre and Konchok Jiatso (2001), in which the possessive and the existential-locational are expressed with the same existential verbs. However, the dialects of Southern Khams, including the dialectal groups of Muli-nDappa, Chaphreng, sDerong-nJol, and Sems-kyi-nyila, possess an analogous system which is related to morphological difference among possessive, existential and locational, to the egophoric, and to animacy (cf. Suzuki 2014).

The usage of a reflex of *snang* as an existential verb stem is attested in many Tibetic languages and dialects (Bartee 2007; Rig-'dzin dBang-mo 2012; Suzuki 2012, 2014; Ebihara 2013, this volume). Because the geographic distribution of *snang* as an existential verb may be important, I provide a map[23] which displays the difference among existential verb stems[24] used in Tibetic varieties spoken in the eastern Tibetosphere below.

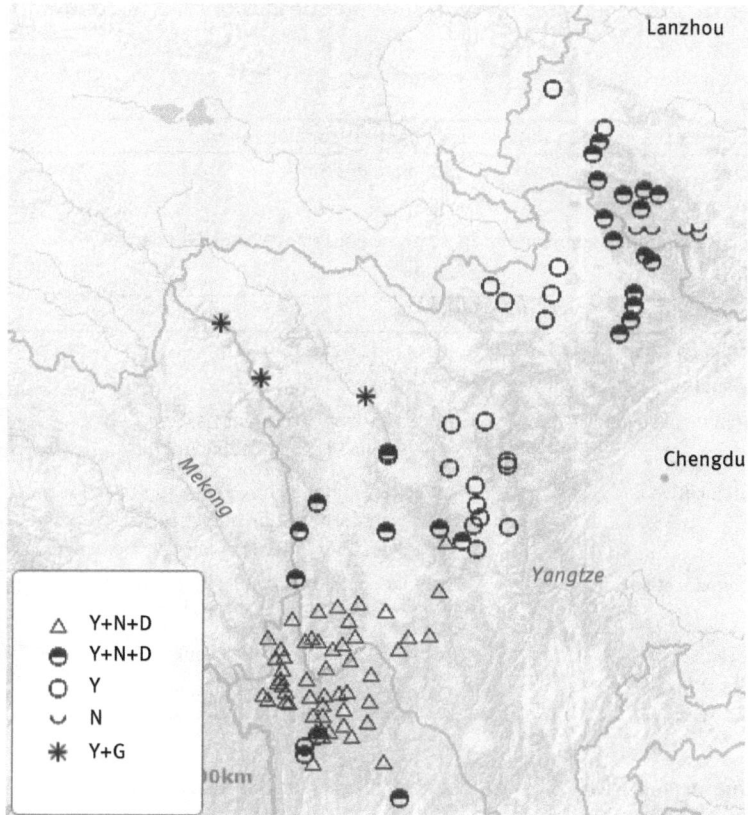

Y *yod*, N *snang*, D *'dug*, G *'gi*

Fig. 1: Geographical distribution of the system of existential verb stems.

---

23 The map was originally designed with ArcGIS online provided by the site: www.arcgis.com/home/webmap/viewer.html, and redrawn with some modifications.
24 All the data represented in the map are based on the author's research.

The geographical position of Zhollam is in the southern area; it seems that Zhollam is geographically peripheral.

13.4 Evidential auxiliaries[25]

The evidentiality expressed with verbal auxiliaries is related to the source and access to information (Tournadre and Lapolla 2014). A list of the main auxiliaries classified into two classes (simple statement expressed by the same forms as copulative verbs, and others) from a morphosyntactic viewpoint is as follows:[26]

Tab. 3: List of main auxiliaries.

Class A: for statement expressed by auxiliaries common to copulative verbs		
form	main function	detailed description
/-jĩ/	egophoric statement	
/-ŋɔŋ/	non-egophoric statement	utterance based on visual experience implied
Class B: for statement expressed by other auxiliaries		
form	main function	detailed description
/-ŋɔŋ/	visual experience	
/-ka˞/	non-visual experience	direct sensory experience except visual perception (endopathic included)
/-ɕɔ̃/	cislocative	speaker cannot be an agent and the action is completed; the action must be related to the speaker (*receptive*; *benefactive/malefactive*)
/-ɕe:/	translocative	speaker must be an agent and the action is completed
/-lʌ/	prediction	supposition for a future event
/-do lʌ/	prediction	supposition for a non-future event

Other than the forms in Tab. 3, there are several auxiliaries employed as T(ense) A(aspect)M(ood) markers, for example, /-tʰũ/ (accomplishment), /-tsʰi:/ (perfect), /-dʑə/ (dubitative), and /-do:/ (progressive). These are mainly related to the T(ense)-A(spect) system and not to evidentiality. The auxiliaries in Tab. 3 can be

---

25 A part of this section was presented in Suzuki (2011, 2012b).
26 The suffixes listed in Class A of Tab. 3 are glossed as CPV, and those in Class B, as EVD.

used in order to express specific evidentiality including access to information, receptivity and action's direction.

The auxiliaries, especially those in Class A of Tab. 3, normally follow a verb connector which represents specific tense and aspect, for example, /-dA-/ 'progressive,' /-pə-, -mə-/ 'perfect,' and /-zə-, -ze-/ 'future'. From the perspective of the typology of Tibetic languages, it should be noted that Class A excludes the existential verb /ˆjʉʔ/.

The summary in Tab. 3 cannot explain the full functions of each suffix, but only the ones with evidential values.[27] For the sake of a facile understanding of the aforementioned auxiliaries, I take two different forms and describe each usage in comparison with the other. Section 4.1 treats the usage of Class A; §4.2 describes the usage of /-n̥ɔŋ/ and /-kaˁ/ in terms of access to information; §4.3 describes the usage of /-kaˁ/ and /-ɕɔ̃/ in terms of receptivity: §4.4 describes /-ɕɔ̃/ and /-ɕe:/ in terms of direction of action; and finally, §4.5 describes /-lA/ and /-do lA/ in terms of indirect source of information.

13.4.1 Simple egophoric statements: /-jĩ/ and /-n̥ɔŋ/

A simple statement, which can represent egophoric evidentiality, is used in a sentence construction with several verbal suffixes, which need a copulative verb to complete a verbal phrase. For example, /-dA-/ 'progressive,' /-pə-, -mə-/ 'perfect,' /-zə-, -ze-/ 'future,' and so on, unless other specific evidential markers appear. However, /-n̥ɔŋ/ has another evidential usage to express source of information (see §4.2). In narrative texts, all the TAM markings tend to be lost, as in (14c).

Example (17) shows the use of /-jĩ/ (cf. (17a)) and /-n̥ɔŋ/ (cf. (17b)). Even though they are the same form as the copulative verbs, they do not bear an independent tone so that we know they here function as auxiliary verbs.

(17) simple statement of verbal phrases
    a ˊŋA-Ø   ˆkəˁ:-kA   ˆjo mA-Ø   ˋɦn̥A-dA-jĩ
       1-ABS   knife-INS vegetables-ABS cut-PRG-CPV
       'I am cutting vegetables with a knife.'
    b ˉkʰy-Ø   ˀɦdʑA nɔŋ-ne: ˊɦoŋ-n̥ɔŋ
       3-ABS   PLN-ABL   come-CPV
       'He is from Weixi Town.'

---

[27] See Suzuki (2012) for the usage of /-n̥ɔŋ/.

The auxiliaries in Class B specify access to information, while /-ŋɔŋ/ is used as a neutral marker of access to information based on old knowledge other than as that of visual perception, which is classified into Class B. Hence, it is uncertain whether /-ŋɔŋ/ in (17b) is employed as a copulative (neutral) auxiliary or as a source of information of visual perception, unless one specifies the context of the utterance.

As an auxiliary /-jĩ/ always carries egophoric meaning, as it does when functioning as a simple copulative verb.

13.4.2 Direct access to information: /-ŋɔŋ/ and /-kaˤ/

Both /-ŋɔŋ/ and /-kaˤ/ (WrT etymon *grag*) are markers indicating source and access to information. The difference between them is whether an utterance is based on information acquired through visual (/-ŋɔŋ/) or non-visual sources (/-kaˤ/), i.e. the other four senses and 'sixth sense' perceptions, i.e. instinctive knowing without the use of reason.

An example of the sixth sense is:

(18) ˊtsʰaː-Ø   ˆpje-kaˤ
    rain-ABS   fall-EVD
    'I feel that it will be raining.' (Based on the speaker's intuition.)

A contrastive usage of /-ŋɔŋ/ and /-kaˤ/ is:

(19) a ˋkoŋ tso-Ø   ⁻ʰtɕĩː-ŋɔŋ
       work-ABS   busy-EVD
       '(I have) a lot of work to do.' (as a general status) (situation: talking about how much the speaker has to work)
    b ˋkoŋ tso-Ø   ⁻ʰtɕĩː-kaˤ
       work-ABS   busy-EVD
       '(I am) busy working.' (working now) (situation: the speaker feels this work makes her busy)

Example (19a) can reflect the amount of work represented by visible things such as documents and planning memos as well as a general knowledge on the work, whereas (19b) is based on the speaker's real experience, which makes her tired.

Visual perception is represented, for example, in the following situations:

(20) a ˊɕiŋ-Ø   ⁻ʰkeː-mə-ŋɔŋ
       field-ABS dry-PRF-EVD
       'The field has become dry.' (situation: the speaker has seen the dry field)

b ˈtʌ mʌ   ˀpʰoŋ-Ø   ˆkʰoŋ tɕʌ-Ø   ˈmʌ-ʰtʌ-n̥ɔŋ
   recently tree-ABS peach-ABS   NEG-bear-EVD
   'The tree did not bear peaches recently.' (situation: the speaker has seen the tree not bearing peaches)

Multiple interpretations are also possible:

(21) ˆɦəˤː-n̥ɔŋ
     well-EVD
     'Alright. / That is good.'
     (situation 1: the speaker has seen and confirmed that is good)
     (situation 2: the speaker has confirmed that is good according to her knowledge)

In situation 2 in (21), the origin of the speaker's knowledge can be any sensory perception, for example, (21) was uttered when a native speaker of Zhollam listened to my pronunciation of a Zhollam word and accepted it.

The use of /-n̥ɔŋ/ for a non-visual source of information is unacceptable, as shown in (22):

(22) a ˈʂoŋ-kaˤ / *ˈʂoŋ-n̥ɔŋ
        tasty-EVD
        'It is tasty.' (After one smelled dishes or took food in the mouth)
     b ˉkẽ ʰto-kaˤ / *ˉkẽ ʰto-n̥ɔŋ
        solid-EVD
        'It is hard.' (After one touched something)

13.4.3 Receptivity: /-kaˤ/ and /-ɕɔ̃/

As seen above, /-kaˤ/ is employed as a non-visual sensory source of information marker, which indicates a direct experience (i.e. a non-future event). In example (23) below, I contrast the usage of /-kaˤ/ with another suffix /-ɕɔ̃/ (WrT etymon *byung*). The two suffixes /-kaˤ/ and /-ɕɔ̃/ are similar to each other in so far as they both indicate direct experience, but differ in terms of receptivity. Receptivity designates the direction of action towards 'ego'; /-ɕɔ̃/ is used as receptive or patientive (cislocative), generally including a benefactive or malefactive feeling caused by an external factor for the speaker. This meaning contrasts with /-kaˤ/, as in (23):

(23) a ˈŋʌ-Ø   ˀʰtuː-kaˤ
        1-ABS   be hungry-EVD
        'I am hungry.' (The speaker really feels hunger.)

b ˆŋA-Ø　ˉʰtuː-ɕɔ̃
　1-ABS　be hungry-EVD
　'I am hungry.' (The speaker maybe does not feel hunger but the dishes makes him/her feel hungry.)

Both examples in (23) express the speaker's experience,[28] but with different points of view. The suffix /-kaˤ/ presents an experience of the speaker from her point of view, whereas /-ɕɔ̃/ presents an experience as an external factor which influences the speaker. This description somehow resembles the egophoric vs. non-egophoric distinction, however, /-ɕɔ̃/ is necessarily receptive or cislocative to 'ego', thus it also includes egophoric evidentiality. Note that endopathic access to information is expressed by /-kaˤ/, not /-ɕɔ̃/. The suffix /-ɕɔ̃/ in Zhollam is always used with a receptive meaning, i.e. benefactive or malefactive feeling obtained from an external source.

The suffix /-ɕɔ̃/ always contains a meaning of receptivity, without which it cannot be used in Zhollam. See the two meanings of example (24).

(24)　ˈtsʰaː-Ø　ˆpje-ɕɔ̃
　　　rain-ABS　fall-EVD
　　a　'It rained.' (It makes me happy/unhappy.)
　　b　'It began to rain.' (It makes me happy/unhappy.)

The expression with /-ɕɔ̃/ can be understood as an inchoative shown in (24b), however, this interpretation in Zhollam can always be taken in the case that the speaker just noticed the rain and has a somewhat benefactive or malefactive feeling.

13.4.4 Direction of action: /-ɕɔ̃/ and /-ɕeː/

The suffixes /-ɕɔ̃/ and /-ɕeː/ (WrT *byas*) are quite different from each other, and they show a pragmatically complementary distribution. /-ɕɔ̃/ does not occur in clauses with an agent (1st person in the declarative sentence and 2nd person in the interrogative sentence), but /-ɕeː/ must appear with an agent.

---

28 However, these receptive and endopathic auxiliaries are employed in the interrogative sentence for the 2nd person subject/agent. This is the anticipation usage. Cf. §2.1, example (5).

Compare the use of /-ɕɔ̃/ and /-ɕeː/:

(25) a ˊŋA-Ø ˋʰtɕiː-ɕɔ̃
    1-ABS be happy-EVD
    'I am happy. / I was happy.'
  b ˋʰtɕiː-ɕɔ̃
    be happy-EVD
    'I am happy.'
  c ˋtɕʰɯ̃ʔ-lɔ̃ ˉmA-Ø ˋʔa-ʰtej-pə-ɕɔ̃
    2-DAT this-ABS Q-give-PRF-EVD
    'Did (he) give you that?' (Do you feel happy thanks to this?)

(26) ˊŋA-Ø ˋʰtej-ɕeː
    1-ABS give-EVD
  a 'I *did* give (the change to you)!' (with anger)
  b 'It is me who gave (the change to you).' (for an explanation of the situation)

The 1st person appears in (25a) and (26), but its role is different in each case: in (25a), the 1st person is in a receptive status of 'happiness', i.e. is undergoer of a 'happiness' that originated from an external factor, whereas in (26) it is an agent of the verb 'give.' Example (25b) is a non-emphatic form of (25a), in which the auxiliary /-ɕɔ̃/ itself designates a cislocative direction. Example (25c) is an anticipatory usage in an interrogative sentence.

13.4.5 Indirect source of information: /-lA/ and /-do lA/

The suffixes /-lA/ and /-do lA/ are used in an utterance based on the speaker's supposition concerning a future and non-future event respectively.

(27) a ˊŋA-Ø ˉjĭ kɛ ˋʱdʑA nɔŋ ˉŋgɣ-ze-lA
    1-ABS certainly PLN go-FUT-EVD
    'I will certainly go to Weixi Town.'
  b ˉtɕʰɯ̃ʔ-Ø ˋjaˤː-pə-do la
    2-ABS tired-PFV-EVD
    'I believe you got tired.'

These two suffixes designate indirect sources of information, mainly hearsay, general judgement based on the speaker's old knowledge obtained via any kind of access to information.

13.5 Concluding remarks

This chapter has provided a description of evidential categories in Zhollam Tibetan. A summary of the description of the evidential categories of Zhollam Tibetan and the morphemes used to mark them is as follows:

Copulative verbs:
    egophoric   /-jĩ/
    non-egophoric   /-ɲɔŋ/

Existential verbs (cf. Tab. 2):
    possessive
        egophoric   /ˆjʉʔ/ (negative: /ˆȵeʔ-ɲɔŋ/)
        non-egophoric   /ˆjʉʔ-ɲɔŋ/ (negative: /ˆȵeʔ-ɲɔŋ/)
    existential-locational
        egophoric   main verbs
        animate factual   /ˉɲɔŋ/ or main verbs
        animate sensory   /ˆjʉʔ-ɲɔŋ/ or main verbs (negative /ˆȵeʔ-ɲɔŋ/)
        inanimate   /ˉɲɔŋ/ (negative: /ˆmA-ɲɔŋ/)

Auxiliaries for general verbs (cf. Tab. 3)
    statement
        egophoric   /-jĩ/
        non-egophoric   /-ɲɔŋ/
specific source and access to information
        visual sensory   /-ɲɔŋ/
        non-visual sensory   /-kaˤ/
        receptive   /-ɕɔ̃/
        indirect for a future event   /-lA/
        indirect for a non-future event   /-do lA/

From the morphological aspect, as also discussed in Suzuki (2012), /-ɲɔŋ/ is widely used as a non-egophoric copulative verb, an existential verb meaning animate factual and inanimate existentiality, and an auxiliary meaning non-egophoric statement and visual sensory access to information within the evidential system in Zhollam Tibetan.

Existential verbs morphologically distinguish the possessive meaning from the existential-locational one, and each meaning has different exponents within the evidential system, in particular the latter is sensitive to animacy and sensory or non-sensory access to information.

When auxiliaries encode source and access to information, they distinguish a visual perception from other sensory and endopathic perceptions. The direction of action, receptivity, is also distinguished, and the receptive meaning always contains a benefactive or malefactive sense. Indirect information such as supposition distinguishes a future event from a non-future one.

An anticipation usage of egophoric, receptive, and endopathic verbs and auxiliaries discussed for example (5) and in Note 28 is also attested in Zhollam, as in many Tibetic languages (Tournadre and LaPolla 2014; Tournadre, this volume).

Abbreviations

1 1st person, 2 2nd person, 3 3rd person, ABL ablative, ABS absolutive, CPV copulative verb, DAT dative, ERG ergative, EXV existential verb, EVD evidential marker, GEN genitive, INE inessive, INS instrumental, LOC locative, NEG negative, NML nominaliser, PRF perfect, PLN place name, PRG progressive, PRS present, PSN person name, Q question marker, TOP topic marker

References

Bartee, Ellen Lynn. 2007. *A Grammar of Dongwang Tibetan*. Doctoral dissertation, University of California at Santa Barbara.

Bartee, Ellen Lynn. 2011. The role of animacy in the verbal morphology of Dongwang Tibetan. In Mark Turin & Bettina Zeisler (eds.), *Himalayan Languages and Linguistics: Studies in Phonology, Semantics, Morphology and Syntax*, 133–182. Leiden: Brill.

Ebihara, Shiho. 2013. Preliminary field report on dPa'ris dialect of Amdo Tibetan. In Tsuguhito Takeuchi & Norihiko Hayashi (eds.), *Historical Development of the Tibetan Languages: Proceedings of the Workshop B of the 17th Himalayan Languages Symposium*, 149–161. Kobe: Kobe City University of Foreign Studies.

Ebihara, Shiho. This volume. Evidentiality of the Tibetan verb *snang*. In Lauren Gawne & Nathan W. Hill (eds.) *Evidential Systems of Tibetan languages*, 41–59. Berlin; Boston: Mouton de Gruyter.

Gawne, Lauren. This volume. Egophoric evidentiality in Bodish languages. In Lauren Gawne & Nathan W. Hill (eds.) *Evidential Systems of Tibetan languages*, 61–94. Berlin; Boston: Mouton de Gruyter.

Huang, Chenglong 黄成龙. 2013. Zangmianyu cunzailei dongci de gainian jiegou 藏缅语存在类动词的概念结构 [Conceptual structure of the locative/existential verbs in Tibeto-Burman languages]. *Minzu Yuwen* 《民族语文》 [Minority Languages of China] 2. 31–48.

de Nebesky-Wojkowitz, René. 1956. *Oracles and demons of Tibet: the cult and iconography of the Tibetan protective deities*. 's-Gravenhage: Mouton.

Post, Mark W. 2013. Person-sensitive TAME marking in Galo: Historical origins and functional motivation. In T. Thornes, E. Andvik, G. Hyslop & J. Jansen (eds.), *Functional-Historical Approaches to Explanation*, 107–130. Amsterdam: John Benjamins.

Sun, Jackson T.-S. 1993. Evidentials in Amdo Tibetan. *The Bulletin of the Institute of History and Philology, Academia Sinica* 63. 945–1001.

Suzuki, Hiroyuki. 2009. Introduction to the method of the Tibetan linguistic geography: a case study in the Ethnic Corridor of West Sichuan. In Yasuhiko Nagano (ed.), *Linguistic substratum in Tibet: New perspective towards historical methodology (No. 16102001) report* Vol.3, 15-34. Suita: National Museum of Ethnology.

Suzuki, Hiroyuki 鈴木博之. 2011. Kamu-Chibetto-go Gagatang-Shaoluo [Zhollam] hōgen no bunpō sukecchi カムチベット語嘎嘎塘勺洛[Zhollam]方言の文法スケッチ [Grammatical sketch of the Zhollam dialect of Khams Tibetan]. *RIHN Descriptive Linguistics Series* 3. 1-35.

Suzuki, Hiroyuki. 2012. Multiple usages of the verb *snang* in Gagatang Tibetan (Weixi, Yunnan). *Himalayan Linguistics* 11(1). 1-16.

Suzuki, Hiroyuki 鈴木博之. 2013. Yunnan Weixi Zangyu de r-jieyin yuyin yanbian — jiantan "erhua" yu "jinhou" zhi jiaocha guanxi 云南维西藏语的r介音语音演变：兼谈"儿化"与"紧喉"之交叉关系 [Sound changes of r-glide in Weixi Tibetan of Yunnan --- with a comment on a crossing relation of "rhotacisation" and "tensethroated"]. *Dongfang Yuyanxue*《东方语言学》13. 20-35.

Suzuki, Hiroyuki 鈴木博之. 2014. Shilun Dongfang Zangqu Zangyu tuhua de yufa ditu: Yi panduan dongci yu cunzai dongci wei li 试论东方藏区土话的语法地图：以判断动词与存在动词为例 [Essay of the grammatical linguistic maps on Tibetan spoken in the eastern Tibetan cultural area: Examples of copulative and existential verbs]. *Di 3 jie Zhongguo Diliyuyanxue Guoji Xueshu Yantaohui Huiyi Lunwenji*《第三届地理语言学国际学术研讨会会议论文集》166-175. Foshan: Foshan Keji Daxue 佛山科技大学.

Tournadre, Nicolas. 2008. Arguments against the concept of 'conjunct' / 'disjunct' in Tibetan. In Brigitte Huber, Marianne Volkart, Paul Widmer & Peter Schwieger (eds.) *Chomolangma, Demawend und Kasbek, Festschrift für Roland Bielmeier zu seinem 65. Geburtstag*, 281-308. Halle: International Institute for Tibetan and Buddhist Studies GmbH.

Tournadre, Nicolas. 2014. The Tibetic languages and their classification. In Thomas Owen-Smith & Nathan W. Hill (eds.), *Trans-Himalayan Linguistics: Historical and Descriptive Linguistics of the Himalayan Area*, 105-129. Berlin: Mouton de Gruyter.

Tournadre, Nicolas. This volume. A typological sketch of evidential/epistemic categories in the Tibetic languages. In Lauren Gawne & Nathan W. Hill (eds.), *Evidential Systems of Tibetan languages*, 95-129. Berlin; Boston: Mouton de Gruyter.

Tournadre, Nicolas & Konchok Jiatso [dKon-mchog rGya-mtsho]. 2001. Final auxiliary verbs in literary Tibetan and in the dialects. *Linguistics of the Tibeto-Burman Area* 24(1). 49-111.

Tournadre, Nicolas & Randy J. LaPolla. 2014. Towards a new approach to evidentiality: Issues and directions for research. *Linguistics of the Tibeto-Burman Area* 37(2). 240-263.

Tournadre, Nicolas & Sangda Dorje [gSang-bdag rDo-rje]. 2009. *Manuel de tibétain standard: Langue et civilisation*. Paris : L'Asiathèque.

Vokurková, Zuzana. 2008. *Epistemic modalities in Spoken Standard Tibetan*. Karel University and University of Paris 8 dissertation.

Zhu, Xiaonong 朱晓农. 2010. *Yuyinxue* 语音学 [Phonetics]. Beijing: 商务印书馆 Shangwu Yinshuguan.

Katia Chirkova
14 Evidentials in Pingwu Baima

14.1 Introduction

Baima is a Tibetic language, spoken by approximately 10,000 people in three counties in Sichuan Province (Pingwu 平武, Songpan 松潘, Jiuzhaigou 九寨沟) and one county in Gansu Province (Wenxian 文县) in the People's Republic of China. The Baima people call themselves /pe^{53}/ *bod* and they are known under the name of Dwags-po in Tibetan. In Pingwu, Songpan, and Jiuzhaigou, they reside in close proximity with Tibetan and Han Chinese groups, whereas in Wenxian, Han Chinese are the Baima's only neighbouring ethnic group. Baima is considered a distinct language by its speakers and it is not mutually intelligible with the Tibetic varieties in its neighborhood.

Baima is little-studied. Linguistic accounts to date have essentially focused on the disputed status of Baima as either a Tibetic language (or a dialect of Tibetan in the Chinese linguistic scholarship) (Zhang 1994a, 1994b, 1997; Huang and Zhang 1995) or a Bodic language distinct from Tibetan (H. Sun 1980a, 1980b, 2003; H. Sun et al. 2007; Nishida and Sun 1990).[1]

---

[1] Officially classified as Tibetans in the 1950s, the Baima advanced claims as an independent ethnic group in the 1960s and 1970s. The main arguments for an independent status included, on the one hand, linguistic differences between the Baima language and its neighboring Tibetic varieties and, on the other hand, major ethnographic differences between the Baima people and Tibetans. Baima generally adopted Chinese lifestyle and customs; they do not drink milk or use milk products, which are essential to the Tibetan diet, and they are also not Buddhists, but practice indigenous animist beliefs. In the 1970s, a group of PRC researchers conducted two surveys in the Baima areas and published two collections of papers, in which the Baima were claimed descendants of the ancient Di 氐 tribe, which set up influential kingdoms in the 3rd through the 6th centuries CE in the areas currently inhabited by the Baima. In the 7th century, the Di territories were occupied by Tibetans and the Di people are believed to have subsequently shifted to the form of Tibetan spoken by their invaders. Despite the conclusion that the Baima constitute a distinct ethnic group rather than a branch of Tibetans, they were never officially reclassified. See Chirkova (2007, 2008c) for an account of the controversy surrounding the ethnicity of Baima Tibetans and their purported link to the Di group as documented in the Chinese historical records.

Note: This chapter builds on my earlier work on Baima evidentials (Chirkova 2008a). I would like to thank Ulatus for preparing an English translation of the original article under the auspices of the European Research Council funded project "Beyond Boundaries: Religion, Region, Language and the State" (ERC Synergy Project 609823 ASIA). Their translation was used as the basis for this study. I am grateful to M Li Degui for his help in checking and discussing the Baima examples cited in this paper.

Baima is spoken in a multi-ethnic area, at the border of the historical Tibetan provinces of Amdo and Khams. This area is home to many language-like Tibetic varieties, such as Zhongu (J. Sun 2003a), Chos-rje (or Dpal-skyid) (J. Sun 2003b), Thebo (or Thewo) (Lin 2014), and Cone (or Chone) (Jacques 2014). In a recent classification of Tibetan languages by Nicolas Tournadre (2014: 121–123), these Tibetan varieties are grouped, together with Baima, into the Eastern section of the Tibetic family. Baima phonology and lexicon readily attest to the complex history of this language and to its intricate relationships with the neighboring Tibetan languages. Multiple sound correspondences between the phonological system of Baima and that of Old Tibetan, as reflected in standard Written Tibetan orthography (hereafter WT), suggest layers of loanwords from different Tibetan languages (Huang and Zhang 1995: 91–92; Chirkova 2008b). To give an example, WT '*gr* has two main reflexes in the basic lexicon of Baima: (1) /ndʐ/, as in /ndʐɔ³⁵/ '*grang* 'be full, be satiated with food', and (2) /ndʑ/, as in /ndʑo³⁴¹/ '*gro* 'walk'. Of these, the former correspondence is typical of Khams Tibetan (respectively, /ndʐõ⁵⁵/ and /ndʐo⁵³/ in 'Ba'-thang Tibetan, Huang et al. 1992: 605), whereas the second correspondence is characteristic of Amdo Tibetan (respectively, /dʑaɣ/ and /ndʑo/ in Bla-brang Tibetan, Huang et al. 1992: 605). The linguistic influence of different donor languages is also detectable in the Baima lexicon. For instance, Baima /ŋgɔ²⁴¹nɑ⁵³ɲi⁵³/ 'human beings, mankind' is shared with Amdo *mgo nag m(y)i*,[2] while Baima /a³³li⁵³/ 'cat' may probably be linked to /le¹³le⁵³/ in Khams Tibetan (as in Sde-dge) (Huang and Zhang 1995: 104). Much like its phonology and lexicon, the grammatical organization of Baima is characterized by a complex, multi-layered structure, as discussed in this chapter in relation to the system of evidentiality. The present overview is based on first-hand fieldwork data on the variety of Baima as spoken in Pingwu County, which has the largest concentration of Baima speakers throughout all Baima-speaking areas. This overview relies on elicited verb paradigms (used as main illustrative examples throughout the chapter) and verbs forms cited from traditional stories (used to address the issues of occurrence frequency and co-occurrence patterns of different markers of evidentiality with various types of verbs).

14.2 Evidentials in Pingwu Baima: An overview

Pingwu Baima has a hybrid evidentiality system that combines (a) specification of speaker's perspective towards the source of, and access to, information (egophoric vs. non-egophoric) and (b) specification of source of information

---

[2] For more on the expression *mgo nag myi*, see Hill (2013), who discusses the use of this formula in Old Tibetan texts.

(direct vs. indirect). The egophoric vs. non-egophoric distinction permeates the entire system, whereas the direct-indirect distinction is restricted to past time reference.[3]

The majority of Baima verbs have two stems: (1) non-past, corresponding to WT present and future stems, and (2) past, corresponding to WT past and imperative stems, as illustrated in Tab. 1.[4] Non-past stems are mostly prenasalized and carry a falling tone (53/341), whereas past stems have a voiceless initial and carry the rising tone (35).

Tab. 1: Examples of past and non-past verb stems in Pingwu Baima.

Pingwu Baima		Tibetan				Meaning
Non-past	Past / Imperative	Present	Future	Past	Imperative	
ko⁵³	kɯ³⁵	rko ba	brko	(b)rkos	rkos	dig
ndzo³⁴¹	ndzɯ²¹³	'tsho ba	gso	(b)sos		graze, herd
ndzu³⁴¹	tsu³⁵	'tshong	btsong	btsongs	tshong	sell
ta⁵³	tʏ³⁵	lta ba	blta	bltas	ltos	look
mo⁵³	me³⁵	rmo ba		rmos		plow, till
ndʐa³⁴¹	tʂe³⁵	dra ba		dras		cut apart, sever
mbe⁵³	pe³⁵	'bod pa		bos		call, shout
ɲɔ⁵³	ɲʏ³⁵	nyo ba		nyos		buy

Evidential markers that combine with non-past verb stems form a simpler system with a binary opposition between egophoric and non-egophoric (or factual) forms. Evidential markers that are used with past verb stems, on the other hand, are more numerous and manifest a richer system of contrasts between egophoric,

---

3 Baima has no specialized marker of reported evidence. Reported speech is marked by the use of various forms of the default verb of speaking /dzo³⁴¹/. Consider the following examples: ɲi⁵³ nɔ²¹³ dzo³⁴¹ də³³. (person exist speak PROG) 'There are reportedly people here.' kʰu⁵³ gje³³pu⁵³ tɛ⁵³ ɲi⁵³-ʁ⁵³-ndu²¹³ uɛ³³ dzɛ³⁵ sə³³. (LOG old.man DEF eye-Q-see PFV.EGO.INT speak.PST PFV) '[The demoness] said: "Have you seen my husband?"'

4 A small number of (high frequency) verbs have three stems: in addition to the non-past and past stems, they also have a separate imperative stem. Verbs with three stems mostly use suppletive forms. Examples include: (1) 'walk, go': present/future: /ndʐo⁵³/ 'gro and /ndʐi⁵³/ mchi, past /tɕʰɛ³⁵/ chas, imperative /ʂʰu³⁵/ song; (2) 'come': present/future /wu⁵³/ 'ong, past /ue³⁵/ 'ongs and /ɕy³⁵/ byung, imperative /ʂuɛ⁵³/ shog; (3) 'make': future/present /zo³⁴¹/ bzo ba, past /ɕɛ³⁵/ byas, imperative /tɕi³⁵/ gyis; (4) 'speak': future/present /dzo³⁴¹/ zlo, past /dzɛ³⁵/ bzlas, imperative /dzɯ²¹³/ zlos. Finally, some verbs have only one stem, e.g. /kʰi⁵³/ 'lead, conduct, bring along', WT 'khrid pa, khrid; /ɲɛ³⁵/ 'sleep', WT nyal ba, nyol; /tsʰə³⁵/ 'look for', WT 'tshal/'tshol-ba, btsol, tshol.

factual, direct, and indirect (inferred) evidential categories. An overview of all markers is provided in Tab. 2.

Tab. 2: Evidential markers in Pingwu Baima.[5]

Verb stem		Marker			
Non-past		Egophoric		Non-egophoric (factual)	
	Prospective	i⁵³ *kyis?*[6]		re²¹³ *red*	
	Durative (stative)	ʐy³⁴¹ *yod*		nɔ²¹³ *snang*	
	Experiential	tʃʰa⁵³ ʐy³⁴¹ *cha? yod*		tʃʰa⁵³ nɔ²¹³ *cha? snang*	
Past		Egophoric intentional	Egophoric receptive (centripetal)	Direct (centrifugal)	Indirect/Factual
		uɛ³³ ?	ɕy³⁵ *byung*	tɕʰɛ³⁵ *chas*	ʂə³³ ?

The basic organization of the system is as follows. Egophoric markers prototypically used in the following two cases:
(i) with first person subjects in statements, in which the speaker is the willful instigator of a situation. Examples include:

(1) ŋa³⁵   ɲɔ⁵³   i⁵³.   ŋa³⁵   ndʑi⁵³   i⁵³.
    1SG   buy.N-PST   PRSP.EGO   1SG   WALK.N-PST   PRSP.EGO
    'I will (definitely) buy (it). I will (definitely) walk.'

---

5 Baima does not have evidentiality distinction in the present progressive and uses one and the same progressive marker /də/ *sdod*? with all types of subjects and verbs. Compare the following examples: /ŋa³⁵ sɔ³⁵ ndu³⁵ də³³/ 'I am eating.' vs. /kʰu³³ɲi⁵³ sɔ³⁵ ndu³⁵ də³³/ 'He is eating.'; /ŋa³⁵ kʰi³⁵ də³³/ 'I am sick.' vs. /kʰu³³ɲi⁵³ kʰi³⁵ də³³/ 'He is sick.'; /nɔ³⁵ mbu⁵³ də³³/ 'It is raining.'

The majority of evidentials can occur in isolation and have etymological tones. Of those evidentials that do not occur in isolation, /i⁵³/ is consistently realized with the high falling tone, whereas /uɛ³³/ and /ʂə³³/ are pronounced with a short, mid-pitch tone, notated here as "33" (neutral tone).

6 The prospective egophoric marker /i⁵³/ does not appear cognate to the egophoric equational copula *yin* in Standard Tibetan. According to regular sound correspondence rules, Pingwu Baima equivalent to *yin* is /ʑi³⁴¹/ (cf. Pingwu Baima /ʐy³⁴¹/, WT *yod*). The form /ʑi³⁴¹/ occasionally occurs as an egophoric (equational/attributive) copula in traditional stories, as in /kʰu⁵³ ndo³³mbu⁵³ ʑi³⁴¹/ 'I am fat.' (where /kʰu⁵³/ is a logophoric pronoun). The default equational copula in the spoken language is /re²¹³/, as in /ŋa³⁵ lɔ³³pe³⁵ re²¹³, wu³³le⁵³ ɕo³³sə⁵³ re²¹³/ 'I am a teacher, he is a student.' (/ɕo³³sə⁵³/ is a loanword from Mandarin Chinese, 学生 *xuésheng*). The prospective egophoric marker /i⁵³/ may be cognate to the prospective marker *kyis* (or one of its allomorphs, *gyis, gis, 'is* or *s*) (cf. Nagano 1995; Häsler 1999: 168, 184–186).

(2) ŋa³⁵   ɲɛ³⁵   ʑy³⁴¹.
    1SG   sleep   DUR.EGO
    'I am sleeping.'

(3) ʂʰu²¹³   ndɛ⁵³   ndʒa⁵³   tʃʰa⁵³ʑy³⁴¹.
    mushroom this   eat.N-PST EXP.EGO
    'I have eaten this type of mushrooms (in the past).'

(ii) with second person subjects in direct questions. This use conforms to the "anticipation rule" in Tibetic languages, whereby the speaker anticipates the access/source available to the hearer and selects the evidential marker accordingly (Tournadre and LaPolla 2014: 245). Consider the following examples:

(4) tɕʰø⁵³   ndu³⁵   ia⁵³?
    2SG   drink   PRSP.EGO.Q
    'Will you drink?'

(5) tɕʰø⁵³   sɔ³⁵   ndu³⁵   mbɔ³³   ua³³.
    2SG   food   drink   CMPL   PFV.EGO.INT.Q
    'Have you eaten?'

Non-egophoric markers are used:
(i) with non-first person subjects in statements and third-person subjects in questions, as in the following examples:

(6a) tɕʰø⁵³ / kʰu³³ɲi⁵³   ɲɔ⁵³   re²¹³.
     2SG / 3SG   buy.N-PST PRSP.N-EGO
     'You / he will (definitely) buy (it).'

(6b) tɕʰø⁵³ / kʰu³³ɲi⁵³   ndʑi⁵³   re²¹³.
     2SG / 3SG   walk.N-PST PRSP.N-EGO
     'You / he will (definitely) walk.'

(7) tɕʰø⁵³ / kʰu³³ɲi⁵³   ɲɛ³⁵   nɔ²¹³.
    2SG / 3SG   sleep   DUR.N-EGO
    'You are / he is sleeping.'

(8) ʂʰu²¹³   ndɛ⁵³   kʰu³³ɲi⁵³   ndʒa⁵³   tʃʰa⁵³nɔ²¹³.
    mushroom this   3SG   eat.N-PST EXP.N-EGO
    'He has eaten this type of mushrooms (in the past).'

(9) ʂʰu²¹³   ndɛ⁵³   kʰu³³ɲi⁵³   ndʒa⁵³   tʃʰa⁵³nɔ²¹³   a³³?
    mushroom this   3SG   eat.N-PST EXP.N-EGO   Q
    'Has he ever eaten that type of mushrooms?'

(ii) with first person subjects in statements, referring to internal (or endopathic) states, such as cold, pain, hunger, or fear, over which the subject does not have control (e.g. Tournadre and Dorje 2003: 167; Tournadre and LaPolla 2014: 242). Examples include:

(10) ŋa³⁵ kʰi³⁵ re²¹³.
     1SG be.sick PRSP.N-EGO
     '(If it continues like that) I will certainly fall ill.'

The system of evidentials allows for interchangeability between the markers so that the speaker is free to choose different markers to signal the degree of her involvement into the situation under description. Not only can first person subjects co-occur with non-egophoric markers (as in the case of endopathic verbs), but non-first person subjects can also co-occur with egophoric markers. The latter use implies that the speaker is responsible for conceptualizing or observing the reported situation and committed to its truthfulness.[7] Consider the following examples:

(11) kʰu³³ɲi⁵³ ndʑa⁵³ i⁵³.
     3SG   eat.N-PST PRSP.N-EGO
     '(I know that) he will definitely eat.'

(12) kʰu³³ɲi⁵³ sɔ³⁵ ndu³⁵ mbɔ³³ ua³³?
     3SG   food drink COMPL PFV.EGO.INT.Q
     '(Do you know whether) he has eaten?'

Evidential markers that co-occur with past verb stems enrich the basic organization of the system with some additional meanings. Notable is also the complex system of oppositions whereby one and the same marker may stand in contrast to several markers depending on the type of verb, with which it combines, and the person of the subject.

(i) /tɕʰɛ³³/ contrasts to /ʂə³³/ in specifying the source of information: direct vs. indirect, respectively.

---

[7] Such use can also be analyzed in terms of empathy, "the speaker's identification, which may vary in degree, with a person/thing that participates in the event or state that he describes in a sentence" (Kuno 1987: 206). By taking the third person actor's viewpoint, the speaker signals her certainty about the person's actions (cf. Häsler's 1999, 2001 analysis of evidentials in Sde-dge Tibetan).

When used with volitional (or controllable) verbs and non-first person subjects,[8] /tɕʰɛ³³/ signals that the speaker witnessed the event under description. By contrast, /ʂə³³/ indicates that the reported event is not directly witnessed by the speaker, but deduced on the basis of available physical evidence. Compare the following sentences:

(13) kʰa³³rə³³-ku⁵³ sɔ³⁵ ndu³⁵ mbɔ³³ tɕʰɛ³³.
    3-PL   food drink COMPL DIR
    '(I saw that) they have eaten.'

(14) kʰa³³rə³³-ku⁵³ sɔ³⁵ ndu³⁵ mbɔ³³ ʂə³³.
    3-PL   food drink COMPL PFV
    'They have eaten.' (inferred, e.g. by empty plates on the table)

When used with endopathic verbs, the direct evidential /tɕʰɛ³³/ is generally used to refer to the speaker's own internal state, whereas /ʂə³³/ is used to report internal states of others (but see also (iv) below). Compare the following sentences:

(15) ŋa³⁵ kʰi³⁵ tɕʰɛ³⁵.
    1SG be.sick DIR
    'I fell ill.'

(16) kʰu³³ɲi⁵³ kʰi³⁵ mbɔ³³ ʂə³³.
    3SG   be.sick COMPL PFV
    'He has fallen ill.'

(ii) /tɕʰɛ³³/ contrasts to /ɕy³⁵/ in specifying the direction of motion.

In addition to being evidential markers, /tɕʰɛ³³/ and /ɕy³⁵/ are also full-fledged verbs of motion: /tɕʰɛ³³/ is the past form of the verb 'go', whereas /ɕy³⁵/ is the past form of the verb 'come, appear'. Examples include:

(17) di³⁵ ka³⁵ tɕʰɛ³⁵ dzɛ³⁵? di³⁵ ɲi⁵³ se⁵³ tɕʰɛ³⁵.
    demon where go.PST say.PST demon person kill go.PST
    '"Where did the demon go?" he asked, "The demon went to kill humans".'

---

8 Volitional or controllable verbs refer to those actions and behaviors that the speaker is able to control through her subjective will, such as 'go', 'eat', or 'look'.

(18) ndʑɛ⁵³   tʰi³³ro³⁵   ɕy³⁵,   tɔ⁵³nɑ³⁴¹   pʰɑ³³gɯ³⁴¹   ɕi⁵³
     demon   ghost   appear.PST   bear   wild.pig   home
     ue³⁵   ʂə³³.
     come.PST PFV
     'Demons and ghosts appeared, bears and wild pigs came home.'

One difference between /tɕʰɛ³³/ and /ɕy³⁵/ as verbs of motion is that the former can be used as a finite verb co-occurring with evidential markers (as in 19), whereas the latter cannot. Finite forms of the verb 'come' make use of the past stem /ue³⁵/ (as in example 18).

(19) tɕʰy⁵³   tʃʰə⁵³   zo³⁴¹   tɕʰɛ³⁵   ue³³?
     2SG   what   make.N-PST   go.PST   PFV.EGO.INT
     'Where have you been up to? [lit. What did you go to do?]'

Both /tɕʰɛ³³/ and /ɕy³⁵/ are also used with verbs of motion as auxiliaries indicating the direction of motion in relation to the speaker. Compare the following sentences:

(20) kʰu³³ɲi⁵³   tse⁵³   tɕʰɛ³⁵.   kʰu³³ɲi⁵³   tse⁵³   ɕy³⁵.
     3SG   arrive   go.PST   3SG   arrive   appear.PST
     'He arrived (there, some place away from the speaker). He arrived (here, towards the speaker).'

(iii) /ɕy³⁵/ contrasts with /uɛ³³/ in specifying the speaker as the voluntary or involuntary participant of the event.

In addition to denoting the actual direction of movement towards the speaker with verbs of motion, /ɕy³⁵/ can be used with non-motion verbs to indicate that the action is directed towards the speaker metaphorically. In such cases, /ɕy³⁵/ indicates that the speaker-subject has undergone the action involuntarily. In this function, Baima /ɕy³⁵/ appears a close counterpart of the auxiliary *byung* in Standard Tibetan (cf. Tournadre and Dorje 2003: 169). Examples include:

(21) ŋa³⁵   jɔ³⁵   ɕi⁵³   ue³⁵   tʃʰa³³pa⁵³   pu³⁵   ɕy³⁵.
     1SG   just   home   come.PST   rain   fall.PST   EGO.RCP
     'Just as I came home it started raining.'

(22) tʃʰə⁵³   iɛ³³ŋgi⁵³   ly³⁵   ɕy³⁵?
     what   matter   happen   EGO.RCP
     'What happened (to you)?'

In neat contrast to /ɕy³⁵/, /uɛ³³/ indicates that the speaker is the willful instigator of a situation, as in the following sentence:

(23) ŋa³⁵ sɔ³⁵ ndu³⁵ mbɔ³³ uɛ³³.
    1SG food drink COMPL PFV.EGO.INT
    'I have eaten.'

(24) ɣa⁵³ se⁵³ mbɔ³³ uɛ³³.
    fox kill COMPL PFV.EGO.INT
    'I killed the fox.'

/uɛ³³/ is also accepted in sentences with endopathic verbs, where it implies, albeit idiosyncratically, that the speaker voluntarily incurred some internal state, e.g.:

(25) ŋa³⁵ kʰi³⁵ mbɔ³³ uɛ³³.
    1SG be.sick COMPL PFV.EGO.INT
    'I have (purposely) fell ill.'

While possible grammatically, such use is, of course, pragmatically implausible, and is generally met with laughter from native speakers.

(iv) /ʂə³³/ can be used a factual counterpart of /uɛ³³/ and /tɕʰɛ³⁵/.

Similar to /uɛ³³/, /ʂə³³/ can be used with first person subjects and endopathic verbs. Compare the following two sentences cited from one and the same traditional story and describing one and the same event:

(26) kʰu⁵³ kʰɔ⁵³ mbɔ³³ tɕʰɛ³⁵.
    LOG lose COMPL DIR
    'I lost (the competition).'

(27) kʰu⁵³ kʰɔ⁵³ mbɔ³³ ʂə³³.
    LOG lose COMPL PFV
    'I lost (the competition).'

The use of the direct evidential /tɕʰɛ³⁵/ in sentence (26) puts an emphasis on the source of information (sensory channels). The use of /ʂə³³/ in sentence (27), on the other hand, represents a factual account of the reported situation.

/ʂə³³/ is also the default perfective marker used with first person subjects and verbs of motion, as in the following example:

(28) ŋa³⁵ tse⁵³ ʂə³³.
    1SG arrive PFV
    'I arrived.'

The distribution of Pingwu Baima past evidential markers in relation to the type of verbs and the person of the subject is summarized in Tab. 3.

Tab. 3: Distribution of Pingwu Baima past evidential markers in relation to the type of verbs and the person of the subject.

	First person subject		Non-first person subject	
	egophoric intentional	egophoric receptive	direct	inferred/ factual
volitional verbs	uɛ³³	ɕy³⁵	tɕʰɛ³⁵	ṣə³³
endopathic verbs		tɕʰɛ³⁵ (sensory source of information) ṣə³³ (factual account)	ṣə³³	
motion verbs	ṣə³³		ɕy³⁵ (centripetal) tɕʰɛ³⁵ (centrifugal)	

As shown in Tab. 3, /ṣə³³/ is the least restricted form, which can co-occur with all types of verbs and all types of subjects. Together with /uɛ³³/, /ṣə³³/ also has high frequency of occurrence in my corpus of traditional stories. /ɕy³⁵/ and /tɕʰɛ³⁵/, on the other hand, occur less frequently. They are chiefly used as verbs of motion or auxiliaries indicating the direction of motion. /ɕy³⁵/ is more restricted in distribution that /tɕʰɛ³⁵/, as it is mostly only used with the verb /tse⁵³/ *slebs* 'arrive', as in the following example:

(29) to³⁵　　ta³³jɔ³⁵　　 dʐa³⁴¹kʰa³³tsʰə⁵³　ṣə³³　na⁵³　tse⁵³　ɕy³⁵.
　　 on　　 just.now　　 beggar　　　　　　 INDF　here　arrive　appear.PST
　　'A beggar just came here.'

/ɕy³⁵/ in its function as the egophoric receptive marker is the least frequent of all evidential markers. Its use has been mainly documented through elicitation.

/uɛ³³/ and /ṣə³³/ also stand in clear contrast to /tɕʰɛ³⁵/ and /ɕy³⁵/ with respect to their degree of grammaticalization. /uɛ³³/ and /ṣə³³/ are etymologically obscure, bound morphs.[9] /tɕʰɛ³⁵/ and /ɕy³⁵/, on the other hand, exhibit a

---

[9] Based on the basic grammatical functions of /uɛ³³/ and /ṣə³³/, Huang and Zhang (1995: 108) argue that the former is a contracted form of *pa-yin* of Standard Tibetan, whereas the latter is a variant of the Proto-Tibetan past tense morpheme *-s. This is not quite in accord with regular sound correspondences between WT and Baima or with the paradigmatic relationship of these two markers to other members of the evidential system, as discussed in this chapter. The etymological origins of /uɛ³³/ and /ṣə³³/ are yet to be determined.

low degree of grammaticalization. They retain their status of autonomous units (as in examples (17–18)) and show no signs of desemanticization, phonological attrition, or loss of morphosyntactic properties (cf. Lehmann 1995: 121–178).

14.3 Pingwu Baima evidentials in the Tibetic context

The system of evidentiality in Pingwu Baima incorporates some very specific categories — such as egophoric, endopathic, and the anticipation rule — all of which are held to be characteristic properties of the evidential systems of the Tibetic family (e.g. Tournadre 1996; Tournadre and Jiatso 2001; Tournadre and LaPolla 2014: 252–256). Overall, evidentiality systems in Tibetic languages are held to be similar in their structure and morphogenesis. When differences occur, they are related to phonological and lexical variation between varieties. A comparative analysis of the final auxiliary verb systems of various Tibetic languages by Nicolas Tournadre also reveals that the range of evidential morphemes across the Tibetic family is limited, while lexical choices in a particular variety can be diagnostic of that variety's group membership (Tournadre 1996; Tournadre and Jiatso 2001: 82–88).

How does Baima fit into this picture? Table 4 provides Pingwu Baima evidentials together with their function equivalents in various Tibetic languages, including Standard Tibetan, two Khams varieties, and three Amdo varieties (comprising two Tibetic languages of the border areas between southern Gansu and northern Sichuan, Thebo and Mdzo-dge) (based on Tournadre and Jiatso 2001: 84–87; J. Sun 1993).

The comparative data in Tab. 4 suggest that the Pingwu Baima system may combine features of different groups of Tibetic languages. On the one hand, Pingwu Baima is similar to Central and Khams varieties in marking a distinction between centrifugal and centripetal evidentials and sharing the receptive egophoric marker *byung*. Interestingly, in Pingwu Baima, these are the markers that are but little grammaticalized and relatively marginal (especially /ɕy³⁵/). For that reason, they are possibly recent additions to the Pingwu Baima system. On the other hand, Pingwu Baima may share some irregular developments with the Tibetic varieties spoken in its neighborhood, at the border of Sichuan and Gansu provinces. One such development is a possible link between the indirect evidential marker and the indefinite marker in Mdzo-dge Tibetan (both /zəɡ/). That is a parallel in Pingwu Baima, where the indirect and factual marker /ʂə³³/ is homophonous with the indefinite marker /ʂə³³/ (as in example 29). In his analysis of Mdzo-dge, J. Sun (1993: 953) proposes a cross-linguistically infrequent grammaticalization path from the indefinite marker to the indirect evidential via the semantic extension referential indefiniteness > evidential indirectness.

Tab. 4: Evidential markers in Pingwu Baima compared to their function equivalents in various Tibetan languages (adapted from Tournadre and Jiatso 2001: 84–87; J. Sun 1993).

Dialect Marker	Pingwu Baima	Ü-Tsang Lhasa	Khams Chunyido	Khams Nakchu	Amdo Labrang	Amdo Thebo	Amdo Mdzo-dge
Prospective egophoric	i⁵³ gyis?	gi-yin	ɟiɟɛ̃n gyi-yin	ɟiɟɛ̃n gyi-yin	ʈi̠ rgyu-yin	ɕi ʔrgyu	jod
Prospective non-egophoric	re²¹³ red	gi-red	lireʔ le-red	lereʔ le-red	ʈireʔ rgyu-red	ɕi gi ʔrgyu-'gi	yod
Durative / Existential egophoric	ʐɤ³⁴¹ yod	gi-yod	ɕɯ bzhin-yod	ɕɯ ʔbzhin-*'od	go gi-yod	yije ʔbzhin-yod / ʔgi-yod	jod jodʰka
Durative / Existential non-egophoric	nɔ²¹³ snang	gi-yod- red	ɕioreʔ bzhin-yod-red	lereʔ le-red	joka/gə *gi-yod-ni-red	yijelegi ʔ*bzhin-yod-le-'gi	ʔyod-'gi
Egophoric experiential	tʰa⁵³ʐɤ³⁴¹ cha yod	myong	ɲɔ̃ŋ myong	ɲɔ̃ŋ myong	ɲɔ̃ŋ myong	ɲɯ myong myong	ɲɔŋ myong
Perfective egophoric intentional	uɛ³³ ?	pa-yin	leɟɛ̃n le-yin	leɟin le-yin	ni/nəjen ni-yin	pu le ?	(ne)¹⁰ ʔni-yin
Direct (centrifugal)	tɕʰɛ³⁵ chas	song	tʰen thal	tʰi thal	tʰa thal	tʰjɛ tʰa	tʰæ thal
Perfective egophoric receptive (centripetal)	ɕy³⁵ byung	byung	? ?	tɕũŋ byung	tʰa thal	tʰjɛ thal	
Indirect	ʂə³³ ?	bzhag	ɕada bzhag-gda'	ɕʌɣda ʔbzhag- gda'	tãŋzək/ ʐogə dang-zug	puɕi ?	zeg ʔzag indefinite marker
Factual	ʂə³³ ?	pa-red	lereʔ le-red	lereʔ gi-red	nəreʔ ni-red	le gi *le-'gi	na re ni-red

10 Jackson Sun (1993: 958) analyzes the enclitic /nə/ as "nothing more than a slot-filler with minimal semantic content or pragmatic function, serving merely to add phonological bulk to monosyllabic predicators." This is quite different from Pingwu Baima, where /uɛ³³/ has a clear function of an evidential.

In contrast to the centrifugal-centripetal distinction shared with Central and Khams varieties, that feature that is common between Pingwu Baima and Mdzodge relates to the etymologically obscure, high-frequency marker /ʂə³³/, which is therefore likely to belong to the core layer of the evidential-aspectual system of Baima. If discovered in other Tibetic languages of northern Sichuan and southern Gansu, the unusual development from the indefinite marker to the indirect evidential marker may be taken as evidence of close historical relationship between these varieties, supporting the Eastern grouping of Tibetic languages. Naturally, more work is required to arrive at a more complete view of Baima, Tibetic varieties in its neighbourhood and their relationship to each other.

Overall, the system of evidentiality in Pingwu Baima appears quite dissimilar to other Tibetic languages in its lexical choices, etymological origins and morphology (note the lack in Pingwu Baima of any nominalizing or connective morphemes commonly attached to verb stems in other Tibetic languages). Whether an idiosyncratic development, a product of competing contact processes, or (most likely) a combination of the two, the system of evidentiality in Pingwu Baima stands out as fairly unique in the Tibetic context, nicely illustrating the diversity of evidential systems among Tibetic languages.

Abbrevations

Abbreviations not included in the Leipzig Glossing Rules are: EGO egophoric, EXP experiential, INT intentional, LOG logophoric, PRSP prospective, RCP receptive. The question mark sign ("?") marks tentative WT glosses.

References

Chirkova, Katia. 2007. Between Tibetan and Chinese: Identity and language in Chinese South-West. *Journal of South Asian Studies* 30(3). 405–417.
Chirkova, Katia. 2008a. Baimayu shizheng fanchou ji qi yu Zangyu fangyan de bijiao 白马语示证范畴及其与藏语方言的比较 [Evidentials in Baima and Tibetan dialects compared]. *Minzu Yuwen* 《民族语文》 [Minority Languages of China] 3. 36–43.
Chirkova, Katia. 2008b. On the position of Baima within Tibetan: A look from basic vocabulary. In Alexander Lubotsky, Jos Schaeken, and Jeroen Wiedenhof (eds.), *Evidence and counterevidence: Festschrift for F. Kortland, Volume 2: General linguistics*, 69–91. Amsterdam: Rodopi.
Chirkova, Katia. 2008c. Baima Zangzu wei Dizu shuo zhiyi 白马藏族为氐族说质疑 [The Baima Tibetans and the Di People of Chinese Historical Records: Challenging the Link]. *Bulletin of Chinese Linguistics* 3(1). 167–180.
Häsler, Katrin Louise. 1999. *A Grammar of the Tibetan Sde.dge Dialect*. Berne: Berne University dissertation.

Häsler, Katrin Louise. 2001. An empathy-based approach to the description of the verb system of the Dege dialect of Tibetan. *Linguistics of the Tibeto-Burman Area* 24(1). 1–34.

Hill, Nathan W. 2013. Come as lord of the black-headed: an Old Tibetan mythic formula. In Christoph Cüppers, Robert Mayer, and Michael Walter (eds.), *Tibet after empire: Culture, society and religion between 850–1000*, 169–179. Lumbini: Lumbini International Research Institute.

Huang Bufan 黄布凡 and Zhang Minghui 张明慧. 1995. Baima zhishu wenti yanjiu 白马话支属问题研究 [A study of the genetic affiliation of Baima]. *Zhongguo Zangxue* 《中国藏学》 [Tibetology in China] 2. 79–118.

Huang Bufan 黄布凡, Xu Shouchun 许寿椿, Chen Jiaying 陈嘉瑛, and Wang Huiyin 王会银 (eds.). 1992. *Zang-Mian yuzu yuyan cihui* 《藏缅语族语言词汇》 [A Tibeto-Burman lexicon]. Beijing: Zhongyang Minzu Daxue 中央民族大学出版社.

Jacques, Guillaume. 2014. Cone. In Jackson T.-S. Sun (ed.), *Phonological profiles of little-studied Tibetic varieties* (Language and Linguistics Monograph Series 55), 269–375. Taipei: Academia Sinica, Institute of Linguistics.

Kuno, Susumu. 1987. *Functional syntax: Anaphora, discourse and empathy*. Chicago: The University of Chicago Press.

Lehmann, Christian. 1995. *Thoughts on grammaticalization* (LINCOM Studies in Theoretical Linguistics 01). München & Newcastle: Lincom Europa.

Lin, You-Jing. 2014. Thebo. In Jackson T.-S. Sun (ed.), *Phonological profiles of little-studied Tibetic varieties* (Language and Linguistics Monograph Series 55), 215–267. Taipei: Academia Sinica, Institute of Linguistics.

Nagano, Yasuhiko. 1995. Function of Written Tibetan instrumental particle, *-kyis*, revisited. In Nishi Yoshio, James A. Matisoff, Yasuhiko Nagano (eds.), *New horizons in Tibeto-Burman morphosyntax*, 133–142. Osaka: National Museum of Ethnography.

Nishida, Tatsuo 西田龙雄 and Sun Hongkai 孙宏开. 1990. *Hakuba yakugo no kenkyū: Hakuba no kōzō to keitō* 《白馬譯語の研究：白馬語の构造と系統》 [A study of the Baima-Chinese vocabulary 'Baima yiyu': the structure and affiliation of the Baima language]. Kyoto 京都: Shokado 松香堂.

Sun, Hongkai 孙宏开. 1980a. Baima ren de yuyan 白马人的语言 [The language of the Baima people]. In Sichuan Institute of Minority Nationalities 四川民族研究所编 (eds.), *Baima Zangzu renshu wenti taolunji* 《白马藏人族属问题讨论集》 [Genetic affiliation of Baima Tibetans], 15–25. Chengdu: Sichuan Institute of Minority Nationalities 四川民族研究所.

Sun, Hongkai 孙宏开. 1980b. Lishi shang de Dizu he Chuan Gan diqu de Baima ren 历史上的氐族和川甘地区的白马人 [The Di people of historical records and the Baima people of Sichuan and Gansu]. *Minzu Yanjiu* 《民族研究》 [Nationalities Studies] 3. 33–43.

Sun, Hongkai 孙宏开. 2003. Baimayu shi Zangyu de yige fangyan huo tuyu ma? 白马语是藏语的一个方言或土语吗? [Is Baima a dialect or vernacular of Tibetan?]. *Yuyan Kexue* 《语言科学》 [Linguistic Sciences] 1(2). 65–75.

Sun Hongkai 孙宏开, Katia Chirkova 齐卡佳, and Liu Guangkun 刘光坤. 2007. *Baima yu yanjiu* 《白马语研究》 [A study of the Baima language]. Beijing: Minzu Chubanshe.

Sun, Jackson T.-S. 1993. Evidentials in Amdo Tibetan. *Bulletin of the Institute of History and Philology* 《中央研究院历史语言研究所集刊》 63(4). 945–1001.

Sun, Jackson T.-S. 2003a. Phonological profile of Zhongu: a new Tibetan dialect of Northern Sichuan. *Language and Linguistics* 4(4). 769–836.

Sun, Jackson T.-S. 2003b. Qiuji Zangyu de yuyin tezheng 求吉藏语的语音特征 [Phonological characteristics of Chos-rje Tibetan]. *Minzu Yuwen* 《民族语文》 [Minority Languages of China] 6.1–6.

Tournadre, Nicolas. 1996. Comparaison des systèmes médiatifs de quatre dialectes tibétains (tibétain central, ladakhi, dzongkha et amdo). In Zlatka Guentcheva (ed.), *L'énonciation médiatisé*, 195–213. Louvain: Peeters.

Tournadre, Nicolas. 2014. The Tibetic languages and their classification. In Thomas Owen-Smith and Nathan W. Hill (eds.), *Trans-Himalayan linguistics: Historical and descriptive linguistics of the Himalayan area* (Trends in Linguistics Studies and Monographs Vol. 266), 105–129. Berlin: Mouton de Gruyter.

Tournadre, Nicolas and Konchok Jiatso. 2001. Final auxiliary verbs in literary Tibetan and in the dialects. *Linguistics of the Tibeto-Burman Area* 24.1: 49–111.

Tournadre, Nicolas and Sangda Dorje. 2003. *Manual of Standard Tibetan: Language and civilization*. Ithaca, New York: Snow Lion Publications.

Tournadre, Nicolas and Randy J. LaPolla. 2014. Towards a new approach to evidentiality: Issues and directions for research. *Linguistics of the Tibeto-Burman Area* 37(2). 240–263.

Zhang, Jichuan 张济川. 1994a. Baimahua yu Zangyu, shang 白马话与藏语（上）[Baima and Tibetan, Part 1]. *Minzu Yuwen* 《民族语文》[Minority Languages of China] 2. 11–24.

Zhang, Jichuan 张济川. 1994b. Baimahua yu Zangyu, xia 白马话与藏语（下）[Baima and Tibetan, Part 1]. *Minzu Yuwen* 《民族语文》[Minority Languages of China] 3. 58–67.

Zhang, Jichuan. 1997. Particularités phonetiqués du baima. *Cahiers de Linguistique Asie Orientale* 26(1). 131–153.

Index

absolutive 278
access to information 2, 63, 65, 96, 98, 104, 108, 114, 120, 125, 161f1, 261, 267, 280f18, 424, 436, 438, 446–447
addressee 66, 98, 110, 121, 124, 319–322, 324
– addressee perspective 269–270, 281–282, 316, 319–321
adjective clauses 44, 97, 194, 197–200, 214, 223, 268–270, 302, 304–305, 316, 319, 329, 399
– comparatives 199–200
– superlatives 199
affirmation 52
Africanist tradition 166
Aikhenvald, Alexandra 1, 2, 8, 11, 13–14, 17, 21f20, 26f24, 42, 97–98, 116, 118, 125–126, 131–132, 180, 235, 261, 262f2, 353
Aktionsart 367–368, 377, 381–382, 395
allomorphy 279, 284
alterphoric 77, 361–363
Amazonian languages 95
Amdo Tibetan 1, 28, 42, 46–48, 55, 61, 67–68, 73–75, 81, 95, 100f5, 105, 107–108, 113, 123–126, 170, 367–418, 446, 455–457
– A rig 378, 389, 392
– Chab cha 370–373, 378, 401
– cross-dialect 370
– dPa'ris 46–48, 55
– Gonghe 73
– Labrang 456
– Mdzo dge 27–28, 73–75, 370–373, 378–387, 404, 456–457
– Mgo log 27–28, 73–75, 370, 379, 381–388, 392–394, 397–403, 405, 407–410, 412–417
– Pari (Hwari) 107
– Reb gong 26, 397
– Them chen 24f21, 27, 73, 346, 370–374, 378, 387–389, 395–396, 398, 406, 409–412
– Thewo 48, 107, 456

Amerindian languages 166
andative 166–168, 170–171, 179
animacy 50, 124–125, 430, 433–435
anticipation rule 66, 83–84, 97–98, 108f16, 113–114, 190f5, 269, 319–320, 357–360, 373, 408, 428, 449, 455
aorist 25f23, 145, 355
aspect 81–82, 97, 116, 139–156, 174–175, 180, 226, 229, 243, 255, 268, 352, 367, 372–373, 381, 383–403, 437
assertion 96, 323f19
assertive 15, 147–148, 336–337
assimilated knowledge 76–77, 120, 310–312, 320–322, 354–356
assumptive 103–104, 109–113, 114, 120f25, 126, 132, 180, 263, 292
attention marker 301, 315, 319, 321, 324, 344f33
attributive 191, 235, 245, 268, 304, 315, 319, 330–331, 354–356
auditory evidence 45, 102, 108, 138, 189, 238, 241, 325
auxiliary verbs 20–28, 43, 46–47, 62–63, 67, 70, 74–75, 81–82, 99, 111, 115, 162, 167f8, 171–173, 175–179, 181, 187–200, 203–222, 226, 229, 235–241, 297, 321, 352, 377, 436–441
Awa Pit 14, 17f15, 66–67, 87

Bacot, Jacques 53
Bailey, T. Grahame 22
Baima, Pingwu 29, 445–457
Balti 2, 14f11, 20, 42–46, 95, 102f6, 105, 261, 292, 313
– Khaplu 46, 55
– Turtuk 45–46, 55, 102f6, 107
– Tyakshi 43–45, 55, 102f6, 107
Baonan 369
Barbacoan languages 14, 66, 84, 87
Barnes Janet 152
Bartee, Ellen 6, 48, 117, 123, 125
Bashir, Elena 14f11
Beckwith, Christopher 5–6, 29

Bell, Charles 4
Bendix, Edward 10–11
benefactive 107, 110, 123–124, 436, 439–440
Bhaichung Tsichudarpo 299
Bhat, D.N.S. 21f20
Bhutia 2, *see also* Denjongke
Bickel, Balthasar 269–270
Bielmeier, Roland 20–22, 43, 102f6, 326
binary features analysis 3, 5–6, 24, 117, 132
Bloomfield, Leonard 134
Boas, Franz 1f1
Bodish 61–62, 80–82, 89
Bogaia 132, 139, 142
Bunan 385f11
Byrne, St. Quentin 25
byung 24, 63, 65, 69–70, 80, 89
– across varieties 89, 456
– in Diasporic Common Tibetan 69–70, 233, 239–240
– historical development 65, 80, 161–181
– in Lhasa Tibetan 188, 191, 205–208, 218, 222–223
– in Middle Tibetan 80, 161–170
– in Pingwu Baima 451–456
– in Zhollam 75–76, 440–443
bzhag 7, 136, 142, 143–149, 225, 227, 241, 250–255

Caplow, Nancy 7, 63, 69–70, 72, 232
case marking 278, 302–304
Causemann, Margret 28
Central Pomoan 87
Central Tibetan 42, 52, 100f5, 125, 145, 455–457 *see also* Lhasa Tibetan
certainty 5, 113, 225–226, 230–234, 241, 246–250, 254, 323f19, 373, 375, 396, 414–416
– non-certainty 225, 231, 233–234, 241–242, 245–246, 254
certantive 279–284
cessative 175, 179
Chafe, Wallace 375
Chang, Kun and Betty Shefts Chang 5–6, 144–145, 148f15
child language 219f25, 299, 320
Chinese 123, 170, 369f3, 448f6
Chirkova, Katia 29

Chochangacha 25, 126
Chonjore, Tsetan 14, 253
cislocative 166–175, 179–181, 436, 440–441, 452
Classical Tibetan 53, 55, 74, 78, 99–100, 105, 107, 112–113, 151, 229f4, 299
clitic 104, 228, 266f9, 303f7, 362–363, 381
co-reference 10, 116–117, 313
Coblin, South W. 54
commands 97
Comrie, Bernard 136, 387, 395
concurring 333–334, 336
conditional 74, 272–273, 411f23
Cone 107
conjecture 132f1, 232–233, 245
conjunct 87, 98, 280 *see* conjunct/disjunct
conjunct/disjunct 5–6, 8, 16–19, 22–23, 26–28, 61–62, 69, 74, 83–84, 98, 115–118, 125, 280f18, 389f15
– historical development 83
– history of scholarship 16–19, 115–118, 126
– and person agreement 10–11, 13–14, 69
– terminology 116–118, 280f18
conjunctive 268, 274
contact 61, 80–81, 457
continuous 150, 192f6, 196, 199, 212f14, 270
control *see* volition
conversation 8, 21, 316, 352, 387f14, 404, 407, 411, 424
conviction 23, 216f22
copula verb 23, 25, 51, 62–63, 65, 74–75, 78, 81–82, 88, 98, 101, 113, 273–275, 287–290, 297–346, 352, 355–361, 364, 381, 416–418, 424–430
corpus 72f5, 105–106, 161–162, 164, 167, 171, 174, 181, 340, 454

Dahl, Östen 15f13, 62f2
Daudey, Henriëtte 81–82
deduction 241, 246, 250, 252, 255, 263, 267, 280, 282
deferred evidence 225–226, 237, 239–240, 250, 254–255
deixis 4, 99, 161–181
– personal 165, 167, 171, 177, 179, 181
– relative 165–168, 171, 176–177, 179, 181
– and speaker 165

Index

DeLancey, Scott 5–6, 8–17, 24, 25, 29–30, 61, 64, 116, 118–121, 124, 131–132, 143–152, 155–156, 250–252, 353, 395f18
demonstratives 292–294
– obviate 263, 293–294
– proximate 263, 292–294
Denjongke 25, 67–68, 72–73, 297–346
Denwood, Philip 6, 13, 30, 148f15, 174, 177
desire 220–221, 238–239
dialogue 293, 301, 381, 388
Diasporic Common Tibetan 67–70, 87, 225–249, 251, 253–255
– comparison to Lhasa Tibetan 225–228
– definition of 225–226
Dickinson, Connie 14f11, 87
Dingri 24, 66
direct evidence 5, 7, 27–28, 48, 75, 131, 136–138, 150, 196–197, 212f17, 225, 233, 235, 240, 262, 266, 276–277, 357, 425, 438, 456
– direct evidential 63, 65, 371, 374–376, 380–394, 400–403, 447–448, 450–451, 453–454
– *see* sensory evidential
– and inference 132, 136–156
– and negation 152
– testimonial 268–269, 272–273
discourse 3, 17, 66, 165, 341, 367f2, 375, 387, 406–407, 413–414
discovery 30, 48–50, 118, 150–151, 154, 205, 359, 363
disjunct *see* conjunct/disjunct
dKon mchog Tshe ring 52
Dorje, Sangda *see* Manual of Standard Tibetan *under* Tournadre, Nicolas
Driem, George van 25, 77, 108–109, 111, 116–118, 121, 124, 319, 351–352, 354–356, 359–361, 364
Drokpa 24, 67, 228, 340 *see also* Diasporic Common Tibetan
Drugchu 107
dubitative 84, 113, 313, 434, 436
'dug 107–108, 114
– in Classical Tibetan 30, 107f12
– correspondence to forms in other varieties 48, 52, 107
– in Denjongke 73, 302–305, 320–326, 331–333, 343

– in Diasporic Common Tibetan 225, 233, 235–247, 249
– in Drokpa 24
– in Dzongkha 25, 354–357, 363–364
– historical development 30, 107
– in Ladakhi 21–22, 43, 108
– in Lhasa Tibetan 4, 5, 6, 7–8, 13–14, 41, 79, 99–101, 103, 107f14, 118–121, 188–190, 196–199, 203–204, 213–214, 217–218, 250–251, 253
– and mirativity 118–121
– in Purik 22, 262, 267–274, 294–295
– in Southern Mustang 23
– in Spiti-Khunu-Garzha 108
– in Tö Ngari 108
– in Written Tibetan 53
– in Yolmo 24
Dulong 180
Duna 14, 132, 138–142, 149
durative 22, 29, 145, 317, 387, 395, 448, 456
Dzongkha 25, 67–68, 76–78, 80, 107–109, 111, 113, 118, 121, 124–126, 298, 310–313, 319, 333, 351–364

Ebihara, Shiho 20, 21, 27, 46–48, 102f6, 370–373, 387, 404
ego 7, 61–62, 63, 110, *see also* egophoric; personal
egophoric 23, 27–30, 4786–91, 104–105, 110–114, 126, 174–179, 181, 253, 310–313, 346, 456 *see also* personal
– across varieties 61–62, 68, 74, 80, 89, 110–113, 126, 311–313, 426–427, 429, 455
– in Amdo 367, 373, 378–382, 384–393, 396–398, 400–418
– broad scope 7, 65, 70, 72, 77, 81, 85–86, 88, 111–113, 353, 426
– and conjunct/disjunct 80, 83–84, 116
– definition 353, 367
– in Diasporic Common Tibetan 66–70
– in Dzongkha 352–353, 361–364
– egophoric/non-egophoric system 423–426, 428–438, 440, 442–443, 446–449
– and egophoricity 80, 83–84
– historical development 72, 78–80, 82, 174, 177–179, 379
– in Lhasa Tibetan 5–6, 8, 15–19, 61–80

- narrow scope 6–7, 65, 70, 72, 79, 111
- and neutral 335f27
- non-egophoric 18, 19, 46–47, 55, 75, 78, 81–82, 89, 346, 374, 384, 390–392, 400–401, 404–418, 423–426, 428–438, 440, 442–443, 449, 456
- other senses of the term 19, 66, 110
- and person 113–114
- in Pingwu Baima 448–455
- scope 6–7, 51, 61, 64–65, 70, 72, 89, 111, 312–313, 346, 353, 429
- similar phenomena in other language families 84–88
- systems 19, 116
- terminology of 110, 116–117, 229, 310–311, 244–425
- typology of 110–113
- zero-marked 75, 378–379, 390
- in Zhollam 423–426, 428–438, 440, 442–443

egophoricity 18–19, 30, 61–62, 66, 80, 83–84
elicitation 17, 227, 300, 340, 368, 381, 424, 433
ELPA (existential, locative, possessive, attributive) 229, 235–237, 243, 303–304, 314 see also existential
empathy 174, 310, 328, 450f7
emphasis 115, 193, 319, 388, 396, 401, 417
endopathic 99, 108, 110, 114, 118, 176, 237–238, 279, 281, 282, 398, 436, 440, 449, 451, 453, 455
English 137, 152, 223, 299
epistemic 3, 95–101, 105–107, 113–114, 225–234, 240, 261, 355–356, 364, 367–368, 373–374, 384, 394, 411, 413–416
- neutral 264, 273, 376
equational copula 51, 63, 73, 101, 243, 262–264, 287–290, 302–317, 326–331, 335, 356, 358–361, 416–418, 424–430
Euchee 180
evidential/epistemic system (E/E) 95–126, 367–418
evidentiality
- and aspect 394–403
- categorization of 5–6, 17, 25, 42, 61, 133, 148–149, 231–232, 235, 303, 312, 313, 335, 345, 356, 359, 370, 430, 454

- choice 72, 75, 82, 98, 119, 233, 327, 412
- context of use 6–7, 17, 72, 81, 118–121, 223, 265, 318, 355, 373, 379, 399, 404
- default 26, 65f4, 109, 113–114, 254, 371
- definition of 2–3, 161f1, 261–262, 310–311, 353
- and dreams 108, 324, 355
- and epistemics 96–99, 105–106, 225–255, 353, 364, 367–370, 373–374, 377, 394
- extension of meaning 234, 262f4, 266–267, 311, 321, 399
- frequency 105–106
- and genre 375, 387f14, 394, 411
- hierarchy 327
- historical development 1–3, 29–30, 42, 54, 56, 65, 72, 78–80, 99–100, 107, 112–113, 161–181, 262
- history of study 1–31, 95–96
- internal states 79, 108, 133, 233, 237–239, 397–398, 402, 450–451, 453
- and images, mirrors, film 108, 121, 362
- morphologically complex forms 233–234, 241, 246–247, 253, 263, 302, 333–345, 356, 380–382, 454–455
- and negation 73, 75, 107f14, 177, 188–189, 191, 194, 200, 211–213, 216–217, 219, 221–223, 263–265, 268, 270–272, 274, 275, 278, 287, 303, 310, 327, 334, 364, 381, 397, 427, 433
- non-evidential 28, 232, 253–254, 370–371, 373–375, 404, 406, 410–412
- obligatoriness 137, 179, 226, 331, 364, 369, 377–378, 384, 399
- and person 14, 65, 97–99, 108–109, 110–113
- pragmatics of use 77, 82, 98–99, 108, 118, 254, 319, 354, 453
- and tense 22, 136–156, 374–375
- terminology 3, 13, 15, 19, 30, 147f14, 148f15, 262f5, 353, 424–425
- translation 140–142, 154–155, 249, 308, 322, 334f26, 344, 354, 388
- typology of 1–2, 25, 67, 95–99, 117–118, 126, 131–133, 223–224, 351–352, 429–430, 434–435, 455–456
- unspecified 230, 232, 240, 244–248, 253, 269f11, 291

– zero marked 27, 75, 378–379, 383f10, 390, 405
existential verb 5, 6, 41, 43, 46, 49, 52, 63, 73, 81–82, 98, 99, 113, 188–191, 235, 262–264, 267–289, 302–308, 317–320, 335, 354–358, 429, 430–436, 456
experiential evidential 5, 21f20, 24, 29, 123

Facetious Tales of the Corpse, The 170–172
factual evidential 62, 72, 85–87, 104, 109, 112, 115, 180, 448, 456
– in Amdo 367, 373–377, 382, 384, 390, 403, 405–415
– in Diasporic Common Tibetan 232–234, 243
– in Lhasa Tibetan 5–7, 23, 24, 27, 29
– in Purik 264, 267, 273, 277–278, 287–288
Fasu 85–86, 262f4
finite verbs 11, 154, 364, 367, 376, 452
first person 4–6, 8–12, 16–17, 20–23, 25, 28–29, 46, 63, 64, 69, 83–85, 99, 108–109, 110–115, 117, 123, 125, 162–163, 198, 204, 218, 312–313, 316, 323, 346, 355, 389–390, 401, 429, 440–441, 448–449, 453–454
– non-first person 22, 69, 77–78, 83–87, 449, 451, 454
Fleck, David W. 132
Floyd, Simeon 18–19, 61
focus 27, 376, 404
Foe 17, 85–86, 132, 156, 262f4
Foley, William and Robert van Valin 373
folk tales 301, 308, 316, 337, 346
Francke, August Hermann 21
future
– action 280
– events 213f20, 279, 281, 285, 415, 436, 441
– non-future 441
future tense 23, 25, 27, 63, 98, 103–104, 110, 123, 162, 376, 437, 447
– in Amdo 371, 374, 406, 412–416
– in Diasporic Common Tibetan 226, 229, 237f15, 241, 246
– in Lhasa Tibetan 189f4, 190, 199, 201, 203f14, 213–216, 218
– in Purik 263, 270

Garrett, Edward 6, 13, 14, 63, 64–66, 116–117, 229
Garzha 68, 108, 121
Gawne, Lauren 20, 65f4, 72, 112, 116–117, 310f12, 332, 429
general knowledge 23–25, 70, 72, 86, 104, 196, 216, 233, 255, 339, 265–266, 282, 338–339, 375–376, 404, 412, 427
generic event 279–280
genitive 304, 356, 401, 417
geographical distribution 20, 41, 55, 56, 67–68, 369, 423, 435–436
gnomic 23, 72, 75–76
Goldstein, Melvyn C. 5, 144, 243f17, 338f28
grammaticality judgements 17, 64, 426, 428
grammaticalization 41, 56, 80, 99, 102, 112–113, 126, 174, 177, 181, 311, 316, 346, 454
Greenberg, Joseph H. 134
Grierson, George Abraham 326f20
Gtsang smyong he ru ka (Tsang Nyön Héruka) 79, 162

Haan, Ferdinand de 96, 154–155, 180
habitual 7, 110, 154, 212, 216f22, 217, 264, 275, 286–287, 338f29, 376, 379, 390–391, 405
Hagège, Claude 15f13, 110
Hale, Austin 8–13, 19
Haller, Felix 24, 27, 76, 116–117, 370–373, 386–389, 392, 395f18, 404–406, 409
Hargreaves, David 10–11, 280f18
Häsler, Katrin Louise 329
Haspelmath, Martin 133, 136
ḥdug see 'dug
hearsay 7, 20, 49, 73, 104, 234, 353, 362–364, 425, 441 *see also* reported speech
Helambu Sherpa *see* Yolmo
Hengeveld, Kees and Hella Olbertz 131–132, 149–152, 156
Hermann, Silke 24
heterophoric 5, 116f22
Hill, Nathan W. 7, 15f14, 30, 63, 72, 79, 103f8, 119–120, 149–152, 353f2
Hiroyuki Suzuki 29, 51–52
Hongladarom, Krisadawan 6, 7, 15f14, 29–30, 49–50, 65f4

honorific 116f22, 202f12, 210f16, 221, 300
Hooper, Robin 180
hortative 378
Hoshi Michiyo 13, 30
Hoshi, Izumi 53, 79
Hualapai 132, 156
Huber, Brigitte 24, 71, 121
Hyolmo *see* Yolmo
hypothetical 96, 165, 289
Hyslop, Gwendolyn 3, 25, 77, 80–81, 83, 319, 353, 362

identification 51, 307, 327–328
immediate evidence 27, 151, 371
imperative 97, 162, 221, 364, 377–379, 411, 447
imperfect 200, 213–214, 218, 220–221, 390–391
imperfective 48, 139–140, 162, 167, 200, 201, 210, 212, 214, 218–221, 371, 381–382, 395–398, 400, 402–403, 406
impersonal verbs *see* volition
inceptive 395–396
inchoative 173, 175–176, 178–179, 265, 402
indirect evidence 5, 7, 27–28, 75, 131, 225, 233, 235, 263, 273, 291, 371–374, 380–389, 393–394, 397–399, 447– 448, 450–451, 456
induction 262, 267
inessive 268, 295
inference 50–52, 53, 71, 96, 102, 104, 109, 120–121, 126, 131–132, 136–156, 213, 225–226, 231, 233, 238, 240–255, 262–264, 284, 357–360, 427
– based on fact 232
– based on new information 275–276
– based on results 99, 109, 121, 131, 137–138, 230, 241–242, 251–252, 451
– based on perception 232, 241, 243, 245, 247, 357–358
– based on personal knowledge 232, 247
– based on reasoning 109, 225, 230, 250, 255, 277f17
– based on unspecified evidence 243, 245–246
– of action 248–249
– of subject 248

inferential evidential 21f20, 22–23, 25, 55, 71, 131, 238, 240–255, 264, 274–276, 353, 371, 389, 454
infinitive 200, 210–222, 268, 270–271, 289, 352
instigator 9–10, 23, 277, 279, 401, 448, 453
intention *see* volition
International Phonetic Alphabet 63f3, 228, 301, 352f1, 425
interrogative 3, 47, 66, 75, 84, 87–88, 97, 107f14, 108f16, 111, 115–116, 120–121, 267
– in Amdo 373, 377–379, 381, 386–387, 396–397, 408–409, 413
– content questions 188, 191, 201–202, 208, 210, 211, 216, 308
– in Denjongke 302, 308–310, 319, 323–325, 327, 329–330
– in Dzongkha 357–358, 360
– in Lhasa Tibetan 9, 11–12, 188, 190–191, 195–196, 201–203, 208, 210, 211, 212, 216, 222–223
– polar questions 188, 191, 201, 208, 210, 211, 216, 288–289, 427–428
– in Pingwu Baima 449
– in Purik 267, 269–270, 273, 274, 281, 284–286, 288–289, 293
– tag 115
– in Zhollam 425–429, 433–434, 440–441
intonation 278
intransitive 88, 265

Japanese 123, 216f22, 223
Jäschke, H.A. 41
Jirel 14, 22, 240

Kagate 240
Kaike 14
Kashaya 17, 84, 86–87, 132
Kham (language of Nepal) 132, 149–153
Kham Tibetan 28, 48–52, 53, 55, 107–108, 123–125, 446, 455–457
– Bathang 48, 50–51, 55, 107
– Brag-g.yab 29, 66
– Budy 48, 51, 55
– Chunyido 456
– Derge 329

- Dongwang 48–49, 55, 100f5, 105, 107, 123, 125–126
- Hor Tibetan 53, 107
- Nakchu 456
- Nangchen 28
- northern 99, 105, 107, 126
- Rgyalthang (or rGyalthang) 48–50, 55, 65f4, 66, 107, 346
- southern 434–435
- Zhollam 29, 48, 55, 66–68, 75–76, 423–443

Khenchen Lha Tsering Rinpoche 297
Khöpokhok 107
Khunu–Töt 68, 108, 121
Kitamura Hajime 7, 13
Koshal, Sanyukta 21
Kretschmar, Monika 24, 68–69
Kurtöp 68, 80–81, 83, 319, 362
Kyirong 24, 67–68, 70–72, 75, 79–80, 81, 86, 87, 95, 105, 121, 126, 318, 323f19, 326

Leipzig Glossing Rules 1, 30, 63f3, 266f9, 457
Lepcha 298
Lhadaki 1, 21–22, 43, 108, 113, 125–126, 261, 313
Lhasa Tibetan 2–19, 20, 27, 29–30, 31, 113, 116, 118, 123–126, 132, 174–181, 187–224, 225–228, 230, 243f17, 249–255, 262f6, 272f15, 299f3, 305, 316, 323, 327, 328, 353, 429, 456 see also Standard Tibetan

colloquial 253
- conjunct/disjunct analysis of 11–14
- evidentiality 2–19, 141f8, 142–149, 161, 174–181
- pedagogical grammars 3–5
- terminology 132, 225, 227f2

Lhoke 126, 298 see also Denjongke
Lhomi 14, 22, 240, 298f1, 326
Li, Fang Kuei 54
lo
- in Denjongke 302, 306f9, 331–333, 345
- in Dzongkha 362–363
- in Purik 263, 269–270, 290–291

locative 235, 268–270, 302, 304, 306, 308, 330–331, 334, 354–356, 431–432, 434–435
Loughnane, Robin 85–86, 142

malefactive 436, 439–440, 443
Mangghuer 369
map 55, 67, 435
Maricopa 132, 156
Matses 132, 156
Mélac, Eric 105–106, 116–117
mi la ras pa'i rnam thar 30, 79, 162–171
Middle Tibetan 80, 162–170, 174, 176, 179, 180
Milarepa 79, 162–170 see also *mi la ras pa'i rnam thar*
mirative 5, 23, 24f22, 25, 49–50, 55–56, 64, 77, 116, 118–121, 126, 149–153, 353, 356–357, 359, 363–364
- non-mirative 5, 64, 356, 359, 363
- as secondary connotation 121, 126, 321
Mithun, Marianne 87
mnemic 101, 115, 122–123
modality 3, 81–82, 99, 105, 310f12, 352, 374–376
Modern Literary Tibetan 30, 160, 170–174, 181
Mongghul 369
motion verbs 80, 99, 161–181, 266–267, 451–453

Nāgārjuna 133
narrative 79, 81, 124, 151, 227, 235, 241, 294, 301, 318, 337, 339, 375, 394, 396, 404, 406, 407, 412, 433, 437, 453–454
Nebesky-Wojkowitz, de (transliteration convention) 30, 423f1
negation 74–75, 152, 177, 377–378
- scope 268, 288, 382
neutral
- in Amdo 375–376, 379, 384, 403, 410–412, 417
- in Denjongke 302–303, 310, 314–315, 326–331, 335–341
- neutral evidential 15, 28–30, 73–74, 438
new knowledge 24–25, 46, 47, 49–50, 71, 118–121, 205, 268, 292–294, 311–316, 321–322, 331, 353–360, 403–404
Newar
- Dolakha 83
- Kathmandu 8–11, 13–14, 17, 115, 280f18, 389f15

Newmeyer, Frederick J. 133–134
newspaper 171, 173–174
nominalization 99, 352
- in Denjongke 297, 302, 311, 313–314, 318, 335–340
- in Lhasa Tibetan 214, 218, 219f24, 223
- in Purik 268, 272, 287
non-finite 272–273, 303, 364, 411–412
Norbu, Kelsang 387–388
Norcliffe, Elizabeth 18–19, 61
Norman, Rebecca 21
Nornang, Nawang 5, 144, 243f17
novels 299, 301, 318, 336
Nuyts, Jan 96

objectivity 63, 189, 193–194, 198, 204, 208–209, 215, 217, 220, 271, 356, 411, 427
obligation 238–239
Oisel, Guillaume 30, 79, 253
Oksapmin 85–86, 132, 139, 141–142, 262f4
old knowledge 24–25, 71, 120–121, 262f6, 292, 310–318, 320–322, 331, 354–360, 438, 441
Old Tibetan 29–30, 31, 53–55, 74, 78, 95, 99, 229f4, 303f7, 370f5, 446
olfactory evidence 45, 102, 254, 325
'ong 163–166, 170–174, 179–181, 190–191, 203
origo 389–390, 398–399, 408, 410–411, 417 see also conjunct
orthography 30, 63f3, 100, 228, 299, 301, 352f1, 368–369, 423f1
Oswalt, Robert L. 86–87

Palden Lachungpa 299
Pāṇini 1
Papuan languages 14, 17, 84–86, 88, 95, 109f18, 139–142, 262f4
participant specific 15, 61 see egophoric
participatory evidential (in PNG) 84, 108, 109f18, 262f4
particle 78, 84, 201–202
passive state 199, 249, 399
past event or state 273, 276–278, 290, 316, 334, 371–372, 387, 405
- completed 276–277, 382, 395
- effect on present 211, 273–274, 277–278, 336, 344, 355, 387–390
- ongoing 395
- recent 320–321
past tense 22, 23, 27–28, 63, 98–99, 103, 107, 109, 123, 139–156, 162, 178, 189–191, 194, 200–205, 211–213, 219, 228, 237, 239, 243, 246, 248, 250, 255, 282, 289–290, 302, 307, 323, 336, 355, 381, 384, 393, 407, 414–415, 453
- completed past 99, 210, 407
- distant 178, 287, 289, 318, 323, 385
- dynamic 266–267
- non-past 447
- recent 178, 323, 385–386, 387
- simple 263–265
- testimonial 276–277
patronising 278
Pear Story 241
pedagogical grammars 3–5, 27
Pema Rinzing Takchungdarpo 299
perception 225, 230, 248–250
- current 225, 230, 235, 237–238, 243, 245–247, 249, 251, 254–255
- past 235, 240, 241, 251
perceptual evidential 61, 63, 198, 232, 235–241, 243 see also sensory
perfect 7, 63, 103–104, 107, 136–140, 142, 149–156, 237–241, 277–278, 381–382, 386–390, 437
- and inference 136–138, 241
- experiential 133, 136–156
- testimonial 250
perfective 48, 139–141, 162, 167, 171, 176, 179, 181, 200–205, 212–213, 264, 371, 382, 384–386, 395, 401–407, 456
performative evidential (in Pomoan) 84, 86–87
person agreement 4–5, 10–11, 16–17, 20–21, 26, 83–84, 116–118, 448–450, 453–454
person sensitive 18
person, subject correlation 123, 162–164, 226, 312–313, 316, 333, 354–355, 426, 440, 448–449
personal evidentials 2, 5–7, 15, 17, 19, 24–25, 27, 29, 61–62, 63, 66, 69–72, 79, 110, 112–113, 147–148, 232–233, 255, 310, 314–320

– in Denjongke 302–303, 312, 317–320, 326, 340–345
– in Kurtöp 80–81, 104
– in Oksapmin 141
Phenpo Tibetan 107
phonology 100f5, 301f5, 370, 446
phyin 162–166, 168, 179–181
plays 299
pluperfect 141, 203f13
poetry 299
Polynesian languages 166f7, 180
Pomoan languages 84, 86–88
possessive 52, 189, 191, 235, 245, 302, 304, 355–356, 431–432, 434
possibility 25, 233, 241, 374
Post, Mark 18f18, 115–116
prediction 113, 190, 279–280, 282, 288, 436
present state or action 263, 273, 316, 317, 320–321, 334, 338–339, 341–342, 344, 355, 362, 388, 390, 402
– ongoing 393
– temporary 311
present tense 25, 27, 29, 63, 98–99, 103, 107, 109, 139, 162, 189, 198, 203, 205, 237, 241, 246–247, 270, 307–308, 336, 399
– present perfect 225, 237, 239, 249, 255
progressive 28, 47, 77–78, 99, 103, 180, 263, 268, 301, 351–352, 361–362, 364, 391–393, 407, 437, 448f5
properties of an entity
– ability 288–289
– intrinsic 275, 288–289
prospective 264–268, 279–184, 280–281, 284–288, 456
protases 289
proverbs 299, 301, 404
proximity, spatiotemporal 312–313, 315, 317–318, 328–330, 343–344, 362, 385
Purik 2, 22, 43, 261–295, 261, 313

questions *see* interrogative
quotative 27, 263, 269–270, 282, 290–291, 371–372 *see also* reported evidential

radio 299
Rangan, K. 22

Read, Alfred F.C 43
realization 77, 118, 190, 240, 321, 359
receptive evidential 24, 63, 65–66, 69–70, 75–76, 80, 89, 110, 161, 175–179, 181, 199, 205–208, 219, 439–443, 448, 454, 456
– historical development 80, 175–179
receptivity 439–443
recognition 121, 239, 282, 359
red 4, 16, 86, 113, 326, 329
– in Amdo 27, 28, 417
– historical development 30
– in Diasporic Common Tibetan 228, 234, 239–240, 242–249
– in Lhasa Tibetan 100, 193–195, 197, 200, 210–216, 218–219, 222
reported evidential 21f20, 27, 104, 105, 232–234, 263, 302, 306f9, 331–333, 345, 351, 353, 362–363, 371
– absence 447f3
– historical development 105
reported speech 10, 12, 114, 116–118, 173, 233, 263, 269–270, 282, 290–291, 325, 447f3
requests 202, 206, 221, 408
resultative 264–265, 271, 277–278, 288–289
Reuse, Willem de 240
revelatory 145, 147–149, 250f18
Rgyal rabs gsal ba'i me long 30, 53–54, 79
rhetorical question 84, 358, 360–361
Rigzin, Karma 25
Robin, Françoise 170
Roerich, George de 26
Rule, W.M. 17, 85–86, 132

Salar 369
San Roque, Lila 18–19, 61, 85–86, 142
Schwieger, Peter 15f14, 29
second person 4–6, 8–12, 21–22, 25–29, 49, 73, 83–84, 99, 108–109, 113–115, 117, 123, 163–164, 192, 219, 316, 319, 354–355, 401, 407–408, 426, 428, 440, 449
self person 27, 73, 110, 424
self-centred 15, 61 *see* egophoric
self-corrective 101, 115, 121
semantic map 41, 55–56

semantic variation 41, 107
sensory inferential 96, 99, 103, 105–106, 109, 253
sensory/sensorial evidential 15, 21–25, 43, 45, 55, 61–62, 64, 70, 73, 99, 102–103, 107–109, 114, 118–121, 126, 139, 161, 171–181, 431, 453
– across varieties 311–313
– in Denjongke 302–303, 310–311, 314, 318, 320–326, 331, 334
– internal 108, 114 see also endopathic
– in Lhasa Tibetan 189–190, 196–199, 204, 208, 213, 217–218, 220, 254
– non-sensory 189, 217
– relationship to deixis 171
– relationship to inference 96, 99, 103, 105–106, 132, 139–156, 225–226, 243, 245, 248–255
– terminology 310–311
Shao, Mingyuan 375, 387, 392, 393, 404
Shar Tibetan 42, 52
shared perception 311, 331
Sharkhok 107
Sharma, D.D. 22
Shefts, Betty see Chang, Kun and Betty Shefts Chang
Sherpa 1, 2, 14, 22, 61, 69, 75, 95, 107, 116, 125–126, 132, 139, 240
Shigatse Tibetan 24, 28, 76, 326, 346
Sikkimese Bhutia see Denjongke
SIL see Summer Institute of Linguistics
simple negated genetic prospective 286
snag 21, 41–57, 75–76, 107–108
– in Amdo 46–48
– in Balti 43–46
– grammaticalisation 41, 56
– historical development 41, 49, 54, 56
– in Kham 48–52
– Ladakhi, absence from 43
– in Pingwi Baima 448–449
– Purik, absence from 43
– in Written Tibetan 53–54
– in Zhollam 51–52, 75–76, 424–439, 442
social media 171
song 21, 24, 80, 108, 125, 143–147, 161–169, 171–175, 177–179
– in Diasporic Common Tibetan 233, 235, 240–241, 248

– in Lhasa Tibetan 250–252
– in Purik 266–267, 291
songs 346
Southern Mustang 23, 69, 240
speaker engagement 69, 226, 323f19
speaker familiarity 188–195, 203, 211, 213, 220, 222
speaker involvement 69, 74, 81–82, 108–109, 111, 125, 174, 178, 209, 295, 311–314, 318, 340–343, 346, 450
speaker knowledge 61, 69, 74, 79, 84, 87, 104, 110–113, 174, 243, 255, 292, 311–314, 318, 339, 356, 362, 242
speaker perspective 2, 3, 43, 117, 267, 269–270, 318, 375–376, 446–447
speaker-performed actions 74, 222, 362, 371
speculative 356–361, 364
speech act participant 62f2, 79, 164f5
Spiti 68, 108, 121, 126
spoken Tibetan 53 see Standard Tibetan
Sprigg, Richard Keith 46
Standard Spoken Tibetan 95–126, 123 see also Standard Tibetan
Standard Tibetan, 31, 47, 62–68, 75–76, 79–81, 87–88, 95, 105, 111, 310–313, 338, 369, 395f18, 455, see also Lhasa Tibetan
– nomenclature 132, 225, 227f2
subjective 197, 223, 410–411
subordinate clauses 65f4, 97, 141f8, 153–154, 273, 289, 379
suffix, evidential 5, 6, 29, 44, 51, 73, 75, 77–78, 81–82, 99, 105–106, 264, 273–274, 290, 292, 381, 433
suffix, non-evidential 228, 355
Summer Institute of Linguistics 8, 22
Sun, Jackson 13, 26–28, 73–75, 81, 116–117, 370–373, 387, 395f18, 396, 404–405
Sung Lha, Kuo-Ming and Lha Byams Rgyal 387–388, 392, 393, 403–410
supposition 234, 425, 436

tactile evidence 45, 46, 102, 189, 205, 235, 262, 325
Takeuchi Tsuguhito 5, 29–30, 80
TAME (tense, aspect, modality, evidentiality), 18, 352, 382, 403

taste evidence 102, 324
tense 5, 7, 20, 83, 97–98, 131–156, 174, 226, 229, 243, 255, 268, 352, 367, 372–373, 383–394, 437
testimonial evidential 63, 250, 262, 264, 267, 276–277, 286, 290, 311 see also sensory evidential
third person 4–6, 9, 16, 21–22, 25–29, 46, 49, 52, 73, 77, 99, 108–111, 113–115, 123, 162–163, 192, 195, 198, 203, 219, 223, 316, 354–355, 361–362, 375, 388, 404, 410, 426–427, 432, 449
Tibetan
– across varieties 41, 95
– Amdo see Amdo
– Balti see Balti
– Central varieties 22–25, 42, 52
– Eastern varieties 26–29
– Kham see Kham
– nomenclature 31
– script 299, 301
– Southern varieties 80, 111, 126
– varieties of 2, 20–29, 53, 61, 67
– western Himalayan 111, 126
– Western varieties 20–22, 42–46, 68
– Western Archaic varieties 42–46
Tibetic 1, 23, 31, 61–80, 88–90, 95–126, 298, 345, 455
– definition of 95–96
Tibetosphere 80, 435
Tö Ngari 108, 126
Tokelauan 180
tone 228, 370, 425, 437, 447
Tournadre, Nicholas 1, 2, 6, 8, 13, 15–19, 25, 29–30, 63–66, 111, 117, 138–139, 147–148, 174–176, 178, 252, 353, 455
– and Konjok Jiatso 47, 52, 78–79, 429
– and LaPolla, Randy J. 2, 20, 63, 65–66, 95–96, 138, 261, 262f2, 373, 242
– *Manual of Standard Tibetan* 8, 63, 64, 121, 143, 147–148, 174–176, 178, 225, 269f11, 310–311, 373f7
transitive 162, 264–265, 274, 404
translocative 166–169, 171–175, 177–178, 181, 436, 452
Tribur, Zoe 27–28

truth value 4, 23, 196, 233, 375–376, 403, 412, 414, 418, 434, 450, 452
Tsafiki 14f11, 87
Tsang 162
Tsang Nyön Héruka 79, 162
Tshering, Karma 3, 25, 77
Tuyuca 151–152
typology 1, 2, 25, 67, 95–99, 110–113, 117–118, 126, 131–136

Ü-Tsang 99, 105, 107, 113, 123–124, 126

Vendler, Zeno 395
ventive 166, 168, 170–171, 176, 179, 180
verb
– dynamic 344, 395
– linking 99, 111, 226, 229, 235–236, 243–244, 302
– secondary 167–170, 173, 181
– serialisation 47, 167
– stative 88, 194, 344, 379, 396–401
– stem 162, 200, 229, 377, 383, 447
– verb clause 47, 97
Vesalainen, Olavi and Marja Vesalainen 22
Villiers, Jill de 320
Visser, Eline 137
visual evidence 13, 20, 22, 44–45, 48, 49, 51–53, 55, 87f6, 102, 108, 132, 139–142, 150–151, 180, 189, 205, 208, 237, 241, 262f4, 274, 325, 357, 402, 425, 431, 436, 438
– non-visual evidential 42–45, 108, 121, 425, 436, 438–439
Vokurková, Zuzana 105–106, 121, 225, 252–253
volition 9–10, 12, 24, 26, 27–29, 49, 64–65, 69, 70, 74–76, 78, 82, 83, 87, 116, 124, 168, 174, 456
– in Amdo 371, 373, 384, 388, 390, 395–396, 398–403, 409–410, 413
– in Diasporic Common Tibetan 226, 229
– in Lhasa Tibetan 200, 204–205, 218, 219f26
– in Pingwu Baima 448–449, 451, 453
– in Purik 267, 280–281, 285
Volkart, Marianne 148f15

Wadu Pumi 67, 80–82
Wang, Qingshan 27

warning 96, 123, 279, 284–285
Watahomigie, Lucille J. 132
Watters, David E. 149–153
Western Apache 240
Widmer Manuel 83
Willett, Thomas 131–132, 235
witnessed 7, 20, 23, 27, 28, 108–109, 118–119, 136, 251, 262, 266, 276–277, 375, 382, 403, 451
Woodbury, Anthony C. 22, 132f3, 139
World Atlas of Linguistic Structures 1
written language 30, 41, 53–54, 56, 228, 233, 262f3, 301
Written Tibetan 30, 41, 53–54, 56, 228, 233, 262f3, 326, 369, 403f20, 446
Wutun 369
Wylie 30, 228, 368

Yamaguchi, Zuihō 53
yin 4, 15–16, 63, 65f4, 67, 79–80, 88–89, 113, 144–147
– across varieties 310, 312–313, 333–335
– in Amdo 27, 28, 379, 406–407
– in Balti 20
– in Denjongke 73, 302–307, 312–317, 327–331, 340–345
– in Diasporic Common Tibetan 69, 228, 233, 242–245, 248–249
– in Drokpa 69
– in Dzongkha 25, 111, 312, 333, 354–356, 359–361, 363–364
– historical development 30, 112–113
– in Kyirong 71
– in Lhasa Tibetan 100–101, 188, 192, 194–195, 199, 210–212, 215, 218–220, 222–223, 312–313
– in Old Tibetan 30, 78
– in Purik 261, 287–290, 294
– in Shigatse 76
– in Southern Mustang 23, 69
– in Yolmo 23, 313
– in Zhollam 425–42, 429
Yliniemi, Juha 25, 63, 72–73
yod 4, 7, 15–16, 63–64, 67, 79, 88–89, 100–101, 111, 113–114, 121, 144–147
– in Amdo 47–48, 100f5, 111, 382
– in Balti 20, 43, 45
– in Brag-g.yab 29
– in Chochangacha 25
– in Denjongke 73, 302–306, 317–322, 326, 330–333, 339–340
– in Diasporic Common Tibetan 69, 233, 242–249
– in Drokpa 24
– in Dzongkha 25, 111, 354–358, 363–364
– historical development 30, 112–113
– in Kham 100f5, 111
– in Kyirong 71, 121
– in Ladakhi 22
– in Lhasa Tibetan 100–101, 111, 121, 180–189, 194–195, 203, 210–211, 213–214, 216–217, 220, 223
– in Purik 22, 267–273, 276, 294–295
– in sKyangtshang 52
– in Written Tibetan 53
– *yo-red* 188–189, 195–196, 204, 214, 217, 220, 234, 338
– in Yolmo 23
Yolmo 2, 65f4, 67–68, 70–72, 75, 79–80, 81, 87, 105, 112, 126, 313, 321, 346
– Lamjung 23, 66, 71–72, 86
– Melamchi Valley 23
yong see *'ong*
Yongning Na 14
Yukawa Yasutoshi 3, 6, 8, 11f10, 70, 81, 144, 148f15

Zeisler, Bettina 22, 121
Zemp, Marius 22
zer 27f26, 105, 169, 234, 371–372

www.ingramcontent.com/pod-product-compliance
Lightning Source LLC
Chambersburg PA
CBHW022102290426
44112CB00008B/522